Duncan Mackenzie

Kent Sharkey

SAMS
Teach Yourself
Visual Basic .NET
in 21 Days

SAMS

201 West 103rd St., Indianapolis, Indiana, 46290 USA

Trademarks

Warning and Disclaimer

ASSOCIATE PUBLISHER
Linda Engelman

ACQUISITIONS EDITOR
Sondra Scott

DEVELOPMENT EDITOR
Todd Meister

MANAGING EDITOR
Charlotte Clapp

PROJECT EDITOR
Carol Bowers

COPY EDITOR
Geneil Breeze

INDEXER
Aamir Burki

PROOFREADER
Plan-It Publishing

TECHNICAL EDITORS
Todd Meister
Sundar Rajan

TEAM COORDINATOR
Lynne Williams

MEDIA DEVELOPER
Dan Scherf

INTERIOR DESIGNER
Gary Adair

COVER DESIGNER
Aren Howell

PAGE LAYOUT
Plan-It Publishing

Contents at a Glance

Table of Contents

About the Author

Duncan Mackenzie is an MCSD, MCSE, and MCT who works for the MSDN (http://msdn.microsoft.com) group at Microsoft out of Redmond, Washington. He is an excited Visual Basic .NET programmer who has an annoying habit of writing the occasional article. Duncan also has been active as a Visual Basic trainer and has taught many courses ranging from intermediate to advanced VB programming. Duncan has written and collaborated on a number of books on Microsoft technologies, including *Platinum Edition Using Visual Basic 6.0* and *Word 2000 VBA Programmer's Reference*. He also speaks at many conferences focused on Microsoft development.

Kent Sharkey is an MCSD, MCSE, MCT, and MCP+SB. He currently works at Microsoft as a Technical Evangelist within its .NET Solutions Group, his current assignment being the .NET Framework and Visual Studio .NET. Before joining Microsoft, Kent had many years of experience as a trainer and consultant, concentrating on architecting and writing n-tier applications using Visual Basic. He has written and collaborated on a number of books on Visual Basic, including *MCSD Fast Track*: *Visual Basic Exam 70 –175; MCSD Fast Track: Visual Basic Exam 70 –176; MCSD Fast Track: 4 in 1;* and *Beginning Visual Basic 6.0 Application Development*. He is a regular speaker at various developer conferences focused on Microsoft development.

Dedication

From Duncan Mackenzie:

While I have been working on this book, almost everything in my life has changed, but it was mostly unrelated to the book itself. I now have a son, Connor, and I have moved to a new country and taken a new job with Microsoft. I would like to dedicate this book to my wife, Laura, who was still supportive about my writing, regardless of how many months over our planned deadline we went, and to my new son, who had no idea I was writing a book, but was very happy and supportive regardless. Finally, I have to thank Kent, because he wrote half the book, and I don't think I would have survived doing the whole thing by myself.

From Kent Sharkey:

I was originally going to be clever and write a poem here, but that side of my brain is having problems these days. So instead, this will be a fairly typical list of all the people who helped me with this book. I want to thank my co-author, Duncan. Thank you for the offer and for never accepting no or "I quit" as a response. Thanks to all the editors who worked on the book, especially Sondra and Todd. Thanks to Squirrel for keeping me honest and alive and thanks to Cica for keeping my lap warm and keyboardless once in a while. Finally, and certainly not least, thanks to Margaret for keeping me while I worked on this, a new job, and a new country. We now have this thing called weekends again!

Tell Us What You Think!

As the reader of this book, *you* are our most important critic and commentator. We value your opinion and want to know what we're doing right, what we could do better, what areas you'd like to see us publish in, and any other words of wisdom you're willing to pass our way.

As an Associate Publisher for Sams Publishing, I welcome your comments. You can fax, e-mail, or write me directly to let me know what you did or didn't like about this book— as well as what we can do to make our books stronger.

Please note that I cannot help you with technical problems related to the topic of this book, and that due to the high volume of mail I receive, I might not be able to reply to every message.

When you write, please be sure to include this book's title and author as well as your name and phone or fax number. I will carefully review your comments and share them with the author and editors who worked on the book.

Fax: 317-581-4770

Email: feedback@samspublishing.com

Mail: Linda Engelman
           Associate Publisher
           Sams Publishing
           201 West 103rd Street
           Indianapolis, IN 46290 USA

Introduction

Welcome to an exciting and informative 21-day lesson in Visual Basic .NET, the newest incarnation of the world's most popular programming language. This book is designed to give you an introduction to the .NET Framework and Visual Basic .NET, and get you started programming real applications as quickly as possible.

Overview

The .NET Framework is the core set of concepts and technology underlying Microsoft's newest set of development tools, and it will form the foundation for the next set of servers, applications, and Web-based services deployed around the world. As you might expect, .NET is not something that can be completely covered in an hour, or even in 21 days, so this book is taking a more focused approach. You need to be productive quickly, and that is exactly what you will get from the next 21 days as you read this book and work through the associated exercises. By providing you with the core elements of the Visual Basic .NET language and enough coverage of the .NET Framework itself, you will be ready to start programming now and prepared to keep learning as you go.

From the beginning, it is important to note a key fact about .NET: The language you use is less relevant than it has been in the past. The Framework (the underlying set of technology that all of .NET is based on) is the true .NET platform, and it can be accessed equally well from any .NET language (including Visual Basic, C#, C++, and others). This is excellent news for Visual Basic and both new and experienced Visual Basic developers. Visual Basic is no longer a second-class language, with certain advanced functionality of the operating system restricted only to programmers who use C++. Now, any system, no matter what type, can be created in Visual Basic.

This language independence also means that you are free to choose to work in whichever language you (or your company) want. Given the choice, many people, including the authors of this book, are going to be picking Visual Basic .NET. Its easy-to-use syntax and style have made it the most popular programming language in the world, even with the limitations the previous version had. Now with .NET, there is nothing stopping it from being used on any project in any company.

If you are interested in learning more than just Visual Basic .NET—perhaps C# seems pretty exciting—then you are still starting at the right place. This book is going to give you an understanding of how to use the .NET Framework, which is knowledge that can be transferred easily to any .NET language.

This book is designed as a series of lessons, each representing some important concept in building applications (such as accessing a database) or a critical piece of knowledge to make you productive (using the IDE, for instance). You can go through these lessons in any order you want, but if you are new to programming in general, then you will find the most benefit from following along from the beginning the first time you go through the book. Most lessons, even the first, include some sample code and a few exercises where you get to write some more code. To get the most out of the time you spend on this book, try all these examples and do all the exercises. Nothing will increase your comprehension of these topics faster than some hands-on coding.

Who Should Read This Book?

Although the primary target of this book is people who are new to programming in general and to Visual Basic .NET specifically, it will be useful to a wider variety of readers. If you are already a Visual Basic programmer, then jump around through the various topics in this book to see some great examples and explanations of all the new features. You will find that there are many differences from the Visual Basic 6.0 world, and the level of coverage given in this book should help you make the transition.

If Visual Basic is new to you, but you are already a seasoned programmer, you will likely be thinking that you can skip or skim large portions of the first few lessons. Regardless of your skill level, you will want to dig into the introduction (Day 1) to understand the overall .NET concept and the coverage of the IDE (Day 2) to get up to speed on working within Visual Studio .NET. Then you can move through the rest of the book at your own pace, skimming over some sections that cover general programming concepts and focusing on the days that explain how Visual Basic .NET accomplishes advanced tasks, such as object creation, database access, and the creation of Internet applications.

What You Will Learn

This book teaches you how to create a variety of different types of applications using Visual Basic .NET, including both client/server and Web-based applications. As you move through the Visual Basic .NET topics, you also will learn a great deal about the .NET Framework and a selection of the .NET Servers, including SQL Server and Internet Information Services.

On the application design and architecture side, you will learn about the object-oriented features of Visual Basic .NET, including creating classes and using objects, along with the basics of inheritance, overloading, overriding, and other advanced OO features.

On the output or interface layer of application development, you will learn how to create "Windows" applications using the new forms features of Visual Basic .NET, how to build Web-page based interfaces using Web Forms, and how to create a simple Web Service that exposes itself on the Web where it can be used from any programming language or platform that can access the Web and understand XML.

Our goal is to prepare you over the next 21 days so that you can create many of your own simple Visual Basic .NET applications and to prepare you to work as part of the team building a large Windows or Web-based application.

What We Won't Cover

Despite the discussion earlier about language independence and the importance of underlying technologies, this is a book on Visual Basic .NET first. As such, we will not cover C# or any other .NET language other than Visual Basic. We will touch on the usage of databases, such as SQL Server, but you will need to refer to books on SQL Server for full details on how to set up and manage your database server.

We do not claim to cover all of Visual Basic .NET in this book either. Visual Basic .NET is a huge language, with many features. Just listing all the features with the syntax to use them would easily fill a book of this size. We will cover Visual Basic .NET in enough detail to make you productive using it and to give you sufficient knowledge to start designing applications to take advantage of the new features of .NET.

Requirements

At the time this book was written, the release version of Visual Studio .NET was not yet available, so the requirements are based on the specifications of the Beta version of that product. The best bet is to check out http://msdn.microsoft.com/vstudio to get the most up-to-date set of system requirements. But this section provides a general guide to what you will need.

As a book on Visual Basic .NET, the first major requirement is a system to run Visual Studio .NET, which needs at least the following basic system specifications:

- Operating system   Windows XP Professional, Windows 2000 (Datacenter Server, Advanced Server, Server or Professional), or Windows NT 4.0 Server. The installation of Visual Studio will take care of installing any required service packs, updated data access files, and version 6 of Internet Explorer, all of which are requirements of Visual Studio .NET.

- Hardware   Pentium II 450Mhz or equivalent, 128 MB of RAM, video card capable of 800x600, 256 colors, and at least 1 GB of hard drive space. A CD-ROM drive is needed to install, but it is possible to put your CDs into another machine and install across a LAN connection.

On top of Visual Studio, the examples in this book assume that you have access to a Web server that is either the same machine as your Visual Studio machine or has the .NET Framework SDK installed onto it. The best bet is to make sure that your main development machine has a Web server running on it, such as with Windows 2000 or Windows NT. Another key requirement used by the examples in the last half of this book is access to a database, specifically SQL Server 7.0 or 2000. If you do not have SQL Server itself, then you can use Microsoft Data Engine (MSDE), which works similarly to the full SQL Server product. An Access database will do, if that is all you have, but you will have to modify some of the examples in the database access lessons to make them work without SQL Server.

Skills You Will Need

This is a book aimed at beginning programmers, but some basic skills are assumed. It is expected that you are familiar with using Windows-based computers, including whichever operating system you have installed to run .NET. Copying files, printing, opening files into Notepad, and basic text editing (cut, copy, paste) skills are all assumed and will not be explained in the lessons. Knowing how to get your machine connected to the Internet and how to browse to Web sites is also a required skill.

Other than this basic knowledge of computers, you will not be expected to be a programmer, or to know how to build databases. Whatever knowledge you do have in these areas will most likely be helpful, but our examples and explanations are designed to be clear even to someone who has never tried coding before.

The Web Site

This book has an associated Web site at `http://www.samspublishing.com/detail_sams.cfm?item=0672320665`. On that Web site, you can find downloadable versions of all the code from this book and any supplementary links or material that we think would be helpful to the reader in understanding Visual Basic .NET. You are, of course, completely able to use this book and follow along with all the examples, without ever visiting this Web site, but for some of the longer examples, it might be nice to save yourself some typing by downloading the code files from the Web.

Chapter Layout

Twenty-one days is a long time, so in addition to breaking the lessons into individual days, we have organized the book into three week-long sections. In Week 1, we will focus on introducing you to the general concepts of .NET and programming, and covering the foundation syntax and techniques of creating programs with Visual Basic .NET. Week 2 will dive into the .NET Framework to provide a deeper understanding of this critical foundation for all your programming, and will also cover the fundamentals for building real programs, such as how to create a user interface (with Windows Forms and with Web Forms) and how to work with databases. The final week will introduce some of the more advanced topics in .NET programming, including creating your own objects, deploying your application to other people's computers, and working with XML and Web Services. As we discussed earlier, try to work through these lessons in order, but feel free to jump ahead if there is a topic you really want to read more about right away.

Feedback

We have worked hard to make this book a useful tool for learning .NET and a valuable addition to your development library. If you wish we had spent more or less time on a particular topic, or if you have suggestions for making this book better, please let Sams Publishing know. We will try to incorporate your suggestions into future books and into the next revision of this same volume.

Conventions Used In This Book

This book uses several conventions to help you prioritize and reference the information it contains:

Note

Notes provide useful sidebar information that you can read immediately or circle back to without losing the flow of the topic at hand.

Tip

Tips highlight information that can make your VB programming more effective.

Caution

Cautions focus your attention on problems or side effects that can occur in specific situations.

Do	Don't
DO/DON'T BOXES emphasize good practices you should adopt...	...and bad ones you should avoid.

New Term | **New Term** icons signal places where new terminology is first used and defined. Such terminology appears in an italic typeface for emphasis.

Input | **Input** icons used in conjunction with code examples point to portions of code the user must input.

Analysis | **Analysis** icons point to discussions of the how and why of code examples.

Code is presented in a monospace font.

WEEK 1

At a Glance

During this week, you will cover several key topics:

- .NET, Visual Basic, and the concept of programming (Day 1)
- How to set up and use Visual Studio .NET to get started writing programs (Day 2)
- The Visual Basic syntax and programming techniques for data types, procedures, and variables (Day 3); controlling program flow—loops and conditionals (Day 4); and error handling (Day 6)
- How to organize and architect a Visual Basic .NET solution (Day 5)
- Important concepts related to object-oriented development that you will be working with throughout the remainder of the book (Day 7)

This week is an important week. It sets up the foundation of basic knowledge on which all other Visual Basic .NET programming will rest. Day 1 prepares you to start exploring and learning Visual Basic by introducing you to the fundamental concepts of programming and the .NET platform along with a brief history of Visual Basic itself. On Day 2, you learn how to use the full-featured development environment of Visual Studio to create projects.

Days 3 and 4 get you programming, with a lot of information on the syntax and concepts (including variables, loops, If statements, and more) that will be part of every Visual Basic program you ever write from this point forward.

On Day 5, you are introduced to all the different project types you can create within Visual Basic .NET and how those different types of projects can fit into an overall system's architecture. Finally Days 6 and 7 return to the hands-on world of coding where you will learn about dealing with errors and using objects in your programs.

This week will provide the information you need to go forward into the rest of the book, giving you all the details that every other topic will build on.

DAY 1

Welcome to Visual Basic .NET

Today, I will be introducing you to the world of Visual Basic programming by answering the following questions:

- What is programming, and why would you want to do it?
- How does Visual Basic fit into all this?
- What is .NET?

These days, computers are common, and many people I know spend their entire day working with them. But, even so, the most common question I get is "What does a computer programmer do?" That question has come up so often, that in today's lesson, I'll spend a little time going over what programming is, and why you would want to do it.

Understanding Computer Programming

Although we often talk about computers in terms of their hardware (you often hear comments like "I have a Pentium III, 600 MHz with 256 MB of RAM," for instance), hardware alone is not very useful. The CPU (Central Processing Unit, or main computer chip, such as the Pentium III in my computer), for instance, is capable of many important tasks such as simple math and the movement of data between the various parts of the system. On its own, however, it isn't even capable of reading a file from the hard drive. A *computer program* is a set of instructions for all these hardware elements, generally written to accomplish some task that the hardware couldn't accomplish on its own. All the basic operations of using disk drives, memory, a monitor, and a printer are complex. A program that had to interact with the basic operations would spend the majority of its time on those issues and only a small percentage of time would actually be spent on the program's true purpose. Written directly against the hardware, a program to calculate the payments on a mortgage would likely contain hundreds or thousands of lines to manage display and other issues and a few lines to do the actual calculation. This is the way programming was done in the past, and it was not very productive because so little time could actually be spent on the real purpose of the application. What was needed was some way for all those details to be handled so that programs could focus on their specific tasks.

The Role of Operating Systems

To provide this basic layer of functionality on top of computer hardware, operating systems were created. These are computer programs themselves, but exist to handle all the details of memory management, disk input/output (I/O) and other low level tasks. When an operating system (OS) exists on a computer, other programs can be written that do not have to worry about all the low-level details; if the programs need to open a file or format a floppy disk, they can ask the OS to perform that function for them. Looking at this graphically (see Figure 1.1) you can visualize the relationships between the computer hardware and the OS, or the OS and other programs, as multiple layers of functionality.

FIGURE 1.1

The operating system becomes the interface between the computer equipment and your program, allowing you to avoid hardware-specific code.

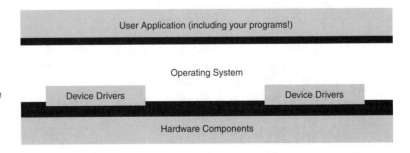

Often, the relationships aren't that clearly defined; a program might need to access the hardware directly (without going through the operating system) to use a hardware feature that the OS doesn't support or in an attempt to boost performance. This was certainly the

1

case early on with one of the first PC operating systems, in which many programs had to interact directly with the hardware. These limitations meant more work for people who wanted to write software for the PC, as each program had to handle its own printers and other details. As successive versions of operating systems provide increased functionality, it becomes easier to write programs for those systems. Eventually, Windows replaced these systems. One of the biggest improvements offered by Windows was that the OS now provided user interface features to other programs. Under Windows, if a computer program needs to show a dialog box on the screen (such as the one shown in Figure 1.2), it simply asks the OS to display a dialog and supply the message to be displayed. To access all the functionality that the operating system provides, a set of Application Programming Interfaces (or APIs) are provided. Those APIs represent all of the exposed OS functionality and might, in turn, be used in your programs.

FIGURE 1.2

Windows handles the display of GUI (Graphical User Interface) elements such as this dialog box as part of the services it provides to programs.

The result of all these improvements is that each individual program has to handle less and less of the generic operation of the computer and can, therefore, focus on its true purpose. Another major benefit of removing the hardware-specific code from applications is that, as hardware changes occur (new printers, new hard drives, faster CPUs), the OS might have to be updated to handle that new equipment, but the programs running on that computer should be unaffected.

What does this mean to you as a Visual Basic programmer? Well, it means that you will be able to create computer programs to accomplish a specific task (like the mortgage calculator example above) without having to know anything about how Windows draws images to the monitor, prints to the printer, or saves files to the hard disk. You can get productive very quickly, with the help of this book.

The Role of Programming Languages

So, now you have an understanding of what the OS provides, but what about the programs themselves—how are they created? Early in the lesson, I defined a computer program as a set of instructions for computer hardware. Because the hardware itself is capable of only relatively simple operations, the instructions also must be simple. The end result of the programs is code that the hardware can understand, often called *machine language* or *native code*. The instructions, after they are loaded into memory by the OS, consist of commands such as "move memory from one place to another" or "perform a mathematical function on values." Thousands of these commands make up a completed program.

It is possible to write programs directly using this native code, creating a file on the hard disk full of instructions, but it would take an enormous amount of work to produce even the simplest program. To avoid that level of effort, and to enable programmers to focus on the purpose of their programs, higher-level programming languages have been created. These languages let you use more powerful and complex instructions that are then translated into the many corresponding machine language instructions required. A single line of such a language could possibly turn into 10 separate machine language instructions.

NEW TERM The process of translating from a higher-level computer language into machine or native code is known as *compiling*. The programs that do this translation are called *compilers*.

Many of these languages have been created over the years. FORTRAN, COBOL, APL, Pascal, C, and BASIC are just a few examples, but hundreds of different languages are available. Each language has its own set of commands, and, over time, new commands are created to simplify the programming effort even more. As computers have evolved over time, so have the languages used to program them, adding new features to existing languages or creating new languages such as C++ (which, as you might have guessed, was based on C) and Java. In general, advancements in programming languages have had the goal of increasing programming productivity, enabling the programmer to create the desired program as easily as possible.

Note

It is a simplification to state that programming languages are evolving simply to make development faster. Speed of development is just one of the motivations behind the improvements that have taken place. Other goals and results include producing faster or more stable (fewer crashes) applications, or even producing applications that are easier to install.

Originally, most programming languages consisted of only one thing, a compiler. You would create the program itself using a text editor, like Notepad, and run the compiler, passing the name of your source file. It would then produce the finished result, an executable program, assuming that there were no errors. You would run the compiled result, test it for errors, and then go back into your text editor to make changes to the code. The

1

code would be compiled again, and the cycle would repeat. This development process (see Figure 1.3) was not language specific; it was a common activity for all programmers.

FIGURE 1.3

Compilers turn source code from higher-level languages into instructions that the computer can understand.

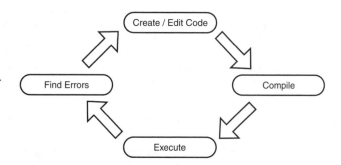

As programming languages have evolved, this development cycle has been improving as well, resulting in the development of more advanced compilers and the concept of an Integrated Development Environment (IDE). The purpose of an IDE is to combine the editing, debugging, and compiling components of software development into a single interface for the programmer (see Figure 1.4). Despite the single interface, the actual technology is very similar. In most cases, code is still being compiled (see the following Note for more information), and the programmer is still creating text files, but the work environment is much more user friendly.

FIGURE 1.4

Visual Studio is an IDE, providing a single interface for any number of languages, including Visual Basic.

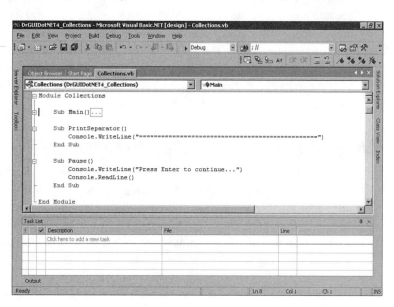

Note

In addition to compiled languages (where the source code must be run through a compiler before it can be executed), another class of languages exists called *interpreted languages*. In these languages, the source code is not compiled. Instead, a special program runs the code by reading the source and executing the appropriate code. In general, because the parsing (the reading through the source for commands) has to occur every time the program is run, interpreted languages run slower than those that are compiled, in which parsing only occurs once, at compile time. At one point in time, Visual Basic was an interpreted language, but that is no longer the case.

The creation of IDEs has led to some confusion between what is a feature of the language being used, and what is a feature of the IDE. This is very true in the case of Visual Basic, for which the IDE provides many features that enable a programmer to easily create advanced functionality. Those features often generate Visual Basic code, and it is that code that performs the work. In such a case, the IDE has added the functionality, not the language, but the two are often seen as the same thing. Today, as I introduce the concept of Visual Studio .NET, you will see that an IDE can support many languages, and it can be valuable to understand the difference between the IDE and its underlying language.

Another important development in the history of programming languages was the creation of "visual" languages, such as Visual Basic. These languages are called "visual" because they enable the creation of programs using a graphical interface. The most common feature of such a language is the ability to place buttons, text, and other items onto a screen to build a user interface (see Figure 1.5). Once again, under the covers, actual code is often being generated, but the programmer has a much easier time creating the graphical portions of her application. I will cover Visual Basic's place as a programming language a little later in today's lesson.

Why Write Computer Programs?

I mentioned before that the most common question I am asked is "What does a computer programmer do?" After I have explained the general concept of the job, I usually get the second most common question, "Why would you want to do that?" The answer, "Because it's fun to write code," has never seemed to satisfy people. So, as we start learning how to write programs, it is worthwhile to spend a little bit of time considering what we are going to write, and why.

FIGURE 1.5

Visual development tools enable you to create interfaces graphically and then generate the required code.

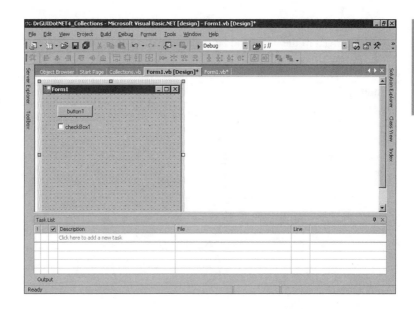

The first thing to understand about computer programming is the type of programs you will be building. If asked to give examples of applications, most people would list programs such as Microsoft Word or Excel, a few might mention computer games, and very few would include Windows itself in the list. All these are definitely computer applications, and someone has to program them, but the biggest category of programs is the one that is almost never mentioned. The most common software programs are the systems that we see all the time. Unless you are interested in (or obsessed by) programming, you don't often think about the months or years of programmer time that goes into building them. These programs, like the rental system at your local video store, or the program that your local government uses to track driver licenses, are developed for either a single customer or a small niche market. Other than in their audience, these programs are not all that different from off-the-shelf software like Microsoft Word. However, their individualized nature means that there is a very large ratio of programming-work-per-customer.

The role of a programmer covers many different aspects of software development, especially in the world of custom software. But the software development life cycle (SDLC) contains several other key stages (see Figure 1.6).

Before the coding begins, there must be an understanding of what the new system is supposed to do, that is, its *requirements*. That information must be turned into a general blueprint for the computer application, that is, the *design*. That blueprint, basically a translation of the customer's needs into the parts of a computer system, becomes the guide by which the programmer works. The desired result is a computer system that meets the needs originally specified by the user. That completed system must then be deployed to the users and be maintained and enhanced. Bugs—problems in the system—must be fixed, and new features must be added.

FIGURE 1.6

The life cycle of a software development project passes through several distinct stages.

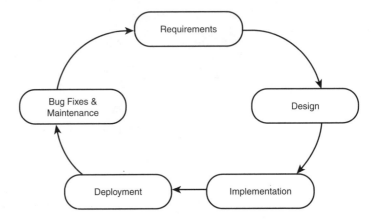

That cycle is the life and work of the software developer. But, for most programmers, *why* they do programming can be stated in simpler terms: They get to write code that does something useful. The entire purpose of programming is to make the computer hardware accomplish useful tasks; this is what drives most software developers. My co-author and I have kept that concept in mind throughout this book, and we will be making sure that almost every program we show you will perform a useful function in addition to providing you with a learning experience. It is this underlying goal, creating useful applications, that points many people towards Visual Basic, as it is considered by many to be the fastest way from idea to application.

A Brief History of Visual Basic

The history of Visual Basic actually starts with the invention of BASIC (Beginner's All-purpose Symbolic Instruction Code) in 1964, a language that is easily learned and used by beginner programmers. This language caught on, and, over the following 15 years, a wide variety of people and companies created compilers and interpreters for BASIC.

In 1975, when Microsoft was a new company, a version of the BASIC language was one of the first products it made, a product that became successful. Microsoft BASIC and its successor, Quick BASIC (or QBASIC, as it is also known), became the most widely available versions of BASIC on the PC. They still have a relatively large following today (if you are interested, check out http://www.qbasic.com for resources and links about this language). Quick BASIC was available for Windows when it was released, but it took quite a bit of effort to code a Windows-style interface, so it was not as well suited to coding in this new environment.

Microsoft came out with a new product, though, a product that combined the popular and easy-to-learn BASIC language with a development environment that enabled programmers to graphically create the user interface for a program. This product, as you might have already guessed, was Visual Basic 1.0. It didn't catch on at first, but it did provide a rapid environment for developing a graphical user interface (GUI). What might surprise you is that Visual Basic actually started out with a DOS version, although it quickly moved into Windows (see Figure 1.7).

FIGURE 1.7

The first version of Visual Basic for Windows provided many of the key features common across many current development tools, with the most important being its visual drag-and-drop form of development.

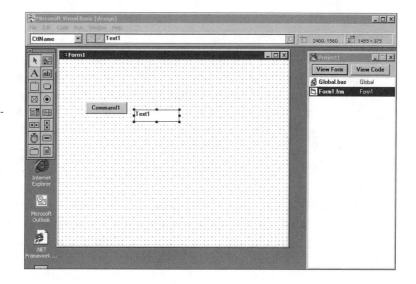

Visual Basic grew in popularity over time. A single feature proved to be critical to its success. This was the capability for Microsoft, the programmer, and third parties to create custom interface components that could be added to programs. Companies quickly jumped into this market, creating components to add a variety of features to Visual Basic applications, such as charting, image editing, modem connections, and many more features. These components enabled the Visual Basic programmer to create more powerful applications by combining various components with their own code. This greatly increased the rapid development possible with Visual Basic, and helped make it into one of the most popular programming languages.

Each successive version of Visual Basic added new features, making it more and more into a fully capable development tool. One particularly important change was how Visual Basic was executed at runtime. Until version 5 was released in 1997, Visual Basic was an interpreted language, which resulted in relatively poor performance as compared to the performance of Visual C++, Delphi, and other compiled languages. Visual Basic 5.0 made it possible to create either compiled or interpreted versions of your program, and performance improved considerably.

Another key change in Visual Basic was the capability to create components. In programming, you often find a segment of code, such as a mortgage calculation routine, that could be used in many places in your program and potentially even in many different programs. Sharing that code within a program is generally accomplished by writing it as a procedure, a block of code that is typed into the program once, but can be called from anywhere within the application. Sharing across programs can be done by simply copying the procedure's code into each new application you are building, but this creates a problem. Whenever you, or someone else, make a change to that block of code (to fix a bug, or improve the way the code works), you would need to copy the code into each and every application that uses it.

A better way of sharing code is to create a library of code that is stored in a file separate from the programs that use it and that can be changed independently. Such a library is known as a *component* and is often created in the form of a .dll file. Using a library is a preferred method of sharing code. As Visual Basic has developed new versions, its capability to create these components has been steadily advancing. Version 4.0 (released in 1996) was the first version to enable the creation of components, and it is now an extremely critical feature in development projects. We'll discuss components in greater detail in Day 14, "Introduction to Object-Oriented Programming."

Many additional features were added to Visual Basic, but everything was being built on top of the existing foundation. This is not unusual. Most development tools progress in this way, but it has the unfortunate side effect of garbage accumulation. New versions of a tool try to stay compatible with all the less-than-perfect aspects of the previous versions. To rewrite a language from scratch is almost unthinkable. The work required would be enormous, and breaking compatibility with the user's existing code is bound to be unpopular. The benefit of such a move would be a completely clean and new implementation that can keep the good and throw away the bad parts of the existing language.

That is exactly what Microsoft has done in the move from Visual Basic 6.0 to Visual Basic .NET. It has rewritten the language to create a clean version that does away with the garbage that built up over a decade of successive language improvements. That means a hard learning curve for people who were experienced in the previous version of the language, but the end result is worth the effort. This radical shift makes this a great time to be new to Visual Basic, as the concepts taught in this book will have a much longer lifespan than what would be learned from material regarding a previous Visual Basic version.

There are many benefits to this change, all of which were motivators for this decision, but the most significant motivation was the need to conform to the new .NET environment. As today's lesson continues, you'll learn more about .NET, what it is, and how Visual Basic fits into it.

What Is .NET?

At first glance, .NET might seem to be just a marketing concept, a way of avoiding yet another number at the end of Visual Basic, but it is much more than that. .NET represents an entire range of technologies and concepts that form a platform on which you can develop applications.

Note

> Visual Basic .NET does have an actual version number, 7.0—the number just isn't used often. Just as Windows 2000 is really Windows NT version 5.0, the simpler or catchier name will generally be the one commonly used. Don't expect to hear Visual Basic 7.0 often though; there was even a cash penalty inside Microsoft for referring to Windows 2000 as NT 5.0 (only 25 cents, but it adds up!).

Earlier in today's lesson, I explained how the operating system provides a level of base functionality to applications (such as the ability to read files from a hard drive or floppy disc). .NET can be thought of in a similar way; it is a layer that exists beneath your programs and provides a set of base services and functions. This layer contains a set of applications and operating systems called the .NET servers; a foundation set of objects called the .NET Framework, and a set of services that support all the .NET languages called the Common Language Runtime (CLR). Each of these parts of .NET (see Figure 1.8) is covered individually.

FIGURE 1.8

.NET is more than just one thing; it is a collection of software and concepts that work together to enable the creation of business solutions.

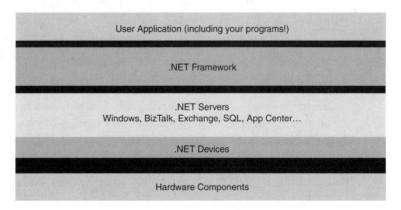

.NET Servers

A major goal of the .NET concept is to decrease the building of distributed systems, in which the work is done in several different locations. For the most part, these types of systems do their work on the back end, at the server level. Microsoft provides a set of software products that together are known as the .NET Enterprise Servers. They are designed to supply the back end features needed by a distributed system. These products include

- The server operating system, Microsoft Windows (Server, Advanced Server, and Datacenter Server)
- Clustering and load-balancing software such as Microsoft App Center and Microsoft Cluster Server
- A database server, Microsoft SQL Server
- An e-mail, collaboration, and free-form information storage system, Microsoft Exchange Server
- A data-transformation engine based around XML (more on XML on Day 20) called Microsoft BizTalk Server
- A server for accessing legacy systems, such as AS/400s, called Host Integration Server
- And more...

Together these servers supply base services to your .NET applications, forming the foundation of your systems. This book will refer to these servers from time to time, illustrating where they can fit into your systems.

.NET Framework

In the move to Visual Basic .NET, many things have changed radically; one of them is the development of a new foundation to all the .NET development tools. This foundation, known as the .NET Framework, provides two key things: the base runtime environment and a set of foundation classes. The runtime environment is similar to the operating system in that it provides a layer between your program and the complexities of the rest of the system, performing services for your application and simplifying access to the functionality of the lower layers. The foundation classes provide a large set of functionality, wrapping and abstracting such technologies as Internet protocols, file system access, XML manipulation, and more.

The true power of this Framework will be explored in more detail in Day 8, "Introduction to the .NET Framework." For now, understand that the .NET Framework is similar in many ways to the operating system, and it provides its own set of APIs to make it easy for programmers to take advantage of its capabilities. Figure 1.9 illustrates the Framework's relationship to your code and to the underlying services of the operating system.

FIGURE 1.9

The .NET Framework provides another layer of abstraction over the operating system, just as the operating system does for the computer hardware.

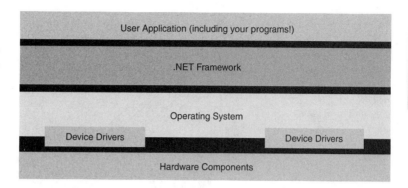

1

For a programming language to take advantage of the runtime environment and other functionality of the .NET Framework, the compiler must produce code that adheres to a certain standard. Microsoft provides this standard, the Common Language Specification, as a way to make any compiler .NET capable. Microsoft has created Visual Basic, Visual C++, and C# compilers that target the .NET Framework, but they have also made the Common Language Specification available outside of Microsoft so that other companies can create compilers for other languages. The result is that, in addition to the languages provided by Microsoft, many other languages exist (such as COBOL, APL, Smalltalk, and more) that are built on the exact same foundation as Visual Basic .NET.

At this point, it becomes important to distinguish between features provided by the language and those provided by the .NET Framework. Visual Basic and COBOL both share all the features of the Framework, but, as different languages, they also have their own unique functions and syntax. As you proceed through the days, you'll learn about both Visual Basic-specific features and those provided by the Framework.

.NET Services

.NET includes certain concepts that extend beyond the details of programming to describe how systems should be built and how they can interact. One such key concept is the idea of Web Services, functionality delivered in a consistent fashion over the Internet. These services enable a company or organization to supply functionality so that the execution of that functionality is completely contained within their environment. An example of this type of service might be a bill payment service, in which a company has servers and applications inside their own organization that can handle bill payment. The company provides that service to others through a Web Service (see Figure 1.10). This is different from simply providing a Web site; this is an interface that other applications or Web sites can access through code.

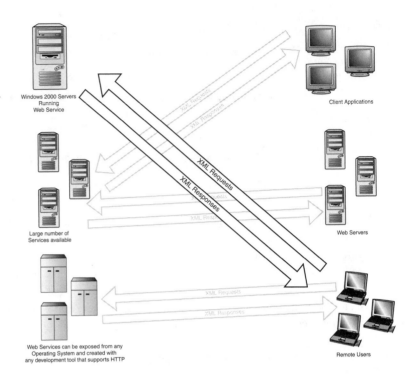

FIGURE 1.10

A Web Service allows companies to provide software-based services over the Internet, and allows other Web sites and/or applications to use them.

There are many possible uses for this technology, but the concept of Web Services is that there are certain base or foundation services that many applications will need, such as authentication, calendaring, messaging (e-mail), and more. By having those kinds of functionality as Web Services, anyone in the world can take advantage of them to reduce the development time of their own system. Microsoft, as part of the .NET initiative, is providing a few of these base services for authentication (known as Microsoft Passport, `www.passport.com`), messaging (hotmail, `www.hotmail.com`), and others.

Later, in Day 21, "Creating Web Services with Visual Basic .NET," we will provide a proper introduction to Web Services and expand on how you can use them in your applications.

.NET Devices

In today's world, there is a wide range of systems that you can use to gain access to the Internet, your company network, or your personal information. Whether they are full PCs, TV-based Internet terminals, thin-clients, or Personal Digital Assistants (PDAs), these devices can all be the means by which a user accesses a .NET application. This trend toward such a large variety of devices forces you, as a programmer, to forget the general assumption of a single type of client, usually a PC, and consider instead that a client could be connecting through one of many possible devices. These devices can be classified as .NET devices—a combination of hardware and software features designed to work with .NET-based services and applications. Currently, the range of available .NET devices includes computers running Windows (Windows 9x, Millennium Edition, and Windows 2000 with the .NET Framework installed) and devices running Windows CE. (The .NET compact Framework is available for this platform, enabling .NET feature support.) There will be continued growth in this area.

Do not worry if there are still parts of .NET that seem confusing; they should be! Throughout the rest of the days, this book's lessons will explain more detail that will help to make it all clear. For now, keep in mind the relationship between .NET and your programs—a layer of functionality that is already provided and that is easy for you to access from your code. Keeping that concept in mind, and knowing that the end result is faster development from concept to finished program, you have learned enough about .NET for today's lesson.

Building Your First Visual Basic .NET Application

It is time to write your first bit of Visual Basic .NET code. Before continuing with this example, and the examples in the rest of the book, you must have Visual Basic .NET installed. In this section, I will walk through getting Visual Basic or Visual Studio (including Visual Basic) on your computer. If you already have it installed, you can skip ahead to "Where's My IDE?"

Getting Ready to Code

Before you can do any work with Visual Basic .NET, you have to install it. You should have either several CDs or a DVD (depending on where you obtained the product) from which you can install. It is also possible that you are installing from a network location, but the process is basically the same in each of the three cases, with the major difference being a bit of CD switching if you happen to have the multiple-CD version.

The first screen you see when you put in Disc 1, or run setup from the DVD or network, is a dialog that lists three separate steps (see Figure 1.11).

The first step is getting the operating system components of your machine up to the level that .NET requires. This is called the Windows Component Update (WCU), and if you click on the first option on the setup dialog (refer to Figure 1.11), you are prompted to supply the WCU disk if necessary, and installation begins. What you see during the WCU setup depends on your system because only those items not already current will be updated. Some of the possible installs include Windows 2000 Service Pack 2, MDAC 2.7 (updated data access components), and Internet Explorer 6.0. One item that will be installed for most systems is the .NET Framework itself, which does not include the Visual Studio .NET IDE, but provides all the Framework classes and supporting files required to run .NET applications. Depending on which components are required, the install program might need to reboot your computer one or more times. When this installation completes, you are returned to the original setup dialog, as shown in Figure 1.11.

FIGURE 1.11

The process of installing Visual Studio .NET is broken up into three main steps.

To install Visual Studio .NET itself, click Step 2 to start the next part of the installation. You are prompted to enter your product key and to accept or reject an End User License Agreement (EULA) before the main installation can start. After you supply the required information and agree to the EULA, you are provided with a screen full of options where you can choose which elements of Visual Studio .NET you want to install (see Figure 1.12).

Figure 1.12 is based on Visual Studio .NET Beta 2, and a few of the options might change, but overall you should see the same list. If you plan on programming mostly in Visual Basic .NET, I would suggest selecting the same options as you can see in Figure 1.12. The first selection worth noting is the choice of Visual Basic and Visual C# in the Language options. Visual C# is not required, but you will find that many code samples will be available in this language, and it is more likely that you will experiment with C# than C++. You can also select Visual C++, but I would do so only if you reasonably expect to use it because it takes up a larger amount of disk space than either of the other languages.

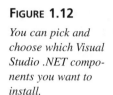

FIGURE 1.12

You can pick and choose which Visual Studio .NET components you want to install.

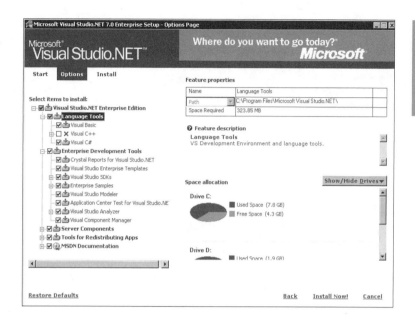

Next, make sure that you select all the options available under Enterprise Tools, Server Components, and Tools for Redistributing Apps. I will not go into what these options contain, but by selecting them all you ensure that you have all the features available in your version of Visual Studio (different Visual Studio versions have different sets of feature options). Finally, select MSDN and either leave it at the default setting of Run From Source, which requires access to your CD, DVD, or Network install location, or if you have enough drive space, switch it to install to a specific path (see Figure 1.13). Running MSDN from the install location is slower than installing it to your local machine, but the decision is usually based on available disk space instead of speed.

After you make all your selections, click on the Install Now! link at the bottom of the dialog to start the installation. Various bits of text describing the features of .NET are displayed as the install progresses, finally ending with a completion screen (see Figure 1.14). If anything goes wrong during the installation, it is displayed on this screen.

FIGURE **1.13**

The MSDN libraries, containing a great deal of useful documentation, articles, and samples can be installed locally for increased speed.

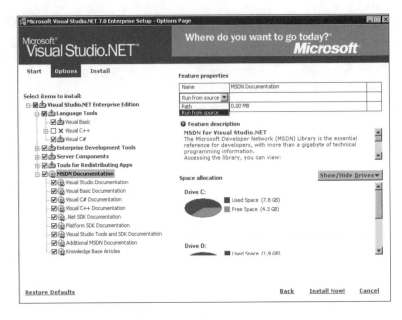

FIGURE **1.14**

If anything goes wrong during installation, you are informed of the problem at this screen.

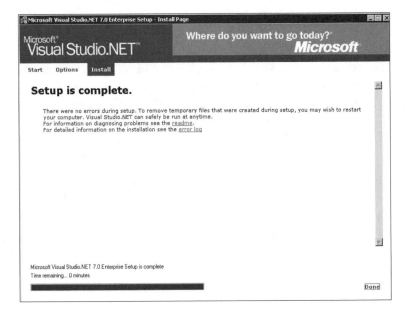

Finally, when you are returned to the initial setup screen, the third choice is available. Clicking on this option, Service Releases, takes you to another dialog (see Figure 1.15), where you can choose to install updates from the Web or from disk. If you have Internet connectivity, I recommend choosing the first option to ensure that you have the most recent list of updates.

FIGURE 1.15

The Visual Studio .NET install program can download and install updates from the Internet.

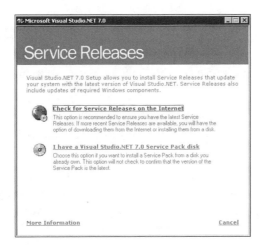

Visual Studio .NET is now installed, and should be ready to run, so you can move onto the next section where you will get started writing a bit of code.

Where's My IDE?

Here you are learning Visual Basic .NET, one of the most advanced development packages available, and your first program is going to be done using Notepad and the command prompt. Yep, you read that right, the command prompt. Earlier in today's lesson, I discussed that many programming languages consisted of just a compiler. In such a language, you would write the programs as text files, and then call the compiler to turn that code (assuming that you have made no mistakes) into an executable. In most languages, this has never changed. The purpose of an IDE is to provide a single environment for you to work in, but it still uses the same sequence of edit/compile/execute as the manual process. In pre–Visual Basic .NET days, you could use the command line to compile your programs, but that was simply running the IDE in a nonvisible mode. Visual Basic .NET has separated the two functions, compiling and editing, by providing the compiler as a completely separate program.

Using the IDE, you never have to see the compiling. It is handled for you, but it is still performing the compilation. The key difference between the compiler in Visual Basic .NET and previous versions is that the Visual Basic .NET compiler is totally independent of the IDE; there is nothing you can do in the IDE that you can't do using just the command-line compiler and Notepad. Because the IDE is a huge and complicated program on its own, it will be simpler to focus on the language and work at the command-line level from time to time. Tomorrow's lesson—Day 2, "Working with Visual Basic

.NET,"—will introduce the IDE and walk through the basics of using it to edit, run, and compile your programs.

A Simple Task

To create your first program, you need to have a goal, something for your program to do. It is my intention to produce no "Hello World!" programs in this book, programs that have no purpose. This is particularly difficult when you are trying to write your first little bit of code.

NEW TERM The phrase *"Hello World!" program* describes a sample program that doesn't do anything useful, or more specifically, nothing more useful than just displaying the message "Hello World!"

You will start off with a program that you can run just from the command line, and have it return a bit of text. Then I will show you how that program illustrates almost everything you need to know to build a useful utility that outputs version information for your operating system (for instance, the release version of Windows 2000 has a version # of 5.00.2195). This might or might not be useful to you as a command-line utility, but it demonstrates the basic concepts of creating one.

Writing the Code

Because you will be starting in a text editor (such as Notepad) instead of in the IDE, nothing is done for you, and the file will start out blank. This means that you have to set up the basic structure of your program before you can start writing code that will correctly compile. To get started, create a new text file somewhere on your computer; for this book's examples create a directory on your computer called `C:\TYVB\C1\`. To create the new text file, right-click in the appropriate folder and choose New, Text Document (see Figure 1.16). This creates a file named `New Text Document.txt`. Rename that file to indicate its eventual contents by changing it from `New Text Document.txt` to `Step1.vb`.

FIGURE 1.16

The Explorer's right-click menu gives you a direct way to create a text file and many other documents.

With the file renamed, and in the right directory, you can go ahead and start setting up your actual code. Open the file in Notepad by right-clicking it and selecting Open With. This brings up a dialog through which you can select Notepad or another text editor (Word Pad, for instance). After you have chosen a program, click OK, and the file opens. There shouldn't be anything in the file at this point; you have to add everything to make it work.

Taking It Step-By-Step

Whenever you are writing code, and especially when you are trying something new, try to approach the problem through multiple steps. This way, when you run into a problem, you know which parts of the program worked and which parts didn't.

In the first step, you will make sure that you can actually create an application using the command-line compiler. To do this, you need some code, but it doesn't have to actually do anything. It just has to have the correct format. The following code represents the basic structure of a Visual Basic .NET program; type it into your Notepad window and then save it as Step1.vb.

```
Public Class Step1
    Shared Sub Main()
    End Sub
End Class
```

Caution

When you try to save your code as Step1.vb, you might end up with some strange results. Because of Notepad's desire to create text files, and depending on your system settings regarding extensions, you might end up with a file called step1.vb.txt on your hard drive. To avoid this, make sure that you have unchecked the option Hide File Extensions for Known File Types (in Folder Options, View, from the Tools menu in Windows Explorer).

Next, launch the command prompt by selecting the Visual Studio .NET command prompt option from the Start, Programs, Microsoft Visual Studio .NET 7.0, Visual Studio .NET Tools menu, as you can see in Figure 1.17.

It is essential that you use this option to access the command line, because only through this command line will you have the correct path(s) set up to run the .NET tools such as the Visual Basic compiler (vbc.exe). If you want to use a regular command line, you must add the appropriate Path setting (do a search for vbc.exe to find the directory that needs to be in your Path) on your machine. This brings up a command console (as shown in Figure 1.18). From there, navigate to the directory containing your Step1.vb file. You are ready to compile your program, creating an executable, but you can break this down a little further by adding an additional step before you compile.

FIGURE 1.17

Selecting the Visual Studio .NET command prompt is the best way to work with .NET from a command line.

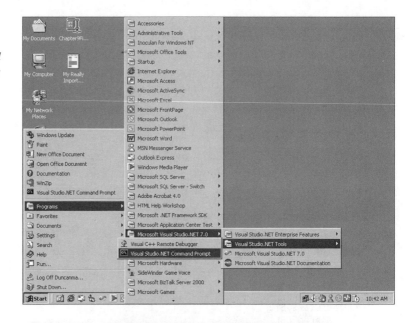

FIGURE 1.18

Using the command-line compiler is done from the console (or DOS prompt, as it is often called).

At the command prompt, type **vbc** and press Enter. You should see the following output

 OUTPUT
```
Microsoft (R) Visual Basic.NET Compiler version 7.00.9254
for Microsoft (R) .NET CLR version 1.00.2914.16
Copyright  Microsoft Corp 2001. All rights reserved.

Visual Basic Compiler Options
```

followed by a large amount of help information about using the Visual Basic compiler. If this works, you have confirmed a number of things:

- You do have Visual Basic .NET installed.
- You have the appropriate permissions to run the compiler.
- The system was able to find the file vbc.exe.

By trying vbc on its own first, you can eliminate it as the source of any problems you encounter trying to compile an actual program. Continuing along, you can now compile your saved program, Step1.vb, by entering a command of vbc Step1.vb /t:exe and then pressing Enter. If everything works, you should get this response:

```
Microsoft (R) Visual Basic.NET Compiler version 7.00.9254
for Microsoft (R) .NET CLR version 1.00.2914.16
Copyright  Microsoft Corp 2001. All rights reserved.
```

This means that the compile was successful, and if you were to look at this folder now, either through Windows or by issuing a DIR command, you would see that there is now a new file Step1.exe. Running this executable (by typing Step1 at the command prompt and pressing Enter) will produce no obvious results at all, which is to be expected because the Step1.vb code didn't really do anything. The fact that it compiled and ran at all demonstrates that the code is correct so far.

The call to vbc can accept a wide variety of optional switches (additional commands added onto the command line, usually separated by slashes [/]), as you can see by running vbc on its own. However, in this case, you only used two. By supplying the name of the source file, step1.vb, you told vbc which code to compile. The second option, /t:exe, specifies the type of compiled application to make. The options for /t (which stands for "target" and can also be entered as /target) can be any one of winexe, exe, a library, or a module. All these options will be covered later, but, for now, only the first two are particularly relevant; winexe creates a Windows application, and exe creates a command-line or console application (which is your goal). By default, when you run vbc, it uses /t:exe.

Let's See Some Output

Now, keeping in mind your ultimate goal of returning the operating system version, try outputting some text. Before you can really do anything in a Visual Basic .NET program, you must tell the compiler which parts, if any, of the .NET Framework you will be using. In this case, you will just be using the root or top-level object from the Framework, System, so add the line Imports System to the top of the code file.

You can now refer to that object, System, and use its features in your code. One of the members or parts of the System Framework class is the Console object. This object allows users to read and write through the command-line interface. For this example, use the Console.WriteLine statement to return some text to the command window. It doesn't matter what text you return; this is simply a test of outputting information. In your code, you used the text *This is where the OS Version Info will go!* to make it clear that this is only a placeholder. Save this new, modified code file (which should look like the following code) as Step2.vb, and then switch back into the command window to compile it:

```
Imports System

Public Class Step2
    Shared Sub Main()
        System.Console.WriteLine("This is where the OS Version Info will go!")
    End Sub
End Class
```

The compile statement will be almost exactly the same as in the previous step, except that you will specify the new source file name, vbc Step2.vb /t:exe. Executing that compile statement produces a file named Step2.exe, which you can then run from the command prompt by typing Step2 and pressing Enter. If your compiling worked, and there were no problems in the code, you should see the following output for your commands:

```
C:\TYVB\C1>vbc step2.vb /t:exe
Microsoft (R) Visual Basic.NET Compiler version 7.00.9254
for Microsoft (R) .NET CLR version 1.00.2914.16
Copyright  Microsoft Corp 2001. All rights reserved.


C:\TYVB\C1>step2
This is where the OS Version Info will go!
```

Adding the Version Information Functionality

You know that the code is correct up to this point (because it worked), so it provides a good starting point for the next step. What you need to do now is to get the actual operating system version information, and then output it instead of the generic bit of text. You are going to have to use the .NET Framework again to get this information, through another feature it provides, access to information about the current operating system, such as Windows 2000. This information is available through that same System object, but, instead of looking at System.Console, you use System.Environment.OSVersion. Modify the code from Step2.vb to look like the following code, and then save the file as Step3.vb.

```
Imports System

Public Class Step3
    Shared Sub Main()
        System.Console.WriteLine(System.Environment.OSVersion.ToString())
    End Sub
End Class
```

Compiling the code vbc step3.vb /t:exe isn't any different than compiling the previous two examples. This compilation produces an executable named step3.exe. Running that exe, by typing Step3 Enter into the open command-line window, produces the following output:

```
C:\TYVB\C1>step3
Microsoft Windows NT 5.0.2195.0
```

Note that the results are from a Windows 2000 (NT 5.0) computer; different results will be produced from different computers. You now have a small exe that will return the version of the operating system, certainly a useful program for network administrators at least. The application is currently named step3.exe, but its name is easily changed to something more indicative of its true purpose.

Using the Command-Line Compiler

In the previous examples, you used the command-line compiler to specify two things, the target of the compiler (/t:exe) and the source file to compile (step1.vb, for instance). The compiler worked just fine with those two options, automatically producing executables with the same name as the source file, but there are many additional options available as part of this command. Here are a few of the command-line switches that you will find most useful as you start experimenting with Visual Basic .NET:

- /target:<winexe, exe, library, or module> (can be called as /t) specifies what type of output should be created by the compiler. The winexe option creates a Windows application. The exe option, used by your examples, creates a command-line or console application, and is the default if no /t switch is used. The remaining two options, library and module, are both used to create output that cannot be used directly, but that is intended to be part of another application. You will learn more about all these output types in later days.

- /out:<filename> is used to specify the name of the created file. In your examples, you omitted this, causing vbc to use the name of your source file (Step1.vb) to create the output file (Step1.exe, for instance).

- /help (or /?) is equivalent to running vbc with no options; either way, the result is a detailed listing of all the available switches.

- /verbose makes the compiler produce more detailed output during compilation, and can help when troubleshooting.

- /reference:<filename> (/r:<filename> for short) is used to indicate to the compiler that your code requires some additional files beyond what is included by default. For instance, if you wanted to work with the System.Web portions of the .NET Framework, you would need to add an Imports System.Web line to the top of your source and then specify /r:system.web.dll when you compile your code.

Summary

Today's lesson covered some of the background of programming, Visual Basic, and .NET before creating a small program. At this point, you are ready to move on to learning the language itself, and writing more complex programs. Visual Basic is one of the most popular programming languages in the world, and you are one day further on the path to mastering it.

Q&A

Q. Why is Visual Basic .NET so different from the previous versions of Visual Basic?

A. Visual Basic has been evolving over time. Each version has been very similar to the previous one, but, at certain points, a major rewrite such as .NET is needed to make sure that the language is keeping pace with other changes in the industry, such as the Internet and distributed computing.

Q. I have heard of another .NET language, C#. Should I learn it instead of, or in addition to, Visual Basic .NET?

A. C# is a great new language, a simpler, easier to use form of C++, but no, you do not have to learn it. All .NET languages are equal in terms of their capabilities; if you can create a certain type of application in C#, you can create it in **Visual Basic .NET**. You might find that many examples from Microsoft will appear in C#, simply because it is a language that both Visual Basic programmers and Visual C++ programmers find relatively easy to read.

Workshop

The Workshop is designed to help you anticipate possible questions, review what you've learned, and get thinking about how to put your knowledge into practice. The answers to the quiz are in Appendix A, "Answers to Quizzes/Exercises."

Quiz

1. What Microsoft product was the predecessor to Visual Basic?

2. Why do all .NET languages (Visual Basic .NET, C#, and so on) share certain common features (the .NET Framework, methods of object creation and use, and more)?

3. What do you call the process of turning source code (your programs) into native machine code (such as an exe file)?

4. Consider the following code:

```
Public Class MyClass
    Shared Sub Main()
    End Sub
End Class
```

If this code was saved into a file called `MySourceCode.vb`, and then you were to execute the following command vbc /t:exe `MySourceCode.vb`, what file would be created?

Exercises

1. In today's examples, you didn't specify an output filename when compiling, which caused the compiler to use the source file's name by default. Recompile `step3.vb`, specifying an output filename of `WhatOS.exe`.

2. To get the version information, you used the `System.Environment` object, which has several more useful properties. Use the help documentation that is installed with Visual Basic (see "Getting Ready to Code" earlier in today's lesson) to find out what else is available and then make another program to output one or more of those additional properties.

DAY 2

Working with Visual Basic .NET

In Day 1, "Welcome to Visual Basic .NET," you learned some general information about programming, Visual Basic, and .NET, giving you the background you need to start building applications. Today you will be creating an actual Windows application using Visual Basic and, in the process, covering the following topics:

- Using the Visual Studio IDE
- Working with solutions, projects, and files
- Creating and running a sample Windows project

I will be starting with a walkthrough of the Visual Studio (VS) IDE. I discussed IDEs in yesterday's lesson, but a quick refresher on the meaning and purpose of an IDE will be included.

The Visual Studio IDE

An IDE (Integrated Development Environment) is intended to be a single work environment for developers. In general, source code is just text and could be entered and edited in any text editor (Notepad, for instance), and compilers can be used from the command-line without too much trouble, so an IDE is technically not required. Despite this, there are few programmers who would agree to work in a language that didn't have some form of IDE. Even the simple tasks of editing and compiling your code are greatly simplified by the Visual Studio IDE, and it provides many additional abilities that are just not possible without it.

Getting Started

Before you can use the Visual Studio IDE, it must be installed onto your machine. The process for doing this was detailed in yesterday's lesson, so check that section if you need to complete the install before continuing.

Profile Settings

The first thing you'll see when you start up Visual Studio .NET is a Web page–style interface (labeled the Visual Studio Home Page) asking you to confirm your profile settings. The concept of a profile is new in this version of Visual Studio, a variation on the concept of user preferences that gives you the capability to set a variety of different options through a single profile. The basic choices provided are designed to ease your transition into this environment depending on your particular background. This setup lead me to quickly choose the settings shown in Figure 2.1. However, within a few hours of use, I had changed the settings into something a little bit different from any of the default profiles. You'll likely end up doing the same.

For now, choose the Visual Basic Developer profile, and you can come back to this dialog later to change these settings if you want. Click Get Started to leave the profile settings page. What you are currently looking at is considered the main work area of the Visual Studio IDE, a general location that holds a variety of content, such as code that you are editing or Web pages that you are designing. It also includes a built-in Web browser, which is open by default; it is used to show a Web-ish interface to Visual Studio.

In this Home Page (see Figure 2.2), you have several useful options. The first, Get Started, is the page that will be shown whenever you open Visual Studio. Designed as a launching pad for your work, this page provides both a list of recently opened projects and a link to create a new project, enabling you to get going with a single click somewhere on this page. For now, you'll choose one of the navigation options along the left side of this page.

FIGURE 2.1

The Visual Studio .NET IDE can be customized to make it easier to transition from other development tools, including the previous version of Visual Basic.

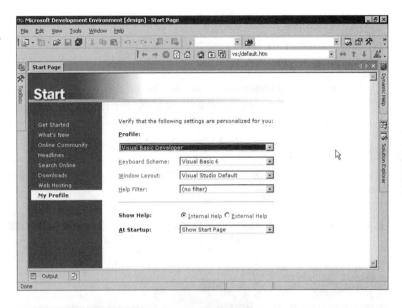

FIGURE 2.2

The Home Page provided by Visual Studio gives a functional view of projects you have recently opened, along with access to a variety of information sources.

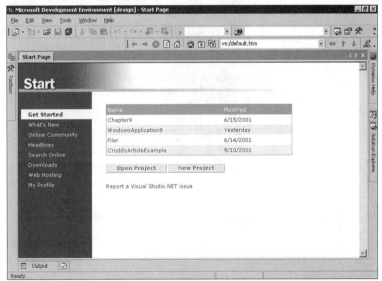

The remaining options along the side include

- Details on the new features of Visual Studio .NET. What's New links to various online resources such as newsgroups (Online Community)
- A live page of news about Visual Studio and other developer-related topics (Headlines, see Figure 2.3)

- A direct link to doing a Web search (Search Online)
- A link back to the profile selection page you were shown by default on the first run of the IDE (My Profile)

All these are valuable resources for a Visual Studio developer, making this home page a good starting point for many people. However, if you feel like adding to these options or totally replacing the entire set of pages, the complete source of the default page is made available for you under \Program Files\Microsoft Visual Studio.NET\HTML. A note of warning though—the default pages are not simple, and it would be easy to damage them beyond repair. Make a copy of the directory as a backup before you start to customize!

FIGURE 2.3

Information relevant to a Visual Basic .NET programmer can often be found on the msdn.Microsoft.com *Web site, the highlights of which are automatically displayed in sections of Visual Studio's home page.*

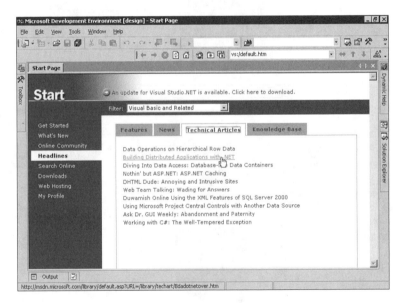

The Main Windows of the Visual Studio IDE

As useful as this home page is, it is only one of the many different windows available as part of Visual Studio, and you are going to walk through most of them in today's lesson. With the Visual Basic Developer's profile chosen, you have several windows visible already: the built-in Web browser already discussed, the Solution Explorer, the Properties, and the Toolbox, along the left side. The other windows, which I'll discuss in today's lesson, but which aren't visible by default in the current profile, are

- Object Browser
- Command/Immediate

- Task List
- Class View
- Server Explorer

There are other windows that I will cover as they become relevant later in the book.

Common Window Features

All the features of these windows, including the entire concept of multiple little windows, revolve around making the most efficient use of space. In any IDE, and especially in Visual Studio .NET, the number of available options and tools is nearly limitless, but the area of your monitor is not. One solution to this problem is to get every developer a 21-inch (or larger!) monitor. For some strange reason, that still hasn't caught on, so other methods have been developed. One such method is to divide the options available to the developer into different windows, which is the approach taken by Visual Studio .NET. Now, the goal is to make the placement of these windows both easy and flexible enough for developers to create their ideal work environment. Each of these individual windows is referred to as a *tool window*. The members of a tool window all share some common features, such as the capability to be docked/undocked, hidden, combined into tabbed groups of windows, and so on. All of them can be resized in various ways.

Docking/Undocking

With the Visual Basic Developer's profile selected, the Solution Explorer and Properties are both flush with the right side of the encompassing Visual Studio, and the Toolbox window is flush to the left side (see Figure 2.4). The placement of a window flush to another boundary is described as *docking* that window. While docked, the window is locked to that boundary along one or two sides (two sides if docked into a corner). Any of the tool windows in Visual Studio .NET can be docked, and there is no limitation as to which edges of the Visual Studio they can be docked to.

To move a docked window to another area of the screen, you can click and hold the mouse on the title bar of the tool window, and then drag the window to the new position. While you are dragging the window, an outline will appear on the screen to show where the window would be placed if you were to release the mouse button. To dock the window to another side of the IDE, simply drag, continuing to hold down the mouse button, the window to a border of the IDE and release the mouse button when the window's outline shows the desired result. On the way, you might have noticed that the outline can look as if it was not docked to any portion of the IDE (see Figure 2.5).

FIGURE 2.4

When Visual Studio .NET is set to the Visual Basic developer's profile, it arranges its windows in a close approximation of Visual Basic 6.0's IDE.

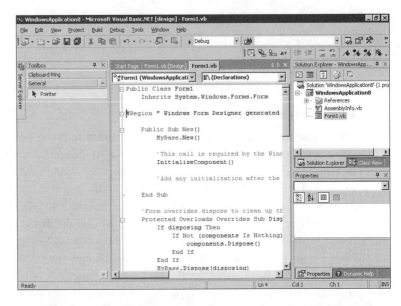

FIGURE 2.5

The outline of a window being dragged changes to indicate what would occur if you were to stop dragging it at any particular point.

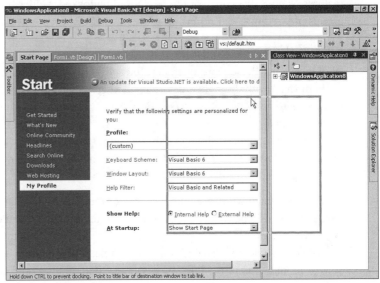

If you were to release at this point, the tool window would become "*undocked*" also known as a *floating* window (see Figure 2.6), at which point it is no longer attached to any of the IDE's borders.

FIGURE 2.6

If you have enough screen space, you can leave your windows undocked.

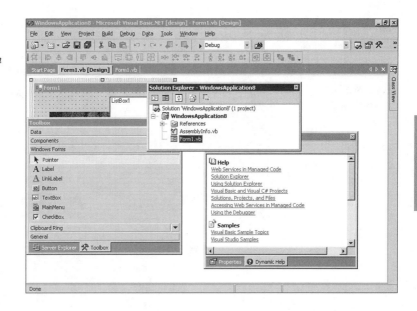

When you are undocked, you can re-dock a window by following the same procedure that you just used.

Note

It can be tricky to get a docked window back into the exact place from which you moved it, so here is a little tip: Instead of dragging a window to dock and undock it, double-click the title bar. This will undock a docked tool window, or take a floating window and put it back into its original place.

Hide

Docked or undocked, the windows still take up space on your screen, but it is possible to hide or close individual windows that you do not want to have visible. Each tool window has an X button on it (see Figure 2.7), similar to the regular close icon on other windows. Clicking this button closes the tool window, removing it from the screen.

To get the window back, you will need to use a menu option. For instance, if you click the X button on the Solution Explorer, it will disappear from view. To get it back, you need to select Solution Explorer from the View menu (or press Ctrl+R). Not too difficult, especially for a window that you don't use often, but what about those windows that you might not be using right at this moment, but do use frequently? The Visual Studio .NET IDE provides a way to recover the screen space used by those windows, while still making them easily accessible—the Auto-Hide feature. Each docked tool window has an icon on its title bar that looks like a small pushpin (see Figure 2.8).

Tool windows can be closed using the little X button, hiding them from view until you need them again.

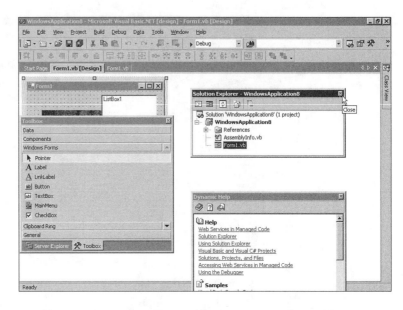

Every tool window has a small pushpin that enables you to lock the window in an open position.

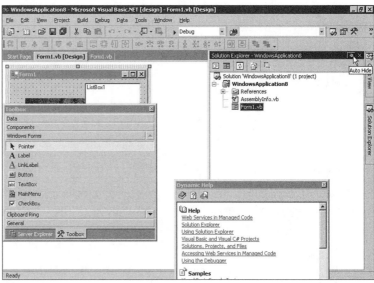

This is a toggle button that controls whether or not the window should be automatically hidden when not in use. By default, the Server Explorer window is set to use this feature and therefore shows up simply as a gray tab or button along the left side of the IDE. Hovering over this tab with the mouse pointer will cause the full Server Explorer to become visible, sliding out into view. Any tool window with the Auto-Hide option turned on will automatically be minimized into a tab along the side of the IDE on which it is docked. The hidden window will be brought into view whenever the user moves the mouse over that tab, meaning that the window will only take up space when it is needed. This feature, along with the menu option Window, Auto Hide All, is what I use to configure Visual Studio to my desired appearance (see Figure 2.9). This leaves maximum space for the main window, where code will appear when you have work open. Such an extreme interface might be unnecessary when working on a large monitor, but, as a laptop user, I find it perfect.

FIGURE 2.9

You can use Auto-Hide to maximize your center work area, which is where you will edit both code and visual objects.

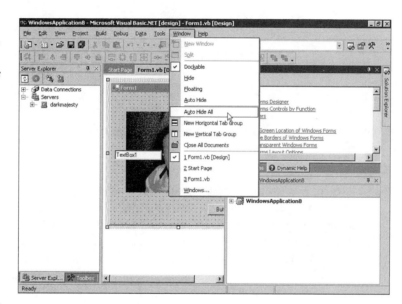

Tabs

Another space-saving feature, multiple tool windows, can be combined into a single area of the screen, where they will automatically become individual tabs in a multi-tab window (see Figure 2.10). In the Visual Basic Developer's profile, several windows have already been combined (the Solution Explorer shares space with the Class View window, and the Properties and Dynamic Help windows are similarly configured), but any combination of tool windows is possible.

To add a window to a group of tabs, or to create a tabbed window, simply drag one tool window (by clicking on its title and dragging) onto another, releasing the mouse button when the outline changes to indicate a tabbed window, displaying a small tab extension at the bottom of the outline. Removing a window is done in a similar fashion. Simply drag one of the tabs away from the group until the outline loses the tab indicator, then drag to the desired new location and release.

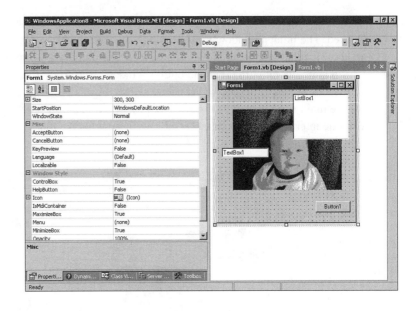

FIGURE 2.10

Tabs enable you to have many different tool windows open while using up the same amount of precious screen space.

Resizing

Any tool window can be resized, but, if the window is docked, it can only be resized along its undocked borders. To resize a window, move the mouse pointer over the edge of the window, until the pointer turns into a resizing indicator, which shows the direction of resizing allowed. When the pointer indicates that you have the mouse in the right position, click and drag to extend or retract the window's border to the desired size. Note that resizing between two docked windows is really changing both windows because one must shrink to allow the other to expand.

Toolbox

One of the more commonly used windows, the Toolbox, provides a listing of various text snippets, user interface elements, and other items that are provided for you to add into your projects. The selection of items shown depends on what is currently being edited in the main window of the IDE. For instance, if nothing, or just the Web browser, is selected in the main window, then the only available item in the Toolbox will be the Pointer icon. This icon, which is always present, is provided as a way to deselect any other item in the Toolbox window. If you were editing something, such as the HTML of the Visual Studio home page (right-click in the Web browser and select View Source), then additional tabs will be added to the Toolbox window. In the case of HTML editing, an HTML tab has been added (see Figure 2.11) containing a variety of items representing different HTML tags.

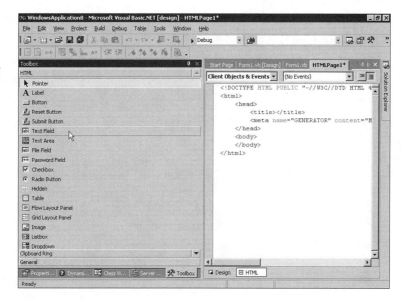

2

Any item, with the exception of the special Pointer item, can be used in one of two ways:

- Click and drag the item into the editing window (releasing when you have moved the mouse to the desired location).

- Double-click the item, which results in the item being added to the editing window at the currently selected insertion point (wherever the cursor was positioned in the editing window when the item was double-clicked).

Both these methods of using items are available for any type of document being edited, but, if a graphic user interface (any visual, nontext document such as a Windows Form) is the current document, then the preceding two options behave slightly differently. A third option also is available:

- Clicking and dragging the item onto the visual document works the same as with text, but, instead of a cursor insertion-point, you are shown an actual outline of the item as you move your mouse over the document.

- Double-clicking also works, but, because a visual document doesn't always have a currently selected insertion point, the new item is generally just created in the center of the document.

- A third option, not available with text editing, is to select the item by clicking on it once, highlighting it in the Toolbox, and then clicking and dragging on the visual document. This outlines the size and location at which you want the item to be added to the document, and the new item is created accordingly (see Figure 2.12).

FIGURE 2.12

You can draw visual elements, such as textboxes, onto a form after you have them selected in the Toolbox.

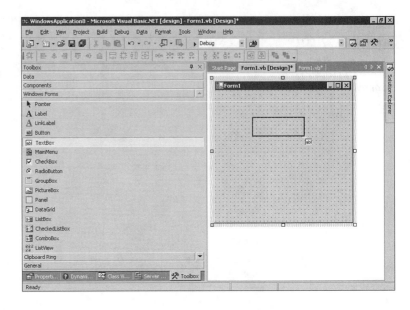

Note

There is a bit of vagueness to the preceding descriptions, which might make you wonder whether the Toolbox is more difficult to use than it seems. Well, the vagueness is a result of the nature of the Visual Studio IDE, which is designed to service a wide variety of programming languages, not all of which are even available today. With this in mind, the exact behavior of the IDE (or any part of it, such as the Toolbox) is difficult to describe. However, you can be confident that it will always work in the general fashion described previously, regardless of the language that uses it.

I will walk through an example of using the Toolbox with a visual document later in today's lesson, as you create a Windows form as part of your first application using the IDE. The Toolbox is capable of holding any arbitrary snippet of text, in addition to the provided parts for HTML editing, forms development, and many other types of work, which means that you can create your own items that represent sections of text. This feature is a useful way to take some piece of text (which can be, and likely will be, code) that you expect to use often, and make it easily available.

To accomplish this amazing feat of productivity, select the desired text in the editing window (which might involve typing the text in first), and drag this selection onto the Toolbox window. Whichever tab you drag, its text will determine where your newly created item will appear. As shown in Figure 2.13, the item will display some boring and fairly meaningless default name, such as HTML Fragment, but you can right-click it and select Rename Item to provide a proper description. Voilá! You now have a new, custom item in the Toolbox, which you can use whenever you want simply by dragging it into the editing window.

FIGURE 2.13

Code, HTML, or other text snippets can be placed on the Toolbox and then used (dragged into code and HTML editing windows) just like any other Toolbox control.

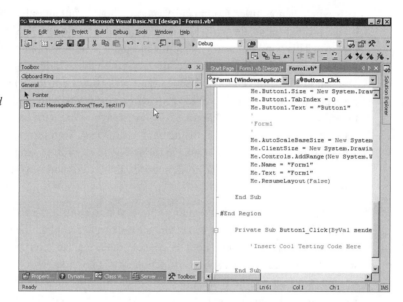

The Toolbox, as with the rest of the IDE, has many additional options that I won't be covering, such as the capability to add more tabs (tabs are those sliding sections of the Toolbox window), rename tabs, and change your view of any section's icon list. These other features are accessible through the context-menu (the right-click menu) of the Toolbox, and also are documented in the IDE help files.

Command/Immediate

Do you ever find yourself running the command console (or *DOS window*, as some like to call it) to accomplish a task? For many people, some tasks can just be done faster using the keyboard and a command-line interface than using the mouse to navigate icons, menus, and dialog boxes. Because programmer productivity is the ultimate goal, any method that might be quicker is worth trying. Visual Studio .NET includes a window that provides two console-based ways to interact with the IDE. One has been part of Visual Basic for some time, the Immediate window, and one has been present in Fox Pro for many years and has finally been added to Visual Studio, the Command window.

In terms of usage, these are really two windows, but they have been combined to make things a little bit more confusing. You can think of them as two windows (I know I am going to), after you have learned two key things: how to switch the mode of the window (from Command to Immediate and back again) and how to tell what mode the window is currently in. First things first—let's make this window visible; select View, Other Windows, Command Window from the menu, bringing up this new window.

This window, now titled Command Window, should contain only a blank line proceeded by a > prompt (almost exactly like the command console, or DOS prompt that you are used to). This window is now in Command mode, and you can enter any command you want and execute it by pressing Return. To switch this window into Immediate mode, you can just type the command `immed` (and press Return or Enter) at the provided prompt. Now, the window will have switched into Immediate mode, distinguishable from the previous state by the addition of – `Immediate` to the window's title bar and the removal of the > prompt from the actual window text. To return to Command mode, type `>cmd` and press Return (yes you have to include the > prompt yourself). Now that you know how to switch back and forth between these two modes, you can look at the purpose and use of each mode.

The Command mode of this window allows you to control the IDE using typed commands—for example, typing `File.NewProject` to accomplish the same task as selecting the File, New, Project menu item. A console interface can often be faster than a graphical user interface. This duplication of functionality is provided as a potential way to speed up your work inside the IDE. A large number of commands are available, but the quickest way to find many of them is to go through the names of the visible menus. After you have typed a name (such as `Edit`, or `File`), add a period, and you will be given a drop-down list of available commands for that menu name. Here's a short list of commands worth knowing:

```
File.NewProject
File.SaveAll
Window.AutoHideAll
```

The Immediate window provides the capability to evaluate code statements directly (immediately!). This enables you to enter a single line of code, and see the results without having to create an entire sample project. This feature is usable when you are in Break mode, which is when you have stopped the execution of a program in progress. Let's create a quick sample project, in which you will use a "breakpoint" to cause program execution to stop on a certain line of code. (The breakpoint will be covered more in Day 6, "What to Do When Good Programs Go Bad, and Making Sure They Don't," because it is really a debugging tool.)

You will use the Command window to start this example, just to get a feel for how it might be useful to you in the future. Make sure that the Command window is visible and in Command mode by selecting View, Other Windows, Command Window from the menu bar. The Command window should now be visible, and have a > prompt showing that is it in Command mode. Type in the following command **File.NewProject** and press Enter. A dialog appears, prompting you to create a new project. Select the folder named Visual Basic Projects from the list on the left and the individual project type labeled Windows Application from the box on the right. Click OK to close the dialog, creating a new blank project.

The project you have created contains only a single Windows Form, and you have yet to add any code of your own. Under the covers though, Visual Basic has placed a small amount of code into your form already, the little bit of work that is required to create and initialize the new blank form. You can see that code by right-clicking on the new form (in the center window of the IDE) and selecting View Code. This will add and select a new tab in the center window, a code window that displays the code associated with this form. Because you have added nothing to this form, the code is fairly limited, but it is enough for the example.

Select the line Form1 = Me, scrolling down to find it if necessary. Now, you want to mark this line as having a breakpoint, so that code execution will pause or "break" when it hits this line. There are three different ways to mark the line. One is to click in the margin (the light gray area on the left side of the code window), another is to right-click on the code line and choose Insert Breakpoint, and the third is to use the keyboard short-cut for this function by pressing F9. Using whichever method you want, add the break-point, and you will see a red dot appear in the margin next to the line. This dot indicates the presence of a breakpoint.

With this breakpoint in place, you can run the project, and the execution will pause when it hits this line. As with the breakpoint, there are three main ways to start a project: One is to use the toolbar button (which looks like the play button on a CD player or VCR—see Figure 2.14); another is to use the menu option Debug, Start; and the third is to use the keyboard shortcut F5. Of course, which option you use is up to personal preference. Many programmers find that, in the long run, the keyboard shortcuts are the easiest way to access the more common functions.

When you start the program running, it will quickly stop and display the line of code that you marked with a breakpoint. Now, you are in Break mode, as indicated by the [break] in the Visual Studio IDE's title bar. The yellow arrow that you can see in the margin of the code window indicates the line that is about to be executed (run). At this point, you can switch the Command window into Immediate mode and try it out.

If your Command window was visible before running the project, it should still be present, although the layout might be slightly changed as certain windows are automatically opened when you are in the midst of a running project. If the Command window isn't visible, open it by using the menu option View, Other Windows, Command Window.

FIGURE 2.14

The toolbar provides buttons to start and stop program execution, using the icons styled after a VCR's interface.

Click the window to select it (making it the active window in the IDE) and type **immed** (followed by the Enter key) to switch the window into Immediate mode. Now you can type in any Visual Basic statement, and it will be evaluated immediately (hence the name). Try the following statements:

```
? Me.Width
Me.Width = 50
? Me.Width
? 3 + 5
? 3 = 5
```

Tip

> Using the up and down arrow keys while you are in the Command/Immediate window does not always move you to different lines within the window. Instead, if you have started entering some text already, you can cycle through commands you have already executed. If you do select a past line (in the window) and start to add text to it, a copy of that line with your new changes will be automatically created at the bottom of the window. This makes any text before the last line of the window effectively read-only.

Notice the ? in front of some of the preceding statements? This indicates "print" and, without it, Visual Basic does not know what to do with statements that return a value. For instance, 3 + 5 will evaluate to 8, but, without the print statement, 8 is not a valid Visual Basic command. On the other hand, statements such as Me.Width = Me.Width * 2 are valid bits of Visual Basic code and do not require the ? in front of them.

Press F5 to make the code execution continue past the breakpoint, and the form will appear on the screen, wider than the original size if you executed the sample statements given previously. As you can see, it is possible to affect parts of your program from the Immediate window, making it an excellent tool for debugging.

Dynamic Help

This tool window is set up as a tab with the Properties window (if you are using the Visual Basic Developer's profile settings), and provides context-based documentation references to Visual Studio's help files. Instead of waiting for you to ask for help, this tool window acts proactively when you press the F1 key or select something from the Help menu. Based on your current selection or task, it displays a list of related topics. In Figure 2.15, the Dynamic Help tool window shows a set of help topics about the HTML tag currently selected in the code-editing window. In addition to the directly related help topics, this window will usually display a link to several more generic topics such as (in this case) the Coding Techniques and Programming Practices section of the documentation. This tool window also provides a quick link to the contents, index, and search sections of the help documentation through the three toolbar icons provided.

FIGURE 2.15

The Dynamic Help window tries to show you useful information even before you ask for it.

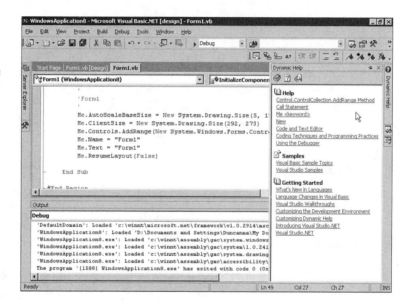

Server Explorer

This tool window (see Figure 2.16) provides a visual listing of two main resources, databases and servers. The first set of resources represents all the connections established between your project and various database servers, and enables you to explore those databases to see tables, stored procedures, and other useful information.

The second set of information, Servers, represents any machines that you can connect to and that provide a visual interface to the resources that those machines can make available to your program. These resources include performance counters, event logs, message queues, and more, all easily found through this tool window.

Day 13, "Using the Server Explorer," goes into depth on using this tool window to find and manipulate server resources.

Figure 2.16

The Server Explorer provides a visual way to view and use resources from both the local server and other machines.

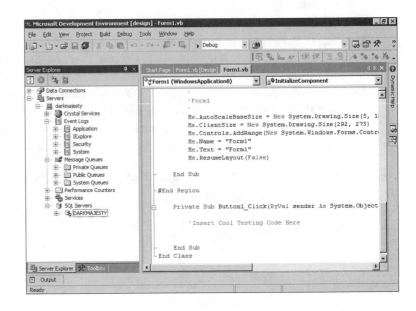

Properties

The Visual Studio IDE enables you to work with many different items, projects, solutions, forms, classes, and more, all of which possess attributes or properties. These properties are pieces of information that describe the item, such as a name for a project. Although properties are usually populated automatically with default values, you need a way to modify them. The Properties window provides this functionality. Whenever an item is selected in the IDE, the attributes of that object will be displayed in this tool window (see Figure 2.17). Some of these attributes might be read-only (they cannot be modified), but, if this is so, then you can click on them in this Properties window and change them as needed.

Solution Explorer

In many ways, the Solution Explorer is similar to the Windows Explorer feature used within Windows. It is the file management interface within Visual Studio .NET. In Visual Studio .NET, the code you create can be organized using different layers of grouping: solutions, projects, and files. The Solution Explorer window enables you to view all these objects that are currently open, in their respective groups or windows. The Solutions window contains projects—that is, individual applications and components, such as an entire system, including components to run on both the client and server. Within each Project window are all of the project's actual files (classes, forms, and other elements).

FIGURE 2.17

*When an object is
selected in the editing
window (a text box on
a form in this case),
then the Properties
window will display all
of its attributes.*

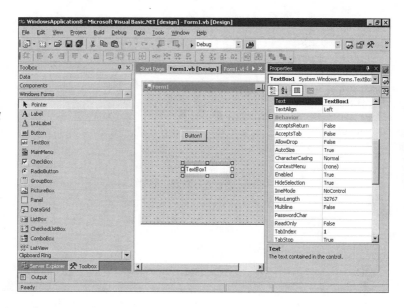

In addition to letting you view what is currently open, the Solution Explorer window
gives you a variety of functionality. Through the window, you can

- Add new files to a project (right-click the project and select Add)
- Remove files (right-click an individual file and select Remove)
- Add and remove entire projects from a Solution group (right-click on the solution
  to add a project, and right-click on a project for the option to remove it from the
  current solution)

Class View

As part of the discussion of the Solution Explorer, I explained that there could be many
different files involved in a single project or solution. Those files often correspond to the
created classes (such as a Vehicle class or an Account class), but there is no requirement
that the file organization must resemble the conceptual organization of the classes in the
project. The Class View window (see Figure 2.18) is designed to let you view the object
structure of your project and use that view to navigate within your code.

Within this window, you can collapse and expand the displayed objects, to access the
various properties and methods they expose. Double-clicking on a particular item in the
Class View will take you to that class, method, event, property, or procedure. If the item
you double-clicked on is not available as a part of your code, Class View takes you to the
definition of that portion of the class within the Object Browser (see the next section).
The Class View is useful as a way to look at your project through its defined classes,
ignoring the physical details of the actual files.

FIGURE 2.18

The Class View window shows your project organized by its objects, not by its physical files, and provides direct access to the internals of those objects.

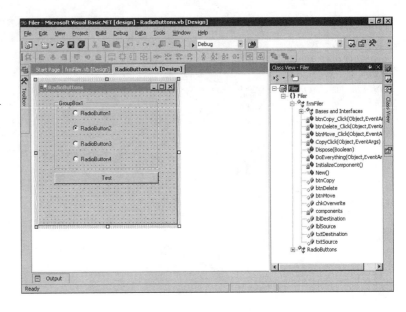

Object Browser

All programming in .NET is based on objects—objects provided for you as part of the .NET Framework, objects you create, even objects that other parts of your own team have created. All of these objects have properties and methods through which you can interact with them, but how do you know what is available? The Object Browser is designed to assist you in working with all of these objects, by enabling you to browse and search through a catalog of available objects. This catalog includes the objects (classes) exposed by any referenced class libraries, along with the classes contained within your own project. Similar in some respects to the Class View, the Object Browser goes beyond the functionality of that other window by including objects outside of your project. This window is most useful as a form of documentation or reference, enabling you to find classes within the .NET Framework or other class libraries and view the details of those classes, such as their properties and methods. In Figure 2.19, you can see the Object Browser being used to browse the contents of the `System.Data` library, displaying detailed information right down to the parameters required for a certain method call.

Task List

In any development project, even completed ones, there are likely to be a variety of outstanding tasks to be completed. Sections of the program might need performance tweaking. There might be known bugs or missing functionality that need to be remedied. When the outstanding tasks can be related to an actual area of the code, a common practice among programmers is to flag that area with comments. When the programmers consistently include certain words such as TODO or BUG in those comments, it is easier to scan through the code looking for those keywords to find the appropriate bits of code. Visual Studio .NET has formalized this process by providing an actual task list that is automatically filled with references to any section of your code that contains one of several keywords such as TODO (but, you can specify any keyword you want). Each comment found is then listed in an easy-to-use list, detailing not only the comment itself, but also the file and line at which it was found (see Figure 2.20).

2

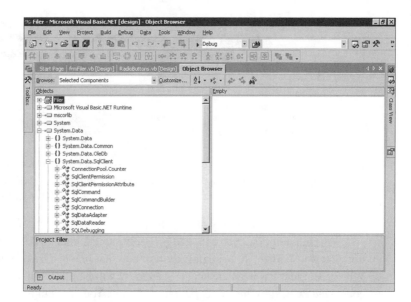

FIGURE 2.19

The Object Browser enables you to walk through the classes provided by the .NET Framework and any other libraries you have created or referenced.

Note

You can add your own keywords to the list of recognized tokens by going through the Options dialog. Under this dialog's Environment\Task List section, you have the ability to add new tokens and to specify settings for the task created when this keyword is found. Keywords will only be considered a match when they are found within comments in your code.

With a quick double-click on a task, you are immediately taken to the code, where you can get to work on whatever the outstanding task indicates. In addition to this functionality—fairly useful on its own—the task list can hold a variety of other types of tasks. Visual Studio adds other tasks automatically, such as referring to compile errors and other notable items. But, it is also possible for you to add two types of tasks to this list: code shortcuts and user-defined tasks.

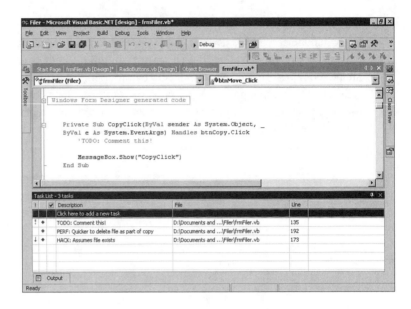

Code shortcuts are similar to comment-based tasks, but are a reference to any line of code. They do not require any special keyword. To add a code shortcut to the task list, right-click in the code-editing window and select the Add Task List Shortcut menu item.

A new task will be added to your task list, with the description defaulting to the line of code selected (although you can, and probably should, change this to whatever description you want). Then, you can quickly return to that line just by double-clicking this task. When a shortcut has been created, a blue arrow will be placed in the left margin of the code window next to the appropriate line of code. You can remove the shortcut by right-clicking on the line of code and selecting Remove Task List Shortcut or selecting the new item in the task list and deleting it directly.

The other type of task that you can create is a *user task*, one that is not associated with any particular bit of code, similar to a standard task in Outlook. A user task is added by clicking the Click Here to Add a New Task section of the task list and filling in the details. Note that, unlike other tasks, these tasks do not have the file/line fields filled in, and therefore only have two fields available, the Description and the Priority (Low, Normal, or High). If you want to create a note about a particular area of code, you likely will find it more useful to create a code shortcut and to change the priority and description to provide more detail on the actual issue.

Solutions and Projects

As discussed in the "Solution Explorer" section, multiple levels exist for grouping your code together. The first level, the solution, represents the overall system being created, whereas the individual components within it are represented by separate projects. Before you can do any code inside the Visual Studio IDE, you must set up the solution and at least one project. In this section, you will go through the basics of organizing your code, creating new projects, and working with existing projects and files. The following is a quick overview of these topics, but, in the section immediately following this one, you will get to practice these skills by creating a complete sample application.

Creating a New Project

A few different ways exist to create a new project, but the most common method uses the menu option File, New, Project. This menu option brings up a dialog showing all the different types of projects that the IDE is capable of creating (see Figure 2.21). Because the Visual Studio IDE works with a variety of languages, the dialog shows options based on the languages you have installed, and might appear differently than the one in Figure 2.21. For now, you will be creating projects based on the choices under the Visual Basic Projects folder.

FIGURE 2.21

Visual Studio has an expandable New Project dialog, which allows for new project types to be added as you install additional templates or languages.

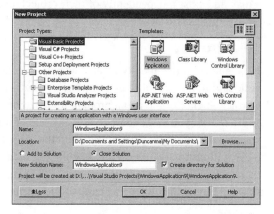

To create an application to run locally on your machine and use a Windows-based user interface (with dialog boxes and other Windows UI elements), select Windows Application from the list of project types. To complete the creation process, enter a name for your new application and, if desired, modify the suggested path. Click OK, and Visual Studio creates your new project. It is a good idea to give your projects meaningful names, even when you are just experimenting; otherwise, you will quickly have a whole group of projects named WindowsApplication1 and WindowsApplication2, making it difficult to find anything that you have been working on.

Opening an Existing Project

When you close Visual Studio, it will ask you whether you want to save what you are working on, and automatically close everything for you. When you want to get back to a previous project, you will need to open it into the IDE. Visual Studio provides a few easy ways to open past projects. One method is to use the menu through either File, Open, Project, or directly through the Recent Projects option near the bottom of the File menu. Another method is through the Get Started section of the Visual Studio home page, an HTML page that lists the projects you have recently worked with. There, you can click the particular project you want to open, or even create a new project through an additional link. Opening a new project closes any other project(s) you currently have open, unless you use the menu option File, Add Project, which adds a new or existing project into the currently open solution.

Files

Solutions and projects exist almost purely for organizational purposes; the actual code resides in one or more individual files. When you create a new project, certain files are usually created for you, such as a new Windows Form (Form1.vb) when you create a Windows application and a new Module (Module1.vb) for a Console application. These files are created on disk and exist independently of their project, enabling a single file to be shared across multiple projects if desired.

Adding Files to a Project

In addition to the files that are automatically created as part of your new project, you might also want to add additional modules, classes, forms, or other types of code files. Through either the Project menu, or the menu brought up by right-clicking the project in the Solution Explorer window, you can choose to add any one of a variety of files. Regardless of the specific menu option you choose, with the exception of Add Existing Item, all of the choices will bring you to the Add New Item dialog (see Figure 2.22). If, instead of creating a new item, you want to add an existing file from disk, the menu option Add New Existing Item will bring up a standard file open dialog for that purpose.

Saving Everything

With all these different groups (solutions, projects, and files), it is important to know how to save any work you have done, even if it is located in more than one file. In the Visual Studio IDE, this is accomplished through two different commands: Save and Save All. These commands, located on the File menu and on the toolbar, enable you to either save just the currently selected file (selected in the Server Explorer window) using the Save command or to save all open files that have been modified using the Save All command.

If you are paranoid about losing work, as I am, you will be especially interested in one of the IDE's options. Under the Options dialog (accessed through the Tools, Options menu item), you can expand the Environment group and select the Projects and Solutions item to see a set of three option buttons under a heading of On Build/Run (see Figure 2.23). These options control whether the IDE saves any modified files before starting to execute a project. This is an important setting because, if the IDE is ever going to crash, it is most likely going to do it when you run your code. This option provides an easy way to ensure that all your changes are saved every time before you run your code.

FIGURE 2.22

Just like the New Project dialog, the interface to add new project items is expandable.

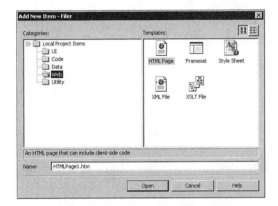

FIGURE 2.23

Always check these Save On Build settings when you use a new computer, to avoid losing a few hours of code.

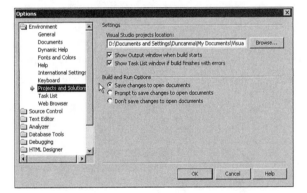

Creating Our First Windows Application

Now that you have learned some of the basics of using the Visual Studio IDE, you can put that information to use building an application without getting into very much code. This exercise will focus on using the IDE itself, which means that you are going to be creating a relatively simple application. For this example, you will make a Windows application (an application that uses the Windows user-interface and runs locally on your machine) that allows a user to enter two numbers. The application will then add the numbers, displaying the final result.

Create the Project

Using the menus, choose the File, New, Project command, bringing up the New Project dialog. Under the Visual Basic category, select the Windows Application icon and change the project name from WindowsApplication(x)—the numbered default name—to **Adder** (unless you are bothered by snakes, in which case you can name the project whatever you want). The new project will already contain a form, which is all you need to get started on the application. Visual Studio automatically creates a Solution folder to hold your new project, naming it Adder as well. Click OK after you have entered the correct project and solution names.

Develop the User-Interface

You need to have three text boxes and a single button on the form. Positioning is not all that important, but you might want to make your interface look something like Figure 2.24. Double-click Form1 in the Server Explorer, bringing it up into the designer window in the center of the IDE. Now, with the form in Design mode, select or open the Toolbox window. This window, which will show all the available objects that can be placed onto your form, contains a TextBox control and a Button control. To place one of these controls onto your form, click and drag the control into position on the form. When it is on the form, select the control and use its handles to resize it to the desired shape and size. Play with resizing and moving these controls until you get all three text boxes and the single button onto the form and looking like the example (Figure 2.24). After everything is in place, you will change a few properties of these controls.

FIGURE 2.24

Arrange the three text boxes and one button on your form to approximate this appearance.

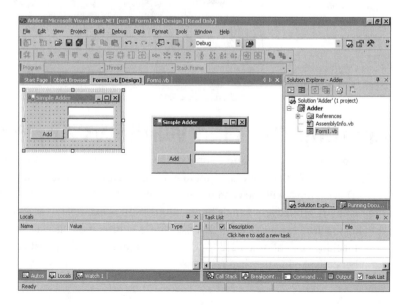

Select the first text box (the one closest to the top on the form) and display the Properties window (press F4 or select View, Properties Window from the menu, if the window is not already visible). Many different properties are listed, but you are only going to change two of them:

- Text (under the Appearance group)　Represents the contents of the text box. Erase the contents of this property to make the text box blank when the program starts.
- (*Name*) (under the Design group)　In the code, you will refer to this text box using the name in this property, which defaults to a relatively meaningless name, such as Text2 or Text1. For the example, change this to **txtFirstValue**.

Continue with the other two text boxes, changing their Text property to blank and their names to **txtSecondValue** and **txtResult**, respectively.

Now select the button to display its attributes in the Properties window. For this object, you will also be changing only two values, (*Name*) to **btnAdd** and Text to **Add**.

Finally, just because you can, you will change one of the properties of the form itself. Select the form (click somewhere on the form that is not another object) and scroll through the list of properties to find the Text property in the Appearance group. For a form, this property represents its caption (the text displayed on the form's title bar), which you can set to **Simple Adder** for the example.

Running the Project

Although you have entered no code, the project can still be run just as it is now. The Visual Studio IDE lets you run the program within the IDE, without creating an actual executable (an .exe file, for instance). You can quickly run the code as much as necessary while developing and, most importantly, perform a variety of debugging tasks while the program is running. More information on debugging applications is provided in Day 6, but, for now, it is important to realize that there is a difference between running your code within the IDE and generating an actual executable file. Creating an executable, or other type of output file from your project, is called *building* and is covered in the next section.

To run a project within the IDE, select Start from the Debug menu, press F5, or use the toolbar button that looks like a right-facing arrow (or the play button on a VCR). Try this now, with the Adder project you already have open, and you will see the form that you have been designing appear in front of the Visual Studio IDE. Without your having written a single line of code, the form appears fairly functional. You can drag it around and minimize it, all because of the underlying .NET Framework and the IDE that allows you to visually create a user interface and that produces the code required to make it work.

Although you have written no code, a great deal of code has already been generated by the IDE, and that is what is being executed when the project is run.

Building the Project

Building a project is the creation of an executable or other output files. For a Windows application like the example, this means compiling your code into an .exe file that can be run outside of the Visual Studio IDE. This is an essential step if you intend for a project to be used by anyone other than other developers, although you can mostly avoid it during development by running your project within the IDE.

Project Build Settings

To build a project, select Build from the Build menu (not very creative menu names, but easy to understand), which will appear to do very little. Without giving you much in the way of information, the default Build settings have created an `Adder.exe` file for you, placing it within the bin subdirectory of your project folder. Unless you chose to customize the displayed path when you created this project, your project should be located at `My Documents\Visual Studio Projects\Adder`, and the executable at `\bin\Adder.exe` within that directory. To see all these default settings, and perhaps to change them, right-click your project in the Solution Explorer window and select Properties from the context menu that appears. The property dialog for your project contains a variety of settings, but the ones that are relevant to the build process are described in the following.

Under Common Properties\General:

- Assembly name   This value provides the first part of the filename for your output file. In the case of the example, it is `Adder`, so `Adder.exe` is created. Change it to **MyAdder**, and `MyAdder.exe` is created when you build.

- Output type   Tells the IDE what type of file is to be created from building this project, an .exe if Windows Application or Console Application is selected, or a .dll, if Class Library is selected.

- Startup object   Indicates the part of the project that should be run when the application is executed, by default. For the example, it should be `Adder.Form1` to indicate that the form should be automatically run. Note that, if you change, even temporarily, the Output Type from Windows Application to anything else, this property will also change and can end up set incorrectly.

Cancel the entire project property dialog (by pressing the Cancel button along the bottom of the form) if you feel you have changed something that you do not know how to fix.

All the Common Properties\Version settings are stored in the output files when the project is built, and are visible as part of the property information for the finished executable (see Figure 2.25). While you are learning Visual Basic, the information entered into this dialog is likely irrelevant, but, when you are creating an application that will be deployed to users, you should consider the information on this page very carefully. At the very least, make sure that you have entered meaningful version numbers into this page because these numbers provide a definitive method for users to check which release of an application they have.

FIGURE 2.25

When you view an executable or DLL's properties, you can see all the information specified before it was built.

Common Properties\Build, despite the name, contains only a single property that is directly relevant to the build process. The Application Icon value determines the appearance of the final .exe in Windows, and allows you to select any icon file (.ico) you want.

Although they are not the only other settings that affect the build, the last items I will mention are under Configuration Properties\Build. There you will find various debug-related settings as well as the Output Directory setting, which determines where the executable or other created files will be placed.

Build Configurations

At the top of the Project property dialog is a drop-down list marked Configuration. Solution Configurations are a useful feature of the Visual Studio IDE, allowing you to create more than one group of settings for the same project. By default, two configurations are provided (Release and Debug), designed to indicate whether you are building output for testing purposes (Debug) or for actual deployment (Release). The settings for these default configurations are a good example of the purpose of Solution Configurations, setting the status of a variety of debugging features and even setting a different output location for each.

Using the Configuration Manager (see Figure 2.26), you can create as many different groups of settings as you want, or even remove an existing configuration. For now, you will likely want to leave the settings as they are, selecting the Release version of the output when you are deploying the project, and the Debug version when you are testing.

FIGURE 2.26

The Configuration Manager allows you to create different configurations for different purposes, (testing, debugging, user acceptance, release, and so on), each of which can have different Build settings.

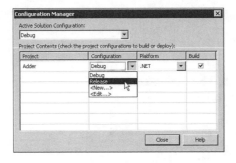

Creating an Executable

The best way to learn about a feature of the IDE is to use it, which means that it is time to build the sample project and produce an executable. Click the Build option on the Build menu, and you see a quick flash of information in the Output window (shown at the bottom of your screen, if you have not moved it around). If all goes well, and there are no errors in any code you have added or changed, the Build process produces an executable file. The file itself, which is named `Adder.exe`, is created in the `bin` subdirectory of your project folder (by default, `My Documents\Visual Studio Projects\Adder\`). Minimize the Visual Studio IDE, use Windows Explorer to find the file, and then double-click it to run your newly created Windows application. The form, with its various text boxes and buttons, appears to show you that the program is running, and it continues running until you close that same form. This executable, along with the .NET Framework, is all that you would need to deploy to a user's machine for the user to be able to run your program.

Adding Our Own Code

Up to this point, the sample project you have been working on has contained only code that was generated by the Visual Studio IDE, which has been great for showing a form but accomplishes no other task. As you might have guessed from the names and layout of the form, this application will add the values in the first and second text box and place the result into the third and final text box. To accomplish this, you will need to add code to the project that will run when the user clicks the Add button.

Using the IDE makes this a very direct process: Double-click the form in the Solution Explorer to make sure its Design view is visible, and then double-click the Add button. This will take you into the form's Code view, and into a subroutine that has been added by the IDE. A control, such as this button or text boxes or other form components, can have events associated with it. Most of a control's events represent actions performed on them such as being clicked, double-clicked, selected, and deselected. It is possible to create procedures that will be executed when one of these events occurs, and, by default, those procedures are designated by their name (the control name, btnAdd, followed by the event, Click). It is possible to associate procedures with events, regardless of their name, but, in this case, the btnAdd_Click procedure will be executed if the user clicks on the button. It is easy to try out this functionality by using a very useful feature of the .NET Framework, the MessageBox class. This class is part of the section of the .NET Framework that provides the forms, buttons, text boxes, and other interface elements, and is therefore available to any project in which you are using those objects. The MessageBox class enables you to display a message in a dialog box with a single line of code, like this:

```
MessageBox.Show("The Button has been clicked")
```

This code displays a dialog like the one shown in Figure 2.27. The simplicity of using this class makes it perfect for use as a testing or debugging tool. Add the preceding code line to the btnAdd_Click subroutine and then run the project by pressing F5. After the form appears, try clicking on the button. Every click should cause the message box to appear, showing you that the code in btnAdd_Click gets executed whenever the button is pressed.

FIGURE 2.27

The MessageBox *class provides an easy way to display information to the screen and is commonly used in the debugging/testing phases.*

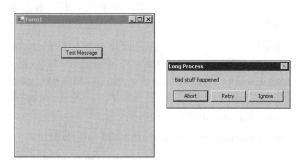

Now that you can see how to execute code in response to a button click, you can create the real code for your project. The code needs to add two values together to produce a result, which sounds easier than it really is. The values you want are the contents of your text boxes, available through the Text property of those controls, but before you can use them in a mathematical equation (adding them together), you have to convert them from strings (text) into numbers. The following code, if put in place of the MessageBox call you added earlier, would accomplish what you need:

```
txtResult.Text = (CInt(txtFirstValue.Text) _
    + CInt(txtSecondValue.Text)).ToString
```

This code converts the contents of the two text boxes into numbers (integers, in this case), adds them together, and then coverts the result back into a string (text), so that it can be placed into the third text box. It takes quite a few steps for something that sounds easy enough when first described, and the end result might seem a little confusing. It will all become clearer as you continue on to Day 3, "Introduction to Programming with Visual Basic .NET."

Summary

The concept of an IDE is to provide an environment in which you can write, edit, execute, and debug your programs, and the Visual Studio IDE provides all those features and more. Today's lesson covered the basic features of the IDE and the purpose of each of its main windows. It also walked you through the creation of a simple Windows application. From this point on, you will be using the IDE frequently, although you will not always be working with any visual elements (such as forms and controls). Hence, you will be learning more about it and its features all the time. Although it might seem a little confusing and overwhelming now, the IDE is the tool that you'll use to do your programming, so over time you will become familiar with it.

Q&A

Q. Do I have to use the IDE, or can I just stick with a text editor and the command line?

A. With Visual Basic .NET, it is possible for you to do everything using just the command-line and a text editor, but the IDE provides a large number of features to make development a much easier process. IntelliSense, statement completion, and color-coded editing all make the creation of code more enjoyable, and the debugging features are hard to do without.

Q. Can I add my own features to the Visual Studio IDE?

A. Most certainly! The IDE supports customization through several different methods, including macros and add-ins. I will not be covering the customization of the IDE in this book, but, for now, take a look at the great sample macros under the menu option Tools, Macros, Macros IDE.

Workshop

The Workshop is designed to help you anticipate possible questions, review what you've learned, and get you thinking about how to put your knowledge into practice. The answers to the quiz are in Appendix A, "Answers to Quizzes/Exercises."

Quiz

1. If you want to see all the files that are a part of your project, what IDE window would you use?

2. What is the default location of new Visual Studio projects?

3. How can you choose an icon for an application you are building in Visual Studio?

4. If the Command window is in Immediate mode, how can I switch it to Command mode, and how can I switch it back?

2

Exercise

Just as you did in today's lesson, use the MessageBox class to add messages into other event procedures and see when they are called. Try selecting txtResult from the first drop-down list in the code editing window and then TextChanged from the second drop-down to work with this event.

DAY 3

Introduction to Programming with Visual Basic .NET

Now that you've become more familiar with the Visual Basic .NET development environment, it's time to begin writing code. Although Visual Basic .NET makes it easy to write a simple program without using much code, any program simpler than a demo will need to keep track of information, and do simple calculations and similar tasks. To write code that performs these tasks, you'll need a good understanding of variables. By understanding the use and types of variables, you're creating the foundation for your understanding of Visual Basic .NET. Similarly, just as when you began learning simple arithmetic, you will need to learn some of the simple operators that can be used to work with number and string variables in your programs. Today, you will learn

- The types of variables you can create with Visual Basic .NET
- Some simple operators and functions available in Visual Basic .NET
- The fundamentals of writing code in Visual Basic .NET, including how to write procedures

Variables and Assignment

Variables and assignment are at the core of every programming language. Variables enable you to store information for later use, and assignment is the way you get information into variables.

What Is a Variable?

A variable is a bucket. It's a place to hold information until you need it. You will use variables throughout your programs to hold temporary values during calculations, to store user input, and to prepare information that will be later displayed to users.

Available Variable Types

Just as with pants, one size does not fit all variables. Although it is possible to create and use a variable that is capable of holding anything, it's not always the best solution. It's easy to imagine that a variable holding strings must do something different from a variable designed to hold numbers. In addition, even different types of numbers require different variable types. Some numbers, such as 1 or 5280, don't have a decimal place, whereas 3.14159265358979 and 16.50 do. A variable made to hold a number with a decimal must do something specifically to keep track of the values after the decimal. Of course, that means that decimal numbers *probably* take up more memory. Any time a computer or program does more work, it usually needs more memory. So, it is important to keep in mind not only the type of information you need to store, but also the amount of memory the computer will have to manipulate to keep track of the variable.

There are three broad types of variables you can create with Visual Basic .NET. The first set encompasses variables that hold simple values, such as numbers or strings. There are many of these, each designed to hold values of various sizes. The second category is complex variables, which hold some combination of simple variables, and include arrays and user-defined types. *Arrays* are variables that hold a series of other variables, and *user-defined types* enable a user to create new types of variables. The third category of variables is object variables.

User-defined types (also known as *structures*) and object variables will be covered later, on Day 7, "Working with Objects." Today's discussion of variables will focus on simple variables and arrays.

Simple Variables

As described previously, the simple variable types "hold" values such as numbers and words. So, you might think that there only needs to be two types of variables: numbers and words. However, there are actually a number of different simple variable types— each made to hold different sizes or kinds of numbers or strings.

Try to use the best variable type for the situation. Sometimes, you only need to keep track of a small number—for example, if you're keeping track of the months of the year. Other times, you need to work with big numbers with many decimal places—for example, if you're writing a program that performs engineering or scientific calculations.

The simple variables can be divided into four subgroups. The first, and largest, group is for integers, numbers that have no decimal places. The second group is used for numbers that have decimal places. Strings and characters make up the third group, and the fourth group is best described as "other." Let's look at each of these groups and see when it is appropriate to use each.

Integer Variables

NEW TERM   The *integer variables* hold the familiar whole numbers (that is, numbers without decimal places). Integers are one of the most common variables you will use in programs, and the easiest for computers to deal with. Because of this ease, they should be your first choice as a variable type when you need to work with numbers. Table 3.1 shows a number of different integer variables, each designed to hold numbers of different sizes, and use different amounts of memory. The amount of memory used is measured in bytes. (One byte contains eight bits, which is just a fancy way of saying that each byte has eight 1's or 0's, or a combination of 1's and 0's.) Although there is no harm in using a variable designed to hold larger values than needed, it wastes memory. In addition, it could cause your program to run slower because it would have to keep track of larger sections of memory, even when that memory is never used.

TABLE 3.1   Integer Variable Types

Data Type	Size (Bytes)	Range	Comments
Byte	1	0 to 255	Rather small, and unlike the other integer data types, the Byte does not support negative numbers. This is because the Byte represents the value that the computer actually stores for each byte in memory. In order to store negative numbers, the computer uses part of each byte to hold the "negative" part. This is useful when keeping track of small numbers that are never negative, such as days in a month, or months in a year.
Short	2	–32,768 to 32,767	A handy, small integer variable. You can use a Short whenever you don't need the full range of an Integer, for example, if you were writing a program to count the number of employees of a company that only had a few thousand employees.

TABLE 3.1 continued

Data Type	Size (Bytes)	Range	Comments
Integer	4	–2,147,483,648 to 2,147,483,647	The standard integer variable. For the most part, the Integer is the fastest type of variable to use, as it requires the computer to do the least amount of work. One use for a variable of this type would be to track the number of sheep in New Zealand (approximately 47,394,000 in 1997).
Long	8	–9,223,372,036, 854,775,808 9,223,372,036, 854,775,807	The perfect variable type for those times when you are working with really, really big numbers (that's –9 quintillion to +9 quintillion, or $\pm 9 \times 10^{18}$, for those keeping track). A Long would be useful if you were tracking the number of stars in the universe (estimated to be about 10^{22}).

Numbers with Decimal Places

A lot of number crunching is done without decimal places. However, more calculations, especially in engineering, finance, and science, require that you also keep a decimal value. Table 3.2 describes the two main decimal variable types. Deciding which to use depends on the degree of accuracy you need to track, rather than the size of values, because they all can hold rather large numbers. In case you don't remember scientific notation from school, the superscript number above the 10 is the number of times you need to multiply by 10 (if positive) or divide by 10 (if negative). Therefore 10^6 is 10 six times, or 1,000,000, and 10^{-6} is 0.000001.

TABLE 3.2 Decimal Variable Types

Data Type	Size (Bytes)	Range	Comments
Single	4	-3.402823×10^{38} to $-1.401298 \times 10^{-45}$ for negative numbers; 1.401298×10^{-45} to 3.402823×10^{38} for positive numbers	Don't worry too much about the size of those numbers in the range. The Single can keep track of very large (or very small) numbers. The important measure for a Single is accuracy. The name Single denotes that this variable type is for *single-precision floating point numbers*. That's computer-speak meaning: "It's really only good at holding seven important digits." Look at each of the numbers in the range.

TABLE 3.2   continued

Data Type	Size (Bytes)	Range	Comments
			Notice that each of them has a number before the decimal place, and six following it, plus the exponent (the number above the 10). So, although the `Single` is good at storing both large and small numbers, it's not as accurate as the others, and could cause rounding errors if you do a lot of calculations with really large, or really small, numbers. The `Single` variable type would be useful in a program where less accuracy is needed.
Double	8	-1.797693134 86231×10^{308} to -4.940656458 41247×10^{-324} for negative numbers; 4.940656458 41247×10^{-324} to 1.797693134 86232×10^{308} for positive numbers	The `Double` is a "double-precision floating point" variable, so it holds twice as many significant digits as the `Single`, or 15 decimal places. Use a `Double` whenever you are doing calculations with large numbers, or when you want to avoid the rounding errors that can happen with the `Single`, such as when doing calculations in engineering or scientific applications.

Strings and Characters

Numbers are fine if you need to track quantities or time, but you also need to deal with words frequently in programming. Visual Basic .NET gives you variables for storing strings: the `Char` and the `String`. The `Char` is good for storing only a single character (thus the name), whereas the `String` can hold strings of great length. Table 3.3 describes the two data types in more detail.

TABLE 3.3   String Variable Types

Data Type	Size (bytes)	Range	Comments
Char	2	One character	Good for holding a single character.
String	10 + 2 per character	Up to 2 billion characters	Use a `String` to hold that novel you always wanted to write. If you assume five characters on average per word, and 250 words per page, a single `String` variable can hold 1.7 million pages of text.

Why does each `Char` and each character in a `String` take up two bytes? After all, there are only 26 characters used in English, plus numbers and symbols—surely, you don't need two bytes (65,536 possible values). You wouldn't if every language used the same character set.

NEW TERM That scenario is what the formerly popular *ASCII* (or ANSI) character set defined. In ASCII, one byte equals one character, and every computer that used ASCII always positioned the same characters at the same position in the list. So the ASCII value 65 was always the letter "A," and the symbol "@" was had the value 64. If you wanted to do the same for all the other symbols people use in writing, however, you needed more characters. To accommodate this, a new system was developed, called *Unicode*.

With Unicode, each character is represented as two bytes. This allows for the storage of all the characters in the ASCII chart, as well as characters for Russian, Greek, Japanese and Thai languages, for mathematics, and so on. In Unicode, 65 still represents the letter "A", but 8800 is the character for . The Japanese Hiragana character "No" is represented as character 12398. Visual Basic .NET uses the Unicode values for all characters, so the `Char` uses two bytes, and each character in a `String` adds two bytes of additional storage space.

Other Simple Variable Types

It never fails when you try to categorize things. Something always defies being categorized (just imagine the first zoologist to come upon the platypus). Likewise, there are some variables that don't fit neatly into the previously described categories. In Visual Basic .NET, there are two such "other" variable types, the `Boolean`, and the `Date`. They are described in more detail in Table 3.4.

TABLE 3.4 Other Simple Variable Types

Data Type	Size (Bytes)	Range	Comments
Boolean	2	True or False	So, if it's just holding a True or False, why is it two bytes? Visual Basic has traditionally used 0 and –1 for False and True. Defining these two values requires two bytes.
Date	8	January 1, 100 to December 31, 9999	The Date variable is capable of holding most dates you will deal with (unless you're a historian or geologist). It also is aware of all the rules for dates (such as adding a day in leap years), so if you add 1 to the Date variable value of "February 28, 2000," you will get "February 29, 2000," but if you do the same for "February 28, 2001," you will get "March 1, 2001." The only real limitation of the Date variable is its size.

Note

You could use another data type to store dates such as a `String`, or an `Integer` representing the number of days after some specific date, but why bother? We all know the problems that can lead to (especially after enjoying all the power outages, nuclear plant explosions and other failures on January 1, 2000).

3

Declaring Variables

Now that you know the types of variables available, how do you create them in your programs? The simplest way is with the `Dim` (short for "Dimension") keyword, followed by the name of the variable, the keyword `As`, and finally the type of the variable. It looks like

```
Dim iSomeNumber As Integer
```

This would create the new variable `iSomeNumber`, which takes up four bytes and can hold a number as large as +/– 2 billion. Here are some more possible variable declarations:

```
Dim sFirstName As String
Dim dblGrossDomesticProduct As Double
Dim bLearned As Boolean
```

One new feature in Visual Basic .NET is the capability to give a value to a variable as you are creating it. You simply assign a value to the new variable on the same line as the `Dim` statement:

```
Dim dtDateOfMagnaCartaSigning As Date = #June 15, 1215#
Dim lPeopleOnEarth As Long = 6000000000
```

We'll look at some other ways of declaring variables later, when we discuss scope.

Arrays

A variable's capability to hold one of anything is handy, even essential, in programming. However, you might need to store a number of related items. For example, if you were writing a program to play chess, the squares on the board would need to be represented as a collection of related items. You use *arrays* to create variables that will store all the related items together. For the chess program, you would likely store the chessboard as an array of positions, each position holding the type of chess piece (or none) at that position. If you did not use an array variable, you would have to use 64 separate variables. You might also need to track a list of strings, for example, a list of the names of students in a class. Whenever you need to store a list of items, you use an array.

As with declaring simple variables, you declare an array with the `Dim` keyword. However, there are some differences between simple variable declarations and array declarations because arrays are collections of variables. Listing 3.1 shows three possible ways of declaring arrays.

LISTING 3.1   Declaring Arrays

```
1  'Simple declaration
2  Dim iValues(3) As Integer
3  Dim dtDates() As Date
4  Dim I As Integer
5  For I = 1 To 3
6     iValues(I-1) = I
7  Next

8  'Changing the size of an existing array
9  ReDim dtDates(4)
10 'fill the list of dates
11 dtDates(0)="6/15/1215" 'Signing of Magna Carta
12 dtDates(1)="8/28/1962" 'Martin Luther King Jr. delivers "I have a dream"
13 dtDates(2)="7/20/1969" 'Apollo 11 lands on Moon
14 dtDates(3)="2/14/1946" 'ENIAC unveiled to public
15 'Declaration with Initialization
16 Dim sMonths() As String = {"Jan","Feb","Mar","Apr","May","Jun", _
17    "Jul","Aug","Sep","Oct","Nov","Dec"}

18 'Using arrays
19 Console.WriteLine("")
20 Console.WriteLine("Second value in iValues = {0}", iValues(1))
21 Console.WriteLine("Third date in dtDates = {0}", dtDates(2))
22 Console.WriteLine("Eleventh month of the year = {0}", sMonths(10))
```

ANALYSIS In the first example, `iValues` is declared as a three-member array. Each item in the array is an `Integer`. That much should make sense. The potentially confusing part is in the way you refer to each member of the array. This is shown in the `For...Next` loop beginning at lines 5 through 7 (Note that we will be covering the `For...Next` loop tomorrow). Notice that the three members of the array are actually numbered beginning with 0 and going up to 2. Therefore, the second member of the array is at position 1, not 2.

Note   It's worth noting that computers, unlike people, always prefer to begin counting at zero. The overall reasons are best left in the recesses of their tiny silicon minds, but we should be aware of this, especially around arrays.

The second array created, the months of the year, is declared and initialized. Just as you can initialize simple variables as you declare them, you can do the same with arrays. In the case of arrays, however, you put each of the elements of the array in a comma-delimited list, wrapped in braces (curly brackets), as shown on line 16. This creates a 12-member array, with each element holding a string. Remember, however, that if you wanted to refer to each element, they are numbered from 0 to 11—so sMonths(10) would be "Nov", not "Oct".

The final declaration is of a dynamically sized array. This array can be resized later to the correct size with the ReDim keyword as shown on line 10. Just as with the other array types, the items of the dynamic array are numbered from 0 to I minus 1. After the array is sized, you can then use it as any other array. This form of declaration is useful if the size of the array depends on the value of another variable, so that it wouldn't be known until runtime.

3

Caution

> I have repeated the fact that all arrays begin with 0 in Visual Basic .NET because, previously, Visual Basic might not have operated that way. In versions of Visual Basic before Visual Basic .NET, you could use the Option Base 1 declaration at the beginning of a module to ensure that all arrays created in that module begin with 1. Alternatively, when declaring arrays, you could define the starting and ending array members, as shown in the following declaration. Neither of these options is available with Visual Basic .NET arrays.
>
> Therefore, the following line of code is not valid in Visual Basic .NET:
>
> ```
> Dim sngValues(15 To 51) As Single
> ```

Assignment

Assignment has been simplified in Visual Basic .NET. Earlier Visual Basic versions (Visual Basic 4.0 to 6.0) had two different ways of assigning a value to a variable—one for simple variables (including structures and arrays) and one for object variables. Fortunately, the developers of Visual Basic .NET decided to remove the assignment method used for object variables, and rely only on the method used for simple variables. You assign values to variables (either simple or object) by putting the variable left of an equal sign, as shown in the following code:

```
iSomeVar = 1234
oObjectVar = New Something()
```

Note

In Visual Basic version 4.0 to version 6.0, the assignment lines shown previously would have appeared like this

```
iSomeVar = 1234
Set oObjectVar = New Something
```

However, the rules of when to use Set were confusing, so Microsoft removed the need for the Set keyword.

Constants

Constants are another class of values that you can use in your Visual Basic .NET programs. *Constants* are values that do not change, either for the lifetime of your program, or ever. For example, the months in a year, the value of pi, and the database server from which your program retrieves data are all constant values. You can define a value as being constant when you declare it. Any attempts to change the value of a constant will be marked as an error while you are still in the IDE (Integrated Development Environment), and before you attempt to run the application. Constants are declared using one of the two forms shown in the following code:

INPUT

```
Const PI = 3.1415 As Double
Const DSN As String = "Random"
```

ANALYSIS If the type of the constant is not described in a declaration, the compiler must use the value type that best fits. However, it does not always select the best possible type. Generally, when declaring constants, if you do not include the type of the value, Visual Basic .NET will create the following variable types

- Long   For any undeclared whole numbers.
- Double   For any undeclared decimal numbers. Note: If the value is actually too large for a Double, it will be truncated.
- String   For any character values.

Note

Declare the type you want when declaring constants, just as you do when declaring variables.

Some Suggested Naming Standards

With all the different types of variables, and so many programmers using them, there are many possible names you can use when declaring variables. This can lead to a problem when you see the variable later. Unless you see the declaration, you might have difficulty knowing the variable's type. Similarly, if you inherit some code another developer has written, you might need to spend some time before you understand how they have named their variables. Naming conventions, preferably shared naming conventions, will reduce both of these difficulties by identifying the type of the variable.

A commonly used naming convention is to add a lowercase prefix to your variable names. The prefix identifies the type of variable. Table 3.5 shows one suggested set of prefixes.

TABLE 3.5 Suggested Naming Conventions

Variable Type	Prefix	Example
Byte	byt	bytAge
Short	sht	shtCount
Integer	i or int	iSheep
Long	l or lng	lPopulation
Single	sng	sngThrust
Double	d or dbl	dblInterest
Char	c	cMiddleInitial
String	s or str	sName
Boolean	b	bIsOpen
Date	dt	dtHireDate
User-defined types	Two or three important characters from the structure name	Variables created, based on Point and Rectangle structures could be called ptLocation and recSize.
Constants	No prefix. Name is all uppercase, with each word separated with underscores (_).	PI, TAX_RATE
Enumerations	Two or three significant characters	dowWeekDay, colBackColor

Note Why this mishmash of single, double, and triple characters? I have to admit that the prefixes I use have changed over the years. My basic philosophy was originally to use a single character, to limit the amount of distraction caused by the prefixes. However, some prefixes would only cause more confusion. For example, what would be the data type of sValue? It could be a Short,

3

`Single`, or `String`. For data types that start with the same letter, I have extended the prefix to multiple characters. I must admit, however, I still tend to use s for strings because it has been used so commonly. (You have to make some sacrifices to avoid carpal tunnel syndrome).

When you first start using these prefixes, you might find they are a little distracting. However, the prefixes quickly become natural, and the information they provide will be invaluable.

Simple Calculations

Just having some values lying around does not make a program. You need to do something with the values. You can perform math on the values, or you can do something more substantial. Similarly, to make your programs more understandable, you will often need to use or create procedures. Visual Basic .NET will provide some of these procedures; you will write others. These procedures range from the operators, which provide many of the common mathematical calculations, to more complex functions that could affect strings or numbers.

Using Operators

In Visual Basic .NET, operators perform simple calculations and similar "functions." Most of the operators in Visual Basic .NET should be familiar to you as common algebraic symbols. However, some of them are unique to programming. Table 3.6 lists the most commonly used operators.

TABLE 3.6 Common Operators in Visual Basic .NET

Operator	Use	Example
=	Assigns one value to another	`X = 6`
+	Adds two values	`Y = X + 7` (Y holds 13)
-	Subtracts one value from another	`Y = X - 4` (Y holds 2)
*	Multiplies two values	`Y = X * 2` (Y holds 12)
/	Divides one value by another	`Y = X / 2` (Y holds 3)
\	Divides one value by another, but only returns a whole number	`Y = X \ 3` (Y holds 1)
Mod	Short for modulus; returns the remainder for a division	`Y = X Mod 3` (Y holds 2)
&	Combines two strings	`S = "Hello " & "World"` (S holds "Hello World")

TABLE 3.6 continued

Operator	Use	Example
+=	Shorthand for adds a value and assigns the result	X += 2 (X holds 8)
-=	Shorthand for subtracts a value and assigns the result	X -= 3 (X holds 5)
*=	Shorthand for multiplies a value and assigns the result	X *= 6 (X holds 30)
/=	Shorthand for divides by a value and assigns the result	X /= 5 (X holds 6)
&=	Shorthand for combines with a string and assigns the result	S &= ", John" (S holds "Hello World, John")
^	Raises one value to the power of an exponent	3^4 (3 to the power of 4, returns 81)

Built-In Functions

In addition to the functions provided by the .NET Framework, Visual Basic .NET has many built-in functions. These functions provide many useful capabilities, including conversion from one data type to another, mathematical calculations, string manipulation, and so on. You should know about some of these functions to be able to get around in Visual Basic .NET.

Conversion Functions

Some of the most important functions available to you in Visual Basic are the conversion functions. They enable you to take one type of data and convert it to another. With Visual Basic .NET, conversion functions have become even more important because this version of Visual Basic is much stricter about data types, and it does not automatically convert one type into another as previous versions did.

 Caution | If you want Visual Basic .NET to automatically convert data types for you, you can turn off the strict type checking by adding Option Strict Off to the top of your files. You should know, however, that this could lead to unexpected results in your code (that is, bugs) if Visual Basic .NET converts a variable when you don't expect it to.

The conversion functions in Visual Basic .NET all begin with the letter "C" (as in conversion), and end with an abbreviated form of the new type. In addition, there is a generic conversion function, CType, which can convert to any type. Table 3.7 describes the main conversion functions.

TABLE 3.7 Conversion Functions

Function	Description
CBool	Converts to a Boolean. Anything that evaluates to False or 0 will be set to False; otherwise, it will be True.
CByte	Converts to a Byte. Any value greater than 255, or any fractional information, will be lost.
CChar	Converts to a single character. If the value is greater than 65,535, it will be lost. If you convert a String, only the first character is converted.
CDate	Converts to a Date. One of the more powerful conversion functions, CDate can recognize some of the more common formats for entering a date.
CDbl	Converts to a Double.
CInt	Converts to an Integer. Fractions are rounded to the nearest value.
CLng	Converts to a Long. Fractions are rounded to the nearest value.
CSht	Converts to a Short. Fractions are rounded to the nearest value.
CStr	Converts to a String. If the value is a Date, this will contain the Short Date format.
CType	Converts to any type. This is a powerful function that enables you to convert any data type into any other type. Therefore, the syntax for this function is slightly different than the others.

▼ SYNTAX

▲

The syntax for CType is

```
oNewVariable = CType(oOldVariable, NewType)
```

in which *oNewVariable* and *oOldVariable* are placeholders for the variables that you're converting to and from, respectively. *NewType* is the type you are converting to. This can be any variable that you could put after the As in a declaration, so you can use this function to convert to enumerations, structures, and object types as well as simple types.

String Manipulation Functions

Most of Visual Basic's earlier string-related functions have been replaced in Visual Basic .NET with the functionality internal to the String class (we'll look at the String class in detail on Day 7). However, you might see some of the functions listed in Table 3.8 in older code, so you should be familiar with these functions.

TABLE 3.8   String-Handling Functions

Function	Description	Example
Len	Returns the length of a string.	iValue = Len("Hello") ('iValue holds 5.)
Chr	Returns the character based on the entered ASCII or Unicode value.	sValue = Chr(56) ('s Value holds the letter A.)
Asc	Returns the ASCII or Unicode value.	iValue = Asc("A") ('iValue holds 56.)
Left	Returns characters from a string, beginning with the leftmost character. Also requires the number of characters to return.	sValue = Left("Hello World", 2) ('sValue holds He.)
Right	Returns characters from a string beginning with the rightmost character (the opposite of Left). Also requires the number of characters to return.	sValue = Right("Hello World",4) ('sValue holds orld.)
Mid	Returns characters not at either end of a string. Mid returns any number of characters. The syntax for Mid is sReturn = Mid(String, Start, Length) in which Start is the character to begin returning from, and Length is the number of characters (including Start) to return. One nice feature is that if you omit Length, you will return all the characters from Start on.	sValue = Mid("Hello World", 4, 5)) ('sValue holds lo Wo.) sValue = Mid("Hello World", 7) ('sValue holds World.)
Instr	Finds one string within another. This is useful when searching a file for some string. The syntax for the Instr function is iReturn = Instr(StartAtCharacter, SearchString, SearchFor, ComparisonType)	iValue = Instr(1,"Hello World", "l")) ('iValue holds 3.) Keep in mind that the string you are searching for could be multiple characters, so a search for "World", as in iValue = Instr(1, "Hello World", "World")) 'iValue holds 7.) StartAtCharacter is the position within the search string, SearchString, where the program begins searching (counting begins at 1). SearchString is the string to search in, and SearchFor is the string being sought.

3

TABLE 3.8 continued

Function	Description	Example
		ComparisonType determines the case sensitivity of the search. If *ComparisonType* is set to 0 (Binary Compare), the search will be case se sitive. If it is ignored, or set to 1 (Text Compare), it will not be case sensitive. iReturn would then hold the position within the *SearchString* where the *SearchFor* begins. If the search for string is not found, iReturn will be 0.
		InstrRev searches from the right side of the string; otherwise, InstrRev is identical to Instr. InstrRev is useful when you are searching a string co taining a directory path, and you want to view the lower directories first. iValue = InstrRev("Hello World", "o") 'iValue holds 8.
LCase	Converts a string to all lowercase.	sValue = LCase("Hello World") 'sValue holds hello world
UCase	Converts a string to all uppercase.	sValue = UCase("Hello World") 'sValue holds HELLO WORLD
LTrim	Removes all leading spaces from a string	sValue = LTrim(" Hello World ") 'sValue holds "Hello World "
RTrim	Removes all trailing spaces from a string	sValue = RTrim(" Hello World ") 'sValue holds " Hello World"
Trim	Removes all leading and trailing spaces from a string.	sValue = Trim(" Hello World ") sValue holds "Hello World"

Other Useful Functions

Finally, some generally useful functions don't fit into the other categories. These include functions that enable you to determine the type of a variable, as well as Date manipulation functions. Table 3.9 describes some of these functions.

TABLE 3.9 Miscellaneous Built-In Functions

Function	Description
IsArray	Returns True if the parameter is an array.
IsDate	Returns True if the parameter is recognizable as a date.
IsNumeric	Returns True if the parameter is recognizable as a number.
IsObject	Returns True if the parameter is some object type.
TypeName	Returns the name of the data type of the parameter, for example, TypeName(sName) would return "String".
Now	Returns the current date and time.
Today	Returns the current date, with the time set to 0:00:00 a.m. (midnight).

Writing Your Own Routines

Although the built-in functions are quite useful, there will always be times when you need to create your own routines. Perhaps you need to select a set of built-in functions that are all called in the same way, or perhaps you need to create some unique functionality. Either way, Visual Basic .NET makes creating your own routines easy.

There are two types of routines used in Visual Basic .NET. One type is a routine that does something, but doesn't return any value. These are called *subroutines* (or *sub* for short). The other type of procedure does something, but returns a value. These are called *functions*.

Subroutines

A subroutine is a block of Visual Basic .NET code that performs some task—for example, the Console.WriteLine method that you see in many of the examples. It prints information to the screen, but does not return any value. You use subroutines to perform tasks in your programs.

Generally, any time you have some code that you perform more than once, you should think about putting it into a subroutine. Similarly, if you have some code that you might use in multiple applications, you should put it into a subroutine. Subroutines let you isolate a small chunk of your program, so that rather than repeating the whole block of code, you simply refer to it by name. This does not mean that the subroutine will always do exactly the same steps, but that it will do some task. For example, a recipe might say, "Add one part vinegar to three parts oil." One time you might mix up one cup of vinegar to three cups of oil, whereas another time it might be only three tablespoons of vinegar to nine tablespoons of oil. Either way, you have performed the CreateVinaigrette subroutine. Yes, I'm making dinner as I write this.

To create your own subroutines, you use the Sub keyword:

SYNTAX

```
Sub SubRoutineName(Parameter1 As Type, Parameter2 As Type, ...
➥ParameterN As Type)
  'Do whatever in here
End Sub
```

In this syntax, each of the Parameters defines a value that is to be passed into the routine. Listing 3.2 shows declaring and using a subroutine.

INPUT   **LISTING 3.2**   Creating and Using a Subroutine

```
1 Sub ShowMessage(ByVal Message As String)
2     Console.WriteLine(Message)
3 End Sub

4 ShowMessage("Hello World from Visual Basic .NET")
```

ANALYSIS   Our subroutine begins with the Sub keyword, as on line 1. The subroutine is called ShowMessage, and takes one parameter when you call it. The subroutine ends with the End Sub keyword (line 3). In between is the actual code executed by the subroutine. In this case, it simply displays the contents of the parameter to the Console window. Line 4 shows one possible way of calling the subroutine, passing in the string "Hello World from Visual Basic .NET".

Functions

Creating your own functions enables you to create new capabilities within your application. Creating a new function is similar to defining new subroutines, except that you define the return value type. Within the procedure, you identify the value to be returned, as shown here:

SYNTAX

```
Function FunctionName(Parameter1 As Type, ... ParameterN As Type) As ReturnType
  'Do whatever in here
  Return ReturnValue
End Function
```

In this syntax, each of the parameters defines a value that is to be passed into the routine, *ReturnType* is the data type the function returns, and *ReturnValue* is the value that will be returned from the function. Listing 3.3 shows the declaration and use of a simple function.

INPUT   **LISTING 3.3**   Creating and Using a Function

```
1 Function Volume(ByVal Length As Integer, _
2         ByVal Width As Integer, ByVal Height As Integer) As Integer
```

LISTING 3.3 continued

```
3    Return Length * Width * Height
4  End Function
5
6  Console.WriteLine(Volume(3,4,5))
```

Scope

NEW TERM   Scope is one of those lovely computer-speak words that means, "Who else can
see me?" Formally, *scope* defines the visibility of variables within a program,
that is, which routines could use a given variable. You might not want all routines to
access all variables. Allowing all routines to see all variables could lead to one routine
"accidentally" changing the value of a variable, introducing a bug in your program.

Up until now, we have usually declared variables using the `Dim` keyword inside of procedures. However, you can also declare variables outside of procedures to make the variable available to multiple procedures. If you do this, you can use two other keywords,
`Public` and `Private`:

- `Public` variables are available throughout an application. These are *Global variables*, which exist *globally*, or throughout, the application. `Public` variables should
  be used sparingly, but are useful when you need some value that will be used at
  many points in your program, such as the connection to a database, or a file.

- `Private` variables are available within the module or class where they are declared.
  `Private` variables are used frequently in applications when you need a single variable that can be used in multiple procedures. By creating it with the `Private` keyword, you allow all the procedures within one module or class to access the variable. Private variables are useful for sharing common information required for a
  task, such as an intermediate value that can be accessed by different functions to
  perform a calculation.

> When you create a variable, you should declare it a newly created variable
> as close as possible to where it is needed. If you only use a variable in one
> procedure, you should declare that variable within that procedure.
>
> Use module-level `Private` and `Public` variables sparingly.

Why Is Scope Important?

Scope enables you to isolate the data used by your applications' procedures. Much
older versions of BASIC did not have the capability for scope, and all variables were

accessible and changeable from all parts of the program. Imagine writing a program back then—you might often reuse (on purpose or accidentally) a variable elsewhere in a program. This could possibly lead to a bug if you changed the value in one spot in the program, only to mistakenly read the changed value later when you expected to get the original value.

Scope and Procedures

Just as variables can have scope, procedures (subroutines and functions) have scope. Scope for procedures means the same as scope for variables: It describes where else in your program you can use the procedure (or outside your program, as you'll see when you begin creating objects).

Procedure scope is defined using the same keywords used for variable scope. Generally, scope has the same meaning here as well.

- `Public`   The procedure can be called from any other part of the application. This is the default if you don't add any other keyword.

- `Private`   The procedure can only be called from another procedure within the same module or class where it is defined. This is useful when you are writing a number of support routines used throughout a calculation, but that other routines would not need to use.

Just as with variables, additional scope keywords apply when you are creating objects in Visual Basic .NET. We'll look at those keywords later.

Sample Application: Calculating a Future Value

Now that you have explored creating and using variables and procedures, you can create an application that performs an investment calculation. This application will enable you to explore the lovely benefits of regular investing and compound interest. This sample Console application will avoid the complexity that a graphical user interface would add. Listing 3.4 shows the output from one run of the program.

INPUT/OUTPUT   **LISTING 3.4**   The Investment Calculator

```
1 InvestCalc.exe
2 Initial Balance: 10000
3 Annual Interest (e.g. for 5%, enter 5): 5
4 Monthly Deposit: 200
5 Years of Investment: 30
```

Listing 3.4 continued

```
 6
 7 If you start with $10,000.00,
 8        and invest $200.00 per month
 9              for 30 years
10              at 5% interest.
11 Your final balance would be: $211,129.17
```

Here we see the result of starting with a $10,000 balance and adding $200 per month for 30 years, at a constant 5 percent interest.

The program requires the user to enter the four values (Initial Balance, Annual Interest, Monthly Deposit, and Years of Investment). In turn, the program calculates the final balance. This calculation is known as the Future Value (FV) calculation, and Visual Basic .NET includes it as one of its built-in functions. The formula for Future Value is

```
FV = MonthlyDeposit * (((1 + MonthlyInterest)^Months - 1 )
➥ / MonthlyInterest ) + StartingBalance * ( 1 + MonthlyInterest )^Months
```

The following steps outline this procedure so that you can better understand how it works:

1. Begin by creating a new project in Visual Basic .NET. Select a new Visual Basic Console Application. Visual Basic .NET creates a new project with one module.

2. Close the file window and rename the file using the Solution Explorer. Right-click on the filename Module1.vb in the Solution Explorer and select Rename. Change the filename to modInvest.vb.

3. Change the name of the Startup Object, also. Right-click on the project in the Solution Explorer and select Properties. On the General page, change the Startup Object to Invest. This should be in the drop-down list.

4. You're ready to begin coding. As a minimum, you need four variables to hold the user's input. Declare the variables as shown in Listing 3.5. Most of these values are floating point numbers, with the exception of Years. These declarations should occur between the Module line and the Sub Main() line because these will be Module-level variables.

INPUT   **Listing 3.5** Declarations for the Future Value Calculation

```
1 Private dblAnnualInterest As Double = 0
2 Private iYears As Integer = 0
3 Private decStartingBalance As Double = 0
4 Private decMonthlyDeposit As Double = 0
```

5. Use the `Main` routine to call each of the routines that will get the user input, do the calculations, and display the output, as in Listing 3.6.

INPUT   **LISTING 3.6**   Main Routine

```
1   Shared Sub Main()
2       Dim decResult As Double
3       'get input values
4       GetInputValues()
5       'calculate
6       decResult = CalculateFV(dblAnnualInterest, _
7         iYears, _
8         decMonthlyDeposit, _
9         decStartingBalance)
10      'output result
11      DisplayResults(decResult)
12  End Sub
```

In Listing 3.7, each of the major functions of the application is a separate subroutine or function. This enables you to more easily change the techniques for getting input or display output later.

6. Add the code in Listing 3.7 to allow the user to enter information. The procedure does not take any parameters, nor does it return a value. Because this is a Console application, you'll use the `Console.Read` routine to get values.

INPUT   **LISTING 3.7**   The Input `Console.Read` Routine

```
1   Private Sub GetInputValues()
2       Console.WriteLine()
3       decStartingBalance = CDec( _
4           GetValue("Initial Balance: "))
5       dblAnnualInterest = CDbl(_
6           GetValue("Annual Interest (e.g. for 5%, enter 5): "))
7       decMonthlyDeposit = CDec(GetValue("Monthly deposit: "))
8       iYears = CInt(GetValue("Years of investment: "))
9       Console.WriteLine()
10  End Sub
11
12  Private Function GetValue(ByVal Prompt As String) As String
13      Console.Write(Prompt)
14      Return Console.ReadLine
15  End Function
```

Notice that the `GetInputValues` subroutine calls the `GetValue` function. This is an example of creating support routines. Rather than rewrite the code to prompt the user many times, pull the code out and create a procedure to perform the task. The resulting code in `GetInputValues` is therefore simplified.

7. Write the routine that will display the output when it is calculated. Eventually, this might be displayed in a window, but for now, use the `Console.WriteLine` procedure, shown in Listing 3.8, to display the information. This procedure should take the value to display, and return nothing.

INPUT   **LISTING 3.8**   The Output Console.WriteLine Routine

```
1  Private Sub DisplayResults(ByVal Result As Double)
2      Console.WriteLine()
3      Console.WriteLine("If you start with {0:c}, ", decStartingBalance)
4      Console.WriteLine(" and invest {0:c} per month", decMonthlyDeposit)
5      Console.WriteLine(" for {0} years", iYears)
6      Console.WriteLine(" at {0}% interest.", dblAnnualInterest)
7      Console.WriteLine()
8      Console.WriteLine("Your final balance would be: {0:c}", Result)
9  End Sub
```

This is a simple routine, consisting of a series of `Console.WriteLine` calls to display the entered values and the result of the calculation.

8. Perform the FV calculation. This routine should take the four values as parameters, and return the result of the calculation. As it has a return value, this procedure is a function. Listing 3.9 shows the `CalculateFV` function.

INPUT   **LISTING 3.9**   The CalculateFV Function

```
1  Private Function CalculateFV(ByVal AnnualInterest As Double, _
2      ByVal Years As Integer, _
3      ByVal MonthlyDeposit As Double, _
4      ByVal StartingBalance As Double) As Double
5      'divide by 1200 to make it percent and per month
6      Dim decMonthlyInterest As Double = CDec(AnnualInterest / 1200)
7      Dim iMonths As Integer = Years * 12
8      Dim decTemp As Double
9      Dim decReturn As Double

10     'we'll need this value in a couple of places
11     decTemp = CDec((1 + decMonthlyInterest) ^ iMonths)
12     decReturn = CDec(MonthlyDeposit * _
13        ((decTemp - 1) / decMonthlyInterest) _
14        + (StartingBalance * decTemp))

15     Return decReturn

16 End Function
```

3

Just as with the `GetInputValues`, you could have pulled out the code that calculated the `decTemp` value. However, because you only need this calculation in this routine, and likely won't need it again, you don't.

Listing 3.10 shows the full code for the sample application.

```
1   Module Invest
2
3       Private dblAnnualInterest As Double = 0
4       Private iYears As Integer = 0
5       Private decStartingBalance As Double = 0
6       Private decMonthlyDeposit As Double = 0
7
8       Sub Main()
9           Dim decResult As Double
10          'get input values
11          GetInputValues()
12          'calculate
13          decResult = CalculateFV(dblAnnualInterest, _
14              iYears, _
15              decMonthlyDeposit, _
16              decStartingBalance)
17          'output result
18          DisplayResults(decResult)
19      End Sub
20
21      Private Function CalculateFV(ByVal AnnualInterest As Double, _
22              ByVal Years As Integer, _
23              ByVal MonthlyDeposit As Double, _
24              ByVal StartingBalance As Double) As Double
25          'divide by 1200 to make it percent and per month
26          Dim decMonthlyInterest As Double = CDec(AnnualInterest / 1200)
27          Dim iMonths As Integer = Years * 12
28          Dim decTemp As Double
29          Dim decReturn As Double
30          'we'll need this value in a couple of places
31          decTemp = CDec((1 + decMonthlyInterest) ^ iMonths)
32          decReturn = CDec(MonthlyDeposit * ((decTemp - 1) _
33              / decMonthlyInterest) _
34              + (StartingBalance * decTemp))
35          Return decReturn
36      End Function
37
38      Private Function GetValue(ByVal Prompt As String) As String
39          Console.Write(Prompt)
40          Return Console.ReadLine
41      End Function
42
```

LISTING **3.10**   continued

```
43     Private Sub GetInputValues()
44         Console.WriteLine()
45         decStartingBalance = CDec(GetValue("Initial Balance: "))
46         dblAnnualInterest = _
47           CDbl(GetValue("Annual Interest (for 5%, enter 5): "))
48         decMonthlyDeposit = CDec(GetValue("Monthly deposit: "))
49         iYears = CInt(GetValue("Years of investment: "))
50         Console.WriteLine()
51     End Sub
52
53     Private Sub DisplayResults(ByVal Result As Double)
54         Console.WriteLine()
55         Console.WriteLine("If you start with {0:c}, ", decStartingBalance)
56         Console.WriteLine(" and invest {0:c} per month", decMonthlyDeposit)
57         Console.WriteLine("for {0} years", iYears)
58         Console.WriteLine("at {0}% interest.", dblAnnualInterest)
59         Console.WriteLine()
60         Console.WriteLine("Your final balance would be: {0:c}", Result)
61     End Sub
62  End Module
```

3

9. Run the application. The output should be similar to that shown at the beginning of this section. You can run the application from the IDE by clicking the Play button on the toolbar. However, it is likely that the window that pops up with the application will go away too quickly for you to see the answer. Instead, run the program from the command prompt by running the executable created.

You can try a frightening experiment with this calculator. Enter deposit values representing the money you would normally spend on a vice (lunch at work, cigarettes, electronic gadgets) each month. The resulting Future Value can often be disturbing.

Summary

Today's lesson covered a lot of ground, looking at the various types of variables you can create in Visual Basic .NET, and how you use them. In addition, it explored the idea of functions and subroutines, both the ones that are built into Visual Basic .NET and ones you can create. These two topics are fundamental to your understanding of Visual Basic .NET and will be used in all types of applications.

Day 4, "Controlling Flow in Programs," will continue the exploration of writing code in Visual Basic .NET by looking at how you can manage the decisions in your programs.

Q&A

Q. **I've read that Visual Basic .NET supports "typeless" programming. What's that?**

A. When you declare the type of a variable or function, you set certain rules: what type of information it represents, where it can be used, and so on. *Typeless programming* occurs when you don't declare the type. All variables are then objects that can hold any kind of information. Visual Basic .NET is the only member of the Visual Studio family that supports this style of programming.

Q. **When you want to create a procedure, should it be a subroutine or a function?**

A. The short answer is, "It depends." You should create the type of procedure that provides the functionality you need. Some procedures are obvious. If you need to create a procedure that performs some calculation or manipulation and returns the result, you should create a function. Other routines—ones in which you might or might not need to return a value—truly lead to a choice. And, there is no correct choice, only opinions. If there is no obvious return value, selecting the type of procedure to create is a matter of personal and/or corporate opinion. Some people and companies always create functions; others will create subroutines as needed.

Q. **How can I find the list of all the built-in functions?**

A. There are two ways you can find out about all the built-in functions:

- Online help   The online help contains descriptions of and code samples for all the built-in functions. You can find these by searching the online help for Visual Basic Language Reference.

- Object Browser   If all you need is a quick description of a built-in function, you can find it in the Object Browser. Open it by selecting View, Other Windows, Object Browser. The built-in functions are contained in the Microsoft.VisualBasic.dll section.

Workshop

The Workshop is designed to help you anticipate possible questions, review what you've learned, and get thinking about how to put your knowledge into practice. The answers to the quiz are in Appendix A, "Answers to Quizzes/Exercises."

Quiz

1. How should I decide which type of variable to use when I am working with numbers?

2. What is the correct way to call this subroutine?

```
Function RaiseToPower(ByVal Number As Integer, ByVal Power As Integer) As
Long
    A: Dim lValue = RaiseToPower(3,4)
    B: RaiseToPower 3,4
    C: Console.WriteLine(RaiseToPower(3,4))
    D: Dim lValue = RaiseToPower 3,4
```

3. If a variable is declared using the `Private` keyword, where can it be used in a program?

Exercises

1. Rewrite the FV Calculator sample application so that it represents a loan payment calculator instead of an investment calculator. It should request the amount of the loan, the annual interest, and the duration of the loan in months, and calculate the amount of your payments. The formula for this calculation is

```
Payment = LoanAmount * (MonthlyInterest * ((1 + MonthlyInterest) ^
Months) / (((1 + MonthlyInterest) ^ Months) - 1))
```

3

DAY 4

Controlling Flow in Programs

So far, this book has covered writing computer programs, but, to write a truly useful program, you need a few more key elements. Up to today, you have been building programs that consisted of a linear series of statements; every line was executed in order when the program ran. For a program to be truly interactive, for it to take different paths through the code depending on the input it receives, you need a new type of statement, a control statement. Almost every programming language has control statements, and Visual Basic .NET is no exception. In today's lesson you will learn about the two categories of control statements:

- Choice statements
- Looping statements

Within each of these categories, I will cover several variations of each type, and you will learn which specific statement is best for a certain situation.

Making Choices with Control Statements

Control statements are those parts of a programming language that exist only to determine what other parts of the program get executed. The determination occurs because of the value of some variable or other circumstance, allowing the program to act differently depending on the situation. The need for this type of behavior is obvious when you walk through most programs using pseudocode.

NEW TERM   When we describe a problem using language that is somewhere between our regular way of speaking and computer code, we call this "almost code" description *pseudocode*. Today's lesson gives several examples of using this type of language to describe what your programs are supposed to do. Many people, including the authors of this book, find this a useful way to work out the general flow of their program in a fashion that non- programmers can still understand. It can be much easier to write an entire program out in pseudocode before composing the actual code (this becomes exceedingly important as you deal with more complicated programs).

For instance, let's consider some code that would form just a small portion of an application, the sign-on greeting. Using regular language to describe what this code does, you might say, "Welcome the user to the program, using the appropriate greeting depending on the time of day." For such a small bit of code, that would likely be the entire description given, and you could start coding right from this point. For this particular task, that pseudocode might look like this:

```
When the program starts...

If it is before noon, display "Good Morning!"
If it is after noon, but before 6 pm, display "Good Afternoon!"
For any other time, display "Good Evening!"

Continue with the rest of the program...
```

Even this simple example shows the need to make some decisions in code, to allow the program to display a different message depending on the time of day. To turn this into code, you use a control statement that allows you to check a condition (in this case, the time) and then choose what action to take.

The If Statement

The simplest control statement—and one that is common to almost every programming language—is the If statement. This statement has several different formats but basically looks like this:

```
If <condition> Then
    Code to execute if the condition is true
End If
```

The `<condition>` is the key part of this statement; it determines whether or not the inner block of code is executed. This condition takes the form of an *expression*, which is a combination of values and operators that is evaluated at runtime down to a single value. Because the `If` statement supports only two possible actions—the code is executed, or it is not—the expression must have only two possible values. This means that any expression used as a condition must have a definite "yes or no" result (`True` or `False`), such as these examples:

- It is before noon.
- It is after noon, but before 6 p.m.
- The number of students exceeds the number of chairs.

Each of those expressions is either true, or it isn't. There is no middle ground, and therefore they fit in as the condition of an `If` statement. If you have any doubts about a particular expression's suitability, simply try it out in pseudocode. For example, consider these expressions:

- 3 + 5
- John
- Wednesday

Now, try one of those expressions in your pseudocode: "If 3 + 5, then end the program." What does that mean? "3 + 5" is not an expression that can be evaluated to a `True` or `False` value, and therefore the entire `If` statement does not make any sense. Expressions that return either `True` or `False` are known as *Boolean expressions*; I will cover them in more detail a little later in today's lesson.

Now let's go back to the original pseudocode example, displaying a greeting at the start of a program.

```
When the program starts...

If it is before noon display "Good Morning!"
If it is after noon, but before 6 pm, display "Good Afternoon!"
For any other time, display "Good Evening!"

Continue with the rest of the program...
```

Before you turn this pseudocode into a Visual Basic .NET program, it might be worthwhile to take these very user-readable lines a little bit closer to code. You can do this by just rephrasing the text to provide more detail:

```
When the program starts...

If the current system time is less than 12:00 noon
then print out "Good Morning!"
```

If the current system time is equal to or greater than 12:00 noon
and the current system time is also less than 6:00 pm
then print out "Good Afternoon!"
If the current system time is equal to or greater than 6:00 pm
then print out "Good Evening!"

Continue with the rest of the program...

Now, to write this program, all you need to know is how to get the current system time; the rest shouldn't be too difficult. The current system time is available through the Now() object, which also includes information on the current date, and it exposes several useful properties such as Hour, Minute, DayofWeek, and Seconds. For our purposes, we can get away with just using Hour, which returns the current hour represented in 24-hour time (values from 0 to 23). Translating as literally as possible from the pseudocode to Visual Basic .NET produces the program in Listing 4.1.

LISTING 4.1   Greeting.vb

```
1 Imports System
2
3   Public Class Greeting
4         'Run the application
5         Shared Sub Main()
6             Dim dtCurrent As System.DateTime
7             Dim iHour As Integer
8
9             dtCurrent = dtCurrent.Now()
10            iHour = dtCurrent.Hour
11
12            If (iHour < 12) Then
13                  Console.Writeline("Good Morning!")
14            End If
15            If (iHour >= 12) And (iHour < 18) Then
16                  Console.WriteLine("Good Afternoon!")
17            End If
18            If (iHour >= 18) Then
19                  Console.WriteLine("Good Evening!")
20            End If
21        End Sub
22
23    End Class
```

You can download Greeting.vb from this book's Web site and try it out on your own. To compile this, and most of the examples in today's lesson, either download this file or create a text file, enter the code from Listing 4.1 into it, and then save the file as Greeting.vb. Go into the command console (DOS prompt) and use the cd (change directory) command to ensure that you are working in the same directory as the

Greeting.vb file, and compile the program by typing **vbc /r:System.dll /t:exe Greeting.vb**. The compiler will, by default, create an executable with the same name as the source file, so, in this case, you will end up with a new file in the same directory called Greeting.exe. Running the newly created executable will produce the appropriate result, depending on what time of day you run it.

To best understand how these three If statements worked, let's step through the code and look at what happens. You could do this stepping through inside the Visual Studio IDE, but we'll just do it on paper and save all that computing power for later.

ANALYSIS The first line to be executed is line 9, which initializes the date variable to the current date and time; line 10 then saves the current hour into another variable, iHour. The first If statement is executed at line 12. At this point, the expression (iHour < 12) is evaluated. iHour equals the current hour value, which is 13 (according to the system clock, for the sake of this example, just assume that the 13th hour is 1 p.m.). Now, the expression, which has been reduced to 13 < 12, will be reduced once more to a simple Boolean value of False (13 is not less than 12, at least not as we understand math). So, a value of False tells the If statement not to execute its block of code, and execution immediately moves on to line 14, the End If. This statement is really just a handy placeholder, so nothing really happens until line 15, the next If. In this case, the If statement, (iHour >= 12) And (iHour < 18) reduces first to (13 >= 12) And (13 < 18) then to True And True. When we And two Boolean values, we only get a result of True if both of the values are True, which happens to be the case here. So, the If statement ends up with a True condition and therefore the inner block of code is executed (line 16), and the very exciting message Good Afternoon! is output to the console. Now, our program has done all its work; we have printed out the right message for this time of day. The code doesn't stop executing, though; there is nothing to tell it that there is no point going on, so execution continues with the End If and then the last If statement at line 18. This statement has the expression (iHour >= 18) as its condition, which becomes (13 >= 18), and ends up as False. Execution happily moves onto the last End If at line 20 and then the program ends.

Extending the If Statement

Although Listing 4.1 was fairly straightforward and certainly not the most complicated program in the world, it does raise one question: Why bother executing any code after you have figured out your answer? That is a good point. Although lines 18 through 20 in Listing 4.1 were only a few extra lines of execution, there could be many more lines left at the end of a real-world program. In this program, I really wanted to continue to the next If statement, only if the current one was False. I could have made that clearer in my pseudo code by writing it like this:

```
When the program starts...

If the current system time is less than 12:00 noon
then print out "Good Morning!"
else
If the current system time is equal to or greater than 12:00 noon
and the current system time is also less than 6:00 pm
then print out "Good Afternoon!"
else
If the current system time is equal to or greater than 6:00 pm
then print out "Good Evening!"

Continue with the rest of the program...
```

This example is almost the same thing as the previous code, but now it clear that you only continue to the next If when the expression's value does not meet the condition of the current one. As you might guess, the capability to nest If statements together like this is a common need in computer programming, so Visual Basic, and most other languages, provides a way to express that exact concept with the If statement. We have been looking at the simple form of this statement:

```
If <condition> Then
    code block
End If
```

If the condition evaluates to True, then the code block is executed; if it is False, then the code block is skipped over, and execution continues after the End If. You can make this a little more complex by adding a new clause, Else. Now, the syntax looks like this:

```
If <condition> Then
    code block #1
Else
    code block #2
End If
```

In this new structure, if the condition evaluates to True, code block #1 is executed, and the program continues after the End If. However, if the condition evaluates to False, then code block #2 is executed, and the program continues after the End If. Because the condition must be a Boolean expression, and all Boolean expressions are either true or false, then either code block #1 or code block #2 must be executed; this statement will never cause them both to execute or neither of them to execute at the same time.

Rewriting the code to take advantage of this new and improved If statement produces Listing 4.2.

LISTING 4.2 Greeting_IFELSE.vb

```
1 Imports System
2
3   Public Class Greeting
```

LISTING 4.2   continued

```
4              'Run the application
5              Shared Sub Main()
6                  Dim dtCurrent As System.DateTime
7                  Dim iHour As Integer
8
9                  dtCurrent = dtCurrent.Now
10                 iHour = dtCurrent.Hour
11
12                 If (iHour < 12) Then
13                     Console.Writeline("Good Morning!")
14                 Else
15                     If (iHour >= 12) And (iHour < 18) Then
16                         Console.WriteLine("Good Afternoon!")
17                     Else
18                         Console.WriteLine("Good Evening!")
19                     End If
20                 End If
21             End Sub
22
23     End Class
```

4

Simpler? No, not really, but Listing 4.2 is more efficient than Listing 4.1. In this new version of the solution, after the correct greeting has been printed out, the program is done. No unnecessary code will be executed.

In this particular program, I nested another If statement within each of the Else clauses, testing another condition if the previous one was false. Code like this is not the only thing that can go inside the Else clause, but these nested If statements are common, and therefore, Visual Basic includes one more enhancement to the basic If statement, the ElseIf statement. This statement combines the functionality of the Else, with the assumption that another If statement will be *nested*, or follow immediately. The syntax of this statement is a compression of what you would have to write using just If and Else. Here is the syntax of an If statement in which the Else clause contains a nested If, followed by the syntax as it would appear using the ElseIf statement:

```
If <condition #1> Then
    code block #1
Else
    If <condition #2> then
        code block #2
    End If
End If
```

becomes

```
If <condition #1> Then
    code block #1
```

```
ElseIf <condition #2> Then
    code block #2
End If
```

Notice the lack of a second `End If` in the second syntax example. The `ElseIf` is considered a single clause and therefore is still part of the original `If` statement. It is still possible to have an `Else` clause for that second condition or even to have another `ElseIf` clause. Examples of both are shown here:

```
If <condition #1> Then
    code block #1
ElseIf <condition #2> Then
    code block #2
Else
    code block #3
End If
```

```
If <condition #1> Then
    code block #1
ElseIf <condition #2> Then
    code block #2
ElseIf <condition #3> Then
    code block #3
End If
```

Even with another `ElseIf` clause, it is all considered part of the original `If`, and only the single `End If` is required. Coming back to the original example, printing out the appropriate greeting depending on the time of day, the `ElseIf` clause (see Listing 4.3) allows you to greatly simplify the code.

LISTING 4.3   Greetings_ElseIf.vb

```
1 Imports System
2
3   Public Class Greeting
4        'Run the application
5        Shared Sub Main()
6            Dim dtCurrent As System.DateTime
7            Dim iHour As Integer
8
9            dtCurrent = dtCurrent.Now
10           iHour = dtCurrent.Hour
11
12           If (iHour < 12) Then
13               Console.Writeline("Good Morning!")
14           ElseIf (iHour >= 12) And (iHour < 18) Then
15               Console.WriteLine("Good Afternoon!")
16           Else
```

LISTING 4.3   continued

```
17                    Console.WriteLine("Good Evening!")
18             End If
19         End Sub
20
21     End Class
```

Single Line and Immediate If Statements

In addition to the block form of the If statement presented previously, in which an inner set of code is enclosed between the If and the End If statements, it is also possible to express an If statement on a single line. Here is an example, in which a condition is checked and an action is taken, all in a single line:

```
If iHour > 11 Then System.Console.WriteLine("It is Not Morning!")
```

This single-line concept can be extended with an Else clause:

```
If iHour > 11 Then DoSomething() Else DoSomethingElse()
```

It can even be used with more than one statement to be executed in the True or False code blocks (or both) as multiple statements can be separated using colons, as follows:

```
If iHour > 11 Then DoSomething(): DoMore() Else DoSomethingElse()
```

I have included this statement more for the sake of completeness than for any real need. There is nothing that you can do with a single-line If statement that you cannot do with the regular block form. Putting all the code onto one line does not execute it any faster. All it accomplishes, in most situations, is to produce source code that takes up less space on disk and is much harder to understand. Occasionally, this single-line version can make your code look nicer, as shown in Listing 4.4. In the listing, a large number of If statements are required, each with only a single code statement to execute if their conditions are True. These situations are too rare to justify the use of another syntax for such a common statement. Please stick to the other form of the If statement and save your fellow programmers the headache.

LISTING 4.4   Single-line If Statements Can Make Some Code Look Better

```
1     If X=5 Then strChar = "A"
2     If X=23 Then strChar = "B"
3     If X=2 Then strChar = "C"
4     ...
```

Boolean Expressions and Boolean Logic

All control statements depend on some form of decision being made, based on the value of some variable, constant, or fact related to the current situation. Regardless of what actual value is being checked, the result can only be True or False. As discussed earlier, all Boolean expressions produce one of two answers: yes or no, true or false. In Day 3, "Introduction to Programming with Visual Basic .NET," you learned about Boolean variables, a type of variable that can only hold True or False values. These are the only types of expressions and values allowed as part of a control statement because a control statement needs to make a decision based on this value. Non-Boolean expressions just wouldn't work; they don't produce a yes/no or true/false answer, and the program wouldn't know what to do.

The two simplest Boolean expressions are True and False; all other Boolean expressions, when they are evaluated, end up as one of these two values. Not many programs will use these values directly, though. Instead, the programs create more complicated expressions that are comparisons between two non-Boolean values, logical operations on Boolean values, or a combination of those two types of expressions.

Comparison Operators

The most common type of expression used in programs is a *comparison*, two non-Boolean expressions with an operator in between. The following comparison operators are available for use in expressions:

- >, greater than
- <, less than
- =, equal to
- <>, not equal to
- >=, greater than or equal to
- <=, less than or equal to

All these operators work with both string and numeric values. An additional comparison operator, Like, is also available for matching the patterns matching of strings. Like allows you to compare a string variable to a pattern of regular text and special wildcard characters. Special characters that can be used with Like include

- *, to indicate any number of additional characters
- ? to represent one character
- # to represent any digit (0–9)
- Ranges ([a-g], for example) to specify that any character within that range should be considered a match

Let's build a small program to experiment with the If statement and the Like operator. This program (see Listing 4.5) will accept a pattern and a test value as input and then check to see whether the test value matches the pattern.

LISTING 4.5   PatternMatcher.vb

```
1 Public Class PatternMatcher
2     Shared Sub Main()
3     Dim sInput As String
4     Dim sPattern As String
5     Dim sMatch As String
6
7         System.Console.Write("Please Enter A Pattern:")
8         sInput = System.Console.ReadLine()
9         sPattern = sInput
10
11        System.Console.Write("Please Enter A String To Compare Against:")
12        sInput = System.Console.ReadLine()
13        sMatch = sInput
14
15        If sMatch Like sPattern Then
16            System.Console.WriteLine(sMatch & " Matched with " & sPattern)
17        Else
18            System.Console.WriteLine(sMatch & " did not Match with "
➥& sPattern)
19        End If
20    End Sub
21 End Class
```

After you have entered it into a text file (or downloaded it), and compiled it (vbc /t:exe PatternMatcher.vb), try running this program with a variety of inputs. For instance, you could use a pattern such as C*T and try test values such as CAT, coat, ct, and so on.

Logical Operators

The other type of expression that can be used as a Boolean expression is one that uses logical operators. These operators work with Boolean values or expressions and produce a Boolean result. Because Boolean values are very similar to bits (binary values, either 1 or 0) the logical operators are often called *bitwise comparisons*. The operators in this category are AND, OR, and XOR, which each compare two values or expressions, and NOT, which works with a single Boolean value or expression.

When you AND two Boolean values, you only get a True result if both of the values being compared equal True. With OR, if either value is True, then the result is True. XOR, also called *exclusive OR*, produces a True result only if one of the values equals True and the other equals False. NOT is simply a *negation operator*: It returns the opposite of whatever value you use it on. Table 4.1 lists all the possible combinations of values and what the

4

various logical operators would produce in each case. In all the examples, the True and False values could be replaced with expressions that can be evaluated down to a Boolean value.

TABLE 4.1 Boolean Combinations

Expression	Result
TRUE AND TRUE	TRUE
FALSE AND TRUE	FALSE
TRUE AND FALSE	FALSE
FALSE AND FALSE	FALSE
TRUE OR TRUE	TRUE
TRUE OR FALSE	TRUE
FALSE OR TRUE	TRUE
FALSE OR FALSE	FALSE
TRUE XOR TRUE	FALSE
TRUE XOR FALSE	TRUE
FALSE XOR TRUE	TRUE
FALSE XOR FALSE	FALSE
NOT TRUE	FALSE
NOT FALSE	TRUE

The availability of logical operators allows you to combine other expressions and values to produce more complicated Boolean expressions, such as: If X > 3 AND X < 8 Then, or If (((X+3) * 5) > (Y*3)) AND (SystemIsRunning() OR iHour < 5) Then. We will use both types of expressions, comparison and logical, later in some exercises involving If statements.

Short-Circuiting

Similarly to an election outcome in the United States, the result of a Boolean expression is often known before the complete expression has been evaluated. Consider this Boolean expression: (X > 1) AND (X < 10). If X is 1, then as soon as you evaluate the left side of the expression (returning False), you know that the right side is irrelevant. Due to the nature of the AND statement, there is no need to evaluate the other side. The entire expression will be False, no matter what value is returned on the other side. This is something that you would do without much thought when you are evaluating Boolean expressions, but it is not always so clear for the computer.

NEW TERM The behavior that we expect, not evaluating any unnecessary portion of an expression, is called *short-circuiting,* but Visual Basic .NET does not work this way by default. To make Visual Basic .NET short-circuit a Boolean expression, you need to use alternative forms of the AND and OR operators, ANDALSO and ORELSE. You do not need to just trust that it behaves in this fashion, though; a simple test program (see Listing 4.6) can be used to see exactly what happens.

LISTING 4.6   ShortCircuiting.vb

```
 1 Public Class ShortCircuiting
 2
 3     Shared Sub Main()
 4         If Test("Left") ANDALSO Test("Right") Then
 5             'do something
 6         End If
 7     End Sub
 8
 9     Shared Function Test(sInput As String) As Boolean
10         System.Console.WriteLine(sInput)
11         Test = FALSE
12     End Function
13
14 End Class
```

4

If the Test() function returns False, as it does in Listing 4.6, then you know what the overall expression will return simply by evaluating the left side. Running the code in Listing 4.6 will produce only one line of output, in this case, "Left". If Test() returns True, then both sides need to be executed, and the program will output both "Left" and "Right". To test the default behavior of Boolean operators, try changing the ANDALSO to just AND and see what results you get.

Dealing with Multiple Possibilities: The Select Case Statement

The IF statement can handle almost any type of decision-making requirement, but it is truly designed for dealing with a single branch type of choice. If a variety of different values need to be checked for, and a different action taken for each, IF statements can become cumbersome. Consider the example of an income tax entry program with separate code routines to handle five different categories of clients. The client category is based on the number of people in a household. You would want to direct users to the correct routine based on that value. Using If statements, the code might look like Listing 4.7.

LISTING 4.7   Using Many Nested IF Statements

```
 1 . . .
 2 If lngNumPeople = 1 Then
 3     Call SinglePersonTaxReturn()
 4 ElseIf lngNumPeople = 2 Then
 5     Call TwoPersonTaxReturn()
 6 ElseIf lngNumPeople = 3 OR lngNumPeople = 4 Then
 7     Call MidSizedHouseholdTaxReturn()
 8 ElseIf lngNumPeople > 4 AND lngNumPeople < 10 Then
 9     Call BigHouseholdTaxReturn()
10 Else
11     Call ReallyBigHouseholdTaxReturn()
12 End If
13 . . .
```

After you start testing more than a few possible choices, all the various If clauses can become overly complex. To handle testing for multiple values, or for multiple sets of values, Visual Basic includes the Select Case statement, which has the following syntax:

```
Select Case <variable or expression being compared>
    Case <value or value range>
        code block
    Case <value or value range>
        code block
    Case Else
        code block
End Select
```

Using the Select Case statement in place of the If statements in Listing 4.7 produces the alternative code shown in Listing 4.8.

LISTING 4.8   The Select Case Command Can Greatly Simplify Your Code

```
 1 Select Case lngNumPeople
 2     Case 1
 3         Call SinglePersonTaxReturn()
 4     Case 2
 5         Call TwoPersonTaxReturn()
 6     Case 3, 4
 7         Call MidSizedHouseholdTaxReturn()
 8     Case 5 to 9
 9        ˙Call BigHouseholdTaxReturn()
10     Case Else
11         Call ReallyBigHouseholdTaxReturn()
12 End Select
```

The `Case Else` clause is used just like the `Else` clause in an `If` statement, except that, in this example, it will execute if none of the conditions are matched. Note that, in Listing 4.8, only one of the conditions could be true at one time. There is no overlap between the various `Case` conditions, which makes a lot of sense. In actual fact, overlaps are not prevented at all by Visual Basic; you are allowed to have overlapping conditions in which more than one `Case` condition might match a particular value. If that is the case, only the first condition that matches will execute because the program exits the `Select Case` statement after a match has been made and the appropriate code block executed. Although it won't cause an error, overlapping conditions can be confusing to a programmer and are worth avoiding for that reason alone.

Do	Don't
DO always cover every possible condition by including a `Case Else` clause. This will catch any unexpected input for which you didn't include another `Case` statement. It will make your program more robust.	**DON'T** use multiple conditions in your `Select Case` if a single value could match more than one of those conditions. This type of code is not an error to Visual Basic, but it will produce difficult to understand code, something very undesirable.

Looping

So far in today's lesson, you have learned how to control which code is executed through the use of `If` and `Select` statements, but there is another very common need—the need to execute the same code a number of times. This requirement is handled through another class of control statement, the loop.

Several different types of loops are available in Visual Basic, any one of which is capable of most tasks, but each is designed around a specific purpose. We will start our exploration of repetition by looking at that most basic of loops, the `For...Next` loop.

For...Next

The goal of a loop is to execute a block of code repeatedly, usually stopping when some condition is true. (Although a loop does not have to ever stop; this situation is referred to as an *endless loop*.). The For loop executes a block of code a specific number of times. The syntax of this control is

```
For <counter variable> = <starting value> to <ending value>
    Code to be executed
Next <counter variable>
```

The inclusion of the counter variable after the ending Next statement is optional, but it helps to indicate which For loop this Next statement belongs to and is good programming practice.

The Counter Variable

The counter variable is incremented each pass through the loop, from the starting value to the ending value. When that ending value is reached, the loop stops execution, and the program continues on the line immediately following the Next statement. To view this concept with some real values in place, let's create a Visual Basic .NET version of the first program I ever wrote (see Listing 4.9).

LISTING **4.9**   Printing Your Name, Over and Over Again

```
1 Dim iCounter As Integer
2 For iCounter = 1 to 10
3     System.Console.WriteLine("Duncan Mackenzie")
4 Next iCounter
```

Of course, I usually use end values up in the thousands... my name would never stop scrolling across the screen!

The counter variable is a real variable, and just as Listing 4.9, it must be declared before you can use it as part of your loop. It is also important to make sure that you use the correct data type for that variable. In Listing 4.9, the variable iCounter would be used to hold the values 1 through 10, making an Integer or Byte the most suitable data type. In other situations, you could be dealing with much larger numbers and might then require a Long Integer. For more information on the various data types, including what range of values each can hold, refer to Day 3. As mentioned earlier, the counter variable is incremented each time through the loop, which often is useful because you can use that variable in your code.

Do	Don't
DO use the most appropriate data type for the situation; do not use a Long Integer when an Integer would do just fine. If the range is close, or could increase greatly, make sure that you use the data type that best handles the largest possible counter range.	**DON'T** change the value of the counter variable inside the loop. The built-in functionality of the For loop is incrementing the counter variable each time the code inside the loop is executed, but you are not prevented from modifying that variable's value yourself. Resist the temptation, it will only result in strange errors and incomprehensible code.

Listing 4.10 shows how you could use the counter variable as part of your code. A little function called WeekdayName produces a listing of the regular business days in the week.

LISTING 4.10   Using the Counter Variable

```
 1 Public Class DaysOfTheWeek
 2
 3     Shared Sub Main()
 4     Dim sDayName As String
 5     Dim iFirstDay As Integer
 6     Dim iLastDay As Integer
 7     Dim iCurrentDay As Integer
 8
 9         iFirstDay = 2
10         iLastDay = 6
11         For iCurrentDay = iFirstDay to iLastDay
12             System.Console.WriteLine(WeekdayName(iCurrentDay))
13         Next iCurrentDay
14
15     End Sub
16
17     Shared Function WeekdayName(ByVal iDayNumber As Integer) As String
18     Dim sWeekdayName As String
19
20         Select Case iDayNumber
21             Case 1
22                 sWeekdayName = "Sunday"
23             Case 2
24                 sWeekdayName = "Monday"
25             Case 3
26                 sWeekdayName = "Tuesday"
27             Case 4
28                 sWeekdayName = "Wednesday"
29             Case 5
30                 sWeekdayName = "Thursday"
31             Case 6
32                 sWeekdayName = "Friday"
33             Case 7
34                 sWeekdayName = "Saturday"
35
36             Case Else
37                 sWeekdayName = "Invalid Day Number"
38         End Select
39         Return sWeekdayName
40     End Function
41 End Class
```

4

Note that in Listing 4.10 Sunday is considered Day 1, so this code would produce the following results:

```
Monday
Tuesday
Wednesday
Thursday
Friday
```

 Note

This example is not quite ready for production because it will produce the list of names in English only, not taking the settings of the machine into account. There are other, slightly more complicated, ways to achieve this functionality complete with support for all the users' regional settings. We will return to this topic in Day 8, "Introduction to the .NET Framework."

Specifying an Increment Using Step

In previous examples, the counter variable was incremented by 1 each time through the loop, but it is possible to specify that increment amount. After the end value portion of the For statement, you can specify Step <*increment value*>, and the counter variable will be incremented by whatever value you supply. Taking the sample code in Listing 4.11 as a starting point, try different values for the First, Last, and Increment values to see the results.

LISTING 4.11   ForExample.vb

```
 1 Imports System
 2 Public Class ForExample
 3
 4     Shared Sub Main()
 5     Dim iCounter As Integer
 6     Dim iFirstValue As Integer
 7     Dim iLastValue As Integer
 8     Dim iIncrement As Integer
 9
10     iFirstValue = 0
11     iLastValue = 100
12     iIncrement = 10
13     For iCounter = iFirstValue to iLastValue Step iIncrement
14         System.Console.WriteLine(iCounter)
15     Next iCounter
16
17     End Sub
18 End Class
```

An interesting and useful feature of having the Step option in the For loop is that it allows you to move through a range of values in reverse. Try values of 10, 0, and 1 for the First, Last, and Increment variables, respectively. Nothing will be output at all, because Last is already less than First, but if you change the Increment value from 1 to –1, a beautiful thing will happen (don't take my word for it, try it!).

Ah, you get a loop that executes the exact number of times you want, and now the numbers are listed backwards. It is hard to believe that it gets better than this, but it does. Wait until we get to the Do loop!

While...End While

The For loop, although useful, is limited. It is designed for situations in which you know how many times you want to loop, which isn't always the case. Knowing this, Visual Basic includes two more flexible loops. The first of these, the While...End While loop, keeps looping while a specified Boolean expression is true, as follows:

```
While <Boolean expression>

    Code to be executed

End While
```

4

The expression can be any valid Boolean expression, just as in an If statement, and therefore can support complex conditions. For example, a While loop can easily duplicate the functionality of the For loop, as demonstrated in Listing 4.12.

LISTING 4.12 WhileExample.vb

```
 1 Imports System
 2 Public Class WhileExample
 3     Shared Sub Main()
 4     Dim iCounter As Integer
 5     Dim iFirstValue As Integer
 6     Dim iLastValue As Integer
 7     Dim iIncrement As Integer
 8         iFirstValue = 0
 9         iLastValue = 100
10         iIncrement = 10
11         While iCounter <= iLastValue
12             '<Insert Code block here>
13             iCounter = iCounter + iIncrement
14         End While
15     End Sub
16 End Class
```

Of course, duplicating the functionality of the For loop is not a useful way to spend your time. You don't have to pick just one loop; you get to use them all! You'll want to use the While loop to do more complicated things, such as to scan an array for a particular bit of data. In Listing 4.13, you will get ready for the search by loading up an array with some string data. Then, using the While loop, you will scan the array until you exceed the size of the array, or you find your match.

LISTING 4.13 WhileSearch.vb

```
 1 Imports System
 2 Public Class WhileExample
 3      Shared Sub Main()
 4      Dim iCounter As Integer = 0
 5      Dim arrList(9) As String
 6      Dim iMatch As Integer = -1
 7      Dim sMatch As String
 8          sMatch = "Winnipeg"
 9          arrList(0) = "San Diego"
10          arrList(1) = "Toronto"
11          arrList(2) = "Seattle"
12          arrList(3) = "London"
13          arrList(4) = "New York"
14          arrList(5) = "Paris"
15          arrList(6) = "Winnipeg"
16          arrList(7) = "Sydney"
17          arrList(8) = "Calgary"
18          arrList(9) = "Orlando"
19          While iCounter <= 9 AND iMatch = -1
20              If arrList(iCounter) Like sMatch Then
21                  iMatch = iCounter
22              Else
23                  iCounter = iCounter + 1
24              End If
25          End While
26          If iMatch <> -1 Then
27              System.Console.WriteLine("Matched " & iMatch)
28          End If
29      End Sub
31 End Class
```

You use the Like comparison in Listing 4.13, which allows you to match using wildcards. If you run through this code, you will see that the program exits out nicely as soon as either one of the exit conditions become true. The While loop is quite useful, but there is still one more type of loop available, the Do loop. If you are like me, you will likely forget all about that While statement, after you have used the Do loop.

Do Loop

The Do loop is both the simplest and the most flexible loop structure available in Visual Basic. Its syntax, in its most basic form, is just

```
Do
    Code to be executed
Loop
```

The syntax doesn't specify any exit condition though, so the code inside will continue to execute forever. This problem is easily solved because the Do statement supports two ways of stating exit conditions. The two available options are While <condition>, which causes the loop to execute as long as the condition is true, and Until <condition>, which makes the loop continue to execute as long as the condition is false.

Which one should you use, While or Until? Technically, it doesn't really matter; you can easily switch between the two options just by negating your exit condition. These two code examples will behave the same way:

```
Do While iMatch = 3

Loop

Do Until Not (iMatch = 3)
'iMatch <> 3 would have also worked

Loop
```

So, While or Until are not that different in effect, but the Do loop offers another option that provides even more flexibility. You can place the exit condition (with the Until or While clause) at either the beginning (with the Do) or the end (with the Loop) of the loop. This means that you can create loops like the following:

```
Do

Loop Until bFound or iCounter > iTotal
```

Unlike the choice between While or Until, the position of your exit condition has a major effect on how your loop executes. If you place the condition at the start of the loop, then that condition is checked before each pass through the code, even before the first time through. If that condition is not met, then the loop will not be entered, and the code will not be executed even once. Conversely, if you place the condition with the Loop statement, then that condition will be checked after each pass through the code. Regardless of the value of the condition, the code will always be executed at least once.

With all these options, there are a total of four different configurations of the Do loop statement, making it by far the most flexible method of looping. You still have to decide between these four options, so let's go over a few things to help with that decision:

4

- You can switch between While and Until just by negating the Boolean expression.

- Choosing between While and Until, use whichever one does not require you to negate your conditional statement. This will lead to a slightly simpler Boolean expression and in code, simpler is usually better.

- The positioning of the conditional statement is very important. If you place it at the beginning of the loop, then the loop will not execute at all if that condition is not met. If you place it at the end, then the loop will be executed the first time, no matter what.

- Choose between the two possible positions by determining if you want the loop not to execute at all if the condition is not met, or if you want it to always occur once.

Note

> The Do While loop can be used instead of the While loop because they have exactly the same effect. It is not unusual for programmers to put aside the While loop completely in favor of this statement.

Exit Conditions

 The *exit condition* of any loop is the expression that is being tested to determine when the loop should end. In the case of a While or Do loop, these exit conditions are clearly defined and appear at the start or end. In a For loop, the exit condition is implied by the setting of upper and lower boundaries. In each of these looping methods though, there is another way to specify when to exit the loop by using the Exit statement. There is a corresponding Exit statement for each loop (Exit For, Exit Do, and Exit While). When the appropriate statement is executed, the loop will be immediately left, and program execution will continue from the line following the end of the loop.

Although you will find many occasions when it seems that these statements are the perfect way to make your program behave correctly, they are one of the many examples of improper programming practices. By using an Exit statement, you have really just specified an additional part to your exit condition, but you have done so in a less-than-obvious way. The best way to do this would be to add this second condition to the main exit condition of your loop. In the following examples, you will see some common ways in which Exit statements are used and the corresponding code that you could use instead.

Example 1: Using a For Loop to Search an Array

With an array of fixed size, you could create a For loop to scan through, aborting the loop with Exit For when the match is found.

```
For i = 1 to 100
    If arrNames(i) = "Joe" Then
        System.Console.WriteLine("Found it at #" & i)
        Exit For
    End If
Next i
```

The real problem here is that you shouldn't have used a For loop at all, but you do not know ahead of time how many loops you will have to perform. A clearer way to write this code would be to use a Do loop that checks for exceeding the upper bound and for finding the match, as follows:

```
i = 1
Do Until i > 100 or arrNames(i) = "Joe"
    i = i + 1
Loop
```

Example 2: Checking for an Escape Value

In loops where you want to get the user's input, but also want to allow them to cancel out, two exit conditions and an Exit statement are often used for one of them:

```
iCurrentGuess = 0
iTarget = 5
Do Until iCurrentGuess = iTarget
    iCurrentGuess = GetNextGuess()
    If iCurrentGuess = -1 Then
        Exit Do
    End If
Loop
```

Once again, the true exit condition is more complicated than this loop makes it seem. A proper solution follows:

```
iCurrentGuess = 0
iTarget = 5
Do Until (iCurrentGuess = iTarget) Or (iCurrentGuess = -1)
    iCurrentGuess = GetNextGuess()
Loop
```

If these Exit statements are bad, you might wonder why I am covering them. Well, although I can count on you to avoid them in your own code, most programmers are often working with code that was written by someone else, and it is important to understand whatever you might find in that code.

Endless Loops

Any loop can have an error, but a particularly annoying error is when a loop executes continuously, forcing you to kill the program to stop it. The fact that you do not have to specify any condition at all in your Do loop makes it a little more prone to this type of error. If you ran the program, and it never seems to end, then, if you are using a DOS-based program, use the key combination Ctrl+C to force it to end. If you are using the Visual Basic IDE, use the key combination Ctrl+Break to force it to cease execution.

Do	**Don't**
DO make sure that you have an exit condition for any loop you create.	**DON'T** make your exit condition too complex; it needs to be evaluated each time through the loop.

Some common causes of endless loops are forgetting to increment a counter variable (in loops other than For), resetting a variable that should be increasing, and using an exit condition that can never occur.

Performance Implications

There are several useful tips to help you get the best performance out of the loops in your code. First, always remember that any performance optimization within a loop is many times more beneficial than performance optimization elsewhere in a program. Because code within a loop will be executed over and over again, any increased performance in that code is magnified by the number of iterations in your loop. As an example, consider the code in Listing 4.14.

LISTING 4.14   LoopPerformance.vb

```
 1 Public Class LoopPerformance
 2
 3     Shared Sub Main()
 4     Dim i As Integer
 5 6        For i = 1 to 1000
 7            System.Console.WriteLine(UserName())
 8        Next i
 9     End Sub
10
11     Shared Function UserName() As String
12     Dim sName As String
13        sName = System.Environment.UserName
14        UserName = sName
15     End Function
16
17 End Class
```

The username is supplied through a little function that uses the .NET Framework to figure out your current security information, but the point of Listing 4.14 is to illustrate a common performance-related mistake. The call to the UserName function occurs inside the loop, which means that the function will be called 1,000 times, each time likely resulting in some form of operating system call to get the current username. Because the current user is not expected to change within this loop, it is much more efficient to create your loop instead, as shown in Listing 4.15. The value of the UserName function does not change, and is therefore not included in this second listing.

LISTING 4.15   LoopPerformance_Better.vb

```
 1 Public Class LoopPerformance
 2
 3     Shared Sub Main()
 4     Dim i As Integer
 5     Dim sName As String
 6     sName = UserName()
 7
 8         For i = 1 to 1000
 9             System.Console.WriteLine(sName)
10         Next i
11
12     End Sub
13
14     Shared Function UserName() As String
15     Dim sName As String
16         sName = System.Environment.UserName
17         UserName = sName
18
19     End Function
20
21 End Class
```

4

Another performance tip that is important whenever you are using Boolean expressions is to ensure that the simplest portions of the expression are placed on the left side of the expression and to then use the short-circuiting ANDALSO and ORELSE. With these versions of the Boolean operators in place, it is possible that only the left side of the expression will be evaluated, so you will want the left side to be the quicker of the two clauses.

Applications of Your New Found Knowledge

Now that you know how to use conditional statements, such as IF and Select Case, and various types of loops, you can take those statements and create some interesting sample programs. To build these examples, you will need something beyond the Visual Basic learned so far; you'll need the .NET Framework Classes. Present to some extent in all the previous examples, these classes are sets of existing code that have been packaged and provided to programs through the fact that Visual Basic is a .NET language. These sets of code are provided as *objects*, basically a way to represent a concept or entity within code. Whenever you use an object such as System.Console or System.Security.Principal, you are working with a part of the .NET Framework. To do so, you often have to tell Visual Basic that you plan on using it by including a line such as Imports System.Security.Principal in your code. Think of these objects as part of .NET; they can bring your programs an enormous set of functionality so that every individual programmer doesn't have to build this functionality himself. This is a critical concept in Visual Basic .NET, but it is also one that I will be covering again in future days, so do not be concerned if it does not seem perfectly clear at this point.

Reading from a File

To read a file from disk is a common need of many programs, so it is provided by .NET Framework. In this lesson, you will use two different objects, both part of the System.IO section of the framework, System.IO.File and System.IO.StreamReader. They represent the actual file on disk and the reading of that file into memory, respectively.

The StreamReader object is created by using the OpenFile method of the File object, specifying the path and filename of the file you wish to open. You can use this StreamReader object to read each line of the file, one at a time, using its ReadLine method until you get to the very end of the file. To check that you have reached the end of the file, compare the last value read in to the special constant Nothing, which is different from a blank line and allows you to distinguish between an empty line in a file and the actual end of all the data. Because Nothing is a special type of value, you use the is operator to compare your string with it, instead of a regular equals operator. In Listing 4.16, the first step is to initialize all your objects, while obtaining the StreamReader object pointing to the file in which you wish to read. You need a sample text file to do this exercise, but any of your other sample .vb program files should do.

LISTING 4.16 Step 1: Set It Up

```
 1 Public Class ReadFromFile
 2
 3     Shared Sub Main()
 4     Dim sFileName As String
 5     Dim srFileReader As System.IO.StreamReader
 6     Dim sInputLine As String
 7
 8         sFileName = "MySampleFile.txt"
 9         srFileReader = System.IO.File.OpenText(sFileName)
10
11     End Sub
12 End Class
```

After you have your `StreamReader` object, which has been initialized to point at the sample file, you can use a `Do While` loop (see Listing 4.17) to read in the file, one line at a time. To make this program produce some output, so that you can tell what it is doing, you will also print out each line as you read it in.

LISTING 4.17   Step 2: Insert This Code Above the End `Sub` Statement in Listing 4.16

```
1       sInputLine = "something"
2       Do Until sInputLine is Nothing
3           sInputLine = srFileReader.ReadLine()
4           System.Console.WriteLine(sInputLine)
5       Loop
```

Before you enter the loop for the first time, you want to make sure that your condition is met, so initialize `sInputLine` to ensure that it is not `Nothing`. In Listing 4.18, you will attempt to output `sInputLine` even when it is `Nothing`, but you could add an `If` statement to check for that possibility.

LISTING 4.18   Adding a Check for Nothing

```
1       sInputLine = "something"
2       Do Until sInputLine is Nothing
3           sInputLine = srFileReader.ReadLine()
4           If Not sInputLine is Nothing Then
5               System.Console.WriteLine(sInputLine)
6           End If
7       Loop
```

Alternatively (see Listing 4.19), you could use a slightly different looping method and ensure that you will not attempt output after the end of the file has been reached.

LISTING 4.19   A Better Loop

```
1 Public Class ReadFromFile
2
3       Shared Sub Main()
4       Dim sFileName As String
5       Dim srFileReader As System.IO.StreamReader
6       Dim sInputLine As String
7
8           sFileName = "MySampleFile.txt"
9           srFileReader = System.IO.File.OpenText(sFileName)
10          sInputLine = srFileReader.ReadLine()
11          Do Until sInputLine is Nothing
12              System.Console.WriteLine(sInputLine)
```

4

LISTING 4.19   continued

```
13                    sInputLine = srFileReader.ReadLine()
14          Loop
15       End Sub
16 End Class
```

Either method will work, but the final application given in Listing 4.19 produces the simplest (and therefore best) code within the actual loop. If you want to run this code, you will have to create a text file with sample content in the same directory as your compiled executable.

A Simple Game

Another common use of a loop is to repeatedly query the user for a response, until you get the response you want. This might sound annoying (somewhat like the queries of a small child), but in the right type of program, it can be useful. For this example, you will create a simple number-guessing game. This particular game was my father's way to keep me occupied while waiting to be served at restaurants, although we played it in a lower technology way. First, he would write a lower and upper bound on the top and bottom of a napkin, 1 and 100, for instance, and then he would pick a number at random (father random, not computer random) and write that on the back of the napkin. I would proceed to guess numbers until I found the right one, being told each time whether I had guessed too high or too low. Although I doubt I was very methodical at it, that information certainly made it easier. As part of the continuing quest to computerize things that don't need to be computerized, let's make a computer program to play "Guess the Number!"

The basics of this program have been outlined above; we could use my little story as the pseudo code for the program. It might be best to quickly rephrase the details into a clearer definition of what the program should do:

1. Ask the user for an upper and lower numeric bound.
2. Determine a random number within that range; this is the target.
3. Ask the user for a guess.
4. If the guess is right, stop the game and tell the user how many guesses it took.
5. Otherwise, tell the user if she is too high or too low and go back to step 3.

This pseudocode is not complex, but there is a new concept in there that you have yet to learn, the generation of random numbers. Luckily for you, the .NET Framework provides a class for just that purpose, `System.Random`. Using this object, you can generate a random number between an upper and lower bound using code like the following:

```
Dim iTargetNumber, iUpperBound, iLowerBound As Integer
Dim objRandom As System.Random = New System.Random
iUpperBound = 100
iLowerBound = 1
iTargetNumber = objRandom.Next(iLowerBound,iUpperBound + 1)
```

Note

This method of generating random numbers returns values that are greater than or equal to the lower bound and less than the upper bound (iLowerBound <= x < iUpperBound). You need to specify an upper value that is one higher than the highest value you want to allow. The code in this example does this already.

After the Random object has been initialized, you can call its Next method as often as you like, and you will get a new random number each time. Now that you know how to get a random number, you can write the code shown in Listing 4.20 to get the bounds from the user and then use those values to get your target.

LISTING 4.20 Getting the Necessary Info from the User

```
 1 Public Class NumberGuesser
 2     Shared Sub Main()
 3     Dim iTargetNumber As Integer
 4     Dim iUpperBound As Integer
 5     Dim iLowerBound As Integer
 6     Dim iCurrentGuess As Integer
 7     Dim iGuessCount As Integer
 8     Dim sInput As String
 9     Dim objRandom As System.Random = New System.Random()
10
11         System.Console.Write("Please enter the lower bound: ")
12         sInput = System.Console.ReadLine()
13         iLowerBound = CInt(sInput)
14
15         System.Console.Write("Please enter the upper bound: ")
16         sInput = System.Console.ReadLine()
17         iUpperBound = CInt(sInput)
18
19         'Figure Out Number
20         iTargetNumber = objRandom.Next(iLowerBound,iUpperBound + 1)
21         System.Console.WriteLine(iTargetNumber)
22
23     End Sub
24 End Class
```

4

In Listing 4.20, you output the number after you generate it. This is useful to test your program, but it would have to be removed or commented out (marked with a beginning comment character (') to indicate that it should not be compiled) in the final version. Next you need to build a loop that will keep asking for a new guess until the target is reached. While the program is looping, you also need to keep another variable around to track the number of guesses it takes to reach the target. This code (see Listing 4.21) would need to be inserted before the End Sub statement to finish the program.

LISTING 4.21   Your Game's Input Loop

```
1        iCurrentGuess = 0
2        iGuessCount = 0
3        Do While iCurrentGuess <> iTargetNumber
4            System.Console.Write("Please Enter A Guess: ")
5            sInput = System.Console.ReadLine()
6            iGuessCount = iGuessCount + 1
7            iCurrentGuess = CInt(sInput)
8
9            If iCurrentGuess < iTargetNumber Then
10               System.Console.WriteLine("Your Guess is Low!")
11           ElseIf iCurrentGuess > iTargetNumber Then
12               System.Console.WriteLine("Your Guess is High!")
13           End If
14       Loop
15       System.Console.WriteLine("You did it in " & iGuessCount & " guesses")
```

Combined, the previous two listings of code produce the completed game that you can compile and try your luck against. You should remove the final WriteLine in Listing 4.21 before playing, or it could seem a little too easy. There is a very methodical and, therefore, boring way to play this game, which guarantees that you will get the correct answer within a certain number of guesses. You can simply guess the middle point in the range every time, using the High/Low information to create a new range (half the size) between your guess and the top or bottom bound. For the sample game using 1 to 100, this method is guaranteed to find a solution in seven guesses (or less), based on a mathematical formula. Do you know what the formula is that will tell you the number of guesses required for any range of values? The answer will be in the exercise section of today's lesson.

Avoiding Complex Loops Through Recursion

Often, there is more than one way to solve a certain problem, and, although a standard loop might work, there can be a simpler way. If a problem is structured just right, or you can restructure it in the right way, then you can use recursion as an alternative to regular loops. In programming, *recursion* occurs when a program or procedure calls itself in an effort to solve a problem. The problems that can be solved through recursion are those in which a subset of the problem has the exact same structure as the entire problem. The best way to explain this concept is through an example, the calculation of a factorial. The formula for a factorial of a value (n!) is n(n-1)(n-2)...(n-(n-1))(1). For a value such as 10, this formula becomes 10 * 9 * 8 * 7 * 6 * 5 * 4 * 3 * 2 * 1 = 3628800. (Note that the result is quite large relative to the value of n.) This formula can be expressed using a For loop, as in Listing 4.22.

LISTING 4.22 Factorial.vb

```
 1 Public Class Factorial
 2     Shared Sub Main()
 3     Dim sInput As String
 4     Dim iInput As Integer
 5     Dim iCounter As Integer
 6     Dim iFactorial As Integer
 7         System.Console.Write("Please Enter A Number: ")
 8         sInput = System.Console.ReadLine()
 9         iInput = CInt(sInput)
10         iFactorial = 1
11         For iCounter = 0 to (iInput - 1)
12             iFactorial = (iInput - iCounter) * iFactorial
13         Next iCounter
14         System.Console.WriteLine(iFactorial)
15     End Sub
16 End Class
```

> **Note**
>
> When experimenting with this program, you will need to keep your test value (10 in our example) less than or equal to 12. Any greater value will produce a factorial that exceeds the maximum size of an Integer variable (see Day 3). If you need support for higher values, use other variable types such as a Long.

This is not the only way to produce the factorial though because this formula can also be expressed as n * (n-1)!, that is, n multiplied by the factorial of n-1. This expression defines the formula recursively; the solution for a factorial includes another factorial. This is a clearer definition than the formula n(n-1)(n-2)...(n-(n-1))(1) though, and, if you write code in this manner (see Listing 4.23), you will produce code that is also simpler than the corresponding routine from Listing 4.22.

LISTING 4.23 RecursiveFactorial.vb

```
 1 Public Class RecursiveFactorial
 2     Shared Sub Main()
 3     Dim sInput As String
 4     Dim iInput As Integer
 5     Dim iCounter As Integer
 6     Dim iFactorial As Integer
 7         System.Console.Write("Please Enter A Number: ")
 8         sInput = System.Console.ReadLine()
 9         iInput = CInt(sInput)
10         System.Console.WriteLine(Factorial(iInput))
11     End Sub
12
13     Shared Function Factorial(n as Integer) as Integer
14
15         If n = 1 Then
16             Return 1
17         Else
18             Return n * Factorial(n-1)
19         End If
20
21     End Function
22 End Class
```

The code produced might not be shorter than Listing 4.22, but it is simpler and that is a worthwhile result all on its own. Note that in the Factorial() function, you check for n = 1. This check ensures that the recursive calls will eventually end, in the same manner as an exit condition in a loop. Without it, just as with a loop, the program will never stop executing. Recursion can be used to solve many problems, and you will see code using it in many different types of systems (and hopefully write your own).

Summary

Today, you learned about control statements, the basis for many of the computer programs you will create in future days. With these statements, you can start to model real-world processes into computer programs by first turning them into pseudo code and then using that to create the actual code you need.

Q&A

Q. My buddy told me that `While` loops are better than `Do` loops, and that I should never use the `For` loop at all! Which loop is the best?

A. Although it is possible to use only one loop for all your programs, there is no benefit in doing so. In the end, all that matters is that your code be as clear and simple as it can be. Use the loop that best fits the problem. Generally, a `For` loop works best when you need a fixed number of iterations; use either a `Do` or `While` loop when this is not the situation.

Q. Are single-line `If` statements faster than the `If...End If` form?

A. No. The Visual Basic compiler turns both forms into the same result, so there is no difference in execution speed between these two formats. The key difference is in code maintainability and readability.

Q. In previous versions of Visual Basic and in Visual Basic for Applications (VBA), I have used a form of the `If` statement called `Immediate If` (IIF). Does this exist in Visual Basic .NET?

A. Yes, it does, but it exists only as part of a special set of objects (Microsoft.VisualBasic) designed to provide access to `IIF` and many other parts of the last version of Visual Basic that are no longer in Visual Basic .NET. The fact that these functions were not built in to the latest version of Visual Basic might mean that they will not be available at all in future versions. `IIF` is a very useful form of the `If` statement; as a function, it can be used in the middle of another expression, such as when outputting a string. However, because future versions of Visual Basic might not include `IIF`, you should avoid using it if possible.

Workshop

The Workshop is designed to help you anticipate possible questions, review what you've learned, and get thinking about how to put your knowledge into practice. The answers to the quiz are in Appendix A, "Answers to Quizzes/Exercises."

Quiz

1. Which of the three available looping methods is best suited to a fixed range of values?

2. Which of the three looping methods is the most flexible?

3. Why should you try to make the inner block of code in a loop as simple as possible?

4. Suppose that you had the following Boolean expression in your program: `CalculatedTotalNetWorth(iCustomerID) < 10000 AND dtCurrentDate.Hour > 12`. What could you do to ensure that this expression would be evaluated as efficiently as possible?

Exercise

1. Write the other side of the NumberGuesser program created earlier in today's lesson—a program with upper and lower bounds that attempts to determine what value has been selected by the user. For each guess that the computer program makes, you will need to allow the user to respond with "H" for too high, "L" for too low, or = for correct. If you choose to use the methodical method for your program's guesses, then the maximum number of tries that are required can be found by solving this equation: $(2^N >=$ Upper Bound – Lower Bound) where N equals the maximum number of tries. For example, for a range of 1–100, the equation works out to 7 because $2^6 = 64$ and $2^7 = 128$.

DAY 5

Application Architecture in .NET

Throughout this book you are learning how to use Visual Basic .NET to create applications, but larger issues are involved at the design phase of the development process. This lesson will cover

- What is "application architecture"?
- What architectural choices does .NET provide?
- What is involved in choosing an application architecture?

In addition to the high-level discussion of these topics, today's lesson also includes a discussion of a few sample scenarios and a walkthrough of determining architectures for each.

What Is Application Architecture?

Before construction begins and long before a building is ready for use, an architect has handled the design phase. After a basic understanding of the project is agreed on, sketches are created that show the broad details of the proposed building, and those sketches form the basis of the detailed blueprints that must be created before any actual construction work begins on the building. Throughout this process, not just at the beginning, an architect, in conjunction with all the project team, is responsible for producing the correct result.

The concept of an architect, both the person and the aspects of a project he is responsible for, has been borrowed by the software development industry. The implied similarity between the two areas must not please real architects, and I do not blame them for being perturbed. If buildings were constructed in the same fashion as the majority of software systems, then I for one would be spending the rest of my days living under the open skies. A lot of business software development is done without sufficient planning, resulting in systems that are unstable, hard to maintain, and almost always over budget.

Role of the Software Architect

Regardless of the appropriateness of using the name of an existing profession, parallels can be drawn. When a building is being designed, the architects use their advanced knowledge of both function and design to envision and plan the overall structure and foundation of a building based on the requirements they have been given. In software, the same process occurs. A software (or system) architect develops a plan for building the system based on the requirements. In both cases, the plan is eventually turned into a detailed design for how the project should be built, and other teams of people take over to handle the actual implementation.

Although some would see it as nowhere near as complex as designing and building a huge skyscraper, software development is complicated, and the role of an architect is definitely needed in almost any size of system. No matter what size of application you are building, or how small your individual part of the system is, an application architecture has been chosen (perhaps informally) and is being used.

 Note

> You might seem to manage without an architect on many smaller projects, but what is actually occurring is that you (or another member of the development team) have unofficially taken on that role. The problem with anyone handling a project role unofficially is that the team is not conscious of who is responsible for any particular aspect of the project.

You might be new to Visual Basic, or new to development altogether. It might be unlikely that you would be chosen to fill the role of system architect in the near future. But that does not change the need for you to understand the process and the architectural decisions being made on any project you are involved in. In the overall software development life cycle, the entire team should be involved throughout the entire process, but the architect is the key driver of the project during the beginning phases of Vision/Scope, Requirements Analysis, and Design (see Figure 5.1).

FIGURE 5.1

In the software development life cycle, architecture fits mainly into the first few phases, where the software is being designed.

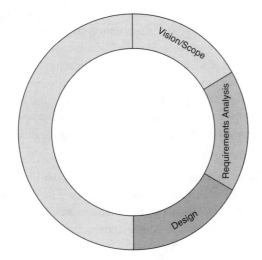

After these initial phases, the focus shifts to the implementation team (software developers) and then to the testing and deployment groups. Ideally, the person handling the role of architect should be highly experienced, with enough technical knowledge to evaluate all the available options and enough business skill to correctly interpret the system requirements. Often, the role of architect is handled by senior members of a development group.

What Parts of a System Are Considered Application Architecture?

The short answer to this question is "everything," but that is a little too broad to be of any use. The architectural aspects of a system are the "big details," such as what type of client interface will be used, Web versus Windows application, and how the code in the Web page will talk to the back-end database. The key is that system architecture is concerned with the foundation and frame of the application, and not with the implementation choices that will be made within that framework.

An architect is involved in the implementation stage, though, even though it would seem that all the "big details" have been determined and only the finer details of the implementation remain. The architect stays involved for two main reasons: to see that the chosen architecture is proving to be correct (adjusting as necessary to handle any problems that appear), and to make sure that the design is being implemented as it was intended. It might be difficult to believe, but sometimes developers will stray from a system design, producing undesirable results.

To answer the question more specifically, in .NET systems, the system architecture should provide a high-level overview of every aspect of the application. The key is the level of detail; most things discussed at the architectural level will be covered again in the detailed design and in the implementation. For example, part of the system architecture might be a discussion of security, and at the architectural level the following statement could be sufficient to cover that topic: "The application will base its security permissions on the Windows 2000 users and groups already in use in the company." This statement is sufficient for a starting point; the next level would get more detailed and could include information on what areas of the application will be secured and who will be given access to each specific area.

In the implementation or build phase, a programmer will have to determine exactly how to find out the current user's Windows logon and group membership, but those details are certainly not part of the system architecture. Although architecture covers everything at a high-level, the following key areas should be addressed as part of every application architecture:

- Logical and physical distribution of code (what code will run where?)
- Technologies used for the user interface, database and business logic
- Communication method between different components of the system and between this system and others within the company
- Security
- Data access
- Scalability and availability

Each of these areas is important in itself, but architecture is the combination of all these factors in a design that works as a whole. The purpose of each of these areas is covered in the following sections.

Logical and Physical Distribution of Code

At the architectural level, decisions can be made about a desired organization, allowing the code to be categorized into groups such as "Data Access Code," "Security Code," "User Interface Code," and others. In reality, any division of code is totally up to the individual programmers and the rest of the project team. Nothing about .NET (or any other development tool) forces you to keep code grouped in an organized fashion. Do not let reality stop you, though; for the purposes of design, it is important to categorize code even if such an organization will never really exist. What must be determined about these groups is where they will be executed; will they all run as part of the single application on a single machine, or will the Data Access Code run on an independent server?

Later in today's lesson, I will discuss the concept of *tiers*, or layers, where all the functionality in an application is logically divided by purpose. Those tiers are then treated as if they were independent sets of code, to be moved around as desired. The decisions about where to run each layer of an application and how many servers to use for each, forms this element of the system architecture.

Technologies

One of the clearer topic areas, this element of system architecture will outline the "general" technologies that will be used. The trick within this area is delivering enough information to be useful, while avoiding details that have not been determined or details that are irrelevant at an architectural level. Consider these two snippets (do not concern yourself with understanding the details, it is merely for example):

Example 1:

The project team will develop the user interface using Visual Basic 6.0 (Service Pack 5) and an ActiveX grid control from Janus. Several windows will be developed, each with menus, a main grid, and several functional buttons. These forms will use DCOM to connect to the middle tier servers, each of which will be running Windows 2000 (Service Pack 2) Advanced Server. The middle tier servers will be hosting five components inside the Windows 2000 COM+ component services environment. These business components will be COM DLLs, built using Visual Basic 6.0 (Service Pack 5) and with their properties set to Public. Each component will consist of…

Example 2:

The user interface will be forms-based and will use DCOM to communicate with the middle tier. Within the middle tier, COM business objects will have been installed into COM+ and will handle communication with the data tier. ADO will be used to connect from the middle tier to the back-end data, and all information will be returned to the presentation layer after passing through the business layer.

Although I cut off Example 1 before it was finished, it wasn't really anywhere near done and had yet to convey as much useful information as Example 2. The key is to keep reminding yourself of the point, which is to gain an understanding of the architecture. There are still detailed design and implementation phases remaining in the project to handle getting into that lower level of detail. Another good rule is to never spend too much time discussing specific technologies. Try to stay focused and only discuss the technology in terms of what it brings to this project.

Communication Between Components

If you are building a distributed system, one that will be executed across multiple machines, then some form of communication needs to exist between the various components. There are many different options, but at the architectural level, you only need to get specific about details that are either already certain, or are relevant due to some other aspect of the project. For this area, you might have to specify the communication protocol if you have to interconnect with another system or if the technical details are crucial to a parallel project such as network/firewall configuration. .NET provides several different options for this type of communication including SOAP.

Security

A vague title for a vague area, security is a topic that must be addressed simply because every discussion will eventually come around to this topic and stay there if it hasn't already been detailed. The architecture should detail how security will be provided (using Windows 2000 Active Directory for instance) and conceptually how it will be implemented ("interface options will be hidden" or "security will be checked on a per page/form basis"). It is not necessary to detail exactly how the programmers will implement these features.

Data Access

What areas of code will access data? How will they do so? This section details how the application will connect to the data (OLEDB provider using SQL Server security, for example). More complex issues, such as the design and organization of the actual database, are best handled in either the detailed design phase or as part of the actual implementation.

Scalability and Availability

This is an important and complex pair of topics and one of the main reasons why application architecture receives so much attention. These two topics are related in many ways; the techniques and architecture used to provide the one service are often used to provide the other.

Scalability describes the capability for a system to handle larger loads, providing the same level of service (response times, number of requests per second, and so on) through an increase in hardware. Keep in mind that this is not a measure of performance; a system can be scalable and have horrible performance. How to ensure that an application scales well is beyond the scope of this lesson and this book, but a link to other resources will be provided at the end of today's lesson if you are interested in deeper coverage of this topic.

Availability is a measure of how often the system is running and capable of processing requests. Now that public-facing Web applications are being built, the need for systems that are available at all times is widespread. Often this concept is described as "uptime" and in terms of the number of "nines" of availability a system has provided. The term "nines" refers to whether the system has an uptime of 99% (two nines), 99.9% (three nines), or greater. As of the time of this writing, some systems in commercial use have been documented with five nines uptime (99.999%). Expressing this in numbers that have more practical meaning, a site with five nines uptime would have been down for only 5 minutes in an entire year (24 hours a day, 7 days a week). This seems almost ridiculous, and it greatly exceeds my uptime at work, but if you are running a site like Amazon.com, then being down at all for any length of time is unacceptable.

Creating a system with this level of availability is a combination of design and process. From the design point of view, the system must be completely free of memory leaks or other flaws that would prevent continuous use, and the system must be able to run across many machines because multiple groups of hardware must be used to supply redundancy. From the process point of view, though, everything is even more complex. For example, software upgrades will have to be done in a rolling fashion so as to never have the entire set of servers down at any time. Discussions of uptime often center on the operating system or the particular database server/Web server/component server technology in use, suggesting for example that Windows 2000 provides a certain number of nines of uptime. This is not a realistic discussion. The operating system or database server is only one part of the system, and everything has an effect on the system's capability to maintain high availability.

Possible Architectures in .NET

5

There is no fixed number of architectures that can be built—all the different options could be combined to produce a multitude of variations—but there are certain general architectures within which the majority of .NET systems will fall.

The Three Elements of Any Application

The differences between all the possible architectures revolve around how the three distinct layers (or tiers) of a computer system are distributed. The three layers, along with a brief description, are listed here:

- Presentation   This layer represents the interface to the user and to other systems, the outward facing aspect of the system.

- Business Logic   All the code not specifically involved in creating the user interface or other aspects of the Presentation layer. This layer represents the core of the application, the code that actually does the work of the system.

- Data   The database (or other data source such as XML) and the code that accesses it is considered to be the Data layer.

These three layers are the logical representation of a complete system, but that system might take on a variety of forms: a single exe, components scattered across any number of servers, or a simple Web site. Regardless of the specific application, it is useful to describe all systems in terms of these three tiers (layers).

How Many Tiers?

One of the most common ways application architectures have been described has been in terms of the number of different machines that are running portions of the system. The simplest architecture has been described as a single-tier system, where the program (presentation, business logic, and data) is all on one machine. This is the architecture used by most consumer applications, such as Microsoft Office, and by many business applications designed to be used by only a few users at a time. Only the number of machines that are performing some form of processing is important. A program where the data files are located on a file server is still considered a single-tier application because all the actual work is being done on the one machine, and the file server is merely providing a network location to store data.

On the other hand, when a database server (such as SQL Server or Oracle) is being used, then that is considered a second tier because the server is actually doing processing. Systems that have client software (usually on more than one person's machine) that connects directly to a back-end database are called two-tier or client/server applications. Client/server is a common architecture for business applications. It enables many users to work against the same set of data while providing much better performance than a file-based system, such as Microsoft Access.

Finally, the most recent form of application architecture is called three-tier, or *n-tier*, and describes systems where code is running in three or more distinct sections. The logical breakdown of such a system still consists of three layers, but the actual physical layout can exceed three distinct groups. Generally, this means that some form of client code, such as an interactive Web site or perhaps a Windows application, which calls code running on another server or set of servers to handle the business logic, and a back-end database are used. This architecture is becoming more popular because it allows for a great deal of flexibility to handle many users and is therefore well-suited to Internet-based applications. There are several different technical ways to create three-tier applications, but the recommended method from Microsoft before .NET became available was called Windows DNA.

Windows DNA

Windows Distributed Network Architecture (or Distributed interNet Architecture, depending on where you find your definition), is the pre-.NET set of technologies and guidelines from Microsoft for creating three-tier systems. Building on the general idea that every application can be broken down into the three layers of Presentation, Business Logic, and Data, Windows DNA outlined the "best" way to build distributed systems. In a Windows DNA application, client code was run as either a standard Windows application or as a Web interface created with Active Server Pages. The client code contained only interface-related logic, accessing all the business logic by calling COM components located either locally or on another server, components that would then take care of interacting with the database.

A key tenet of the Windows DNA model for building applications is that everything flows through the three layers, so that the Presentation layer communicates only with the business objects, and the business objects handle all communication with the database. The Presentation layer never goes directly to the database, and therefore the three layers are abstracted, allowing the possibility of switching the database without having to rewrite the entire user interface, or to create a totally new interface without having to modify the business layer or the database. The flexibility gained from this model more than makes up for any extra work involved to ensure that the three layers are properly independent.

Now, although the Windows DNA model is fairly detailed, the actual implementation can be any one of a multitude of different configurations. In one case, the application could be running all on one server, with Active Server Pages (Web interface) communicating with components (likely written in Visual Basic 6.0), which then work with a local install of SQL Server. Only one machine is used, but the three layers are still distinct, and the Windows DNA model is maintained. Alternatively, the model can also be scaled out to as many machines as are needed to handle the system load. A possible system might use a farm of 20 Web servers all serving out Active Server Pages that connect to a load-balanced cluster of machines all running the same set of COM components that connect to a pair of servers running SQL Server in a clustered configuration. Despite the much larger scale of the implementation, the same model is being followed, demonstrating the flexibility and scalability of the Windows DNA/three-tier model that has made it so popular.

Where Does .NET Fit In?

.NET is a radical shift in development, but the same general architectural concepts apply. Many .NET systems follow the models and examples discussed previously and can be classified as single-tier, client/server, or even Windows DNA applications. The technology might change (ASP.NET instead of ASP, .NET classes instead of COM objects,

5

and so on), but the architecture is still the same. A few more choices are available, though, to enhance the Windows DNA architecture when using .NET.

The first new concept revolves around communication between the layers. In traditional Windows DNA, the Web pages communicated with the COM business objects using DCOM (Distributed COM), which is a binary standard used to connect COM-aware applications together across a network connection. The abstraction between the layers is limited by this method of communication because only COM-capable technologies can be used in the Business and Presentation layers. In traditional Windows DNA, you could rewrite your business objects without having to change the Presentation or Data layer, but only as long as you were using a COM-capable language (generally Visual Basic or VC++). .NET introduces a new way to communicate that can allow true abstraction between the layers, SOAP (Simple Object Access Protocol).

SOAP communication is all done using XML, instead of a binary format, and runs on top of the widespread HTTP protocol. For the development of distributed applications, this means that any language/tool could be used to create the layers of your system. Your company could have existing components written with Java, which could provide the Business layer of your system, while the front-end is still .NET using either ASP.NET or a Windows application. The .NET version of Windows DNA is even better than it was using the previous set of development technology.

Choosing a Client Technology

One of the most noticed choices when designing a system is what type of client will be created, which is generally a discussion of whether to go thick or thin. The main options under .NET are the same as have been available for some time now, either ASP.NET to create a Web application or Windows Forms to create a Windows application. The trick is determining which one is best suited for a particular system or project. The following sections describe each of the two technologies, covering their benefits and issues. Can I give you a simple rule to tell you what technology to use when? No, but later on in today's lesson I will provide a general list of questions that you can use to help make a variety of architectural choices, including what type of client to use.

Thin Client Systems (ASP.NET)

Active Server Pages are developed using standard .NET languages (such as Visual Basic .NET) and are designed to process incoming requests from users and return the appropriate output to their browsers. The code that you write for an ASP.NET page is executed at the Web server, not at the client, which is the most important point when you are comparing this type of interface with any other. ASP.NET does not have any client requirement beyond network access and some form of browser. You can build ASP.NET pages that output fancy HTML and end up with output that requires the latest and greatest version of Internet Explorer, but that is totally up to you. You also can write your pages so that they return the plainest HTML you have ever seen, enabling even the original Mosaic browser to view your Web pages. The operating system of the client is not an issue either. Just like for the Web, your pages can be viewed from any platform where the Internet is available.

To continue to drive this same point home, the lack of client requirements means that for your application to run, nothing (beyond the basic requirement for a Web browser of some sort) needs to be installed onto the user's computer. When you update your site, changing the pages that are stored on your server, the next user to hit the site will see the new version, no upgrade or other deployment issues at all. All these benefits that result from the lack of client requirement make the choice of a Web interface a relatively easy one except for two issues:

- The user experience using a Web browser is still not quite as good as it is with a Windows application. Consider some of the Windows applications you have used, such as Microsoft Office, Visual Studio .NET, Adobe Photoshop, and so on, and you will realize that almost nothing on the Web comes close to that level of user interface. It is possible to produce a Web interface that is close, but the work required is much greater than for a comparable Windows application.

- An ASP.NET application, for the most part, works only when the user is connected, and its functionality is affected by the speed of the user's connection.

Some things just won't work in a Web-based system, such as an equally functional and rich offline experience. For example, Outlook can handle being online or offline, but its Web counterpart, Outlook Web Access has absolutely no offline functionality. A program designed to work with files or other "local" aspects of your system will not transfer well to a Web-based user interface.

In the end, it is difficult to find reasons against using a Web interface, and there are many advantages to building a system this way.

Windows Applications (Windows Forms)

It is often difficult for me to explain what I mean by a "Windows application" because this is really the only type of application most people have seen. Basically, a Windows application is anything that you can create using a combination of windows and dialog boxes to run on the Windows platform. Almost every application that you are used to using—Microsoft Office, Quicken, even Solitaire—is an example of what you can build using the Windows Forms features of .NET.

After reading the previous section on ASP.NET, you might be wondering why you wouldn't always use a Web interface, and you are not alone. A Windows Forms application has a few requirements for the client machine:

- The .NET Framework must be installed on the client, whereas in the case of ASP.NET, it is required only on the Web server.
- The Framework only runs on Windows platforms.
- Your application must be installed.
- Updating your application generally means touching each and every desktop in some way (automated tools or downloadable patches might remove some of this effort).

The dependence on the client machine has a nasty side-effect when you are dealing with public applications; your application's performance is dependent on a machine that you have absolutely no control over.

All these requirements might make it seem like the decision between thick and thin is no decision at all. In reality, though, there are still several big advantages to Windows Forms applications that are worth mentioning. The number one big advantage is that a developer using Windows Forms can create rich and responsive user interfaces and can do so much quicker than using ASP.NET. Despite all the advances in Web technology, it is still more difficult to create a complex interface on the Web than on Windows.

> **Note**
>
> Many Web developers would disagree with my comments that ASP.NET is more difficult to develop in than Windows Forms, but despite its many virtues, that is one place where it becomes a difficult.

A second advantage is in user-interface performance, a Windows interface is generally more responsive (faster to respond to clicks and other user actions). Finally, the remaining advantage of using Windows Forms is that there are those things (offline use, faster processing of local objects such as files) that just can't be done using the Web.

> **Note**
>
> Using Dynamic HTML, ActiveX controls, and other more complex Web technologies, it is possible to improve on some of the issues described previously. In doing so, though, a certain amount of the benefit of ASP.NET is lost as you create an application that has restricted support for platforms (ActiveX controls only run on certain operating systems and processors, and Dynamic HTML is not supported by every browser) and might even have some deployment requirements.

Deciding Which Architecture to Use

Making the actual choice of architecture, even before the application-specific modifications are made, is probably worth whatever you need to pay an experienced system architect. If you make the wrong decision at this point, the entire project could be doomed to failure. Of course, mistakes can always be corrected, but in this case, you would likely be scrapping a large amount of work if a new architecture needed to be chosen.

Key Factors Influencing Your Decision

The most important factor in deciding on the best architecture is the actual system requirements. These details, gathered from the business drivers of a project, and from its future users, should detail exactly what the system needs to do. Given the details of what it needs to do, the trick is to design a system that can handle those needs. You can walk through the brief system requirements in the section "Sample Scenarios" to get a feel for making these decisions, but first I will give you a set of questions to ask when compiling system requirements or to consider when you are reading through a preexisting set of requirements.

 Note

Based on personal experience, and through watching the painful experiences of others, I would recommend that you never build a system (or estimate on the building of one) based on requirements that someone else compiled. By someone else, I mean someone other than you or a member of your team whose work you trust. Incorrect requirements will generally result in an incorrect system and will definitely result in an invalid estimate. After the fact, blaming the requirements you were given will not help, so make sure that you or a member of your team is involved in the documentation of the system requirements. If that is not possible, then allow time in your plan to review the existing requirements analysis and to investigate any unclear portions by going directly to the source (the business people behind the project, the users, or even a previous software system that performed the same action).

Client Platform

As part of your planning, you need to know a few details about the platform that your system will be running on:

- What operating systems are installed on the target systems?
- What are the hardware specifications of the target machines (CPU/RAM/disk space)?

- How much control does the company/organization have over the target machines? Does it control the configuration, software install, antivirus protection? The extreme answers to this question would be a full terminal-server with dumb terminals at the one end, and public computers owned by the users at the other.
- Are any of the client computers laptops? Is offline or remote access required? Are dial-up services needed or already in place?

Networking

Many architectural choices, such as the type of client, database replication, and protocol used, are dependent on the network that the system will be running on:

- What speed of connection is available between the users and the back-end servers (or what would be available, if the back-end servers do not exist yet)?
- Are remote access services needed and/or provided? VPN? Dial-up?
- Do the client computers have access to the Internet?
- Is there any firewall hardware/software between the users and the back-end servers?
- What type (TCP/IP, IPX, NetBEUI, and so on) of network is in use?

Security

Any system needs to have at least some security specifications; even an unprotected application should state that it is intended to be unprotected. An important piece of information that needs to be determined, but is not easy to turn into a simple question, is how important is the security of the application and its data? A financial system and a golf-score tracking system both care about security, but the degree of concern is likely a bit higher for one of them. Beyond that bit of information, the following questions are useful starting points for determining the security needs of the application:

- How are the users authenticated to the existing network?
- Do the client machines belong to a NT/Windows 2000 domain?
- If public-facing, will access be anonymous or will the users have to log in?
- Will this application be responsible for password changes or other security administration?
- Will users have different levels of access, perhaps with restrictions on application features they can use?

Other Considerations

Other important factors in developing an architecture are listed here, but it is in these areas that the experience level of the architect is of major importance. In these areas, there are really no firm answers. It is more a matter of coming up with sufficient information to include it into the architectural planning.

- Rate of change to business logic—If the business logic driving the system is changing rapidly, that will affect how often the client in a client/server system would have to be updated. Major changes to the business logic would likely require even a client update as well.

- Skill set of development team—Some forms of development are more complex and, therefore, more difficult than others. In most cases, a client/server system is simpler to write than a full three-tier system. When choosing an architecture, you can either attempt to architect to the skill level of the team, or you can base the required skill on the architecture you choose.

- Future requirements/plans—When developing the architecture for a system, you have to look beyond the exact requirements of today and consider the requirements of tomorrow. At the least, even if you have no information on what the future plans are, architect a system that can be built on. If you do know specific details, document those in your requirements and architect appropriately. As an example of this type of information, consider a system that is meant to be used by two people today but opened up to the public Web in a few months.

Sample Scenarios

The preceding discussions about the key factors focused on what you need to look for during the requirements analysis phase, but that usually involves reading through a variety of narrative-style descriptions and trying to find the information they contain. In this section, I will show you some small examples of system requirements and the architectural information that you can obtain for them.

Video Store System

Narrative Requirements:

"A chain of video stores needs a new system for tracking videos, customers, and rentals. All sites are currently connected to the head office using modems. Each store has one or more computers acting as point-of-sale terminals. The computers are new, Pentium IIs. Sales/Customer/Video data from each store does not have to be available at the head office in real time; the current system does nightly batches, which are often enough for the store's purposes."

Discussion:

This is a fairly common scenario—multiple sites or branch offices doing data entry and a head office that wants to be updated regularly with the site data (see Figure 5.2). The machines at the client site sound (from this brief discussion) standard enough and new enough that a Windows Form application is a possibility, and an ASP.NET application is always an option. In this case, the deciding factor ends up being the statement that says nightly data updates are fine. With this comment in place and a relatively slow link back to the head office, I would be considering a system where the data is stored at the head office and is replicated out to each site during slow periods or at night, after each site closes.

The system at each site would be Windows Forms applications, removing the need for a Web server. A local database of some sort (MSDE or Access) would be installed at each site, and a scheduled upload of that data would be sent to the head office on a nightly basis. Using a central database instead, with all the offices doing all their work across the dial-up connection, would provide the benefit of having all the different stores' data available and up-to-date at the head office, but the performance over a modem connection would likely be an issue. A Web-based front-end that supported the functions a video store likely needs (more investigation would be needed to determine) such as printing receipts and possibly membership cards would be difficult to create.

FIGURE 5.2

The video store has a common architecture, with many branch locations connecting in to a head office. The key decision is whether the clients should connect directly to the head office or use some form of local data store.

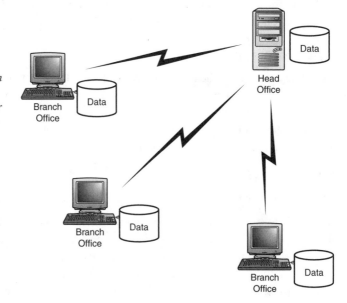

Public Access

Consider what would be different if the following line was included in the video store requirements: "Eventually we hope to create a public Web site for our customers, where they could search for movies and check whether a certain movie was in stock at a specific store."

This statement changes more things than you might expect. As a "future requirement," you could just ignore it and design the system based on the rest of the information. This would produce a system that would have to be rebuilt as soon as the company moved onto the next stage of its plans. Instead, you want to try to develop an architecture that both covers the current plans and can handle the future requirements.

Without going into too much detail, because you would really need to gather more details about the future plans to make a proper architecture for the public Web site, consider the basic changes that would be required (see Figure 5.3). The comment about "nightly batches" is likely incorrect now. If the Web site provided availability information on movies but was a day behind, it wouldn't be all that useful. Real-time is not necessarily required, but an acceptable amount of delay would have to be determined (15 minutes perhaps).

If the expected delay is not too short, then perhaps the system can still be designed with local data storage and more frequent batch updates. To a computer system, 15 minutes is a long time, and it would require much less bandwidth than a full-time connection. With this new requirement, a Web application looks more worthwhile because all the data would be stored in the head office, and some of the system code could be shared between the two systems. But a Web site still wouldn't be as responsive as a Windows Forms application with data storage onsite at the store.

FIGURE 5.3

The decision to have a public Web site has modified the video store architecture to ensure that up-to-date data exists at the head office.

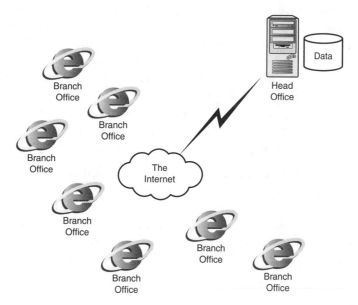

5

Listing Service for Real Estate

Narrative Requirements:

"A large national Real Estate company wants to computerize its real estate listings. The agents would add listings directly to a computer system and a public Web site would be provided for the customers to browse the available listings and send messages to the appropriate agents. The agents would require the listing service as well as the capability to enter new listings, and would access both from their laptops. Because these agents are usually traveling all day, they will be using their laptops remotely most of the time."

Discussion:

Given the preceding description, you can pull out a few key elements right away: There will be a Web site, which is not in doubt at all, at least for the public-facing element. The question is "how to handle the interaction with the agents." They need to be able to access the listings and add, update, and remove listings they have placed into the service, all while being roaming agents all day. You could have them synch with the system when they are in the office, downloading the listings to their machine and uploading any new listings they have added. It is likely, though, that they would hit the office only occasionally, and so a new listing wouldn't get to them, or their new listings wouldn't get uploaded, for about a day. Is that acceptable? Perhaps, you need more information.

Alternatively, the agents could be provided with wireless modems (using cellular technology such as CDMA), which can connect them to the head office or to the Internet from wherever they are. Using this option, you now have two choices: still use the offline application but perform your synch using the wireless connection (resulting in more frequent updates), or build the add/edit/delete functionality into a secured portion of the public real estate Web site, `http://www.thesitename.com/agents`, which the agents access and log in to using a regular browser over the cellular modem. Due to the (current) low speed of these cellular modems, I would want to consider both options and perform some tests, but the public site could be started on without delay.

As you can see, application architecture is not a definitive science, especially when you are dealing with only a limited amount of background information. Often you will need to collect all the requirements you can, analyze them, and then go back to the various stakeholders and request additional information. This can simply be clarification on the original questions, or perhaps new questions came up based on the answers they provided.

Personal CD Library

Narrative Requirements:

"As a practice project, you are building a personal CD library that users will be able to install on their machine to track their CD collection. It will support looking up CD names and tracking titles from the Internet. All the details of the user's CD collection will be stored, and the system will support generating some simple reports against this data."

Discussion:

This system is fairly simple, and the architecture for building it should be too. The only real unknown about this system is the lookup of CD details from the Internet, but that is not an architectural concern. A Windows Forms application would be the most suitable, but you should choose a database other than SQL Server because you want to be able to distribute this without requiring any additional software on the users' machines. Either an Access file (.mdb) or an MSDE database would suit this project well. Alternatively, you could store all the information simply as XML persisted from a DataSet.

Summary

The world of .NET is new and powerful, but everything needs a foundation. The design and architecture of your systems is critical to success. Despite the new features and radical changes to the underlying technology, the architecture of a .NET system is not all that different than it was for a Visual Basic 6.0 system; many of the same choices still exist. Always be sure to base your choices on the requirements you have, and don't forget to plan for the future!

As mentioned earlier, many aspects of system architecture go beyond the scope of today's lesson, but MSDN has devoted a section of its Web site to the architecture of .NET applications. Go to http://msdn.microsoft.com/library/ en-us/dnbda/html/bdadotnetover.asp to find many useful resources.

5

Q&A

Q. I have been told Windows DNA is dead and that it no longer applies now that .NET is here. You say it still applies, but isn't it old stuff?

A. Windows DNA represents both concepts and technologies. Some of the technologies embodied in Windows DNA, such as Visual Studio 6.0, are replaced by .NET equivalents, but the concept of Windows DNA (distributed n-tier computing with distinct Presentation, Business, and Data layers) is still valid. Systems that have been already built on the Windows DNA model will be easy to move into the .NET world.

Q. In the .NET world, will all my components talk to each other using SOAP (XML over HTTP), instead of the old binary standard of DCOM?

A. You are correct that DCOM is no longer the preferred method, but .NET provides more than just SOAP as a means for two applications to communicate. SOAP is excellent for communication with .NET or non-.NET systems and is especially good when you are attempting to work between two networks because it easily passes through a firewall. Within your own system, between two .NET components, SOAP is one option, but there are several other forms of communication including binary formats.

Workshop

The Workshop is designed to help you anticipate possible questions, review what you've learned, and get you thinking about how to put your knowledge into practice. The answers to the quiz are in Appendix A, "Answers to Quizzes/Exercises."

Quiz

1. Name a major advantage of using a Web-based user interface instead of a Windows application.

2. If an application uses an Access database file located on a server, is it considered a client/server or a single-tier system?

3. What has to be installed for a computer to run an application created with .NET (not just browse to a Web site created with it)?

DAY 6

What to Do When Good Programs Go Bad, and Making Sure They Don't

There is an old Robbie Burns quote—often changed to suit the author's purpose—that states, "The best-laid schemes o' mice an' men, Gang aft agley." Although I haven't a clue what "Gang aft agley" really means, it doesn't sound like it's a good situation. Just as with "schemes o' mice an' men," your (and my) Visual Basic .NET programs will likely "Gang aft agley." If it happens when your program is running, something bad will happen (usually causing the end to your program). If it happens when a customer is running your program, even worse things might happen (perhaps you won't get paid). So, it's best if you can prevent these problems before they happen.

There are two main techniques that will help you when you're trying to avoid errors. First, you should detect when errors happen in your programs and deal with them instead of allowing the default error message to handle them. Second, you should make sure that your application has as few errors as possible.

Today, you will learn two main ways to prevent problems with your code:

- Structured Exception Handling
- Debugging

Structured Exception Handling

Older versions of Visual Basic used error handling to protect an application. Visual Basic .NET is the first version to support a better concept in programming languages—Structured Exception Handling.

What Is Structured Exception Handling?

 Before you can really look at what Structured Exception Handling (SEH) is, you should look at just what a *structured exception*—or even *a non-structured exception*—is. Otherwise, you won't know what you're handling. An *exception* is something that happens out of the ordinary (and usually unexpectedly) in your applications. There are two kinds of exceptions—hardware exceptions and software exceptions. A hardware exception, of course, is one caused by hardware—for example, when your program tries to access memory it shouldn't, or a similar event occurs based on hardware. A software exception occurs when you try to assign an incompatible value to a variable, or a similar error occurs.

Structured Exception Handling is a strategy for handling either hardware or software exceptions. By dealing with both types of exceptions in the same way, the code required to process exceptions is easier to write and more consistent. You perform Structured Exception Handling by "protecting" sections of code that are likely to experience exceptions. For example, when you are about to make a division, you could protect the code that does the division. If—either because of an error you've made in the program, or a value the user has entered—the program attempts to divide by zero, the protected code could deal with the resulting exception. Other times when you should use SEH include when reading from databases; when opening, reading from, or writing to files; or at any other time you think that an error could occur.

Note

I'm of the belief that it is difficult to overuse SEH. The benefits you get by protecting yourself, your programs, and your users from errors far outweigh the minimal slowdown that results from using SEH. On the other hand, be reasonable. If there really isn't any possibility (and I mean, *really* isn't *any* possibility) for an error to occur, don't bother with the extra typing.

Errors and Exceptions

So, how is an exception different from an error? If you're familiar with other versions of Visual Basic, or indeed most other programming languages, you've likely come across the idea of an error, but not an exception. What's the difference? Why do you need a new word, and something as fancy sounding as Structured Exception Handling?

First, an exception really is an error. Part of the problem, though, is that an error is so much more. An error could be that the function returned a result that you weren't expecting, or that the programmer used the wrong algorithm. An exception is more formal. An exception, to repeat the previous definition, is when something happens in your code outside the normal flow of control. SEH defines a particular way of dealing with exceptions, ensuring that everything gets cleaned up after the fact. In addition, one other nice feature of exceptions is that they are now shared between all the languages supported by the .NET platform. This means that you could possibly have code that causes an exception in one language, but deal with it in another.

Most errors in Visual Basic have traditionally been dealt with using the `On Error` statement. `On Error` is *unstructured* and can lead to confusing code that jumps around in a procedure. Exceptions are dealt with using a more structured, or organized, approach, as you will see.

The `Try` Block

You protect a section of code to trap whenever an exception occurs with the `Try...End Try` block. Begin the code you want to protect with `Try`, and end the section with `End Try`.

The Syntax for `Try...End Try`

▼ SYNTAX

The following code shows the syntax for the `Try...End Try` block:

```
Try
.
Catch Ex As Exception
.
End Try
```

where `Try` is the beginning of the section of code to protect, and `End Try` ends the block of code. The `Catch` line marks the section of the block that actually deals with any exceptions that might occur.

▲

The `Catch` Section

Simply marking a section of code with `Try...End Try` does not actually do anything. If an exception occurs in the protected code, it must be "caught" and dealt with. You catch the exception with the `Catch` keyword.

6

Each `Try...End Try` block can have one or more `Catch` sections. Each `Catch` section is usually targeted at one or more types of exceptions. If you decide to have multiple `Catch` sections in your `Try` blocks, each `Catch` section should catch different types of exceptions. You might want to do this to allow each type of exception to be handled differently. If you decide to have multiple `Catch` sections, you should also have one generic `Catch` section that will catch all exceptions that might have fallen through the others. This form of the `Try...End Try` block would look similar to that shown in Listing 6.1.

INPUT   **LISTING 6.1**   Catching Multiple Exceptions

```
1  Try
2  '
3  Catch eNoFile As FileNotFoundException
4  ' deal with file not found exception here
5  Catch eIO As IOException
6  ' deal with input/output exception here
7  Catch Ex As Exception
8  ' deal with generic exceptions here
9  End Try
```

ANALYSIS   This `Try Block` is designed to trap errors for a file processing procedure. There are separate sections for handling `FileNotFoundExceptions`, `IOExceptions`, and other exceptions. If there were only a single `Catch` section, you would need to have some code that determined the actual exception. This way, it is more obvious which code is used for each type of exception.

Let's create a program with an intentional exception, so you can see how it works. You'll look at the results of the exception, and what it does to your program. Then, you'll add exception handling, and see how it can protect the program.

1. Create a new console application. Call it Exceptions.
2. Change the created Module name to **modExceptional**.
3. Bring up the Project Properties dialog by right-clicking on the project name in the Solution Explorer and selecting Properties.
4. Set the Startup Object to **modExceptional**. The final settings should be as shown in Figure 6.1.

For the purpose of this example, you'll use a simple, but surprisingly common exception—a Division by Zero exception, which occurs when you divide by zero. You can easily demonstrate this error by dividing any number by an uninitialized variable. (This is one of the more common causes for this exception.)

Listing 6.2 shows how the final code should look.

FIGURE 6.1

Project Properties for a program with an exception.

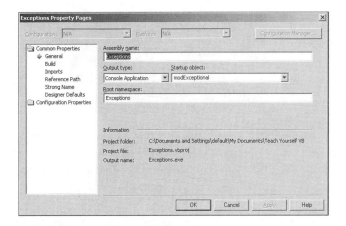

LISTING 6.2 An Exception Program

```
1 Module modExceptional
2
3     Sub Main()
4         '***This code contains an exception,
5         'and so will not run to completion
6         Dim dDividend As Decimal = 5
7         Dim dDivisor As Decimal = 0
8         Dim dResult As Decimal = 0
9         'This line is the culprit
10        'will lead to a DivisionByZero Exception
11        dResult = dDividend / dDivisor
12        System.Console.ReadLine()
13     End Sub
14
15 End Module
```

ANALYSIS Lines 6, 7, and 8 declare your variables. You're using `Decimals` here, but you could use other numeric variable types as well. The values also are initialized.

Before the division at line 11, the divisor has never been changed from the value it was initialized to: `0`. So, when the computer attempts to perform the division, an exception occurs. If you run this program in the IDE, you should see an error as shown in Figure 6.2.

If you select Break, the program will still be running, but in Debug mode. You'll look more at Debug mode later today, so select Continue for now. This causes the program to continue running. In this case, the program ends.

6

FIGURE 6.2

Default exception message.

If you build the example and try to run it in a command prompt window, the end result is similar, but less easily fixed. First, on a development computer (one that has Visual Basic .NET installed), you should see the Just-In-Time Debugging dialog. Select No; your program will continue, and you should see this result:

OUTPUT
```
1  Unhandled Exception: System.DivideByZeroException:
2  An exception of type System.DivideByZeroException was thrown.
3     at System.Decimal.Divide(Decimal d1, Decimal d2)
4     at Exceptions.modExceptional.Main() in
5  C:\Work\Day06\Exceptions\modExceptional.vb:line 11
```

ANALYSIS
This is the default message you will see when an exception occurs. Many exception error messages will be much longer, however, they all contain similar information. The first line always identifies the type of the exception that has just occurred. In this case, you see that the exception was a `System.DivideByZeroException`. The exception type is usually a great indication of the error's nature, and might even give you ideas as to how to fix the exception. Here, the exception type, `System.DivideByZeroException`, tells you two main things:

- The exception that has just occurred is one of the "normal" exceptions. That is, they are part of the System namespace (and not another namespace, such as `System.IO.FileNotFoundException`).

- The exception that has just occurred involves division. So, you should look for a possible cause in your code where you're doing some division.

Similarly, the remainder of the exception tells you a good deal of information. The remaining lines are an upside-down list of the actual procedures that were being executed when the exception occurred. In the sample output, you see that the actual exception occurred in the procedure `System.Decimal.Divide`. This procedure was called by `Exceptions.modExceptional.Main`.

The main use for all this information is to locate likely candidates for the error. When you get an exception, you should first look at the code in each of these procedures. Usually (but, not always), the error should be in one of these. Start at the first item on the list that you've written (in this case, `modExceptional.Main`) and work your way down the list. Later today, you'll look at some tools that will make doing this easier.

Some other common exceptions are described in Table 6.1.

Note

This isn't a complete list of all the possible exceptions. There are many others; please look in the Visual Basic .NET help for more details. In addition, you can create your own exceptions to add to this list if you need to, as you'll see later today.

TABLE 6.1   Common Exceptions

Exception Type	When Does It Occur?
ArgumentException	General category for errors that occur when the wrong type (or value) is passed to a method. Includes ArgumentNullException and ArgumentOutOfRangeException. Can occur because of programmer error or user data entry.
ArgumentNullException	Occurs when you pass a null to a method when it will not accept it.
ArgumentOutOfRangeException	Occurs when you pass a variable that is either too large or too small for the method, for example, if you pass the number –1 to a method that is designed to expect a month number (that is, between 1 and 12).
DivideByZeroException	Occurs when attempting to divide by an uninitialized variable, or a variable holding zero. Usually only occurs because of programmer error.
IndexOutOfRangeException	Occurs when attempting to access the member of an array that does not exist. Usually occurs because of programmer error, but could also be caused by invalid user entry.
NotImplementedException	Usually used as a placeholder when a developer is first working on a program. You can create the shell for your application, and then throw this exception from all methods. As you continue on the application, you replace the exception with the actual code. This ensures that you complete each of your procedures.
OutOfMemoryException	Occurs when your program runs out of memory. This can happen when you are filling large arrays, or performing a loop.
OverflowException	A fairly common exception that occurs when you try to put a value that is too large into a variable, for example, if you attempt the following assignment: `Dim iSmallishNumber As Short = 50000`

6

TABLE 6.1 continued

Exception Type	When Does It Occur?
FileNotFoundException	An example of an error that is not defined in the System namespace. In this case, the exception is defined in the System.IO namespace (see Day 8, "Introduction to the .NET Framework," for more information on namespaces). This exception occurs when you attempt to access a file that does not exist. It could be because it has not been created, or because the path is incorrect.

Now that you've seen an exception, and have (hopefully) a better idea of what they are, you should add SEH to your program to give the user more information when an error occurs.

Open the Exceptions project in Visual Basic .NET. You will copy the earlier project and make changes to trap the exception, as shown in the following steps:

1. Change the name of the project to **Exceptions2**. Do this by selecting the project in the Solution Explorer and then selecting File, Save Exceptions As from the menu.

2. Change the name of the file containing the code to **Exceptions2.vb**. Do this by selecting the file in the Solution Explorer and then selecting File, Save Exception.vb As.

3. Add a Try...End Try block around the code that does the calculation. Use a generic exception Catch statement to catch the Division by Zero exception.

4. Add code to display a friendlier message when the exception occurs.

The new code should look similar to the code in Listing 6.3.

INPUT   **LISTING 6.3**   Adding the Try...End Try Block

```
1   Module modExceptional
2
3       Sub Main()
4           '***This code contains an exception,
5           'and so will not complete
6           Dim dDividend As Decimal = 5
7           Dim dDivisor As Decimal = 0
8           Dim dResult As Decimal = 0
9           'This line is the culprit
10          'will lead to a DivisionByZero Exception
11          Try
12              dResult = dDividend / dDivisor
13          Catch Ex As Exception
```

LISTING 6.3   continued

```
14              System.Console.WriteLine("A division by zero error has occurred.")
15              System.Console.WriteLine("Please check the divisor.")
16          End Try
17
18          System.Console.ReadLine()
19      End Sub
20
21  End Module
```

ANALYSIS   Line 11 begins the `Try` Block; therefore, code from there to the first `Catch` block at line 13 is protected. In this case, the only executable line is the one causing the division by zero exception at line 12. When this exception occurs, the program will stop and search for something to handle the exception. Because the `Catch` section at line 13 is a generic one, it will catch any type of exception. The variable `Ex` will be used to store the created exception, and you can use the properties of this variable to view more information about the exception. It then displays an error message, and the code continues to completion, beginning with the line following the `End Try` statement.

Nesting `Try...End Try` Blocks

You might have a situation in which you want to protect two sections of code with `Try...End Try` blocks, but want to deal with the exceptions differently. If the two are separate blocks of code, this is not an issue. However, if one of the blocks of code is contained within another (see Listing 6.4), this is not an option. In this case, you must nest `Try...End Try` blocks, as shown in Listing 6.4.

INPUT   **LISTING 6.4**   Nesting `Try...End Try` Blocks

```
1   Sub WriteToFile(ByVal FileName As String)
2       Dim fsOut As System.IO.FileStream
3       Dim strOut As System.IO.StreamWriter
4       Try
5           'Open the File
6           fsOut = _
7               New System.IO.FileStream(FileName, _
8                   System.IO.FileMode.OpenOrCreate, _
9                   System.IO.FileAccess.Write)
10          Try
11              'Write to the file
12              strOut = _
13                  New System.IO.StreamWriter(fsOut)
14              strOut.Write(DateTime.Today.ToString())
15          Catch eIO As Exception
16              Console.WriteLine("Couldn't write to file: {0}.", FileName)
```

6

LISTING **6.4**   continued

```
17              End Try
18          Catch eFile As Exception
19              Console.WriteLine("Couldn't open file: {0}.", FileName)
20          End Try
21      End Sub
```

ANALYSIS   Listing 6.4 is an example of writing to a file. You'll look at this in more detail in Day 8. However, there are two Try...End Try blocks in this example. One of the Try blocks (the one beginning at line 10) is entirely contained within the other Try block (that starts on line 4). The inner Try block, therefore, is *nested* in the other block. If an exception occurs at the write on line 14, the Catch statement at line 15 will catch the exception, and the user will see "Couldn't write to file SomeFile.out". However, if the file cannot be opened, the catch block at line 18 will catch the exception, showing "Couldn't open file: SomeFile.Out".

Just as with If...End If and other blocks, there is no limit to how far you can nest these blocks. Sometimes, nesting blocks enables you to write your code in a more organized fashion than if you didn't nest them.

The Finally Section

As you write Try blocks, you sometimes come across situations in which, even if an exception occurs, you *must* do something. For example, if you are writing code that writes information to a file, you should close the file, whether an error occurs during the write or not. You add this functionality with the Finally section. This section appears after all the Catch sections and should contain only code that must always be performed. This is a good place to close files, set variables to Nothing, and otherwise clean up after yourself. Listing 6.5 shows the addition of a Finally section to the code in Listing 6.4.

INPUT   **LISTING 6.5**   Using the Finally Section

```
1   Sub WriteToFile(ByVal FileName As String)
2       Dim fsOut As System.IO.FileStream
3       Dim strOut As System.IO.StreamWriter
4       Try
5           'Open the File
6           fsOut = _
7               New System.IO.FileStream(FileName, _
8                   System.IO.FileMode.OpenOrCreate, _
9                   System.IO.FileAccess.Write)
10          Try
11              'Write to the file
```

LISTING 6.5　continued

```
12                strOut = _
13                    New System.IO.StreamWriter(fsOut)
14                strOut.Write(DateTime.Today.ToString())
15            Catch eIO As Exception
16                Console.WriteLine("Couldn't write to file: {0}.", FileName)
17            Finally
18                strOut.Close()
19            End Try
20        Catch eFile As Exception
21            Console.WriteLine("Couldn't open file: {0}.", FileName)
22        Finally
23            fsOut.Close()
24        End Try
25
26    End Sub
```

ANALYSIS　Here, the StreamWriter and File will both be closed, even if errors occur. Although this is not absolutely necessary, it's good practice to always clean up after you're done with a variable.

Raising Exceptions

Occasionally, you might want to notify a user that something drastic has gone wrong. This might be something related specifically to your application, or it might be a "normal" exception. For example, you might have two objects you've created in your application, an Employee and a Customer. You might want to create an exception if the program attempts to assign an instance of an Employee to a variable designed to hold Customer objects (wouldn't want them shopping here, anyway). Rather than create a brand-new type of exception, you can reuse the InvalidCastException. You can then create a new InvalidCastException, and use it to notify the application by using the Throw statement. This is shown in Listing 6.6.

INPUT　**LISTING 6.6**　The Throw Statement

```
1 Dim oCust As Customer = New Customer("Bob", "Sjerunkl")
2 Dim oEmp As Employee = New Employee("Phil", "Barr")
3 Dim oSomething As Object
4 oSomething = oEmp
5 If TypeOf oSomething Is Customer Then
6    oCust = oSomething
7 Else
8    Throw New InvalidCastException("Cannot assign an Employee to a Customer.")
9 End If
```

6

ANALYSIS The important line in the sample is line 8. Here, you create a new instance of an `InvalidCastException` object, and "throw" it. This generates a new exception that must be caught by a `Catch` statement, or the default exception handler will deal with it, leading to the debugger appearing (if they have a development environment installed), or an error message.

Exception handling provides a structured, clean way to protect your programs from errors due to hardware problems, invalid user entry, or your own errors. Any program will be more robust if you add exception handling around code that could create an exception.

Debugging

NEW TERM Equally important to properly dealing with errors and exceptions is *debugging*—the act (and art) of trying to find and fix errors in code. Of course, this often leads to the question, "Why are there errors in the code in the first place? Aren't those developers supposed to be smart?" And, although it is true that all developers are smart (you are reading this book, aren't you?), sometimes mistakes happen. Before you look at how you can remove bugs from your programs, let's spend some time examining how they can get there.

The Source of Bugs

A bug (in a computer program) can be many things. It could be

- A mistake in the strategy used to perform some task. These bugs are usually called *logic errors*, and are sometimes the hardest bugs to fix. They occur when you write code the wrong way. Perhaps you are attempting to sort a list of names, but the way you are doing it doesn't take into account all possible names. For example, should someone with the last name St. Jean come before or after someone with the name Santana?

- A mistake in entering the code, a typo. These can be either easy to solve or difficult. In one sense, these errors should disappear almost entirely, as Visual Basic .NET will check the spelling of key words. Typos can become a problem, however, if you don't have `Option Explicit` set for your modules. If you don't, you could accidentally mistype a variable name later, causing Visual Basic .NET to automatically create a new variable for you. This new variable would be initialized to 0 (for numeric variables), which might not be what you wanted. For example, without `Option Explicit`, the following code would compile, but always return nothing.

```
1 Imports System
2 Module Typo
3
```

```
4  Sub Main
5    Dim sName As String
6
7    Console.WriteLine("Enter name: ")
8    Name = Console.ReadLine()
9    Console.WriteLine("Entered name was {0}", sNmae)
10     End Sub
11 End Module
```

As stated previously, `Option Explicit` would cause Visual Basic .NET to catch
this error. Without it, you could also catch it fairly easy. However, there is a subset
of these types of errors that, for reasons I cannot answer, your brain will always
read correctly. I've stared for minutes at a section of code in which I knew that
there was a typo, but didn't see anything. Every time I read the misspelled word, it
read "correctly." In these situations, you invariably call another person over, who
looks over your shoulder, immediately noticing the typo, causing some embarrassment. After a few moments of ribbing, you both get back to work.

* A mistake caused by user entry or by the data. These are difficult errors to correct
  after the fact. The best solution for incorrect entry or data is to reduce the chance
  of the user entering bad information. You'll look at some of the controls that can be
  used for this later in the book. In addition, being a "defensive programmer" will
  also help. Assume that the data is bad—you should check for values, to make certain that they are appropriate, and protect sections of code that might generate
  exceptions using Structured Exception Handling.

Do	Don't
DO use Option Explicit for all modules. It helps Visual Basic .NET to detect many errors you might accidentally add to your code by mistyping variable names.	**DON'T** forget to also turn on Option Strict. This option ensures that you are always aware when a value is being passed to a variable of a different type. Automatic conversion can lead to insidious bugs. By being made aware of the need for conversion, you can perform the task more appropriately.

6

So, there are many possible sources for bugs in your programs. Some of them are under
your control, whereas others are not. Either way, Visual Basic .NET gives you a great
number of tools to assist you in correcting, or debugging, your programs.

Learning Debugging by Doing it

As stated earlier, debugging is almost as much art as science. It requires a certain knack sometimes to figure out what might be causing an error. Therefore, I feel that one of the best ways to learn debugging is to not simply talk about the tools (which can be rather abstract), but to debug an actual program. For this, you'll debug a program that calculates a mortgage table. It shows the various monthly payments that would be required for loans of various lengths and interest rates. Listing 6.7 shows the output you are looking for with a loan of $100,000.

OUTPUT   LISTING 6.7   Desired Output from a Mortgage Table Calculator

```
Enter loan amount:
100000


          Years  10      15      20      25      30
Interest
5.00             1060.66 790.79  659.96  584.59  536.82
5.25             1072.92 803.88  673.84  599.25  552.20
5.50             1085.26 817.08  687.89  614.09  567.79
5.75             1097.69 830.41  702.08  629.11  583.57
6.00             1110.21 843.86  716.43  644.30  599.55
6.25             1122.80 857.42  730.93  659.67  615.72
6.50             1135.48 871.11  745.57  675.21  632.07
6.75             1148.24 884.91  760.36  690.91  648.60
7.00             1161.08 898.83  775.30  706.78  665.30
7.25             1174.01 912.86  790.38  722.81  682.18
7.50             1187.02 927.01  805.59  738.99  699.21
7.75             1200.11 941.28  820.95  755.33  716.41
8.00             1213.28 955.65  836.44  771.82  733.76
8.25             1226.53 970.14  852.07  788.45  751.27
8.50             1239.86 984.74  867.82  805.23  768.91
8.75             1253.27 999.45  883.71  822.14  786.70
9.00             1266.76 1014.27 899.73  839.20  804.62
9.25             1280.33 1029.19 915.87  856.38  822.68
9.50             1293.98 1044.22 932.13  873.70  840.85
9.75             1307.70 1059.36 948.52  891.14  859.15
10.00            1321.51 1074.61 965.02  908.70  877.57
```

Listing 6.8 shows the initial attempt at creating this program, and the output from the program, confirming that you need to do some debugging.

 LISTING 6.8   The Program Needing Debugging

```
1 Option Explicit On
2 Imports System
3 Imports Microsoft.VisualBasic.ControlChars
```

LISTING 6.8   continued

```
 4
 5  Module modMain
 6
 7      Sub Main()
 8
 9          Dim sInput As String
10          Dim dblReturn As Double
11
12          'Get User Input
13          Dim dblPayment As Double
14          Console.Write("Enter loan amount:")
15          sInput = Console.ReadLine()
16          dblReturn = CDbl(sInput)
17
18          'Create the table
19          OutputMortgageTable(dblReturn)
20          Console.Write("Press ENTER to continue")
21          Console.ReadLine()
22      End Sub
23
24      Private Sub OutputMortgageTable(ByVal Principal As Double)
25
26          Dim iYears As Integer
27          Dim iRate As Integer
28          Dim dblAnnualInterest As Double
29
30          Console.WriteLine(Tab & "Years" & Tab & "10" & Tab & "15" & _
31              Tab & "20" & Tab & "25" & Tab & "30")
32          Console.WriteLine("Interest")
33
34          For iRate = 500 To 1000 Step 25
35              dblAnnualInterest = iRate / 100
36
37              For iYears = 10 To 30 Step 5
38                  Console.Write(Format(dblAnnualInterest, "0.#0") & Tab & Tab)
39                  'iYears * 12 to get the number of months (assumes monthly
                     ➥payments)
40                  Console.Write(Format(Payment(Principal, _
41                      dblAnnualInterest, iYears * 12), "0.00") & Tab)
42              Next
43              Console.WriteLine()
44          Next
45
46      End Sub
47
48      Public Function Payment(ByVal Principal As Double, _
49          ByVal AnnualInterest As Double, _
50          ByVal Periods As Integer) As Double
51          Dim dblMonthlyInterest As Double = AnnualInterest / 1200
52          Return Principal * dblMonthlyInterest * 1 + _
```

6

LISTING 6.8 continued

```
53                  dblMonthlyInterest ^ Periods / 1 + _
54                  dblMonthlyInterest ^ Periods - 1
55      End Function
56
57 End Module
```

```
Enter loan amount: 100000
          Years  10      15        20        25        30
Interest
5.00             415.67  5.00                415.67    5.00          415.67  5.00
          415.67 5.00              415.67
5.25             436.50  5.25                436.50    5.25          436.50  5.25
          436.50 5.25              436.50
5.50             457.33  5.50                457.33    5.50          457.33  5.50
          457.33 5.50              457.33
5.75             478.17  5.75                478.17    5.75          478.17  5.75
          478.17 5.75              478.17
6.00             499.00  6.00                499.00    6.00          499.00  6.00
          499.00 6.00              499.00
6.25             519.83  6.25                519.83    6.25          519.83  6.25
          519.83 6.25              519.83
6.50             540.67  6.50                540.67    6.50          540.67  6.50
          540.67 6.50              540.67
6.75             561.50  6.75                561.50    6.75          561.50  6.75
          561.50 6.75              561.50
7.00             582.33  7.00                582.33    7.00          582.33  7.00
          582.33 7.00              582.33
7.25             603.17  7.25                603.17    7.25          603.17  7.25
          603.17 7.25              603.17
7.50             624.00  7.50                624.00    7.50          624.00  7.50
          624.00 7.50              624.00
7.75             644.83  7.75                644.83    7.75          644.83  7.75
          644.83 7.75              644.83
8.00             665.67  8.00                665.67    8.00          665.67  8.00
          665.67 8.00              665.67
8.25             686.50  8.25                686.50    8.25          686.50  8.25
          686.50 8.25              686.50
8.50             707.33  8.50                707.33    8.50          707.33  8.50
          707.33 8.50              707.33
8.75             728.17  8.75                728.17    8.75          728.17  8.75
          728.17 8.75              728.17
9.00             749.00  9.00                749.00    9.00          749.00  9.00
          749.00 9.00              749.00
9.25             769.83  9.25                769.83    9.25          769.83  9.25
          769.83 9.25              769.83
9.50             790.67  9.50                790.67    9.50          790.67  9.50
          790.67 9.50              790.67
9.75             811.50  9.75                811.50    9.75          811.50  9.75
          811.50 9.75              811.50
10.00            832.33  10.00               832.33    10.00         832.33  10.00
          832.33 10.00             832.33
```

The Modes in the Life of a Program

When you are creating programs with Visual Basic .NET, the program will go through three distinct modes. When you first start Visual Basic .NET and are working on a program, it is in Design mode. You can confirm this by looking at the title bar of the window. After the words "Microsoft Visual Basic," you will see [design]. Similarly, when you are running a program in the IDE, you will see a [run], denoting that you are in Run mode. The final mode is Break, or Debug, mode. This mode kicks in if the running program is interrupted in any way. This interruption might be due to an exception occurring in your program, or you might intentionally put the IDE into Break mode. See Figure 6.3 for an example of the IDE in Break mode. Notice that the title bar includes the marker [break].

FIGURE 6.3

Visual Basic .NET in Break mode.

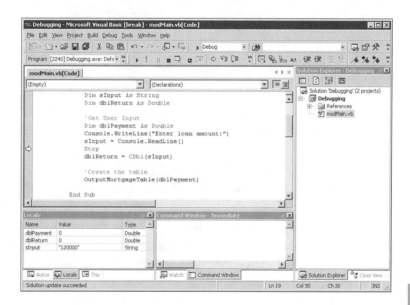

You use Break mode to assist in debugging your programs. During this mode, a number of tools become available with which you can view the contents of variables, watch or change the flow of the program, or test blocks of code. These tools will become invaluable to you for uncovering and fixing bugs in your programs. If you want to intentionally enter Break mode, use the Stop keyword, as shown in Figure 6.3.

Alternatively, you can place a breakpoint at the line on which you'd like to have the program stop. The program will run normally until it reaches the line, and then switch to Break mode and return to the IDE. Your program is still running in the background, but it is paused. You can place a breakpoint into your code in one of three ways:

6

- Click in the colored left margin of the code window next to the line on which you'd like the breakpoint. A red circle should appear in the margin.

- Right-click on the code line and select Insert Breakpoint. A red circle should appear in the margin.

- Select Debug, New Breakpoint from the menu. This opens the New Breakpoint dialog (see Figure 6.4). This is the most flexible means of creating a breakpoint. Not only does this dialog allow you to create a breakpoint that stops the program when a line is reached, it also allows you to create breakpoints when a variable changes or reaches a specified value, or simply when a specified condition is True.

FIGURE 6.4

New Breakpoint dialog.

Using Breakpoints to Examine the Sample Program

Load the initial version of the program in the IDE (from the OriginalMortgage directory), so you can experiment with breakpoints. With the modMain.vb module open in the editor, click in the colored margin next to the line

```
dblReturn = CDbl(sInput)
```

You should see a red circle appear next to the line. If so, start the program in the IDE. The console window should appear, allowing you to enter a loan amount. Enter **100000** and press Enter. You should be back in the IDE, and a yellow arrow should have been added to the red circle, as you see in Figure 6.5. The yellow arrow always shows the next line to be executed.

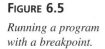

FIGURE 6.5

Running a program with a breakpoint.

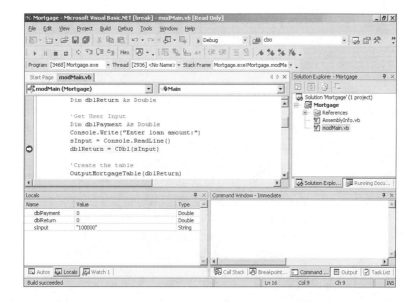

Stepping Through Your Code

One of the most useful features available in Break mode is the capability to step through the code. This enables a user to view the flow of logic in a program, possibly finding errors in loops, or during procedure calls. After you have entered Break mode, you can begin stepping through your code one line at a time. This lets you watch the effect of each line on the variables, or make sure that the program is actually performing the steps you had intended. There are four main step functions, available from the Debug menu, or on the debug toolbar. They are

- Step Into   This is the most commonly used step command. Each time you select it, the next available action is performed. Select it from within the OutputMortgageTable procedure, and you should see the yellow arrow move to the line

```
OutputMortgageTable(dblReturn)
```

Select it again, and you should go into the OutputMortgageTable procedure. Once more, and you should be at the line

```
Console.WriteLine(Tab & "Years" & Tab & "10" & Tab & "15" & _
Tab & "20" & Tab & "25" & Tab & "30")
```

Notice that the yellow line does not stop at the variable declaration statements. This is because they are not considered executable code. The yellow arrow will only stop at lines that do something, not at lines that declare new variables.

6

- Step Out   This command is occasionally useful if you step into a procedure that you know has no bugs. It causes the rest of the procedure to run, and moves the yellow arrow to the first line after the original call. Select it from within the `OutputMortgageTable` procedure, for example, and you should be returned to the `Sub Main` procedure.

- Step Over   Also useful when debugging around procedures that you know have no bugs. Step Over will treat a procedure as though it were only a single line of code. For example, if the yellow arrow were on the `OutputMortgageTable` line in `Sub Main` and you select Step Over, all of the code in `OutputMortgageTable` will run, and you will move to the next line in `Sub Main`.

- Run To Cursor   Another useful command when you know a section of code does not have bugs. Run To Cursor will let you execute all of the code up to the selected line. To use this mode, select the line that you want to run up to, and select Run To Cursor from the Debug menu, or the right-click menu.

Using Stepping to Examine the Sample Program

Stepping through a program can sometimes show you errors caused by the developer. These might be loops that end too soon, or that are not performed enough, or logic tests that are not producing the expected results.

To step through the sample program, do the following:

1. Stop the program by selecting the Stop Debugging button from the toolbar, or select Stop Debugging from the Debug menu.

2. Remove the breakpoint you created earlier by clicking on the red circle in the margin, and create a new one at the beginning of the first `For Loop` inside `OutputMortgageTable`.

3. Start the program. When prompted, enter **100000** as the loan amount. The program should enter Break mode on the line

   ```
   For iRate = 500 To 1000 Step 25
   ```

4. Step through the code (or select Run To Cursor) until you reach the line

   ```
   Console.WriteLine()
   ```

5. Look back at the console window (see Figure 6.6). Notice that there are actually ten items on the line, instead of the five you wanted (one for each column from 10–30). The Interest rate value is being repeated each time through the loop when it should only be run once before the loop.

FIGURE 6.6

Displaying the header.

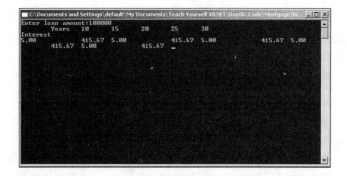

6. Stopping the program, cut the line that writes the interest rate for each row to just before the beginning of the second For loop. The result should look like

Before:

```
For iYears = 10 To 30 Step 5
Console.Write(Format(dblAnnualInterest, "0.#0") & Tab & Tab)
```

After:

```
Console.Write(Format(dblAnnualInterest, "0.#0") & Tab & Tab)
For iYears = 10 To 30 Step 5
```

7. Press Step Into to continue the program. Notice that the yellow arrow is again at the beginning of the OutputMortgageTable procedure. Visual Basic .NET has recompiled and reloaded the procedure with the changes.

8. Now if you step through the code to the line as in step 4, you should see only five values written on the line, as in Figure 6.7. They still have the wrong values, but at least you've fixed one of the bugs.

FIGURE 6.7

First Fix.

6

9. Run the program to completion by first using Step Out to return to the Sub Main. Look at the console window to see the wrong values (they are all the same for each row). Then return to the IDE and select Continue to end the program.

Watching Variables

In addition to watching the flow of logic in your application, Visual Basic .NET provides tools that let you view the contents of variables. This enables you to determine if their contents are what you intended, and that the calculations are accurate.

Just as with stepping, there are a number of tools that you can use to monitor variables. Some of the more useful ones are shown in Figure 6.8 and described here:

- Pop-up watch   If you hold the mouse cursor over a variable in the current procedure, a small tag will appear showing you the current value. You can see this in Figure 6.8, where the dblReturn variable is currently holding 100000. This is a useful and handy tool if you just want to quickly check a value occasionally. One other benefit of this tool is that you can select part of a calculation to determine its value, without requiring that the whole calculation be performed.

- Locals window   This window usually appears at the bottom of the screen when in Break mode. If not, select it from the Debug, Windows menu. The Locals window shows all the current procedure's variables as well as their type and current value. This is handy when stepping through a procedure because the values will turn red as they change. The Locals window is useful any time you are debugging a procedure that changes variable values.

- Watch window   This window usually appears at the bottom of the screen when in Break mode. If not, select it from the Debug, Windows menu. The Watch window shows variables that you are interested in. Right-click on variables and select Add Watch to add them to this window. If they are in scope, the current value will be displayed. Otherwise, you will be told that, "The name [*your variable name*] is not declared." This window is useful for monitoring a group of variables. Instead of only seeing them when they are in the Locals window, you can monitor them throughout the debugging session.

Examining Variables to Debug the Sample Program

Because you've made the layout of the mortgage table look better, the only bug that is likely to remain now would be in the calculation of each variable. You should debug the Payment function to make certain that all the correct values are being used. Follow these steps:

1. End the program if it is currently running. Remove all the existing breakpoints, and add one to the first line in the Payment function. This should be the line

   ```
   Dim dblMonthlyInterest As Double = AnnualInterest / 1200
   ```

2. Add a second breakpoint on the End Sub line of Sub Main to let you view the table before the program ends.

FIGURE 6.8

Watching variable values.

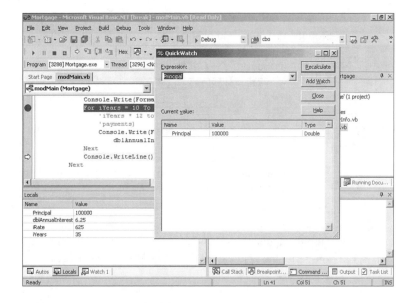

> **Note**
>
> Even though this line begins with a declaration, it is an executable line because of the assignment.

3. Run the program until it reaches the breakpoint. Enter **100000** for the amount of the loan.

4. When the program enters Break mode, look at the Locals window. Notice that it includes all the values for Principal, AnnualInterest, and Periods. Similarly, if you hold the mouse cursor over a variable (for example, AnnualInterest) in the IDE, you should see a Pop-up tag showing the current value.

5. Step once to execute that line. Notice that the dblMonthlyInterest variable changes in the Locals window, and turns red.

6. Select the code

   ```
   1 + dblMonthlyInterest ^ Periods
   ```

   Then hold the mouse cursor over the selected text. A Pop-up tag should appear, telling you that the value is 1. A quick calculation elsewhere confirms that this is correct if you perform the power operation first, and then add 1. However, the correct value should be about 1.647 because the addition should happen first, and then you should raise the result to the number of periods. This error is repeated in the second half of the function. Add parentheses to the calculation so that the additions happen first and then test the value again.

6

7. Similarly, the calculation in general suffers from an extreme lack of parentheses. Stop the program, and change the line of the calculation to be like

```
Return Principal * (dblMonthlyInterest * _
  ((1 + dblMonthlyInterest) ^ Periods) / _
  (((1 + dblMonthlyInterest) ^ Periods) - 1))
```

Tip

Parentheses don't cost anything. When you are writing a mathematical function, don't skimp on the parentheses—use as many as you need to make sure that the operations happen in the correct order. Alternatively, you can move each step to its own line, although this would require more temporary variables in the calculation.

8. Stop the application, remove the breakpoint on the line in the Payment function, and rerun the application. You should see the correct mortgage table, as shown in Figure 6.9.

FIGURE 6.9

Correct mortgage table.

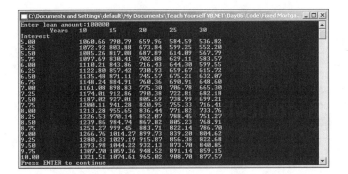

Finishing Touches with the Sample Program

There are a few other minor changes you can make to clean up the sample program. For example, the code that is used to ask the user a question could be wrapped up into a function. This would allow you to replace that code later with code that would perform a similar function, but with WinForms or WebForms or some other screen.

Tip

A good idea is to isolate sections of code that are operating system- or user-interface specific in procedures. Then, when you need to change the user interface, you only have to change the procedure, not the code that uses it.

Another similar change is to simplify the calculation in the mortgage payment function. Because the expression (1 + dblMonthlyInterest) ^ Periods) appears twice in the calculation, you can move it to its own calculation. Declare a temporary Double variable to hold the contents and replace the calculation with the temporary variable.

After you have made all the changes to the sample program, it should look similar to the sample shown in Listing 6.9.

INPUT   **LISTING 6.9**   Debugged Code

```
1  Option Explicit On
2 Imports System
3 Imports Microsoft.VisualBasic.ControlChars
4
5 Module modMain
6
7     Sub Main()
8
9         Dim sInput As String
10         Dim dblReturn As Double
11
12         'Get User Input
13         Dim dblPayment As Double
14         Console.Write("Enter loan amount:")
15         sInput = Console.ReadLine()
16         dblReturn = CDbl(sInput)
17
18         'Create the table
19         OutputMortgageTable(dblReturn)
20         Console.Write("Press ENTER to continue")
21         Console.ReadLine()
22     End Sub
23
24     Private Sub OutputMortgageTable(ByVal Principal As Double)
25
26         Dim iYears As Integer
27         Dim iRate As Integer
28         Dim dblAnnualInterest As Double
29
30         Console.WriteLine(Tab & "Years" & Tab & "10" & Tab & "15" & _
31             Tab & "20" & Tab & "25" & Tab & "30")
32         Console.WriteLine("Interest")
33
34         For iRate = 500 To 1000 Step 25
35             dblAnnualInterest = iRate / 100
36
37             Console.Write(Format(dblAnnualInterest, "0.#0") & Tab & Tab)
38             For iYears = 10 To 30 Step 5
39                 'iYears * 12 to get the number of months (assumes monthly
```

6

LISTING 6.9 continued

```
                         ➥payments)
40                   Console.Write(Format(Payment(Principal, _
41                       dblAnnualInterest, iYears * 12), "0.00") & Tab)
42               Next
43               Console.WriteLine()
44          Next
45
46      End Sub
47
48      Public Function Payment(ByVal Principal As Double, _
49          ByVal AnnualInterest As Double, _
50          ByVal Periods As Integer) As Double
51          Dim dblMonthlyInterest As Double = AnnualInterest / 1200
52          Return Principal * (dblMonthlyInterest * _
53              ((1 + dblMonthlyInterest) ^ Periods) / _
54              (((1 + dblMonthlyInterest) ^ Periods) - 1))
55      End Function
56
57 End Module
```

Other Tools for Debugging

Many other tools are available that might help you in debugging. Most of these are advanced tools that are beyond the scope of this book, but you should at least know that they exist. The other tools include

- Immediate Window   Available from the Debug, Windows menu at all times. Opens a window that lets you enter a line of code that will be run immediately. This enables you to test small fragments of code. Because it is available whether or not you are debugging, you might want to try using the Immediate window to test small calculations while you are writing your programs. One common use for the Immediate window is to display the contents of variables by "printing" them in the window, for example:

  ```
  ? dblMonthlyInterest
  4.16666666666667E-03
  ```

- Quickwatch Window   Available from the Debug menu when in Break mode. Opens a window showing the value of variables. This feature has been somewhat superceded by the pop-up tag that shows the value of variables. However, the Quickwatch window is also useful to test for expressions as well as variables.

- Call Stack   Available from the Debug, Windows menu when in Break mode. Opens a window showing the list of procedures that are currently active. For example, if your Sub Main has called OutputMortgageTable, the Call Stack will show the two procedures (in reverse order). You can use this to navigate between the two. This could allow you to see the line in Sub Main that called the second procedure. You might use this window to debug issues where the wrong decision is being made in an If statement.

- Disassembly   Available from the Debug, Windows menu when in Break mode. This is an advanced tool that shows the actual machine language created for the program, really only useful if you know Assembly.

- Threads   Available from the Debug, Windows menu when in Break mode. This is an advanced tool that shows the active threads in a program. Useful when you are doing multithreaded programming in Visual Basic .NET.

Visual Basic .NET provides a large number of tools that will assist you in releasing bug-free programs. The best way to learn the tools, and to learn which tools will help you the most, is to experiment with them. Rather than trying to solve bugs by simply staring at the source code, step through your code, look at the values for the variables you use, and try to isolate the errors using these tools.

Summary

All programs have bugs. Sometimes, the bug is the person running the program. Other times, there is an actual bug or error in the code. It might be because the author of the program didn't test for all possibilities of input, or didn't protect the program from missing files or databases. In any case, it is up to you, the developer, to try to ensure that none of these errors cause the user to lose information. You should strive to make your programs as bug-free as possible. The debugging tools of Visual Basic .NET will help here. Make sure that you use them to walk through your code and that the flow is what you had planned. Make sure that variables hold the correct values and that calculations are accurate.

Similarly, you can protect the program from errors by adding Structured Exception Handling to critical sections of code. Possible fail points—such as where code opens files, reads or writes information, or makes calculations—should be wrapped in Try...Catch...End Try blocks. These blocks should gracefully deal with the errors, ideally allowing the user to continue using the program.

Tomorrow, you will look at how you can work with objects. As you will see, you already have been working with objects; however, you will examine this in more detail in Day 7, "Working with Objects."

6

Q&A

Q. What if I have some old code that uses On Error? Do I have to rewrite it to use Structured Exception Handling?

A. No. If you include the Microsoft.VisualBasic reference, you can continue to use On Error Goto and On Error Resume Next. In addition, the Err object is available to you.

Workshop

The Workshop is designed to help you anticipate possible questions, review what you've learned, and get thinking about how to put your knowledge into practice. The answers to the quiz are in Appendix A, "Answers to Quizzes/Exercises."

Quiz

1. Name three tools that can be used to view the contents of a variable while you are in Break mode.

Exercises

1. You've just inherited the following block of code. It prompts the user for two values. It then will calculate and display a multiplication table of all the values between the two entered numbers. For example, if the user enters 5 and 9, the output should look similar to

OUTPUT

```
Multiplication Table (5 to 9)
      5     6     7     8     9
5    25    30    35    40    45
6    30    36    42    48    54
7    35    42    49    56    63
8    40    48    56    64    72
9    45    56    63    72    81
```

Add exception handling and debug the code in Listing 6.10 to ensure that it generates the desired output.

INPUT **LISTING 6.10** Multiplication Table Code

```
1 Imports System
2 Imports Microsoft.VisualBasic.ControlChars
3
4 Module modTable
5
6     Sub Main()
```

LISTING 6.10   continued

```
 7          Dim iLow, iHigh As Integer
 8          Dim sInput As String
 9
10          'Allow multiple runs through the table generation
11          Do
12              'prompt for values
13              Console.Write("Low value (maximum of 20, 0 to end): ")
14              sInput = Console.ReadLine()
15              iLow = CInt(sInput)
16
17              If iLow <> 0 Then
18                  Console.Write("High value (maximum of 20): ")
19                  sInput = Console.ReadLine()
20                  iHigh = CInt(sInput)
21
22                  OutputTable(iLow, iHigh)
23              End If
24          Loop Until iLow = 0
25          Console.Write("Press ENTER to continue")
26          Console.ReadLine()
27      End Sub
28
29      Private Sub OutputTable(ByVal MinValue As Integer, _
30        ByVal MaxValue As Integer)
31          Dim iCount, iCount2 As Integer
32
33          Console.WriteLine()
34          Console.WriteLine("Multiplication Table ({0} to {1})", _
35            MinValue, MaxValue)
36
37          'write header
38          For iCount = MinValue To MaxValue
39              Console.WriteLine(Tab & CStr(iCount))
40          Next
41          Console.WriteLine()
42
43          'Write each of the lines of the table
44          For iCount = MinValue To MaxValue
45              For iCount2 = MinValue To MaxValue
46                  Console.Write(CStr(iCount) & Tab & CStr(iCount * iCount2))
47              Next
48              Console.WriteLine()
49          Next
50      End Sub
51
52 End Module
```

6

2. As you continue with the book and have problems with your code, try to use the debugging tools to correct the program. Use breakpoints to isolate sections you think might have errors, step through the code, and use the Locals and Watch windows to monitor variables.

3. If you receive exceptions in your programs, add exception handling. Search the online help for the keyword "Exception" to see the various types of exceptions. Alternatively, you can explore the list by selecting Exceptions from the Debug, Windows menu.

4. Use the sample application to explore the different types of breakpoints. Try setting a breakpoint when the payment goes below a certain value.

Day 7

Working with Objects

Objects, both using and creating them, are key to development in Visual Basic .NET. Although you have already been working with objects throughout this book, today's lesson will focus on this topic and cover:

- What are objects
- How objects work
- Where objects fit into your programs

We will start with the basic definition of objects and all the terms and concepts that they bring along with them.

Getting Started: What Is an Object?

To define the term "object," we could go all the way back to Medieval Latin, "obiectum" or "thing put before the mind," but the simplest definition starts instead with just the word "thing." An object is a generic description of anything we might want to discuss or work with. In regular conversation, object is usually intended to describe only material objects, but in programming, where very little is truly material, this definition is expanded to include any entity. We can refer to a car, person, or building as an object, but it is also acceptable to use this term to describe something less tangible like an interest rate or a rule that will be applied to incoming e-mail.

The use of objects allows your programs to be focused on the entities you are working with, the end goal of which is to produce systems that are easier to understand and to enhance. Instead of a program where all the information and code related to a single entity are scattered throughout the entire application, an object-based approach consolidates this information by bringing it into the definition of the object.

Classes and Instances

To understand objects requires you to quickly move to the concept of a class. Classes, as in classifications, describe a group or type of entity, and all objects are one member of a certain class. Classes are the description of an object, providing details that define its behavior and telling what types of information are available about an object. We could, for instance, have a Car class. This class would tell us that the following information is available about a car: its color, speed, weight, make, model, and year. All these things are attributes of the object, descriptive pieces of information referred to as the object's properties. In addition to these properties, the class also describes what the object can do, and how it does it. These behaviors are often called the object's methods, and a car object might have methods such as "TurnLeft," "GoForward," "BackUp," and so on. Using this class, which provides information on the object's properties and methods, along with some other details, as a template, actual objects are then created.

Returning to the car example, the class would be the specification of the car, the blueprint that describes how it works and looks. That class is then used to create many cars, each of which exists on its own, but all of which are based on that same specification. Each individual car has the same properties because those come from the specification, such as color, but each one might have a different value for those properties (blue car, red car, yellow car, and so on). All the cars would also share the same behaviors or actions (the methods of the class), such as "GoForward," and all the cars built to the same specification would perform this action in the same way.

When we create a car based on the specification, it is equivalent to creating an object based on a class. So, whereas the Ford Thunderbird would be a class, Bob's blue T-Bird would be an object. Each of those individual objects is an *instance* of the class, and there is no limit to the number of these instances you can create. Every instance shares the template, or description, provided by its class. This means that every single instance of the Car class will have the same properties and methods and will behave in the same general fashion. Each individual instance has its own values for its properties, though; all cars have a color property, but each car might be a different color.

References

In programming, an additional concept is introduced, that of *referencing* an object. An object variable, any variable declared as an object of some type (`Dim myCar As Car`), does not hold the object itself, but merely a reference to that object. This is different from regular variable types, such as Integers or Strings, where the variable directly holds the value. This means that more than one object variable can refer, or point, to the same object. Generally, this isn't the case. You create one object and use it with one variable, but it is important to understand the difference between objects and other variable types in this regard.

Turning Concept into Code

Let's turn some of these concepts into code. First, to create objects, you must have a class. Many classes are available that have been created by other people; in fact, the entire .NET framework is really a "class library," a set of preexisting classes that you can use in your programs. For our example, though, we'll just make our own class, Car, because it is really not that complex to make a simple class.

Note

The purpose of today's lesson is not to teach you everything you need to know to create your own classes; it is to teach you enough about building classes so that you will understand ones that have already been created. You will need this knowledge to dig into the .NET Framework in Day 8, "Introduction to the .NET Framework," and it will give you a head start on developing your own objects in Day 15, "Creating Objects in Visual Basic .NET."

Open up Visual Studio .NET, and create a new Empty Project from under the Visual Basic Projects folder (see Figure 7.1).

This project contains no files of any sort, so we need to add one to it; Choose Project, Add Class from the menu. This adds a new, empty class to the project (name it `clsCar.vb`), a great starting point for this exercise. The shell of a class has been created into this file now, providing the following code:

```
Public Class clsCar

End Class
```

At this point, a class has been created, but it is completely blank. Now, within this shell of code, we can begin to describe the properties and methods of our Car objects. Whatever we place in this class will be part of every object instance created from it. For now, let's add `Make`, `Model`, and `Color` properties.

7

FIGURE 7.1

An empty project starts out containing no files at all.

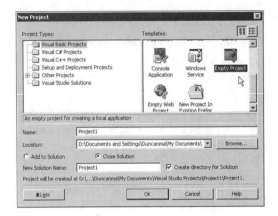

Properties

Properties are attributes about an object you can retrieve and set, and can be added to a class in one of two ways. The first, and the simplest, method is to declare a variable as `Public`. As discussed back in Day 3, "Introduction to Programming with Visual Basic .NET," `Public` describes the *scope* of the variable. In the case of a class, anything that is declared as `Public` is therefore available to anyone using that class. In our class, simply including the line `Dim Year As Integer` would not create an exposed property because `Year` would only be available internally to our class. If we were to declare `Year` as `Public Year As Integer`, then suddenly it is exposed through every instance of this object.

Property Statements

Alternatively, properties can be declared using a special `Property` syntax:

```
Dim myVar as <Property Data Type>
Public Property <Property Name>() As <Property Data Type>
    Get
        Return myVar
    End Get
    Set(ByVal Value As <Property Data Type>)
        myVar = value
    End Set
End Property
```

The two parts of the property definition, `Get` and `Set`, represent the retrieval of the property value, and the setting of that value. Generally, the `Get` code simply returns the value of an internal variable (a class-level variable that represents the property, usually prefixed with `m` to indicate a member value), and the `Set` code places a value (which is provided through the special keyword `value`) into that same internal variable. To implement the color property in `clsCar`, we could use code like Listing 7.1

INPUT **LISTING 7.1**   Creating Properties in Classes

```
 1 Public Class clsCar
 2     Dim m_sColor As String
 3     Public Property Color() As String
 4         Get
 5             Return m_sColor
 6         End Get
 7         Set(ByVal Value As String)
 8             m_sColor = value
 9         End Set
10     End Property
11 End Class
```

Now, add property code for each of Make and Model, remembering to add two addition-al internal variables as well (both of these properties should use String as their data type). Overall, this second way for declaring properties can produce similar results, but it is much more flexible because it allows you to define whatever code is required to prop-erly control the setting and retrieval of a property value.

ReadOnly and WriteOnly Properties

It is not unusual to have a property that you want to be read-only, such as a version prop-erty, or perhaps a creation date. It is much less common, though not impossible, that you might have a property that can be changed but cannot be read, such as a password field. In previous versions of Visual Basic, you could create these read-only or write-only properties simply by choosing not to implement either the Set or the Get portion of the property definition. That is partially what you do in Visual Basic .NET. If you are creat-ing a read-only property, you do not create the Set portion of the property definition, but you must also specify ReadOnly as an additional keyword. This is shown in the following code with the Description property, which is a computed value and therefore it would-n't make much sense to have it be writable. You wouldn't want to set a property like Description because it is really just the result of a calculation.

```
1 Public ReadOnly Property Description() As String
2     Get
3         Return m_sColor & " " & m_sMake & " " & m_sModel
4     End Get
5 End Property
```

For a write-only property, the keyword used is WriteOnly, and you supply only the Set portion of the property definition:

```
1 Dim m_sPassword As String
2 Public WriteOnly Property Password() As String
3     Set(ByVal Value As String)
4         m_sPassword = Value
```

7

```
5     End Set
6 End Property
```

Creating an Object Instance

After we have this class, we can create an instance of it in another part of our project. Add a module to your project (choose Project, Add Module from the menu) named Main.vb and create a Sub Main() inside it. Your module should look like the code in Listing 7.2 at this point.

INPUT   **LISTING 7.2**   Creating a New Module for Testing

```
1 Module Main
2     Sub Main()

3     End Sub
4 End Module
```

This new Main() procedure is the starting point of our solution. The code in it will be executed when we run this application, and this is where we will start writing the code to work with our new class. To get started using our new class, we have to first create a variable of the appropriate type:

```
Dim objCar As clsCar 'or Chapter7.clsCar, more on this later
```

This declaration looks like declaring a regular variable, such as a String or Integer, but it is very different. At this point, we have a variable that could hold a reference to an object of type clsCar, but that is current holding nothing. When we declare a String variable, the string itself has been created. Although it might not have any data in it, it does exist. In this case, we do not have anything in objCar at all. So, the next step is to create an instance of our class, which we can do with the New keyword:

```
objCar = New clsCar()
```

So, we now have created an instance of clsCar and assigned a reference to that new object to the objCar variable. We can now, through objCar, access the properties of the new object:

```
1 objCar.Color = "Red"
2 objCar.Make = "Ford"
3 objCar.Model = "Escort"
```

These properties can be retrieved just as easily:

```
Dim sCarDesc As String
sCarDesc = objCar.Color & " " & objCar.Make & " " & objCar.Model
```

Because objects work by reference, we can create additional variables, all pointing at the same location:

```
1 Dim objCar As clsCar
2 Dim objCar2 As clsCar
3 Dim sMake As String
4 objCar = New clsCar()
5 objCar2 = objCar
6 objCar.Make = "Ford"
7 objCar2.Make = "Chevy"
8 'objCar2.Make is equal to objCar.Make
```

Contrast this with a non-object variable, such as a `String`, where the actual value is moving between locations:

```
1 Dim sFirstValue As String
2 Dim sSecondValue As String
3
4 sFirstValue = "Dog"
5 sSecondValue = sFirstValue
6 sSecondValue = "Cat"
7 ' sFirstValue <> sSecondValue
```

Normally, when dealing with variables, as soon as the variable goes out of scope (see Day 3 for more information on variables and scope), it ceases to exist. Because multiple variables can point at a single object, the rules controlling object destruction are a little different. When all the variables that reference the object are gone, the object becomes inaccessible and is eventually destroyed by the background services of .NET. This process, which is called *garbage collection*, allows the program to freely create and release objects knowing that the system is following along behind cleaning up any mess. In this way, .NET cleans up on behalf of your program, providing another underlying service so that individual programs do not have to worry about such things.

Encapsulating Code into Your Classes

Now you have seen, in code, the creation of a class, the instantiation of objects based on that class, and the manipulation of those object properties. Moving along, consider the idea that a class, unlike a UDT (again, see Day 3 for more information on Structs or User-Defined Types), describes more than just a set of values, but also can include behavior. To provide this implementation of behavior, a class includes more than just simple code to set and retrieve property values; it can also include code to perform property validation and other actions. With our `clsCar`, we can demonstrate this feature by adding some valida-tion code to our properties. Currently, you could set the property `Color` to any string value, even if it isn't even a color at all (`objCar.Color = "John"`). To make our represen-tation of a Car object a little bit smarter, we can add a bit of code that checks any value submitted against a list of colors and rejects anything that does not match. This involves rewriting the routine for the `Color` property as shown in Listing 7.3.

7

INPUT **LISTING 7.3**   Adding Validation to the Color Property

```
1 Public Class clsCar
2     Dim m_sColor As String
3
4     Public Property Color() As String
5
6         Get
7             Return m_sColor
8         End Get
9
10        Set(ByVal Value As String)
11
12            Select Case Value.ToUpper()
13                Case "RED"
14                    m_sColor = Value
15                Case "YELLOW"
16                    m_sColor = Value
17                Case "BLUE"
18                    m_sColor = Value
19                Case Else
20                    Dim objException As System.Exception
21                    objException = New System.ArgumentOutOfRangeException()
22                    Throw objException
23            End Select
24        End Set
25    End Property
26
27 End Class
```

Now, an attempt to set the property to an invalid color (invalid by our code's internal list, which considers the popular color "mauve," for instance, to be invalid) results in an exception being raised. For more information on exceptions and exception-based error handling, see Day 6, "What to Do When Good Programs Go Bad, and Making Sure They Don't." As described in that day's lesson, we can correctly deal with this exception by rewriting our test code (contained in `Sub Main()`) to include a `Try...Catch` structure. This modified code is shown in Listing 7.4.

INPUT   **LISTING 7.4**   Including Error Handling in Our Test Code

```
1 Sub Main()
2     Dim objCar As clsCar
3     Dim sColor As String
4
5     objCar = New clsCar()
6     objCar.Year = 1999
7
```

LISTING 7.4   continued

```
 8      Try
 9          objCar.Color = "Green"
10      Catch objException As System.ArgumentOutOfRangeException
11           'whoops! Handle the error!
12           System.Console.WriteLine("Whoops!")
13      End Try
14      sColor = objCar.Color
15
16      objCar.Make = "Ford"
17      objCar.Model = "Escort"
18      System.Console.WriteLine(objCar.Description)
19 End Sub
```

Other than property validation, which is powerful in itself, a class can contain a code function or subroutine that is not part of any of the property retrieval or setting code, commonly referred to as a *method*. Methods are designed to provide related functionality to an object and often act based on property information (because it is available). For our clsCar, a useful method might be to produce an age of the car by comparing the current date and time to a property of the car representing its manufacturing date. Creating the manufacturing date property is relatively straightforward. It is just like the earlier properties we created except that it is a date, and adding this method is actually as easy as creating a public function inside our class definition.

First, the new property:

```
 1 Dim m_dtManufactured As Date
 2
 3 Public Property Manufactured() As Date
 4     Get
 5         Return m_dtManufactured
 6     End Get
 7     Set(ByVal Value As Date)
 8         m_dtManufactured = value
 9     End Set
10 End Property
```

Note

If we created this function as private, it would still be usable from inside this class but would not be available from any other code. Alternatively, we can also declare elements of our class (properties, functions, subroutines) as Friend. This declaration ensures that code within the same assembly can access these portions of the class as if they were public, but that they would be hidden (private) to any code external to the class's assembly. (Assemblies will be covered in detail as part of deployment in Day 19, "Deploying Your Application"; for now, consider them to be all the other parts of the same solution.)

7

Listing 7.5 shows the new method.

INPUT   **LISTING 7.5**   The GetAge Method

```
1 Public Function GetAge() As Long
2     Dim lngDays As Long
3     Dim dtCurrent As Date
4     dtCurrent = System.DateTime.Today
5     lngDays = dtCurrent.Subtract(m_dtManufactured).Days
6     Return lngDays
7 End Function
```

After we have added that code to our class, we can call it through any instance,
(objCar.GetAge()), as in Listing 7.6.

INPUT   **LISTING 7.6**   Using Our New Method

```
1 Dim objCar As clsCar
2 objcar = New clsCar()
3 objCar.Manufactured = #1/30/2000#
4 System.Console.WriteLine(objCar.GetAge())
```

In some ways, the new method just created would be better suited as a property (which
we would then rename Age, because it is an attribute not an action) because it does not
actually perform any action and returns only a value. For our Car class, a better method
example might be something action-related, such as StartEngine, a sample implementation of which is provided in Listing 7.7.

INPUT   **LISTING 7.7**   Our New Action-Oriented Method

```
1 Public Sub StartEngine()
2     System.Console.WriteLine("Vroom, Vroom...!!!")
3 End Sub
```

With this code added to clsCar, we would have a more action-oriented method available.
Through a combination of properties (some with code, and some without) and methods,
it is possible to create complex objects. Keep in mind that the objects that make up the
.NET Framework (such as System.Console and others) are built according to these same
rules and have all the same characteristics as objects that you can create. The only real
difference between the .NET Framework and your objects is that you didn't have to write
the ones in the Framework!

Advanced Topics

Although properties and methods allow you to create powerful and complex objects, the object support in .NET has many more features beyond those basics. These advanced features make it easier for you to represent concepts and entities in our code, producing a system that is easier to use, maintain, and extend. Although the object support in .NET is extensive, we will provide a brief overview of five main areas: overloading, inheritance, constructors, namespaces, and static class members.

Overloading

This section covers the basics of overloading; further details will be covered in Day 15, when we create our own objects. Overloading allows a single function or subroutine to be called with a variety of different parameters. This allows a single method, for instance, to accept parameters in different combinations or using different data types. So, returning to our clsCar example, we could design the GetAge method so that it could work in any one of several different ways. The existing implementation takes no parameters and returns the difference in days between the current date and the manufactured date, but perhaps we would also like to allow a user of our object to request the difference between the manufactured date and any arbitrary date, and also to allow the user to specify the unit of time to measure the difference in. To do this without this concept of overloading, we would have to create a different function for each possible call, as in Listing 7.8.

INPUT   **LISTING 7.8**   Building Many Variations on a Single Method

```
1 Public Function GetAge() As Long
2     Dim lngDays As Long
3     Dim dtCurrent As Date
4     dtCurrent = System.DateTime.Today
5     lngDays = dtCurrent.Subtract(m_dtManufactured).Days
6     Return lngDays
7 End Function
8
9 Public Function GetAgeAtDate(ByVal dtPointInTime As Date) As Long
10     Dim lngDays As Long
11     lngDays = dtPointInTime.Subtract(m_dtManufactured).Days
12     Return lngDays
13 End Function
14
15 Public Function GetAgeInUnits(ByVal sUnit As String) As Long
16     Dim lngUnits As Long
17     Dim dtCurrent As Date
18     Dim tsDifference As System.TimeSpan
19     dtCurrent = System.DateTime.Today
```

7

LISTING 7.8   continued

```
20      tsDifference = dtCurrent.Subtract(m_dtManufactured)
21      Select Case sUnit
22          Case "Hours"
23              lngUnits = tsDifference.Hours
24
25          Case "Days"
26              lngUnits = tsDifference.Days
27
28          Case "Minutes"
29              lngUnits = tsDifference.Minutes
30
31          Case "Years"
32              lngUnits = tsDifference.Days \ 365
33      End Select
34      Return lngUnits
35 End Function
```

All these functions are really just variations on GetAge, but each different parameter list and different corresponding code, needs its own function name. With overloading, we remove this restriction and can create all these functions using the same name GetAge. To use this feature, all we need to do is add the Overloads keyword in front of each (including the original) function declaration (before the Public) and change each function name to be the same:

```
Public Overloads Function GetAge() As Long
End Function

Public Overloads Function GetAge(ByVal dtPointInTime As Date) As Long
End Function

Public Overloads Function GetAge(ByVal sUnit As String) As Long
End Function
```

In our example code that uses this function, we can now choose between any one of the three possible declarations for this function (see Figure 7.2).

 Note

> Each function declaration must be different in some way—number of parameters, data type of parameters, or the data type of the return value—or it will not be allowed.

Overloading represents the concept that the same action or request can be used in a variety of ways and allows you to model that in your object without having to resort to creating multiple distinct methods (GetAge, GetAgeFromDate, and so on). This technique is used throughout the .NET Framework to allow you to call functions with a variety of different parameter sets. Consider, for instance, the `System.Console.WriteLine` method, which can be called using any one of 18 different parameter lists. As the Framework demonstrates, this is a useful way to simplify objects and provide the most options to programs using them.

FIGURE 7.2

All the available versions of a function are shown through IntelliSense when you are using Visual Studio .NET to create a client.

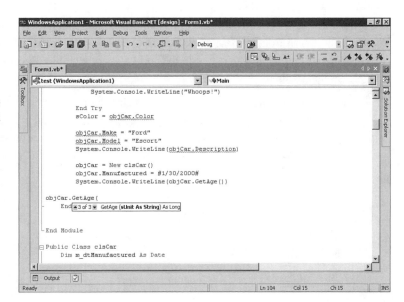

Inheritance

To some people, this is one of the most exciting features of Visual Basic .NET—a feature that is considered fundamental to the creation of object-based systems and that has been missing from Visual Basic until this version. I am not going to argue with this opinion, but somehow I managed to build systems for many years before .NET arrived, without inheritance. Regardless, the addition of inheritance to the Visual Basic language is an important feature and worth a little discussion.

As discussed earlier in today's lesson, objects are ways for you to represent concepts or entities in code, and each of the object features of Visual Basic is designed to help you make the most useful representation possible. In many situations, one entity or concept is really what we would call a subobject of a more basic entity or concept. Many examples of this are used in programming books, and sadly I am not going to come up with anything too revolutionary. Consider our class of objects designed to represent cars, such as a Ford Mustang, Toyota Celica, or Chevy Cavalier. The class would have various properties, such as `Doors` (number of doors the car has), `MaxSpeed`, `Color`, and others.

7

This general Car class really contains several subclasses of objects, such as Hatchbacks and Convertibles. Those classes would, of course, have all the properties of their parent class, Car, such as Doors, MaxSpeed, and Color, but they could also have unique properties of their own. A hatchback could have properties that described the size and behavior of its rear door. This relationship, between Car and its subclasses of Hatchback and Convertible, would be considered to be a parent-child relationship, and the method for representing this relationship in our systems is called *inheritance*. The class Hatchback is said to inherit from its base class Car. This relationship means that, in addition to any properties and methods created in the child class, the child will also possess all the properties and methods of the parent.

The previous example started with our Car class and headed downwards. Let's take the same starting point of Car and head upwards for a more detailed example of inheritance. To start, we could have a base class of Vehicle, which could represent any type of vehicle (boat, car, truck, plane) and has the properties of MaxSpeed, NumberOfPassengers, Color, and Description. We could easily represent this class in Visual Basic code, as shown in Listing 7.9.

INPUT   **LISTING 7.9**   Our Vehicle Class

```
 1 Public Class Vehicle
 2
 3     Public Property MaxSpeed() As Long
 4         Get
 5         End Get
 6         Set(ByVal Value As Long)
 7         End Set
 8     End Property
 9
10     Public Property NumberOfPassengers() As Long
11         Get
12
13         End Get
14         Set(ByVal Value As Long)
15         End Set
16     End Property
17
18     Public Property Color() As String
19         Get
20
21         End Get
22         Set(ByVal Value As String)
23         End Set
24     End Property
25
26     Public Function Description() As String
27     End Function
28 End Class
```

The code that goes within the various procedures in that class is not really relevant to our example, so we will just leave it blank for now. If we were to jump to some code to try using our object (for instance, in the Sub Main() of our project, as in our earlier examples), we would see that we can create objects of type Vehicle and work with their properties, as in Listing 7.10.

INPUT   **LISTING 7.10**   Working with Our Vehicle Class

```
1 Module UseVehicle
2     Sub Main()
3         Dim objVehicle As Vehicle
4         objVehicle = New Vehicle()
5
6         objVehicle.Color = "Red"
7         objVehicle.MaxSpeed = 100
8     End Sub
9 End Module
```

Now, by adding an additional class to our project (see Listing 7.11), we can create a class (Car) that inherits from Vehicle, just like the real class of object Car is a subclass or child of the Vehicle class of objects. Because we are creating a class designed to deal with just cars, we can add a couple of properties (NumberOfDoors and NumberOfTires) specific to this subclass of Vehicle.

INPUT   **LISTING 7.11**   Creating a child Class

```
 1 Public Class Car
 2     Inherits Vehicle
 3
 4     Public Property NumberOfTires() As Integer
 5         Get
 6
 7         End Get
 8         Set(ByVal Value As Integer)
 9
10         End Set
11     End Property
12
13     Public Property NumberOfDoors() As Integer
14         Get
15
16         End Get
17         Set(ByVal Value As Integer)
18
19         End Set
20     End Property
21
22 End Class
```

7

The key to this code is the line `Inherits Vehicle`, which tells Visual Basic that this class is a child of the `Vehicle` class and therefore should inherit of all that class's properties and methods. Once again, no code is actually placed into any of these property definitions because they are not really relevant at this time. After that code is in place, without having to do anything else, we can see the effect of the `Inherits` statement.

Returning to our `Main()` procedure, we can create an object of type `Car`, and we'll quickly see that it exposes both its own properties and those of the parent class (see Figure 7.3).

When an inherited class adds new methods or properties, it is said to be *extending* the base class. In addition to extending, it is also possible for a child class to *override* some or all of the functionality of the base class. This is done when the child implements a method or property that is also defined in the parent or base class. In such a case, the code in the child will be executed instead of the code in the parent, allowing you to create specialized versions of the base method or property.

For a child class to override some part of the base class, that portion must be marked `Overridable` in the base class definition. For instance, in the version of `Vehicle` listed earlier, none of its properties had the keyword `Overridable` and therefore child classes would be unable to provide their own implementations. As an example of how overriding is set up in the base and child classes, the code in Listing 7.12 marks the `Description()` function as being overridable, and then overrides it in the `Car` child class. Note that non-relevant portions of the two classes have been removed for clarity.

FIGURE 7.3

Classes expose all their public properties and methods, along with the public properties and methods of the class they are based on.

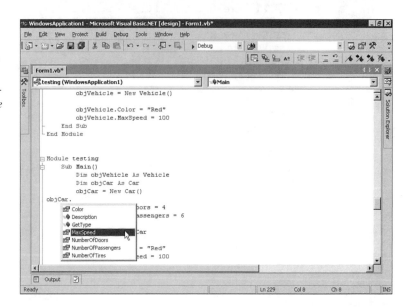

```
 1 Public Class Vehicle
 2
 3      'Code removed for simplicity....
 4
 5      Public Overridable Function Description() As String
 6          Return "This is my generic vehicle description!"
 7      End Function
 8 End Class
 9
10 Public Class Car
11      Inherits Vehicle
12
13      'Code removed for simplicity....
14
15      Public Overrides Function Description() As String
16          Return "This is my Car Description"
17      End Function
18
19 End Class
```

When overriding a method or property, as we did in Listing 7.12, you can refer back to the original member of the base class by using the built-in object MyBase. For example, to refer to the existing Description() method of the Vehicle class, we could call MyBase.Description() from within the Description method of Car. This functionality allows you to provide additional functionality through overriding without having to redo all the original code as well.

In addition to marking code as Overridable, it is also possible to mark a method or property as MustOverride and a class as MustInherit. The MustOverride keyword indicates that any child of this class must provide its own version of this property or method, and the MustInherit keyword means that this class cannot be used on its own (you must base other classes off of it). It is important to note that if a class contains a method marked MustOverride, then the class itself must be marked as MustInherit.

Inheritance is a big topic, and we haven't covered it all, but with the information provided in today's lesson, you are ready to start designing some applications that take advantage of this object feature.

The Base of All Base Classes

If you look at the list of what is exposed by this new instance of the Car class, you will see more than simply the properties of Vehicle and of Car. The methods ToString() and GetType() are exposed by this object, but are not part of its class or its parent class. These methods are actually another result of inheritance. Whereas Car inherits from Vehicle, both Vehicle and Car (and every other class in .NET) inherit from the base

7

class `System.Object`. This ultimate base class provides a few methods that are automatically part of every class we create.

One additional result of inheritance, one that is certainly worth mentioning, is in the area of data types. As discussed way back in Day 3, every variable is of a certain data type, and objects are no exception. When we declare a variable to be of type `Car`, that is just as strict of data typing as with Integers and Strings. If we make a function parameter of that type, then only that type of object can be passed to that function. In an inheritance situation, the child class can act as if it was an instance of the parent class. This means, in our example, that we can put our `Car` objects into variables and procedure arguments that are of type `Vehicle`. Listing 7.13 shows an example of this.

INPUT   **LISTING 7.13**   A Child Class Acting as an Instance of the Parent Class

```
 1 Sub Main()
 2     Dim objVehicle As Vehicle
 3     Dim objCar As Car
 4     objCar = New Car()
 5
 6     objCar.NumberOfDoors = 4
 7     objCar.NumberOfPassengers = 6
 8
 9     objVehicle = objCar
10
11     objVehicle.Color = "Red"
12     objVehicle.MaxSpeed = 100
13 End Sub
```

The instance of `Car` represented by `objCar` was easily placed into the variable `objVehicle`, and from that point on could be treated just like a `Vehicle` object. This fact, that a child object can be used as if it was an instance of the parent class, allows for the creation of generic code that will work with a class or any of its subclasses. This is just one way that inheritance can be used to create better solutions, but there are many others. This has been a rapid overview of the subject of inheritance, and it deserves further discussion from both a design and implementation point of view. For that reason, this topic and other object-related discussions will be covered in more detail in the rest of the book.

Constructors

When you want to use an object, you have to either work with an existing instance, or create your own. Creating an object instance is done through the `New` keyword, which takes the specified class and establishes an area in memory for this instance of that class. *Constructors* are a way to provide information to the class at this creation time to allow it to initialize itself or perform other configuration tasks at this point. If a class has a constructor, and many of the .NET Framework classes do, then you can usually supply parameters at creation time, as part of the call to New. The following code shows this working with the creation of a new exception object (see Day 6 for more information on exceptions and other error handling topics), supplying an error message as a parameter to its constructor. This error message will be used automatically by the new object to populate one of its properties.

```
Dim exError As System.Exception
Dim sMessage As String
sMessage = "This will be the error message."
exError = New System.Exception(sMessage)
```

The creation of a constructor for our Vehicle class is relatively easy. You first have to create a method named New that is public and has no parameters.

```
Public Sub New()
End Sub
```

With this completed constructor (that doesn't do anything yet) in place, you will see little difference in your code, and until we add some functionality into this New() subroutine, nothing different happens at all. The constructor, even without parameters, can be used as a place to initialize internal variables, such as the Manufactured Date in our Vehicle class (see Listing 7.14).

INPUT   **LISTING 7.14**   Using a Constructor to Initialize the Members of a Class

```
1       Public Sub New()
2           m_dtManufactured = System.Date.Now()
3
4       End Sub
```

Just like any other method of an object, it is possible to overload that method and provide more than one way to call it. Unlike other methods, though, overloading the constructor does not require the use of the Overloads keyword. You can just create multiple versions of the New procedure, and each will be treated as an available version of the constructor. In our case, we could quickly create a few useful constructors (shown in Listing 7.15) just by thinking of the different ways in which someone might want to initialize our object.

INPUT   **LISTING 7.15**   Overloading a Class's Constructor to Provide Ways to Initialize Objects

```
1       Public Sub New()
2           m_dtManufactured = System.Date.Now()
3
```

7

LISTING 7.15   continued

```
4          End Sub
5
6          Public Sub New(ByVal sColor As String)
7              m_dtManufactured = system.Date.Now
8              m_sColor = sColor
9
10         End Sub
11
12         Public Sub New(ByVal dtManufactured As Date, _
13             ByVal sColor As String)
14             m_dtManufactured = dtManufactured
15             m_sColor = sColor
16
17         End Sub
```

In the case of a child class, one that inherits from another class, you might want to call the base class's constructor from your New procedure. You can accomplish this easily using the special object MyBase, using code such as MyBase.New().

Namespaces

A *namespace* is an abstract concept used to group a number of classes or modules together, allowing you to logically categorize all these objects within a single higher-level object. So, by having a Namespace Chapter7 at the top of our classes and a corresponding End Namespace at the bottom, we effectively create a grouping called Chapter7 that contains all our classes within it. After this namespace exists, it is used by default for object references made in code within the same namespace, but can also be explicitly stated (Dim objCar as Chapter7.Car).

There are many reasons why you might want to create and use namespaces, not the least of which is the basis for the moniker "namespace," as a way to create a private area to ensure that your class names are unique. By defining a namespace, our class Car becomes Chapter7.Car, and therefore will no longer conflict with any other class created with the name Car.

Another, subtler, reason to use namespaces is because they produce easier code to maintain. The grouping of classes under higher-level namespaces leads to code that is clearly defined by some categorization scheme and is therefore more readable and easy to maintain.

For our examples throughout this book, we could have created namespaces based on the lesson name (for instance, all the code from this day's lesson would be placed under the Day7 namespace), all of which could then be located under a bookwide namespace of TeachYourselfVB. Our classes would be creatable as simply Day7, but to ensure no

ambiguity, we could also refer to them as their fully qualified name
(TeachYourselfVB.Day7.Car, for instance).

This method of grouping classes is similar to the concept of scope that was discussed on
Day 3; a class only has to be unique within its particular namespace. If you do happen to
make a class that shares its name with a class that exists in another namespace, then you
will need to make sure that you are specifying the full name of the class whenever you
reference it from outside its own namespace.

Namespaces are hierarchical, which allows you to create a multiple level scheme for
grouping your classes and objects, just like within the .NET Framework itself. There are
two ways to create a lower-level namespace: Either define the namespace using the fully
qualified name (see Listing 7.16) or nest namespace definitions (see Listing 7.17).

INPUT   **LISTING 7.16**   Declaring a Multipart Namespace

```
 1 Imports System
 2 Namespace MyApp.Console
 3     Module Main
 4         Sub Main()
 5             Dim objHW As New MyApp.Console.Utilities()
 6             objHW.PrintOut()
 7         End Sub
 8     End Module
 9
10     Public Class Utilities
11         'Run the application
12         Public Sub PrintOut()
13             Console.WriteLine(Environment.MachineName)
14             Console.WriteLine(Environment.SystemDirectory)
15             Console.WriteLine(Environment.GetLogicalDrives())
16             Console.WriteLine(Environment.Version.ToString())
17         End Sub
18     End Class
19 End Namespace
```

INPUT   **LISTING 7.17**   Using Nested Namespaces to Create Object Hierarchies

```
 1 Imports System
 2 Namespace MyApp
 3     Namespace Console
 4         Module Main
 5             Sub Main()
 6                 Dim objHW As New MyApp.Console.Utilities()
 7                 objHW.PrintOut()
 8             End Sub
```

7

LISTING 7.17 continued

```
 9        End Module
10
11        Public Class Utilities
12            'Run the application
13            Public Sub PrintOut()
14                Console.WriteLine(Environment.MachineName)
15                Console.WriteLine(Environment.SystemDirectory)
16                Console.WriteLine(Environment.GetLogicalDrives())
17                Console.WriteLine(Environment.Version.ToString())
18            End Sub
19        End Class
20    End Namespace
21 End Namespace
```

Within your applications, you can use namespaces as a way to group conceptually related code together, but other than their effect on the scope of classes, namespaces are not really required for building a system.

Shared Objects and Members

Earlier today, when we described the relationship between classes and objects, you learned that to use any method or property described in a class you would have to obtain or create an instance of that class. In general, this is the case; you cannot work directly with a class, only with instances of the class that you create. There is a way to expose certain functionality through the class itself, though, independently of any particular instance of that class, through the use of the Shared keyword. Shared, like the other access descriptors you have seen (such as Public, Private, and Friend), denotes that part of a class is available without the creation of an instance. The .NET Framework uses this feature in its classes, such as the exposed property Today of the System.DateTime class (an example of which is shown in Listing 7.18).

 LISTING 7.18 Built-In Functions from Visual Basic 6.0 Have Been Replaced with Shared Methods in Visual Basic .NET

```
1 Imports System
2 Module Main
3     Sub Main()
4         Dim dtToday As Date
5         dtToday = DateTime.Today()
6     End Sub
7 End Module
```

e: AKBAS FAKHRI

       04-Apr-03 07:00 PM

       Sams teach yourself Visual Basic NET in
       21 days / Duncan Mackenzie, Kent
       Sharkey

       QA76 73.B3 M335 2002

…ted in your own code when you want a particular
… at all times, without the overhead of object creation.
… unless you really require it because having many
… as simply creating a module full of procedures and
…s. Note that Modules are a special type of Class, all
…d Shared by default.

…f classes that you can use in your applications, all
…ated programming principles common to the .NET
…ncept of classes, instances, properties, methods, inher-
…dation of creating your own classes within Visual
…pplication beyond the simplest example, you will need
…ou will also generally have to create your own classes,
…ill for any .NET programmer. In today's lesson we
…classes as examples, basic object-oriented concepts
…t those concepts in your own code. In the next lesson,
…es available in the .NET Framework and illustrate how
you will use those classes to build great .NET applications.

Q&A

Q. I have never worked with an object-oriented programming language before; can't I just stick with procedures and modules?

A. You do not have to make objects in Visual Basic, but you will find it difficult to use this language without using at least some objects, such as the .NET Framework. For that reason, the initial focus for a developer new to objects is to become familiar with using objects before moving on to building them yourself.

Q. I have read that, in Visual Basic .NET, you cannot tell exactly when an object will be destroyed and that fact will limit you in many ways. What is meant by these comments, and are they true?

A. When working with objects, their destruction does not always occur at a set point in the code, so it is difficult to have a certain piece of code that runs whenever an object is terminated. In some languages, including previous versions of Visual Basic, there was a mechanism available to add code to a "termination event" procedure. Code placed in such a procedure would be guaranteed to run whenever the object is destroyed. In Visual Basic .NET, the garbage collection subsystem will

7

destroy objects when necessary, but it is not possible to create code to run at the time of that destruction. In general, this "limitation" should not cause you much trouble, but sometimes (especially when migrating old Visual Basic code) there is an expectation of running code at the end of the object's life cycle, and this will not be easily transferred into a Visual Basic .NET implementation.

Workshop

The Workshop is designed to help you anticipate possible questions, review what you've learned, and get thinking about how to put your knowledge into practice. The answers to the quiz are in Appendix A, "Answers to Quizzes/Exercises."

Quiz

1. If a class contains a method marked `MustOverride`, what else must be true?

2. What is the keyword that you can use in a constructor to call the constructor of a base class?

3. What is wrong with the overloaded constructors in this code (see Listing 7.19)?

LISTING 7.19 Different Versions of Constructor Available for the
INPUT `Vehicle` Class

```
1 Public Class Vehicle
2     Dim m_dtManufactured As Date
3     Dim m_lngNumberOfPassengers As Long
4     Dim m_sColor As String
5
6     Public Sub New()
7         m_dtManufactured = System.DateTime.Now()
8     End Sub
9
10    Public Sub New(ByVal sColor As String)
11        m_dtManufactured = System.DateTime.Now()
12        m_sColor = sColor
13    End Sub
14
15    Public Sub New(ByVal sName As String)
16    End Sub
17
18    Public Sub New(ByVal dtManufactured As Date, _
19                   ByVal sColor As String)
20        m_dtManufactured = dtManufactured
21        m_sColor = sColor
```

LISTING 7.19   continued

```
22        End Sub
23
24 End Class
```

Exercises

Using classes, properties, methods, and inheritance, create an example class hierarchy starting with Animal at the top and going a few levels down with some example classes.

7

WEEK 1

In Review

Now that you have worked your way through the first week of lessons, you should have a good understanding of programming, Visual Basic, .NET, and how it all fits together (Days 1 and 2). You have created a few sample programs in .NET, using both the IDE and the command line to compile them. With that experience, you are now able to try out all the examples in this book, and you can even do some experimenting on your own.

The lesson on data types and the basic programming techniques used in creating Visual Basic .NET applications (Day 3) has given you a good introduction to simple programming. Day 4 introduced conditionals (including If statements) and loops, two things used in almost every single program you will ever write. Because Visual Basic .NET allows the creation of so many different types of programs, using a wide variety of projects and individual source files, Day 5 covered the architecture options to build all the different types of systems that .NET can be used to create.

No matter how good you are at programming, errors will always happen in programs. Regardless of whether the error was avoidable, the error handling techniques covered on Day 6 will allow you to deal with the problem gracefully. Finally, because most of the .NET Framework is based on objects, the focus of Day 7's lesson was on the terms and concepts needed for you to work with objects in your own programs.

All this information, and the hands-on coding that accompanied it, should have you ready to tackle the first bonus project (The Game of Life). This bonus project, which you can find by going to the Web site for this book (`http://www.samspublishing.com/detail_sams.cfm?item=0672320665`), in addition to walking you through the creation of a complete working program, illustrates the use of conditionals, arrays, loops, variables, and even error-handling techniques shown through the lessons you just completed. Read the bonus material, build the project, and play around with the results for a while. When you are ready to move on, try modifying the code to change how the program works, making your own variation of the program.

WEEK 2

At a Glance

During this week, you will really dive into the exciting world of the .NET Framework. The week starts with a lesson in the Framework itself (Day 8), including details on using the Console, Math, Random, and Environment classes, and information on all the great array and list functionality provided by the Framework. In addition to all these specifics, this lesson also includes an introduction on how to find the functionality you need in the .NET Framework on your own—invaluable information when you start your own projects using .NET.

The next two lessons, Days 9 and 10, focus on the creation of a user interface for your applications, either for Windows (using Windows Forms, Day 9) or for the Web (using the Web Forms technology, covered in Day 10). Few programs run without some user interface, making these two lessons absolutely essential.

Almost every business application in existence uses some form of a database, so you will spend two lessons on just that topic. Day 11 covers the underlying concepts of databases and walks you through the creation of a database for a CD-tracking application. Day 12 continues the lesson on data by showing you how to connect to your sample database and build an application that allows you to add, edit, and delete CDs in your collection.

Working with databases introduces you to the Server Explorer, but Day 13 shows you how to use its many features. In this lesson, you will work with Performance Counters and Event Logs, and learn an easier way to set up a database connection.

8

9

10

11

12

13

14

Finally, in Day 14, you learn about some of the more advanced object-oriented features of Visual Basic .NET, including inheritance, overriding, and overloading. This lesson really makes the power of this version of Visual Basic clear and shows you how you can use these features to architect systems that are easier to maintain and extend.

At the end Week 2, you will have learned about so many features of Visual Basic .NET that you will be ready to create complex applications. Bonus project 2 will provide practice using a few of these new techniques.

DAY **8**

Introduction to the .NET Framework

The .NET Framework is not specifically a new feature in Visual Basic .NET because it is shared across many languages (more than 20 as of this writing). The Framework provides a powerful set of components for you to use in your programs. It contains an immense number of classes that perform various functions, from manipulating strings or numbers, to encryption and network access. Learning the .NET Framework is an ongoing process, but knowing key terms and the way that the Framework is organized are invaluable skills that will assist you as you develop more applications with Visual Basic .NET.

Today, you will learn

- What the .NET Framework is
- Some important classes in the .NET Framework
- How to find what you need in the .NET Framework

What Is the .NET Framework?

The *.NET Framework* is the name given to a variety of components and services that combine to create a powerful development environment. It includes a huge number of classes (more than 6,000) that provide most of the functionality previously included in Visual Basic or the Windows API. These allow you to write Windows-based and Web applications, access the network, create graphics, and much more.

In addition, the .NET Framework includes the *Common Language Runtime* (*CLR*), which is responsible for running your code. The CLR offers a number of important innovations that affect developers of .NET applications in Visual Basic .NET, or other supported languages. The most important change is that now all these languages compile to Microsoft Intermediate Language (MSIL). This is then converted by the CLR into native code when it is first executed. The end result is that you get the performance of fully compiled code, not code that is interpreted at runtime.

In addition, all languages supported by the CLR use the same data types. This means that it is much easier for two (or more) languages to interoperate. Previously, if you needed to pass information from one language (such as C++) to another (perhaps Visual Basic), you might have needed to perform some conversions to properly interpret the variable. Now, as both languages will use the same data types, this is trivial. The CLR enables developers to use the language they are most comfortable in, and still be able to communicate with other languages.

Although the CLR is important, it generally works in the background. The important, visible part of the .NET Framework you should examine is some of the classes that make up the Framework.

Important Classes in the .NET Framework

You will use many classes within the .NET Framework as you build applications in Visual Basic .NET. However, you will use some classes more frequently than others. Some of the most useful classes are

- `Console`   Enables reading and writing to the command-line.
- `Environment`   Enables reading and writing to the system environment variables.
- `Random`   Enables the generation of random numbers.
- `Math`   Includes a number of mathematical calculations.
- `Collections`   Provides a number of classes for different strategies for storing collections of items.

Console

You have already seen some of the Console class while building previous applications. The WriteLine and ReadLine methods of the Console class have been frequently used to write output and read input from the various console, or command-line, applications you have created thus far in the book. That is the most important use of the Console class. However, there are some less used features of Console worth investigating. Some of the important methods of the Console class are shown in Table 8.1.

TABLE 8.1   Methods of the Console Class

Method	Description
Read	Reads information from the command-line (or other input). Does not require the line to end with Enter.
ReadLine	Reads information from the command-line (or other input). Reads all characters up to, but not including Enter.
SetError	Changes the destination for error messages displayed while your program is running. This could be used to create a simple error logging mechanism for your application.
SetIn	Changes the source of the input for Read and ReadLine. This could be used to change a command-line application to read from a file or network location. See the section "Redirection," later in today's lesson.
SetOut	Changes the destination for Write and WriteLine methods. This could be used to change the destination for output for logging or other use. See the section "Redirection," later in today's lesson.
Write	Writes information to the command-line (or other output). Does not end with a new line.
WriteLine	Writes information to the command-line (or other output). Ends the output with a new line.

Simpler Output

As the Console class is often used for output, it would be nice if it made your life easier when you perform this task. Fortunately, it does. When you are using either the Write or WriteLine methods to display information, you can take advantage of these methods' capability to use placeholders for your variables. Normally, if you want to display a string that contains information stored in variables, you would use a technique known as concatenation.

NEW TERM *Concatenation* is yet another lovely word for "adding strings together." Rather than adding the strings with the + symbol, as you do with numbers, you use the & symbol, as in

```
Console.WriteLine("Please enter " & ITEM_COUNT & _
  "items. Press ENTER between items.")
```

If you have a complicated string, it's sometimes difficult to manage all the quotation marks and ampersands. Instead of building a complicated string using concatenation, you can use these placeholders in the correct spots, and then include the variables used to fill them later, as follows:

```
Console.WriteLine("Please enter {0} items. Press ENTER between items.", _
ITEM_COUNT)
```

The {0} is a placeholder for the variable you include after the end of the string. This is the ITEM_COUNT in the previous statements. You can include multiple placeholders (or even use the same placeholder multiple times) in the string. Then, the variables you include after the string will be plugged into the string in order, beginning with the "zero-th" (first) item, and continuing up through the variables and placeholders ({0}, {1}, {2}, and so on). Listing 8.1 demonstrates this use.

INPUT **LISTING 8.1** Using the Console Class for Input and Output

```
1   Imports System
2   Public Class ConsoleTest
3     Private Const ITEM_COUNT As Integer = 10
4     Shared Sub Main()
5       Dim I As Integer
6       Dim sItems(ITEM_COUNT) As String
7       Console.WriteLine("Please enter {0} items. " & _
8         Press ENTER between items.", ITEM_COUNT)
8       For I = 0 To ITEM_COUNT-1
9         sItems(I) = Console.ReadLine
10      Next
11      Console.WriteLine()
12      Console.WriteLine("Items in reverse order:")
13      For I = ITEM_COUNT - 1 To 0 Step -1
14        Console.WriteLine(sItems(I))
15      Next
16    End Sub
17 End Class
```

ANALYSIS The code in Listing 8.1 is quite simple and only meant to demonstrate some of the ways you have been using Console for seven days now.

Line 1 imports the System namespace. This is where the Console class is defined, as well as many other important classes. Therefore, you should always import this namespace in most apps. The Visual Basic .NET IDE will do this for you for applications you create while using it.

Within the single class defined in your file, you declare a single constant, ITEM_COUNT, (line 3) and a subroutine, Main (line 4). The constant is used instead of simply putting the number 10 throughout, in case you decide to change the value later. It is much easier to change a single constant's value, rather than to have to search for all the occurrences of the value throughout the application. Using a constant also shows that the developer knows that the values are related. If you had put the number 10 everywhere, and you looked at this code six months later, you might not remember whether all the 10s should be the same value, or whether it was only a coincidence.

The Shared Sub Main procedure is, as you've seen many times in the past, the first method run in an application. Within the procedure, you declare an array of strings (line 6) and populate it with the Console.ReadLine method.

Line 7 is worth noting. Within the item you write with Console.WriteLine (or Console.Write), you can include a number of *tokens*, such as the {0} item in the middle of the string in line 7. Each of these tokens will then be populated with variables. These are included after the string in the Console.WriteLine call, as you did with the ITEM_COUNT constant.

Note

Using the token approach of building a string can be useful, but whether or not it makes sense depends somewhat on personal taste. With this technique, each of the values replaces a token in the order that they appear, beginning with the "zero-th" token. The variables can be numeric, strings, or any other type that can be converted to a string. For example, if you wanted to use this technique to write a string with four variables included, it would look like

```
Console.WriteLine("{0} + {1} = {2} : {3}", 1, 1, 2, _
  "Bertrand Russell, 1912")
```

More experienced developers of Visual Basic might be somewhat more familiar with an alternative approach. In this approach, you build the string by concatenating the strings and variables. The previous string could be built and displayed with the code:

```
Console.WriteLine(value1 & "+" & value2 & "=" & result & ": " &
  sSource)
```

Although this might seem more "natural," you might forget to include a concatenation ("&") character when adding strings. Your program would fail to compile or run.

Each line of the input is read in (line 9) and written to one of the elements of the array. Notice that the elements of the array are numbered from 0 to 9 (line 8).

Finally, the elements are printed to the screen in reverse order. This is done using the Step clause of the For...Next statement (line 13). Each is written in turn to the current output, as seen in line 14. Listing 8.2 demonstrates this type of output.

INPUT/ OUTPUT   **LISTING 8.2**   Running the Console Application

```
 1  [c:\work\console]Console1.exe
 2  Please enter 10 items. Press ENTER between items.
 3  Aardvark
 4  Bandicoot
 5  Cassowary
 6  Dugong
 7  Echidna
 8  Finch
 9  Giraffe
10  Hippopotamus
11  Iguana
12  Jackalope

13  Items in reverse order:
14  Jackalope
15  Iguana
16  Hippopotamus
17  Giraffe
18  Finch
19  Echidna
20  Dugong
21  Cassowary
22  Bandicoot
23  Aardvark
```

Redirection

Redirection simply means "to send something to a different location." When dealing with the Console class, it means that you can change the location you read from or write to. For example, this could be used to write an application that either takes input from the command-line, or from a file. Similarly, you could use Console.WriteLine when debugging the application in testing, and then redirect it to a file to create a simple logging tool for your application.

You can redirect the input, the output, or error information from your program. This information can be redirected to any destination for which there is a TextReader (for input) or TextWriter (for output and error). Note that you cannot create either of these two classes directly, as they are abstract. Instead, you must create one of the classes that implement or inherit from TextReader or TextWriter (see Day 7, "Working with Objects," and Day 14, "Introduction to Object-Oriented Programming with Visual Basic .NET," for more details on abstraction and inheritance). Some of the implementations of these two classes allow you to read and write from files, network feeds, and more. Listing 8.3 shows how you can modify the example shown in Listing 8.2 to write to a file instead of to the command-line window. Notice that the commands to Console.WriteLine haven't been changed; only the destination was changed.

INPUT   **LISTING 8.3**   Redirecting Console Output

```
1  Imports System
2  Imports System.IO

3  Public Class ConsoleTest
4      Private Const ITEM_COUNT As Integer = 10

5    Shared Sub Main()
6      Dim I As Integer
7      Dim sItems(ITEM_COUNT) As String
8      Dim oFile As TextWriter = File.CreateText("Output.txt")
9      Dim oOut As TextWriter = Console.Out

10     Console.WriteLine("Please enter {0} items. Press ENTER between
       ➥items.", _ITEM_COUNT)
11     For I = 0 To ITEM_COUNT-1
12         sItems(I) = Console.ReadLine
13     Next

14     Console.WriteLine()
15     Console.SetOut(oFile)
16     Console.WriteLine("Items in reverse order:")
17     For I = ITEM_COUNT - 1 To 0 Step -1
18         Console.WriteLine(sItems(I))
19     Next

20     oFile.Close()

21     Console.SetOut(oOut)
22     Console.WriteLine("Done")
23     Console.ReadLine()

24   End Sub
25 End Class
```

Running the application:

```
1 [c:\work\console]Console2.exe
2 Please enter 10 items. Press ENTER between items.
3 Aardvark
```

```
 4 Bandicoot
 5 Cassowary
 6 Dugong
 7 Echidna
 8 Finch
 9 Giraffe
10 Hippopotamus
11 Iguana
12 Jackalope
13
14 Done
```

ANALYSIS The only lines that have changed between Listing 8.1 and Listing 8.3 are the addition of lines 2, 8, 9, 15, 20, 21, and 22. These are the lines that create the file, cause the redirection of the output, and end the redirection. Line 2 imports the System.IO namespace. This will be needed as it contains the definition for the TextWriter and File classes you use later. Line 8 creates the file Output.txt using the CreateText method of the File class. Notice that you did not need to create an instance of the File class, as the CreateText method is Shared. If there is an existing file of that name, it will be deleted. If you would rather continue adding to an existing file, you should use AppendText instead. Line 9 is used to save the original destination for the output, so you can set it back at line 21. Line 15 causes the redirection to your file. All output using Console.Write and Console.WriteLine after this redirection will be sent to your file instead of the command-line window. The last important line is line 20. If you fail to close the file, the contents cannot be written, and you will end up with a 0 byte (empty) file.

The code in Listing 8.3 should produce a file Output.txt with the following contents:

OUTPUT
```
 1 Items in reverse order:
 2 Jackalope
 3 Iguana
 4 Hippopotamus
 5 Giraffe
 6 Finch
 7 Echidna
 8 Dugong
 9 Cassowary
10 Bandicoot
11 Aardvark
```

Environment

Knowing where you stand can often mean the difference between success and embarrassment. And knowing where you stand often comes from your surroundings, or environment. Similarly, when programming, you are surrounded by a particular environment. The environment your programs run in is made up of information about the operating system, as well as a variety of variables and other settings that affect your computer. This environment allows you to query settings for the user, such as the location of his temp files directory, the contents of his search path, or even the other items on the command-line. Some of the important properties and methods of the Environment class are listed in Table 8.2. Note that all these properties and methods are shared.

TABLE 8.2 Methods and Properties of the Environment Class

Member	Description
Properties	
CommandLine	Represents the complete command-line that began the application.
CurrentDirectory	Returns the path of the current directory.
OSVersion	Returns information about the current operating system, for example, if it is Windows 9x, Windows NT, or Windows 2000.
SystemDirectory	Returns the path of the system directory (\winnt\system32 under Windows NT or 2000).
Version	Returns information on the version information for an assembly.
Methods	
Exit	Ends an application, optionally returning an error code that might be used by the operating system.
GetCommandLineArgs	Returns all the items listed on the command-line when the application was started. This is returned in the form of a string array. The executable itself is the zero-th (0th) element in the array.
GetEnvironmentVariable	Returns the value for a requested environment variable. This returns information stored in the environment with the Set command, such as the search path (path), directory for temporary files (temp), or other settings.
GetLogicalDrives	Returns the list of available drives. This is returned in the form of a string array. The first (zero-th) element is usually A:\.

The Environment class is useful when you need information about the system running *around* your program, such as when you need to know where to write your temporary files, or what operating system you're running under.

Random

Random is a simple class, intended to create random numbers, generally either an Integer or Double. The important methods of this class are listed in Table 8.3.

TABLE 8.3 Methods of the Random Class

Method	Description
Next	Returns an integer between 0 and the maximum possible value for an integer (approximately 2 billion).
Next(MaxValue)	Returns an integer between 0 and the MaxValue value (some integer).
Next(MinValue, MaxValue)	Returns an integer between the minimum and maximum values. This is the most commonly used variant if you need 1 as your minimum value.
NextDouble	Returns a double between 0 and 1.

For example, if you want to generate a random integer between 1 and 100 (inclusive), you would write

```
Dim oRand As New Random
Dim iValue As Integer = oRand.Next(1, 100)
```

Math

The Math class contains many of the important mathematical constants and functions. Most of these are shared methods, and therefore can be used without creating an instance of the Math class. The most important methods are outlined in Table 8.4. If you look at the Math class in Help, you will see that there are far more methods available.

TABLE 8.4 Methods of the Math Class

Method	Description
Abs	Returns the absolute value of a number (if negative, it returns the positive value of the number).
Cos	Returns the cosine of an angle (measured in radians; see following Note).
E	Returns a double representing the value of e (2.7182818284590451).
Max	Returns the maximum of two values.
Min	Returns the minimum of two values.
PI	Returns a double representing the value of pi (3.1415926535897931).
Round	Rounds a number to the nearest whole number.

Note

For those of us who slept through geometry, one radian is approximately 57.296 degrees. Why such a round number? Radians are related to the circumference of a circle—the exact measurement is

```
# Radians = (# degrees * pi)/180
```

The reason radians are used in computing is due to calculus, and therefore is beyond the scope of this book. Simply remember to convert your angles from degrees to radians before using any of the Math methods related to angles.

The Math class is generally useful for calculating values. Even if you don't remember (or never learned) what a hyperbolic tangent is, the Math class is where you will find it.

Collection Classes in the .NET Framework

You already learned about the Array data type back in Day 3, "Introduction to Programming with Visual Basic .NET." The .NET Framework includes a number of other collection classes that add extra capabilities to the Array. These classes allow you to store a list of information just as the arrays do, plus, they have features such as list sorting and easier addition to, and retrieval from, the list. A number of collection classes (most in the System.Collections namespace) are available. Some are described later today. If you need other types of collections, look in that namespace before you look elsewhere.

ArrayList

The ArrayList is the collection most like the Array. The main difference is that the ArrayList is designed to allow for easy growth as you add more elements. Like the other classes in the System.Collections namespace, ArrayList is designed to hold a collection of Object variables. Therefore, it can be used to hold any type of data. The ArrayList is a good collection to use if you have a very dynamic collection that might grow or shrink as time goes on, and if you don't need the features of the other collections.

You can create a new instance of an ArrayList using one of the available constructors. One version allows you to define the initial capacity of the collection, and another sets the initial size to 16:

```
Dim arrList As New ArrayList
'creates a new ArrayList, with 16 members initially
Dim arrList2 As New ArrayList(20)
' creates a new ArrayList, with 20 members initially
Dim arrList3 As ArrayList
Set arrList3 = New ArrayList(52)
' creates a new ArrayList, with 52 members initially
```

The other important properties and methods of the ArrayList are used to add, retrieve, or delete members from the collection. Table 8.5 outlines some of the more important members.

TABLE 8.5 Methods and Properties of the `ArrayList` Class

Member	Description
	Properties
Capacity	The current size of the `ArrayList`. Initially set when the `ArrayList` is created (16 by default), but might increase as more elements are added.
Count	The actual number of items in the `ArrayList`.
Item	Returns a specific element from the `ArrayList`.
	Methods
Add	Adds a new item into the `ArrayList`. If this would cause the `Count` to go above the `Capacity`, the `Capacity` is increased (by the amount of the initial `Capacity`—16 by default).
Clear	Removes all items from the `ArrayList`. `Count` is set to 0, but `Capacity` is not changed.
IndexOf	Returns the position in the `ArrayList` for a given object. This is useful after you have performed a `Sort`.
Insert	Adds a new element into the `ArrayList` at a requested position.
Remove	Removes the requested object from the `ArrayList`.
RemoveAt	Removes the element at the requested position.
Sort	Sorts the members of the `ArrayList`.
ToArray	Copies all or part of an `ArrayList` to an array.
TrimToSize	Shrinks the `ArrayList` so that the `Count` and `Capacity` are both equal to the current number of elements in the `ArrayList`.

The `ArrayList` is best suited as a replacement for the array when you know the size will increase, but you don't know how large the collection will be. Its open-ended growth allows you to add items as needed.

Queue and Stack

The `Queue` and `Stack` collections are similar. They are two of the "classic" types of collections and are useful in many programming endeavors. Both are collections that allow you to easily add new items. Both generally remove the item from the collection as you view it because they are designed for holding the collection temporarily. They differ in how items are added to each collection and, more importantly, in how items are removed from collections.

A `Queue` is a "first-in, first-out" (FIFO) collection. That means that items are removed from the queue in the same order that they are added. This is similar to most queues (or lineups) that you might experience. Generally, whether it is at a bus stop, in the lunch line, or in passing through customs, those who get there first are served first. Queues are often used in programming when you want this behavior. For example, when two programs (or objects) are communicating, the messages are placed on a queue for the receiving object. It then can process the messages in the order that they are received. Table 8.6 describes some of the important methods and properties of the Queue.

TABLE 8.6   Methods and Properties of the Queue Class

Member	Description
Properties	
Count	The number of items in the queue.
Methods	
Clear	Removes all items from the queue.
Dequeue	Pulls an object off the queue and returns it.
Enqueue	Puts a new object on the queue.
Peek	Allows you to look at the next item in the queue without removing it from the queue. This is useful because removing the item from the queue could prevent another method from dealing with the queue properly.

Note

So, why are the methods called Dequeue and Enqueue? Why not Add and Remove? It's simply a matter of keeping traditional names. Programmers have always referred to the act of adding an item to a queue as *enqueuing* the item, so that term, as well as *dequeue*, has stuck.

The Stack is a "first-in, last-out" (FILO) collection. That means that items are removed from the stack in the reverse order from which they were added. FILO order is analogous to a stack of plates: the most recently added plate is always removed first. Stacks are the classic solution to deal with problems that require you to reverse an order of operations. Many calculations are processed internally with the aid of stacks. Table 8.7 describes some of the important methods and properties of the Stack.

TABLE 8.7   Methods and Properties of the Stack Class

Member	Description
Properties	
Count	The number of items in the stack.

TABLE 8.7   continued

Member	Description
Methods	
Clear	Removes all items from the stack.
Pop	Removes the next item from the stack and returns it. Just as the queue has Enqueue and Dequeue, the two methods used traditionally for dealing with stacks are Pop and Push.
Push	Puts a new object on the stack.
Peek	Allows you to look at the next item in the stack without removing it. Queue and Stack are interesting collections partly from an historical perspective, but also because they solve particular programming problems. When you need a collection with the behavior of these two objects, you should remember them.

SortedList

The SortedList Class has characteristics of both the ArrayList and the NameValueCollection as well as some additional useful characteristics of its own. Similar to the ArrayList, the SortedList can grow, and it has the same Count and Capacity properties as the ArrayList. Like NameValueCollection, each item is identified by a name. In addition, the SortedList values are sorted on the basis of the name given to each item. As such, SortedList is useful any time you need a "growable" list of organized items, such as the attendees at a conference, or the results of a number of tests for a class of students. Table 8.8 describes some of the significant methods and properties of the SortedList.

TABLE 8.8   Methods and Properties of the SortedList Class

Member	Type	Description
Properties		
Capacity		The current size of the SortedList. Initially set when the SortedList is created (16 by default), but can increase as more elements are added.
Count		The actual number of items in the SortedList.
Methods		
Add		Adds a new item into the SortedList. If this would cause the Count to go above the Capacity, the Capacity is increased by the amount of the initial Capacity—16 by default.

TABLE 8.8 continued

Member	Type	Description
Properties		
Clear		Removes all items from the SortedList. Count is set to 0, but Capacity is not changed.
IndexOfKey		Returns the position in the SortedList for a given object. This is very useful after you have performed a Sort.
Item	Property	Returns a specific element from the SortedList.
Keys	Property	Returns all the Keys stored in the SortedList.
Remove	Method	Removes the requested object from the SortedList.
RemoveAt	Method	Removes the element at the requested position.
TrimToSize	Method	Shrinks the SortedList so that the Count and Capacity are both equal to the current number of elements in the SortedList.
Values	Property	Returns all the Values stored in the SortedList, in order of their key.

Often when you are working with lists, you need to keep the lists in order because you must display them to the user in sorted order. In these situations, the SortedList can be useful.

Finding What You Need in the .NET Framework

With more than 6,000 classes in the .NET Framework, finding what you need is sometimes the most difficult part of using the Framework. However, just as with finding a book in your favorite bookstore, or finding a site on the Internet, knowing a few basic rules will assist you in finding the one class you need to finish your application. This section helps you find a number of different classes in the Framework, to show you how I go about discovering classes. Hopefully, this will help you in your own hunts.

The Rules of the Hunt

In most libraries, the books are organized. Libraries might use the Dewey Decimal System, some other cataloging system, or simply alphabetical organization (by title or author's last name). If a library weren't organized, imagine trying to find a book in it. You would have to wander randomly until you accidentally bumped into the book you wanted. Many people try to find classes within the .NET Framework in a similar way.

They might get lucky occasionally, but they will spend more time frustrated.

The .NET Framework is organized in a hierarchical fashion. The name for each namespace is created by a series of parts, each part divided from others by a dot. Lower namespaces (ones with more parts) are not contained within higher namespaces, but they are related. For example, the `System.Data.SqlClient` namespace is related to the `System.Data`, but not contained within it because `System.Data.SqlClient` exists at a lower hierarchical level than `System.Data` namespace.

In the .NET Framework, there are two top-level names, `System` and `Microsoft`. The `System` namespaces are those that are part of the .NET Framework, and are available to users of Visual Basic .NET, as well as to users of the other languages that employ the Framework. The Microsoft classes are generally specific to Visual Studio, and are targeted at one or more environments. For example, there is a `Microsoft.VisualBasic` namespace that contains many of the features that existed in Visual Basic before this version.

The Quest for the Golden Class

To demonstrate some of the techniques that you can use to find functionality within the .NET Framework, I'll show the search for three procedures. I'll try to show you some of the mistakes I made when trying to find the functionality and the result I ended up with. There might be other ways to track down needed functionality, or other answers within the .NET Framework, but these are the answers I found.

What Color Is That Brush in the Window? Naming Colors

This search was initiated for a common need, the need to describe a color. Controls can be colored, and the color can change at runtime. Changing the color at design time is easy; simply select the color from the appropriate drop-down list (for example, `BackColor` or `ForeColor`). However, to change a color at runtime, you will need to know how to identify a color.

Each color in Visual Basic .NET can be described on the basis of the percentages of red, green, and blue that make up the color. In Visual Basic .NET, each of the three colors ranges in value from 0 to 255, raising the total number of available colors to 16,581,375. Therefore, you can identify any color through its proportions of red, green, and blue. A color composed of each of the three colors at 50 percent saturation, or a value of 128, would be a light gray in color.

At other times, you want to identify a color by name—that is, when "Red" might be more significant than knowing that the color was -65536.

You'd think with color being so important that named colors would appear within the `System` namespace. However, if you thought that (and I did, at first search), you'd be wrong. The named colors and the capability to create new colors are found in the System.Drawing namespace.

Within the System.Drawing namespace, there are two sets of colors: the Color structure and the SystemColors class.

The Color structure has two main purposes. The first is the "functional" aspect of the structure. Two methods, described in Table 8.9, enable you to create a color and find out its numeric value.

TABLE 8.9 Methods of the Color Structure

Method	Description
FromARGB	Creates a new color based on the red, green, and blue values (each from 0 to 255). There are other versions of this function as well. One variant takes an Alpha value in addition to the red, green, and blue values, whereas another is used to add the Alpha value to an existing color. The Alpha value represents the transparency of the color. Like the other values, Alpha ranges from 0 to 255, with 255 being completely opaque. The last variant of the FromARGB takes the integer value for a color and returns the color.
ToARGB	Returns the integer that represents a color's composition of Alpha, red, green, and blue.

In addition to the capability to create and convert colors, the Color structure contains a number of named colors. These represent a wide variety of different colors, many with helpful, evocative names, such as PapayaWhip, Gainsboro, and BurlyWood. These are useful shortcuts if you want to color something but aren't sure of the exact numeric value that you want. Even more of a shortcut is that you do not have to create a new instance of the Color structure before using these colors. So, you can use them in a program using code similar to

```
frmMain.BackColor = Color.SeaShell
```

One problem with defining your own colors, either by the RGB (red, green, blue) values, or by selecting a named color is that your perception of the color might be different from that of your users. I have met people who set up their computer desktops with the most garish colors, and others who never change from the defaults. Similarly, I have met programmers who have created weird, multicolored applications, and others who have hard-coded all colors to shades of gray. If you hard-code the colors, your program might stand out on users' desktops, possibly being irritating. To avoid this, polite programmers set the color of screen elements with the system colors (the ones defined in Control Panel). The system colors are available in the SystemColors class, which has a number of properties that represent the different elements that appear within Windows (such as `WindowText`, `Control`, or `Menu`). Coloring the parts of your application using these colors means that they will take up whatever color the user has selected for that item.

Using the `SystemColors` class is similar to using the `Color` structure. You do not have to create a new instance of the class before using the values. Therefore, you could color the background of a form to the defined `Desktop` color with the following code:

```
frmMain.BackColor = SystemColors.Desktop
```

Colors are everywhere in Windows, so knowing the way to create color is important.

Who Am I? Finding Your Computer's Name

Many programs must know the name of the computer they are running on. For example, you might be attempting to access some system features or services, as you will do in Day 13, "Using the Server Explorer." Or, you might want to log or store the computer name for database access. This search for a solution was initiated by such a need. Unfortunately, this one also took the longest. Fortunately for you, I found many ways that you can use to determine your computer's name. Depending on what namespaces you already have imported, or the type of application you are running, at least one way (and probably all) should be available to you.

You've already looked at the first of three easy ways to get the name of a computer where a program is running: `System.Environment`. Under Windows 2000 and later, the computer name is stored as an environment variable called `COMPUTERNAME`. If this is the case, you can retrieve the local computer name with

```
Console.Writeline("Using Environment: {0}", _
System.Environment.GetEnvironmentVariable("COMPUTERNAME"))
```

However, relying on an environment variable, even one set by the operating system, seems a bit too trusting. So, I dug deeper.

The network often needs the computer name, so `System.Net` was my next stop. After a couple of failed attempts, I found `GetHostName` in the `DNS` class. This basically makes sense—the DNS (Domain Naming Service) is a service used to track computer names on the Internet (or on local networks). Therefore, the DNS class would need to know who the current computer is. You can use the DNS class to retrieve a computer's name by including the `System.Net` namespace in your project and accessing it with code similar to

```
Console.WriteLine("Using Net.DNS: {0}", DNS.GetHostName)
```

This solution might not work, however, if you were using it on a computer that did not have TCP/IP installed (which, with the popularity of the Internet, would leave about two computers). And so, you search onward.

8

Deep in the heart of System.Windows.Forms is a treasure of a class: SystemInformation. Strangely enough, SystemInformation contains information about the current program and the operating system within which it is running. If you look at the class, you will see that it has properties that represent all the measurements that are important to applications, especially to Windows Forms–based applications: FrameBorderSize, CaptionHeight, MenuHeight, and MousePresent. More importantly for your current search, SystemInformation class has a ComputerName property, which you can use to retrieve the computer's name if you include the System.Windows.Forms namespace in your application, as follows:

```
Console.WriteLine("Using SystemInformation: {0}", _
SystemInformation.ComputerName)
```

Don't let the fact that this class is hidden within the System.Windows.Forms namespace put you off. You can use it in any application type by loading the namespace.

So, why have three ways get the name of the computer where a program is running instead of simply one? Well, not being one of the people who decided these things, I would suggest a couple of reasons:

- Different groups working on different sections created different ways of solving the same problem.
- Each of the solutions is only appropriate in certain situations (such as, if the environment variable has been set, if you're running with a TCP/IP network, if you're using WinForms, and so on).

In searching through the .NET Framework, you often will find multiple solutions. Use whichever solution fits your needs best, until you find a better one.

That Day in History

This search for a solution was initiated for a function that existed in Visual Basic 6, WeekDayName. This function returns the name of the day of the week. You can determine the day of the week for any date by using

```
sDayName = WeekDayName(WeekDay(CDate("May 6, 1937")))
```

For the record, the Hindenburg disaster was on a Thursday.

This function, like many others that existed in older versions of Visual Basic, can be found fairly easily, in the Microsoft.VisualBasic namespace. This namespace is automatically loaded when developing with the IDE, allowing you to run code written for older versions of Visual Basic. So, if all you want is a function that "used to exist," likely it's in that namespace.

Summary

It is often difficult to understand where the .NET Framework ends and Visual Basic .NET begins. Most of the functionality of Visual Basic .NET actually comes from the Framework, including features that previously were part of the Windows API, or that were not available to Visual Basic programmers before this version. It is an understatement to describe the .NET Framework as being important to Visual Basic .NET developers. In Day 17, "Using the .NET Framework," you will spend more time with the .NET Framework collection of classes. In addition, you can get more information on the .NET Framework on the .NET section of the MSDN (Microsoft Developer Network) at `http://msdn.microsoft.com/net`.

In Day 9, "Building a User Interface with Windows Forms," you will look at another family of classes in the .NET Framework, the classes that allow you to build Windows user interfaces. You will use these classes frequently as you create applications that use the rich user interfaces of standard applications.

Q&A

Q. Should I use the .NET Framework or an old function I read about that Visual Basic supports?

A. If you've programmed in Visual Basic in the past, or if you read "How to" books or magazine articles that target earlier versions of Visual Basic, you'll see a number of the "old" ways of performing tasks. Many of these functions still exist, within the `Microsoft.VisualBasic` namespace. You can import that namespace to make use of some of the older functions or constants, such as the math functions, or `vbCrLf` (a constant that means "Add a new line here."). However, if possible, it would be better to make use of the newer capabilities of the .NET Framework.

Q. Why didn't you cover the `"Fill-in-My-Favorite"` namespace? I really need to know how to use it in my program.

A. With 6,000 classes available within the .NET Framework, a lesson like today's can hardly cover even a sliver of them with the detail they need. You'll look at more of the .NET Framework in Day 17. In addition, you will also be using the Framework in the remaining days of this book.

Workshop

The Workshop is designed to help you anticipate possible questions, review what you've learned, and get thinking about how to put your knowledge into practice. The answers to the quiz are in Appendix A, "Answers to Quizzes/Exercises."

8

Quiz

1. How could you make use of the `Console` class if you are writing a Windows- or Web-based application?

2. Why would you choose the `SortedList` collection over the `ArrayList` collection if the `ArrayList` has a `Sort` method?

3. What would be the result of the following code executing?

```
Dim oRand As New System.Random
Dim iValue As Integer = oRand.Next(1, 6) + oRand.Next(1, 6)
Console.WriteLine(iValue)
```

Exercises

1. Write a short console program that will accept a number of words on the command line and print them to the screen in alphabetical order.

DAY 9

Building a User Interface with Windows Forms

Back on Day 5, "Organizing Programs," you learned about the different ways in which .NET applications could be architected. One key decision was what type of user interface to create. The choice usually comes down to either Web or a Windows-style application. In .NET, the way to create a Windows application is through the Windows Forms technology. In today's lesson you will learn

- How to add and manipulate controls on a form
- How to handle user-interface events in code
- How to accept and validate user input
- How to use dialog boxes

In addition to these topics, you will learn about a variety of the special visible and nonvisible controls used in Windows Forms.

An Overview of Windows Forms

Windows Forms are used to create applications using the user interface common (with small variations in the actual appearance) to all the Windows operating systems (see Figure 9.1). Using this set of classes and functions, you can add this style of user interface, including windows and dialog boxes, to your applications.

FIGURE 9.1

The majority of Windows applications share the same interface style because the OS handles drawing the windows and other interface features.

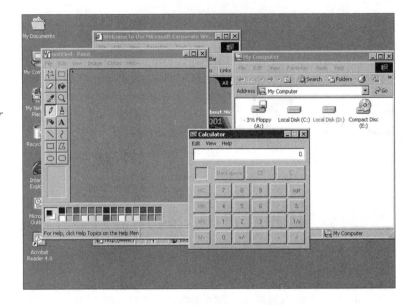

Before you dive into the creation and configuration of a Windows application, a refreshment of the key Windows Forms related terms is in order. The first and most difficult to define term is "window." A *window*, in the computer sense, is an area of the screen used by an application to display information. A single application might have more than one window, but each window belongs to one and only one application. Windows can be moved and resized (including maximizing and minimizing), but these options can be turned off by the application that owns the window, allowing a window to be of a fixed size or to stay in a fixed position. Subelements of a window, such as a button, text box, list, or an image (see Figure 9.2) make up the interface of an application and are called *controls*.

These controls provide the interface to the application because they can be manipulated (clicked, typed into, or whatever else is appropriate) to provide input to the program. They also display information back to the user. Windows exist in one of two states—modal or nonmodal. Modal windows must be dealt with and closed before the user can work with any other aspect of that application—for example, a window asking whether you want to save changes to a document. Nonmodal windows allow the user to interact in a less structured manner, moving between all the nonmodal windows in an application as desired, more like a document window in Microsoft Word or a Toolbox window in Visual Studio .NET. Modal windows are also known as *dialog boxes*, and in .NET they have specific features to make it easy to use them to obtain some form of information from a user. Dialog boxes will be covered in more detail later in today's lesson.

FIGURE 9.2

All the elements on a window are called controls.

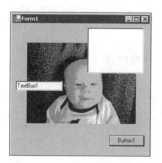

Creating a Windows Forms Application

For example, you can build a simple Windows Forms application that accepts user input and demonstrates how these user-interface objects function. Along with teaching about Windows Forms, this example also shows you how to perform some simple file manipulation using the System.IO classes within the .NET Framework. First, I will walk you through the creation of this simple example and then cover the individual topics of controls and event procedures directly.

Setting Up the Project

The first step in building a Visual Basic .NET project that uses Windows Forms is to create a new project, selecting the Windows Application project type. A new project will be created containing a single form object, all ready for you to start working. The new form will be named Form1 by default, but you do not want to leave this default name because that name has no meaning in your application.

Because you are building a program that will work with files, rename the form frmFiler, which takes two steps:

1. Rename the file by right-clicking on Form1.vb in the Solution Explorer window, selecting Rename, and then typing in a new value of frmFiler.vb.

2. Right-click on the new blank form in the design window that is displaying it and select Properties. This should display the Properties Toolbox window, through which you can find and change the (Name) property (which you can find under the

Design section of the properties) from Form1 to frmFiler. It is best to do this before you start any other coding, avoiding any situation where you had already written some code referring to Form1.

At this point, notice that the form's title is still Form1, not frmFiler as you might expect. This is because the title is not connected to the form's name, but the IDE happens to use the form's name as the default title at creation. Simply bring up the form's property window again and find the Text property, which represents the form's title. Change it to whatever you want—Filer would be fine—and notice that the title changes accordingly.

Adding Controls to the Form

Before a form can be of much use, you need to place some controls onto it. All the built-in Windows Forms controls are available through the Toolbox window. Just bring the Toolbox window into view and find the Windows Forms section (see Figure 9.3).

FIGURE 9.3

The Windows Forms section of the Toolbox provides a wide variety of controls for your forms.

On that section of the Toolbox, you will find a variety of controls, but for now all you will need is the button and text box controls. Add a control to the form by either double-clicking it (which adds the control onto the form at the upper-left corner), clicking and dragging the control onto the form, or selecting the control (click once and release) and then clicking and dragging on the form to outline the desired location. Using any of these methods will produce the same result: The control is placed onto the form. Using one of the methods just described, add three buttons, two labels and two text boxes to the form. Arrange the controls onto the form into the general layout shown in Figure 9.4, using the Text property of the buttons and labels to make your interface match the one in the figure.

9

FIGURE 9.4

One possible way to arrange the interface of the sample application.

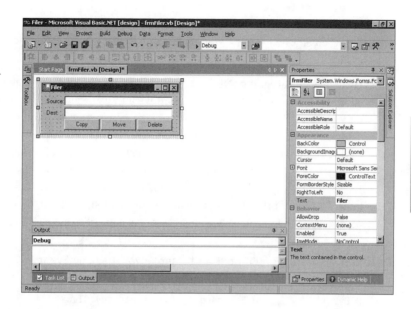

Naming Your Controls

Before you create an event handler, rename all your controls from their default names (`Button1`, `Button2`, `TextBox1`, and so on). You will need to use the control names to access the control and its attributes, so you want to ensure that each control has a meaningful name. You can use any name you want, but I recommend using some form of naming convention. Here are my suggestions for these controls, based on the naming convention that I (and many others) have used in Visual Basic for years:

- `txtSource` and `txtDestination` for the two text boxes, in order from the top down.
- `btnCopy`, `btnMove`, and `btnDelete` for the buttons. In Visual Basic 6.0 and before, buttons were called *command buttons* (instead of just "button" as it is in Visual Basic .NET), so many people used the prefix `cmd` when naming their button controls.
- `lblSource` and `lblDestination` for the labels.

Renaming a control is just like renaming the form: Select the control, bring up its properties, and then change the (`Name`) property. Rename all the controls before moving onto the next part of the example.

Event Handling

When you are programming a user interface, you must understand the concept of events and event-driven programming. Whenever the user takes an action, such as clicking on a button, or typing a value into a text box, these are called *events*. If you want to have code run when an event occurs, you must create an event handler for the event you are interested in.

Using the Visual Studio .NET IDE, it is easy to create an event handler for one of your controls. A common event that you will want to have code for is the clicking of a button on your form. This is called the `Click` event of a button, and you can add or edit the code associated with this event by double-clicking the button. You will be switched into the Code editing window and placed inside a new subroutine called *<button name>*_Click (see Listing 9.1). The name of the routine is not really important, but that is the default format the IDE uses. Double-click on the Copy button to switch into the appropriate code. Notice that if you hadn't renamed your button, your new `Click` event would be named something such as `Button1_Click`, instead of `btnCopy_Click`.

LISTING 9.1   Listing an Empty Event Handler for the Copy Event

```
1 Private Sub btnCopy_Click(ByVal sender As System.Object, _
2 ByVal e As System.EventArgs) Handles btnCopy.Click
3
4 End Sub
```

Now, any code you place inside this routine will be run when the user clicks on the button. For this example, you will be adding code to all the buttons (`btnCopy`, `btnMove`, and `btnDelete`), but you have to start with one, so double-click `btnCopy` and bring up the associated code. In this event handler, you want to add code that will copy the file specified in `txtSource` and to the file specified in `txtDestination`. To accomplish this, you will need to work with the `System.IO` namespace. This namespace is already referenced in your project because it is part of the `System.DLL`, but you can make your code much easier to read and type if you add an `Imports System.IO` statement to the top of your form's code.

After that statement is in place, you can refer to objects within that namespace without having to include the entire reference. To accomplish a file copy, you can use the static method `Copy` on the `System.IO.File` class, but you will need the source and destination filenames first. To access the contents of a text box, you use its `Text` property, referring to the specific object using its name.

LISTING 9.2   Copying files using the static methods of the File object

```
1 Private Sub btnCopy_Click(ByVal sender As System.Object, _
    ByVal e As System.EventArgs) Handles btnCopy.Click
2     Dim sSource As String
```

LISTING 9.2   continued

```
3     Dim sDestination As String
4     sSource = txtSource.Text()
5     sDestination = txtDestination.Text()
6     File.Copy(sSource, sDestination)
7 End Sub
```

ANALYSIS With the values you need stored into String variables, the actual file copy can take place. Because Copy is a static method of the File class, you do not need to create an instance; you can just call File.Copy. That single line (line 6 in Listing 9.2) is not the entire process, though, because proper error handling must be added. In the case of a file copy, many different errors could occur, ranging from "the destination file exist" to "not enough disk space." Whatever error happens, you can just inform the user using the static Show method of the MessageBox class. The MessageBox, which was used earlier in this book, is part of the System.Windows.Forms namespace and is a quick and easy way to put up a dialog box. Listing 9.3 provides an example of using the MessageBox.Show method in response to an exception.

LISTING 9.3   Using the MessageBox Class to Display an Error

```
1     Private Sub btnCopy_Click(ByVal sender As System.Object, _
2     ByVal e As System.EventArgs) Handles btnCopy.Click
3       Dim sSource As String
4       Dim sDestination As String
5       sSource = txtSource.Text()
6       sDestination = txtDestination.Text()
7       Try
8         File.Copy(sSource, sDestination)
9       Catch objException As Exception
10        MessageBox.Show(objException.Message)
11      End Try
12    End Sub
```

Creating Multiple Event Handlers for a Single Event

The important part of the event handler routine is not its name, btnCopy_Click, but the Handles btnCopy.Click that has been added at the end of the declaration. This statement tells Visual Basic .NET that this routine is the event handler for the event. Unlike in previous versions of Visual Basic, which used only the name of the routine to associate code to specific events, it is possible in Visual Basic .NET to have a single procedure handle multiple events, or to have a single event with multiple event handlers. Copy the entire btnCopy_Click routine and rename it to CopyClick, leaving the parameter list the same and the Handles btnCopy.Click in place.

The procedure's signature (which consists of its parameter list and return value, if any) must match exactly what you see on the original procedure to act as an event handler, but the code can be just about anything. Now, change the code of this second procedure to just pop up a message instead of all the file copy work (see Listing 9.4). Try running your project and clicking on the Copy button. Both event handlers are called, doing the file copy and popping up the MessageBox dialog.

LISTING 9.4   The Handles Statement Links a Routine with a Specific Event

```
1    Private Sub CopyClick(ByVal sender As System.Object, _
2    ByVal e As System.EventArgs) Handles btnCopy.Click
3      MessageBox.Show("CopyClick")
4    End Sub
```

Remove the CopyClick routine by selecting and deleting the text, and move onto the event routines for the other two buttons.

Finding Objects and Events Using the Code Editor

Instead of going back to the design window and double-clicking on each of the other two buttons, you can get to the Click event handling routine directly in the code window. Select the name of the object (btnMove, for example) from the first (left side) drop-down list above the code editor, and then select the desired event (Click) from the second drop down. This has the same effect as double-clicking the object in the designer, so both methods are available to you. The code for the Move and Delete buttons will use the corresponding static methods of the File object. Listing 9.5 shows one way in which these two buttons could be coded.

LISTING 9.5   Moving and Deleting Files Using the Static Methods of the File Object

```
1     Private Sub btnMove_Click(ByVal sender As System.Object, _
2       ByVal e As System.EventArgs) Handles btnMove.Click
3       Dim sSource As String
4       Dim sDestination As String
5       sSource = txtSource.Text()
6       sDestination = txtDestination.Text()
7       File.Move(sSource, sDestination)
8     End Sub
9
10    Private Sub btnDelete_Click(ByVal sender As Object, _
11      ByVal e As System.EventArgs) Handles btnDelete.Click
12      Dim sSource As String
13      sSource = txtSource.Text()
14      File.Delete(sSource)
15    End Sub
```

Multiple Events with One Event Handler

Alternatively, you can handle all three `Click` events through one procedure by modifying the `Handles` statement to include all of them. Just the declaration of that event handling routine is shown in Listing 9.6; the details are left to today's exercises.

LISTING 9.6   Using the `Handles` Keyword to Link Multiple Events with a Single Event Procedure, or Multiple Event Procedures with a Single Event

```
1 Private Sub DoEverything(ByVal sender As Object, _
2 ByVal e As System.EventArgs) _
3 Handles btnCopy.Click, btnMove.Click, btnDelete.Click
```

9

The only restriction on the number of events you can handle with a single routine is that the events must all use the same set of parameters. The `Click` event of a button, for instance, receives two parameters (a `System.Object` and a `System.EventArgs`), whereas the `ChangeUICues` event of the same button receives different parameters (a `System.Object` and a `System.Windows.Forms.UICuesEventArgs`). Therefore, the two events could not be handled by a single routine. The purpose of these parameters is to give your handler information about the event, and some events supply different types of information than others.

More About Controls

The example you just worked through had you adding text boxes, labels, and buttons to a new form, but many more controls are available.

Here is a list of several of the more commonly used built-in controls, along with a quick description:

- `Label/Link Label`   Both of these provide a way to place static (noneditable) text onto a form. The `Link Label` control adds some additional functionality, which can have some or all of its text look like an HTML link and has an additional event (`LinkClicked`) to indicate when the user has clicked on the hyperlinked portion of the label.

- `Button`   The standard button, with much more functionality than it had in previous versions of Visual Basic. Using the button's properties, you can add an image, change the layout of the text and image, set the caption, and much more.

- `Text Box`   Provides a text entry area on a Form, and supports basic editing. Can be made multiline by setting the `Multiline` property to `True` and provides a simple default context (right-click) menu that gives the user cut/copy/paste functionality.

- `Main Menu` and `Context Menu` Although not together on the Toolbox, these two controls are used to create a menu system for your window. Day 16, "More Windows Forms," details how to build menus for your systems using these two controls.

- `Check Box/Radio Button` These two controls are used to display and input simple yes/no or true/false values. Both controls are often used to show a list of options that must be turned on or off, but the difference between them is how they handle the selection of another control of the same type within their group. In a group of radio buttons, the intention is that only one of them will be on at any time. Check boxes, on the other hand, are multiselect, meaning that you can check off any number of them.

- `Picture Box` Allows you a place to either display an existing image or to draw images using the graphic library.

There are many more, but all of them work in the same basic fashion. You place them onto your form, manipulate their properties either through code or the Properties window, and write code to handle their events. Although I will not be covering each control individually, I will go through the use of two of them to provide a demonstration.

Creating Groups of Radio Buttons

As mentioned previously, radio buttons and check boxes are used to represent settings that can be either on or off, but the two types of controls have an important difference. Radio buttons are only intended to be used in groups of two or more, and only one button in a group can be selected at a time. Clicking a radio button selects it and automatically unselects the previously selected button. Check boxes on the other hand are also turned on and off through clicking, but any number of them can be selected at the same time in a group. Think of these two types of controls in terms of a multiple-choice exam: Check boxes would be suitable for a question where the answer is phrased as "Select all the correct answers," whereas radio buttons would only fit for questions phrased as "Select the best answer."

To create a group of radio buttons, you will first make a new form because the first form `Filer` is already pretty full. With the project containing `Filer` already open, right-click on the project in the Solution Explorer window. Choose Add, Add Windows Form from the menu that appears, and a dialog box appears allowing you to enter a name for your new form (you could type in **RadioButtons**, for example). Click OK to add that new form to the current project. Now, on the new form, use the Toolbox to add a `Group Box` control. This control, which looks like a rectangle with a caption and nicely chiseled-looking edges, is used to group and contain other controls. Move and resize the box to fill most of the screen. To create a radio button group, you just have to start adding `Radio`

`Button` controls into this group box. Add four of these controls to the group box, and position them in a somewhat proper layout. You do not have to do anything else to these controls to make them understand that they form a group together; that is handled by the fact that they are contained within the same group box.

If you ran your project at this point, your new form would not appear because the project is set up when it is created to display the first form. To change the project so that your new form is run instead, right-click the project in the Solution Explorer window (just like when you added a file earlier) and select Properties from the context menu. This brings up a large dialog containing a variety of options and settings (see Figure 9.5). The value we need to change is on the first page (Common Properties, General) and is called Startup Object. The Startup Object setting determines which of the forms, or other code, will be run when the project is executed. Currently, this should be equal to `frmFiler` (the name of the first form in this project). Change it to `RadioButtons` or whatever you named the form you added last.

FIGURE 9.5

Using the project properties dialog, you can control a variety of settings, including the Startup Object.

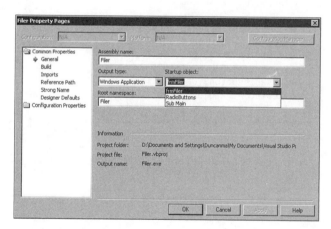

Now, if you run the project, your new form (with its four radio buttons) will be displayed (see Figure 9.6).

FIGURE 9.6

A group of radio buttons is an excellent way to allow the user to choose one option out of many.

After it is up and running, try clicking the radio buttons and notice that only one button is selected at a time. To determine whether a radio button is selected using code, you can use the Checked property. To try accessing these controls using code, you can add some test code to your new form. Close the form (using the X button in the upper-right corner) and go back to the Design view of your new form. Add a regular button from the Toolbox, change its name to btnTest and its caption to "Test" and then double-click it to switch to Code view for its default event (Click). The code in Listing 9.7 demonstrates how you could check which set of radio buttons was selected and display the appropriate value using a MessageBox. Enter this code into the Click event of btnTest and then run your project to try it out.

LISTING 9.7   Using Radio Buttons When Only One Option Can Be Chosen

```
 1    Private Sub btnTest_Click(ByVal sender As System.Object, _
 2    ByVal e As System.EventArgs) Handles btnTest.Click
 3      Dim sSelected As String
 4
 5      If RadioButton1.Checked Then
 6        sSelected = "RadioButton1"
 7      ElseIf RadioButton2.Checked Then
 8        sSelected = "RadioButton2"
 9      ElseIf RadioButton3.Checked Then
10        sSelected = "RadioButton3"
11      ElseIf RadioButton4.Checked Then
12        sSelected = "RadioButton4"
13      End If
14
15      MessageBox.Show(sSelected, "Selected Radio Button")
16    End Sub
17 End Class
```

Adding a Check Box to the Filer Sample

If you replaced the radio buttons in the previous example with check boxes, you would find that you could select any number of them at one time (including none). The test code would still work, though, (assuming that you either named the check boxes the exact same as the radio buttons, or you modified the code to account for the new names) because check boxes also provide the Checked property.

A more useful example of a check box can be created by modifying the first form you created (Filer). On this form, if the user entered a destination filename that already existed, and then clicked the Copy or Move buttons, an error would occur. Alternatively, the code could just overwrite the existing file whenever one was found, without any error message appearing. You can add a check box to this form to support the toggling on and off of this Automatic Overwrite feature.

First, bring up the first form (Filer) in Design view and then add a new Check Box control from the Toolbox. Change the caption to "Overwrite Existing" by changing the Text property through the Properties window. At this point, you can also set the default or starting value of the check box by setting the Checked property through the Properties window. Move the new control into position beneath the destination field and then double-click the Copy button to switch into code editing. You will need to make a small modification in both btnCopy_Click and btnMove_Click before the check box will have any actual effect. Currently, the call to Copy and the call to Move use only two parameters (source and destination), but Copy supports an additional option (overwrite) which determines whether it should delete an existing file if one is found. By setting this new property equal to the Checked property of the check box, you can control how an existing file is handled. Listing 9.8 shows you the modified btnCopy_Click that handles the new check box.

LISTING 9.8 Adding a Check Box

```
 1 Private Sub btnCopy_Click(ByVal sender As System.Object, _
 2  ByVal e As System.EventArgs) Handles btnCopy.Click
 3    Dim sSource As String
 4   Dim sDestination As String
 5    sSource = txtSource.Text()
 6    sDestination = txtDestination.Text()
 7    Try
 8      File.Copy(sSource, sDestination, chkOverwrite.Checked)
 9    Catch objException As Exception
10      MessageBox.Show(objException.Message)
11    End Try
12  End Sub
```

Handling this same situation for the case of the Move command is a bit trickier. Instead of just changing one parameter, you have to respond to the existing file error and either abort the Move attempt or delete the offending file. Listing 9.9 shows one way of handling the btnMove_Click event.

LISTING 9.9 Handling the btnMove_Click Event

```
 1    Private Sub btnMove_Click(ByVal sender As System.Object, _
 2    ByVal e As System.EventArgs) Handles btnMove.Click
 3      Dim sSource As String
 4      Dim sDestination As String
 5      sSource = txtSource.Text()
 6      sDestination = txtDestination.Text()
 7      If File.Exists(sSource) Then
 8        If File.Exists(sDestination) Then
```

9

LISTING 9.9   continued

```
 9          If chkOverwrite.Checked Then
10             File.Delete(sDestination)
11          Else
12             MessageBox.Show("Move aborted, destination exists")
13             Return
14          End If
15        End If
16        File.Move(sSource, sDestination)
17      End If
18    End Sub
```

Input Validation

As the name "form" might suggest, windows and dialogs are often used to allow data entry into your application. Often, when information is being entered into the system, you will want to go through some form of validation (checking for valid dates, the correct number of digits in phone numbers, and so on). The .NET Framework provides a model for coding that validation.

Given a form with several entry fields on it (text boxes, for example), there is likely to be a button or two as well. At least one of those buttons indicates that the user thinks she is finished entering data. So, when the user clicks OK, you want to run through your validation code, checking all the fields for correctness. When the user clicks the Cancel button, there is no reason to bother validating the data because she intends to cancel out of the form.

Checking for valid data only when the user clicks OK (or Save, or whatever is appropriate in your application) avoids the problem where the user has to have entered valid data before you will allow her to cancel your application. I have worked with many applications that forced me to enter a proper phone number before they would let me exit an unwanted dialog box, even though the phone number was being thrown away because I clicked Cancel!

Several aspects of the Windows Forms classes work together to provide this validation: the CausesValidation property and the Validating/Validated events, which both exist on every control. The general process to use these properties and events is to set CausesValidation to True on every actual data entry control (text box, radio button, combo box, and so on) and also on any button that causes the data to be used or saved (OK, Save, Continue, Next, and so on). On buttons, such as Help, Cancel, Previous, or other buttons where you do not care whether the data is valid when it is clicked, set the CausesValidation property to False. Next, place code to check whether a field is valid in the Validating event. When the user attempts to switch the focus to a control where CausesValidation = True, then the Validating event will be raised on each of the edit controls that have received focus since the last time you hit a control where CauseValidation equals True. That was a little complex, so here is a walkthrough of what happens:

You have a form to enter/edit addresses (see Figure 9.7), with an OK button, a Cancel button, and several text boxes for data entry. You have set the CausesValidation property of all the text boxes to True. You have set this property to True on the OK button as well, but not on the Cancel button.

FIGURE 9.7

This dialog, designed for entering and editing addresses, is an example of a data entry form and is available for download from this book's Web site.

The focus is currently on the txtStreet text box, and the user presses Tab to move to the txtCity text box. At this point, because of the CausesValidation property of txtCity, the Validating event of txtStreet fires. Now, the Validating event should be checking the contents of txtStreet and making sure that it is valid. It can cancel the validation if the data is not correct.

If the data is correct (so the event is not canceled), then the Validated event of txtStreet will be called to indicate that validation succeeded. If the data was not correct, and the event is canceled, then the attempt to move the focus will be canceled as well, leaving the focus on the txtStreet text box.

So, any time the focus hits a control where CausesValidation = True, then the Validating event will be raised on any control that has been visited since the last time you hit a control where CausesValidation = True. This is not dependent on direction, so if the user was to Tab or click back to txtStreet after moving to txtCity, then the Validating event would be called on txtCity.

Still confused? Listing 9.10 contains the code for the various validation events of the Address Form, which might help a bit. The entire form is downloadable from this book's Web site as well, to save you time re-creating it.

LISTING 9.10   Validation Events of the Address Form

```
1    Private Sub txtZip_Validating(ByVal sender As Object, _
2     ByVal e As System.ComponentModel.CancelEventArgs) _
3     Handles txtZip.Validating
4      'cast sender to a System.Windows.Forms.Control
5      Dim ctlSender As Control
6      ctlSender = CType(sender, Control)
7      Dim bValidPostalCode As Boolean = False
8      'Validate for US/Canada postal code format only.
9      'Check if txtCountry = Canada, otherwise assume US
10     'Handle 3 possible formats,
11     'US short #####, US long #####-####, Cdn A#A#A#
12
13     Dim sPostalCode As String
14     Dim sPattern As String
15     Dim objRegEx As Regex
16
17     sPostalCode = ctlSender.Text.Trim.Replace(" ", "")
18     If txtCountry.Text.Trim.ToUpper = "CANADA" Then
19       If sPostalCode.Length = 6 Then
20         sPattern = "[ABCEGHJKLMNPRSTVXY]\d[A-Z]\d[A-Z]\d"
21       End If
22     Else
23       If sPostalCode.Length = 10 Then
24         sPattern = "\d\d\d\d\d-\d\d\d\d"
25       ElseIf sPostalCode.Length = 5 Then
26         sPattern = "\d\d\d\d\d"
27       End If
28       objRegEx.IsMatch(sPostalCode, "")
29     End If
30
31     If sPattern <> "" Then
32       If objRegEx.IsMatch(sPostalCode, sPattern) Then
33         bValidPostalCode = True
34       End If
35     End If
36     If bValidPostalCode = False Then
37       e.Cancel = True
38       errAddress.SetError(ctlSender, "Invalid Postal Code")
39     End If
40   End Sub
41
42   Private Sub GenericValidated(ByVal sender As Object, _
43    ByVal e As System.EventArgs) _
44    Handles txtStreet.Validated, txtCity.Validated, _
45    txtCountry.Validated, txtZip.Validated, _
46    txtState.Validated
47      'cast sender to a System.Windows.Forms.Control
```

Listing 9.10 continued

```
48    Dim ctlSender As Control
49    ctlSender = CType(sender, Control)
50    'Clear Error, if any exists
51    errAddress.SetError(ctlSender, "")
52  End Sub
53
54  Private Sub GenericNotEmpty(ByVal sender As Object, _
55  ByVal e As System.ComponentModel.CancelEventArgs) _
56  Handles txtStreet.Validating, txtCity.Validating, _
57    txtState.Validating
58
59    'cast sender to a System.Windows.Forms.Control
60    Dim ctlSender As Control
61    ctlSender = CType(sender, Control)
62    If ctlSender.Text.Trim = "" Then
63      e.Cancel = True
64      errAddress.SetError(ctlSender, "Must not be empty")
65    End If
66  End Sub
```

When combined with the ErrorProvider control, discussed later in today's lesson, the validation features of .NET make it easy to create data entry forms.

Using the MessageBox Class

A dialog box is a special kind of form that is displayed modally, which means that the user has to deal with it before he can interact with any other part of the application. Dialog boxes are usually used to inform the user of something (such as an error) or to obtain some information. Dialog boxes are not used for displaying status or progress information, simply due to their modal nature; they should be used only when you need to communicate with the user immediately, before doing anything else.

You can build dialogs of your own just like any other Windows Form, and I will cover exactly how to do that later in today's lesson. Often you don't need anything complex, though; you just want to ask a simple question (with a yes/no or OK/cancel answer) or display a message to the user. That is where the MessageBox class comes in. This class is used to display text in a simple dialog box and to display a selection of buttons from which the user can choose his response (see Figure 9.8 for an example). You cannot create an instance of this class, but it exposes a single static method, Show, through which you can configure the dialog as desired and display it all in one single call.

FIGURE 9.8

The MessageBox *is a
useful tool capable of
displaying a message
along with a variety of
button combinations.*

Parameters

The Show method accepts seven different parameters, but you can supply only the values that you have. This method has 12 different overloads to support a wide variety of parameter combinations. Each of the possible parameters is listed here, with a quick description of its purpose:

- Text   Representing the message displayed by the MessageBox, this parameter is not optional; every overload of Show includes it.

- Caption   Another string, like Text, this parameter determines the title bar that is shown by the MessageBox.

- Buttons   Accepting one of the possible enumerated values, this parameter controls the buttons shown on the MessageBox. MessageBoxButtons.AbortRetryIgnore will make the dialog display Abort, Retry, and Ignore buttons; MessageBoxButtons.YesNo displays Yes and No buttons; and so on.

- Icon   Controls which, if any, picture is displayed along with the message. Can be any one of nine values, but the current versions of operating systems only provide images for four of these values, and so all nine options map to one of the four images.

- DefaultButton   When you have more than one button on the dialog, only one of them can be the default. If the user presses Return or Enter when the MessageBox opens, it will be treated as if she had clicked on the default button. This parameter can be set to Button1, Button2, or Button3, which maps to one of the appropriate buttons.

- Options   These options control the appearance of the MessageBox and are especially useful when your application is being localized to another country/region. The options include making the text right-justified, making it read right to left, and ensuring that the message box appears only on the primary desktop of the OS.

- OwnerWindow   This parameter specifies a window within your application that the MessageBox should appear in front of. In general, this functionality is not needed, but it is available.

Figures 9.9 and 9.10 show some sample calls to MessageBox.Show() and the resulting dialogs.

FIGURE 9.9

The default
MessageBox, *called*
with just the message
text (the minimum).

FIGURE 9.10

A more customized
MessageBox, *specifying*
the text, caption, and
the button parameters.

Getting Results

After you have chosen the buttons you want to display, you will want to know which one the user clicked (assuming that you displayed more than just an OK button). That information is returned from the Show method as a DialogResult value, which you can store in a variable, or you can use the method call directly in an expression or conditional. Listing 9.11 shows how to ask the user a question using the MessageBox class and the two ways to handle the result.

LISTING 9.11   Using the MessageBox to Ask Simple Questions and Then Act on the Answer

```
1    Private Sub btnTest_Click(ByVal sender As System.Object, _
2   ByVal e As System.EventArgs) Handles btnTest.Click
3      Dim drResult As DialogResult
4      drResult = MessageBox.Show("Whattya wanna do?", _
5      "Sample", MessageBoxButtons.RetryCancel)
6
7      If drResult = DialogResult.Retry Then
8        'retry
9      Else
10       'cancel
11     End If
12
13     Select Case MessageBox.Show("Bad stuff happened", _
14     "Long Process", MessageBoxButtons.AbortRetryIgnore)
15       Case DialogResult.Abort
16         'abort
17       Case DialogResult.Retry
18         'retry
19       Case DialogResult.Cancel
```

LISTING 9.11   continued

```
20          'cancel
21       Case Else
22          'hmm... how'd I get here?
23     End Select
24  End Sub
```

To demonstrate the use of MessageBox in a real system, you can add a bit of functionality to the original Filer form. This form, which allowed you to copy, move, and delete files, didn't include any confirmation messages ("Are you sure you want to delete c:\test.txt?"), even when you ask it to delete a file completely. To add this feature to the Filer Form, you could use a MessageBox to display the confirmation and Yes/No buttons and then perform or cancel the action accordingly. Listing 9.12 shows the three event routines, modified to include the confirmation step.

LISTING 9.12   Using the MessageBox.Show Method to Ask for Confirmation

```
1   Private Sub btnCopy_Click(ByVal sender As System.Object, _
2   ByVal e As System.EventArgs) Handles btnCopy.Click
3     Dim sSource As String
4     Dim sDestination As String
5     sSource = txtSource.Text()
6     sDestination = txtDestination.Text()
7
8     If File.Exists(sSource) Then
9
10      Dim sConfirm As String
11      sConfirm = _
12      String.Format("Are you sure you wish to copy {0} to {1}?", _
13          sSource, sDestination)
14      If MessageBox.Show(sConfirm, _
15        "Confirm Copy", _
16        MessageBoxButtons.YesNo, _
17        MessageBoxIcon.Question, _
18        MessageBoxDefaultButton.Button2) = DialogResult.Yes Then
19
20        Try
21          File.Copy(sSource, sDestination, chkOverwrite.Checked)
22        Catch objException As Exception
23          MessageBox.Show(objException.Message)
24        End Try
25      End If
26    End If
27  End Sub
28
29  Private Sub btnMove_Click(ByVal sender As System.Object, _
30  ByVal e As System.EventArgs) Handles btnMove.Click
```

LISTING 9.12   continued

```
31    Dim sSource As String
32    Dim sDestination As String
33    sSource = txtSource.Text()
34    sDestination = txtDestination.Text()
35    If File.Exists(sSource) Then
36      Dim sConfirm As String
37      sConfirm = String.Format( _
38        "Are you sure you wish to move {0} to {1}?", _
39        sSource, sDestination)
40
41      If MessageBox.Show(sConfirm, _
42        "Confirm Move", MessageBoxButtons.YesNo, _
43        MessageBoxIcon.Question, _
44        MessageBoxDefaultButton.Button2) = DialogResult.Yes Then
45
46        If File.Exists(sDestination) Then
47          If chkOverwrite.Checked Then
48            File.Delete(sDestination)
49          Else
50            MessageBox.Show("Move aborted, destination exists")
51            Return
52          End If
53        End If
54        File.Move(sSource, sDestination)
55      End If
56    End If
57
58    End Sub
59
60    Private Sub btnDelete_Click(ByVal sender As Object, _
61    ByVal e As System.EventArgs) Handles btnDelete.Click
62      Dim sSource As String
63      sSource = txtSource.Text()
64
65      If File.Exists(sSource) Then
66        Dim sConfirm As String
67        sConfirm = String.Format( _
68        "Are you sure you want to delete {0}?", _
69        sSource)
70
71        If MessageBox.Show(sConfirm, _
72          "Confirm Delete", MessageBoxButtons.YesNo, _
73          MessageBoxIcon.Question, _
74          MessageBoxDefaultButton.Button2) = DialogResult.Yes Then
75
76          File.Delete(sSource)
77        End If
78      End If
79    End Sub
```

Nonvisible Controls

All the controls used in today's lesson so far have been visible when you run your project. That is the standard type of control that you will work with. However, .NET also includes controls that are the same as regular controls in almost every way, except that they have no visible interface at runtime. These controls still have properties, methods, and events and are designed as an easy modular way to add specific functionality to a form.

Back in pre-.NET Visual Basic, nonvisible controls were still placed on your form, cluttering up the design-time interface but totally invisible at runtime. Visual Studio .NET has a much better way of handling this type of control, placing them into a separate area below the design area of the Form (see Figure 9.11). You can still drag, select, click on, and delete them, but they are not interfering with your design view of the Form.

FIGURE 9.11

In Visual Studio .NET, nonvisible controls are placed into a special area of the designer, to avoid confusion with actual interface elements.

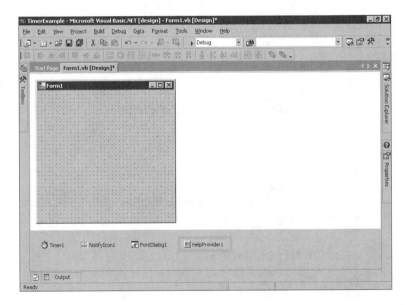

There are a variety of these design-time controls, but I will cover a few of the more commonly used ones in this section: `Timer`, `NotifyIcon`, `ErrorProvider`, and the `Dialog` controls.

Timer

The `Timer` control is designed to allow you to run code at certain time-based intervals. The control, if enabled, will just fire its own `Tick` event at regular intervals. By placing some code into a handler for that `Tick` event, you can execute whatever tasks you want on a regular basis.

Using the `Timer` control involves only a few steps:

1. After you add this control to your form, you have to set its properties; set `Enabled` to `True` to indicate that you want it to be active and set the `Interval` property to the length of time (in milliseconds, 1000ms equals 1s) that you want between events.

2. Add your code to the `Tick` event (double-click the `Timer` control to quickly access this event handler).

That's all that is required, and the code you placed into the `Tick` event handler will be run once every `Interval` milliseconds.

You can try out this control in a project of your own by following these steps:

1. Create a new blank project—a Windows application. A blank form will have been added to the project, `Form1`. Make sure that you are viewing the Design view of this blank form.

2. Drag a `Timer` control from the Toolbox (under Windows Forms) onto the form. It will be added as a control in the nonvisible control area (which is now shown) with the name `Timer1`.

3. Click once on `Timer1` to select it and then view the properties window, which should show you the `Enabled` and `Interval` values that determine the timer's behavior.

4. Set `Enabled` to `True` and `Interval` to `1000` (1 second).

5. Double-click the `Timer` control to switch to Code view and access the event-handling routine for the `Tick` event.

Add the code shown in Listing 9.13 to the `Tick` event handler.

LISTING 9.13   Code That Causes the Form's Caption to Act Like a Clock

```
1   Private Sub Timer1_Tick(ByVal sender As System.Object, _
2   ByVal e As System.EventArgs) Handles Timer1.Tick
3
4     Me.Text = DateTime.Now.ToLongTimeString()
5
6   End Sub
```

Run the project (by pressing F5 or selecting Start from the Debug menu), making sure that it is the startup project (right-click on the project in the Solution Explorer and select Set as StartUp Project) if you have more than one project open.

When the project is run, the form should appear, and its caption will reflect the current time right down to the second. Experiment with different `Interval` values to see how this property affects the firing of the `Tick` event. For a little bit more fun, add a button to the form and place this line of code into its `Click` event:

```
Timer1.Enabled = Not Timer1.Enabled
```

Try running the project again and clicking the button a few times to see what happens.

NotifyIcon

When a program wants to be running all the time and needs some means of visual notification, a common method is to place an icon into the system tray or notification area on the far right side of the taskbar. This might not be the best place to put every application, this area is already getting pretty crowded, but it is useful for certain special-purpose utilities.

In the old days, before .NET, adding an icon to the system tray involved the use of several Win32 API calls and a technique called subclassing that tended to make your Visual Basic application unstable. In .NET, all you need to do is to add a `NotifyIcon` control to your form and set its properties. The most important property is `Icon`, which you can set to any icon file to control what appears in the notification area. If you want to have a menu appear when the user right-clicks your icon, you can add a `ContextMenu` control to your Form and set the `NotifyIcon`'s `ContextMenu` property. Be careful to only use this control when it is appropriate; so many applications are placing icons into this area that Windows XP has added an auto-hide feature!

ErrorProvider

As another great feature for designing data entry forms, the `ErrorProvider` control allows you to visually indicate (see Figure 9.12) which controls on a form have errors associated with them.

To use this control, just add it to your form and set the properties. In fact, you can get away with even less work because the default values should be fine for most purposes, unless you want to use a different icon. Then, whenever you want to indicate that a control has an error associated with it, call the `SetError` method of the `ErrorProvider` control:

```
errorProvider1.SetError(txtStreet, "Invalid Street Address")
```

When the error has been fixed, you can clear it from the `ErrorProvider` by setting the error to an empty string:

```
errorProvider1.SetError(txtStreet, "")
```

FIGURE 9.12

With an
`ErrorProvider` *control*
on your form, data
entry errors are easy
to indicate to the user.

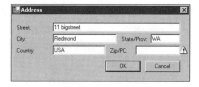

The dialog example (an address entry/edit dialog) covered briefly earlier in today's lesson (and downloadable from this book's Web site) uses this nonvisible control in its code and is a good example to look at.

Dialog Controls

The final type of nonvisible control covered in today's lesson actually refers to an entire group of controls ranging from Open and Save dialogs to font selection dialogs. These controls allow you to use a variety of standard Windows dialogs from your program (see Figure 9.13), which is much nicer than having to create your own.

FIGURE 9.13

The Open File dialog
handles all the commu-
nication with the OS
and the file system,
without you having to
write any code.

Like the other nonvisual controls, you can just drag whichever dialog control you want to use onto your form or into the nonvisual control area. After you have an instance of the control on your form, start working with the properties to configure the control for your application. I will walk you through an example program that uses the Open File dialog and the Save File dialog, and I might as well use the Font and Color dialogs too, just to be complete.

The form itself contains a variety of controls including a Rich Text Box, four Buttons, and a Panel control, which is used to hold the buttons. By using a Panel control in this way, and then setting it to dock right and the Rich Text Box control to Fill the Form, you get an interface that will scale correctly as you resize or even maximize the form. I will not cover the details of setting up these controls, but you can download the entire form from this book's Web site.

In addition to the visible controls, I have placed the four dialog controls (Open, Save, Font, and Color) onto the form as well. Each of the four buttons uses one of the dialogs to open a file, save a file, change the font or change the font color, and their code is listed in the following individual sections. Note that I set up the dialog controls within the button click procedure, even though I could have set many of these properties using the dialog control's property window. This is only being done because this is an example; any control property that will be the same throughout the life of the form should be set only once, which is what occurs when you manipulate properties through the properties window. I will now go through the code behind each of the four buttons and discuss how the dialog control was used in each case.

Open Dialog

The event handler for the Open button (see Listing 9.14) allows the user to select a filename using the Open dialog and then reads that file into the form's Rich Text Box control.

LISTING 9.14   Event Handler for the Open Button

```
1    Private Sub btnOpen_Click(ByVal sender As System.Object, _
2    ByVal e As System.EventArgs) Handles btnOpen.Click
3      Dim sNewFile As String
4      Dim trNewFile As System.IO.TextReader
5      If MessageBox.Show("Overwrite current contents?", _
6       "Open New File", MessageBoxButtons.YesNo, MessageBoxIcon.Question, _
7       MessageBoxDefaultButton.Button2) = DialogResult.Yes Then
8        With dlgOpen
9          .Filter = "Text files (*.txt)|*.txt"
10         .AddExtension = True
11         .CheckFileExists = True
12         .CheckPathExists = True
13         .InitialDirectory = IO.Path.GetDirectoryName(sCurrentFile)
14         .Multiselect = False
15
16         If .ShowDialog() = DialogResult.OK Then
17           sNewFile = .FileName
18           If IO.File.Exists(sNewFile) Then
19             trNewFile = New IO.StreamReader(sNewFile)
20             rtfContents.Text = trNewFile.ReadToEnd()
21             sCurrentFile = sNewFile
22           End If
23         End If
24       End With
25     End If
26   End Sub
```

ANALYSIS Lines 2 to 7, after declaring the variables needed, confirm that the user wanted to load a new file, therefore overwriting the current contents of the text box. A MessageBox dialog is used to ask this question because it is a simple Yes/No. If the user answers Yes, go ahead and overwrite the current contents. Then the Open dialog is prepared in lines 8 to 14. A filter is set to restrict the file types to text files only. The dialog is told to return the extension along with the filename, to check whether the path and file exist and to start in the same folder as the file that was loaded last. The property MultiSelect is also set to False, indicating that you only want the user to be able to select a single file at a time.

Line 16 displays the dialog and checks whether the result is okay. If it is, lines 18 to 20 ensure again that the file exists and then load it in a single read into the rich text box. More error handling should be added here in a production system because file opening is a common location for failure due to security privileges and other reasons.

Save Dialog

When you need the user to supply a destination filename, you need the Save dialog. It is a part of the OS, so it understands drives, folders, file shares, shortcut links, and everything else that Windows might throw at it. Writing your own dialog like this would be difficult and would require ongoing maintenance as the file system features of the OS changed over time. Using the built-in dialogs makes your system better integrated into the OS (see Listing 9.15).

LISTING 9.15 Using the Built-in Dialogs

```
1    Private Sub btnSave_Click(ByVal sender As System.Object, _
2    ByVal e As System.EventArgs) Handles btnSave.Click
3
4        Dim sNewFileName As String
5        Dim swOutput As IO.StreamWriter
6
7        sNewFileName = sCurrentFile
8
9        If MessageBox.Show("Save As Different File Name?", _
10        "Save File", MessageBoxButtons.YesNo, MessageBoxIcon.Question, _
11         MessageBoxDefaultButton.Button2) = DialogResult.Yes Then
12            With dlgSave
13                .FileName = sCurrentFile
14                .CheckFileExists = False
15                .CheckPathExists = True
16                .DefaultExt = "txt"
17                .Filter = "Text files (*.txt)|*.txt"
18                .AddExtension = True
19                .InitialDirectory = IO.Path.GetDirectoryName(sNewFileName)
20                .OverwritePrompt = True
```

9

LISTING 9.15   continued

```
21                       .CreatePrompt = False
22
23                   If .ShowDialog() = DialogResult.OK Then
24                       sNewFileName = .FileName
25                       swOutput = New IO.StreamWriter(sNewFileName)
26
27                       swOutput.Write(rtfContents.Text)
28                       swOutput.Close()
29                       sCurrentFile = sNewFileName
30                   End If
31              End With
32          End If
33      End Sub
```

ANALYSIS   Using the Save dialog is similar to the Open dialog. After the user has confirmed
that he wants to save the file (line 9), the dialog properties are set to create the
proper image. The filename is set to the last used filename as a starting point. The dialog
is told that the file doesn't have to already exist (CheckFileExists = False), but the
folder does (CheckPathExists = True). By default, the file will be saved as a .txt file
(line 16), but the dialog will not stop the user from saving it as something else. An interesting pair of options, OverwritePrompt and CreatePrompt, don't apply to the Open dialog but are important in saving. OverwritePrompt controls whether the dialog will warn
the user before allowing him to save using the path and name of an existing file.
CreatePrompt determines whether the user should be warned if he tries to do the exact
opposite (use a path and name that doesn't already exist).

With the dialog prepared, it is displayed (line 23), and if the user exits the dialog by
clicking OK, then the contents of the Rich Text Box are written out to the file (lines 24
to 28).

Font Dialog

The names, available sizes, and styles of fonts on a user's machine can be quite a set of
information, and this dialog handles all that for you while providing an interface that
likely appears in many of the programs the user works with. Listing 9.16 shows how the
Font dialog can be used to allow the user to select a font face and style.

LISTING 9.16   Using the Font Dialog

```
1    Private Sub btnFont_Click(ByVal sender As System.Object, _
2      ByVal e As System.EventArgs) Handles btnFont.Click
3        dlgFont.Font = rtfContents.Font
4
```

LISTING 9.16 continued

```
5          If dlgFont.ShowDialog() = DialogResult.OK Then
6              rtfContents.Font = dlgFont.Font
7          End If

8      End Sub
```

ANALYSIS The Font dialog is simple to use: just load the current font settings into it (line 3) and then show the dialog (line 5). If the user clicks OK, then take the new font settings and put them back into the target (the rich text box in this case, line 6). That's it; works perfectly.

Color Dialog

Unless you need some advanced functionality, the Color dialog is exactly what you need to allow the user to choose a color (see Listing 9.17). The user can pick a standard, predefined color, or mix their own all through this dialog.

LISTING 9.17 Adding Graphical Color Picking to an Application

```
1      Private Sub btnColor_Click(ByVal sender As System.Object, _
2          ByVal e As System.EventArgs) Handles btnColor.Click
3          dlgColor.Color = rtfContents.ForeColor
4
5          If dlgColor.ShowDialog() = DialogResult.OK Then
6              rtfContents.ForeColor = dlgColor.Color
7          End If
8
9      End Sub
```

ANALYSIS The Color dialog functions exactly the same as the Font dialog: just load the current Color values (line 3), show the dialog (line 5), and set the target to use the values chosen in the dialog—as long as the user clicked OK (line 6).

Building Your Own Dialog Boxes

The MessageBox class provides a way to display simple dialogs, showing a message and/or asking the user to make a choice between one of a fixed set of options (Yes/No, OK/Cancel, Abort/Retry/Ignore). But there will be times when you need a dialog with more complex capabilities. It is possible to turn any Windows Form into a dialog, giving it the appearance and behavior of a dialog, and to use it in your program. There are several distinct stages, and I will walk through them as I show you how to build a

9

userid/password dialog for use as an application login screen. To follow along with this example as you go through this section, create a new project (of type Windows Application).

Creating the Dialog Box

A dialog box doesn't just behave differently than a regular Windows Form, it looks different as well. Add a new form to your project, called `LogonDialog`, and bring it up in the Design view. Click on the form and bring up the properties window. To make this form look like a dialog, set the following properties:

- `FormBorderStyle = FixedDialog`   This will prevent the dialog from being resized.
- `Text = "Logon"`   This is the title caption and `Logon` is more appropriate than `LogonDialog`.
- `MaximizeBox` and `MinimizeBox` both set to `False`   No need to minimize or maximize a dialog box.

Now add the controls needed to create a logon dialog, two text boxes (userid and password), two labels (one for each of the text boxes), and two buttons (OK and Cancel). How you arrange them is not all that important for the purposes of an example, but Figure 9.14 shows how I did it.

FIGURE 9.14

This form has been resized to appear normal with only a few controls on it.

Name the controls using the naming conventions you have seen throughout today's lesson, producing `lblUserid`, `lblPassword`, `txtUserid`, `txtPassword`, `btnOK`, and `btnCancel`. Finally, as the last part of the cosmetic setup, view the properties for `txtPassword` and set `PasswordChar = "*"`. With `PasswordChar` set, any text entered into this field will be shown as a string of that character.

Now that the two buttons have been added to the form, you can go back to the form's properties and set two properties that you couldn't set without any buttons available. Set `AcceptButton` and `CancelButton` to `btnOK` and `btnCancel`, respectively. The result of setting these two properties is that if the user presses Enter on this dialog, it will have the same effect as clicking the OK button. If the user presses the Escape key, it will have the same effect as clicking the Cancel button.

Setting Up the Dialog Result

When the dialog box has been shown, and the user closes it by clicking OK or Cancel, your program will need to determine two things: First, whether the user clicked OK or Cancel, and second, what the user entered into the Userid and Password boxes. The first piece of information, which button was pressed, is similar to what is returned from a call to MessageBox.Show(), and your new dialog handles it in the same way. There is a DialogResult property of the form, and whatever that property is set to is returned to the program that displayed the MessageBox. You can set this property using a single line of code like the following:

```
Me.DialogResult = DialogResult.Cancel
```

There is another way to set this result value, though, and that is to set the DialogResult property of btnOK and btnCancel (to OK and Cancel, respectively). If those values are set, then the dialog is automatically closed when the user clicks either one of the buttons, and the dialog result is set to the button's dialog result value. It is all a question of control, and where you plan on doing validation.

If you set the CausesValidation property on txtUserid, txtPassword, and btnOK to True (and False on btnCancel), then you can use the Validating event of txtUserid and txtPassword to check the user's entry. Alternatively, you might want to do all the checking in the Click event of btnOK, in which case you would want btnOK.DialogResult to be set to None so that the dialog would not be automatically closed when the button is clicked. In code, you can always close the form yourself by setting the DialogResult property directly. Using either method, you can leave the DialogResult property of btnCancel set to Cancel because no validation should occur if the user clicks Cancel.

Which of these two ways is better? On a form with only two text fields, it probably doesn't matter, but if you had a large dialog with a lot of validation, then you should use the validation events and the CausesValidation property.

Listing 9.18 shows the code for the Click event of btnOK, validating the data entered into the two dialogs and setting the form's dialog result property. This code assumes that CausesValidation equals False for everything on the form, and the DialogResult property of btnOk equals None.

LISTING 9.18 Using Validation Properties

```
1    Private Sub btnOK_Click(ByVal sender As System.Object, _
2        ByVal e As System.EventArgs) Handles btnOK.Click
3    Dim sUserID As String
```

LISTING 9.18   continued

```
 4     Dim sPassword As String
 5
 6     sUserID = txtUserid.Text
 7     sPassword = txtPassword.Text
 8
 9     If sUserID.Trim() = "" Then
10       MessageBox.Show("UserID cannot be blank," _
11         & " please enter a proper UserID.", "Error", _
12           MessageBoxButtons.OK, MessageBoxIcon.Error)
13       txtUserid.Select()
14     Else
15       If sPassword.Trim() = "" Then
16         MessageBox.Show("Password cannot be blank, " & _
17           "please enter a proper Password.", "Error", _
18           MessageBoxButtons.OK, MessageBoxIcon.Error)
19         txtPassword.Select()
20       Else
21         Me.DialogResult = DialogResult.OK
22       End If
23     End If
24  End Sub
```

ANALYSIS   The `Click` routine does not perform any complex validation; it simply checks whether the user has entered a userid and a password (lines 9 and 15) and sets the dialog result to OK (line 21) if she has. Setting the form's `DialogResult` property in line 21 closes the dialog to hide and to return this result back to the calling program. Note that if `btnOK.DialogResult` had been set to OK (using the properties window), then the dialog would have closed at the end of this `Click` event regardless of the userid/password entered.

Set the `btnCancel.DialogResult` property to `Cancel` (so that it always causes a `Cancel`, and no event handling is needed) using the properties window, and this logon dialog is ready.

Showing the Dialog Box

To use your new `LogonDialog`, you need it to be displayed. Setting this form as the start-up object for your project would not be useful because it would run the dialog, but the application would just end when the user entered a userid and password. You need to call the `LogonDialog` before displaying `Form1`, which is the startup object of this project. Just like buttons, forms have events as well, and one particular form event, `Load`, is perfect for this purpose because it is called before the form is displayed. View the code for `Form1` and select Base Class Events from the left drop-down at the top of the code editing window. Selecting this option populates the right drop-down with the list of events that this form supports. Select Load from the right drop-down, and you will be editing the Form1_Load event procedure.

In this procedure, you will need to create an instance of your LogonDialog, display it as a dialog, and then check the userid/password the user entered. Listing 9.19 provides an example of how this event procedure could be written.

LISTING 9.19   Display a Form as a dialog

```
1    Private Sub Form1_Load(ByVal sender As Object, _
2      ByVal e As System.EventArgs) Handles MyBase.Load
3      Dim frmLogon As New LogonDialog()
4      Dim bLogonSuccessful As Boolean = False
5      Dim sFailureMessage As String
6
7      If frmLogon.ShowDialog() = DialogResult.OK Then
8
9        If frmLogon.txtUserid.Text = "Duncan" Then
10         If frmLogon.txtPassword.Text = "password" Then
11           bLogonSuccessful = True
12         Else
13           sFailureMessage = "Invalid Password!"
14         End If
15       Else
16         sFailureMessage = "Invalid User ID!"
17       End If
18     Else
19       sFailureMessage = "Logon Attempt Cancelled"
20     End If
21
22     If Not bLogonSuccessful Then
23       MessageBox.Show(sFailureMessage, "Logon Failed", _
24       MessageBoxButtons.OK, MessageBoxIcon.Error)
25       Me.Close()
26     End If
27   End Sub
```

ANALYSIS   A new instance of LogonDialog is created (line 3), which is needed before you can display this form. Two variables are used (lines 4 and 5) to track the success/failure of the logon attempt. Line 7 uses the ShowDialog method of the form to display it in a modal fashion. Using ShowDialog, the next line of code in this procedure will not execute until the form is hidden or closed, but using just Show would have displayed the form nonmodally, and code execution would have continued before the user had completed logon.

ShowDialog, just like the Show method of the MessageBox class, returns a DialogResult value, as discussed earlier while you were creating the LogonDialog. Line 7 checks the value returned, because if the user canceled the dialog, then the userid and password should not be processed. The text box controls on the `LogonDialog` are then accessed, and their values checked against a hard-coded userid and password (lines 9 and 10). In your real programs, you would likely be checking these values against some sort of security list or database. Finally, if everything is correct, `bLogonSuccessful` is set to `True` (line 11), or the appropriate failure message is placed into `sFailureMessage` (lines 11–19). If the logon was not successful, the failure message is displayed in a `MessageBox` (line 23), and `Form1` is closed (line 25) to prevent access to the program.

Summary

Windows Forms are used to build .NET applications with a Windows interface, which are one of the two main types of applications you will be creating (the other being Web-based systems). Containing many major advances over previous versions of Visual Basic, and providing a common system for Form development across all of .NET, the Windows Forms system will allow you to build whatever interface your application needs. Day 16 will continue this topic and provide more information on using these Forms in your programs.

Q&A

Q. Can I have more than one Windows Form in a project/application?

A. Yes, you can have as many as you want. Only one form can be the "startup" form, though, so you will have to create instances of the other forms within your code and then call their `Show` method when you want to display them.

Q. I want to use a `MessageBox` from a Console application I created, but I can't get it to work. It doesn't seem to recognize the class name.

A. `MessageBox` is a part of the `System.Windows.Forms` namespace, so you must have namespace available to you before you can use this class. When you create a Windows application using Visual Studio, it automatically adds the necessary reference, but it doesn't do that for a Console application. Using the Solution Explorer, right-click on the `References` folder inside your project and select Add Reference. From the dialog this brings up, select `System.Windows.Forms.dll` in the list. Another good idea is to add an `Imports System.Windows.Forms` line to the top of your module or class file so that you can refer to `MessageBox` without having to prefix it with `System.Windows.Forms` every time.

Workshop

The Workshop is designed to help you anticipate possible questions, review what you've learned, and get thinking about how to put your knowledge into practice. The answers to the quiz are in Appendix A, "Answers to Quizzes/Exercises."

Quiz

1 What is the difference between a modal and nonmodal form?

2. Why wouldn't you set the CausesValidation property of a Cancel button to True?

3. What statement is added at the end of a procedure declaration to indicate that it is an event handler?

Exercises

1. Given that a single procedure can handle multiple events (Sub myhandler() Handles btnOpen.Click, btnClose.Click, btnSave.Click), how could you rewrite these three event procedures into a single procedure?

   Hint: You have to cast (using CType) the sender parameter into a System.Windows.Forms.Control or a System.Windows.Forms.Button before you can access the regular set of control properties.

LISTING 9.20 Using the Handles Keyword to Create a Single Procedure Called for Multiple Events

```
1    Private Sub btnCopy_Click(ByVal sender As System.Object, _
2      ByVal e As System.EventArgs) Handles btnCopy.Click
3      Dim sSource As String
4      Dim sDestination As String
5      sSource = txtSource.Text()
6      sDestination = txtDestination.Text()
7      File.Copy(sSource, sDestination)
8    End Sub
9
10   Private Sub btnMove_Click(ByVal sender As System.Object, _
11     ByVal e As System.EventArgs) Handles btnMove.Click
12     Dim sSource As String
13     Dim sDestination As String
14     sSource = txtSource.Text()
15     sDestination = txtDestination.Text()
16     File.Move(sSource, sDestination)
17   End Sub
18
19   Private Sub btnDelete_Click(ByVal sender As Object, _
20       ByVal e As System.EventArgs) Handles btnDelete.Click
```

LISTING 9.20 continued

```
21    Dim sSource As String
22    sSource = txtSource.Text()
23    File.Delete(sSource)
24  End Sub
```

Day 10

Building the User Interface with Web Forms

More applications today are being written as browser-based applications. Before Visual Basic .NET, it was difficult to create these browser-based applications using Visual Basic. With Visual Basic .NET, these become as easy to create as traditional Windows-based applications. Today, you will look at how you can create browser-based user interfaces. The tools within Visual Basic .NET assist the developer in creating Web pages that provide fairly rich user interfaces across any browser type. In particular, today's lesson will focus on

- How the Web programming model differs from the traditional Windows-based model
- Using standard Web Forms controls
- Using advanced Web Forms controls
- Using the `Validator` controls

The Web Programming Model

Some days, I think that everyone in the world is on the Internet, especially when my access speed is in the painfully slow mode because everyone is browsing, chatting, and e-mailing (but not doing business). (As a tip, I somehow find that the best time to be online is during *Star Trek*—probably just a coincidence.) Obviously, one of the most important, or at least popular, aspects of the Internet is the World Wide Web (WWW or just Web). However, there has generally been a shortage of really good programming tools for creating Web "programs," rather than just simple Web pages. This is at least partly because creating applications for the Web is different from creating applications for a desktop computer, with which you have more control. In addition, Web applications must deal with the network more frequently.

So, what is the "Web Programming model"? It is just a term used to describe how you can design, or architect, a program that uses Web pages in a browser to allow the user to enter information. These Web pages are designed using HTML (HyperText Markup Language).This book won't be covering HTML, but there are plenty of books on the market that do.

A *browser* is an application that knows how to read HTML and display it on the screen. Usually (but not always), most of the work of an application is done on the Web Server. The Web Server is another program running on a computer that knows how to return HTML on demand. In Windows NT and 2000, this program is called Internet Information Server (IIS). The information is carried between the browser and the server using a protocol, or language, called HTTP (Hypertext Transfer Protocol).

Note

The actual name of IIS has changed with the different versions. In Windows NT 4.0 Server, it is called Internet Information Server. In Windows 2000, it is called Internet Information Services, whereas in Windows NT 4.0 Professional, it is Personal Web Server.

In the "beginning" of the World Wide Web, Web pages were static. That is, they never really changed. Things got more interesting when people started to create dynamic, or changing, Web pages. This was the dawn of the Web program. With Web programs, rather than simply returning the same HTML every time, the Web server can perform some task and return HTML appropriate to the result. For example, the user might request the sales information for a particular date range. This information is passed to the server. The server, in turn, might look up that information in a database and then write the HTML to display it to the user. The whole process looks similar to Figure 10.1.

FIGURE 10.1

Web programming model.

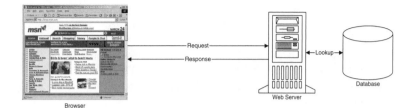

Alternatively, the server (or Web page designer) might add programming information to the page itself, creating a page that is a little program in its own right. This is often called Dynamic HTML (or DHTML). With DHTML, the page includes some JavaScript (a programming language, like Visual Basic .NET that runs in Web pages) or other language. The code can run in the browser without needing to send any information back to the server. Figure 10.2 shows this model in action.

FIGURE 10.2

Dynamic HTML programming model.

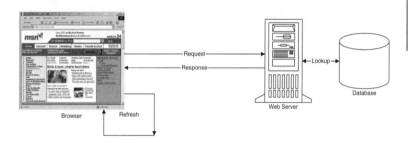

There are a variety of techniques that can be used to create a Web program. Some of the most common techniques used in the past have been ASP (Active Server Pages), Perl (another programming language), or JSP (Java Server Pages). The technique used by Web Forms is an improvement of ASP, ASP.NET.

ASP.NET

ASP.NET is Microsoft's name for its improved version of ASP. Although ASP was an easy method for building dynamic Web pages, it had some problems that ASP.NET solves:

- ASP often required too much code to get something done. ASP.NET requires less code (often much less code) for common programming tasks.

- ASP still suffered from the limited number of controls that HTML suffers from. ASP.NET adds the idea of "server-side controls" that can generate HTML appropriate to the browser requesting them. Although these controls are just HTML in the browser, they can represent a great deal of HTML and code, saving you from having to write it.

- ASP only allowed programming in a language such as VBScript. VBScript is interpreted at runtime, not compiled as real Visual Basic is. ASP.NET allows you to write Web pages in real, fully compiled Visual Basic .NET.

ASP.NET is also designed to solve other problems with ASP that aren't appropriate to this discussion of building user interfaces, such as improvements in scalability and memory use.

How Creating Web-Based Programs Is Different from Creating Windows-Based Programs

When you are designing a Web-based program using Web Forms, there are a number of differences you must keep in mind. Some of the differences include

- Web-based applications tend to have more code on the server, rather than on the client. That is, the look and feel of your program comes from the browser, but the "smarts" are on the server.
- Web-based applications are dependent on the capabilities of the browser used to view them. Sadly, each browser has different capabilities, and many Web developers have had to struggle with these differences as they designed their programs.
- When you receive a Web page, it tends to be static. Although there are ways you can update the page without returning to the server (that is, to make it dynamic), these methods make creating the page more complex. Therefore, producing animated forms (or any kind of response to the user) is more difficult with Web-based applications.
- Many operations of a Web-based application require a "network round-trip". This is because of the separation of code and design. In order to have a button or other control do something, it is often necessary to send information to the server. The server then responds appropriately. You should keep this in mind when you are creating Web applications. This back-and-forth communication might take a while, so you should only do it as necessary.

Web-based applications are limited, both by the limitations on the browser itself, and on the number of browsers available on the market. Browsers are limited in the types of controls that can be used, as well as by their limited drawing capabilities—that is, you typically can't draw on the Web page. In addition, if the user has installed an older version of a browser, or has disabled certain features, the Web page can react in different ways. This is one of the main reasons that Web-based applications tend to place most of the code on the server. In addition, this has meant that traditionally Web-based applications have required a lot of code to be added to change the appearance of the Web page based on the browser viewing it.

Fortunately, the Web Form controls hide most of those details from you. They are written to produce dynamic output (that is, the page can change without needing to send information back to the server) if the controls detect that the browser is capable of using dynamic output. If they do not recognize the browser being used, or if the browser does not support dynamic updating, only plain HTML is returned to the client browser. This ensures the developer that the client browser will receive the Web page designed, within the limitations of the browser.

In addition to the limits caused by the browser, Web-based applications also require the developer to consider the fact that the client and server are separated, possibly by great distances by a network. This means that operations that might only take a few seconds if the client and server were close (or even the same machine) could take a long time. So, operations like animations might be jerky, or not display at all until the download is completed. Also, the speed of the connection comes into play. If you are accessing the Web page using a slower modem, this difference is made even more significant.

With all these issues to keep in mind, you might ask "Why bother creating Web applications?" Although there is a downside to creating Web applications, there are many benefits:

- Installation   To make your application available, all you need to do is point someone at the URL. The application is immediately usable by the client. This saves you from having to visit each of those client machines, or from having your users all install the application.

- New Versions and/or bug fixes   When you want to upgrade to a newer version of part of your application, you only need to install the upgrades at the server, not at every client.

- Performance   Improving the performance of Web applications is much easier than improving the performance of *regular* applications. You can improve the performance of Web applications by adding more servers and distributing the requests across all the servers.

- Knowledge   If you already know some HTML, Web applications can be much easier to create than Windows applications. Alternatively, they can be easier to learn, if you know neither HTML nor Windows.

So, when designing an application, should you create a Windows-based or Web-based program? The easy (but unsatisfying) answer is, "It depends." Many applications fit either type, but people are starting to create more Web-based applications. The capability to easily make upgrades and fixes available is compelling, so you might want to at least consider creating your programs as Web applications first.

Some applications are not candidates for Web applications, however. Any programs that require a continuous link between client and server are not appropriate, nor are applications that require a lot of graphics (such as games). Finally, if you only have a single computer involved (that is, not a client/server application like a database program), or if the app is only for yourself, it might make sense to create a Windows-based application.

Using Standard Web Forms Controls

Designing a Web page using Visual Basic .NET is similar to designing a normal Visual Basic .NET application. The only difference is what happens behind the scenes. Rather than code being added to create the controls and set their properties, HTML tags are added to the ASP.NET page, and code is added to a Visual Basic .NET file that works behind the scenes.

The controls available to you in creating a Web application are similar to those available in Windows applications. They include all the common controls you're used to using (see Figure 10.3). Table 10.1 describes these controls in brief.

FIGURE 10.3

Standard controls for Web Forms.

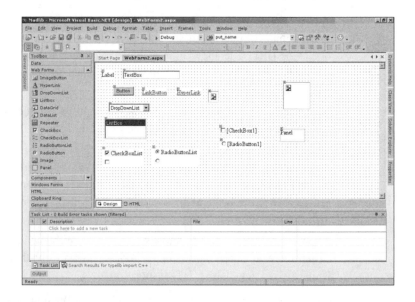

TABLE 10.1   Standard Web Forms Controls

Control	Description
Label	Use to place text on the Web Form. Alternatively, you can simply click on the Web Form and start typing. The Label gives you better control over formatting, and allows you to place the text where you want it. Finally, the Label control

TABLE 10.1   continued

Control	Description
	also allows you to dynamically change the contents inside of your application, something not possible with text added to the form.
TextBox	Use to give the user a field to enter information into. This will often be the most common control added for a Web application.
Button	Use to give the user something to click to carry out some action.
LinkButton	Similar in action to the normal Button control, the LinkButton is something for your Web application's users to click. The difference is that the Button looks like a button, whereas the LinkButton is a hyperlink. (That is, the user sees a nice blue, underlined pointer somewhere.)
ImageButton	Similar in action to the normal Button control, the ImageButton is something for your users to click to perform some action. The difference is that the ImageButton is a graphic that your users can click.
Hyperlink	This is similar to the LinkButton, except that the LinkButton has a Click event, whereas the Hyperlink does not. This means that you can write code only to deal with LinkButton clicks, whereas the Hyperlink can be used only to send the user elsewhere.
DropDownList	DropDownList controls are quite common in Web Forms. They are a list that initially only takes a single line. You can click on the drop-down arrow to open them and see the full list. When you select an item from the list, the list again closes, and only a single line is shown, containing your selection. You would use these controls when your user needs to select a single item from a list, and when you want to save screen space—for example, when selecting a state or country code.
ListBox	ListBox controls allow the user to select one or more items from a list of choices. They differ from DropDownLists in that the list is always visible. One other difference is that it is possible to select multiple items in a ListBox. Use the ListBox when you need this multiple selection capability (although see CheckBoxList), when you want the user to always see the choices, or when screen space is plentiful.
CheckBox	The CheckBox represents the answer to a yes or no question. It is either checked, or unchecked, and therefore is used when you want the user either to select an option or not. It differs from the RadioButton, in that the CheckBox is independent of other CheckBox controls, whereas the RadioButton is generally one possible option out of many.
CheckBoxList	The CheckBoxList is a series of CheckBox controls. Each one is independent of the others, but the CheckBoxList control is a handy way of adding a number of CheckBox controls to a page. This control is especially useful if you have a collection of items (perhaps retrieved from a database) from which you want the

10

TABLE 10.1 continued

Control	Description
	user to select. The CheckBoxList is also a handy replacement for the ListBox when you want the user to select a number of items. However, you should still use the ListBox if you have more than about six items.
RadioButton	The RadioButton is similar to the CheckBox in that its value is either True or False. It differs from the CheckBox in that RadioButton controls tend to "travel in packs." Although each CheckBox on a form can be set independently to either True or False, only one RadioButton in a set can be True. So, you can think of a CheckBox as posing a Yes/No question, whereas a RadioButton (or rather a group of RadioButtons) is more like a multiple-choice question to which only one answer is correct.
RadioButtonList	The RadioButtonList is a group of RadioButton controls. It makes creating this group easy, if you already have a list from some other location (like a database).
Image	The Image control allows you to place a graphic on the page.
Panel	The Panel control is similar to the Label control in that it is just a placeholder for text. The difference is that the Panel control can hold other controls. As such, it is a great control to use when you need to separate or highlight information or controls. Similar, or related, controls can be grouped in a Panel control to make them stand out from the other controls.

Just as with Windows controls, you use the Web Form controls by double-clicking them in the toolbox, or by dragging them onto your form. In this case, however, the form is a Web page.

Let's create a simple Web Form application to see how these controls make it easy to write Web programs.

Start the development environment if it is not running and create a new Web application. Call this one Madlib. You'll use it to create a simple Web application to see many of the standard controls in action. Select File, New, Project to open the New Project dialog. Open the Visual Basic Projects folder and select the Web Application project template. Change the name of the project to **Madlib** and click OK to build the project.

Note Before you create a Web application, you should first install or have access to Internet Information Services (or Internet Information Server).

Just as with Windows-based applications, your first step is to lay out the controls you will be using in your application (see Figure 10.4 for the final result). You'll start by adding a graphic to your page.

FIGURE 10.4

Madlib *form.*

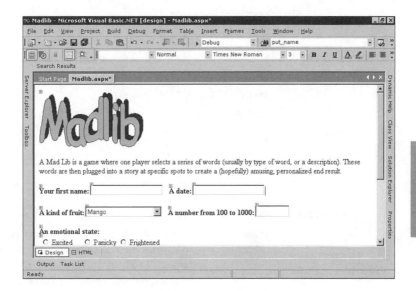

Drag an Image control onto the form. Initially, it should look like a blank square (or rather a missing graphic) because you need to set the path to the graphic. Go to the property window and find the ImageUrl property. When you click in the Property window for the ImageUrl property, you should see a button with three dots appear. Just as with Windows applications, this means that a dialog will help you set this property. Click the button, and find a nice graphic. (I created one that said Madlib in the Paint program that comes with Windows 2000.) Click OK, and the graphic should now be showing on the form.

Explaining your program is generally considered good form. Add a Label control and add a simple explanation to the Text property. The text I entered was

```
A Mad Lib is a game where one player selects a series of words (usually
by type of word, or a description). These words are then plugged into a
story at specific spots to create a (hopefully) amusing, personalized
end result.
```

Next, you'll add the controls to the page for the various items you'll plug in. Table 10.2 describes the controls and property settings used.

TABLE 10.2 Controls Used in the Madlib Web Form

Control	Property	Value
Label	(ID)	lblName
	Text	Your first name:
	Font Bold	True
TextBox	(ID)	txtName
Label	(ID)	lblDate
	Text	A date:
	Font Bold	True
TextBox	(ID)	txtDate
Label	(ID)	lblFruit
	Text	A kind of fruit:
	Font Bold	True
DropDownList	(ID)	cboFruit
	Items	The DropDownList has a dialog that assists you in adding items to it. Click the Items property, and then the resulting Build button. See Figure 10.5 for the resulting dialog. Add a number of fruits, by clicking the Add button, and then set the Text property. Repeat for about 10 items. I added Mango, Orange, Banana, Currant, Berry, Kumquat, Peach, Kiwi, Apricot, and Plum.
Label	(ID)	lblNumber
	Text	A number from 100 to 1000:
	Font Bold	True
TextBox	(ID)	txtNumber
	Text	500
Label	(ID)	lblEmotion
	Text	An emotional state:
	Font Bold	True
RadioButtonList	(ID)	rlstEmotion
	Items	The Items property of the RadioButtonList is similar to the Items property of the DropDownList, and has the same editor. Add a few of your favorite emotional states here. I added Excited, Frustrated, Intrigued, Saddened, Panicky, Ecstatic, Angry, Jealous, Frightened, Happy, Shocked, and Blue.

TABLE 10.2 continued

Control	Property	Value
	RepeatColumns	3
Label	(ID)	lblVerb
	Text	A verb:
	Font Bold	True
TextBox	(ID)	txtVerb
Label	(ID)	lblOccupation
	Text	An occupation:
	Font Bold	True
TextBox	(ID)	txtOccupation
Button	(ID)	cmdWrite
	Text	Write Story
Button	ID	cmdClear
	Text	Clear
Label	(ID)	lblResult
	Text	Leave this field blank (that is, clear out the value in the Text property)
	BorderStyle	Groove
	Width	75%

In addition, you might want to start a new line periodically to arrange the controls better on the page. See Figure 10.5 for one example. If you're familiar with HTML, you might want to put the controls in a table for even better formatting possibilities.

Note

There is another technique you can use to put controls on a Web Form. If you look at the properties of the Web Form (look for the DOCUMENT in the drop-down list of objects at the top of the Property window), you will see one called pageLayout. By default, this is LinearLayout. The alternative, GridLayout can help you create rich Web Forms. If the pageLayout is set to GridLayout, you can place controls on the Web Form just as you can on a Windows Form.

10

FIGURE 10.5

Adding items to the
DropDownList.

Most of the properties used should make sense; however a few likely need extra explanation. Many controls that work with lists are able to be "bound" to a collection of items. Often, this means that they can be attached to information retrieved from a database, however, they can also be attached to other collections, such as arrays. Controls capable of this can be identified easily, as they have an Items collection. This Items collection appears in the Property window, and allows you to add items without binding the control to an array or other collection. This is the easiest way to add the items if they will not be changing. If they will likely change, you should keep them in a database and retrieve them at runtime, then bind them to the control. You will see this in action in Day 12, "Accessing Data with ADO."

The RadioButtonList has a relatively rare property: RepeatColumns. You can set this to control the number of columns used to display the list of items. This can be a great way to save some space on the screen, while still showing all the items. Behind the scenes, the RadioButtonList writes HTML to make this work. This is one of the features that make these controls easier to use than writing your own HTML.

Your next step in writing your Web application is to add code. You will only be adding code to the two buttons. You'll start with the Clear button. This button will clear the information in the various TextBox controls, and in the results Label. Double-click on the Clear button and add the code shown in Listing 10.1.

INPUT   **LISTING 10.1**   Code for the Clear Button

```
1  Private Sub cmdClear_Click( _
2    ByVal sender As System.Object, _
3    ByVal e As System.EventArgs) _
4    Handles cmdClear.Click
```

LISTING 10.1   continued

```
 5        txtName.Text = ""
 6        txtDate.Text = ""
 7        txtVerb.Text = ""
 8        txtNumber.Text = ""
 9        txtOccupation.Text = ""
10        lblResult.Text = ""
11   End Sub
```

ANALYSIS   The code for this button is simple. All it does is sets the `Text` property of all the `TextBox` controls and the results Label to `""`. This clears those controls.

The code in Listing 10.2 also is simple. The basic idea is that you build a long string containing the entire story, and this is written to the results `Label`.

INPUT   **LISTING 10.2**   Code for the Write Story Button

```
 1   Private Sub cmdWrite_Click( _
 2     ByVal sender As System.Object, _
 3     ByVal e As System.EventArgs) _
 4     Handles cmdWrite.Click
 5     'here's were we combine the selections
 6     'the user has made into the final story
 7       Dim sTemp As String
 8       sTemp = "Diary of " & txtName.Text & _
 9         " for " & DateTime.Today.ToString & "<br>"
10       sTemp &= "On " & txtDate.Text & _
11         " I started to program in Visual Basic.NET. "
12       sTemp &= "I'm " & rlstEmotion.SelectedItem.Text & "! "
13       sTemp &= "I think I'm going to go out and " & txtVerb.Text
14       sTemp &= " my new " & txtNumber.Text
15       sTemp &= " PicoHertz " & cboFruit.SelectedItem.Text
16       sTemp &= " and become a " & txtOccupation.Text & "."
17       'the final story goes into the Label control
18       lblResult.Text = sTemp
19   End Sub
```

ANALYSIS   The process begins on line 7, where you declare the string. The string is then built through lines 8–16, and the result is put into the `Text` property of the `lblResult` control on line 18. One symbol that likely seems strange is the `&=` that appears on lines 10–16. A new feature of Visual Basic .NET, this is a shortcut when adding to a string. The code on lines 10 and 11, for example,

```
10       sTemp &= "On " & txtDate.Text & _
11         " I started to program in Visual Basic.NET. "
```

is equivalent to:

```
10      sTemp = sTemp & "On " & txtDate.Text & _
11         " I started to program in Visual Basic.NET. "
```

You can use the &= operator to make your code shorter when you are adding more information to the end of an existing string.

After you have added the code, you're ready to build and experiment with this program. Select Build from the Build menu and then run the program. This should start a browser and load your page. Enter a few items and click the Write Story button to see your story. Figure 10.6 shows the Web Form in action.

FIGURE 10.6

Madlib *form in action.*

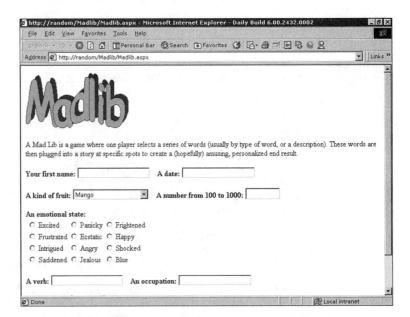

Using Advanced Web Forms Controls

Although it is easy to build a form with controls that are available as part of HTML, Web Forms become even more useful (and colorful, and easy to use) when you apply some of the more advanced controls, such as the Calendar, AdRotator, or Data controls. Although they are built using more simple controls, they make building user interfaces easier.

The Calendar control shows, strangely enough, a monthly calendar. This control allows the user to view and select dates more easily than by using a TextBox. In addition, by using the Calendar, you reduce the chance of the user entering a date in an invalid format. The `Calendar` control has a huge number of properties, however, most of them affect how the `Calendar` control is displayed. Just about everything visible on the control can be adjusted—the colors, whether the weekday or month names are abbreviated, and so on. Table 10.3 outlines a couple of the most useful properties of the `Calendar` control.

TABLE 10.3 Important Properties of the `Calendar` Control

Item	Property	Description
SelectedDate	Property	The date that will be returned by this control.
VisibleDate	Property	The date showing in the control. Although this is generally the same as the SelectedDate, it might be different, particularly if you are trying to set the date through code.

Let's update the `Madlib` project to use a `Calendar` control instead of the `TextBox` for the date entered. You can either edit the old form, or create a copy if you want to view both.

Delete the Date text box and add a `Calendar` control. At this point, you have the choice of either playing with the properties that affect the appearance of the `Calendar`, or being lazy and selecting the AutoFormat link that appears at the bottom of the Properties window when you select the `Calendar` control. I clicked the link and selected `Colorful 2`. (Why fuss and make something ugly when a professional already has made something look good—one of my programming strategies?) Set the `Calendar`'s `Name` property to `calDate`.

You will also need to change the code from Listings 10.1 and 10.2 slightly because of the change in the name of the control. Listings 10.3 and 10.4 show the new, changed code.

INPUT **LISTING 10.3** Altered Code for the Clear Button

```
 1  Private Sub cmdClear_Click( _
 2    ByVal sender As System.Object, _
 3    ByVal e As System.EventArgs) _
 4    Handles cmdClear.Click
 5      txtName.Text = ""
 6      calDate.SelectedDate = DateTime.Today
 7      txtVerb.Text = ""
 8      txtNumber.Text = ""
 9      txtOccupation.Text = ""
10      lblResult.Text = ""
11  End Sub
```

ANALYSIS Only a single line of code is changed. Because you no longer have the TextBox txtDate, you cannot set it to "". Instead, you can reset the Calendar to select today (DateTime.Today), as you do in line 6.

INPUT   **LISTING 10.4**   Altered Code for the Write Story Button

```
 1  Private Sub cmdWrite_Click( _
 2    ByVal sender As System.Object, _
 3    ByVal e As System.EventArgs) _
 4    Handles cmdWrite.Click
 5    'here's were we combine the selections
 6    'the user has made into the final story
 7      Dim sTemp As String
 8      sTemp = "Diary of " & txtName.Text & _
 9        " for " & DateTime.Today.ToString & "<br>"
10      sTemp &= "On " & calDate.SelectedDate & _
11        " I started to program in Visual Basic.NET. "
12      sTemp &= "I'm " & rlstEmotion.SelectedItem.Text & "! "
13      sTemp &= "I think I'm going to go out and " & txtVerb.Text
14      sTemp &= " my new " & txtNumber.Text
15      sTemp &= " PicoHertz " & cboFruit.SelectedItem.Text
16      sTemp &= " and become a " & txtOccupation.Text & "."
17      'the final story goes into the Label control
18      lblResult.Text = sTemp
19  End Sub
```

ANALYSIS Again, the only change in Listing 10.4 is on line 10. Rather than retrieving the date in the TextBox, the code retrieves the selected date from the Calendar with calDate.SelectedDate.

Doesn't this property thing make sense? That's why they didn't call it Visual Complex .NET.

Using the Validator Controls

When you are writing data entry forms for the Web, you often need to make certain that the form is filled out correctly. This could mean that certain fields are filled in, or that some fields are filled in, but with values that fit into a range. In the past, this could be done by writing code at either the server or the client. If the code is at the server, it might cause the information to be passed between the client and server needlessly. If you would rather place the code at the client, you run into the problem with cross-browser incapability.

A number of `Validator` controls come with Visual Basic .NET that make form validation much easier. The controls will either process the validation at the server, or at the client if the control determines that the browser is capable of it. Five validation controls are available in Visual Basic .NET:

- `RequiredFieldValidator`   Ensures that a field has been filled in. You can use it any time that you want to make certain that the user completes a form before submitting it.

- `CompareValidator`   Ensures either that two fields match, or that a field is compared to some value. In the first case, matching fields is useful when you want the user to enter his password twice. Comparing a field to some value is useful if you wanted the user to enter a positive number, or if the user's entry must be a particular type of information (for example, a date).

- `RangeValidator`   Ensures that the value entered in a field is within a range. The range could be between two values (for example, a starting and ending date), or two controls. For example, you might have one control where the user enters a minimum value, and a second for the maximum value. The Validator would then ensure that the value entered in a third control was between these two values. This is useful as part of a report, in which you might want the user to select a date that is within the range of information stored in a database.

- `RegularExpressionValidator`   Ensures that the value entered "looks" like it should. The value is compared to a Regular Expression. If it matches, the value is considered valid. This can be useful for values that must have a certain structure, such as phone numbers, ISBNs, or part numbers.

- `CustomValidator`   Allows you to add your own code to validate the field. The most flexible of the validators, this code could run either at the server or on the client. This would be useful when one of the other validators does not fit your purpose, or valid information must be determined through some process—for example, if the value must be one of a number of entries that are in a database.

In addition to these five controls, there is also the `ValidationSummary` control, which displays all the error messages from all the `Validator` controls on the same page. This is useful to provide a single location for all this information.

The five validation controls have a number of important properties in common. These relate to the control they monitor, and how the error is displayed. The most important of these properties are described in Table 10.4.

TABLE 10.4 Common Properties for the Validation Controls

Property	Description
ControlToValidate	This is the most important property of all the validation controls. It should be set to point to another control (by name) on the same form. This is the control that will be monitored by the validator. Use the drop-down in the Property window to select the monitored control.
ErrorMessage	This is the message to display if there is an error with the validator, for example, if the field is left blank. This should be enough information to allow the user to determine what is wrong, and how to fix the error.
Display	This is a rather odd property that defines how the Validator control appears on the Web page. By default, it is Static; however, there are two other choices, Dynamic or None. If the value is Static, the space taken up by the ErrorMessage will always be taken up, even if the ErrorMessage is not being shown. This is useful if you want to guarantee how your Web page will be laid out. Dynamic means that the control takes up no space until the ErrorMessage property is shown. This is useful if you don't want blank spaces on your form. Finally, if this property is set to None, the ErrorMessage will never be shown. This is really only useful in conjunction with the ValidationSummary control (which will show the error).

You can use some of these controls to finish the Madlib sample application. You can use the RequiredFieldValidator control to ensure that the user has entered information in certain fields, and the RangeValidator to make certain that an appropriate number has been entered in the txtNumber field. Finally, you can summarize all errors with a ValidationSummary control.

Again, either copy the old project or form, or open the existing project to edit it. You'll add the Validator controls to this existing form.

Drag a RequiredFieldValidator next to each of the remaining TextBox controls (txtName, txtNumber, txtVerb and txtOccupation). Add a RangeValidator next to the RequiredFieldValidator you added to the txtNumber field. Finally, add a ValidationSummary control on a line of its own between the buttons and the lblResult control. Set the properties of each of these controls as shown in Table 10.5.

TABLE 10.5 Properties for the Validator Controls in the `Madlib` Form

Control	Property	Value
RequiredFieldValidator	ID	reqName
	ControlToValidate	txtName
	ErrorMessage	Please enter a name
RequiredFieldValidator	(ID)	reqNumber
	ControlToValidate	txtNumber
	ErrorMessage	Please enter a number
	Display	Dynamic
RangeValidator	(ID)	rngNumber
	ControlToValidate	txtNumber
	ErrorMessage	Please enter a number from 100 and 1000
	Display	Dynamic
	Type	Integer
	MaximumValue	1000
	MinimumValue	100
RequiredFieldValidator	(ID)	reqVerb
	ControlToValidate	txtVerb
	ErrorMessage	Please enter a verb
	Display	Dynamic
RequiredFieldValidator	(ID)	reqOccupation
	ControlToValidate	txtOccupation
	ErrorMessage	Please enter an occupation
	Display	Dynamic
ValidationSummary	(ID)	valSummary

10

You should take a moment to describe the three properties of the `RangeValidator` you haven't assigned previously. Although the `MaximumValue` and `MinimumValue` *should* make sense in terms of something called a `RangeValidator`, the `Type` property is not so obvious. Because the `RangeValidator` might be used to test a number of different types of values (such as integers, financial values, or dates), the `Type` property identifies the type of information to compare. It can have one of the following values:

- `String` The default, this causes the control to test whether the value is alphabetically between the two extremes.

- `Integer`   Compares the value to the two extremes to make certain that the value fits. Only `Integer` (whole) values are used.

- `Double`   The same as with `Integer` but includes the decimal part of the value and extremes.

- `Currency`   The same as with `Integer` but includes the first four decimals of the value.

- `Date`   Compares the values as though they were dates, so a value of August 27, 1964, would be allowed with a range between November 23, 1963, and April 1, 1986.

Now on to why the `Validator` controls are so useful. To make them work, you don't have to add any additional code. Build and view the new Web page (see Figure 10.7). Try leaving some fields blank, and delete the 500 that is the default value for the number field. You should see red error messages appearing on the form. If not, try clicking the Write Story button. You should see something like the form that appears in Figure 10.8. Try entering a value outside of the range for the number field. Finally, enter in correct values for all the fields and select the Write Story button. All error messages should go away, and our story should be written.

FIGURE 10.7

`Madlib` *form showing validation controls.*

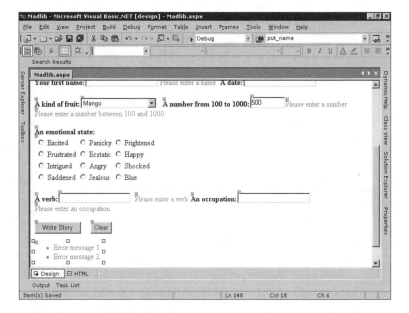

FIGURE 10.8

Madlib *form showing*
validation errors.

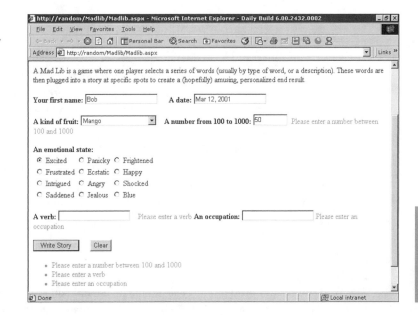

10

Summary

Web applications are becoming more and more important as time goes on, and Web
Forms make creating them incredibly easy. They enable you to use the same techniques
that you would use to build a desktop application to build a Web application that would
work in any Web browser. By moving the code back to the server (that you can control),
you get the best of both worlds that Web developers have striven for—a rich user interface and cross-browser capabilities.

Although simply re-creating a Windows-like experience would be good enough for most,
Web Forms go one step further, helping you more easily create validation routines and
complex controls.

Tomorrow, you will start examining object-oriented programming. You will look at what
OOP has to do with Visual Basic .NET, and with programming in general. You will see
that you have been looking at objects all along, in the form of the .NET Framework, as
well as the forms and controls you have been using.

Q&A

Q. Do I need to have a Web server available to use Web Forms?

A. Yes, Web applications need a Web server that knows about ASP.NET, such as
Internet Information Server (IIS). IIS comes with a free Web server that is part of
Windows NT Server or Windows 2000 Server.

Q. Can I use Windows 98 or Windows Me to create and deploy Web applications?

A. These operating systems either come with, or have available, Personal Web Server (PWS). You cannot use PWS to create Web applications. Windows 9x can be used for creating Web applications, but are not great platforms for deploying them. You must create Web applications using IIS on either Windows NT 4 Server or Windows 2000.

Q. How can I learn more about writing HTML?

A. Although Web Forms make knowing HTML almost optional, having a good working knowledge of HTML will help. Take a look at one of the fine books out on the market (*Sams Teach Yourself HTML in 21 Days* would be a good start) to learn more.

Workshop

The Workshop is designed to help you anticipate possible questions, review what you've learned, and get you thinking about how to put your knowledge into practice. The answers to the quiz are in Appendix A, "Answers to Quizzes/Exercises."

Quiz

1. If you can simply add text to a Web page by typing, why do you need `Label` controls?
2. What controls help you to navigate between pages in a Web application?
3. How can I display graphics on a Web Form?

Exercise

Create a registration application. This new Web application should allow the user to enter

- His name. Must be filled in.
- A username to use on your site (Alias). Must be filled in and no more than 10 characters long.
- A new password (remember to keep the password a secret). The user should enter his password twice to make certain he has entered it correctly. Both fields must be filled in and match.

After the information has been entered, the user should click a button. The information will then be shown to the user.

DAY 11

Introduction to Databases

Computers are good at working with data, especially large amounts of data, and, throughout the history of these devices, most programs have been written to do just that. Even today, with computers being used for an enormous variety of tasks, data processing is still part of almost every business application, and many non-business applications. In today's lesson, you will learn about databases, including

- Important database terms
- Basic SQL
- Database design tips
- Quick introduction to data in .NET

A Database Is the Solution to All of Life's Problems

Over the past few years, one of the authors of this book has become increasingly confused about his CD collection. Just recently, he realized that he was almost always playing just one or two particular CDs because he didn't really know what else he had, or, if he knew what he had, he didn't know where it was. All his CD collection concerns turned into reality when he decided to tidy up his large pile of discs and try to organize them in some semblance of order.

Now, organizing CDs into a single binder is not as simple a task as it might seem because there are many different ways to arrange them. Perhaps by artist would be best, (making sure that Barenaked Ladies comes before Boney M), or by category, dividing the discs into groups for pop, rock, Christmas music, and more. There are so many decisions to be made. Should Brian Adams be sorted into the A's (using last name), or into the B's (using the first name)? What about new CDs? After you have placed that same Brian Adams CD into one of the first few spots in your CD binder, what if he comes out with a new album? Do you have to move all the other CDs forward to make room, or should you just stick it at the end and ruin your nice alphabetical positioning system? In the end, it might be simpler to decide not to buy any more music, which seems to have been the choice taken by the author's parents in the early '70s.

The need to make a decision became obvious when, during the aforementioned CD tidying, your friendly neighborhood author came upon two (2!) "Queen: Classic Hits, Volume 1" CDs. Now—and this nothing against Queen—, no one needs two of the same greatest hits CD, no matter how much he likes to listen to "Bohemian Rhapsody." Something had to be done soon.

The Decision Is Made

All the choices ended up being too much stress, and the author came to a startling conclusion: The CD information should go into a computer program! Actually, it isn't all that startling—he comes to that conclusion about a great many things (perhaps too many, if you ask his wife or one of his few remaining friends). The idea of storing data in a computer is not a new idea though; in fact, it always has been one of the most common purposes of computer systems.

You can organize data in many ways, but the advantage of using a computer to do the organizing is that, after that data is in the system, it can be viewed in a variety of different ways. This removes many of the problems faced by the poor author in the previously described scenario. If a new CD has to be entered, it can be added at the end of the data file, but will be displayed in its proper location based on the view selected. If you want to view CDs by artist, just sort the data by an Artist field. If you would prefer to see them sorted by CD Title, resorting is easily done.

In this case, let's assume all the data has been entered into a text file on the computer, with each line of the file representing one CD. Possible fields and entries would look like this:

```
ArtistName, ArtistFirstName, ArtistLastName, CDTitle, CDReleaseYear,
➡ MusicCategories
Sting, Sting, -, Brand New Day, 2000, Pop
Queen, Queen, -, Classic Hits Volume 1, 1987, Rock/Pop/Best Of
Sting, Sting, -, Fields Of Gold, 1994, Pop/Best Of
```

> **Note**
>
> In many databases, spaces are not allowed in table or field names, so these field names have been modified to avoid compatibility issues.

The first line of this file, called a *header row*, indicates which individual pieces of information are being stored in each row. A new line marks the start of each individual album. Commas are used to separate the fields, making this a *comma-separated* (or *comma-delimitated*) file. As simple as it is, this file is a database and could be used by a computer program that tracked albums. Because this is a database, you can use it to learn some of the terms that you will be using from here on to refer to the different parts of a database:

NEW TERM Each CD listed in this file is an individual *record*, sometimes referred to as a *row* because records are often stored or displayed as separate lines of information.

NEW TERM Within each record, multiple pieces of information about each CD are being tracked and each one of those items is referred to as a *field* (in this case, the ArtistName, CDTitle, CDReleaseYear, and others). Like records, fields are often called by another name, columns, because they are often stored and displayed as individual columns of information.

NEW TERM The entire group of records (all with the same set of fields) is called a *table*, and a database can contain many of these tables, although the example in today's lesson currently consists of only one.

The Move to a Real Database

Okay, so now you have all the terms you need to describe your little database, which contains a single table of CD records that you will call Disc. (I hope that my use of the term "record" to describe both musical releases and a part of a database won't get confusing.) With your terms and database established, how do you go about working with this data from your computer programs?

As mentioned earlier, the sample database is just a text file, and it is relatively easy to read a text file. (Check out Day 4, "Controlling Flow in Programs," for an example of reading from a file, or Day 17, "Using the .NET Framework," for more details on the wonderful file reading classes in the Framework.) However, as the example stands now, you would have to parse each line of the data yourself and handle all the columns. Even if you could read the file, you would want to be able to manipulate it in a few standard ways, including finding specific records, adding new records, deleting records, and modifying all or part of a record. To implement all this functionality, you would be writing a lot of code, but you won't have to handle any of these things if you place your data into a database format such as Access or SQL Server. These database management systems can handle storing your information and can also respond to requests to retrieve and modify that data, managing all the details of storage and file layout for you. Database systems possess a wide variety of features, but the common service that these systems provide to handle the details of data storage and to relieve you of all physical interaction with the data.

An Introduction to SQL

After data is stored in a database system, you still need to be able to manipulate it from the program, but you no longer have to handle all the details yourself. To provide a common language for accessing databases, SQL (Structure Query Language) was developed. This language contains commands for manipulating records in database tables, and is supported to some degree in almost every piece of database management software available. Many different commands are available in SQL, but the ones I will be covering here handle

- Retrieving data records
- Adding new records
- Modifying existing records
- Deleting records

Retrieving Records with the SELECT Statement

In SQL, you use the SELECT statement to retrieve data from a database. This statement, in its basic form, looks like this:

```
SELECT <field names> from <Table>
```

Using the CD database as an example, if you wanted to retrieve all the CD titles along with their artists' names, you could execute this SQL statement:

```
SELECT ArtistName, CDTitle FROM Disc
```

This would return a set of data with two fields and one row returned for every record in the Disc table. Alternatively, if you wanted to obtain all the columns in a table, you can use * instead of a list of fields, producing a statement like this:

SYNTAX ▼

```
SELECT * FROM Disc
```

Although you are likely to see SQL statements like this in many examples and even in applications, it is not recommended practice to retrieve all fields at once. You always want to retrieve the smallest possible amount of information, and that is not usually all the fields. Always be careful not to hurt the long-term performance of your code just to obtain a savings in the time it takes to type in your program.

Do	Don't
DO specify each field you want to retrieve in a SQL statement.	**DON'T** use * to indicate all fields, unless you are sure that you need every single field that exists in the table and any fields that might get added later.
DO retrieve the smallest amount of data or number of fields and records possible to provide the best performance.	

Ordering the Results

The order of the records returned has not been specified in the two queries shown so far, but you can add a clause to the SQL statement to set the sort order. This clause, ORDER BY, takes a list of fields, allowing you to specify more than one field to use for sorting. The following SQL statement retrieves the ArtistName and CDTitle fields from all the records of the Disc table, sorting them first by ArtistName, and then by CDTitle within each artist's set of records:

```
SELECT ArtistName, CDTitle FROM Disc ORDER BY ArtistName, CDTitle
```

By default, a field specified in the ORDER BY clause will be sorted in ascending order (increasing in value, or alphabetical position, towards the end of the records returned), A to Z if the field contains text. If you want the sort order to be reversed, descending from Z to A, then specify a DESC keyword next to the part of the ORDER BY clause that you want sorted in reverse. The following example will sort by Artist in reverse alphabetical order, and then by CDTitle in the regular order.

```
SELECT ArtistName, CDTitle FROM Disc ORDER BY ArtistName Desc, CDTitle
```

The default order, ascending, can also be specified explicitly using the ASC keyword just as the Desc keyword is used. The following SQL statement has the exact same effect as the previous one, but is more explicit about what is happening.

```
SELECT ArtistName, CDTitle
FROM Disc
ORDER BY ArtistName Desc, CDTitle ASC
```

11

Do	**Don't**
DO specify ASC if you are also using DESC; it will help avoid confusion.	**DON'T** sort on any more fields than needed because it will impact performance.

Specifying Criteria

All the SELECT statements shown so far have retrieved all the records from the Disc table, but what if you only want to retrieve a certain record or a set of records based on certain criteria? Another clause can be added to a SELECT statement to take care of this, the WHERE clause. In the WHERE clause, you can specify as many criteria as you want to restrict which rows will be returned. Using this feature, this SELECT statement will only retrieve CDs by Sting:

```
SELECT CDTitle, CDReleaseYear FROM Disc
WHERE ArtistName = 'Sting'
```

Note that the field used to restrict the results was not one of the ones returned; you can use any field you want. It is possible to combine multiple criteria using the operators AND/OR and to use parentheses to determine how these criteria will be applied. To retrieve those discs that were released after 1984 and had an artist name of Sting, and those that were before 1984 by The Police, the following SELECT statement could be used:

```
SELECT CDTitle, CDReleaseYear FROM Disc
WHERE (ArtistName= 'Sting' AND CDReleaseYear => 1984)
      OR (ArtistName= 'The Police' AND CDReleaseYear < 1984)
```

This query raises an issue that has always plagued databases: Should a disc be entered with an ArtistName field value of Police or Police, The? I will dive into this and other common database issues, along with the best ways I know to solve them, later in today's lesson under "Common Database Problems and Solutions."

Adding New Records

The order in which today's lesson covers these SQL statements is a little backwards. You learned how to retrieve data from the database before you learned how to put it in! Although some databases are read-only, in most cases new records are added to tables on a regular basis. The SQL command used to add these new records is called INSERT and follows this basic format:

```
INSERT INTO <Table> (field 1, field 2,...) VALUES (value 1, value 2,...)
```

Returning to the CD library example, you could use an INSERT statement to add a new disc:

```
INSERT INTO Disc (ArtistName, ArtistFirstName, ArtistLastName, CDTitle,
➡CDReleaseYear, MusicCategories) VALUES ('Lenny Kravitz', 'Lenny',
➡ 'Kravitz', 'Greatest Hits', 2000, 'Rock/Pop/Best Of')
```

Notice the single quote marks use around all the values except the CDReleaseYear. These marks are required to surround any text values used in the SQL statements to distinguish between the value and the SQL itself. Because the CDReleaseYear is not a text value, it does not have to be placed into quotes.

It is possible to skip the list of field names, as long as your list of values is in the correct order. But, this is another example of how you can save a little bit of time in code entry, but produce code that is harder to maintain and more likely to break in the future.

Modifying Records

SQL provides the UPDATE statement for making modifications to existing records, allowing you to change one or more fields on any number of records at once. This statement has the following basic syntax:

```
UPDATE <Table Name> SET <field name> = <new value>
```

▼ SYNTAX

As with the SELECT statement used earlier, the UPDATE statement can have a WHERE clause. Without such a clause, the statement will perform its update on all the records in the table. So, this statement

```
UPDATE Disc SET CDTitle='New Title'
```

would set every single CDTitle field to 'New Title', which is likely not the intended result. Although you will often be updating only a single record, it is useful to be able to modify multiple records with a single UPDATE statement. New values set using this statement can be based on the existing contents of the field. As an example, consider this update on a fictional table that gives every employee a 10% raise:

```
UPDATE Employee SET Salary = Salary * 1.1
```

In most cases, though, you will want to specify a WHERE clause to narrow the affected records down to a smaller selection or even to a single item. The following SQL statement updates all the Barenaked Ladies records in the Disc table to change their MusicCategories value to Pop":

```
UPDATE Disc SET MusicCategories = 'Pop' WHERE ArtistName = 'Barenaked Ladies'
```

This sort of re-evaluating categories and groupings in a database is something you might want to do from time to time to prevent confusion.

Although today's examples have been simple, the UPDATE statement is capable of more complex actions. For instance, you can update multiple fields at once, separating each assignment with a comma, and you can use as complicated a WHERE clause as you want.

11

```
UPDATE Disc SET ArtistName = 'Sting',
                ArtistFirstName= 'Gordon',
                ArtistLastName = 'Sumner'
WHERE ArtistName = 'Sting' OR ArtistName = 'Mr. Sting'
```

Removing Unwanted Records

You have retrieved, added, and modified your records, leaving one basic operation, deletion. SQL provides a DELETE statement that uses simple syntax:

```
DELETE <Table> WHERE <criteria>
```

In this case, as with UPDATE, the WHERE clause is optional but important because without it, you will delete all the records in the specified table.

In the Disc table, you could use this statement to remove a certain selection of records, or, more commonly, to delete a single record. The SQL statement shown here would remove all the Gordon Lightfoot discs (except one):

```
DELETE Disc
WHERE ArtistFirstName = 'Gordon'
      AND ArtistLastName = 'Lightfoot'
      AND CDTitle != 'Summertime Dream'
```

Where to Go from Here with SQL

SQL is really important, but it is also a large and complex topic all to itself. You will be learning more bits and pieces of SQL throughout the rest of today's lesson and the rest of this book, but these samples do not provide complete coverage of the topic. Almost every database product uses SQL to some degree, and there are a number of books that are completely devoted to this single language. A couple of particularly good ones are

- *Sams Teach Yourself SQL in 10 Minutes* from Sams Publishing
- *SQL in a Nutshell* from O'Reilly

Another good source, and one that you likely already have, is the materials in the Microsoft Solution Developers Network (MSDN) library, which was installed as part of your Visual Studio installation. Try searching on the SQL commands described earlier to track down the SQL reference section of the MSDN library. If you want to practice your SQL outside of the examples you will be doing in this book, you should be able to do so with whatever database program(s) you have available to you. If you have SQL Server installed, run the Query Analyzer (see Figure 11.1), which is one of the tools that come with SQL Server and is available as an icon in the SQL Server program menu folder. This tool is designed to enable you to execute queries and view the results, although you should be careful running anything other than SELECT queries until you are a bit more comfortable with specifying WHERE clauses.

FIGURE 11.1

*The Query Analyzer
allows you to execute
SQL statements
against your database,
but its true power lies
in its capability to ana-
lyze the performance
and structure of your
queries.*

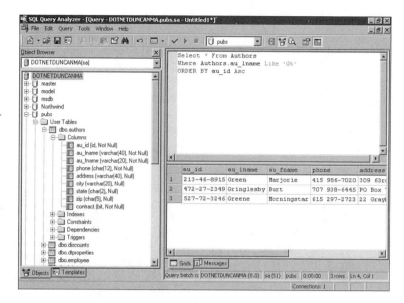

Common Database Problems and Solutions

Database software will keep track of your tables, fields, and records, but how you structure the data is completely up to you, and is therefore where most of the problems occur.
There are many different ways in which you can organize the same set of data, but only a
few of those ways will work well in a database system. The goal is to produce a database
that is efficient for searching but that makes it difficult to introduce inconsistent data.
Inconsistency is the biggest problem of databases. If different parts of the database disagree, the data is unreliable. Consider a sample table, in which you have intentionally
made a few of the more common mistakes. In this table, it is easy for you to create
inconsistent data because it is not structured to prevent or even minimize these issues. I
will walk through each of the main problems with such a table and show you how to
avoid the same problems in your own databases.

Update Inconsistencies

Suppose that a user decides to update a row in the Disc table because the Artist value is
incorrect. Perhaps Sting was specified when it was supposed to be Bruce Willis. The user
could execute this SQL statement:

```
UPDATE Disc SET ArtistName = 'Bruce Willis'
WHERE ArtistName = 'Sting' and CDTitle = 'The Return Of Bruno'
```

This is a perfectly good SQL statement, but, if the original row of data looked like this:

```
ArtistName, ArtistFirstName, ArtistLastName, CDTitle, CDRelaseYear,
➡MusicCategories
```

```
Sting, Gordon, Sumner, The Return Of Bruno, 1986, Rock/Pop
```

then it will now be this:

```
Bruce Willis, Gordon, Sumner, The Return Of Bruno, 1986, Rock/Pop
```

`ArtistName` reflects the correct information, but `ArtistFirstName` and `ArtistLastName` do not, and that is an inconsistency. This could have been avoided by updating all three fields at once, but that relies upon the user or the software to ensure that the data is consistent. You want to do everything you can at a database-design level to prevent inconsistency.

Do	**Don't**
DO structure your database to avoid inconsistency.	DON'T rely on your users, including your own programs, to work with the data exactly as you expect.

Another common inconsistency that can occur when using a database structure like the Disc table is that several different variations can exist in data that should be identical. Here are three rows from the Disc table:

```
Barenaked Ladies, - , - , Maroon, 2000, Pop
The Barenaked Ladies, - , - , Gordon, 1993, Pop
Barenaked Ladies, - , - , Stunt, 1999, Rock/Pop
```

A SQL query designed to find all the albums by the Barenaked Ladies would likely be written like this:

```
SELECT * FROM Disc WHERE ArtistName = 'Barenaked Ladies'
```

This code would return the first and the last of the three rows listed above, but wouldn't find the CD named "Gordon." This wouldn't result in any error shown to the user, or anything like that. The user just wouldn't get the correct information.

The third problem regarding these Artist fields occurs if an artist changes his name. (This situation is not common in music, but if you were dealing with company departments or product names in other databases, it would be much more of an issue.) Suppose that an artist, let's pick "Prince" at random, changes his name from the simple word "Prince" to an unpronounceable symbol (which, sadly, isn't part of the ASCII code and therefore you won't be able to enter it into your database). You would have to update every single record that currently has Prince's name in it. Of course, this is a single statement:

```
UPDATE Disc SET ArtistName = 'The Artist Formerly Known As Prince'
WHERE ArtistName = 'Prince'
```

Assuming no one has misspelled Prince anywhere, this SQL statement would update all the required records. Once again though, you are relying on the user or the software knowing that they need to make multiple changes. It is possible that they would not use an UPDATE statement like the preceding one. They might just change a single entry to the new value, instead of all the Prince discs, making the database once again inconsistent. It gets even worse when you find out that you have to change the records all back to "Prince" in the end!

All these issues are a result of one problem in the structure of the database—the artist information is stored with the record for each and every disc, even though the artist's name is actually an independent set of data. To prevent the problems described above, you should break the artist information out into its own table, and store only a single value with the disc to link the two tables together. For this value, you could use the ArtistName field, but that will cause you trouble if that value ever changes.

It is always best if you choose a value that is certain not to be modified unless the linked record, in the Artist table, is deleted. Looking at the current set of artist information—the values for ArtistName, ArtistFirstName, and ArtistLastName—you do not have anything that is completely guaranteed not to change. Hence, you will add a special field just for this purpose. This is often the case, an additional field has to be created purely to act as a unique identifier for a record, and the most common method is to create a field that contains an auto-incrementing number. Adding this field to your set of artist information, you get the following Artist table:

```
ArtistID, ArtistName, ArtistFirstName, ArtistLastName
1, Sting, Gordon, Sumner
2, The Barenaked Ladies, - , -
3, Bon Jovi, - , -
4, Queen, - , -
5, The Police, - , -
...
45, Janet Jackson, Janet, Jackson
```

Each record of the Disc table still needs to be associated with an artist, so you will add a field to that table that will contain an ArtistID value for each record.

The Disc table would now look like this:

```
ArtistID, CDTitle, CDReleaseYear, MusicCategories
1, Brand New Day, 2000, Pop
4, Greatest Hits, 1988, Rock/Pop
...
```

The ArtistID is called a key because it is being used to identify an individual entity. In the Artist table, where the ArtistID uniquely identifies a specific artist, this field is referred to as the *primary key*. In the Disc table, it is called a *foreign key* because it is being used as a link back into a different table (see Figure 11.2). A table will usually contain several foreign keys, linking it to other tables, but a table has only one primary key (although more than one field can be used together to form a primary key).

FIGURE 11.2

The Artist and Disc tables contain key fields that link them together.

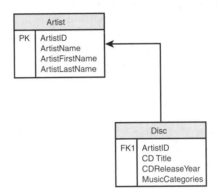

A *key* is a value, generally a field, that identifies an entity, such as a student ID, author name, or Social Security number. When one field of a table uniquely identifies each record of that table, it is called the *primary key* of the table. A *primary key* from one table that is placed into a field of another table to link the two entities is referred to in the latter table as a *foreign key*.

NEW TERM

When two tables are linked through the use of primary and foreign keys, they are said to be *related*.

NEW TERM

By moving the Artist field data into a separate table, the statements required to add and retrieve information will have to change. For adding data, you will have to do two INSERTs, one into the Artist table and one into the Disc table, but the INSERT into the Artist table will occur only once per artist, not for every single disc. The creation of separate, linked tables has removed the issues discussed previously, but has created a new way to introduce inconsistent data—invalid foreign keys. If a user or program removes an Artist field value, then all the discs that reference that ArtistID will suddenly be referencing a record in the Artist table that does not exist. I will discuss how to deal with this problem a little later in today's lesson under the section "Referential Integrity." The means of retrieving data you need from the database has also changed, as the information you want is now spread across two tables. The methods you will use to get at this data will also be covered later today, under the section "Joins: Querying Multiple Tables at Once."

Place Inconsistency Versus Incorrect Data

In the new table layout, the Artist information is stored in the Artist table, separate from the CD information, which is stored in Disc. The goal of this separation is to prevent inconsistent information. You want to avoid situations in which two different parts of the database disagree on the same piece of data. You are not trying to avoid incorrect data, although it is certainly a problem.

It is not really a database design issue if the First Name field for Sting is set to George instead of his real name Gordon, as long as the entire database is consistent and is storing only the one value George. This might seem a little odd because incorrect data is pretty important, but the goal of database design is to avoid introducing errors due to the data layout. The software and its users can concern themselves with avoiding incorrect data.

Multivalued Fields

One of the fields, MusicCategories, could contain more than one value at one time, in this format: Rock/Pop. This type of field has to be removed from your database, or you will have a wide variety of problems with it. The first problem occurs when the user is attempting to retrieve data based on information in this field:

```
SELECT * FROM Disc Where MusicCategories = 'Rock'
```

This would bring back discs with a MusicCategories value of Rock, but not those with Rock/Pop, Best Of/Rock, or anything else that is more than just the single category. You have to know a bit about the objective of the database. In this case, the point of the MusicCategories field was to group the CDs by one or more types of music. If the user wanted to find all of his pop discs or all of his discs that were both rock and "best of" collections (is it Rock/Best Of, or Best Of/Rock?), the resulting problems would make this categorization fairly useless. Updating the data in a multivalued field is almost as hard. You end up having to add your new value onto the existing one, making sure that it was not already there! Things get even more complicated if you ever decide to rename a category, changing Pop to Popular perhaps, a task that would be extremely difficult to do using an UPDATE statement.

To fix this multivalued statement, and avoid all the problems associated with it, you will separate the data into another table. Unlike with the Artist information though, a single, new table cannot handle the relationship between the categories and the discs. Each artist can be associated with any number of discs (or none at all). This relationship is called *one-to-many* or more correctly *zero-to-many*. The disc and category relationship is more complex; a single category can be associated with many discs *and* a single disc can be associated with many categories. This produces a many-to-many relationship which you

11

can model using two new tables. One table will hold the categories themselves, another table will link discs to categories (see Figure 11.3).

FIGURE 11.3

To model a many-to-many relationship requires three tables: the two entities that are related and a special table that exists only to connect them.

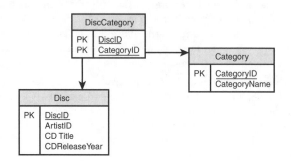

The resulting tables follow a pattern that you can always use to represent a many-to-many relationship. I will detail how to query against both the one-to-many and many-to-many relationships in the following section "Joins: Querying Multiple Tables at Once."

Joins: Querying Multiple Tables at Once

Now that you have separated your data nicely into multiple tables, it will take more than the simple SELECT queries you have done earlier to get the data you want. You have several distinct tables now, but each of them is related to the other through the use of *key* fields. Using those same key fields, you can now join the data from one table with the corresponding data from another table, or tables, and produce a single set of output. There are a variety of ways to form the SELECT statement when you want to work with multiple tables, but here is one sample:

```
SELECT Artist.ArtistName, Disc.CDTitle FROM Artist, Disc
WHERE Artist.ArtistID = Disc.ArtistID
```

```
Sting                Nothing Like The Sun
Sting                Brand New Day
The Barenaked Ladies    Maroon
The Barenaked Ladies    Gordon
    ...
```

> **Note**
>
> When you have more than one table involved in a SELECT, it is possible for the same field name to exist in multiple tables. In such a case, you need to specify the field as table.field in your SELECT statement to ensure that the database understands which field is intended. You can use this syntax at any time though, even when working with only one table.

This statement tells the database to retrieve all the records from the Disc table and, for each of those records, to do a lookup (using the `ArtistID` stored in the Disc table) against the Artist table for the corresponding `ArtistName`. This sounds fairly labor intensive, but, luckily for you, all of the actual work is handled by the database, and it can do this type of work very, very quickly. So, although you carefully removed the `ArtistName` from the Disc table, you can still produce the same output results by joining the Disc and Artist tables.

NEW TERM   Linking two tables in a query to retrieve related data from both is called *joining*.

The last SQL statement used a `WHERE` clause to join the two tables, which will certainly work, but it is not the preferred way to perform joins. Instead, you will learn a new syntax in which you can specify the join information as a part of the `FROM` clause in your SQL. Redoing the previous statement to use the correct syntax will produce

```
SELECT Artist.ArtistName, Disc.CDTitle
FROM Disc INNER JOIN Artist ON (Artist.ArtistID = Disc.ArtistID)
```

This statement will produce the same results as the earlier example with the `WHERE` clause, and is referred to as an *inner join*. It is possible to specify `Disc JOIN Artist`, and the "skipped" `INNER` is assumed, but Access won't accept this shorter form.

Inner Versus Outer Joins

With an inner join, the query returns only records in which a match is found between the two tables. In the example, this means that if an artist was listed in the Artist table, but did not have *any* corresponding records in the Disc table, that artist would not be part of the result. If that is not the desired result, if instead you wanted every single artist listed in the Artist table in your results (even if you didn't have any discs by some of the artists), you could use an outer join. Outer joins link the tables using the same information, but, if they cannot find any matching values in one of the tables, they still bring back the fields from the first table and null (empty) values for the fields that are in the second table. You can precede the `OUTER` keyword with `LEFT` or `RIGHT` to specify in which direction the join should work.

Wondering which table is first, and which is second? Well, if you specify `RIGHT OUTER JOIN`, then the first table is considered the table on the right of the `JOIN` statement. If you specify `LEFT OUTER JOIN`, then the table on the left is the first table.

Let's assume that, in the sample database, you had the artist Limp Bizkit in the Artist table, but you didn't have any records in the Disc table performed by this artist. Now, the `INNER JOIN` shown in the following code would produce a set of records, but the artist Limp Bizkit wouldn't be mentioned in the results.

11

```
SELECT Artist.ArtistName, Disc.CDTitle
FROM Disc INNER JOIN Artist ON (Artist.ArtistID = Disc.ArtistID)
ORDER BY Artist.ArtistName
```

On the other hand, if you used an OUTER JOIN as shown in the following, the ArtistName field would come back with Limp Bizkit in it. Because no corresponding record would be found in the Disc table, CDTitle would be null for that record.

```
SELECT Artist.ArtistName, Disc.CDTitle
FROM Disc LEFT OUTER JOIN Artist ON (Artist.ArtistID = Disc.ArtistID)
```

As you have seen in the examples, the results of an inner join can be misleading because they include only those values in which a match was found between the two tables. Still, this type of join is suitable for most queries.

Many-To-Many Relationships

To model the many-to-many relationship of CDs to categories, you ended up with three distinct tables: Disc, Category, and a third designed just for this relationship, called DiscCategory. To query against these tables, you will need to use two joins—one join between Disc and DiscCategory, and one between DiscCategory and Category. For example, the SQL to retrieve all CDs that have been assigned to the Pop category is shown here:

```
SELECT Disc.CDTitle
FROM Category INNER JOIN
    (Disc INNER JOIN DiscCategory ON Disc.DiscID = DiscCategory.DiscID)
    ON Category.CategoryID = DiscCategory.CategoryID
WHERE Category.Category = "Pop"
```

When you have multiple related tables, you can use nested join statements like the ones shown in the preceding code, in which one table is actually being joined to the result of the join of two other tables.

Referential Integrity

When you have multiple tables, you have the possibility for inconsistencies. As discussed earlier, if an artist is referenced by their ID in one or more Disc records, then you will have inconsistent data if that artist is deleted. To avoid this, you make the database aware of the links between your tables by defining the keys and the relationship (see Figure 11.4). When the database knows about the relationships in your system, it can enforce them by preventing the deletion of a record if it has related records in other tables. In your specific system, placing the relationships into the database would prevent (the database would return an error) a user from deleting a record from the Artist table if the Disc table contained any records with that Artist's ID.

FIGURE 11.4

Inside your database program, whether that is Access or SQL Server, you can create relationships that the database can then enforce.

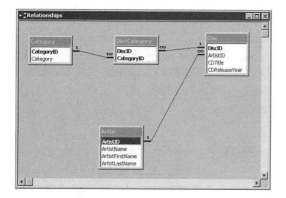

Creating Primary Keys

In the example, you have ended up with numeric keys for all of the tables (`ArtistID`, `CategoryID`, `DiscID`), but what you have not discussed is that you have to obtain or generate those keys whenever you insert a new record. There are several different ways in which you can handle this requirement: Built-in feature of the database, calculated at insert time, using GUIDs instead of simple numbers, or a system to manage and increment keys called a key manager.

Database Feature

The first method for managing keys is built in to many databases, a special type of field that automatically increments its value when a new row is added. These fields are always numeric; they can be set to increment by a set amount, usually 1, and to start at a specific value, usually 1 as well. This is a good way to handle keys because the database will handle all the work, but, under certain circumstances, an auto-generating key can cause problems. For example, if you had a new CD to add to the collection, and that CD was by an artist who was not in your database, you would have to do two INSERTs—one into the Artist table and then one into the Disc table. Using auto-generated keys, you wouldn't insert a value for ArtistID for the first insert; instead, one would be automatically generated. However, for the second insert (into Disc), you would need that new ArtistID value to link your new CD with the new artist. Using just SQL, that ID is not returned to you.

You could do another query on the database, but you would have to use fields such as ArtistName to find them again, and this would be prone to error. This problem is one reason why you need an alternative method of obtaining keys; another reason is discussed later in the section "Globally Unique Identifiers (GUIDs)."

11

Calculated Keys

As an alternative to database-generated keys, you can use SQL statements to determine the next ID in the sequence before doing the actual INSERT. This involves the use of a special type of SQL operator called an *aggregate*, which retrieves a computed value based on all the fields found by a SELECT clause. There are several of these aggregates, but you will use one named MAX, which returns the highest value for a field out of all the records selected.

To determine the next ID, you could execute this statement (using the Artist table as an example):

```
SELECT MAX(ArtistID) FROM Artist
```

This statement would return a single record with a single field containing the highest ID value currently in the table. Add one to this value and you have the next ID, which you go on to use in an INSERT.

This approach, although valid in some circumstances, has two main problems. The first problem occurs because more than one program could be running against this database at once—it is possible that two or more users could be adding artists at the same time. In such a situation, it would be possible for additional users to have executed the first SELECT before the first user had executed the INSERT, therefore all these users would have obtained the same ID value.

This problem can be avoided through the use of transactions, another one of those database concepts that I won't be going into in today's lesson.

The second problem is not so easily avoided. This problem occurs when one or more records from the end of the table (the highest IDs) are deleted. Any new records added will first select the MAX(ArtistID) and will be given ID values previously assigned to the deleted records. In a system in which ID values are intended to be unique, having different records share the same ID at different points in time is not always advisable.

Globally Unique Identifiers (GUIDs)

In some situations, an incrementing key—whether created by the database or through your own calculations—is not suitable. One example of when this would be a case with distributed databases, in which multiple copies of the database exist and are merged back together on a regular basis. Inserts can occur in any of the copies. If you used an incrementing key, then any time inserts occurred at more than one location, you would produce duplicated IDs. A solution is to use some form of randomly generated ID that is random enough so that IDs could be created at multiple locations with little or no chance of duplication. The generally accepted method for creating random IDs is to use a GUID

(Globally Unique Identifier), a 128-bit random number generated by the database, or by the operating system. A GUID is sufficiently random to use in a distributed database scenario.

Key Manager

The final ID creation scheme I will discuss is suitable for systems that are not distributed (see the previous section on GUIDs), but for which you do need to obtain the key immediately upon adding the record. (This makes a database-generated key problematic.) This method, called a Key Manager system, uses an additional table in your database to hold the current highest ID values for all of your other tables (see Figure 11.5).

FIGURE 11.5

The Key Manager method of generating keys requires an additional table that holds the highest ID value for each table that will use this method.

Key Manager	
TableName	HighestID
Disc	35
Artist	7
Category	12

To obtain new IDs using this method, you will have to query the Key Manager table for the current ID value, increment that by one, insert your new record, and update the Key Manager table with the incremented ID value. The four individual actions mean that this method shares the multiuser problem with the Calculated Key method. The problem of reusing keys due to deletions is avoided because the ID value stored in the Key Manager is never decremented, and IDs are never reused.

> ### Stored Procedures and Auto-Generating Keys
> While describing the auto-incrementing data type as an option for creating keys, I mentioned that it is difficult to obtain the key after an INSERT, and that this is a major reason to choose an alternative method of key generation. Although these earlier comments are certainly true, there is a commonly used method for obtaining a system-generated key after an INSERT. This method is only available if you use a stored procedure to insert your records, which I will not be covering in any detail in this book. If you want more information on this method of inserting records and obtaining the newly created ID, search MSDN on @@IDENTITY.

Creating the Sample Database

For the examples in the rest of today's lesson, and for the code you will be writing in Day 12, "Accessing Data with .NET," you will need your own copy of the sample database. Although you could go through the process of creating the database manually—and that isn't a bad idea if you are new to databases—I will try to make it a bit easier by providing you with three different database options you can set up on your machine.

The three versions are designed to target three different database systems: Microsoft SQL Server (2000), Microsoft Database Engine (MSDE 2000), or Microsoft Access. SQL Server and MSDE will support the same downloaded file, allowing you to provide a single setup for both systems. All these options will work, but the best possible product for you to have for this and future practice is SQL Server. It is a popular database server and is likely to be what you will be working against when you start building real systems. MSDE is free, which is a great price for a fairly complete database system, but it gives you only a few tools to work with data from outside your program. Access comes with several different versions of Office 2000/XP, and provides a variety of tools for viewing data, creating and modifying tables, and even building your SQL statements (the Query Builder), so it is not a bad option if you already have it.

Determine which product you have and then follow the appropriate directions in the following sections. If you do not have Access, MSDE, or SQL Server, you can just download the .mdb file (covered in the following section on Access) and use it without the rest of the database software being installed.

Downloading the Necessary Files

If you visit the Web site for this book (at `http://www.samspublishing.com/detail_sams.cfm?item=0672320665`), you will find a file called Chapter11.zip. Download this file to your machine and extract it into a directory on your machine. (You will need WinZip for this, which you can obtain at `http://www.winzip.com`.) Inside that file, you should find the following files:

- `CD.mdf` and `CD.ldf`   Together these two files contain all the data for use with SQL Server or MSDE.
- `AttachDB.vbs`   Before the mdf and ldf files can be used from your code, this VBScript file (`.vbs`) must be run to attach them to your local SQL Server or MSDE.
- `CD.mdb`   The Access database, which you can use if you don't have SQL Server or MSDE.

- `TestDB.vb`   A sample program in Visual Basic .NET that you can use to test the setup of your database.
- `Orders.txt`   This file is used by Exercise #2 at the end of today's lesson.

Access 2000 or Access 2002

For users with Access, or without any database system, no real setup is required; you will simply need to know the path to the `.mdb` file for use in the examples. If you want to use Access to work with the data, the only issue you might have is whether you have a different version of Access than the one that the sample was created with. If this is the case, by default, you will only be able to view and not edit the various tables and other objects in your database through Access. Feel free to use the database conversion tools in Access to upgrade the database to the same version that you are running, if you want.

MSDE and SQL Server 2000

For both MSDE and SQL Server, the two files (`cd.mdf` and `cd.ldf`) represent a detached database. It is possible to reattach this database into your own copy of SQL or MSDE. Code provided in the `AttachDB.vbs` script file will link those two files to your database system. Although the file should work "as is" for most people, it does contain the system administrator userid and password inside its code, set to a default of `sa` and a blank password. If your system does not have a blank password for the `sa` account, you will need to edit this file. This script file also is intended to be run (by double-clicking it) from the same directory as the `.mdf` and `.ldf` files and on the same machine as your database system. Go ahead and double-click this file, after you have made any necessary modifications to the userid and password stored in the code.

Testing the Setup with `System.Data`

Now that you have your sample data downloaded and set up, you can do a quick little console application in Visual Basic .NET to confirm that everything is working as intended. To do this, you will need to use the `System.Data` namespace with the .NET Framework. These classes contain everything you will need to access data in almost any type of database, divided into two main areas—classes designed to access Microsoft SQL Server (including MSDE) and classes designed to access any database that has an OLE DB driver (which is pretty much every database).

I won't go into too much detail on how these classes work. Instead, the following example will simply test that your database is set up correctly before moving onto tomorrow's lesson, in which I will be diving deeply into data access through .NET.

11

The code you are going to use to test the database will establish a connection to the database using the OLE DB set of classes from `System.Data.OLEDB`. You could use the `System.Data.SqlClient` classes if you have SQL Server or MSDE, but, because it is also possible that you have Access, it would be simpler to use the classes that can access both types of databases. When using either method of database connection, the key piece of information is called the *connection string*, text that provides all the information needed to connect to your database. This is the only piece of code that will have to be modified to fit your particular setup. Listing 11.1 contains the entire procedure, and I will provide additional information on the connection string values after this listing.

LISTING 11.1 TestDB.vb

```
 1 'Replace Connection String with the appropriate value
 2 'for your setup (explained in Day 11)
 3 'and then compile with:
 4 '   "vbc /r:System.DLL /r:System.Data.DLL TestDB.vb"
 5 Imports System
 6 Imports System.Data
 7 Module TestDB
 8     Sub Main()
 9         Dim sConnectionString, sSQL As String
10         sConnectionString = < see below >
11
12         sSQL = "SELECT CDTitle FROM Disc ORDER BY ArtistID Asc"
13
14         Dim connCD As New OleDb.OleDbConnection(sConnectionString)
15         Dim cmdCD As New OleDb.OleDbCommand(sSQL, connCD)
16         Dim drCD As OleDb.OleDbDataReader
17         connCD.Open()
18         drCD = cmdCD.ExecuteReader()
19         Do While drCD.Read()
20             Console.WriteLine(drCD.Item("CDTitle"))
21         Loop
22
23         drCD.Close()
24         connCD.Close()
25         Console.ReadLine()
26     End Sub
27 End Module
```

If you are using the Access database (`CD.mdb`), your connection string will include the full path to that file like this:

```
Provider=Microsoft.Jet.OLEDB.4.0;Data Source=c:\chapter11\cd.mdb
```

Make sure to modify this connection string to indicate the proper path to `CD.mdb` on your machine.

If, on the other hand, you are using SQL Server or MSDE, and have already successfully run `AttachDB.vbs`, then the following string should work on your machine:

```
Provider=SQLOLEDB.1;User ID=sa;Initial Catalog=CD;Data Source=(local)
```

This SQL connection string (which is broken into two lines in this book but should be only a single line in your code) assumes a blank password for the `sa` account, but you can modify this string to specify a password if required:

```
Provider=SQLOLEDB.1;User ID=sa;Password=peanutbutter;
➥Initial Catalog=CD;Data Source=(local)
```

Place the appropriate connection string into Listing 11.1. Note that this code is included, as `testdb.vb`, in the Chapter11.zip that you downloaded earlier from the book's Web site. Now compile the code as directed in the comments at the beginning of the file, and you should have an `.exe` that you can use to test your database connection. If all goes well, you should receive the following output:

OUTPUT

```
Left Of The Middle
the tragically hip
Road Apples
Day for Night
Phantom Power
Brand New Day
Mercury Falling
Fields of Gold
Classic Queen
20 Greatest Christmas Songs
Gordon
Born on a Pirate Ship
Maroon
Tails
Firecracker
Janet
The Velvet Rope
Design Of A Decade 1986-1996
Mad Season
Music
```

11

With this output, you have created an application that connects successfully to a database, and you are ready to move on to more advanced database topics.

Summary

Today's lesson covered an introduction to databases and their role in building .NET applications. As you continue building Visual Basic .NET systems, you will be using a database often, regardless of the industry for which you are creating your programs. Often, you will be writing programs that will use a database which already exists.

Sometimes, your job will include designing and implementing that database yourself, a task that can be quite complex to do correctly. In tomorrow's lesson, you will continue working with databases, moving from the theoretical to the directly practical and writing some programs that use the System.Data classes.

Q&A

Q. In today's lesson, you mentioned three different types of databases, but are Microsoft databases the only kind I can connect to?

A. Not at all. Any database for which you have an OLE DB (or ODBC) driver is available for you to connect to with the System.Data.OleDB classes. If you do not have an OLE DB provider, but have an ODBC driver, you can still connect by going through an additional layer and using the OLE DB provider for ODBC connections.

For more information on OLE DB, check out http://www.microsoft.com/data.

Q. In the CD database, you moved the Artist information out of the Disc table, but then you have to bring it back into almost any output using a join in your SQL statement. Wouldn't it be better to just keep a copy of the Artist information with each Disc record?

A. Storing data in more than one location means that, to avoid inconsistencies, you have to be sure to update all the possible locations at once. The benefits you get by avoiding the join in your queries are lost by the added work necessary whenever you update records in the Disc or Artist table.

Q. XML is designed for storing data. Does it replace databases?

A. XML is one way to store data, and, although it is certainly a replacement for some flat-file–based database systems, it does not replace relational database systems such as SQL Server. XML will most often be used as a way to interchange data between systems, and will be the output you create from your traditional database systems.

Workshop

The Workshop is designed to help you anticipate possible questions, review what you've learned, and get you thinking about how to put your knowledge into practice. The answers to the quiz are in Appendix A, "Answers to Quizzes/Exercises."

Quiz

1. In a database table, one or more fields is used to uniquely identify each record. What are those fields, or field, called?

2. Given the two tables shown in Figure 11.6, what would the result be of the SQL statement shown here?

```
SELECT Make.MakeName, Model.ModelName
FROM Make LEFT OUTER JOIN Model ON Make.MakeID = Model.Make
```

FIGURE 11.6

Exhibit for Quiz Question #2.

Make	
MakeID	MakeName
1	Ford
2	Audi
3	BMW
4	Pontiac
5	Toyota

Model		
ModelID	Make	ModelName
1	1	Mustang
2	1	Explorer
3	4	Grand Am
4	4	Grand Prix
5	4	Aztek
6	5	Rav 4
7	5	Camry

11

3. Looking at the tables from Figure 11.6 again, what would the output be of this SQL statement?

```
SELECT Make.MakeName, Model.ModelName
FROM Make INNER JOIN Model ON Make.MakeID = Model.Make
```

Exercises

1. If you wanted to expand your CD library to track more than one user's collection of CDs, how would you modify your database? Consider that you would need to track information about the users themselves and ownership information for the discs.

2. Given the set of data contained in Orders.txt (part of the Chapter11.zip download file), how would you design a database to hold the same information?

DAY 12

Accessing Data with .NET

In yesterday's lesson you were introduced to databases and shown how they can be used in a variety of applications. Today, you will learn how your programs will work with data from within Visual Basic .NET. This lesson will include:

- Overview of the .NET data access architecture
- How to connect to a database
- How to execute SQL statements
- Using data binding with Windows and Web forms

In addition to these topics, at the end of today's lesson, you will learn a few of the more advanced concepts and techniques for working with databases from .NET.

An Overview of Data Access in .NET

Databases are used in almost every business application ever created, and in many personal and desktop systems as well. They have existed in one form or another since before Visual Basic was even created. This long history of databases and their use in computer programs has ensured that Visual Basic programs have been accessing data and databases since Visual Basic's first versions. Accordingly, data access technology for Visual Basic has evolved over time, passing through many different versions before .NET came onto the scene.

ADO and OLEDB

There is little value in going through the complete history of Visual Basic and data access, but a brief look at the most recent (pre .NET) data access technology is worthwhile. Prior to .NET, and used extensively by Visual Basic 6.0 programmers, a data access library called ActiveX Data Objects (ADO) was considered the primary means of connecting your Visual Basic or Visual Basic for Applications (VBA) systems to almost any back-end database. ADO was a COM library that encapsulated the functionality of the real data access technology, OLE DB, and was designed as an easy-to-use way to work with this new technology.

To avoid the need to write code to work with every database you might encounter, ADO/OLEDB used a similar approach as ODBC (`http://www.microsoft.com/data/odbc`), providing a single programming interface regardless of the database, and then using database-specific *drivers* to work with each database. This same concept had already become popular, and almost every database system had an ODBC driver available. ADO requires drivers to function as well, although they are referred to as OLEDB *providers*, and many of the most popular databases have the required provider(s) available. But because ADO is newer than ODBC, not as many of these drivers exist. Having just the ODBC driver is enough, though, because ADO ships with an OLEDB provider for ODBC drivers. With the combination of the available OLEDB providers and all the available ODBC drivers, ADO could be used to connect to almost every database system in existence.

The overall architecture of ADO is that your code worked only with ADO, and not with the database system itself, and then ADO used an OLEDB provider to translate and transport your requests to the actual database system (see Figure 12.1). ADO exposed several key objects to represent the database connection, commands against the database, and the results obtained from queries—all designed to be easy to use as part of your Visual Basic program.

ADO.NET

ADO.NET is the data access technology that is part of the .NET Framework. It will be your means for getting at data when programming in Visual Basic .NET and is the next step beyond ADO/OLEDB. The underlying OLEDB technology is still in place, and OLEDB providers are still the primary method by which ADO.NET communicates with specific database systems, but above that layer there is very little resemblance to the older ADO objects.

FIGURE **12.1**

ADO exists as a layer above OLEDB, which itself uses OLEDB and ODBC drivers to connect to the actual databases.

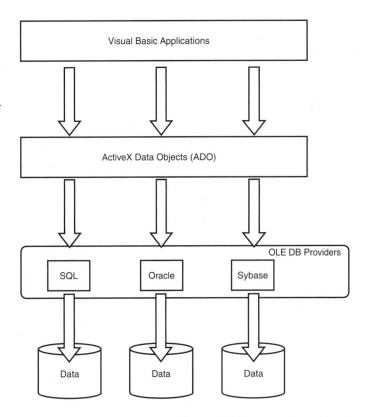

In .NET, database access is handled by the classes in and under the System.Data namespace. That namespace is divided into two distinct areas: the System.Data.OleDB set of classes and the System.Data.SQLClient classes. The first set, System.Data.OleDB, is designed to allow you to connect to any database for which you have an OLEDB provider or (through the OLEDB provider for ODBC) an ODBC driver, and is technically the equivalent of the original ADO data access layer. The second area, System.Data.SQLClient, is designed to work only with Microsoft SQL Server, but otherwise provides a similar set of functionality as the OLEDB classes. The general architecture of the .NET data access classes is shown in Figure 12.2, illustrating the two main systems.

In the examples in today's lesson, you will learn how to work with both OLEDB databases and SQL Server or MSDE systems. Even if you only have SQL Server, you will still be able to experiment with both methods because you can connect to SQL Server through its OLEDB provider as well as through the new .NET classes. In addition to the SQLClient and OLEDB classes for accessing databases, System.Data also includes a variety of other classes designed for working with data independent of its particular source. You will learn about these other classes, the DataSet class in particular, as part of today's examples as well.

12

FIGURE 12.2

ADO.NET is broken into two main sections, OLEDB and SQL, which allow you to connect to a wide variety of data sources.

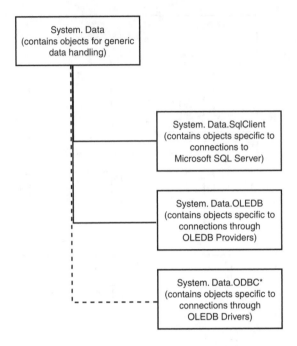

*As of Beta 2. not shipping with Visual Studio .NET but available as a Web download

Standard Database Tasks

Instead of approaching the System.Data classes in a class-by-class reference format, this section focuses on the common tasks that you will want to perform. These tasks, such as connecting to a database, executing a SQL statement, or retrieving data, provide a natural starting point for coverage of the underlying objects.

Connecting to the Database

Before you can start working with any data, you need to establish a connection. The connection to the database represents and holds all the settings required to find and log on to your database. In previous releases of ADO, this connection involved two main things, the connection object and a connection string. The connection string, a line of text that includes some or all the information necessary to connect to your database, is still the key to setting up a database connection in ADO.NET, although there are now two different connection objects (one for OLEDB and one for SQL Server). Before you can start coding, you should obtain the proper connection string for your database. Although this is just a text value, and you could create it manually, the easiest way to obtain a correct string is to be a little tricky.

Just by having ADO installed on your computer—and it is installed as part of the .NET installation so you do—a special file type, Microsoft Data Link, has been registered. Files of this type are designed to hold database connection information, and if you create a blank one, then a nice graphical user interface is provided to create and edit all the details of the connection. After you have worked with the graphical user interface and made the appropriate selections for your database, the file will contain the connection string that you can copy out and use in your Visual Basic .NET application. Follow these steps to use this trick for yourself:

1. Create a blank Microsoft Data Link file by creating a new text file (right-click on the desktop and select New, Text Document from the menu that appears) and renaming it to something with a `.udl` file extension (New.udl would be perfect). If you do not have file extensions visible, which you can turn on using the Folder Options control panel, this will be difficult to accomplish. You should notice the icon of the file change after you have changed its extension, indicating its new file type.

2. Double-click the new file, and a dialog appears with a set of four tabs for creating and editing the connection information for your database.

3. Using the dialog that has just opened (see Figure 12.3), start with the first tab, Provider, and set up the correct information for your database:

   - For the Access database `CD.mdb`, select the Microsoft Jet 4.0 provider.
   - For either SQL Server or the MSDE database, select the Microsoft OLEDB Provider for SQL Server.

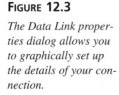

FIGURE 12.3

The Data Link properties dialog allows you to graphically set up the details of your connection.

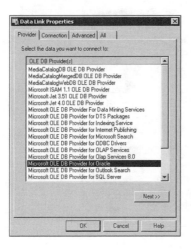

12

4. On the Connection tab, you see different options depending on which of the two possible providers you selected in the previous step. For Access, you only need to enter the path to the CD.mdb file (see Figure 12.4).

FIGURE 12.4

The Connection tab is different depending on the provider you select; the options for Access include the path to the database file.

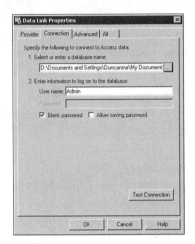

For SQL, you need to supply the server name or (local) if your SQL Server is the same computer, the userid/password, and which specific database (CD in this case) you want to connect to. Figure 12.5 shows the Connection tab configured for a local SQL server database that uses "sa" as its userid with a password that is entered but not visible.

FIGURE 12.5

For SQL Server, the connection details include the server name, the specific database name, and the userid/password needed to connect.

5. Although there are two more tabs, you are finished entering information. Click the Test Connection button to see whether the information you have entered is correct. If the test is successful, then close the dialog by clicking OK. Now, use Notepad or some other text editor to open the .udl file so that you can examine the contents of the file. The exact contents will depend on the information you entered into the dialog, but you should see text like the following

```
[oledb]
; Everything after this line is an OLE DB initstring
Provider=Microsoft.Jet.OLEDB.4.0;
    Data Source=C:\CD.mdb;
    Persist Security Info=False
```

The last line of this file, starting with `Provider`, is an OLEDB connection string, which is what you will need to use in your Visual Basic .NET program. If you are using an Access database, then the string preceding should be the same as yours except for the path. The contents of a .udl file configured for SQL Server is shown in the following example, but you might need to change the `userid`, `password`, and `Data Source` values for this string to work on your system:

```
[oledb]
; Everything after this line is an OLE DB initstring
Provider=SQLOLEDB.1;Password=password;
    Persist Security Info=True;User ID=sa;
    Initial Catalog=CD;Data Source=(local)
```

Note that the last line is actually a single long line of text, but it has been broken into several lines to maintain clarity.

After you have your connection string, which you know is correct because the Test Connection button performed a successful test based on this information, you can start writing some code to connect to your database.

To create a connection, you need to create a new instance of either the `System.Data.OleDB.OLEDBConnection` or the `System.Data.SqlClient.SQLConnection` object. If you are connecting to MSDE or to SQL Server, then the connection string requires a little modification before you can use it with the `SQLConnection` object. The string is used with OleDB, and therefore with any type of database, so it includes a Provider section. Specifying a provider is not necessary and should be removed when connecting through the SQL classes.

Listing 12.1 creates a new instance of `OLEDBConnection` and provides the connection string in the constructor, producing a Connection object that is already set up with all the information it needs to talk to your database.

12

LISTING 12.1 A Connection String

```
 1 Module Module1
 2     Private Const sConnection As String = "Provider=SQLOLEDB.1;" & _
 3                                            "Password=password;" & _
 4                                            "Persist Security Info=True;" & _
 5                                            "User ID=sa;" & _
 6                                            "Initial Catalog=CD;" & _
 7                                            "Data Source=(local)"
 8
 9     Sub Main()
10         Dim objConn As New System.Data.OleDb.OleDbConnection(sConnection)
11     End Sub
12 End Module
```

At this point, you have created the connection object and loaded it with the details of your system, but no actual communication has occurred with the database server. To establish the link with the database, you need to call the Open method of the OleDBConnection object:

objConn.Open()

This particular line is the first one that will cause interaction with your database, and you should wrap it in an error handling structure. Listing 12.2 shows a complete example of opening the connection with simple error handling.

LISTING 12.2 Opening a Connection

```
 1 Module Module1
 2     Private Const sConnection As String = "Provider=SQLOLEDB.1;" & _
 3                                            "Password=password;" & _
 4                                            "Persist Security Info=True;" & _
 5                                            "User ID=sa;" & _
 6                                            "Initial Catalog=CD;" & _
 7                                            "Data Source=(local)"
 8     Sub Main()
 9         Dim objConn As New System.Data.OleDb.OleDbConnection(sConnection)
10         Try
11             objConn.Open()
12         Catch myException As System.Exception
13             Console.WriteLine(myException.Message)
14         End Try
15         Console.ReadLine()
16     End Sub
17 End Module
```

For more information on error handling, see Day 6, "What to Do When Good Programs Go Bad, and Making Sure They Don't." If you want to try this code yourself, just create

a new Console Application using Visual Basic .NET and place this code into
Module1.vb. Remember to replace the sConnection value from the Listing 12.2 with the
string that you created earlier in today's lesson. For even more fun, try changing values,
such as the password, in the connection string to cause the connection attempt to fail.
Your error handling should produce a nice line of output showing you what went wrong
with your program.

For this particular task, opening a connection, the SQLClient classes can be used with
only a few small modifications. First, remove the Provider section from your connection
string and then change your objConn declaration to refer to the
System.Data.SQLClient.SQLConnection object instead of the OLEDB class. Listing
12.3 shows the completed code, which produces essentially the same result.

LISTING 12.3   Error Handling Is Essential when Dealing with Databases

```
 1 Imports System
 2 Module Module1
 3    Private Const sConnection As String
 4       sConnection = "Password=password;" & _
 5                     "Persist Security Info=True;" & _
 6                     "User ID=sa;" & _
 7                     "Initial Catalog=CD;" & _
 8                     "Data Source=(local)"
 9    Sub Main()
10       Dim objConn As New Data.SqlClient.SqlConnection(sConnection)
11       Try
12          objConn.Open()
13       Catch myException As Exception
14          Console.WriteLine(myException.Message)
15       End Try
16       Console.ReadLine()
17    End Sub
18 End Module
```

12

Establishing a connection will be a common first step, but on its own it is not particularly
useful, you will need to use some other database objects to starting working with data.

Executing a SQL Statement

Now that you have a connection established, you will most likely want to be able to add,
delete, modify, and retrieve records. To accomplish any of those tasks, you can use a
command object (SQLCommand or OleDBCommand) to represent and then execute a SQL
statement. Before you can use a command object, you will need the SQL statement you
want to execute and a connection (SQLConnection or OleDBConnection) object. The connection object does not have to be open when you create your command object, but it
does need to be open before you actually execute the command. If you have your SQL

and your connection, then all that you need to do is create a new instance of the appropriate type of command object. You have the option of passing the SQL and the connection object into the constructor when you create the object (see Listing 12.4) or setting them after the fact (see Listing 12.5).

LISTING 12.4   Executing Queries Against the Database

```
 1 Module Module1
 2     Private Const sConnection As String = "Provider=SQLOLEDB.1;" & _
 3                                            "Password=;" & _
 4                                            "User ID=sa;" & _
 5                                            "Initial Catalog=CD;" & _
 6                                            "Data Source=(local)"
 7     Sub Main()
 8         Dim sSQL As String
 9         sSQL = "INSERT INTO CATEGORY (CategoryID, Category)" & _
10                "VALUES (7, 'Electronic')"
11         Dim objConn As New _
12             System.Data.OleDb.OleDbConnection(sConnection)
13         Dim objCmd As New _
14             System.Data.OleDb.OleDbCommand(sSQL, objConn)
15         Try
16             objConn.Open()
17         Catch myException As System.Exception
18             Console.WriteLine(myException.Message)
19         End Try
20
21         Console.Write("Press Return to Execute Query: {0}", sSQL)
22         Console.ReadLine()
25
26         If objConn.State = ConnectionState.Open Then
27             Try
28                 objCmd.ExecuteNonQuery()
29             Catch myException As System.Exception
30                 Console.WriteLine(myException.Message)
31                 Console.ReadLine()
32             End Try
33         End If
34
35     End Sub
36 End Module
```

LISTING 12.5   Setting Properties Individually

```
1 Dim objCmd As New OleDbCommand()
2 objCmd.Connection = objConn
3 objCmd.CommandText = sSQL
```

The execution of the INSERT statement is accomplished by the ExecuteNonQuery method of the command object (line 28), but this method is only designed for use with SQL commands that return no rows.

Retrieving Data

If you want to execute a SQL query that returns data rows, such as SELECT, then you need to use the ExecuteReader method. This method exists on both variations of reader objects and returns an OleDBDataReader or a SQLDataReader, as appropriate. After the reader object has been returned, it can be used to loop forward through the data to retrieve the values from any or all of the fields and rows in the results of your query. The reader object has many methods and properties, but the key members are Read() and the collection of data retrieval methods GetString, GetDouble, GetDateTime, and so on, all of which take an ordinal to indicate which field they should return their data.

The Read method advances the data reader to the next record and returns a Boolean value indicating whether any more rows are available. After you are on a record (after you have called Read()), you can then use the various Get<*data type*> methods to retrieve the values of individual fields. The code shown in Listing 12.6 has been expanded to include the execution of a new SELECT query and a loop to move through and output the results of the query to the console.

LISTING 12.6   Accessing the Results of a Database Query

```
 1 Module Module1
 2     Private Const sConnection As String = "Provider=SQLOLEDB.1;" & _
 3                                            "Password=;" & _
 4                                            "User ID=sa;" & _
 5                                            "Initial Catalog=CD;" & _
 6                                            "Data Source=(local)"
 7
 8     Sub Main()
 9         Dim sSQL As String
10         sSQL = "SELECT Artist.ArtistID, " & _
11                "Artist.ArtistName, Disc.CDTitle " & _
12                "FROM Artist INNER JOIN Disc ON " & _
13                "Artist.ArtistID = Disc.ArtistID;"
14         Dim objConn As New _
15             System.Data.OleDb.OleDbConnection(sConnection)
16         Dim objCmd As New _
17             System.Data.OleDb.OleDbCommand(sSQL, objConn)
18         Dim objReader As _
19             System.Data.OleDb.OleDbDataReader
20
21         Try
22             objConn.Open()
23         Catch myException As System.Exception
```

12

LISTING 12.6   continued

```
24              Console.WriteLine(myException.Message)
25         End Try
26
27         Console.Write("Press Return to Execute SQL: {0}", sSQL)
28         Console.ReadLine()
29
30         If objConn.State = ConnectionState.Open Then
31             Try
32                 objReader = objCmd.ExecuteReader()
33                 Do While objReader.Read()
34                     Console.WriteLine("{0} {1} - {2}", _
35                     objReader.GetInt32(0), _
36                     objReader.GetString(1), _
37                     objReader.GetString(2))
38                 Loop
39                 Console.ReadLine()
40             Catch myException As System.Exception
41                 Console.WriteLine(myException.Message)
42                 Console.ReadLine()
43             End Try
44         End If
45     End Sub
46 End Module
```

Data readers are fast, forward-only and read-only ways to retrieve data, but they are fully connected sets of data as well. This means that when you create a data reader and loop through its rows, each row is being retrieved directly from the database. In fact, while you are working a data reader, your connection to the database is busy and cannot be used for any other purpose. This is not a real problem, and it is a major part of why these readers are so fast (nothing is stored in the client's memory), but sometimes you need to obtain data that gives you a bit more control. As an alternative to data readers, a disconnected model of working with data is also available using DataSets.

Working with Data Sets

In the previous section, you used a Data Reader to retrieve data from your database. This was a connected style of data access, where you had to be connected to the database throughout the process. As a result, this style of data access is best used when you want to quickly retrieve a set of information and have no plans to continue using that information over a longer (more than a few seconds) period of time. Alternatively, if you retrieve data and then proceed to modify, output, filter, process, or otherwise manipulate this data over a longer period of time, or even just hold on to it as a form of cache, then a connected style of data access is not the best choice.

As an alternative, .NET provides a totally disconnected model of data access through the Data Set (`System.Data.DataSet`). Data Sets are capable of having information, usually from a database, although it could come from anywhere, loaded into them where the data becomes independent of its original source. This independence from the data source is why this information is considered disconnected and can be kept for as long as needed in a totally offline environment. If you have used the previous version of ADO, then this might sound similar to that technology's disconnected `Recordset` object. It is similar to that object in several ways, but it is capable of much more functionality. A Data Set can hold multiple tables of information, track relationships between those tables, and even maintain multiple different views for each single table of data. These objects are like complete databases that sit in memory while still being capable of simple usage with a single set of results.

In the following sections, you will learn how to load data into a DataSet and then, after it is there, how to navigate through that information. After those basics have been covered, you will use some of the more complex functionality, including multiple tables, views, and relationships. Finally, you will learn how to take your dataset, after rows have been edited, deleted, and added, and send all your changes back to the database.

Getting Data into a `DataSet`

To load data from your database into a `DataSet`, you will need to use another type of object, a data adapter. The data adapter objects, `SQLDataAdapter` and `OleDBDataAdapter`, are designed to provide the glue or link between your database and a `DataSet` object. This link works in two parts, filling the `DataSet`, and then sending changes to the `DataSet` back to the data source to update the original. You will learn about the update stage of this process a little later in today's lesson, but before you can update anything, you must load the data. First, you must create a connection object, exactly as in the previous examples. A new instance of the appropriate data adapter class (OLEDB or SQL) should be created next. Use the desired SQL statement, or a command object that refers to the correct SQL, and the connection object in the constructor of the data adapter, and it will be completely set up.

```
Dim sSQL As String
sSQL = "SELECT Artist.ArtistID, " & _
       "Artist.ArtistName, Disc.CDTitle " & _
       "FROM Artist INNER JOIN Disc ON " & _
       "Artist.ArtistID = Disc.ArtistID;"
Dim objConn As New OleDb.OleDbConnection(sConnection)
Dim objDataAdapter As New OleDb.OleDbDataAdapter(sSQL, objConn)
```

Because you want to fill a dataset with the results of your query, a `DataSet` object must also be created. This line of code creates an instance and supplies a name for the `DataSet` as part of the constructor:

12

```
Dim objDS As New DataSet("CDs")
```

To load the data into the DataSet, you can use the Fill method of the DataAdapter, but before that will work, the connection object must be opened successfully:

```
objConn.Open()
objDataAdapter.Fill(objDS, "Disc")
```

After the preceding code has executed, a table has been created inside the DataSet, with the name "Disc", and filled with the results of your SQL query. After this table exists, you can work with its contents through the DataSet's Tables collection:

```
Console.WriteLine("{0} Rows", objDS.Tables("Disc").Rows.Count)
```

More details on accessing data stored within a DataSet will be provided later in today's lesson. Note that because the DataSet is a disconnected object, you could have completely closed the connection to your database before working with the DataSet's contents:

```
objDataAdapter.Fill(objDS, "Disc")
objConn.Close()
Console.WriteLine("{0} Rows", objDS.Tables("Disc").Rows.Count)
```

The full code shown in Listing 12.7, with proper error handling, uses an OLEDBDataAdapter to load the results of a SELECT query into a new DataSet object.

LISTING 12.7   Filling a DataSet with the Results of a Query

```
 1 Module Module1
 2     Private Const sConnection As String = "Provider=SQLOLEDB.1;" & _
 3                                            "Password=;" & _
 4                                            "User ID=sa;" & _
 5                                            "Initial Catalog=CD;" & _
 6                                            "Data Source=(local)"
 7
 8     Sub Main()
 9         Dim sSQL As String
10:        sSQL = "SELECT Artist.ArtistID, " & _
11             "Artist.ArtistName, Disc.CDTitle " & _
12             "FROM Artist INNER JOIN Disc ON " & _
13             "Artist.ArtistID = Disc.ArtistID;"
14
15         Dim objConn As New _
16         OleDb.OleDbConnection(sConnection)
17         Dim objDataAdapter As New _
18           OleDb.OleDbDataAdapter(sSQL, objConn)
19         Dim objDS As New DataSet("CDs")
20
21         Try
```

LISTING 12.7   continued

```
22            objConn.Open()
23        Catch myException As System.Exception
24            Console.WriteLine(myException.Message)
25        End Try
26
27        If objConn.State = ConnectionState.Open Then
28            Try
29                objDataAdapter.Fill(objDS, "Disc")
30                objConn.Close()
31              Console.WriteLine("{0} Rows", _
32              objDS.Tables("Disc").Rows.Count)
33            Catch myException As System.Exception
34                Console.WriteLine(myException.Message)
35            End Try
36            Console.ReadLine()
37        End If
38    End Sub
39 End Module
```

As with all the examples so far in today's lesson, you can run this code yourself by placing it into the module of a new Console Application.

Navigating Data

After you load some data into your DataSet, you will most likely want to move through that information. The object that you actually will work with is not the DataSet itself, because it potentially represents a number of different tables, but the DataTable object corresponding to the loaded data you are interested in. The following code shows how you can obtain a DataTable from the DataSet that contains it:

```
Dim objTable As DataTable
objTable = objDS.Tables("Disc")
```

Because the code that loaded the data into the DataSet provided the name "Disc" for the newly loaded table, you can use that name to access the same table. The DataTable object provides two collections that are particularly useful: The Rows collection, which contains all the records from the table, and the Columns collection, which contains a collection of DataColumn objects describing each individual field in the table. The Rows collection can be used in one of several ways to loop through all the records of the table:

Using a For Each loop

```
Dim objRow As DataRow
For Each objRow In objTable.Rows
    Console.WriteLine(objRow.Item("CDTitle"))
Next
```

12

Using a regular `For` loop

```
Dim i As Integer
Dim objRow As DataRow

For i = 0 To objTable.Rows.Count - 1
    objRow = objTable.Rows(i)
    Console.WriteLine(objRow.Item("CDTitle"))
Next
```

Either method produces the same results in this case. Each individual record of the table is represented by a `DataRow` object. This object gives you access to its fields through the `Item` property (into which you can supply the index or name of the field you want to retrieve), and also supplies a variety of useful properties, such as `RowState`, that returns the current editing state of the record.

The `Columns` collection contains details of the fields of the `DataTable`, each one represented as a `DataColumn` object. Through this collection, and the objects contained within it, you have all the information about the structure of your table. As with the previous `Rows` collection, you can loop through the table's fields using either a `For Each` or a `For` loop:

```
Dim objColumn As DataColumn
For Each objColumn In objTable.Columns
    Console.WriteLine("Column Name: {0} Data Type: {1}", _
                        objColumn.ColumnName, _
                        objColumn.DataType.FullName)
Next
```

The `DisplayTable` sample procedure code in Listing 12.8 shows how you could use the `Rows` and `Columns` properties of a `DataTable` to write a generic procedure to output all the table's information with column headers.

LISTING 12.8 Displaying the Contents of a DataTable

```
1    Sub DisplayTable(ByRef objTable As DataTable)
2        Dim objRow As DataRow
3        Dim objCol As DataColumn
4        Dim i, j As Integer
5
6        For j = 0 To objTable.Columns.Count - 1
7            objCol = objTable.Columns(j)
8            Console.Write("{0}:{1} ", _
9                objCol.ColumnName, _
10               objCol.DataType.Name)
11       Next
12       Console.WriteLine()
13
```

LISTING **12.8**   continued

```
14          For i = 0 To objTable.Rows.Count - 1
15              objRow = objTable.Rows(i)
16              For j = 0 To objTable.Columns.Count - 1
17                  Console.Write("{0} ", objRow.Item(j))
18              Next
19              Console.WriteLine()
20          Next
21      End Sub
```

You can try out this procedure by modifying the sample for loading a DataSet to include a call to this new procedure, as shown in Listing 12.9.

LISTING **12.9**   The DisplayTable Function

```
 1 Private Const sConnection As String = "Provider=SQLOLEDB.1;" & _
 2                          "Password=;" & _
 3                          "Persist Security Info=True;" & _
 4                          "User ID=sa;" & _
 5                          "Initial Catalog=CD;" & _
 6                          "Data Source=(local)"
 7
 8 Sub Main()
 9     Dim sSQL As String
10     sSQL = "SELECT Artist.ArtistID, " & _
11     "Artist.ArtistName, Disc.CDTitle " & _
12     "FROM Artist INNER JOIN Disc ON " & _
13     "Artist.ArtistID = Disc.ArtistID;"
14
15     Dim objConn As New _
16         OleDb.OleDbConnection(sConnection)
17     Dim objDataAdapter As New _
18         OleDb.OleDbDataAdapter(sSQL, objConn)
19     Dim objDS As New _
20         DataSet("CDs")
21
22     Try
23         objConn.Open()
24     Catch myException As System.Exception
25         Console.WriteLine(myException.Message)
26     End Try
27
28     If objConn.State = ConnectionState.Open Then
29         Try
30             objDataAdapter.Fill(objDS, "Disc")
31             objConn.Close()
32             Dim objTable As DataTable
33             objTable = objDS.Tables("Disc")
34
```

12

LISTING 12.9 continued

```
35              DisplayTable(objTable)
36
37          Catch myException As System.Exception
38              Console.WriteLine(myException.Message)
39          End Try
40          Console.ReadLine()
41      End If
42 End Sub
```

The DataRow object is important; in addition to being the means by which you access field values (as was done in Listing 12.8), it is also used when you edit, delete, and add records to a DataTable. In the following section, you will learn how to modify the contents of your DataSet using both the DataTable and DataRow objects.

Editing Data (Add, Edit, Delete)

In this section, you will be writing code to modify your database through the DataSet object. The database itself knows nothing of these DataSets, though, and in the end, the database is modified through the use of SQL statements. The changes you make to the DataSet will be translated by the DataAdapter into the SQL statements that need to be executed against the database. You could, of course, simply execute all the individual UPDATE, INSERT, and DELETE statements directly, but the DataSet model has the benefits of being disconnected (avoiding the use of server resources while waiting for user interaction) and being simple (using object methods, such as Delete, instead of custom-built SQL statements).

Taking the three types of data modifications—add, edit, and delete—one at a time you will see how you can easily manipulate your data through the methods of the DataTable and DataRow objects.

Adding Records

After you have created a connection, created a data adapter, and loaded some data into your DataSet, you can directly access a DataTable object:

```
objDataAdapter.Fill(objDS, "Disc")
Dim objTable As DataTable
objTable = objDS.Tables("Disc")
```

After you have that DataTable, you can access its contents through the Rows collection, which returns a DataRowCollection object:

```
Dim drRows As DataRowCollection
drRows = objTable.Rows
```

This object represents all the records in the table as a collection of `DataRow` objects. The collection itself provides a method, `Add`, to create new records. This method can be called in one of two ways: either with an array of field values for the new record, or with a single `DataRow` object representing the information to add. The second method, calling it with a `DataRow`, requires a way to obtain a new row object that has the same schema (the same fields, with the same data types and sizes) as the rest of the rows in the table, and the `DataTable` itself provides that through a `NewRow` method. You will see an example of both styles in Listings 12.10 and 12.11. Listing 12.10 shows the use of an array, which forces you to know the order of the fields and results in code that is much less clear than the second method. Listing 12.11 shows the second method—using a `DataRow` object.

LISTING 12.10   Using an Array (partial code listing)

```
 1 Dim drRows As DataRowCollection
 2 Dim objNewRow As DataRow
 3 drRows = objTable.Rows
 4
 5 'In this case, we have 3 columns
 6 'ArtistID
 7 'ArtistName
 8 'CDTitle
 9
10 'Using the array method produces
11 Dim arrFields(3) As Object
12 arrFields(0) = 10
13 arrFields(1) = "Sting"
14 arrFields(2) = "Dream of Blue Turtles"
15 objNewRow = drRows.Add(arrFields)
```

12

LISTING 12.11   Providing a `DataRow` Object as the Parameter to the `Add` Method

```
 1 Dim drRows As DataRowCollection
 2 Dim objNewRow As DataRow
 3 drRows = objTable.Rows
 4
 5 'In this case, we have 3 columns
 6 'ArtistID
 7 'ArtistName
 8 'CDTitle
 9
10 objNewRow = objTable.NewRow()
11 objNewRow("ArtistID") = 3
12 objNewRow("ArtistName") = "George Orwell"
13 objNewRow("CDTitle") = "Party like it's 1984"
14 drRows.Add(objNewRow)
```

In each case, the data was added to the table, but that does not mean it is going to end up back in the database. Changes in the server database since the data was loaded into this DataSet could prevent these added records from being valid (you could be specifying an Artist that has been deleted from the Artist table, for instance), but you won't see those kinds of errors until the update stage. Because you are working in a disconnected, or offline, state when you work with a DataSet, any server-related issues will not be discovered until you attempt to update the server.

Editing Records

Editing records is similar adding; you work through the DataRow objects that represent the table's records. In the case of editing though, you want to work with an existing DataRow, instead of creating a new one as you did in the previous "Adding Records" section. As with the previous examples, you must first create a connection, a command, and a data adapter, and then load data into a DataSet to create a DataTable. After you have that DataTable, you have access to its DataRowCollection, and you are ready to start editing records.

```
objDataAdapter.Fill(objDS, "Disc")
Dim objTable As DataTable
objTable = objDS.Tables("Disc")
Dim drRows As DataRowCollection
Dim objRow As DataRow
drRows = objTable.Rows
objRow = drRows(5)
```

Each individual DataRow object has several methods that directly affect editing: BeginEdit, EndEdit, and CancelEdit. BeginEdit and EndEdit put the DataRow into and out of edit mode, which is a special state in which the row maintains information about the in-progress edit, and therefore change events will not fire for each individual field modification. You will learn more about change events in the "Data Binding" section later in this lesson. BeginEdit is optional, but it clearly indicates your intention. You can access and change the values through the Item property using the field's name or position:

```
objRow.BeginEdit()
objRow("au_lname") = "Exciting"
objRow.EndEdit()
```

When EndEdit is called, if BeginEdit was used, then the row is committed into the DataTable, at which point any errors that have occurred throughout the edit will be thrown by ADO.NET. Without using BeginEdit and EndEdit, any errors that occur will happen when each individual field is edited.

You will learn how to take a DataSet containing modified fields, new records, and even deleted records, and update the original source database later in today's lesson.

Deleting Records

Deleting a record from a data table is accomplished using the Delete method of the specific DataRow object. This is straightforward to accomplish, but there is one issue to watch for. The Delete method marks the row as deleted but doesn't actually remove the DataRow object from the DataRowCollection. This is critical because it allows the object to be undeleted and provides the necessary information to update the source database by deleting this record back in the original table. There are other methods, Remove and RemoveAt, of the DataRowCollection class that do actually take the specific DataRow object right out of the collection. Using Remove or RemoveAt is fine when you are using a DataTable object without a back-end database, but when the intention is to take all the changes made to the DataSet and update the source table(s), you need to use the Delete method.

Listing 12.12 gives an example of looping through a table, finding certain specific rows, and then deleting them. None of these deletions will affect the source data, SQL Server for instance, until you update the server.

LISTING 12.12   The Delete Method Marks a Row as Deleted

```
 1 Module Module1
 2     Private Const _
 3     sConnection As String = _
 4         "Provider=SQLOLEDB.1;" & _
 5         "Password=;" & _
 6         "Persist Security Info=True;" & _
 7         "User ID=sa;" & _
 8         "Initial Catalog=CD;" & _
 9         "Data Source=(local)"
10
11     Sub Main()
12         Dim sSQL As String
13         sSQL = "SELECT ArtistID, DiscID, CDTitle From Disc"
14
15         Dim objConn _
16             As New OleDb.OleDbConnection(sConnection)
17         Dim objDataAdapter _
18             As New OleDb.OleDbDataAdapter(sSQL, objConn)
19         Dim objDS _
20             As New DataSet("CDs")
21
22         Try
23             objConn.Open()
24         Catch myException As System.Exception
25             Console.WriteLine(myException.Message)
26         End Try
```

12

LISTING **12.12**   continued

```
27
28          If objConn.State = ConnectionState.Open Then
29              Try
30                  objDataAdapter.Fill(objDS, "Disc")
31                  objConn.Close()
32                  Dim objTable As DataTable
33                  objTable = objDS.Tables("Disc")
34                  Dim drRows As DataRowCollection
35                  Dim objCurrentRow As DataRow
36                  drRows = objTable.Rows
37
38                  DisplayTable(objTable)
39
40                  Console.Write("About to Delete, press return to start!")
41                  Console.ReadLine()
42
43                  For Each objCurrentRow In drRows
44                      If CType(objCurrentRow("ArtistID"), Integer) = 3 Then
45                          objCurrentRow.Delete()
46                      End If
47                  Next
48
49                  Console.Write("After Deletion, press return to view")
50                  Console.ReadLine()
51
52                  DisplayTable(objTable)
53
54              Catch myException As System.Exception
55                  Console.WriteLine(myException.Message)
56              End Try
57              Console.ReadLine()
58          End If
59
60      End Sub
61      Sub DisplayTable(ByRef objTable As DataTable)
62          Dim objRow As DataRow
63          Dim objCol As DataColumn
64          Dim i, j As Integer
65
66          For j = 0 To objTable.Columns.Count - 1
67              objCol = objTable.Columns(j)
68              Console.Write("{0}:{1} ", _
69                  objCol.ColumnName, _
70                  objCol.DataType.Name)
71          Next
72          Console.WriteLine()
73          For i = 0 To objTable.Rows.Count - 1
74              objRow = objTable.Rows(i)
75              Select Case objRow.RowState
```

LISTING 12.12   continued

```
76                     Case DataRowState.Deleted
77                         Console.Write("[Deleted]    ")
78                     Case DataRowState.Modified
79                         Console.Write("[Modified]   ")
80                     Case DataRowState.Added
81                         Console.Write("[New]        ")
82                     Case DataRowState.Unchanged
83                         Console.Write("[Unchanged] ")
84                 End Select
85                 For j = 0 To objTable.Columns.Count - 1
86                     If objRow.RowState <> DataRowState.Deleted Then
87                         Console.Write("{0} ", _
88                             objRow.Item(j))
89                     Else
90                         Console.Write("{0} ", _
91                             objRow.Item(j, DataRowVersion.Original))
92                     End If
93
94                 Next
95                 Console.WriteLine()
96            Next
97     End Sub
98 End Module
```

Note that in line 90, inside the DisplayTable routine, a different syntax is used to access the value of a field. By including the second parameter, DataRowVersion.Original, this code specifies that the value of the field after the most recent update, or at the time it was loaded, should be displayed instead of the current field value (the default). In this case, this is particularly important because a deleted row has no valid current field values, and an error will be generated if you attempt to access them.

Updating the Database

After you have added, edited, or deleted records, you must update the original data source (the database) before those changes will take affect. The procedure to take a modified DataSet and update the source database is the same regardless of the changes you have made and involves the use of the data adapter class.

Specifying Update, Insert, and Delete Commands

When you originally created a data adapter to load data into your DataSet, you provided a SQL statement or command object that the adapter then used to retrieve data from the database. This command is actually one of four that the Data Adapter can support, each designed to handle a different task in relaying data between the database and DataSets. Only one of the commands, the one you supplied already, handles pulling data from the

12

database and is called the SelectCommand. The other three (UpdateCommand, DeleteCommand, and InsertCommand) handle edits, deletions, and additions to the database. Each of these commands must contain a proper value, either a SQL statement or a call to a stored procedure on the server, before its corresponding action can be performed. Each of these properties represents a Command object of the appropriate type (OleDBCommand or SQLCommand), which you create and initialize before assigning to the property.

NEW TERM   To create these commands yourself, you will need to use a type of query that has not been covered so far in this lesson, a *parameterized command*. This type of command leaves special placeholders in its SQL—parameters—which are filled in with specific values before the command is executed. Question marks are used in the SQL statement to represent parameters, as shown in Listing 12.13:

LISTING 12.13   Data Adapters Require Placeholder Commands

```
1 Dim objDeleteCommand As New OleDb.OleDbCommand()
2 Dim sDeleteSQL As String
3
4 sDeleteSQL = "DELETE FROM Artist WHERE ArtistID = ?"
5
6 objDeleteCommand.Connection = objConn
7 objDeleteCommand.CommandText = sDeleteSQL
```

Details must be given for each placeholder by adding a parameter object (OleDBParameter or SQLParameter, depending on which world you are working in) to the command's parameters collection. Each parameter object is linked to a specific field within the DataSet by using the SourceColumn property, and can also be associated with a specific version of the field by using the SourceVersion property. Listing 12.14 shows the code required to add a parameter and set some of the available properties.

LISTING 12.14   Creating Parameters on a Command Object

```
1 Dim objParam As OleDb.OleDbParameter
2
3 objParam = objDeleteCommand.Parameters.Add( _
4         "@ArtistID", OleDb.OleDbType.Integer)
5
6 objParam.SourceColumn = "AristID"
7 objParam.SourceVersion = DataRowVersion.Original
```

In this example, the single "?" in the SQL provided has been associated with this new parameter object. Placeholders are associated with parameters based on position: The first placeholder is linked to the first parameter. After the parameter object is created, the corresponding field and field version are specified in lines 5 and 6. Because we are dealing with deleted rows here, just like in Listing 12.12 earlier, it is important to specify the SourceVersion. The default version is the current (DataRowVersion.Current) value, which is not available for a deleted row. The final step you have to do before this command will be used by the Adapter is to assign it to the DeleteCommand property:

```
objDataAdapter.DeleteCommand = objDeleteCommand
```

Listing 12.15 shows a complete, and very large, example, creating a database connection and a data adapter, and then setting up individual commands for UpdateCommand, DeleteCommand, and InsertCommand. Finally, to test these commands, a data set is created, loaded with data, and modified, and then the data source is updated using the adapter's Update method.

LISTING 12.15   Changes Do Not Take Effect until Update Is Called

```
 1 Module Module1
 2     Private Const _
 3     sConnection As String = _
 4         "Provider=SQLOLEDB.1;" & _
 5         "Password=;" & _
 6         "Persist Security Info=True;" & _
 7         "User ID=sa;" & _
 8         "Initial Catalog=CD;" & _
 9         "Data Source=(local)"
10
11     Sub Main()
12         Dim sSQL As String
13         sSQL = "SELECT ArtistID, ArtistName From Artist"
14         Dim objConn _
15             As New OleDb.OleDbConnection(sConnection)
16         Dim objDataAdapter _
17             As New OleDb.OleDbDataAdapter(sSQL, objConn)
18         Dim objDS _
19             As New DataSet("Artists")
20         Dim objDeleteCommand _
21             As New OleDb.OleDbCommand()
22         Dim objUpdateCommand _
23             As New OleDb.OleDbCommand()
24         Dim objInsertCommand _
25             As New OleDb.OleDbCommand()
26         Dim sDeleteSQL As String
27         Dim sUpdateSQL As String
28         Dim sInsertSQL As String
29
30         sDeleteSQL = "DELETE FROM Artist WHERE ArtistID = ?"
```

LISTING 12.15   continued

```
31
32          objDeleteCommand.Connection = objConn
33          objDeleteCommand.CommandText = sDeleteSQL
34
35          Dim objParam As OleDb.OleDbParameter
36          objParam = objDeleteCommand.Parameters.Add( _
37                  "@ArtistID", OleDb.OleDbType.Integer)
38          objParam.SourceColumn = "ArtistID"
39          objParam.SourceVersion = DataRowVersion.Original
40
41          objDataAdapter.DeleteCommand = objDeleteCommand
42
43          sUpdateSQL = "Update Artist SET ArtistName = ? " & _
44                  "WHERE ArtistID = ?"
45
46          objUpdateCommand.Connection = objConn
47          objUpdateCommand.CommandText = sUpdateSQL
48
49          objParam = objUpdateCommand.Parameters.Add( _
50                  "@ArtistName", OleDb.OleDbType.Char)
51          objParam.SourceColumn = "ArtistName"
52          objParam.SourceVersion = DataRowVersion.Current
53
54          objParam = objUpdateCommand.Parameters.Add( _
55                  "@ArtistID", OleDb.OleDbType.Integer)
56          objParam.SourceColumn = "ArtistID"
57          objParam.SourceVersion = DataRowVersion.Original
58
59          objDataAdapter.UpdateCommand = objUpdateCommand
60
61          sInsertSQL = "INSERT INTO Artist " & _
62                  "(ArtistID, ArtistName) " & _
63                  "VALUES (?,?)"
64
65          objInsertCommand.Connection = objConn
66          objInsertCommand.CommandText = sInsertSQL
67
68          objParam = objInsertCommand.Parameters.Add( _
69                  "@ArtistID", OleDb.OleDbType.Integer)
70          objParam.SourceColumn = "ArtistID"
71          objParam.SourceVersion = DataRowVersion.Current
72
73          objParam = objInsertCommand.Parameters.Add( _
74                  "@ArtistName", OleDb.OleDbType.Char)
75          objParam.SourceColumn = "ArtistName"
76          objParam.SourceVersion = DataRowVersion.Current
77
78          objDataAdapter.InsertCommand = objInsertCommand
79
```

LISTING 12.15   continued

```
 80        Try
 81            objConn.Open()
 82        Catch myException As System.Exception
 83            Console.WriteLine(myException.Message)
 84        End Try
 85
 86        Try
 87            Dim sNewArtistSQL As String
 88            sNewArtistSQL = "INSERT INTO Artist " & _
 89                "(ArtistID, ArtistName, " & _
 90                "ArtistFirstName, ArtistLastName)" & _
 91                "VALUES (11, 'Weird Al Yankovich'," & _
 92                " 'Al', 'Yankovich')"
 93
 94            Dim objNewArtistCmd _
 95                As New OleDb.OleDbCommand(sNewArtistSQL, objConn)
 96            objNewArtistCmd.ExecuteNonQuery()
 97        Catch e As Exception
 98            'Might cause an error because
 99            'ArtistID #11 already exists
100            'But if so, then that is ok.
101            Console.WriteLine(e.Message)
102        End Try
103
104        If objConn.State = ConnectionState.Open Then
105            Try
106                objDataAdapter.MissingSchemaAction _
107                    = MissingSchemaAction.AddWithKey
108                objDataAdapter.Fill(objDS, "Artist")
109                objConn.Close()
110                Dim objTable As DataTable
111                objTable = objDS.Tables("Artist")
112                Dim drRows As DataRowCollection
113                Dim objCurrentRow As DataRow
114                drRows = objTable.Rows
115
116                DisplayTable(objTable)
117
118                Console.Write("About to Delete," & _
119                    " press return to start!")
120                Console.ReadLine()
121
122                'Delete the row with primary key = 11
123                drRows.Find(11).Delete()
124
125                Console.Write("After Deletion," & _
126                    " press return to view results")
127                Console.ReadLine()
128
```

12

LISTING 12.15 continued

```
129                         DisplayTable(objTable)
130
131                         Console.Write("About to Insert," & _
132                             " press return to start!")
133                         Console.ReadLine()
134
135                         Dim drRow As Data.DataRow
136                         drRow = objTable.NewRow
137                         drRow("ArtistID") = 40
138                         drRow("ArtistName") = "Kent Sharkey"
139                         objTable.Rows.Add(drRow)
140
141                     Console.Write("After Insert," & _
142                         " press return to view!")
143                         Console.ReadLine()
144                         DisplayTable(objTable)
145
146
147                     Console.Write("About to Update," & _
148                       " press return to start!")
149                         Console.ReadLine()
150
151                         'Get Row with Primary Key of 7 (Lisa Loeb)
152                         drRow = drRows.Find(7)
153
154                         drRow.BeginEdit()
155                         drRow("ArtistName") = "John Doe"
156                         drRow.EndEdit()
157
158                     Console.Write("After Update," & _
159                       " press return to view results")
160                         Console.ReadLine()
161                         DisplayTable(objTable)
162
163                         objConn.Open()
164                         objDataAdapter.Update(objDS, "Artist")
165
166                     Catch myException As System.Exception
167                         Console.WriteLine(myException.Message)
168                     End Try
169                     Console.Write("Press Return to End.")
170                     Console.ReadLine()
171                 End If
172         End Sub
173         Sub DisplayTable(ByRef objTable As DataTable)
174             Dim objRow As DataRow
175             Dim objCol As DataColumn
176             Dim i, j As Integer
177
```

LISTING **12.15**   continued

```
178     For j = 0 To objTable.Columns.Count - 1
179        objCol = objTable.Columns(j)
180        Console.Write("{0}:{1} ", _
181           objCol.ColumnName, _
182           objCol.DataType.Name)
183     Next
184     Console.WriteLine()
185     For i = 0 To objTable.Rows.Count - 1
186        objRow = objTable.Rows(i)
187        Select Case objRow.RowState
188           Case DataRowState.Deleted
189              Console.Write("[Deleted]    ")
190           Case DataRowState.Modified
191              Console.Write("[Modified]   ")
192           Case DataRowState.New
193              Console.Write("[New]        ")
194           Case DataRowState.Unchanged
195              Console.Write("[Unchanged] ")
196        End Select
197        For j = 0 To objTable.Columns.Count - 1
198           If objRow.RowState <> DataRowState.Deleted Then
199              Console.Write("{0} ", _
200                 objRow.Item(j))
201           Else
202              Console.Write("{0} ", _
203                 objRow.Item(j, DataRowVersion.Original))
204           End If
205        Next
206        Console.WriteLine()
207     Next
208  End Sub
209 End Module
```

ANALYSIS The code in Listing 12.15 is available for download from this book's Web site, so don't type it in manually unless you really want to. The first section of the code is fairly standard to all the code written in today's lesson. The connection string is created, and you should replace this with the values appropriate for your system, and used to instantiate a new OleDBConnection object (line 14). An OleDBDataAdapter and DataSet are also created and initialized, so that you can connect to the database and bring the results of the SELECT statement back to your program. As part of the initialization code, three new OleDBCommand objects are also created, which will be used to represent the UPDATE, DELETE, and INSERT commands for the OleDBDataAdapter. These command objects are not actually created at this point though, that step is handled as each command is set up later.

12

Lines 30–41 create and set up the Delete command object, adding the single parameter object for the ArtistID (the primary key). Note how line 39 specifies the SourceVersion to be DataRowVersion.Original because the current data is not valid for a deleted row. Lines 43–59 set up the Update command, and then lines 61–78 handle the Insert command. Note that for Update and Insert, many parameters are needed, due to the fact that all the table's fields must be sent into these commands.

Moving back to the code that is common throughout today's examples, lines 80–84 set up the connection to the database. Next, a single row of data is inserted into the database using the ExecuteNonQuery() method of a command object. This row is added so that it can be deleted later, because attempting to delete any other Artist record would fail due to the existence of child records (CDs by that Artist in the Disc table). Instead of working through the data set and the data adapter in disconnected mode, this insert is done immediately through a direct execution.

Line 106, which occurs after the connection is open and the single new record has been inserted, tells the data adapter how to handle setting up a table when no schema (the layout and data type information about the data) exists. This particular setting, AddWithKey, tells the data adapter to automatically create the basic schema (field information) and to include the primary key information as well. Next, on line 108, the DataSet is loaded with the data using the Fill method and with an additional parameter to specify the name of the newly created table, "Artist".

Just to make sure it is clear that this is a disconnected process, line 109 closes the connection to the database before the actual data manipulation occurs. After this point, the code deletes, modifies, and adds records to the DataTable to provide a test of all three types of changes that can occur to a DataTable. To find the correct row to delete (line 123) and to edit (line 152), the Find method of the DataRowCollection object is used. This method returns a DataRow given a valid primary key value to look up, a process that requires the DataTable to contain primary key information (see preceding paragraph for an explanation of how line 106 provides this information).

Finally, after all the edits, line 164 uses the OleDBDataAdapter's Update method to apply all the data changes to the DataSet. This method takes a DataSet as a parameter, along with a string indicating which table within the DataSet should be used to update the database. If the table name is not provided, the adapter attempts to update the database with all the available tables.

The result of this code should be a sequence of SQL statements being executed against the database, each corresponding to one of the adapter's commands. If you are using SQL Server, and you want to see what happens, you can use the Profiler to watch all the commands being executed against the server while this code is running. Providing details on how to use the Profiler is beyond the scope of this book, but the output should be similar to what is shown here:

```
INSERT INTO Artist (ArtistID, ArtistName, ArtistFirstName, ArtistLastName)
VALUES (11, 'Weird Al Yankovich', 'Al', 'Yankovich')
go
SELECT ArtistID, ArtistName From Artist
go
exec sp_executesql
N'Update Artist SET ArtistName = @P1
WHERE ArtistID = @P2', N'@P1 char(8),@P2 int', 'John Doe', 7
go
exec sp_executesql
N'DELETE FROM Artist WHERE ArtistID = @P1', N'@P1 int', 11
go
exec sp_executesql
N'INSERT INTO Artist (ArtistID, ArtistName) VALUES (@P1,@P2)',
N'@P1 int,@P2 char(12)', 40, 'Kent Sharkey'
go
```

In this example, only one record was being inserted, modified, and deleted, but the Update method would simply call the appropriate commands once per modified record.

Using Automatically Generated Commands

As an alternative to specifying the commands yourself, you can let ADO.NET automatically create the necessary commands for you, which can be simpler, although there are a few steps to follow to accomplish this. The first requirement for auto-generated commands is that your DataSet must contain at least primary key information for the relevant tables. This information can be provided in one of several ways, all of which will produce the desired effect.

First, you can manually specify it using the PrimaryKey property of a DataTable. This property is set to the appropriate field, which you can obtain using the DataTable's Columns collection:

```
Dim PK(0) As DataColumn
PK(0) = objTable.Columns("ArtistID")
objTable.PrimaryKey = PK
```

You also can let the data adapter obtain the appropriate information from the data source, including the primary key and many more details about the table, by using the FillSchema method. This method creates the DataTable object prior to loading it and populates the table with its list of columns, primary key information, and any other constraints it could discover from the data source:

```
objDataAdapter.FillSchema(objDS, SchemaType.Mapped, "Artist")
```

Finally, you can have the adapter create the required schema information during the load of data, by setting the value of the MissingSchemaAction property before calling Fill.

12

This property has a few interesting settings, but `AddWithKey` is required for this purpose. `Add` (the default value) automatically creates the column information (names and data types) if those details don't already exist in the table, whereas `AddWithKey` adds that same column information and also sets the `PrimaryKey` property for each table it fills.

```
objDataAdapter.MissingSchemaAction _
    = MissingSchemaAction.AddWithKey
objDataAdapter.Fill(objDS, "Artist")
```

Regardless of which method you use, after the `DataTable` that is being updated contains primary key information, the `Update`, `Insert`, and `Delete` commands can be automatically generated. An instance of the appropriate command builder class (`OleDBCommandBuilder` or `SQLCommandBuilder`) must be created and initialized first, and then when the adapter's `Update` method is called, any missing commands will be created if they are needed. Listing 12.16 demonstrates these concepts by loading some simple data into a `DataSet`, making a few modifications, and then calling `Update`.

LISTING 12.16   The Update Method Executes the Corresponding Commands Against the Source Database

```
 1 Module Module1
 2    Private Const _
 3    sConnection As String = _
 4       "Provider=SQLOLEDB.1;" & _
 5       "Password=;" & _
 6       "Persist Security Info=True;" & _
 7       "User ID=sa;" & _
 8       "Initial Catalog=CD;" & _
 9       "Data Source=(local)"
10
11    Sub Main()
12       Dim sSQL As String
13       sSQL = "SELECT ArtistID, ArtistName From Artist"
14       Dim objConn _
15          As New OleDb.OleDbConnection(sConnection)
16       Dim objDataAdapter _
17          As New OleDb.OleDbDataAdapter(sSQL, objConn)
18       Dim objCommandBuilder _
19          As New OleDb.OleDbCommandBuilder(objDataAdapter)
20       Dim objDS _
21          As New DataSet("Artists")
22
23       Try
24          objConn.Open()
25       Catch myException As System.Exception
26          Console.WriteLine(myException.Message)
27       End Try
28
```

LISTING **12.16** continued

```
29          If objConn.State = ConnectionState.Open Then
30              Try
31                  objDataAdapter.MissingSchemaAction _
32                      = MissingSchemaAction.AddWithKey
33                  objDataAdapter.Fill(objDS, "Artist")
34
35                  objConn.Close()
36                  Dim objTable As DataTable
37                  objTable = objDS.Tables("Artist")
38                  Dim drRows As DataRowCollection
39                  Dim objCurrentRow As DataRow
40                  drRows = objTable.Rows
41
42                  DisplayTable(objTable)
43
44                  Console.Write("About to Edit," & _
45                      " press return to start!")
46                  Console.ReadLine()
47
48                  'Delete the row with primary key = 11
49                  drRows.Find(7)("ArtistName") = "Kent Sharkey"
50
51                  Console.Write("After Edit," & _
52                      " press return to view results")
53                  Console.ReadLine()
54
55                  DisplayTable(objTable)
56
57                  objConn.Open()
58                  objDataAdapter.Update(objDS, "Artist")
59
60              Catch myException As System.Exception
61                  Console.WriteLine(myException.Message)
62              End Try
63              Console.Write("Press Return to End.")
64              Console.ReadLine()
65          End If
66      End Sub
67      Sub DisplayTable(ByRef objTable As DataTable)
68          Dim objRow As DataRow
69          Dim objCol As DataColumn
70          Dim i, j As Integer
71
72          For j = 0 To objTable.Columns.Count - 1
73              objCol = objTable.Columns(j)
74              Console.Write("{0}:{1} ", _
75                  objCol.ColumnName, _
76                  objCol.DataType.Name)
77          Next
```

12

12.16 continued

```
,8      Console.WriteLine()
79      For i = 0 To objTable.Rows.Count - 1
80          objRow = objTable.Rows(i)
81          Select Case objRow.RowState
82            Case DataRowState.Deleted
83                Console.Write("[Deleted]   ")
84            Case DataRowState.Modified
85                Console.Write("[Modified]  ")
86            Case DataRowState.Added
87                Console.Write("[New]       ")
88            Case DataRowState.Unchanged
89                Console.Write("[Unchanged] ")
90          End Select
91          For j = 0 To objTable.Columns.Count - 1
92            If objRow.RowState <> DataRowState.Deleted Then
93                Console.Write("{0} ", _
94                    objRow.Item(j))
95            Else
96                Console.Write("{0} ", _
97:                   objRow.Item(j, DataRowVersion.Original))
98            End If
99          Next
100         Console.WriteLine()
101     Next
102    End Sub
103 End Module
```

As with all the examples in today's lesson, this code could be switched to work with the SQLClient classes with only minor changes. The connection string would need to be modified by removing the Provider section, and all the objects declared as OLEDB classes would have to be changed to the SQLClient equivalents.

Working with Multiple Tables

When data is loaded into a DataSet, it is placed into individual tables, allowing a single DataSet to hold the results from many different queries. After you have a DataSet with more than one table, it is possible to specify relationships between those tables, such as between an Artist table and a Disc table (based on our examples so far). All the relationships that exist inside a DataSet are represented by objects within the Relations collection, which is accessible as a property of the DataSet object itself. To create a relationship between two tables, use the Add method of the Relations collection. This method has many parameter options, allowing you to call it in seven different ways, but if you want to set up a simple relationship based on a single field (column) in the parent table and a single field in the child table, then this syntax works well:

```
objNewRelation = objDS.Relations.Add(RelationName,ParentColumn,ChildColumn)
```

As an example of this, Listing 12.17 creates a database connection and loads the Artist and Disc tables into a new `DataSet`. After everything is loaded, a relationship is established between the two tables.

LISTING 12.17   DataSet Closely Reflects the Source Data

```
 1 Module Module1
 2
 3    Private Const _
 4     sConnection As String = _
 5      "Provider=SQLOLEDB.1;" & _
 6      "Password=321dweksp302axn;" & _
 7      "Persist Security Info=True;" & _
 8      "User ID=sa;" & _
 9      "Initial Catalog=CD;" & _
10      "Data Source=(local)"
11
12    Sub Main()
13       Dim sSQLArtist As String
14       Dim sSQLDisc As String
15
16       sSQLArtist = "SELECT ArtistID, ArtistName From Artist"
17       sSQLDisc = "SELECT ArtistID, CDTitle From Disc"
18
19       Dim objConn _
20          As New OleDb.OleDbConnection(sConnection)
21       Dim objDataAdapterArtist _
22          As New OleDb.OleDbDataAdapter(sSQLArtist, objConn)
23       Dim objDataAdapterDisc _
24          As New OleDb.OleDbDataAdapter(sSQLDisc, objConn)
25       Dim objDS _
26          As New DataSet("CD")
27
28       objDataAdapterArtist.MissingSchemaAction = _
29          MissingSchemaAction.AddWithKey
30       objDataAdapterDisc.MissingSchemaAction = _
31          MissingSchemaAction.AddWithKey
32
33       objDataAdapterArtist.Fill(objDS, "Artist")
34       objDataAdapterDisc.Fill(objDS, "Disc")
35
36       objDS.Relations.Add("DiscArtist", _
37       objDS.Tables("Artist").Columns("ArtistID"), _
38          objDS.Tables("Disc").Columns("ArtistID"))
39    End Sub
40 End Module
```

12

With relationships in place, it is possible to use this information to allow structured access from a parent data row to any related rows in the child table. The code in Listing

12.18, which can be added just before the end of the procedure in Listing 12.17, loops through the records in the Artist table and displays the CDs associated with that artist.

LISTING 12.18   Accessing Child Rows of any Specific Parent Row Using the `GetChildRows` Method

```
1      Dim objDRParent As DataRow
2      Dim objDRChild As DataRow
3      Dim objChildRows() As DataRow
4
5      For Each objDRParent In objDS.Tables("Artist").Rows
6          Console.WriteLine("{0} {1}", _
7          objDRParent("ArtistID"), _
8          objDRParent("ArtistName"))
9          objChildRows = objDRParent.GetChildRows("DiscArtist")
10         For Each objDRChild In objChildRows
11             Console.WriteLine("      {0}", _
12         objDRChild("CDTitle"))
13         Next
14     Next
15     Console.ReadLine()
```

The key part of this code sample is line 9, where the `GetChildRows` method of the `DataRow` is used to return an array of `DataRows` from the child table. This array includes all the rows from the child where the `ArtistID` fields from the parent and the child matched.

Views

ADO.NET includes the concept of views against data, the capability to specify sort order, a filter on rows, and a filter based on `RowState` (Modified, Deleted, Unchanged, or New). This view (`DataView`), when created, is accessible through the `DefaultView` property of the table itself, or through the `Relations` collection, which is a property of the `DataSet` itself.

Listing 12.19 has the standard code for opening a database, filling a table with data, and then creating a `DataView` object using the table as its constructor. After the view is created, it can be configured with any combination of three different properties: `RowStateFilter`, `Sort`, and/or the `RowFilter`. The view itself can be bound to a windows forms control (see the next section for information on data binding), or you can access its contents directly as a collection of `DataRowView` objects.

LISTING 12.19   Multiple DataView Objects Pointing at the Same DataTable

```
 1 Module Module1
 2    Private Const _
 3     sConnection As String = _
 4      "Provider=SQLOLEDB.1;" & _
 5      "Password=;" & _
 6      "Persist Security Info=True;" & _
 7      "User ID=sa;" & _
 8      "Initial Catalog=CD;" & _
 9      "Data Source=(local)"
10
11    Sub Main()
12       Dim sSQLArtist As String
13       sSQLArtist = "SELECT ArtistID, ArtistName From Artist"
14       Dim objConn _
15          As New OleDb.OleDbConnection(sConnection)
16       Dim objDataAdapterArtist _
17          As New OleDb.OleDbDataAdapter(sSQLArtist, objConn)
18       Dim objDS _
19          As New DataSet("CD")
20       objDataAdapterArtist.MissingSchemaAction = _
21          MissingSchemaAction.AddWithKey
22       objDataAdapterArtist.Fill(objDS, "Artist")
23
24       Dim objDR As DataRow
25       Console.WriteLine("Through Table")
26       For Each objDR In objDS.Tables("Artist").Rows
27          Console.WriteLine("{0} {1}", _
28                   objDR("ArtistID"), _
29                   objDR("ArtistName"))
30       Next
31
32       Dim objDV As DataView
33       objDV = New DataView(objDS.Tables("Artist"))
34       objDV.Sort = "ArtistName"
35       objDV.RowFilter = "ArtistID < 8"
36
37       Dim objDRV As DataRowView
38       Console.WriteLine("Through DataView")
39       For Each objDRV In objDV
40          Console.WriteLine("{0} {1}", _
41                   objDRV("ArtistID"), _
42                   objDRV("ArtistName"))
43       Next
44       Console.ReadLine()
45    End Sub
46 End Module
```

12

Up to line 22 is not all that different from the other examples so far in today's lesson: a database connection was opened, and data was loaded into a `DataSet`. After the data is loaded, a quick loop (lines 26 to 30) prints out the data without seeming to go through a `DataView` (it is actually going through the default data view). A `DataView` object is then created and set up with a sort and a filter on the values in the rows (lines 32 to 35). Finally, that `DataView` is used to access the rows (lines 39-43), this time printing them out with the `DataView`'s sort and filter applied. The output from this code, assuming that you have done all the examples up to this point, should look like this:

```
Through Table
1 Natalie Imbruglia
2 The Tragically Hip
3 Sting
4 Queen
5 Boney M.
6 Barenaked Ladies
7 Kent Sharkey
8 Janet Jackson
9 Matchbox Twenty
10 Madonna
40 Kent Sharkey
Through DataView
6 Barenaked Ladies
5 Boney M.
7 Kent Sharkey
1 Natalie Imbruglia
4 Queen
3 Sting
2 The Tragically Hip
```

Even if your output is not exactly the same as the preceding text, notice that in the `Through Table` list, 11 rows are printed out in `ArtistID` order. In `Through DataView`, the rows are accessed through the newly created view, and the output reflects both the filter and the sort.

Data Binding

Data binding provides a way to link a user interface element, such as a grid, with a data source, such as a `DataTable` or `DataSet`. After an interface element is bound to a data source, changes to that data source will be reflected in the user interface, and changes made to the data through the user interface will in turn be propagated back to the data source. For the developer, data binding wraps up all the complex issues of handling a user's interactions with data and removes the need to write all that code just to provide a means for user interaction with your data. An interesting and powerful feature of data binding in .NET is that it is not limited to working with `DataSet`s. In fact, a wide variety of objects can be data bound, including `Arrays`, `Collections`, `DataViews`, `DataSets`, `DataTable`, and more. In our examples, we will be working only with `DataSets`, `DataViews`, and `DataTables`, but the potential is there to bind all sorts of information.

> **Note**
>
> When a `DataSet` or `DataTable` object is bound to a user interface control, the actual binding is occurring with the default view (`DataView` or `DataSetView` object) of the `DataTable` or `DataSet`.

In the world of .NET, two main types of user interfaces can be created: the rich Windows client (`System.Windows.Forms`) and the `WebForms` Internet client. The binding details for Windows Forms are covered in the following section along with a step-by-step example of binding a dataset to a grid. Data binding in `WebForms` and general ASP.NET data access is not detailed in today's lesson.

Data Binding with Windows Forms

All Windows Forms controls that support data binding come in two main flavors: those that support simple binding and those that can handle complex binding. Simple binding is when a property of a control is associated with a field of a data source. Complex binding is when the control is associated with a complete data source (such as a `DataTable`), and among the built-in objects it is supported only by the `DataGrid` and the `ComboBox` controls.

Simple Binding

Controls that support simple binding expose a `DataBindings` collection that can be used to link properties to data fields. Listing 12.20 gives an example of this type of data binding as part of a Windows Forms application. To try out this code yourself, create a new Visual Basic Windows application and place a single text box and button onto the form. Leave the controls with their default names (`textbox1` and `button1`) and place this code into the `Click` event for the button.

LISTING 12.20 Data Binding Can Be Created Dynamically in Code

```
1     Private Sub button1_Click(ByVal sender As System.Object, _
2                         ByVal e As System.EventArgs) _
3                         Handles button1.Click
4         Dim sConnection As String = _
5         "Provider=SQLOLEDB.1;" & _
6         "Password=;" & _
7         "Persist Security Info=True;" & _
8         "User ID=sa;" & _
```

LISTING **12.20**   continued

```
 9          "Initial Catalog=CD;" & _
10          "Data Source=(local)"
11
12          Dim sSQL As String
13          sSQL = "SELECT ArtistID, ArtistName From Artist"
14          Dim objConn _
15              As New OleDb.OleDbConnection(sConnection)
16          Dim objDataAdapter _
17              As New OleDb.OleDbDataAdapter(sSQL, objConn)
18          Dim objDS _
19              As New DataSet("Artists")
20          Dim objDV _
21              As DataView
22
23          Try
24              objConn.Open()
25          Catch myException As System.Exception
26              Windows.Forms.MessageBox.Show(myException.Message)
27          End Try
28
29          If objConn.State = ConnectionState.Open Then
30              Try
31                  objDataAdapter.Fill(objDS, "Disc")
32                  objConn.Close()
33                  Dim objTable As DataTable
34                  objTable = objDS.Tables("Disc")
35                  objDV = objTable.DefaultView
36                  textBox1.DataBindings.Add("Text", _
37                                    objDV, _
38                                    "ArtistName")
39              Catch myException As System.Exception
40                  Windows.Forms.MessageBox.Show(myException.Message)
41              End Try
42          End If
43      End Sub
```

In addition to all the code that you should recognize (lines 1 to 34) opening the database connection and obtaining a DataSet, the line at the end of the procedure (line 37) does the actual data binding. The Add method of the DataBindings collection allows you to specify a property of the control and the data source (in this case the default data view of the table). After this is done, the value of the ArtistName field will be displayed (see Figure 12.6).

This isn't all that useful, considering you are viewing only the first record and you have no way to move backwards or forwards through the data. To provide functionality like that when you are using simple data binding, you have to access the BindingContext collection of the parent Form. By specifying the particular data source that you are interested in, you can obtain a BindingContext object for that data source.

Figure 12.6

Simple data binding can be done with many different controls at once, allowing you to display the fields of your data in a variety of ways.

In the following example, the original data source was not a form level variable, so the code accesses it by going through the text box's DataBindings collection. There is only one data binding, so specifying an index of zero returns the only data source available. With this context object, you have access to several properties and methods for creating an interface for working with bound data. One particular property, Position, is useful because it allows you to move back and forth through the data as desired. If you add a second button to the form and place the following code into it, you will have the capability to move forward through the list of Artists. Note that there is absolutely no intelligence to this code; it will crash if you try to move beyond the end of the available data:

```
Private Sub button2_Click(ByVal sender As System.Object, _
                          ByVal e As System.EventArgs) _
                          Handles button2.Click
    Me.BindingContext(textBox1.DataBindings(0).DataSource).Position += 1
End Sub
```

This context object exposes other functionality such as AddNew and CancelCurrentEdit, making it an object that you will likely work with often.

Complex Data Binding

New Term Binding controls to an entire data source, instead of a single field, is called *complex data binding*. This type of data binding is supported by two of the controls that ship with Visual Studio .NET, the DataGrid and ComboBox. To set up data binding with one of these controls, you set the control's DataSource property to the appropriate object (DataView in this case, could be an Array, Collection, DataSet, and so on). If the DataSource contains more than one object that could be bound to (such as a DataSet with more than one table in it), then specify the appropriate item as a string value into the DataMember property. So, if you bind the DataGrid to a DataSet, you have to provide the name of the table as the DataMember property. The code to do this would be identical to Listing 12.20, except that you would need to replace lines 36–38 with the following:

```
dataGrid1.DataSource = objDS
dataGrid1.DataMember = "Disc"
```

12

To try complex binding for yourself, create a new Windows application and place a button and a `DataGrid` onto the form (both are available from the Toolbox). Leave everything with the default names and place the code from Listing 12.20, including the modifications described previously, into the `Click` event of your button. The result of this code is that, after the button is clicked, the `DataGrid` will be bound to, and will therefore display, the Artists table within your `DataSet`. Your form might not look exactly like Figure 12.7, but it should be similar.

FIGURE 12.7

A DataGrid creates a professional-looking environment without much coding.

Summary

Data access has been totally redesigned for .NET, but it still supports the underlying technology of OLEDB. Using OLEDB providers (drivers), you can create code that will run against almost any database you need, while still learning only a single way to program against all of them. Using the disconnected nature of `DataSets`, you can create fully interactive systems that do not tie up valuable database connections. When you are building actual user interfaces, data binding provides you with a quick and easy way to display your data onto a Windows Form.

Q&A

Q. In all of today's examples, my connection string was hard-coded into the code. Because this includes my userid and password, this doesn't seem very secure.

A. Excellent point. In today's code, the connection string has been right in the `.vb` file, which is fairly unsafe. A better idea, for when you aren't just writing samples, would be to place the connection string value into the Registry or into a settings file on disk. This is done for more than just security reasons; by not having your connection string in your code, it is possible to change databases and other connection parameters without recompiling your system.

Q. **When you update the database, what happens if the record you are trying to update was modified since you pulled down your original data?**

A. When dealing with updates against a database, you must be aware of concurrency issues, where two or more people could be modifying the same data during the same time period. In the case of `DataSets`, because they are designed to be used offline, it is likely that the time between the load of data and the update back will be relatively long. During this time in between load and update, another user could have modified that same data in some way. If you use the automatically generated update commands, they include code to check for these issues before updating. Otherwise, if you are building the commands manually, you will have to check the original data against the current data in the database yourself.

Workshop

The Workshop is designed to help you anticipate possible questions, review what you've learned, and get you thinking about how to put your knowledge into practice. The answers to the quiz are in Appendix A, "Answers to Quizzes/Exercises."

Quiz

1. What property do you need to set (and to what value) to force the data adapter to create primary key information when it loads data into a `DataSet`?

2. What is the difference between the `Delete` method of a `DataRow` and the `Remove` method of the `DataRowCollection`?

3. How should you execute this SQL statement?

```
DELETE FROM Artist Where ArtistID=3?
```

Exercises

1. Create a Windows application that uses the classes you learned about in today's lesson to provide a user interface for viewing, modifying, adding, and deleting from your CD database.

12

DAY **13**

Using the Server Explorer

One of the main goals of an Integrated Development Environment (IDE) is to provide tools that are not available to developers using the command-line compilers with a text editor. These might be improved editing and debugging features—tools that allow programmers to develop faster and better code. In addition, a good IDE might include features that assist developers by generating code without them having to write it themselves. The add-ins and wizards that are part of the Visual Basic .NET IDE are all of this type. The Server Explorer is also in this category. The Server Explorer is a feature of Visual Basic .NET that allows easy control of the various services that are part of the operating system. In addition, it allows the developer to quickly and painlessly create code to use those various services. Today, we will learn

- What is the Server Explorer?
- Exploring services
- Working with services
- Writing programs that use services

What Is the Server Explorer?

The Server Explorer is a tool available within the Visual Basic .NET IDE. Like the Explorer and Internet Explorer, it is a tool that allows you to browse a set of features. Instead of browsing folders on a hard drive or Web site, the Server Explorer allows you to browse the various servers on your network and view the services running on them. In addition, with some services, you can control the service, or write code to use that service, all from within the Server Explorer. Figure 13.1 shows the Server Explorer. If it is not visible, it could be because it was closed earlier. Open it by selecting View, Server Explorer from the menu.

FIGURE **13.1**

The Server Explorer.

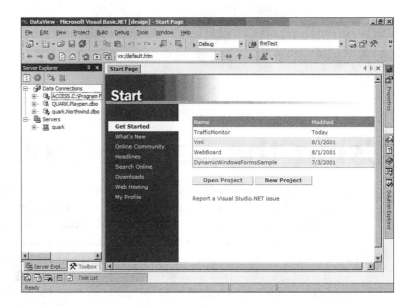

The Server Explorer shows a hierarchical list of services available on the selected computer. By default, it only shows the services on the development computer, but you can add others as needed. These can be broken down into two broad categories:

- Data connections   This is similar to the data environment available in Visual Basic 6 (assuming you used that version). It allows you to connect to and view databases without leaving the Visual Basic .NET environment. This has obvious uses if you do a lot of programming to access and update databases, which is one of the main uses for Visual Basic .NET.

- Servers   This is the list of servers you are connected to and the services running (or available on) each of them. The information in this section includes the capability to access the event logs and performance monitoring on these computers, as well as other services, such as message queues, SQL Server, and others.

We will use the Server Explorer today for two of its main functions: viewing information and writing programs.

What Is a Service?

NEW TERM A *service* is a program that runs in the background, providing some service to supplement the operating system. These services can include programs that are traditionally considered servers, such as database servers (such as Microsoft SQL Server), Web servers (such as Microsoft IIS), or mail servers (such as Microsoft Exchange). Alternatively, the service might provide some added functionality that other programs can leverage, such as performance monitoring or event logging. Windows 95, 98, and ME provide far fewer Services than Windows NT or 2000.

Usually services have a program that is used to view information about it. For example, the Event Viewer tool allows you to view the Event Logs on a computer, or SQL Server Enterprise Manager allows you to view and administer a SQL Server. The Server Explorer supplements these tools by allowing you to work with the services without leaving the IDE.

Exploring Services

To view the Server Explorer, select it from the View menu. By default, it appears on the left side of the IDE. Like other views, it can be "pinned open," or set to automatically slide out of the way when you no longer need it. On a computer running Windows 2000, and with Microsoft SQL Server installed, it appears as shown in Figure 13.2. On another computer, with different services installed, different services might appear.

Data Connections

The Data Connections section of the Server Explorer is where you view and administer databases from within Visual Basic .NET (see Figure 13.3). From this section, you can connect to any data source.

Initially, only an Add Connection link should be available under the Data Connections folder. Double-clicking this option brings up the Data Link Properties dialog (see Figure 13.4). This dialog allows you to configure a new data connection. The actual options you will complete for this dialog vary depending on the type of data you are attempting to connect to. The settings are divided between multiple tabs on the resulting Data Link Properties dialog.

13

FIGURE **13.2**

Server Explorer.

FIGURE **13.3**

Viewing data connections with the Server Explorer.

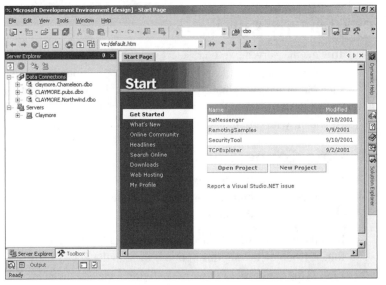

The Provider tab is used to select the provider that will be used to connect to the database. Depending on which providers you have installed, there could be many possible providers. Figure 13.4 shows the available providers on my machine.

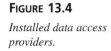

FIGURE 13.4

Installed data access providers.

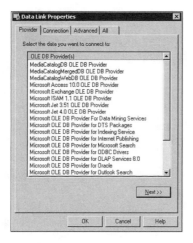

Some of the more commonly used data access providers are

- Microsoft Jet 4.0 OLE DB Provider   Allows access to Microsoft Access databases (.mdb files).

- Microsoft OLE DB Provider for ODBC Databases   Allows access to any database that has an ODBC driver installed. Many ODBC drivers are available, so this provider could be used to access almost every possible database. However, this provider should be used only as a last resort because it accesses information using both OLE DB and ODBC. Because there are more layers between your program and the database, this is generally the slowest provider.

- Microsoft OLE DB Provider for Oracle   Allows access to Oracle databases.

- Microsoft OLE DB Provider for SQL Server   Allows access to Microsoft SQL Server databases.

Depending on the provider you select at this step, different options are available on the other tabs. Table 13.1 outlines some of the options available under the Connection tab.

13

TABLE 13.1   Data Link Properties Options

Field	Provider	Purpose
Select, or enter a database name	Access	This field identifies the Access database (MDB file) to connect to.
User name	Common	The user account to use to connect to the database.
Password	Common	The password to use to connect to the database.

TABLE 13.1   continued

Field	Provider	Purpose
Select, or enter a server name	SQL Server	This field identifies the server to connect to. Select "(local)" to connect to your own computer if you are running SQL Server locally.
Select the database on the server	SQL Server	Because a single SQL Server might contain multiple databases; this field identifies the database on the server to connect to.
Test Connection	Common	This button allows you to test the connection parameters. This causes the IDE to attempt to connect to the database. A successful connection guarantees that the database is accessible.

The Advanced and All tabs are rarely used. The Advanced tab holds settings that most users don't need to make, based on the selected provider. The All tab is just another way of accessing all the properties. Rather than having a number of fields to edit, the All tab is a list of all the properties, allowing you to edit them from this list.

After you have entered all the information needed to access your database, click the Test Connection button to confirm. If the result is a dialog saying "Test Connection Succeeded," you can click OK to close the dialog and continue. If not, the dialog should suggest a way of fixing the error (usually it is because you missed a setting somewhere). Fix the error and try testing the connection again.

After you have connected to a database, it should appear in the Data Connections section of the Server Explorer. Depending on the type of database, the entry will have a number of sections. Figure 13.5 shows the available items for some of the available database types.

Table 13.2 outlines the types of items you should see for the various databases you might typically connect to.

FIGURE 13.5

Data Connections.

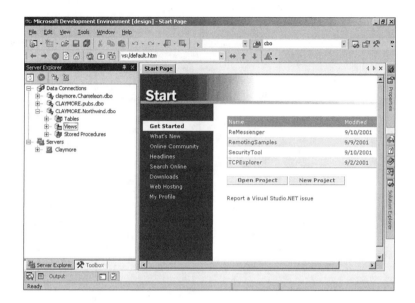

TABLE 13.2   Database Objects

Object	Description
Tables	Contains a list of all the tables stored in the database. A table is a grouping of information. For example, it might contain information about the employees of a company, the products it sells, or similar related items. Generally, this is the most important section of the Data Connections available.
Views	Contains a list of the views of data in the database. A view is a way of looking at the information—for example, it might not display all the fields, might sort information in a different way, or include information from multiple tables.
Stored procedures	Contains a list of the programs stored in the database. These include queries that might return information, as well as programs that might delete, update, or insert information.
Functions	Similar to stored procedures, however, functions are specific to some databases. They usually are used to return small amounts of information and are, for now, similar to the functions we use in Visual Basic .NET.
Database diagrams	Usually you will only see this with SQL Server. They are used to document the database and to give you a visual description of the tables in the database. (See Figure 13.6 for an example.)

13

FIGURE 13.6

Database diagram.

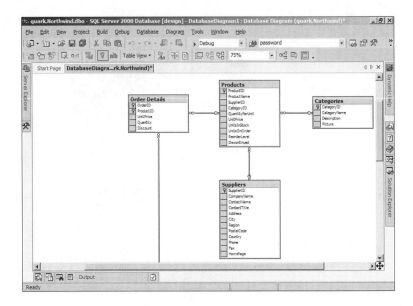

Walkthrough for Connecting to a Database

As described previously, the most important section in the Data Connections are the tables. Tables represent a set of information stored in the database. With the tables, you can view the data in the database, change the tables, and more. Let's use the Data Connections to connect to and view a database. We'll use the Northwind database that comes with Visual Basic .NET as an example.

1. Double-click on Add Connection to bring up the Data Link Properties dialog.

2. Select the Provider tab and select Microsoft Jet 4.0 OLE DB Provider. Click Next.

3. Click the button next to the Select or Enter a Database Name field. Navigate to find an Access database. There should be one at `%directory to Visual Basic.NET%\Common7\Tools\Bin\nwind.mdb`. Click OK to accept this database.

4. Click the Test Connection button. A dialog should popup telling you that the connection succeeded. If not, make sure that you have a database in the location selected. Click OK to accept this data connection.

5. The resulting connection has a number of tables, views, and stored procedures. Open the Tables folder and double-click on the Employees folder. A new window should open, showing you the list of employees of the Northwind Company. You should also be able to click on other tables to open them and view the data stored in them.

Do	Don't
	DON'T make any changes to the database now. If you change this database, other samples or applications could stop working. Just look at the information for now. If you want to try making changes to a database, create a new one for experimentation.

Working with Services

In addition to allowing you to view databases, the Server Explorer also makes accessing, viewing, and controlling services easy.

So, what's a service? A service is an application that runs in the background, providing some capability to the operating system. They will be familiar to developers who have used Windows NT and Windows 2000. However, developers who use Windows 95, 98, or ME might be less familiar because those operating systems tend to have fewer services running. Some of the services that run on Windows NT and 2000 include the Event Log (a central log for the system, security, and applications), Performance Counters (tracks a number of significant values for the operating system and other applications), and the Print Spooler (manages print jobs). In addition, other services can be installed, such as IIS, SQL Server (database) or Message Queue Server (allows asynchronous, or detached, application-to-application communication, similar to e-mail).

In Windows 95, 98, and ME, services are either part of the operating system itself or are programs that typically appear in the taskbar.

Viewing Services

Just as with the Data Connections, the services shown in the Server Explorer vary, based on what is installed and running on the computer. Some of the items that may appear in the Server Explorer are described in Table 13.3. These are the ones available as I write this; many others might be available later.

13

TABLE 13.3   Services in the Server Explorer

Service	Description
Event Logs	Provide access to the Application, Security, and System log files of Windows NT or 2000. These log files contain errors and other information from the applications running on the computer. This provides the same functionality as the Event Viewer application, without having to leave the Visual Basic .NET IDE.

TABLE 13.3 continued

Service	Description
Loaded Modules	Provides a list of all the DLLs loaded in memory and the programs using them. This can be a long list, depending on what you have running at any one time. This can be useful if you want to see whether a particular DLL is loaded in memory, and if so, whether it is being used by an application.
Management Data	Provides access to the Windows Management Information (WMI) for the server. WMI is a means of querying a computer for information. This information ranges from simple values, such as the installed operating system or CPU, to the programs running, and is precise as the settings for the installed printers. WMI is a powerful tool, and best used to retrieve information, not to change it.
Performance Counters	Provides access to the performance of the computer. Windows NT and 2000 constantly track information as you run your programs. This includes information on the time required to carry out tasks, the memory used, and much more. You can access the Performance Counters to measure CPU usage, memory, and so on.
Processes	Provides a list of all the running applications. You might be surprised to see just how many programs are running on your computer.
Services	Shows a list of the services running on the computer. These are the background applications running. One nice feature is that you can use this section to start or stop the services (depending on security).
SQL Server Databases	Provides another way (the Data Connections section is the other) of accessing SQL Server databases. This provides similar information to the Data Connections (however, only for SQL Server databases).
Web Services	Provides a list of Web Services installed on the computer (for more details, see Day 21, "Creating Web Services with Visual Basic .NET").
Message Queues	Provides a list of message queues available. These are used when creating message-based applications (not e-mail applications, however).

Connecting to Another Server

To see some of the services listed in Table 13.3, you might need to connect to a server. Double-click on the Add Server item in the Server Explorer, enter a valid server name in the dialog (see Figure 13.7), and click OK. You should be able (depending on network security) to view the services loaded on that machine as well as your own. You can specify another user account to use if that user has rights to access the other computer.

FIGURE 13.7

Adding another server.

You can use this feature to connect to the servers you commonly work with. For example, many developers need to access a database server, test server, and possibly a Web server as they develop a program. The Server Explorer would let you connect to all three as you need to monitor and/or use the services.

Writing Programs that Use Services

One of the most exciting features of the Service Explorer is that it allows you to not only view the Services and graphically work with them, but also to easily write applications that communicate with these services. For example, you can use the objects made available through the Service Explorer to add data access to an application. In addition, you can add objects to your application that can control or interact with the services—for example, to read performance counters, or to read or write information in the event logs of Windows NT or Windows 2000. These are capabilities that previously required a great deal of code and now can be done in a few lines, modifying the properties and running the methods of the objects that represent these features.

Writing Data Access Code with the Server Explorer

Although the Server Explorer is useful when you want to view services, it becomes much more useful when you want to access them. You can use the Server Explorer to write a great deal of code, saving you from having to write it yourself. One area where this becomes useful is when writing data access applications. Usually, this requires writing (as you saw on Day 11, "Introduction to Databases," and Day 12, "Accessing Data with .NET") the same type of code to retrieve information and display it to the user. Why spend your time writing this, if your computer can do it for you?

Let's create a simple application to view the data in one table of a database. I'll use the Northwind database; you can select any database you have a connection to from your machine.

After you have a valid connection to a database in Server Explorer, create a new Windows application project. Mine is called DataView; you can use that name (it's not

13

copyrighted, or anything), or pick your own. After the project is created, delete the original form by right-clicking on it in the Solution Explorer and selecting Delete. Accept the warning. Next, right-click on the project and select Add, Add Windows Form. Name the resulting form Customers. Right-click on the project one last time and select Properties. Set the Startup object to Customers and select OK.

As always, the first step in building a Visual Basic .NET application is to add the controls to the form. In our case, we will have a simple user interface—nothing but a grid. Select the DataGrid control from the toolbox and add it to your form. Set the properties as shown in Table 13.4.

TABLE 13.4 Properties for Data Grid

Control	Property	Value
Form	Text	Customer listing
DataGrid	Name	dbgCustomers
	Dock	Fill
	CaptionText	Customers

You also might want to use the AutoFormat feature (or manually set values) to make the grid pretty.

Next, we want to add the data access code. Rather than doing it manually, however, we'll use the Server Explorer. Select a table in your database (I've chosen the Customers table in Northwind), drag it from the Server Explorer, and drop it on the form. Two new objects appear under the form—OleDbConnection1 and OleDbDataAdapter1 (see Figure 13.8).

The OleDbConnection1 is, as you probably guessed, the connection to the database. The OleDbDataAdapter1 is the component that extracts (and saves) information from the database. Change the name of the controls as shown in Table 13.5.

TABLE 13.5 Properties of the Connection and Command

Control	Property	Value
OleDbConnection	Name	conNW
OleDbDataAdapter	Name	cmdCustomers

Now comes the fun part. Right-click on the cmdCustomers Data Adapter and select Generate DataSet; set the name to CustomerSet and place a check in the box to add an instance to the designer (see Figure 13.9). You should hear more hard drive grinding, and a new `CustomerSet1` is added to the window (see Figure 13.10). Change the name to `dsCustomers`.

FIGURE 13.8

Connection objects added.

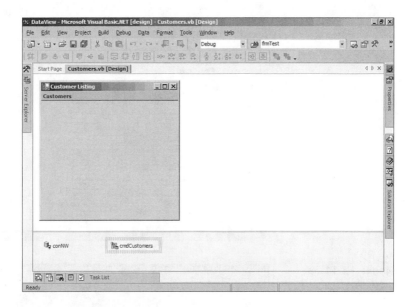

FIGURE 13.9

Adding the `DataSet`.

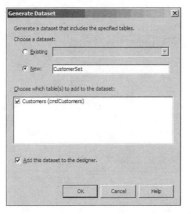

Before writing code, we should now connect the database and `DataSet` to the `DataGrid`. Set the `DataSource` of the `DataGrid` to `dsCustomers` and the `DataMember` to `Customers`. When you do this, the column headers should appear in the `DataGrid` (see Figure 13.11).

INPUT Now comes the hard part—we actually need to write some code. Find the `Form_Load` procedure and update it to fill the `DataSet` as shown in Listing 13.1.

13

FIGURE **13.10**

The DataSet *added.*

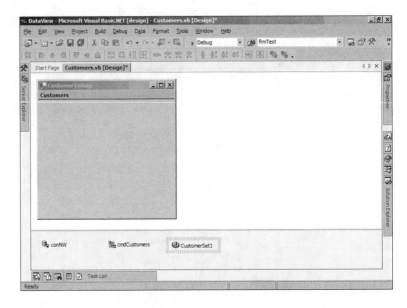

FIGURE **13.11**

Connecting DataSet *and* DataGrid.

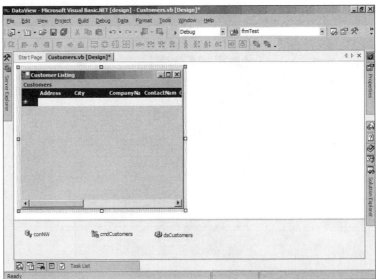

INPUT **LISTING 13.1** Changes to the New Procedure

```
1    Private Sub Customers_Load(ByVal sender As System.Object, _
2      ByVal e As System.EventArgs) Handles MyBase.Load
3        cmdCustomers.Fill(dsCustomers)
4    End Sub
```

ANALYSIS   The `Form_Load` procedure is standard for Windows applications, with the addition of line 3. Line 3 calls the `Fill` method of the `cmdCustomers` Data Adapter. `dsCustomers` is the `DataSet` created when we selected Generate DataSet. In other words, other than having to type in this one line, everything is generated for us. Build and run your program. If everything works out, it should appear as in Figure 13.12.

FIGURE 13.12

Running the `DataView` *application.*

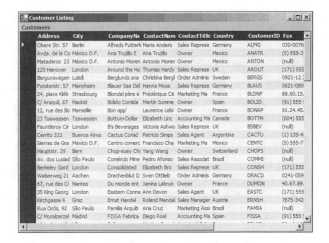

Accessing Performance Counters and Event Logs

To see the benefits of the tools in the Server Explorer, we'll build a small application that will monitor some of the performance counters that the operating system keeps about itself. In addition, we will record the date and time that the program begins and ends in the Application Event Log. The end result should look similar to Figure 13.13.

FIGURE 13.13

PerfLite in action.

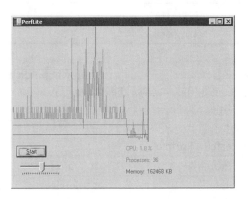

13

Create a new Windows application. Call the new project PerfLite because it will be a light (or 'Lite' in marketing-speak) version of the Performance Monitor application that comes with Windows NT and Windows 2000. When the project is ready, close the default form and rename it frmMain.vb. Next, right-click on the file and select View Code. Change all references of Form1 to frmMain. Using the Replace command will help (remember to select Search Hidden Text. Finally, right-click on the project in the Solution Explorer, select Properties, and change the Startup Object on the resulting form to frmMain (see Figure 13.14).

FIGURE 13.14

PerfLite properties.

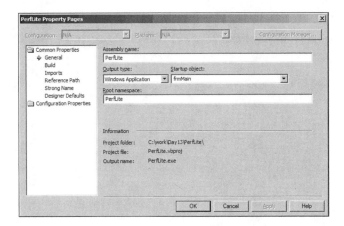

Build the application to make sure that all changes are made.

After everything compiles, we're ready to begin adding controls and setting their properties. Set the properties of the form as shown in Table 13.6.

TABLE 13.6   Properties for PerfLite Form

Property	Value
Text	PerfLite
Size	480, 360

We will display some performance information by drawing it on a panel. In addition, we will need to be able to control the speed of the drawing. Add the controls listed in Table 13.7, and set their properties as shown in the table.

TABLE 13.7   Controls for PerfLite Form

Control	Property	Value
Panel	Name	pnlSweep
	Dock	Top
	Height	240

TABLE 13.7 continued

Control	Property	Value
Button	Name	cmdSweep
	Text	&Start
	Location	8, 248
	Size	64, 24
TrackBar	Name	trkSpeed
	Location	8, 280
	Size	104, 42
	Minimum	1
	Maximum	20
	Value	10
Label	Name	lblCPU
	Location	240, 248
	Autosize	True
	Text	CPU:
	Forecolor	Red (or something you like/can see)
Label	Name	lblProc
	Location	240, 272
	Autosize	True
	Text	Processes:
	Forecolor	Green (again, or something appealing)
Label	Name	lblMem
	Location	240, 296
	Autosize	True
	Text	Memory:
	Forecolor	Blue
Timer	Name	tmrClock
	Interval	1000

To display the performance information, we need to add the appropriate performance counters to the application:

1. Open the Server Explorer and select a server (possibly your own computer).
2. Open the Performance Counters section.

3. Scroll down until you find the Processor item and open it.

4. Open the % Processor Time item and select the _Total item.

5. Drag this item over the form and drop it on the form. An item called PerformanceCounter1 should be visible in a new section below the form (see Figure 13.15).

FIGURE 13.15

After adding the Performance Counter.

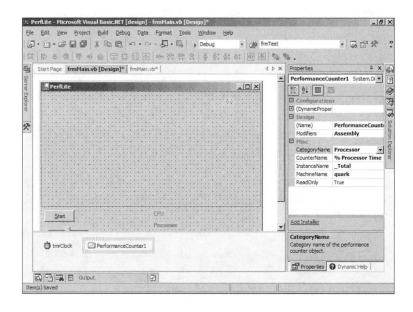

There is another way to add an item from the Server Explorer to your application. Find the System\Processes Performance Counter. Notice that it does not have any items under it, like the _Total under the % Processor Time item. Right-click on the Processes counter and select Add to Designer. You should then see another Performance Counter object added next to the first.

To finish adding our Performance Counters, select and add the Memory\Committed Bytes Performance Counter.

Rename the three Performance Counters prfCPU, prfProcs, and prfMem.

In addition to Performance Counters, we can also add objects to make accessing the Event Log much easier than ever before. Open the Event Logs section of the Server Explorer and select Application. Either drag the Application item to the Form, or right-click and select Add To Designer (whichever you prefer). A new item should appear next to the three Performance Counters. Set the properties of this new object as in Table 13.8. The final form should appear as shown in Figure 13.16.

TABLE 13.8 Properties of the `EventLog` Object

Property	Value
Name	logApp
Source	PerfLite

FIGURE 13.16

PerfLite, ready for coding.

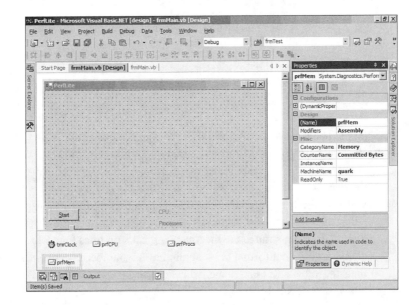

Now that the user interface is in place, it's time to start adding some code to make our program do something. For this application, we will add code to three of the controls and another procedure to assist. The end result will show a "sweep" line moving across the panel, with three colored lines trailing behind it (see Figure 13.17).

FIGURE 13.17

The sample, running.

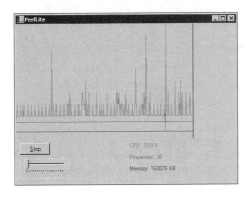

13

To draw the sweep line periodically, we will use the `Timer` control's `Timer` event. This code is in Listing 13.2.

LISTING 13.2 The Code for the Timer Control

```
1    Private Sub tmrClock_Tick(ByVal sender As System.Object, _
2      ByVal e As System.EventArgs) Handles tmrClock.Tick
3        Dim sngCPU As Single = prfCPU.NextValue() / 100
4        Dim sngProcs As Single = prfProcs.NextValue()
5        Dim sngMem As Single = prfMem.NextValue / 1024
6        'draw the sweep panel
7        DrawSweep(sngCPU, sngProcs, sngMem)
8        'update the labels
9        lblCPU.Text = "CPU: " & sngCPU.ToString("p")
10       lblProc.Text = "Processes: " & sngProcs
11       lblMem.Text = "Memory: " & sngMem.ToString("f0") & "KB"
12   End Sub
```

The code in this procedure is basically interested in two things: converting the values from the Performance Counters into Single variables and updating the Label controls. Lines 3–5 retrieve the values from each of the Performance Counters. Notice that we are assigning the values to the variables as we create them. We then pass these values to the DrawSweep routine (line 7—see Listing 13.3) to display. Finally, each of the values is formatted and displayed on each of the Label controls (lines 9–11). Two items that might seem strange are the ToString calls on lines 9 and 11. The ToString method allows an optional format to be applied as the number is converted to a string. Line 9 formats the value as a percentage, whereas line 11 formats it as a fixed decimal place number, with 0 decimal places.

LISTING 13.3 Drawing the Sweep Line

```
13   Private Sub DrawSweep(ByVal CPU As Single, _
14     ByVal Processes As Single, _
15     ByVal Memory As Single)
16       Dim oGrafix As Graphics = pnlSweep.CreateGraphics()
17       Dim sngHeight As Single = pnlSweep.Height
18       'for the points
19       Dim sngCPUY As Single
20       Dim sngProcsY As Single
21       Dim sngMemY As Single
22       'erase previous sweep line
23       oGrafix.DrawLine(penBack, m_sngX, 0, m_sngX, sngHeight)
24       'draw data points
25       sngCPUY = sngHeight - (CPU * sngHeight) - 1
26       oGrafix.DrawLine(penCPU, _
27           m_sngX - increment, m_sngCPUY, m_sngX, sngCPUY)
28       m_sngCPUY = sngCPUY
29       sngProcsY = sngHeight - Processes
30       oGrafix.DrawLine(penProcs, _
31           m_sngX - increment, m_sngProcsY, m_sngX, sngProcsY)
```

LISTING 13.3   continued

```
32        m_sngProcsY = sngProcsY
33        'the 10000 is for my machine, to get the memory to a nice value
34        '   you may need to change it if the memory line
35        '   isn't drawing correctly
36        sngMemY = sngHeight - (Memory / 10000)
37        oGrafix.DrawLine(penMem, _
38            m_sngX - INCREMENT, m_sngMemY, m_sngX, sngMemY)
39        m_sngMemY = sngMemY
40        'increment x
41        m_sngX += increment
42        If m_sngX > pnlSweep.Width Then
43            'reset back to start
44            m_sngX = 0
45            'and clear the drawing surface
46            oGrafix.Clear(SystemColors.Control)
47        End If
48        'draw new line
49        oGrafix.DrawLine(penFore, m_sngX, 0, m_sngX, sngHeight)
50   End Sub
```

ANALYSIS   As you might expect, this routine is the heart of the application. Don't be frightened off, either by the length, or by the graphics calls—it is a fairly easy routine.

We begin by retrieving the Graphics object from the Panel control (line 16). All graphics in Visual Basic .NET are created on a Graphics object. Any control that can be drawn on (such as Image and Panel controls, or forms) exposes this Graphics object with a CreateGraphics method. The object in turn exposes objects and methods for drawing on it (and in turn, the container control).

Before we discuss the actual code, let's determine what it is intended to do. The end result is to have a vertical line that moves across (horizontally) the Form. As it moves, it trails behind it three colored lines, each representing one of the three Performance Counters. When the vertical (sweep) line gets to the end of the form, it should start over at the left side of the form, clearing the form for the next sweep. The end result should look a little like a heart monitor (without the "ping"). So, we will need code to draw the vertical line (and move it across the form), and the three performance lines.

To move the sweep line, we need to draw a new line (in the background color) to erase the old line, move over a bit, and draw a new line. In the preceding code, we erase the old line at line 23, and the new line is moved and drawn from lines 25–41. The reason it takes so long is that we also need to test to see whether we will be moving past the right-hand side of the form. If this is the case (the If statement at line 42), we clear the form and move back to the left-hand side to begin a new sweep.

13

The Performance Counter lines are drawn as well in this routine. One difference with these calls is that we also need to determine where to draw the line, and we also need to remember the old value, to allow us to connect the new line to the old. Using the first Performance Counter as an example (lines 25–28), it boils down to three steps:

1. Decide what the new Y value (the height) should be for the new line. Line 25 does this for the CPU counter by determining what percentage of the total height is taken up by the CPU (remember, the CPU counter is a percentage counter).

2. Draw the line, connecting the old line to this one. Lines 26–27 do this by drawing a line in the CPU color from the old values for X and Y to the new ones. The new X is determined by adding the increment (15 units) to the old one, while the new Y was calculated in step 1.

3. Store the newly calculated Y value for the next loop through (line 28). This will be used for drawing the next line.

The routines for drawing the other two Performance Counter lines (lines 29–35 and lines 36–39) are similar—differing only in the way that the new Y value is calculated.

INPUT   **LISTING 13.4**   Turning the Sweep Line On and Off

```
51      Private Sub cmdSweep_Click(ByVal sender As Object, _
52          ByVal e As System.EventArgs) Handles cmdSweep.Click
53          'Toggle the button text and timer (on or off)
54          If cmdSweep.Text = "&Start" Then
55              cmdSweep.Text = "&Stop"
56              tmrClock.Enabled = True
57          Else
58              cmdSweep.Text = "&Start"
59              tmrClock.Enabled = False
60          End If
61      End Sub
```

ANALYSIS   The purpose of this routine is to allow the user to start and stop the sweep. As such, it is relatively simple. Based on the text on the button, we will "toggle" it and our timer. That is, if the timer is active, we will stop it. If the timer is not active, we will activate it. We could use another variable to track this status, but we will instead use the caption on the button. If the Text property of the button is &Start (the initial value), we will start the timer and change the Text to &Stop (notice that the two have the same access key, the letter S). Alternatively, we will stop the timer and set the text back to &Start.

Next, we need to allow the user to change the speed of the sweep line. This is done in Listing 13.5.

INPUT **LISTING 13.5** Setting the Speed

```
62    Private Sub trkSpeed_Scroll(ByVal sender As Object, _
63       ByVal e As System.EventArgs) Handles trkSpeed.Scroll
64          Dim iValue As Integer
65          iValue = CInt(trkSpeed.Value)
66          'set the timer interval to the selected time
67          tmrClock.Interval = iValue * 100 'ms
68    End Sub
```

ANALYSIS The code for setting the speed is fairly basic. Lines 64 and 65 simply make sure that the value we use (the current speed setting) is an integer. We then use the speed to adjust the interval for the Timer (line 67). Smaller intervals mean that the sweep arm will travel faster.

Finally, there are some variables that we will need throughout the application. These will store the current X and Y coordinates used when drawing and the Pens used to draw the lines. Add the code in Listing 13.6 to the form, just under the region marked Windows Form Designer generated code, and before any of your other code.

INPUT **LISTING 13.6** Form-Level Variables

```
69    Dim m_sngX As Single
70    Dim m_sngY As Single
71
72    Dim m_sngCPUY As Single
73    Dim m_sngProcsY As Single
74    Dim m_sngMemY As Single
75
76    Dim penCPU As New System.Drawing.Pen(Color.Red)
77    Dim penProcs As New System.Drawing.Pen(Color.Green)
78    Dim penMem As New System.Drawing.Pen(Color.Blue)
79    Dim penFore As New System.Drawing.Pen(SystemColors.WindowText)
80    Dim penBack As New System.Drawing.Pen(SystemColors.Control)
81
82    Const INCREMENT As Single = 1
```

13

ANALYSIS The variables from lines 69–74 are used to store the current pen positions when not drawing the lines. One variable stores the current X position, and the others the current Y positions for each performance counter. The pens are used to draw each performance line and the sweep line. Finally, the constant in line 82 is used to space the sweep line as it moves across the form.

After the code is in place, build the program and run it. Click the Start button and watch for a few seconds. You should begin to see the sweep bar move from left to right on the form, leaving behind three lines—one each for CPU (% usage), Processes (programs running), and Memory (in use). The text on the button should change to Stop. Change the track bar (set it higher or lower) to watch how it affects the sweep; try clicking the Stop button to watch it change back to Start. You might want to try adding a few other counters to the display as an exercise.

Summary

Most modern operating systems like Windows include a number of services. These services provide functionality that extends the operating system, adding functionality, such as databases or logging, that enriches the core functionality. The Server Explorer allows you to view and change the state of these services on either your own development computer or another computer without leaving the Visual Basic .NET IDE. In addition, for many of the available services, the Server Explorer makes writing code to use these services trivial.

Tomorrow, we will begin our quest into discovering the true object-oriented nature of Visual Basic .NET by learning what it takes to be "really" object-oriented.

Q&A

Q. I've got some things in my Server Explorer that weren't mentioned (or I don't have some that are mentioned). What are they?

A. It is possible for other companies to create components to "plug into" the Server Explorer. This would enable the developer to work with these services directly, just as you can with the normal services. Alternatively, if the server you connect to doesn't provide a given service, it might not appear in the list.

Q. If I change the data in the Server Explorer, does it change the database?

A. Yes, please be careful.

Workshop

The Workshop is designed to help you anticipate possible questions, review what you've learned, and get you thinking about how to put your knowledge into practice. The answers to the quiz are in Appendix A, "Answers to Quizzes/Exercises."

Quiz

1. Name two sections in the Server Explorer that would tell you what programs are running on your computer.

2. What is a service?

3. What would be displayed if the following code were added to a program and run?

```
Dim prfCPU As New PerformanceCounter("processor", _
    "% Processor Time", "_total")
Console.WriteLine(prfCPU.NextValue())
```

Exercises

1. Use the Data Connections to connect to an available database and explore the Tables and other items made available (remember not to make any changes, unless you really know you should).

2. Explore the Server Explorer to find out what is available on your computer, as well as servers you normally use for development.

13

DAY **14**

Introduction to Object-Oriented Programming

In the .NET release, Visual Basic has been rewritten from the ground up. One of the main reasons why this was done was to add deeply integrated object-oriented features. This lesson will cover:

- An overview of object-oriented programming (OOP)
- Important OOP concepts
- How to incorporate OOP into your own systems

In addition to these topics, at the end of today's lesson you will learn techniques to help you build applications using these OOP techniques.

Overview of Object-Oriented Programming

Object-oriented programming (OOP) is not a particular technology or language; it is a way to design and build applications. To make it even more abstract, you could consider it a way to think about designing and building applications. OOP has an academic history, and I won't try to give you an exact date on which it was first conceived, but it really started to catch on with the software industry at large in the 1980s. Now it is almost assumed that you are using OOP, but often the term is used with little understanding of what it really means.

At the heart of OOP is the concept of an *object*, a programming construct that combines specific information and a set of related behaviors. In OOP, scenarios are thought of in terms of these objects instead of the linear step-by-step approach that was (and still is) used in the majority of computer programs. Objects are usually used to describe entities, which can be real (a vehicle) or abstract (a itinerary booked with a national airline). These entities have attributes, such as the color of the vehicle or the departure date of the itinerary, that describe the object. These objects also have certain actions that can be performed on them, such as "Selling" for the car and "Canceling" for the itinerary. In OOP, the entities become objects, the attributes are known as *properties* (which you can set or retrieve), and the actions are called *methods*.

NEW TERM   An *object* is a representation of a real or abstract entity along with the properties of that entity and the related actions that can be performed.

Comparing Linear to Object-Oriented

The difference between linear or procedural programming and OOP might seem simple, but it is a complex concept that is often misunderstood. I will show you two descriptions of the process for calculating a mortgage payment. One process is described in linear steps (also called *procedural programming*), and the other is described from an object-oriented point of view.

The linear process follows these steps:

1. Get the principal amount.
2. Get the annual interest rate.
3. Get the length in years.
4. Calculate the interest rate per month.
5. Calculate the number of payments (years * 12).
6. Calculate the payments.

The object-oriented process includes these steps:

1. Create a new mortgage.
2. Set the principal, interest rate, and duration properties of the mortgage.
3. Retrieve the payment property.

In code, the two approaches also look different. Consider the two sets of code shown in Listing 14.1 and Listing 14.2, both of which could run behind a Windows Form or Web Form to calculate mortgage payments.

LISTING 14.1   Procedural View of a Mortgage Calculator

```
1    'Linear Style
2    Private Sub btnCalc_Click(ByVal sender As System.Object, _
3    ByVal e As System.EventArgs) Handles btnCalc.Click
4        Dim iYears As Integer
5        Dim iMonths As Integer
6        Dim dblInterestRate As Double
7        Dim curPrincipal As Decimal
8        Dim curPayment As Decimal
9
10       iYears = CInt(txtPayments.Text)
11       iMonths = iYears * 12
12       dblInterestRate = CType(txtInterest.Text, Double)
13       curPrincipal = CType(txtPrincipal.Text, Decimal)
14
15       'divide interest rate by 12 to obtain monthly rate
16       dblInterestRate /= 12
17
18       curPayment = curPrincipal * _
19           ((1 - (1 + dblInterestRate)) _
20           / (1 - ((1 + dblInterestRate) ^ iMonths)) _
21           + dblInterestRate)
22       lblMonthlyPayment.Text = curPayment.ToString()
23   End Sub
```

LISTING 14.2   Object-Oriented View of Mortgage Calculator

```
1    'Object Style
2    Private Sub btnCalc_Click(ByVal sender As System.Object, _
3    ByVal e As System.EventArgs) Handles btnCalc.Click
4        Dim iYears As Integer
5        Dim dblInterestRate As Double
6        Dim curPrincipal As Decimal
7        Dim curPayment As Decimal
8
9        iYears = CInt(txtPayments.Text)
10       dblInterestRate = CType(txtInterest.Text, Double)
11       curPrincipal = CType(txtPrincipal.Text, Decimal)
12
13       Dim objMort As New Mortgage()
14
15       objMort.AnnualInterestRate = dblInterestRate
```

14

Listing **14.2** continued

```
16          objMort.NumberOfYears = iYears
17          objMort.Principal = curPrincipal
18
19          lblMonthlyPayment.Text = objMort.PaymentAmount.ToString
20      End Sub
```

Listing 14.2 creates an instance of the Mortgage object to do its calculations, but the underlying calculations are the same. Note that because the Mortgage object has not yet been defined, you will not be able to run the code from Listing 14.2. Although a similar end result could be obtained if you wrote a function with the procedural code, such as CalculateMortgagePayment(), that still would not be OOP. Only by using the Mortgage object, which combines the information about the mortgage and the code to process that information, have you really used OOP.

This style of programming is not new to you, if you have been following along with the first half of this book; almost everything in Visual Studio .NET is built in this manner. Consider the code used to work with controls on a Windows Form: txtPayment.Text = lblResult.Text. Both controls are objects, with a Text property, just like the Mortgage object from the previous example. Using the objects provided by Visual Basic .NET and the .NET Framework does not make your code object-oriented, although many people will tell you it does. You can use objects and still program in a procedural step-by-step style.

Using Objects for Code Organization

In procedural programming, not using OOP techniques, it is common to break functionality into subroutines or functions that can then be called from any other part of the program. It is also common to take these subroutines and group them together (usually with other related subroutines) into modules, DLLs, or other form of code structure. You then add these groups of subroutines into your program as individual units and call any of them as needed. So, all your mathematical functions could be grouped into a math.dll, and all your string functions in string.dll, creating an organized system.

This form of coding is still procedural rather than object-oriented. That doesn't reduce its value as a good way to organize code, but it is starting to look a lot like OOP with calls such as Math.SquareRoot(x) being made. When you are programming with .NET, you need to use objects to group procedures in this fashion. Placing 20 different procedures together as methods of an object is a useful technique, but keep in mind that this style of grouping is not OOP; it is merely how code is organized in .NET. Your code is only truly object-oriented when you are using objects to represent the entities and concepts that make up your application.

In .NET, objects that do not represent an abstract or real entity, existing just to group code, usually designate themselves and all their methods as static or shared. You will learn more about these types of objects in tomorrow's lesson (Day 15, "Creating Objects in Visual Basic .NET"), but just remember that there is a particular way to build these procedural libraries of code.

Important Concepts in OOP

Terms have been defined for use in OOP, and these terms are relatively universal across all programming languages and technologies. In this section, I will explain the most common terms and provide an example of how each of them works.

Classes, Objects, and Instances

The first terms that need discussion are those that will be used throughout any material involving OOP: class, object, and instance. These concepts are the foundation of your work with OOP, and as such must be clear before moving on.

A *class* is a template for an object; it describes the basic structure of the object. Many different analogies are used to describe the relationship between class, object, and instance. One of the more common is to think of these concepts in terms of houses and house building. In such an analogy, the class is the blueprint for the house, and the house itself is an object. Many houses can be created based on the same blueprint, and many objects can be created based on the same class. Each object created from a class is called an *instance* of that class. To look at this in Visual Basic terms, consider Listing 14.3.

LISTING 14.3 Placing Multiple Classes into a Single File

```
1 Module AllAboutObjects
2     Sub Main()
3         Dim x As myFirstClass
4         x = New myFirstClass()
5     End Sub
6 End Module
7
8 Public Class myFirstClass
9 '<class definition and code goes in here>
10 End Class
```

14

The statement `Public Class myFirstClass` (line 8) defines a new class, a blueprint for objects. Line 3 creates a variable of type `myFirstClass`, a variable capable of holding an instance of `myFirstClass`. Line 4 creates a new instance of `myFirstClass` (creating an object) and assigns it to the variable x. Now x refers to an instance of the `myFirstClass` class. Another example of using objects is shown in Listing 14.4.

LISTING 14.4   Variables and Instances Are not the Same Thing

```
1 Module AllAboutObjects
2     Sub Main()
3         Dim x As myFirstClass
4         Dim y As myFirstClass
5         x = New myFirstClass()
6         y = New myFirstClass()
7     End Sub
8 End Module
```

In Listing 14.4, two variables of type `myFirstClass` are declared (in lines 3 and 4) and then two new instances of `myFirstClass` are created (lines 5 and 6). One instance is referred to by each variable. x holds a reference to a different object than y, but both objects are instances of `myFirstClass`. This concept, instances compared to variables, is explored further using another sample in Listing 14.5.

LISTING 14.5   Instances Compared to Variables

```
1 Module AllAboutObjects
2     Sub Main()
3         Dim x As myFirstClass
4         Dim y As myFirstClass
5         x = New myFirstClass()
6         y = x
7     End Sub
8 End Module
```

Listing 14.5 makes things a little more confusing. Now two variables have been declared, both capable of referring to an instance of the `myFirstClass` class. One new instance of that class then is created (using the New keyword), and a reference to the new object is placed into x. Next, y is assigned x, and the result is that y now holds a reference to the same instance of `myFirstClass` that x does. There is only one object, and therefore one area of memory, but two variables that refer (or point) to it. This will be demonstrated in the next section as you learn about properties.

Properties

Classes can define properties that every one of their instances should have. A *property* is a value that exists as part of an object, and you can retrieve or set it through the object.

Listing 14.6 adds a property to the definition of myFirstClass by adding a public variable. This is not the only way to add a property, but we will cover the other methods in Day 15.

LISTING 14.6   Adding a Property to the Definition of myFirstClass

```
 1 Module AllAboutObjects
 2     Sub Main()
 3         Dim x As myFirstClass
 4         Dim y As myFirstClass
 5         x = New myFirstClass()
 6         y = New myFirstClass()
 7         x.Name = "Fred"
 8         y.Name = "Joe"
 9         Console.WriteLine("x.Name = {0}", x.Name)
10         Console.WriteLine("y.Name = {0}", y.Name)
11         Console.ReadLine()
12     End Sub
13 End Module
14
15 Public Class myFirstClass
16     Public Name As String
17 End Class
```

As before, two variables are declared, x and y; two new instances of myFirstClass are created; and references are placed into the two variables. Next, in lines 7 and 8, a value is placed into the Name property of each instance of myFirstClass, accessing this property through the variables that refer to the object. The Console.WriteLine statements (lines 9 and 10) produce the following output:

```
x.Name = Fred
y.Name = Joe
```

Each individual instance of a class has its own memory associated with it, and therefore property values are stored independently with each instance. Returning again to the house analogy, every instance of a house is created from the same blueprint, but each instance might be painted a different color. The color of the house is a property, and its value is not determined by the blueprint; it is an attribute of each instance. Listing 14.7 should help illustrate how properties are associated with an individual instance of a class.

LISTING 14.7   x and y Point to a Single Object Instance

```
 1 Module AllAboutObjects
 2     Sub Main()
 3         Dim x As myFirstClass
```

14

LISTING **14.7**   continued

```
 4          Dim y As myFirstClass
 5          x = New myFirstClass()
 6          y = x
 7          x.Name = "Fred"
 8          y.Name = "Joe"
 9          Console.WriteLine("x.Name = {0}", x.Name)
10          Console.WriteLine("y.Name = {0}", y.Name)
11          Console.ReadLine()
12      End Sub
13 End Module
```

The only difference between Listing 14.7 and Listing 14.6 is in line 6, where y is assigned a reference to x instead of to a new instance of myFirstClass. This difference means that in lines 7 and 8, the code is working with the Name property of the same instance, and the output from this routine will be

```
x.Name = Joe
y.Name = Joe
```

Both WriteLine statements produce the same property value because both x and y refer to the same object instance. This particular concept, where multiple variables refer to the same object, is another important but confusing topic. Check out section 6.1 of the Visual Basic Language Specification (part of the .NET documentation; search on "Value Types and Reference Types" to find it) for more details.

In .NET, properties can be read-only, write-only, or read/write, allowing control over how these values are accessed. You will learn how to control access to properties of your own classes on Day 15.

Methods

In addition to properties, classes also can have behaviors or actions associated with them. Referred to as *methods*, these actions allow a class to include some logic in addition to the information being stored by its properties. A house is not the best example when you want to talk about methods, but a house class created for use by a real-estate application might have methods to list the house on the Web (myHouse.List()), sell the house (myHouse.Sell()), or perhaps to print out a brochure (myHouse.PrintBrochure("Printer1"). These methods are just like any other procedure; they can accept parameters when you call them and provide return values as well.

In Listing 14.8, a method (DoSomething) has been added to myFirstClass by adding a Public procedure (Sub) to the class definition.

LISTING 14.8 Adding a Method to `myFirstClass`

```
1 Module AllAboutObjects
2     Sub Main()
3         Dim x As myFirstClass
4         x = New myFirstClass()
5         x.DoSomething()
6     End Sub
7 End Module
8
9 Public Class myFirstClass
10     Public Name As String
11     Public Sub DoSomething()
12         'code would go here
13     End Sub
14 End Class
```

Calling this method (line 5) can then be done from any instance of the class. Just as with properties, though, the method is defined in the class but called in the instance. This means that if the method uses any of the properties (private or public) of the class, then it will be using the information stored in the particular instance.

Inheritance

A key concept in OOP, but one that has not been easy to implement in Visual Basic prior to .NET, is inheritance.

NEW TERM *Inheritance* is the idea that you can base a class on another class, generally to modify or add to the features available on the original class.

I have just finished lunch, so I think I will move away from the house analogy and try to confuse you with one based on burgers. Consider the basic hamburger: a bun with a beef patty stuck in between it.

When the restaurant decides to start offering a cheeseburger, it doesn't start from scratch. The restaurant tells the cook to "make a hamburger, but add a slice of cheese." The cook has created a new class of burger, the cheeseburger, which inherits from the hamburger class. To continue stretching this analogy until even I get sick of burgers, the restaurant could now decide to offer a deluxe burger, which inherits from the cheeseburger and adds lettuce and tomato. In each case, the base class is being used as a foundation.

In this way, you can create an object hierarchy, where the class you are using might be at the end of several layers of inheritance. You can have as many classes based on a single class as you want, so the restaurant could offer a vegetarian burger or a chicken burger, both of which are derived from the hamburger class and override the type of patty.

14

NEW TERM *Overriding* is a term used to indicate that a child class is providing its own implementation of a feature of the base class, as compared to simply adding new features.

On Day 15, you will learn about creating your own objects in Visual Basic .NET using overriding, inheritance, and other features, but for now I will provide a simple example of using inheritance in Listing 14.9.

LISTING 14.9   Using Inheritance to Create Object Hierarchies

```
 1 Module AllAboutObjects
 2     Public Sub Main()
 3
 4         Dim mySnippet As CodeSnippet
 5         mySnippet = New CodeSnippet()
 6
 7         With mySnippet
 8             .Contents = "txtEntry.Text = lblInfo.Text"
 9             .Author = "Joe"
10             .Language = "VB.NET"
11             .Purpose = "Get Label Caption Into Text Box"
12         End With
13     End Sub
14 End Module
15
16 Public Class Snippet
17     Public Contents As String
18     Public Author As String
19 End Class
20
21 Public Class CodeSnippet
22     Inherits Snippet
23     Public Language As String
24     Public Purpose As String
25 End Class
```

As you can see, `CodeSnippet`, which is derived from `Snippet`, adds two new properties. When you create a new instance of the `CodeSnippet` class (line 5), it has the properties of both classes available.

Often your new class needs to override some functionality of the base class, simply because the base functionality does not take into account the other modifications you have made to the class. Consider a method, called `GetSnippet()` that exists on the `Snippet` class and is designed to return the complete `Snippet` as a `String`, as shown in Listing 14.10.

LISTING 14.10   Take into Account All the Features of Your New Class

```
 1 Public Class Snippet
 2     Public Contents As String
 3     Public Author As String
 4     Public Function GetSnippet() As String
 5         Dim sTmp As String
 6         sTmp = "Author: " & Author _
 7             & System.Environment.NewLine _
 8             & Contents
 9         Return sTmp
10     End Function
11 End Class
```

This function outputs only the two properties of the base class, so if you do not override
it in the new class, your two new properties would not be handled. The CodeSnippet
class in Listing 14.11 handles this by overriding the base class's GetSnippet function.

LISTING 14.11   Override a Function to Customize it to Handle New Features of
Your Class

```
 1 Module AllAboutObjects
 2     Public Sub Main()
 3
 4         Dim mySnippet As CodeSnippet
 5         mySnippet = New CodeSnippet()
 6
 7         With mySnippet
 8             .Contents = "txtEntry.Text = lblInfo.Text"
 9             .Author = "Joe"
10             .Language = "VB.NET"
11             .Purpose = "Get Label Caption Into Text Box"
12         End With
13     End Sub
14 End Module
15
16 Public Class Snippet
17     Public Contents As String
18     Public Author As String
19     Public Overridable Function GetSnippet() As String
20         Dim sTmp As String
21         sTmp = "Author: " & Author _
22             & System.Environment.NewLine _
23             & Contents
24         Return sTmp
25     End Function
26 End Class
27
28 Public Class CodeSnippet
```

14

LISTING **14.11**   continued

```
29    Inherits Snippet
30    Public Language As String
31    Public Purpose As String
32
33    Public Overrides Function GetSnippet() As String
34        Dim sTmp As String
35        sTmp = MyBase.GetSnippet() & _
36                System.Environment.NewLine & _
37                "Language: " & Language & _
38                System.Environment.NewLine & _
39                "Purpose: " & Purpose
40        Return sTmp
41    End Function
42 End Class
```

To override this function, it must be marked as Overridable in the base class (line 19) and then you must supply a new implementation in the derived class (marked with Overrides, line 33). To obtain the results from the base class's function as a part of this class's implementation, you can use the special keyword MyBase (line 35) to access the properties and methods of the base class. Another special keyword, although it is not used in this example, is Me. Me refers to the current object, so Me.Name used in the GetSnippet procedure would refer to the Name property of the current instance of this class.

A useful feature of inheritance is that classes that derive from a specific base class can be used as if they were that base class. Instances of the new class can be placed into variables that use the data type of the old class and can be passed as parameters into procedures expecting the old data type, as shown in Listing 14.12.

LISTING **14.12**   Use an Inherited Class Anywhere its Base Class Is Supported

```
 1 Option Strict On
 2 Option Explicit On
 3
 4 Module AllAboutObjects
 5     Public Sub Main()
 6
 7         Dim mySnippet As CodeSnippet
 8         mySnippet = New CodeSnippet()
 9         With mySnippet
10             .Contents = "txtEntry.Text = lblInfo.Text"
11             .Author = "Joe"
12             .Language = "VB.NET"
13             .Purpose = "Get Label Caption Into Text Box"
14         End With
```

LISTING **14.12** continued

```
15          PrintSnippet(mySnippet)
16          Console.ReadLine()
17      End Sub
18
19      Public Sub PrintSnippet(ByVal objSnippet As Snippet)
20          Console.WriteLine(objSnippet.GetSnippet())
21      End Sub
22 End Module
```

When an object is passed as its base type, as in line 15 in Listing 14.12, the properties and methods added by the inherited class are not available. So, `objSnippet.Language` would not compile if you placed it into line 20 because it is not a valid property for the `Snippet` class. Overridden methods are available because they exist in the definition of the base class, but the implementation in the derived class will be called instead of the base implementation. Listing 14.12 would produce the following output:

```
Author: Joe
txtEntry.Text = lblInfo.Text
Language: VB.NET
Purpose: Get Label Caption Into Text Box
```

You will learn more about inheritance and the capability to treat a derived object as if it were its base class, during tomorrow's lesson (Day 15).

Constructors

Another object-oriented feature new to this version of Visual Basic is the addition of constructors for objects.

NEW TERM A *constructor* is a routine called when an instance of a class is created, and your class can specify what parameters can be supplied at creation time. This concept provides a way of initializing your object at creation time.

In Visual Basic .NET, the constructor is represented by a `New` procedure in the class definition, and (just like any procedure) you can have any number of overloaded versions of this procedure, providing multiple ways in which the object can be created. In Listing 14.13, a variety of constructors are added to the `Snippet` and `CodeSnippet` classes, allowing you to initialize these objects in a variety of ways.

LISTING **14.13** Constructors Create and Initialize Your Object

```
1 Option Strict On
2 Option Explicit On
3
```

14

LISTING 14.13   continued

```
 4 Module AllAboutObjects
 5     Public Sub Main()
 6         Dim mySnippet As CodeSnippet
 7         mySnippet = _
 8             New CodeSnippet("txtEntry.Text = lblInfo.Text", _
 9             "Joe", "VB.NET", "Get Label Caption Into Text Box")
10         PrintSnippet(mySnippet)
11         Console.ReadLine()
12     End Sub
13     Public Sub PrintSnippet(ByVal objSnippet As Snippet)
14         Console.WriteLine(objSnippet.GetSnippet())
15     End Sub
16 End Module
17
18 Public Class Snippet
19     Public Contents As String
20     Public Author As String
21
22     Public Sub New()
23
24     End Sub
25
26     Public Sub New(ByVal Contents As String)
27         Me.Contents = Contents
28     End Sub
29
30     Public Sub New(ByVal Contents As String, _
31             ByVal Author As String)
32         Me.Contents = Contents
33         Me.Author = Author
34     End Sub
35
36     Public Overridable Function GetSnippet() As String
37         Dim sTmp As String
38         sTmp = "Author: " & Author _
39             & System.Environment.NewLine _
40             & Contents
41         Return sTmp
42     End Function
43 End Class
44
45 Public Class CodeSnippet
46     Inherits Snippet
47     Public Language As String
48     Public Purpose As String
49
50     Public Sub New()
51         MyBase.New()
52     End Sub
```

LISTING **14.13**   continued

```
53
54      Public Sub New(ByVal Contents As String)
55          MyBase.New(Contents)
56      End Sub
57
58      Public Sub New(ByVal Contents As String, _
59              ByVal Author As String)
60          Me.New(Contents)
61          Me.Author = Author
62      End Sub
63
64      Public Sub New(ByVal Contents As String, _
65              ByVal Author As String, _
66              ByVal Language As String)
67          Me.New(Contents, Author)
68          Me.Language = Language
69      End Sub
70
71      Public Sub New(ByVal Contents As String, _
72              ByVal Author As String, _
73              ByVal Language As String, _
74              ByVal Purpose As String)
75          Me.New(Contents, Author, Language)
76          Me.Purpose = Purpose
77      End Sub
78
79      Public Overrides Function GetSnippet() As String
80          Dim sTmp As String
81          sTmp = MyBase.GetSnippet() & _
82                  System.Environment.NewLine & _
83                  "Language: " & Language & _
84                  System.Environment.NewLine & _
85                  "Purpose: " & Purpose
86          Return sTmp
87      End Function
88 End Class
```

Lines 22–34 are the constructors for the Snippet class, and they illustrate the standard way of initializing an object. Lines 50–77 are the constructors for the CodeSnippet class, and they contain a few tricks in how they initialize the class. First, you can call the base class constructor using the MyBase keyword (lines 51 and 55), which ensures that any actual code is being executed in the base class routine, and then it will be executed for your derived class as well. The second trick, which is used throughout the rest of the constructors, is to call your own simpler constructors from the more complex ones. Using this style of coding makes it easier for you to avoid duplicate code; generic initialization goes into the first constructor, and any additional code that you need for handling

14

each new parameter can be placed into only the first constructor where each new parameter appears.

Designing an Application Using OOP

Object-oriented programming is not a technical concept, and it isn't related only to the programming of a system. OOP is involved in the creation of a system from the conceptual design onward. You should decide whether you are going to design a system using object-oriented techniques, and the implementation is not involved in that decision. Prior to .NET, Visual Basic did not have features to allow inheritance, procedure overloading, and other OOP concepts, but programmers could still design an application using those concepts and then implement them using multiple steps or workarounds to achieve what Visual Basic .NET has built-in today. After you have your Vision/Scope phase and your Requirements Analysis work done on a project, you move into Conceptual Design. During the design phase, you start to incorporate objects into your application. Follow these steps to create this design:

1. Identify entities.
2. Determine properties and methods.
3. Create object hierarchies.
4. Model your objects.

Each step is covered individually as I take you through the process of describing a blackjack game using objects. It would be helpful for you to understand the game of blackjack, which is a card game, before reading these sections. If you do not know anything about the game, check out the rules by searching for "BlackJack" on Encarta (`http://encarta.msn.com`).

Identifying Objects

The first task is to lay out the requirements of your system, which is a much bigger task than it might seem. In this stage, you need to outline the proposed system, application, or application component in enough detail to determine all the major entities. A trick that I like to use to get this process started is simply to grab all the nouns out of my system descriptions. Taking blackjack as our example, take a look at this brief, and possibly inaccurate, description of the game (refer to the Encarta site given previously for better info).

Blackjack is a card game played with two or more players, one of which acts as the dealer. The goal of the game is to have the value of your cards come as close as possible to 21 without going over that value, and the game is being played between each player and the dealer. Any tie (where the dealer and the player both get equally close to 21) goes to the dealer. Before each round, the players bet; putting money on their likelihood of beating the dealer's hand. One or more decks of cards are shuffled together and then the dealer deals one card out to each of the players and to himself.

At this point, the players place their bets after looking at the single card. The dealer then deals one more card to each player and to himself. The round ends if anyone produces a total of 21 with just two cards. If no one produces this result, a so-called "natural," then the dealer goes to each player in order and deals him cards, one at a time, until the player decides to stop at or under 21. If the player exceeds 21 with the new cards being dealt, then he immediately loses this round. Each player goes through this process, requesting additional cards until he decides to stay or until he busts by exceeding 21.

After all the players have decided to stop receiving cards or have been removed from the round, the dealer proceeds to deal cards to himself, deciding whether to hit or stand based on fixed rules. After the dealer and the players have all their cards ready, then the dealer has to pay out to all players with higher hands than the dealer, and the players with lower hands have to pay the dealer. Therefore, since the dealer always wins on a tie, if the dealer ends up with 21, everyone pays the dealer.

This is a brief description, of course, not covering doubling of bets, splits, and other features of the game, but it is detailed enough for this discussion. Taking this as a portion of a requirement statement for your work, you can start looking for entities that could be turned into objects. Remember my advice about nouns and try to come up with a list of objects on your own before looking at the list I have found.

Running through and just looking at the nouns produces more entities than I want, but I can select from that list and obtain the following suggestions for objects:

- Player
- Dealer (also a player perhaps?)
- Round (one time around)
- Game (the whole game)
- Deck of Cards
- Hand (player or dealer's cards)
- Card (a single playing card)
- Bet (representing a player's bet)

Given this list, I would move on to determining the properties and methods of these objects, which often helps determine which objects, if any, are related.

14

Determining Properties and Methods

Sticking to only a subset of the found entities, I start to look at Player, Dealer, Deck of Cards, Hand, and Card. Each of these has several attributes that can turn into properties, and several likely actions that can become methods. A Player might have Name, Current Hand, Position (because the dealer goes in a specific order through the players, position might be necessary), and Money Balance as properties. Methods of the Player object could include Stand, Hit, Bet, and others. The Dealer might have Name, Current Hand, and Money Balance as well, along with the Stand and Hit methods of the Player object. Two objects in and already you are seeing a bit of a pattern. With the similarities between Player and Dealer, perhaps it would be best if they were just one object, or there was an inheritance relationship between them.

Seeing these relationships is a key part of the process of identifying objects and can greatly affect the resulting application. If the Dealer and Player objects are both inherited from the same base object, or Dealer is inherited from Player, then you will be able to write code that deals with both entities simply by treating them as instances of the base class.

Continuing through the list of objects, the Deck of Cards would have a collection of individual Card objects and a Count property (to indicate the quantity of cards currently in the deck, shrinking as cards are dealt). Similarly, the Hand object, representing the cards a player or dealer is currently holding, also would have a collection of individual Card objects and a Count property. Possibly you would want a Sum property on the Hand object as well, to indicate the total value of the cards, but the "ace can be 1 or 11" rule makes this a difficult property to implement and more design work could be required. Methods of the Deck object would include Add/Remove for the collection of individual cards and a Shuffle method to randomize that same collection. Add/Remove would apply to the Hand object, although Shuffle wouldn't likely be useful.

The Deck and Hand objects are not just similar, they are almost completely identical. Instead of looking at inheritance, one option would be to make them both the exact same class, but containing different numbers of cards. Alternatively, you could create Hand and Deck both as derived classes from a more generic CardCollection class. The Card class is fairly easy to define: suit (Heart, Diamond, Spade and Club) and value (2-10, K, Q, J, A), and there is really no need for it to inherit from any other object.

Modeling Your Objects

As you work through the process of determining objects from the requirements analysis, it is useful to create diagrams or models to illustrate the objects and their relationships. Visual Studio .NET Architect Edition provides modeling tools, and they also are available through a standalone copy of Microsoft Visio. For now, to illustrate the look of an object model diagram, check out Figure 14.1.

FIGURE 14.1

FIGURE **14.1**

UML (Unified Modeling Language) modeling serves a design purpose, giving you a view of the current state of your application's object model, and provides documentation of the internals of your system.

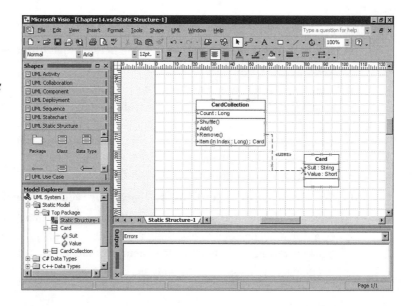

The diagram shown in Figure 14.1 has been created using a model style called UML or Universal Modeling Language. This type of diagram can be created using any one of several different tools, including Visio and Rational Rose. The benefit of modeling your application is to provide a visual diagram of your initial object design and to use that diagram as you make changes over time. In a large team environment, the code generation features of most modeling tools also can be helpful, allowing you to create the skeleton code for any set of objects in your diagrams. Related to the code generation, Visio and Rational Rose (and likely others) both support reverse engineering existing code and can use this technology to produce an object diagram from existing code. Reverse engineering is a great way to document a system when you haven't been using modeling right from the start.

Summary

Objects are a major part of Visual Basic .NET, but an object-oriented approach is different from a regular procedural one. You must focus first on design, attempting to view the concepts and entities of your system as objects, before worrying about the details of implementing these object concepts. In Day 15, you will learn more about creating your own objects using the various OOP features discussed throughout today's lesson.

14

Q&A

Q. I have heard that C# and C++ provide better object-oriented programming features than Visual Basic .NET. Is that the case?

A. Before .NET, this was true about C++; it provides OOP features (such as inheritance) that Visual Basic did not. Now, all the .NET languages have the same OOP functionality because that functionality is being provided by the Common Language Specification (which all .NET languages must conform to) instead of being each individual language. This means that in .NET, Visual Basic .NET is just as good a language for OOP as C++ or C#.

Q. Is OOP better or faster than the "linear" or regular style of programming?

A. Not necessarily. OOP doesn't produce different results in an application; it is merely a different approach to designing and building that application. For the most part, OOP is believed to produce systems that are more easily maintained and extended, but that is most certainly dependent on your particular code.

Workshop

The Workshop is designed to help you anticipate possible questions, review what you've learned, and get you thinking about how to put your knowledge into practice. The answers to the quiz are in Appendix A, "Answers to Quizzes/Exercises."

Quiz

1. What keyword allows you to refer to the base class when writing code inside a derived class?

2. What is it called when you create multiple versions of the same method with different sets of parameters?

3. What would the output of this code be?

```
1 Module AllAboutObjects
2     Sub Main()
3         Dim x As myFirstClass
4         Dim y As myFirstClass
5         x = New myFirstClass()
6         y = x
7         y.Name = "Fred"
8         x.Name = y.Name
9         Console.WriteLine("x.Name = {0}", x.Name)
10        Console.WriteLine("y.Name = {0}", y.Name)
11        Console.ReadLine()
12    End Sub
```

```
13 End Module
14
15 Public Class myFirstClass
16     Public Name As String
17 End Class
```

Exercises

Describe a possible object design for tracking events at a major stadium. Take into account a variety of different types of events and produce a small list of the objects you could design for this purpose.

14

WEEK 2

In Review

In Week 2, you covered a lot of ground, going from an introduction to a good selection of the .NET Framework classes to details on the advanced object-oriented features of Visual Basic .NET. Overall, you have learned enough to create a complete working application with a user interface, database connections, and even some connections to server functions such as event logging.

Day 8 started the week off with coverage of several of the more useful pieces of the .NET Framework and also walked you through the process of exploring the Framework on your own. This knowledge will allow you to find whatever functionality you need in the Framework; an invaluable skill when you need to do something that this book didn't have time to cover.

Although Web applications are the hip and trendy thing to build these days, Windows applications are still common, and Day 9 showed you how to build them in Visual Basic .NET. This coverage of Windows Forms introduced you to the original reason why the "Visual" was tacked onto Visual Basic— drag-and-drop user interface creation. Using controls, properties, and a bit of code, you can now create your own Windows application.

Of course, you had to learn how to build a Web-based user interface as well, and Day 10 was just the lesson you needed. Day 10's introduction to Web Forms showed you how to create a Web application that you could program in the same event-driven model as Windows applications have used for years.

Through Days 11 and 12, you learned about databases—some theory but a lot more hands-on. These lessons showed you how `System.Data` framework classes can be used to connect to a database, retrieve the information you need, and then manipulate that data as necessary. Along the way, you managed to learn more than you likely wanted to about at least one of the author's musical tastes (and we are not telling you which one).

On Day 13, you covered another one of the major new features of the Visual Studio IDE, the Server Explorer, and how you can use it from Visual Basic .NET to connect to servers, view and create performance counters, and work with the Windows XP/2000/NT Event Logs. Now the applications you create can act like enterprise-level programs, providing performance, auditing, and error information using the tools that system administrators are already familiar with.

On the last day of Week 2, Day 14, you returned to the subject of objects in Visual Basic .NET, which we started on back in Day 7. In this advanced lesson, you learned about the structure and features of objects and how you can use them to build applications. More information on objects is still coming. Check out Day 15 for details on how you can build your own objects and object-based systems in Visual Basic .NET.

At the end of Week 2, you now have a substantial understanding of Visual Basic .NET, allowing you to create systems that go beyond just samples into the area of real applications. Week 2's bonus project, an online CD/DVD library, takes your increased knowledge and puts it to the test as you build an application with a more complicated internal structure and a user interface in both Windows and on the Web. Check out all three bonus projects on the Web at `http://www.samspublishing.com/ detail_sams.cfm?item=0672320665`.

WEEK 3

At a Glance

During this final week, you will cover a variety of advanced topics to round out your knowledge of Visual Basic and the .NET Framework. First, you learn how to create your own components and library classes in Day 15. Day 16 covers the details of creating more complex user interfaces for Windows applications using the Windows Forms classes. This day includes coverage of menus, multiple document interface (MDI) applications, and several of the more complex controls provided by the Windows Forms classes.

As you have seen through the first 14 days of this book, the .NET Framework is large and complex, but this framework provides all the functionality you will need in your applications. For that reason, Day 17 is an exploration of more areas of the Framework, including working with the graphics and file handling functionality of .NET.

Days 18 and 19 provide the wrap up information you need to be able to package up your application and install it onto the final destination machine, whether that is a Web server or several thousand user desktops. A discussion of the redistributable .NET Framework and the basic client requirements is also included in these days.

Day 20 is an introduction into XML, the common language for data that flows throughout .NET. This day covers both XML itself and those parts of .NET (System.Xml) that make it easy for your code to read, write, and manipulate XML information.

The final day in this book, Day 21 is a discussion of Web Services, code that can be called across the Web using industry standard technologies such as SOAP, XML, and HTTP.

15

16

17

18

19

20

21

The place of Web services in your systems was discussed on Day 5, but Day 21's material shows you how to make and test a simple Web Service using Visual Basic .NET.

Finally, there is the book's third and last bonus project, Hangman, a complex program that uses the XML concepts from Day 20, requires a bit of work with files and graphics (Day 17), and involves the creation of an advanced user interface (Day 16). This program should also be fun. You write a game that you can show to your family, friends, and co-workers, and have them get enjoyment out of a program that you created!

DAY 15

Creating Objects in Visual Basic .NET

In previous lessons, you have learned how to use objects and how to design them, but at some point you will want or need to start building your own. Today's lesson will cover:

- Defining objects in Visual Basic .NET
- Using your own objects in your code
- Building your classes into assemblies and using those assemblies from another application

To illustrate these concepts, today's lesson will include the creation of several sample classes and the generation of an assembly containing them.

Creating Objects

You do not create objects directly in Visual Basic .NET; instead you build classes that become the definition of the object. Objects are then created from the class, becoming an instance of the class. The steps to defining your own objects therefore start with creating a new Visual Basic .NET class.

Declaring a New Class in Visual Basic .NET

Creating a new class is as easy as typing `Public Class Test` into your code editing window (inside a Visual Basic .NET file) and pressing Enter. Assuming that you didn't try this inside an actual procedure (sub or function), you can tell it was successful because Visual Basic .NET adds an `End Class` line for you automatically. These statements declare a new class and indicate the start and end of the class definition. Inside this class you define properties, methods, and events, but first you need to understand the class declaration itself.

Scope

Typing `Public Class Test` creates an empty class with `Public` scope, which means that anyone with a reference to this project can create an instance of `Test` just by executing myTest = `New Test()`. This is normally what you want, so you will likely create classes with `Public` scope, but it is not your only option. You also can create `Private` classes, by using the `Private` keyword, producing a class that you can only use from other code at the same scope level as the declaration, which usually means within the same file. If you have declared your class within the declaration of another class (nesting classes together), then any other code within the containing class can access the new object. `Private` is used when you have a class that you do not want created outside your current set of code. Finally, the other scope option I will mention is `Friend`. Classes, variables, and procedures declared with the `Friend` scope can be accessed by any other code within the same program (assembly, Web service, windows application and so on) but cannot be accessed at all by any other code.

Inheritance

As part of the class declaration, you can specify a single base class for the new class to inherit from, if the class will be derived from any other class. Listing 15.1 shows an example of this.

LISTING 15.1   A Class Can Inherit from One Other Class

```
1 Public Class Snippet
2 'class definition
3
4 End Class
5
6 Public Class CodeSnippet
7     Inherits Snippet
8 'class definition
9 End Class
```

Additionally, you also can specify that your class cannot be inherited from by adding a `NotInheritable` keyword after the scope portion of the class declaration. If you specify this keyword, then no one will be able to create a new class derived from this class. This is equivalent to the term "Sealed," which is used in C# to indicate that this new class cannot be inherited from and is used in the definition of many .NET objects such as `System.String`.

Directly opposite from creating sealed classes, you can create abstract classes, which must be used as base classes and cannot be created directly. If you are defining base objects that you do not want to be used on their own, only as a part of their object hierarchy, then the `MustInherit` keyword is perfect. A common use of this keyword is when the base class would not be functional on its own and one or more key methods need implementing in derived classes before you have anything useful.

Listing 15.2 illustrates the use of the `MustInherit` keyword. It is useful to note that you can supply the `MustOverride` keyword as part of the declaration of methods to force those methods to be included in every inherited version of this class. If you use `MustOverride`, you do not have to provide any implementation for that method or property.

LISTING 15.2   `MustInherit` and `MustOverride` Allow You to Specify that a Class Cannot Be Used Directly

```
 1 Public MustInherit Class BaseShape
 2     Public MustOverride ReadOnly Property NumSides() As Integer
 3     Public MustOverride Sub Draw()
 4 End Class
 5
 6 Public Class Square
 7     Inherits BaseShape
 8     Public Overrides Sub Draw()
 9         'draw a square
10     End Sub
11     Public Overrides ReadOnly Property NumSides() As Integer
12         Get
13             Return 4
14         End Get
15     End Property
16 End Class
```

ANALYSIS   This `Shape` class is useless on its own; it is simply laying out the general template for all objects that share this as a base class. This is a useful base class because it allows you to code various routines around the single base class and automatically support all the derived classes. By marking this class as `MustInherit`, you ensure that programmers are unable to go against your intentions and create an instance of Shape directly. It is likely that no one would try to create an instance of Shape—and if someone did, there isn't really any problem with that—but you make your intentions clear by preventing the incorrect type of use. Marking the Draw method as MustOverride indicates that when this class is inherited from that method it has to be provided in the new derived class. Once again, this is a way of clearly indicating your intent using the features of Visual Basic .NET instead of relying on other programmers to always do the right thing.

Adding Properties

There are two main ways to add properties to a class: creating public variables (which become properties directly) or creating complete property routines. Creating properties using public variables will work, but you have absolutely no control over these exposed variables and no way of running code when their values are changed. Listing 15.3 shows this method of defining properties, which is suitable when you are just playing around with classes in Visual Basic .NET.

LISTING 15.3 Public Variables Become Properties When Declared Within a Class

```
1 Public Class Person
2     Public Name As String
3     Public FirstName As String
4     Public SecondName As String
5 End Class
```

Creating properties through the creation of a property routine is a more complex method that gives you complete control over the property itself. First, you determine the name and data type of the property you want to add and then type this line inside the boundaries of a Class (making the appropriate substitutions for the property name and the data type):

```
Public Property Name() As String
```

When you press Enter at the end of this line, Visual Basic .NET creates the skeleton of a complete property procedure for you:

```
Public Property Name() As String
    Get

    End Get
    Set(ByVal Value As String)

    End Set
End Property
```

The two halves of this procedure, Get and Set, handle the assignment of a property value and the receiving of a value (objTest.Name = "Fred"), respectively. Because you are not using a public variable when you use this type of property routine, you likely will need a private variable declared to hold the property value itself. Adding this, m_sName, to your sample class allows you to create the code to go within your property Get/Set routine. The private class variable is prefixed with m_ (which stands for *member variable*) to indicate that it is the internal representation of an exposed property. In its simplest form, the code within the property routine (see Listing 15.4) will just be used to exchange values into and out of the internal variable.

LISTING 15.4 Property Procedures Are an Alternative to Using Public Variables

```
 1 Public Class Test
 2     Private m_sName As String
 3
 4     Public Property Name() As String
 5         Get
 6             Return m_sName
 7         End Get
 8         Set(ByVal Value As String)
 9             m_sName = Value
10         End Set
11     End Property
12 End Class
```

The property routine in Listing 15.4 is Public, which is what you most likely would want, but you also could mark it as Private, therefore restricting it from use outside the class itself.

The true advantages of property routines over just using a public variable are that you can create read-only or write-only properties and you can perform data validation with every attempt to write into a property.

Creating Read-Only and Write-Only Properties

Property routines are made read-only or write-only through the property declaration. If the property is declared with no additional keywords, as in Listing 15.4, then it is a read/write property and you must supply both the Get and Set portions of the routine. Alternatively, you can specify Public ReadOnly Property in the declaration to create a property that can only return values or specify Public WriteOnly Property to create one that cannot be read. Read-only properties, although they might not be as common as read/write properties, can be useful in a variety of situations. Listing 15.5 shows how three properties, two of which are read/write and one that is read-only, can be used to produce a useful class.

LISTING 15.5 Properties Can Be Read/Write, Read-only or Write-only

```
 1 Option Strict On
 2 Option Explicit On
 3
 4 Module AllAboutObjects
 5     Public Sub Main()
 6
 7         Dim objSample As New Person()
 8
 9         objSample.FirstName = "Fred"
10         objSample.LastName = "Jones"
11         Console.WriteLine(objSample.DisplayName)
12         Console.ReadLine()
13     End Sub
14 End Module
15 Public Class Person
16     Private m_sName As String
17     Private m_sFirstName As String
18     Private m_sLastName As String
19
20     Public ReadOnly Property DisplayName() As String
21         Get
22             Return String.Format("{0} {1}", m_sFirstName, m_sLastName)
23         End Get
24     End Property
25
26     Public Property FirstName() As String
27         Get
28             Return m_sFirstName
29         End Get
30         Set(ByVal Value As String)
31             m_sFirstName = Value
32         End Set
33     End Property
34
35     Public Property LastName() As String
36         Get
37             Return m_sLastName
38         End Get
39         Set(ByVal Value As String)
40             m_sLastName = Value
41         End Set
42     End Property
43 End Class
```

Write-only properties are a bit more confusing; I personally do not see many reasons for a property that the user can set but cannot see. If the user can set it, then he should have the value already, and then why would you want to stop him from viewing it? The one situation I can imagine in which a write-only property could be useful is when dealing with passwords. Consider a class that is going to be used to connect to a back-end database and one of its properties is the database password. In some situations, you might want to pass an instance of this object to another routine, with its properties already populated, without exposing any secure information.

Using Property Routines to Validate Data

The use of property routines versus public variables has another main benefit; with a property routine, you get to run code whenever the user wants to retrieve or set the value of that property. This allows you to do several things, including validation of data on the way into your objects. Listing 15.6, for instance, checks a credit card number on its way into an object, making sure that it is valid and rejecting the attempt if it is not.

LISTING 15.6   Property Procedures Allow for Data Validation

```
 1 Option Explicit On
 2 Option Strict On
 3
 4 Public Class CreditCardValidation
 5     Public Enum CardTypes
 6         ccvVisa
 7         ccvMasterCard
 8         ccvDiscover
 9         ccvAMEX
10         ccvDinersClub
11         ccvEnRoute
12         ccvUndefined
13     End Enum
14
15     Private Const Numbers As String = "0123456789"
16     Private Const sInvalidCheckSumError As String _
17         = "Credit Card Number contains an error " & _
18             "in one or more digits (Checksum Error)"
19     Private Const sLengthError As String _
20         = "Credit Card is not the correct length " & _
21             "for its type (Length Error)"
22
23     Private sErrorMsg As String
24     Private mCardType As CardTypes
25     Private sCardNumber As String
26     Private bValid As Boolean
27
28     Public Property CardNumber() As String
29         Get
30             Return sCardNumber
31         End Get
32         Set(ByVal Value As String)
```

LISTING **15.6**   continued

```
33              bValid = ValidCreditCard(Value)
34              If bValid Then
35                  sCardNumber = Value
36              Else
37                  Throw New System.ArgumentException(sErrorMsg, _
                        "CardNumber")
38              End If
39          End Set
40      End Property
41
42      Private Function CTPrefix(ByVal sCard As String) As CardTypes
43          If CType(Left(sCard, 2), Integer) > 50 AndAlso _
44                  CType(Left(sCard, 2), Integer) < 56 Then
45              Return CardTypes.ccvMasterCard
46          ElseIf Left(sCard, 1) = "4" Then
47              Return CardTypes.ccvVisa
48          ElseIf Left(sCard, 4) = "6011" Then
49              Return CardTypes.ccvDiscover
50          ElseIf Left(sCard, 2) = "34" OrElse _
51                  Left(sCard, 2) = "37" Then
52              Return CardTypes.ccvAMEX
53          ElseIf Left(sCard, 2) = "36" Then
54              Return CardTypes.ccvDinersClub
55          Else
56              Return CardTypes.ccvUndefined
57          End If
58      End Function
59
60
61      Private Function Prefix(ByVal sTest As String, _
62              ByVal sArg As String) As Boolean
63          If Left(sArg, Len(sTest)) = sTest Then
64              Prefix = True
65          Else
66              Prefix = False
67          End If
68      End Function
69
70      Private Function ValidCreditCard(ByVal sNumber As String) _
71              As Boolean
72          Dim sTemp As String
73          Dim iTemp As Integer
74          Dim sCreditCard As String
75          Dim iCardLength As Integer
76          Dim Checksum As Integer
77          Dim i As Integer
78
79          sTemp = sNumber
80          sCreditCard = ""
```

LISTING **15.6**   continued

```
81          Checksum = 0
82
83          For i = 1 To Len(sTemp)
84              If InStr(Numbers, Mid(sTemp, i, 1)) <> 0 Then
85                  sCreditCard = sCreditCard & Mid(sTemp, i, 1)
86              End If
87          Next
88
89          mCardType = CTPrefix(sCreditCard)
90          sCardNumber = sCreditCard
91          iCardLength = Len(sCreditCard)
92
93          Select Case mCardType
94              Case CardTypes.ccvAMEX
95                  If iCardLength <> 15 Then
96                      ValidCreditCard = False
97                      sErrorMsg = sLengthError
98                  End If
99
100             Case CardTypes.ccvVisa
101                 If (iCardLength <> 13) AndAlso (iCardLength <> 16) Then
102                     ValidCreditCard = False
103                     sErrorMsg = sLengthError
104                 End If
105             Case CardTypes.ccvMasterCard, CardTypes.ccvDiscover
106                 If iCardLength <> 16 Then
107                     ValidCreditCard = False
108                     sErrorMsg = sLengthError
109                 End If
110         End Select
111
112         sCreditCard = Right("0000000000000000" & sCreditCard, 16)
113
114         For i = 1 To Len(sCreditCard) - 1
115             iTemp = CInt(Mid(sCreditCard, 16 - i, 1))
116             iTemp = iTemp * (1 + (i Mod 2))
117             If iTemp >= 10 Then
118                 iTemp = iTemp - 9
119             End If
120             Checksum = Checksum + iTemp
121         Next i
122         Checksum = (10 - (Checksum Mod 10)) Mod 10
123         If Checksum = CInt(Right(sCreditCard, 1)) Then
124             ValidCreditCard = True
125             sErrorMsg = ""
126         Else
127             ValidCreditCard = False
128             sErrorMsg = sInvalidCheckSumError
129         End If
```

LISTING **15.6** continued

```
130    End Function
131
132    Public Function CardTypeName(ByVal sCardNumber As String) As String
133        Dim sTmp As String
134
135        If ValidCreditCard(sCardNumber) Then
136            Select Case mCardType
137                Case CardTypes.ccvAMEX
138                    sTmp = "American Express"
139                Case CardTypes.ccvVisa
140                    sTmp = "Visa"
141                Case CardTypes.ccvMasterCard
142                    sTmp = "MasterCard"
143                Case CardTypes.ccvDinersClub
144                    sTmp = "Diners Club"
145                Case CardTypes.ccvDiscover
146                    sTmp = "Discover Card"
147                Case CardTypes.ccvEnRoute
148                    sTmp = "enRoute"
149                Case CardTypes.ccvUndefined
150                    sTmp = "Unknown"
151            End Select
152        Else
153            Throw New ArgumentException(sErrorMsg, "Card Number")
154        End If
155        Return sTmp
156    End Function
157 End Class
```

ANALYSIS This code is only checking whether it is a valid credit card number, not whether it actually is a credit card number. This number can also refer to a canceled, expired, or otherwise invalid credit card account. The Set portion of this property routine accepts a string and then uses a checksum to determine whether it is a valid credit card number, adding up the digits in a specific way so as to check them against the last digit. If the string supplied is invalid, then an exception is raised. This exception should be caught by the program setting the CardNumber property just like it is in this example.

In general, you should not use public variables as properties; it will work, but you end up with no control and no options. The best bet is to always use property routines and use copy/paste to handle the extra typing.

Creating Methods

To add methods to your class, you will be creating Sub and Function procedures, the exact type dependent on your particular situation. Just as with classes (see the "Scope" section earlier in today's lesson), you can create methods that have `Public`, `Private`, or `Friend` scope. Methods declared with `Public` scope can be accessed by anyone using an object of this type. `Private` methods are available only inside the class itself, and `Friend` methods are available only to other code within the same assembly or executable. Listing 15.7 shows the same class as from the earlier examples (with a few unrelated pieces of code removed, such as the `Property` routines) with a `Public` method added to connect to Outlook and try to find an e-mail address for this person.

> **Note**
>
> To use this code, you must add a reference to Outlook to your project (and you must have Outlook 2000 or XP installed and working). To add this reference to your own project, follow these steps:
>
> 1. Right-click on the References folder in your project in the Solution Explorer and click Add Reference on the context menu.
> 2. Click on the COM tab and find Microsoft Outlook in the list.
> 3. Click the Select button and then close the dialog by clicking OK. You will likely be prompted to create an Interop Assembly, and you should click Yes to this question.

LISTING 15.7 This Function Retrieves Information from Outlook

```
1 Public Class Person
2 'unrelated code removed from listing
3     Public Function LookUpInOutlook() As String
4         Dim objOutlook As New Outlook.Application()
5         Dim objSession As Outlook.NameSpace
6         Dim objPerson As Outlook.Recipient
7         Dim sEmailAddress As String
8
9         objOutlook.Session.Logon(NewSession:=False)
10        objSession = CType(objOutlook.Session, Outlook.NameSpace)
11        objPerson = objSession.CreateRecipient(Me.DisplayName)
12        Try
13            sEmailAddress = String.Format("{0}:{1}", _
14                objPerson.AddressEntry.Type, _
15                objPerson.AddressEntry.Address)
16            Return sEmailAddress
17        Catch objException As Exception
18            'Address Not Found
19            Return ""
20        End Try
21    End Function
22 End Class
23 Module AllAboutObjects
24     Public Sub Main()
```

LISTING 15.7   continued

```
25
26          Dim objSample As New Person()
27          objSample.FirstName = "Joel"
28          objSample.LastName = "Semeniuk"
29          Console.WriteLine(objSample.DisplayName)
30          Console.WriteLine(objSample.LookUpInOutlook())
31
32          Console.ReadLine()
33    End Sub
34 End Module
```

ANALYSIS   When you run this code, Outlook might give you a warning (see Figure 15.1) that a program is attempting to access e-mail addresses, which is certainly true because that is exactly what this Sub does.

FIGURE 15.1

The new security features in Outlook warn you and allow you to prevent programmatic access to your e-mail and contact information.

If you are sure that this code is the cause of the warning, then you can click OK if you want it to successfully obtain an e-mail address. You have to provide a name that exists in your Contacts folder or one of your address lists or this code will fail to find anyone and the address won't be resolved. Line 4 creates a new instance of Outlook; then line 9 obtains the current MAPI Session. Line 10 obtains an Outlook Namespace object, which is a key object in the Outlook object model, and one that exposes everything that you need to access. Using the CreateRecipient method (line 11) is the equivalent of typing the name value you have into the To box of an e-mail and letting Outlook resolve that name. If CreateRecipient fails (the user could not be resolved), then the Try/Catch block around obtaining the address should prevent any visible errors from occurring.

If you want to allow derived classes to override a method defined in their base class, then the base method must be marked with the Overridable keyword, and the derived class's method must specify the Overrides keyword. In Listing 15.8, the class Mortgage is defined to handle mortgage calculations (this class also was used in Day 14, "Introduction to Object-Oriented Programming"), and then in Listing 15.9 a new class, AccelMortgage, has been derived from Mortgage. In these listings, the keywords

Overridable and Overrides are both used so that the new class can accommodate a
payment schedule other than monthly.

LISTING 15.8   Inheritance Is a Good Way to Add Functionality

```
 1 Public Class Mortgage
 2     'Very simple Mortgage Calculator
 3     'Set AnnualInterestRate, NumberOfYears and Principal
 4     'Then retrieve PaymentAmount property
 5     Private m_dblInterestRate As Double
 6     Private m_iDuration_Years As Integer
 7     Private m_curPrincipal As Decimal
 8
 9     Public Property AnnualInterestRate() As Double
10         Get
11             Return m_dblInterestRate
12         End Get
13         Set(ByVal Value As Double)
14             m_dblInterestRate = Value
15         End Set
16     End Property
17
18     Public Property NumberOfYears() As Integer
19         Get
20             Return m_iDuration_Years
21         End Get
22         Set(ByVal Value As Integer)
23             m_iDuration_Years = Value
24         End Set
25     End Property
26
27     Public Property Principal() As Decimal
28         Get
29             Return m_curPrincipal
30         End Get
31         Set(ByVal Value As Decimal)
32             m_curPrincipal = Value
33         End Set
34     End Property
35
36     Public Overridable Function PaymentAmount() As Decimal
37         Dim iNumPaymentsPerYear As Integer = 12
38         Dim iPayments As Integer
39         Dim dblFractionalInterestRate As Double
40         Dim curPayment As Decimal
41
42         iPayments = m_iDuration_Years * iNumPaymentsPerYear
43         dblFractionalInterestRate = m_dblInterestRate / iNumPaymentsPerYear
44
```

LISTING **15.8**   continued

```
45          curPayment = m_curPrincipal * _
46              ((1 - (1 + dblFractionalInterestRate)) _
47                / (1 - ((1 + dblFractionalInterestRate) ^ iPayments)) _
48                + dblFractionalInterestRate)
49
50          Return curPayment
51      End Function
52 End Class
```

ANALYSIS   The details of Listing 15.8 are not very relevant, except for how this class has to have been written to allow you to base a new accelerated mortgage class on it. On line 36, the function PaymentAmount is declared using the Overridable keyword. Without that keyword, AccelMortgage (see Listing 15.9) wouldn't be able to supply its own version of the PaymentAmount function.

LISTING **15.9**   AccelMortgage Adds the Capability to Calculate a Faster Mortgage Payment Plan

```
1 Public Class AccelMortgage
2      Inherits Mortgage
3      Private m_iNumberOfPaymentsInYear As Integer = 12
4
5      Public Property PaymentsInYear() As Integer
6          Get
7              Return m_iNumberOfPaymentsInYear
8          End Get
9          Set(ByVal Value As Integer)
10             m_iNumberOfPaymentsInYear = Value
11         End Set
12     End Property
13
14     Public Overrides Function PaymentAmount() As Decimal
15         Dim iPayments As Integer
16         Dim dblFractionalInterestRate As Double
17         Dim curPayment As Decimal
18
19         iPayments = Me.NumberOfYears * Me.PaymentsInYear
20         dblFractionalInterestRate = _
21            Me.AnnualInterestRate / Me.PaymentsInYear
22         curPayment = Me.Principal * _
23             ((1 - (1 + dblFractionalInterestRate)) _
24               / (1 - ((1 + dblFractionalInterestRate) ^ iPayments)) _
25               + dblFractionalInterestRate)
26
27         Return curPayment
28     End Function
29 End Class
```

ANALYSIS Listing 15.9 illustrates overriding a method in a derived class, and line 14 does just that by declaring a method that exists in the base class and specifying the Overrides keyword. The PaymentAmount function itself has been rewritten to support payments other than monthly. In this revised version of the function, the required properties of the class are accessed using the Me keyword (lines 19, 20, and 22), instead of using the internal variables directly, because a derived class has no access to the private variables of the base class. Listing 15.10 is a quick and simple client for these two classes, designed to compare a regular mortgage (with monthly payments) to the same mortgage done with accelerated biweekly payments.

LISTING 15.10 Client Program Calls Both Mortgage Calculators

```
 1 Module Main
 2    Sub Main()
 3       Dim objMortgage As New Mortgage()
 4       With objMortgage
 5          .AnnualInterestRate = 0.07
 6          .NumberOfYears = 25
 7          .Principal = 140000
 8          Console.WriteLine("{0:C}", .PaymentAmount())
 9       End With
10
11       Dim objNewMortgage As New AccelMortgage()
12       With objNewMortgage
13          .AnnualInterestRate = 0.07
14          .NumberOfYears = 25
15          .PaymentsInYear = 26
16          .Principal = 140000
17          Console.WriteLine("{0:C}", .PaymentAmount())
18       End With
19       Console.ReadLine()
20    End Sub
21 End Module
```

Deciding what should be a property and what should be a method is not always easy, and many developers make the wrong choice. There is no "rule" that tells you what to do, but I can offer you the guideline I use and the logic behind it. I use a simple test as I design my objects: "properties shouldn't cause anything to happen." I like to write classes so that setting a property three times has the same end result as setting it once.

This single guideline avoids situations where the order of setting an object's properties can affect the outcome. In the Mortgage class, for example, you could write the code so that setting the Principal property caused the payment amount to be recalculated. If that was the case, then you would want to make sure that you had set the other properties (AnnualInterestRate, NumberOfYears) before Principal. I avoid putting any code in to a property routine that changes other internal parts of my class, other than changing its corresponding internal variable. PaymentAmount, the function in the Mortgage class, could reasonably be a property or a method because it doesn't change anything about the class when it does its calculation. I made it a method in today's lesson, but a property in Day 14; there are often situations where either choice is fine.

Adding Events

Events are a major part of objects in .NET, especially in the GUI world, but in the rest of the Framework as well. Events allow an object to announce to anyone who is interested that something has happened, which is a much more active interaction between an object and the code using it than the alternative where the object's properties are polled repeatedly. Events don't fit into every situation, for instance the Mortgage and AccelMortgage classes have no real need for events; their code is self-contained and only runs on demand. When you do have a need for your object to inform its users about something, events are a wonderful mechanism to do so.

Consider a class designed to talk to a mail program and alert you when new mail arrives that meets certain specific criteria. When that new mail message comes in, a property could be set as a flag, but then your program would have to keep checking that value. Instead, you can create an event that your class is capable of raising along with a few pieces of data to describe what has occurred. Your main program doesn't do any polling of the object; you just write code into an event handler for that event of your object. To create an event, you add a declaration to your class, such as the example in Listing 15.11.

LISTING **15.11**   Adding an Event Declaration

```
1 Public Class OutlookMessageWatcher
2
3     Public Event EmailArrived(ByVal From As String, _
4         ByVal Subject As String, _
5         ByVal Message As Outlook.MailItem)
6
7 End Class
```

When this event is raised, you can supply values for each of these parameters, and those values will be sent to any routine that has chosen to handle this event. To raise the event, which you will do from your class, use the RaiseEvent statement, as shown in Listing 15.12 (the complete OutlookMessageWatcher class).

LISTING 15.12   Complete Listing of Outlook Message Watcher

```
1 Imports System
2 Imports System.Windows.Forms
3
4 Public Class OutlookMessageWatcher
5     Private WithEvents objInboxItems As Outlook.Items
6     Private objOutlook As Outlook.Application
7     Public Event EmailArrived(ByVal From As String, _
8         ByVal Subject As String, _
9         ByVal Message As Outlook.MailItem)
10
11    Public Sub New()
12        objOutlook = New Outlook.Application()
13        objOutlook.Session.Logon(NewSession:=False)
14        objInboxItems = objOutlook.Session.GetDefaultFolder _
15            (Outlook.OlDefaultFolders.olFolderInbox).Items
16    End Sub
17
18    Private Sub objInboxItems_ItemAdd(ByVal Item As Object) _
19            Handles objInboxItems.ItemAdd
20        Dim objNewMail As Outlook.MailItem
21        Try
22            objNewMail = CType(Item, Outlook.MailItem)
23            RaiseEvent EmailArrived(objNewMail.SenderName, _
24                objNewMail.Subject, _
25                objNewMail)
26        Catch objException As Exception
27            MessageBox.Show(objException.Message)
28        End Try
29    End Sub
30 End Class
```

After you have created an event in your class, you can write code to handle those events in other classes by declaring your object with the WithEvents keyword and then creating an event routine using Handles. For instance, Listing 15.13 shows how this new class could be used as part of a Windows Form.

LISTING 15.13   Trying Out the Message Watcher

```
1 Public Class Form1
2     Inherits System.Windows.Forms.Form
3     Private WithEvents objOMW As OutlookMessageWatcher
4
5 'Windows Form Designer generated code omitted
6
7     Private Sub Form1_Load(ByVal sender As System.Object, _
8 ByVal e As System.EventArgs) Handles MyBase.Load
```

LISTING **15.13**   continued

```
 9          objOMW = New OutlookMessageWatcher()
10     End Sub
11
12     Private Sub objOMW_EmailArrived(ByVal From As String, _
13            ByVal Subject As String, _
14            ByVal Message As Outlook.MailItem) _
15            Handles objOMW.EmailArrived
16          lbMailItems.Items.Add(Subject)
17     End Sub
18 End Class
```

The two requirements for using the event(s) of your object are to declare the object using WithEvents and to create an event handler using the Handles keyword. If you are working in the Visual Studio IDE, it can create the event procedure for you if you declare your object using WithEvents, select it from the right-hand drop-down list, and then select your event from the left-hand drop-down list.

Defining and Using Interfaces

One of the more powerful features of object-oriented programming (OOP) is the capability to treat an object as if it was an instance of another class. When you are dealing with inheritance, this means that you can treat any derived class as if it was any one of its ancestors. This is useful and is often a key motivator of creating base classes, but it is limited to use with classes with an inheritance relationship.

Another way to produce a similar result, classes that can be treated as if they were other classes, is to use interfaces. An *interface* is a special type of class that contains no code but is used instead as a way of describing the appearance of an object. Other classes then can implement one or more of these interfaces, allowing them to be treated as if they were an object of one of those types.

Interfaces are used throughout the .NET Framework, allowing any number of classes to state that they all provide a specific set of functionality. One of the interfaces defined in the .NET Framework is IComparable (interface names often are prefixed by a capital I), which provides a single method (CompareTo) that is used to compare the current object to another instance of the same class. Any class that implements the IComparable interface is essentially stating that two instances of that class can be compared and a greater than, less than, or equal to relationship can be determined.

To implement an interface, a class usually has to provide its own version of one or more methods. Classes that want to implement IComparable just have to write their own version of the method CompareTo. Listing 15.14 shows a class that has decided to implement IComparable and the custom version of CompareTo that it has provided.

LISTING 15.14   IComparable Allows Your Class to Work

```
 1 Public Class Person
 2     Implements IComparable
 3     Private m_sName As String
 4     Private m_sFirstName As String
 5     Private m_sLastName As String
 6
 7     Public ReadOnly Property DisplayName() As String
 8         Get
 9             Return String.Format("{0} {1}", _
10 m_sFirstName, m_sLastName)
11         End Get
12     End Property
13
14     Public Property FirstName() As String
15         Get
16             Return m_sFirstName
17         End Get
18         Set(ByVal Value As String)
19             m_sFirstName = Value
20         End Set
21     End Property
22
23     Public Property LastName() As String
24         Get
25             Return m_sLastName
26         End Get
27         Set(ByVal Value As String)
28             m_sLastName = Value
29         End Set
30     End Property
31
32     Public Function CompareTo(ByVal obj As Object) As Integer _
33         Implements System.IComparable.CompareTo
34         'Compare this instance to obj, return a number
35         'less than zero to indicate obj < me, 0 to indicate
36         'obj = me, and greater than zero to indicate obj > me
37         Dim objOtherPerson As Person
38         objOtherPerson = CType(obj, Person)
39
40         If objOtherPerson.LastName < Me.LastName Then
41             Return -1
42         ElseIf objOtherPerson.LastName > Me.LastName Then
43             Return 1
44         Else
45             If objOtherPerson.FirstName < Me.FirstName Then
46                 Return -1
47             ElseIf objOtherPerson.FirstName > Me.FirstName Then
48                 Return 1
49             Else
50                 Return 0
```

LISTING **15.14**   continued

```
51              End If
52           End If
53      End Function
54 End Class
```

By implementing IComparable, the Person class can now be passed into functions as if it was an object of type IComparable and used with other objects that require this interface to be implemented. An example of how this could be useful can be found in the .NET Framework class SortedList. This class allows you to build a list of objects, each with an associated key, and it keeps the list sorted by the key values. The catch is that the objects you supply as keys must support IComparable because the SortedList depends on the CompareTo method exposed by that interface to perform its sorts. This requirement is not a problem if your key is a simple data type, such as a String, Integer, or Date, because all these support the IComparable interface, but if you want to use a class of your own as the key, then it will not work unless that class implements IComparable. Listing 15.15 shows how you could now build a sorted list using instances of the Person class as key values.

LISTING **15.15**   Implementing IComparable Allows a Class to Work in a Sorted List

```
 1 Option Strict On
 2 Option Explicit On
 3
 4 Module AllAboutObjects
 5    Public Sub Main()
 6        Dim objPerson1 As New Person()
 7        Dim objPerson2 As New Person()
 8        Dim objPerson3 As New Person()
 9        Dim Val1, Val2, Val3 As Integer
10
11        Val1 = 234
12        Val2 = 13
13        Val3 = 500
14
15        objPerson1.FirstName = "John"
16        objPerson1.LastName = "Adams"
17        objPerson2.FirstName = "Quincy"
18        objPerson2.LastName = "Wallace"
19        objPerson3.FirstName = "Arlene"
20        objPerson3.LastName = "Ratuski"
21
22        Dim slPeople As New SortedList()
23
24        slPeople.Add(objPerson1, Val1)
```

LISTING 15.15   continued

```
25        slPeople.Add(objPerson2, Val2)
26        slPeople.Add(objPerson3, Val3)
27
28        Dim objDE As DictionaryEntry
29
30        For Each objDE In slPeople
31            Console.WriteLine("{0} {1}", _
32                CType(objDE.Key, Person).DisplayName, _
33                CType(objDE.Value, Integer))
34        Next
35        Console.ReadLine()
36    End Sub
37 End Module
```

Interfaces should be used instead of inheritance when your intention is to indicate that a class provides some form of common functionality (such as the capability to be compared). The Person class from the previous examples has a purpose completely unrelated to its support for being compared, so that support is best indicated using an interface.

The .NET Framework provides a wide variety of interfaces, but you also can create your own in a manner similar to defining a new class. The definition of an interface starts with Public Interface <interface name>, ends with End Interface, and contains declarations for methods, properties, and events between the start and end. No code goes into an interface no matter what you are doing, so the method and property declarations consist of only the first line of a regular declaration. Listing 15.16 defines a simple interface, IDebugInfo, to provide some general information about the class for the purposes of debugging.

LISTING 15.16   Interfaces Look Like Empty Classes

```
1 Option Explicit On
2 Option Strict On
3
4 Public Interface IDebugInfo
5     ReadOnly Property ClassName() As String
6     ReadOnly Property Author() As String
7     ReadOnly Property SourceFile() As String
8     ReadOnly Property Description() As String
9 End Interface
```

Interfaces are similar in some ways to classes, but as you can see from Listing 15.16, quite different in others. Inside the Interface declaration (lines 4–9), the members are defined with their declarations only, and no implementation code is provided. Scope also is not included as part of these declarations, but `Public` is the default when you implement this interface in one of your classes. Regardless of the scope you choose in your class, these members will be available through the `IDebugInfo` interface. In the case of this interface, these properties will be the same for each instance of a single class, and they are intended to describe that particular class. The nature of these properties allows for read-only values, but interfaces can include any form of property needed. An example logging routine, shown in Listing 15.17, records trace information from any class that supports `IDebugInfo`.

LISTING 15.17   A Logging Procedure Accepts Any Class that Implements IDebugInfo

```
 1 Option Explicit On
 2 Option Strict On
 3
 4 Imports System
 5 Imports System.IO
 6
 7 Public Class LoggingRoutine
 8     Const DefaultLogFile As String = "C:\LogFile.txt"
 9     Shared Sub LogMsgToFile(ByVal Message As String, _
10             ByVal FileName As String, _
11             ByVal Source As IDebugInfo)
12         Dim objLogFile As StreamWriter
13         If File.Exists(FileName) Then
14             objLogFile = File.AppendText(FileName)
15         ElseIf Directory.Exists _
16                 (Path.GetDirectoryName(FileName)) Then
17             objLogFile = File.CreateText(FileName)
18         Else
19             'error, use default log file
20             objLogFile = File.AppendText(DefaultLogFile)
21         End If
22
23         objLogFile.WriteLine("---------------------------")
24         objLogFile.WriteLine(Message)
25         objLogFile.WriteLine("From {0} ({1}) by {2}", _
26             Source.ClassName, Source.SourceFile, Source.Author)
27         objLogFile.WriteLine("Description: {0}", _
28             Source.Description)
29         objLogFile.WriteLine("---------------------------")
30
31         objLogFile.Flush()
32         objLogFile.Close()
33     End Sub
34 End Class
```

ANALYSIS   This logging class shows how the use of a common interface across multiple objects can be part of an application design. The shared procedure `LogMsgToFile`

15

(line 9) accepts several parameters including an object of type `IDebugInfo`, therefore allowing any instance of a class that implements that interface to be passed into this routine. The routine itself is not doing anything radical, but some of it might be interesting. The classes `Path`, `File`, and `Directory` are all from the `System.IO` namespace, and each one of them exposes a variety of shared or static functions, so you can use these objects without ever creating an instance of them. The code in Listing 15.18 shows a sample class that implements `IDebugInfo`.

LISTING 15.18   Using the `IDebugInfo` Interface

```
1 Option Explicit On
2 Option Strict On
3
4 Module Main
5     Sub Main()
6         Dim objPerson As New Person()
7         objPerson.FirstName = "Duncan"
8         objPerson.LastName = "Mackenzie"
9         Console.WriteLine(objPerson.DisplayName())
10     End Sub
11 End Module
12
13 Public Class Person
14     Implements IComparable
15     Implements IDebugInfo
16
17     Private m_sName As String
18     Private m_sFirstName As String
19     Private m_sLastName As String
20
21     Public Sub New()
22         LoggingRoutine.LogMsgToFile _
23             ("Started Up", "C:\test.txt", Me)
24     End Sub
25
26     Public ReadOnly Property DisplayName() As String
27         Get
28             LoggingRoutine.LogMsgToFile _
29                 (String.Format("DisplayName called, {0} {1} output", _
30                     m_sFirstName, m_sLastName), "C:\test.txt", Me)
31
32             Return String.Format("{0} {1}", m_sFirstName, m_sLastName)
33         End Get
34     End Property
35
36     Public Property FirstName() As String
37         Get
38             Return m_sFirstName
```

LISTING **15.18**   continued

```
39          End Get
40          Set(ByVal Value As String)
41              m_sFirstName = Value
42          End Set
43      End Property
44
45      Public Property LastName() As String
46          Get
47              Return m_sLastName
48          End Get
49          Set(ByVal Value As String)
50              m_sLastName = Value
51          End Set
52      End Property
53
54      Public Function CompareTo(ByVal obj As Object) As Integer _
55          Implements System.IComparable.CompareTo
56          'Compare this instance to obj, return a number
57          'less than zero to indicate obj < me, 0 to indicate
58          'obj = me, and greater than zero to indicate obj > me
59          Dim objOtherPerson As Person
60          objOtherPerson = CType(obj, Person)
61
62          If objOtherPerson.LastName < Me.LastName Then
63              Return -1
64          ElseIf objOtherPerson.LastName > Me.LastName Then
65              Return 1
66          Else
67              If objOtherPerson.FirstName < Me.FirstName Then
68                  Return -1
69              ElseIf objOtherPerson.FirstName > Me.FirstName Then
70                  Return 1
71              Else
72                  Return 0
73              End If
74          End If
75      End Function
76
77      Public ReadOnly Property Author() As String _
78          Implements IDebugInfo.Author
79          Get
80              Return "Duncan Mackenzie"
81          End Get
82      End Property
83
84      Public ReadOnly Property ClassName() As String _
85          Implements IDebugInfo.ClassName
86          Get
87              Return "Person"
```

LISTING 15.18   continued

```
88              End Get
89      End Property
90
91      Public ReadOnly Property Description() As String _
92              Implements IDebugInfo.Description
93          Get
94              Return "The Person is designed to represent" _
95                  & " a customer or employee"
96          End Get
97      End Property
98
99      Public ReadOnly Property SourceFile() As String _
100             Implements IDebugInfo.SourceFile
101         Get
102             Return "\\liquidsoap\bigproject\Source\Person.vb"
103         End Get
104     End Property
105 End Class
```

ANALYSIS   To use this code, place the IDebugInfo interface (from Listing 15.16), the logging routine (Listing 15.17), and this code (Listing 15.18) together into a project, each into a separate file. Go into the project properties and make sure that the Main routine from Listing 15.18 is selected as the Startup object, and everything should work fine. Remember that this code is downloadable from the Web (http://www.samspublishing.com/detail_sams.cfm?item=0672320665) as well, so you can always avoid the typing if desired.

Listing 15.18 includes two things: a sample class (Person) that implements IDebugInfo (lines 13–105) and a bit of sample code (lines 4–11) that create an instance of the Person class and then call the DisplayName method. As described above, if you put all this code into a project—three separate .vb files is fine—and make Sub Main the startup object for the project, then the code should run without trouble and produce a file (c:\test.txt) containing your trace information.

Interfaces and Inheritance both provide the capability to have many different objects share common attributes, but two key differences make them suitable for different roles. Interfaces do not include any implementation along with those attributes; the Interface definition contains no code, and the classes that implement that interface must provide all the functionality themselves. That is certainly an advantage of Inheritance, the sharing of implemented functionality from the base to the derived classes, but interfaces make up for that difference by greatly increased flexibility, allowing a single class to implement as many interfaces as desired.

In the end, the two technologies have some similarities, but they are intended for different purposes. Use interfaces when you want to indicate that a class has certain (often more than one) capabilities, equating to a relationship such as "myClass supports the IDebugInfo interface." Inheritance, on the other hand, indicates an "is a" relationship. Phrases such as "Customer is a Person" and "Employee is a Person" could describe the relationship between two derived classes and their base class.

Using the Objects You Create

After you have defined a set of classes and interfaces, you likely will want to use them as part of an application. In the examples so far, only a single project has been involved, so using your classes was as simple as declaring new variables. This might be the case in your real systems, but requiring the class definitions to be part of each project is not useful and certainly does not work well when you want many different projects to share the same set of class and interface definitions. To make your code easily available to any project that needs to use it, you need to create a Class Library project. This type of project is not designed to be run on its own, but instead holds code for use by other projects.

1. Select File, New, Project from the menu, which should bring up the New Project dialog (see Figure 15.2).

2. Select the Class Library project template, and notice the nice text description ("A project for creating classes to use in other applications") that confirms this template's purpose.

3. Provide a name for this new project, instead of the default ClassLibrary1, and click OK to create the project.

Projects of this type consist of as many code files full of classes as you want to add and no startup object. You can spread your classes around, with as little as a single class in a file, or you can combine all your code together; the end result is the same.

Namespaces

One useful way to add organization to your classes is to use namespaces. The defining of namespaces is really a mechanism for code organization, but when you are creating libraries of classes, organization is important. The .NET Framework makes deep use of namespaces, producing the neatly organized classes and their containing namespaces (System, System.Data, System.IO, and so on), and you can do the same simply by adding namespace definitions around your code. Namespaces are declared around your code using Namespace <namespace name> and End Namespace. Nested namespaces (allowing you to have Namespace1.Namespace2.Namespace3) are accomplished by actually specifying the complete name (Namespace1.Namespace2) as you cannot nest the

Namespace declarations. When defined around a class (see Listing 15.19), or multiple classes, those classes are considered a part of that namespace and can be referenced as *Namespace1.Class1* in your code.

FIGURE 15.2

The New Project dialog includes templates for creating class libraries.

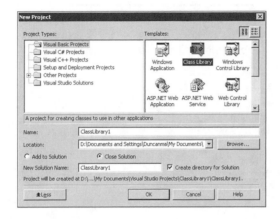

LISTING 15.19 Namespaces Provide Organization to Your Classes

```
1 Option Explicit On
2 Option Strict On
3 Namespace libPerson
4     Public Class Class2
5
6     End Class
7 End Namespace
8
9 Module mod1
10     Sub main()
11         Dim objClass2 As libPerson.Class2
12
13     End Sub
14 End Module
```

You also can use the same namespace name across multiple code files, even across code libraries, and Visual Studio .NET considers each individual definition of that namespace to be part of the whole. Listings 15.20 and 15.21 illustrate this, representing two separate files.

LISTING 15.20 The Same Namespace Can Be Used in Multiple Files

```
1 Option Explicit On
2 Option Strict On
3 Namespace libPerson
4     Public Class Class1
```

LISTING 15.20 continued

```
5
6     End Class
7 End Namespace
```

LISTING 15.21 To the Programmer Using Your Code, Everything Will Appear to Be Part of a Single Namespace

```
 1 Option Explicit On
 2 Option Strict On
 3 Namespace libPerson
 4     Public Class Class2
 5
 6     End Class
 7 End Namespace
 8
 9 Module mod1
10     Sub main()
11         Dim objClass2 As libPerson.Class2
12         Dim objClass1 As libPerson.Class1
13     End Sub
14 End Module
```

At the end of Listing 15.21, you can see code declaring and using the two classes (lines 11–12). When you decide to build a code library and compile it into a DLL, you can wrap all your code in Namespace declarations to make it easy for the user to find your classes. As you will see a little later on, your classes will already appear to be grouped together after you have built them into a library and referenced that library in another project.

Creating and Using a Library DLL

After you have added all your classes and interfaces to your library project, building the final DLL just requires you to select Build from the Build menu or click Ctrl+Shift+B. This creates a DLL, usually *<name of project>*.dll, located in the bin directory under your project. That location and name are fine, but to test your new library, you will have to close this solution and open a new console application project.

1. Select New, Project from the File menu and create a new Visual Basic .NET Console Application.

2. After you have the new project open, right-click on the References folder in the Solution Explorer view of your project.

3. Select Add Reference from the menu that appears, and you see the Add Reference dialog (see Figure 15.3).

4. Click the Browse button and go out and find the libPerson.dll that has been created.

FIGURE 15.3

The Add Reference dialog can be used for adding component references and references direct to other projects.

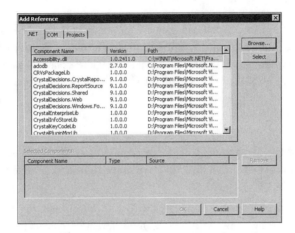

5. After you have found the DLL you want, click OK to bring it back into the Add Reference dialog; then click OK again to return to your code with the newly added reference available to your project.

To use this library of classes, you can just treat them like any part of the .NET Framework. The classes themselves will be found under through the path of *<name of the project>.<namespace>.<class>*. Assuming that your project was called libPerson, and you have added a reference to libPerson, then Listing 15.22 illustrates how you can create instances of classes from your library.

LISTING 15.22   Using Your Library

```
1 Option Explicit On
2 Option Strict On
3
4 Module Module1
5     Sub Main()
6         Dim objClass As libPerson.libPerson.Class1
7     End Sub
8 End Module
```

Note that the use of a `libPerson` namespace has resulted in a secondary grouping that likely is unnecessary. Use namespaces in your libraries to create more granular groupings than just the entire library.

Summary

Making OOP work for you, in your applications, is not a technical issue; it is a design issue. When you create the conceptual design for your application, you need to be thinking in terms of objects. If you can manage that, then building the system using objects will not be a complete paradigm shift but merely a translation from the conceptual to the implementation. For more information on all the OOP concepts available in Visual Basic .NET, search your .NET documentation for "Introduction to Objects in Visual Basic."

Q&A

Q. I heard the term "polymorphism" related to object-oriented programming. Does this mean that I have to have more than one spouse to work with Visual Basic .NET?

A. Never fear, this has nothing to do with your family relationships. Polymorphism describes the capability to treat many different objects as if they were of the same type, allowing you to have different classes, such as `Circle`, `Square`, and `Triangle`, but to treat them all as type `Shape`. This concept is useful and is provided by the technologies of inheritance and interfaces.

Q. Do I have to program with objects to use Visual Basic .NET?

A. In short, yes. Visual Basic .NET, and the entire .NET Framework, is built around objects, and whenever you use any of the .NET Framework classes, you are working with objects. Your own programs, however, can use objects as much or as little as you want. All the code you create will be contained in classes (or modules, which are just a slightly odd form of classes) and therefore you cannot avoid objects completely, but the choice of building your entire system with entities represented as objects is totally up to you.

Workshop

The Workshop is designed to help you anticipate possible questions, review what you've learned, and get thinking about how to put your knowledge into practice. The answers to the quiz are in Appendix A, "Answers to Quizzes/Exercises."

Quiz

1. If you have entities in your business that serve a variety of purposes (Orders, Customers, OrderItems, Events) but all share some common features or capabilities, what OOP concept should you use when building them?

2. When you have an inheritance relationship, such as Employee and Customer both derived from Person, how do you ensure that certain methods or properties of the base class are implemented in the derived classes?

3. Again, in an inheritance relationship, how do you make a base class that cannot be created, forcing the users of your code to create only classes that have been derived from the base?

4. How do you indicate that a class cannot be inherited from at all? What is this also known as?

Exercises

Create an object, or object hierarchy, intended to represent a customer. Try to build it using one or more classes with a focus on reusing your code across other parts of your application.

DAY 16

Advanced Windows Forms

On Day 9, "Building a User Interface with Windows Forms," you saw how to build applications using Windows Forms. As you might imagine, there are many more things to learn in this area. Today, you will see other topics related to building Windows Forms applications. In particular, today we will focus on

- Menus
- Multiple document interface programs
- Advanced Windows Forms controls

Menus

If you've used any version of Windows, you should be familiar with menus. Almost every application has them; they provide access to most of the functionality of the program. You will want to add menus to many of your programs.

Adding a Menu to a Form

You add a menu to your application the same way you add any other control, with two small differences. When you double-click the MainMenu control on the Toolbox to add a new menu to your form, you should see the first difference. Instead of seeing an instance of the menu on the form, you will see the control appear in a new section of the IDE (see Figure 16.1). The second difference between adding a MainMenu control and adding most other controls is that you usually only add a single MainMenu control to each form.

Note

Although you can actually add multiple MainMenu controls to a form, only one can be active at any one time. You can alternate between the MainMenu controls by setting the Menu property of the form to the desired menu.

```
Me.Menu = mnuSecond
```

You might want to do this in cases where you use a single form to perform multiple tasks—for example, if you load different types of files into a control on the form. You could change the menus to reflect the operations that might be performed on the file. However, an easier solution to this problem might be to hide and show menu items as they are needed.

FIGURE 16.1

The form after adding the MainMenu *control.*

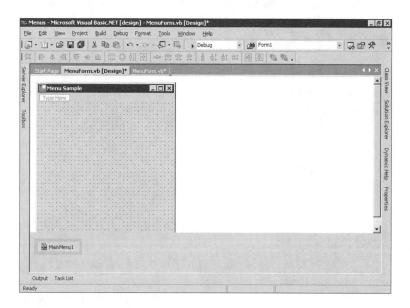

Although the MainMenu control does not appear on the form, it does change the form. After adding a MainMenu control, you should see a new band appear on the form, just under the title bar, as shown in Figure 16.1.

You add items to the menu by building the menu visually. When the MainMenu control is selected in the IDE, you should see a text area with the words "*Type Here*" in the top left-hand corner of the form you are designing, where the File menu would normally be. Click in this space and type the text you want to appear in the menu. As you do this, two more text areas will appear: One beside the new item you have just created, and one below (see Figure 16.2). The items you add to the menu band will be the top-level menu items for your application, whereas the items you add under them will be the menu items. For example, type **File** in the initial box. Below it, add **New** and **Exit** items. Click in the space next to the File menu and type **View** to create a new menu. Below View, enter new items **Red**, **Green**, and **Blue**. As you work on each menu, other top-level menu menus will close. However, they can be reopened if you need to add new items.

FIGURE 16.2

In-place menu editing.

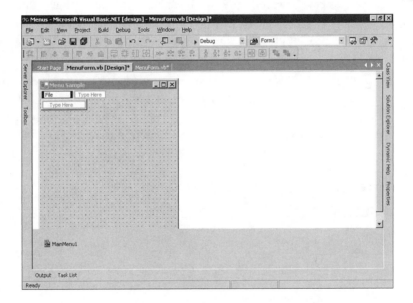

Just as with other controls, you should have a common naming convention for your menu items. A suggested naming convention is the one used in today's lesson:

- Top-level menu items should be named using the three letter prefix **mnu**, followed by the text for the menu—for example, **mnuFile**, **mnuEdit**, mnuHelp.

- Child menu items should be named based on the top-level menu they are contained in, followed by the text of the menu item. You might want to abbreviate or select only part of the text, assuming that the resulting name is still unique. For example, mnuFileOpen, mnuHelpAbout, mnuWindowHorizontal. Duplicate menu items, such as separators (the horizontal lines used to group sections of a menu), should be named by adding a number after them, unless you can rename them something unique.

Keyboards and Menus

Although menus provide access to functionality, they actually can limit access to some users. Menus by themselves are useful, but they can prevent users who lack the coordination or ability to use a mouse. Alternatively, advanced users might not want to constantly switch between using the keyboard and the mouse. When designing menus for your applications, keep these two groups in mind.

Keyboard support can be added to menus in two ways. First, access keys should be added to all menu items. *Access keys* are the underlined menu items, for example, the F for the File menu. Access keys allow those who cannot use a mouse, or those without a mouse, to use your menus. Generally, the first letter of a menu or menu item is the access key. However, to avoid having multiple items with the same access key, you might need to use another letter in the word. For example, in many Microsoft products, the access key for the File menu is usually the F key, whereas the Format menu uses the O key.

Click on the File menu created previously. Change the Text property to **&File**. An underline appears under the F. You also can add this underscore by clicking on a menu item to select it, waiting briefly, and then clicking again to allow you to edit the text. Add an ampersand (&) before the letter you want to be the access key for that menu item. Add access keys to the menus created previously as shown in Table 16.1.

TABLE 16.1 Access Keys in the Menu Sample

Menu Item	Access Key
File	F
New	N
Exit	x
View	V
Red	R
Green	G
Blue	B

Note

As you look at the list of access keys, you should see that most of them are the first character, with the exception of Exit. In this case, the standard is to use the X key as the access key.

The second way to add keyboard support to menus is through the use of shortcut keys or, as they are sometimes known, hotkeys. Shortcut keys are usually associated with Function keys (such as F1 for help) and keys pressed at the same time as the Ctrl key—for example, Ctrl+C is usually a shortcut key for the Copy command. Shortcut keys give users a fast way of accessing frequently used commands. They are not required but provide shortcuts to assist users, particularly those used to dealing exclusively with keyboards or advanced users. Although a shortcut key usually will not be associated with each menu item, you should have them on commonly used menu items. In addition, you should add them to menu items where they would be commonly found, such as on the Cut, Copy, and Paste commands.

You add shortcut keys to menu items with the Shortcut property. Select the Shortcut from the drop-down list. Add the shortcut keys as shown in Table 16.2.

TABLE 16.2 Shortcut Keys

Menu Item	Shortcut
New	CtrlN
Exit	CtrlQ
Red	CtrlR
Green	CtrlG
Blue	CtrlB

Note   As you look at the list, you should again notice that only one seems out of place—the Exit shortcut key. Ctrl+Q was selected instead of Ctrl+X because the latter is generally associated with the Cut command.

The selected keys do not appear on the menu items at design time (see Figure 16.3); however, they do appear when the application is running (see Figure 16.4).

Adding Code

Both top-level menus and menu items support a number of events. However, typically, you will only use the Click event. This event occurs when the user selects the menu item. Add code to this event handler to carry out whatever action is needed. Double-click the menu items to open the code window to add code to the Click event. Add the code in Listing 16.1 to the form.

FIGURE 16.3

Shortcut keys at design time.

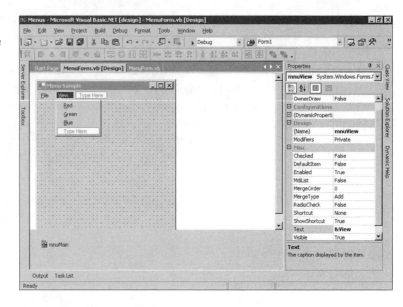

FIGURE 16.4

Shortcut keys at runtime.

LISTING 16.1 Code for the Menu Sample

```
1    Private Sub mnuFileNew_Click(ByVal sender As System.Object, _
2      ByVal e As System.EventArgs) Handles mnuFileNew.Click
3        Dim frmNew As New frmMenu()
4        frmNew.Show()
5    End Sub
6    Private Sub mnuFileExit_Click(ByVal sender As Object, _
7      ByVal e As System.EventArgs) Handles mnuFileExit.Click
8        Me.Close()
9    End Sub
10   Private Sub mnuViewRed_Click(ByVal sender As System.Object, _
11     ByVal e As System.EventArgs) Handles mnuViewRed.Click
12       Me.BackColor = Color.Red
13   End Sub
```

LISTING **16.1** continued

```
14    Private Sub mnuViewGreen_Click(ByVal sender As System.Object, _
15      ByVal e As System.EventArgs) Handles mnuViewGreen.Click
16        Me.BackColor = Color.Green
17    End Sub
18    Private Sub mnuViewBlue_Click(ByVal sender As System.Object, _
19      ByVal e As System.EventArgs) Handles mnuViewBlue.Click
20        Me.BackColor = Color.Blue
21    End Sub
```

16

ANALYSIS The mnuFileNew_Click event handler relates to the File, New menu item. The code for this event (lines 1–5) creates a new instance of the current form and displays it. This allows you to see multiple copies of the form simultaneously. Alternatively, the code for the mnuFileExit_Click event (File, Exit lines 6–9) closes the active form. The application ends when the last form is closed. The last three event handlers relate to the Red, Green, and Blue menu items. They simply change the background color of the active form to the desired color.

Build and run the application. Use the File, New menu item (or press Ctrl+N) to open multiple views of the menu. Try changing the color of the forms using the Red, Green, and Blue menu items (remember that there are also shortcut keys for these items). Figure 16.5 shows the application running. Finally, close all the forms using the Exit menu item to end the application.

FIGURE 16.5

Running the Menu sample.

A Few Suggestions

As you have seen, menus provide a common view into the functionality of your program. However, menus become more useful when people find the menu commands in the same locations from program to program. Therefore, it is good practice to set up your menus similarly to other applications. This assists your users in learning your application because they will find commands more quickly if they are located where they expect them.

This means that you should have some common menus and that they should be located in the same place other programs place them. Figure 16.6 shows some common main menus from programs such as Word, Excel, PowerPoint, Calculator, and Visual Basic .NET. Try to emulate applications such as these, if appropriate for your application. Therefore, a common top-level menu structure should include File, Edit, View, Tools, and Help menus, in that order.

FIGURE 16.6

Common main menus.

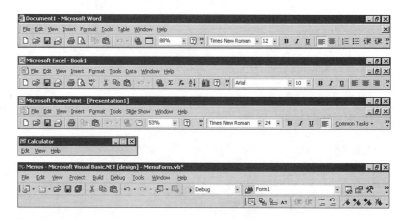

Of course, if your application does not use files, or have alternate views, you might not find some of these menus appropriate. For example, the Calculator application that comes with Windows does not have a File menu. Similarly, many applications have no need for other common menus, such as Edit, Tools, or Help. It is not necessary to include these menus if you have no need for them; however, if they do exist, they should be in their expected locations.

Just as there are common top-level menus, you also should construct menus for your applications so that they are similar to other applications your users might have used. For example, the File menu should generally contain New, Open, Save, and Exit items. Similarly, the Edit menu should have Cut, Copy, and Paste items.

Do	**Don't**
DO look to other applications to suggest common menu structures when defining your menus. Use these common menu structures to assist your users in finding needed menu commands.	**DON'T** feel that this is an absolute rule. If a menu is not appropriate, don't hesitate to leave it off. For example, if your application does not use files, you can avoid using the File menu. You might still want to include the Exit item as the last item on the first menu, however.

16

Multiple Document Interface Programs

Often, you will need to create a program that deals with multiple similar items, such as a text editor that needs multiple windows open, or a database tool that allows the user to view the results of various queries. Although not required, these types of programs can be designed as an MDI (Multiple Document Interface) application to assist your users in viewing the relationship between the open windows. Figure 16.7 shows an MDI application.

FIGURE 16.7

Multiple document interface application.

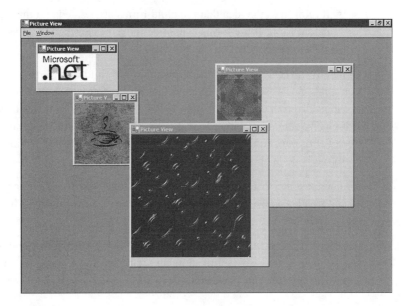

What Is Multiple Document Interface?

To describe MDI, you should compare it to a normal, or an SDI (Single Document Interface) application. In a normal application, such as NotePad, each open document is shown in its own window. Thus, one form holds a single document. In an MDI application, you might assume that one form might hold multiple documents. Basically, this is true. However, a better definition is that one window contains a number of other forms, each of which holds a single document. Older versions of Microsoft Word used this strategy. Similarly, Visual Basic .NET itself is an MDI application. You can have multiple documents open at the same time. Each is displayed in its own window within the parent window of Visual Basic .NET.

Adding the Parent Form

The one difference between creating a normal Windows application, and creating an MDI application is the MDI container. The container or parent form is the one form in your application that contains its children. Any contained forms cannot be moved outside the MDI parent. This serves two purposes:

- It decreases the chance that one or more forms might be misplaced by novice users. Users who are less familiar with navigating Windows can sometimes lose a form by selecting another and are often unable to locate the previous form using the taskbar.

- It reinforces the idea that the child forms are related and that they are related to the parent form. If the forms cannot be moved independently, they will be thought of as being dependent on one another.

Generally, all other forms in the application are children of this parent form. However, you might not want some of them to be a child. You would want to do this if the form is not logically contained by the parent. For example, in Visual Basic .NET, a code window is logically contained within Visual Basic .NET and therefore should be a child form. An open file dialog, on the other hand, is not logically contained within the application and therefore is not a child window.

You create a new MDI parent form by setting the IsMdiContainer property to True. Doing so adds a new control to the form, an MdiClient control. This control fills the entire form and is the container for the child forms.

After you have an MDI parent form, you can make other forms children of this form by setting their MdiParent before showing them. Set this property to point to the parent form. Listing 16.2 shows an example of this.

LISTING 16.2 Creating a Child Form

```
1      Private Sub mnuFileOpen_Click( _
2          ByVal sender As System.Object, _
3          ByVal e As System.EventArgs) _
```

LISTING **16.2**   continued

```
4          Handles mnuFileOpen.Click
5
6              Dim oForm As New frmView()
7              oForm.MdiParent = Me
8              oForm.Show()
9      End Sub
```

16

ANALYSIS To display another form, the first step is to create a new instance of the desired form (line 6). Next, the MdiParent property is set to the parent form. This form must have its IsMdiContainer set to True. Finally, the form is shown (line 8). It cannot be moved outside the bounds of the parent form.

Note

> Although MDI applications provide many benefits, you might not want to use them for most of your applications. Microsoft has reduced its own use of MDI applications greatly, stating that many novice users are confused by them. For example, Microsoft Word and Excel both used to be MDI applications. However, now they are SDI applications and create one window per document.
>
> Therefore, like any technology, use MDI where appropriate and when your users will understand it.

MDI and Menus

As you might expect, when a single window could hold multiple, different child windows, MDI applications have special menu settings. These allow you to organize the child windows easier. Generally, MDI applications will have a Window menu that provides access to these commands.

The standard Window menu has four commands:

- Tile Horizontally   Organizes the child windows so that each is a horizontal band across the screen (see Figure 16.8). This is useful when you need to compare information that needs the whole line in view, such as two word processing documents.
- Tile Vertically   Organizes the child windows so that each is a vertical band side-by-side across the screen (see Figure 16.9). This is useful when comparing small areas of two or more documents, or when you are performing a quick scan of two documents for changes.

FIGURE 16.8

Tile Horizontally applied to child forms.

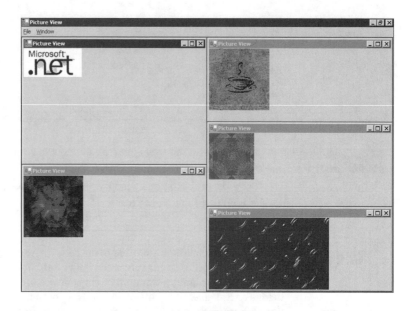

FIGURE 16.9

Tile Vertically applied to child forms.

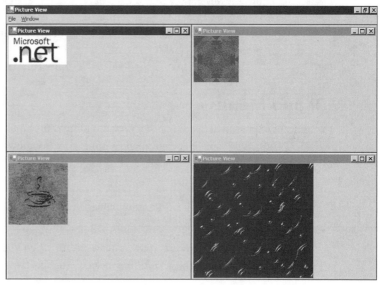

- Cascade   Organizes the child windows so that they are all the same size. Each
  window is positioned slightly below and to the right of the ones behind it, leading
  to an arrangement where you can view all the title bars of each child window
  (see Figure 16.10). This is useful to determine which documents you have open
  currently.

FIGURE **16.10**

Cascading child forms.

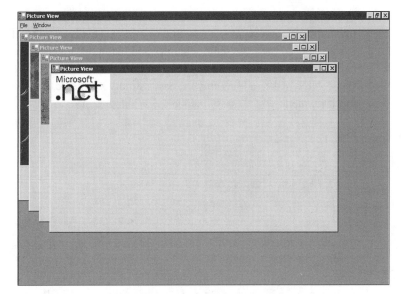

- **Arrange Icons**   Organizes all minimized windows so that they are arranged in rows along the bottom of the parent window (see Figure 16.11). This is useful to organize child windows not currently in use.

FIGURE **16.11**

Arrange Icons applied to child forms.

16

In addition to the common Window menu items, the Window menu typically also has a
list of all the child windows (see Figure 16.12). This is usually referred to as the Window
List. It lists all the open child windows and maintains a check mark next to the active
child window. Rather than build and maintain the code to produce this yourself, Visual
Basic .NET makes adding this list easy. Simply set the MdiList property to True for the
top-level menu you want to include the Window List.

FIGURE 16.12

Window List menu.

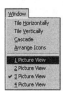

To see how to create an MDI application, you will create a simple MDI graphics viewer
application. Create a new Windows application and call it MultiPicView. Change the
form's name in the Solution Explorer to MdiParent. Open the code view for the form
and change the class name from Form1 to MdiParent. Finally, open the project properties
and set the Startup Object to MdiParent. Set the properties of the form as shown in
Table 16.3.

TABLE 16.3   Properties for the MDI Parent Form

Property	Value
Size	480, 360
Text	Picture View
IsMdiContainer	True

The user will have a menu to allow him to open new files to view. Add a MainMenu control and OpenFileDialog to the MDI parent form. Rename the MainMenu object mnuMain
and build the menu as shown in Table 16.4. Set the properties of the OpenFileDialog as
shown in Table 16.5.

TABLE 16.4   Menu Structure for MDI Parent Form

Menu Item	Property	Value
Top level	(Name)	mnuFile
	Text	File
Under File	(Name)	mnuFileOpen
	Text	&Open
	Shortcut	Ctrl+O

TABLE 16.4 continued

Menu Item	Property	Value
Under Open	(Name)	mnuFileSep
	Text	-
Under separator	(Name)	mnuFileExit
	Text	E&xit
	Shortcut	Ctrl+Q
Top-level menu	(Name)	mnuWindow
	Text	&Window
	MdiList	True
Under Window	(Name)	mnuWindowHorizontal
	Text	Tile &Horizontally
Under Tile Horizontal	(Name)	mnuWindowVertical
	Text	Tile &Vertically
Under Tile Vertically	(Name)	mnuWindowCascade
	Text	&Cascade
Under Cascade	(Name)	mnuWindowArrange
	Text	&Arrange Icons

TABLE 16.5 Properties of the `OpenFileDialog`

Property	Value
(Name)	DlgOpen
Filter	Graphics files|*.gif;*.bmp;*.jpg|All files|*.*

The File menu will be used to open new graphics files and to end the application. Add the code in Listing 16.3 to the form for the menu items.

LISTING 16.3 Code for the File Menu Commands for `MultiPicView`

```
1    Private Sub mnuFileOpen_Click( _
2        ByVal sender As System.Object, _
3        ByVal e As System.EventArgs) _
4        Handles mnuFileOpen.Click
5
6        If dlgOpen.ShowDialog() = DialogResult.OK Then
7            Dim oForm As New frmView()
8            oForm.MdiParent = Me
9            oForm.Picture = Image.FromFile(dlgOpen.FileName)
```

LISTING 16.3   continued

```
10              oForm.Show()
11          End If
12      End Sub
13
14      Private Sub mnuFileExit_Click( _
15          ByVal sender As System.Object, _
16          ByVal e As System.EventArgs) _
17          Handles mnuFileExit.Click
18
19          Me.Close()
20
21      End Sub
```

ANALYSIS   The code should be similar to what you've seen already. The File, Open event handler displays the `OpenFileDialog` (line 6). If the user selects a file, the code creates a new `frmView` form, which we will create in a moment, and sets its `MdiParent` property to the current form (line 8). It then sets its `Picture` property to the graphics file and displays the new form (line 10). The graphic is loaded in line 9 using the `FromFile` method of the `Image` class to retrieve the graphic stored in a file.

The File, Exit event handler is even more simple, closing the current form. This causes all open child windows to also close, ending the application.

In addition to writing code for the File menu, you should also write the code for the commands of the Window menu. Listing 16.4 shows this code.

LISTING 16.4   Code for the Windows Menu Commands for `MultiPicView`

```
22      Private Sub mnuWindowHorizontal_Click( _
23          ByVal sender As System.Object, _
24          ByVal e As System.EventArgs) _
25          Handles mnuWindowHorizontal.Click
26
27          Me.LayoutMdi(MdiLayout.TileHorizontal)
28      End Sub
29
30      Private Sub mnuWindowVertical_Click( _
31          ByVal sender As System.Object, _
32          ByVal e As System.EventArgs) _
33          Handles mnuWindowVertical.Click
34
35          Me.LayoutMdi(MdiLayout.TileVertical)
36      End Sub
37
38      Private Sub mnuWindowCascade_Click( _
```

LISTING 16.4   continued

```
39              ByVal sender As System.Object, _
40              ByVal e As System.EventArgs) _
41              Handles mnuWindowCascade.Click
42
43              Me.LayoutMdi(MdiLayout.Cascade)
44          End Sub
45
46          Private Sub mnuWindowArrange_Click( _
47              ByVal sender As System.Object, _
48              ByVal e As System.EventArgs) _
49              Handles mnuWindowArrange.Click
50
51              Me.LayoutMdi(MdiLayout.ArrangeIcons)
52          End Sub
```

16

ANALYSIS   Each of the four Window menu items simply execute the LayoutMdi method of the MDI parent form, setting the desired arrangement for the child forms.

You are now ready to create the form that will be used to display the graphics. Add a second form to the project by selecting the Project, Add Windows Form menu item. When prompted for a name, name the new form PictureView. Change the Text property of the form to Picture View. Add a PictureBox control to the form and set the properties of this control as shown in Table 16.6.

TABLE 16.6   Properties for the PictureBox Control

Property	Value
(Name)	picView
Dock	Fill

Enter code view, and add a public property to the form called Picture that represents the Image property of the PictureBox. This should be similar to the code in Listing 16.5.

LISTING 16.5   Picture Property

```
1          Public Property Picture() As Image
2              Get
3                  Return picView.Image
4              End Get
5              Set(ByVal Value As Image)
6                  picView.Image = Value
7              End Set
8          End Property
```

ANALYSIS Just as you might have properties that represent private values stored within the Form class, you can also have properties that represent controls on the form, or properties of those controls. In this case, the Picture property is used to access the Image property of the picView control. Although this could have been solved by making the picView control itself Public, that would have allowed too much access to the control. This allows the code to easily read or change the image, without allowing the code on another form to change other information about the PictureBox.

Run the application. You should be able to open multiple graphics files, as shown in Figure 16.13.

FIGURE 16.13

MultiPicView *in action.*

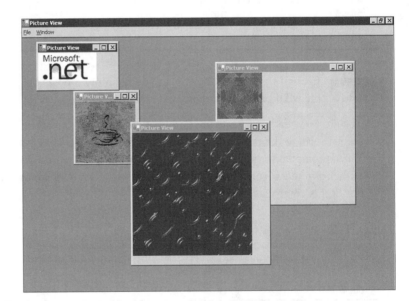

Advanced Windows Forms Controls

Although it is often possible to build an application using only the most common controls, such as the Label, TextBox, and PictureBox controls, you will likely need other controls at times. Many controls are available with Visual Basic .NET that have not been covered in this book, and many others are available for purchase. It would be difficult, if not impossible, to cover all the available controls in a single book, let alone during part of one day's lesson. Therefore, I will to show you a few of the more important controls and how to use these controls.

TreeView

The TreeView control should be familiar to anyone who has used Windows for any length of time. It is the control that appears on the left-hand side of the window in

Explorer, as well as anywhere else a hierarchical display is shown. It allows you to show the user a list of items and their relationships. The graphics shown for each item in the list can be changed, or not shown at all. Similarly, the lines that connect the items can be customized or removed. `TreeView` should be considered whenever you need to display many related items and show that relation to users—for example, to allow the user to browse directories, browse folders of e-mail, or create the outline for an article. Figure 16.14 shows the `TreeView` control in use, showing a list of folders on a hard drive.

FIGURE 16.14

The `TreeView` control in action.

The `TreeView` control has many properties, methods, and events. Table 16.7 describes the most commonly used ones.

TABLE 16.7 Members of `TreeView`

Member	Description
	Properties
Checkboxes	Adds check boxes next to each item in the `TreeView`. This makes creating multiple selection easier.
FullRowSelect	If this property is `True`, the entire row will be selected when an item is selected. Alternatively, only the text for the selected item will be selected.
Nodes	This is the most important property of the `TreeView`. It contains the list of all the top-level items in the `TreeView`.

16

TABLE 16.7   continued

Member	Description
PathSeparator	Used when retrieving the path to a node in the TreeView. This character is used between each of the nodes. It defaults to the backslash (\) character.
SelectedNode	The currently selected node in the TreeView.
ShowLines	Determines whether lines are drawn between the nodes in the TreeView.
ShowPlusMinus	Determines whether + and – characters are shown next to nodes in the TreeView.
ShowRootLines	Determines whether lines are drawn to connect top-level nodes in the TreeView.
Sorted	Determines whether items added to the TreeView should be sorted when added.

Methods

Member	Description
CollapseAll	Closes all tree nodes.
ExpandAll	Expands all tree nodes.

Events

Member	Description
BeforeCollapse	Occurs before a subtree is closed. This can be used to cancel the event, or to update other controls.
BeforeExpand	Occurs before a subtree is opened. This is a great event handler to call to update the items in the subtree before displaying to the user.
BeforeSelect	Occurs before a node is selected.
AfterCollapse	Occurs after a subtree is closed. This is a good location if you need to free resources used by the subtree, such as to close database connections.
AfterExpand	Occurs after a subtree is opened. This can be used to update other controls with the newly shown tree nodes.
AfterSelect	Occurs after a tree node is selected. This can be used to update other controls based on the selected node.

As described in Table 16.7, Nodes is the most important property for the TreeView. Each of the items in this collection is a TreeNode object, and this object is the focal point of most work with the TreeView. Table 16.8 describes the important properties and methods of the TreeNode class.

TABLE 16.8 Properties and Methods of the `TreeNode`

Member	Description
Properties	
Checked	Used in cooperation with the `Checkboxes` property of the `TreeView`. This property is `True` if the `TreeNode` is checked.
FullPath	This returns a string containing each of the nodes down to the selected node, each separated by the `PathSeparator` property of the `TreeView`. Generally, this creates a pathlike string.
Nodes	The collection of `TreeNodes` of this `TreeNode`.
Text	The text for this `TreeNode`.
Methods	
Collapse	Collapses the tree beginning with the current node.
Expand	Expands the tree beginning with the selected node.
Toggle	Changes the tree beginning with the selected node to either collapsed or expanded, whichever it isn't currently.

Not only are the individual `TreeNode` objects and the whole `TreeView` important, an additional object is important when dealing with the `TreeView` control. This is the collection represented by the `Nodes` properties—TreeNodeCollection objects. One of these collections is at the topmost level of the `TreeView`, reflected in the `Nodes` property of the `TreeView`. In addition, each `TreeNode` in this collection has its own `Nodes` collection, representing all the child nodes of that `TreeNode`. Table 16.9 describes some of the properties and methods of this important collection.

TABLE 16.9 Methods and Properties of the `TreeNodeCollection`

Member	Description
Properties	
Count	Determines how many items are in the collection.
Item	Returns one of the `TreeNodes` from the collection. This can be nested—for example, `tvwFolders.Nodes.Item(3).Nodes.Item(1)` would be the second node under the fourth node in the `TreeView`. (Remember that collections begin at 0).
Methods	
Add	Adds a new node to the end of the current collection. This can either be an actual `TreeNode` object, or simply the text to display for the new node.

16

TABLE 16.9   continued

Member	Description
Clear	Removes all nodes from the selected collection.
IndexOf	Returns the position number of the selected node in the collection.
Insert	Adds a new TreeNode to the list of nodes at a defined position.
Remove	Removes a requested node from the collection.
RemoveAt	Removes a node by index from the collection.

ListView

The ListView control should also be familiar to most Windows users as the left side of the Explorer window, as well as many other locations. The ListView is similar to the ListBox control, in that it can hold multiple items. It provides more functionality, however, in that it allows you to display the items in multiple ways. The items in the list can be displayed as a list, associated with large or small icons. In addition, a list with extra details for each item can be displayed. Finally, the ListView can be used in place of a grid control because it also can display grid lines. Table 16.10 shows some of the more important properties, methods and events of the ListView control.

TABLE 16.10   Important Properties, Methods and Events of the ListView Control

Member	Description
Properties	
Checkboxes	Determines whether check boxes are shown next to each item in the list. This is an excellent way to create a multiselect list.
CheckIndices	Returns the index values for each of the selected items in the ListView. This allows you to know the items selected when using the ListView for multiselect lists.
Columns	When the ListView is in Detail view, columns can be shown to organize the list.
FullRowSelect	Determines whether the entire row, or only the text for the item, is selected when an item is selected.
GridLines	Determines whether grid lines will be shown when the ListView is in Detail view. This allows you to make a ListView look like a simple Grid control.
Items	Represents the collection of all items in the ListView.

TABLE 16.10 continued

Member	Description
View	Determines how the ListView will be shown. This can be one of Large Icons, Small Icons, List, or Detail.
Methods	
Clear	Removes all the items from the ListView.
Events	
ColumnClick	Occurs when the user clicks on a column header. This can be used to alter the sort order for the column.
SelectedIndexChanged	Occurs when the user selects a new item in the ListView. This would allow you to update other controls based on this selection.

Just as with the Nodes collection of the TreeView control, the most important property of the ListView control is the Items collection. Each of the individual items in the Items collection is a ListViewItem object. This object in turn has methods and properties that represent what is possible with each of the individual items in the ListView. Table 16.11 describes the most important of these properties.

TABLE 16.11 Properties of the ListViewItem

Member	Description
Properties	
Checked	Used in cooperation with the Checkboxes property of the ListView, this property is True if the individual item has been checked.
Index	Returns the position of the item in the ListView.
Selected	Determines whether the ListViewItem is selected.
SubItems	Used in cooperation with Detail view and Columns. This property contains the information to display in the additional columns.

As the TreeView has TreeNodeCollection objects reflecting the collections of TreeNode objects, the ListView has ListViewItemCollection objects. This collection is less important than the corresponding property of the TreeView, however, because the ListView does not have the same hierarchy of nodes. Instead, there is basically only one ListViewItemCollection. Table 16.12 describes some of the important properties and methods of this collection.

TABLE 16.12   Properties and Methods of the `ListViewItemCollection`

Member	Description
Properties	
Count	The number of items in the `ListViewCollection`.
Item	Returns the `ListViewItem` at the requested position.
Methods	
Add	Adds a new `ListViewItem` to the collection at the end. The new item can either be a `ListViewItem` object, or the text to display for the item.
Clear	Removes all the items from the collection.
IndexOf	Returns the index, or position, for the requested `ListViewItem`.
Insert	Adds a new `ListViewItem` to the collection at a requested position.
Remove	Removes a `ListViewItem` from the collection.
RemoveAt	Removes an item from the collection by position.

Splitters

Although you have probably seen the `TreeView` and `ListView` controls, you are less likely to have seen the `Splitter` control; however, you might have used it. The `Splitter` control is used to resize child controls in a window at runtime. For example, in Explorer, if you move the mouse over the gray line separating the `TreeView` and `ListView`, you can drag this separator from side to side, changing the relative size of the two controls (see Figure 16.15). This is the `Splitter` control. It is a simple control, whose sole purpose is to enable this type of dynamic resizing. It is used in cooperation with two docked controls. One of the two controls is docked to one of the sides of the parent form, whereas the other has its `Dock` property set to `Fill`.

It is rare to need to use any of the properties of the `Splitter` control. However, there are some properties that you might want to set to customize the behavior of the control. These are described in Table 16.13.

TABLE 16.13   Important Properties of the `Splitter` Control

Member	Description
BackColor	As with other controls, this defines the background color for the `Splitter`. It is useful for the `Splitter` control to assist the user in noticing the existence of the `Splitter`.

TABLE 16.13   continued

Member	Description
Dock	Sets the direction of the Splitter. If set to a side, the Splitter is used to change the height of the two controls. If the Splitter is docked to the top or bottom of the form, it is used to change the width of the two controls.
MinSize	Sets a minimum size for the control not set to Fill. This is useful if you do not want information on one side of the Splitter to be obscured.

FIGURE 16.15

Using the Splitter *control.*

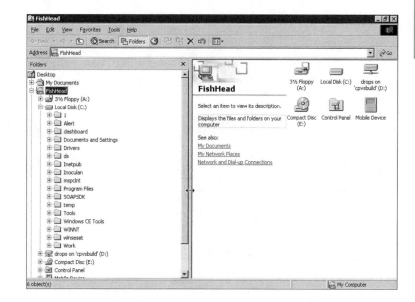

To see how these three controls can be used to quickly build up an application, we will create an Explorer clone, allowing the user to navigate through the drives, seeing the files stored on them.

Create a new Windows application. I called mine Pioneer, but you can call yours whatever you want. Change the filename of the created form to PioneerForm, and the class created to frmPioneer. Set the Startup Object of the Project to frmPioneer using the Project Properties dialog. Build the application once to ensure that there are no errors.

The user interface will be Spartan—consisting of a TreeView, ListView, and Splitter controls (see Figure 16.16).

Resize the form to make it larger than the default. Set this and other properties as shown in Table 16.14.

FIGURE **16.16**

*User interface for
Pioneer.*

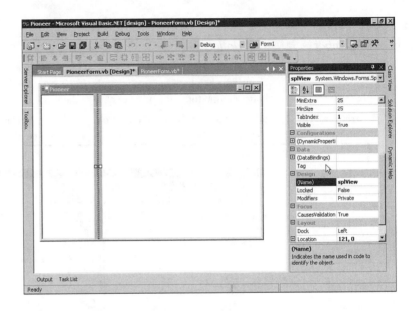

TABLE 16.14   Properties for the Pioneer Form

Property	Value
Name	FrmPioneer
Text	Pioneer
Size	480, 330

Add a TreeView control to the form. Set the properties as in Table 16.15.

TABLE 16.15   Properties for the TreeView Control

Property	Value
Name	TvwFolders
Dock	Left
Width	121

Add the Splitter control to the form, change the name to splView. Other properties are fine as their defaults. Add a ListView control to the form. Set the properties as shown in Table 16.16.

TABLE 16.16   Properties for the `ListView` Control

Property	Value
Name	LvwFiles
Dock	Fill
View	List

When the form first loads, the `TreeView` control should display the available drives (see Listing 16.6). As each drive is selected, the directories in that drive should be shown in the `TreeView`, and the files in each directory in the `ListView`. Initially, however, only the `TreeView` will be populated with the available drives. Because this code uses the `Directory` object, you should also add an `Imports System.IO` to the top of the code view. This allows you to use the `Directory` object without having to fully qualify it (that is, without having to write `System.IO.Directory`).

LISTING 16.6   Adding the Drive List to the `TreeView`

```
 1    Private Sub PioneerForm_Load(ByVal sender As System.Object, _
 2        ByVal e As System.EventArgs) _
 3        Handles MyBase.Load
 4
 5        'add drives to the treeview
 6        Dim sDrives() As String = Directory.GetLogicalDrives()
 7        Dim sDrive As String
 8        Dim tvwNode As TreeNode
 9
10        For Each sDrive In sDrives
11            tvwNode = tvwFolders.Nodes.Add(sDrive)
12            'add a dummy node
13            tvwNode.Nodes.Add("dummy")
14        Next
15
16    End Sub
```

ANALYSIS   The `GetLogicalDrives` method of the `Directory` class is a shared method that returns an array containing all the names of all the available drives on the computer. This includes floppy drives, CD-ROM drives, mapped network drives, and other devices that look like a hard drive. Line 6 fills this array, and the `For Each...Next` block loops through the array. We add this as a `TreeNode` to the TreeView (line 11), and add a child node with the text `dummy` to this node at line 13. This child node serves two purposes: It marks those nodes that we have not yet opened, and it ensures that there is a + next to all nodes. If no child nodes are in a `TreeView`, the control does not add a plus symbol, and it is not obvious that there could be children. Adding a single dummy node that we will remove later is a common strategy to make each node seem like it has children.

The `TreeView` serves two functions. As each directory is selected, the files in that directory are added to the `ListView`. Second, as each node is expanded in the `TreeView`, the child directories of the selected directory are added to the `TreeView`. Listing 16.7 shows these two event handlers.

LISTING 16.7   `TreeView` Event Handlers

```
17    Private Sub tvwFolders_BeforeExpand(ByVal sender As Object, _
18        ByVal e As System.Windows.Forms.TreeViewCancelEventArgs) _
19        Handles tvwFolders.BeforeExpand
20
21        'see if we already know what the children are
22        '   (we don't if there is still a dummy there)
23        Dim oNode As TreeNode = CType(e.Node, TreeNode)
24        If oNode.Nodes(0).Text = "dummy" Then
25            'remove the dummy
26            oNode.Nodes(0).Remove()
27            'add the real children
28            GetChildren(oNode)
29        End If
30    End Sub
31
32    Private Sub tvwFolders_AfterSelect(ByVal sender As Object, _
33        ByVal e As System.Windows.Forms.TreeViewEventArgs) _
34        Handles tvwFolders.AfterSelect
35
36        Dim sFiles() As String
37        Try
38            sFiles = Directory.GetFiles(tvwFolders.SelectedNode.FullPath)
39        Catch ex As Exception
40            'just ignore the exception
41            'the most likely cause of the exception
42            ' is 'Drive not ready' if you're accessing a floppy
43            ' without a disc in the drive
44        End Try
45
46        If Not IsNothing(sFiles) then
47            Dim sFile As String
48            Dim oItem As ListViewItem
49
50            lvwFiles.Items.Clear()
51
52            For Each sFile In sFiles
53                oItem = lvwFiles.Items.Add(StripPath(sFile))
54            Next
55        End If
56    End Sub
57
58    Private Sub GetChildren(ByVal node As TreeNode)
```

LISTING **16.7**   continued

```
59          Dim sDirs() As String = Directory.GetDirectories(node.FullPath)
60          Dim sDir As String
61          Dim oNode As TreeNode
62
63          For Each sDir In sDirs
64              oNode = node.Nodes.Add(StripPath(sDir))
65              'add a dummy node as a child
66              oNode.Nodes.Add("dummy")
67          Next
68      End Sub
69
70      Private Function StripPath(ByVal path As String) As String
71          'removes the leading path from the filename
72          Dim iPos As Integer
73          'find the last \ character
74          iPos = path.LastIndexOf("\")
75          'everything after it is the actual filename
76          Return path.Substring(iPos + 1)
77      End Function
78 End Class
```

ANALYSIS   One of the features of the TreeView control is that for each of the operations affecting the nodes in the tree, there is a Before and an After event. The Before events, such as the BeforeExpand event handler (lines 17–30 in the code listing) provide a chance to either cancel the event or make changes before the effects of the event are shown. In the case of the BeforeExpand event, you can change the contents of the children of the node before the list is expanded. Recall that earlier, you added a dummy node to guarantee that each node had a plus next to it, implying that it could be expanded. The BeforeExpand event handler is the best place to remove this dummy node and to add the actual nodes. Later, if there is no dummy node, you do not have to make any changes because the TreeView will remember the added nodes. The routine begins by assigning the affected node to a temporary variable. This is not absolutely necessary because the code could have been written using e.Node instead of oNode. However, using a temporary variable like this, or using the With...End With block is a good habit because it is slightly more efficient. Next, the code tests for the existence of the dummy node (line 24). If it exists, it is removed, and the real children are added with the GetChildren subroutine (described later). If the dummy node does not exist, nothing is done because we have already populated the TreeView with the appropriate child nodes.

The tvwFolders_AfterSelect event handler is where the ListView is populated with the files in the selected TreeNode. This begins by retrieving the names of all the files using the shared method GetFiles of the Directory class (lines 21–22). This method returns the full path to all the files in a requested directory. The second parameter to the AfterSelect event handler, e, has two properties of interest:

- Action   Why was the node selected? That is, is this during an expand operation, a collapse, or simply the user selecting the node?

- Node   The node that was selected. This is an easier way to retrieve the selected node than the alternative tvwFolders.SelectedItem.

Each node in a TreeView can retrieve its path in the TreeView. This path consists of each of the parents, beginning with the root node, separated by the PathSeparator character of the TreeView control. Because this defaults to the backslash character, this is an easy way to retrieve a path similar to the path on the drive. For example, if the node System32 is a child node of the node Winnt, which is a child node of C:\, the FullPath property of the System32 node would be C:\Winnt\System32. This path is passed to the GetFiles method, which is a shared method of the Directory class that returns a string array of all the files in the directory. A For Each...Next loop (lines 27–29) is used to populate the ListView with each filename, after first clearing the ListView of all contents (line 25). Note that the contents for each directory are retrieved each time the TreeNode is selected; no attempt at storing this list is made.

The GetChildren procedure is used to populate a TreeNode with its child nodes (lines 58–68). The node to add to is passed into the routine to assist in determining the subdirectories and to identify the TreeNode to add to. Notice that the existing path of the selected node is not passed in because this can be determined using the FullPath method of the node (line 59) as done earlier in the AfterSelect event handler. The shared method Directory.GetDirectories is used to retrieve a string array containing the subdirectories of the selected directory. The remaining code is similar to that used when the drives were added to the TreeView. The path is removed from the retrieved directory name (line 64), and a dummy node is added to ensure that the node looks like it can be expanded (line 66).

The StripPath function is used by other procedures to remove the path from a filename, leaving only the name. This routine (lines 70–78) uses the LastIndexOf method of the string object to find the last position for a requested character, in this case the backslash "\" character. Everything in the path leading up to that last backslash should be the path, whereas everything after the last backslash should be the actual filename. Finally, line 76 extracts and returns the text starting with the character following the last backslash.

Build and execute the application. You should see something similar to Figure 16.17, depending on your own set of drives and directories. You should be able to navigate through the directories, and the files in each directory should be shown. You now have a starting point to create your own file Explorer. You might want to extend Pioneer to add other features, such as the capability to add directories, change the view of the files, add graphics, and so on.

FIGURE 16.17

Pioneer in action.

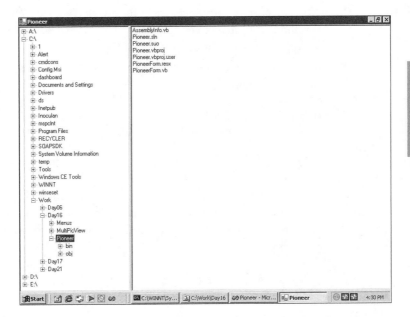

16

Summary

There are obviously many more topics related to Windows Forms to learn about. In addition, many other controls are available in the Toolbox that have not been described. Experiment with these to see how they can help you with your applications. If you see a feature in another application that you like, try finding the control, or possibly the property setting, that will allow you to reproduce the feature in your own applications.

You should see that we have in fact been using objects all along in our applications. However, you should learn how to create your own objects. Tomorrow, we will continue our look at the .NET Framework and some other important classes you will use frequently.

Q&A

Q. How would you associate Ctrl+B with a menu item so that pressing that key combination would run the code for the menu item?

A. You add shortcut key to a menu item using the ShortcutKey property. Select the CtrlB item from the drop-down list for the ShortcutKey property.

Q. **What happens if you do not set the `MdiParent` property of a form before showing it?**

A. If you do not set the `MdiParent` to a form with the `IsMdiContainer` property set to `True`, the new form will not be contained within the `MdiParent` form and will be able to be moved outside the bounds of the parent form.

Q. **What would be the result of this code running if `tvwFolders` was a `TreeView` control on a form?**

```
Dim oItem as TreeNode
oItem = tvwFolders.Nodes.Add("One")
With oItem.Nodes.Add("Two")
    .Nodes.Add("Three")
    .Nodes.Add("Four")
End With
```

A. Four items would be added to the `TreeView`. The root node would have the text `One`. It would have one child node, `Two`, which would have two child nodes, `Three` and `Four`. The `With...End With` block is an alternative to storing a node in a `TreeNode` variable when adding child nodes.

Workshop

The Workshop is designed to help you anticipate possible questions, review what you've learned, and get you thinking about how to put your knowledge into practice. The answers to the quiz are in Appendix A, "Answers to Quizzes/Exercises."

Quiz

1. How can you arrange the child windows of an MDI application best to see the title bars of all children?

Exercises

1. Find examples of MDI and SDI applications that you typically use. Do they make it easier, or more difficult to keep track of multiple documents as you work with them?

2. Update the Pioneer application you built during today's lesson to show the files using the Detail view of the `ListView` control. Add columns to display the `ReadOnly`, `Hidden`, and `System` attributes for each file. In addition, show the last time the file was modified in another column.

DAY 17

Using the .NET Framework

Back on Day 8, "Introduction to the .NET Framework," you first learned about the .NET Framework and some of the classes it makes available. As you might guess we discussed classes during that lesson. Today, we will examine some of the more common groups of classes that you will work with regularly. They include:

- Files and the related classes
- Drawing with the graphics classes

Streams and Files

Many Visual Basic .NET applications you write will have to deal with files of some sort. Either you will create files, or you will need to read configuration files or find files on the user's drives. Therefore, learning how to work with files is an important skill you will need as a Visual Basic .NET developer.

When you start working with the classes of the .NET Framework, especially when you write applications to work with files, you will frequently come across something with "Stream" in it, for example: `FileStream`, `TextStream`, `StreamWriter`, and `NetworkStream`. As you might have guessed, these are related. The designers of Visual Basic .NET and the .NET Framework tried to make using the Framework easier by making everything as consistent as possible. One way they tried to do this is by using the same types of objects in many places. One group of these objects is the `Stream` object, its children, and the classes used to work with Streams. These other classes include a variety of `Reader` and `Writer` classes, `Encoders`, and many others. We'll focus on the essentials, but as you become more advanced, you'll see that any other classes in this family will seem familiar.

What's a Stream?

The term "streams," like many computer terms, is an attempt to name something to remind you of a real-world counterpart. A stream in the real world is a small amount of water, flowing. A computer stream is similar—it is a flow of information that passes in some sequential manner. However, unless you have a file about the rivers of the world, I'm sure that you might not think of water when you're looking at the files on your hard drive. However, imagine yourself as the part of your hard drive that reads files. All it sees is a series of information, flowing sequentially past it—a stream.

After you make the abstraction of files as a stream, working with files is easier. Now, whether the file is binary or contains text, you can deal with it in the same way. You open the file, move through the file, and write to the file using the same methods because they are all streams. In addition, these skills also apply to other things that look like streams. We won't be covering them in this book, but they include network communications, the memory in your computer, encrypted data, and many other locations. By learning how to read and write simple text files, you will already know how to work with any of these streams.

Files and Directories

Before you start creating streams, however, let's spend some time looking at how to find, create, and delete directories and files. This will allow you to locate files and make directories to store your applications.

As you saw on Day 8, the .NET Framework is divided into a series of namespaces. Each of the namespaces contains a number of classes that are related somehow. Recall that on Day 8, we worked with collections (such as `ArrayList` and `Queue`), and they were bundled into the `System.Collections` namespace. Similarly, all the file and directory (and stream) classes are bundled into the `System.IO` namespace. The `System.IO` namespace is not, as you might think, related to the highly volcanic moon of Jupiter (`http://photojournal.jpl.nasa.gov/cgi-bin/PIAGenCatalogPage.pl?PIA00292`), but instead to input and output. The `System.IO` namespace is one of the most heavily used namespaces in the .NET Framework for this reason. Although a namespace relating to Jupiter's moon might be useful, it is not a heavily used namespace. Anytime you want to open, read from, write to, or otherwise deal with a file or stream, you will need this namespace. Fortunately, Visual Basic .NET always includes it when you create a new Windows application, so it should generally be available.

If you look in the online help at the `System.IO` namespace, you will see two classes that shouldn't be surprising—`File` and `Directory`. These two classes map to files and directories. They have properties and methods that represent what you would expect from files and directories. For example, the `Directory` class has methods for retrieving subdirectories, getting the list of files in the directory, and so on. Similarly, the `File` class has methods for copying the file, opening it, and retrieving information about the file. Table 17.1 lists the important methods of the `Directory` object, whereas Table 17.2 shows the important methods of the `File` class.

17

TABLE 17.1 Methods of the `Directory` Class

Method	Description
CreateDirectory	Creates one or more directories. One of the more powerful uses for this class is to create an entire tree of directories.
Delete	Removes a directory.
Exists	Returns `True` if the directory exists.
GetCurrentDirectory	Returns the full path to the current directory.
GetDirectories	Returns an array containing the child directories of the desired directory.
GetFiles	Returns an array containing the files in the requested directory.

TABLE 17.2 Methods of the `File` Class

Method	Description
Copy	Copies a file.
Create	Creates a new file.
CreateText	A special version of `Create` that creates a text file.
Delete	Deletes a file.
Exists	Returns `True` if the file exists.
Open	Opens a file for reading, writing, or both.
OpenRead	Specialized version of `Open` that always opens the file for reading.

TABLE 17.2   continued

Method	Description
OpenText	Specialized version of Open that opens text files only for reading. This would be a handy shortcut if you were writing an application that needed to read configuration information, or a log file.
OpenWrite	Specialized version of Open that always opens the file for writing.

Creating Files

As you can see from Tables 17.1 and 17.2, many methods of the File and Directory classes can be used to browse and create files and directories. This is a great example of object-orientation in action—classes that represent real-world objects acting like that object. For example, a directory should know what child directories it has. Similarly, you should be able to ask a file to open itself.

Note

Many of the methods of File and Directory classes are Shared. This means that you don't have to create an object to use them; you simply use the class to access them. For example, the Exists method of the File class is Shared. To determine whether a file exists, you do not need to declare an instance of a File; you just use the File class itself. So, rather than writing this:

```
Dim oFile As New File()
bExists = oFile.Exists("somefile.txt")
```

you determine whether a file exists with the following code:

```
bExists = File.Exists("somefile.txt")
```

Reading from a Text Tile

After you create a file, you need to be able to read from it. This is where Stream classes come in, as well as the various Reader and Writer classes. After you open a file, you will invariably be passed one of these classes, usually a Stream of one sort or another. You then can read the information from the file using the Stream, or by applying a StreamReader to the Stream. Because the most likely Stream you will be dealing with is a FileStream, we'll spend the most time with it.

The FileStream is a Stream you get by reading in a file. This could be a text file or a binary file. The FileStream has a number of methods that allow you to read from the file and properties that relate to the file. Table 17.3 describes the most important of these.

TABLE 17.3 Methods and Properties of `FileStream`

Name	Description
`CanRead` (Property)	`True` if you can read from the file. This is a good property to test to avoid an exception that might occur if the file is locked, or open for write-only.
`CanSeek` (Property)	`True` if you can seek (that is, move forward and backward) through the file. This is a good property to test to avoid an exception caused when reading a file that you cannot move backward through. This is rare with files, but frequent with some of the other types of `Streams`.
`CanWrite` (Property)	`True` if you can write to the file. This is a good property to test to avoid an exception that might occur if the file is locked, or open for read-only.
`Length` (Property)	Number of bytes in the file.
`Position` (Property)	The current position in the file.
`Close` (Method)	Closes the `FileStream`. Always close the `FileStream` (or any `Stream`) when you are finished with it.
`Read` (Method)	Reads a number of bytes from the `FileStream`. These come back to you as an array.
`Seek` (Method)	Moves forward or backward through the file.
`Write` (Method)	Writes a number of bytes to the `FileStream`.

The problem with the `Read` methods of the `FileStream` class is that they tend not to be overly convenient because they all deal with bytes. Instead of using these, you can apply a `StreamReader` to the `FileStream` to read the information in the file in a more natural way. Table 17.4 shows the important methods of the `StreamReader`.

TABLE 17.4 Important Methods of the `StreamReader`

Name	Description
`Close`	Closes the `StreamReader`. Always close your `StreamReaders` when you are finished using them.
`Read`	Reads the next character from the `Stream`. This is handy if you are reading the information one character at a time.
`ReadBlock`	Reads a block of characters from the `Stream`. This can be a fast way of reading information from a `Stream`.
`ReadLine`	Reads the next line from the `Stream`. This is a nice way of handling files that provide information organized by lines.
`ReadToEnd`	Reads all the characters from the `Stream` at once. This is the fastest way to get all the information out of the `Stream` and into a variable.

17

Listing 17.1 shows a typical way of opening a text file and reading the contents into a string variable.

INPUT **LISTING 17.1**   Reading from a File

```
1 Dim oFile As FileStream
2 Dim oReader As StreamReader
3 Dim sContents As String
4 oFile = New FileStream("MyFile.txt", FileMode.OpenOrCreate, FileAccess.Read)
5 oReader = New StreamReader(oFile)
6 sContents = oReader.ReadToEnd()
7 oReader.Close()
8 oReader = Nothing
9 oFile = Nothing
```

Writing to a Text File

Just as with reading, you can use the `Stream` object to write to itself. However, it is much easier to use a `StreamWriter` to do this. Just as with a `StreamReader`, you apply a `StreamWriter` to an existing `Stream` and use the `Write` and `WriteLine` methods to add information. Table 17.5 outlines the significant methods of the `StreamWriter`.

TABLE 17.5   Important Methods of the `StreamWriter` Class

Name	Description
Close	Closes the `StreamWriter`. Always close any `StreamWriter` you create. Failing to do so could cause you to lose any changes you have made to the file.
Write	Writes to the `Stream`.
WriteLine	Writes to the `Stream`, ending the added information with a new line.

Listing 17.2 shows a typical example of writing to a text file.

INPUT **LISTING 17.2**   Writing to a File

```
 1 Dim oFile As FileStream
 2 Dim oWriter As StreamWriter
 3 oFile = New FileStream("MyFile.txt", _
 4     FileMode.OpenOrCreate, FileAccess.Write)
 5 oWriter = New StreamWriter(oFile)
 6'Writes the Integer 123 to the file
 7 oWriter.Write(123)
 8'Writes the String "Customer" to the file
 9 oWriter.Write("Customer")
10'Writes the String "John Bull" to the file, next writes will be on a new line
```

LISTING 17.2   continued

```
11 oWriter.WriteLine("John Bull")
12 oWriter.Close()
13 oWriter = Nothing
14 oFile = Nothing
```

The methods of the StreamWriter should look familiar; they are the same methods we used from the Console class. The Console class is a StreamWriter—one designed to write to the console.

Now put the reading and writing together and create a simple application that uses the three main classes we've discussed: FileStream, StreamReader, and StreamWriter. As an example, we'll create a simple Notepad replacement that allows you to read and write text files. You can later extend it to allow for the creation of other types of information.

Create a new Windows application and call it Note. It is your program, after all. As always, the first step after creating the project is to make sure that the main form is not called Form1. Open the Form in Code view, and search and replace Form1 with frmMain. Similarly, rename the file to frmMain.vb. Finally, open the project properties dialog and set the Startup Object to frmMain. Perform a build to make sure that there are no errors.

Add a TextBox control to the form and set its properties as shown in Table 17.6.

TABLE 17.6   Properties for the TextBox

Property	Value
(Name)	TxtText
Multiline	True
Text	(leave blank)
Scrollbars	Vertical
Dock	Fill

To make your notepad like Windows' Notepad, you'll need a menu. Double-click on the MainMenu item in the Toolbox to add one. As always, change the name to mnuMain. Add the items shown in Table 17.7.

TABLE 17.7   The Main Menu

Item	Property	Value
Top-level menu item	Caption	&File
	Name	mnuFile

TABLE 17.7   continued

Item	Property	Value
Under &File	Caption	&New
	Name	mnuFileNew
	Shortcut	CtrlN
Under &New	Caption	&Open...
	Name	mnuFileOpen
	Shortcut	CtrlO
Under &Open...	Caption	&Save
	Name	mnuFileSave
	Shortcut	CtrlS
Under &Save	Caption	Save &As...
	Name	mnuFileSaveAs
Under Save &As...	Caption	-
	Name	mnuFileSep
Under -	Caption	E&xit
	Name	mnuFileExit
	Shortcut	CtrlQ
Top-level item	Caption	&Edit
	Name	mnuEdit
Under &Edit	Caption	Cu&t
	Name	mnuEditCut
	Shortcut	CtrlX
Under Cu&t	Caption	&Copy
	Name	mnuEditCopy
	Shortcut	CtrlC
Under &Copy	Caption	&Paste
	Name	mnuEditPaste
	Shortcut	CtrlV
Top-level item	Caption	&Help
	Name	mnuHelp
Under &Help	Caption	&About
	Name	mnuHelpAbout

The final result should look like the menus shown in Figure 17.1.

To complete the form, add a FileOpenDialog and a FileSaveDialog to the form, and set the properties as shown in Table 17.8.

FIGURE 17.1

Running the Note sample.

TABLE 17.8 Other Controls on the Form

Object	Property	Value
FileOpenDialog	Name	dlgOpen
	Filter	Text Files|*.txt|All Files|*.*
FileSaveDialog	Name	DlgSave
	Filter	Text Files|*.txt|All Files|*.*
	FileName	note1

Now that the user interface is set up, we need to add the code.

First, we'll add the System.IO namespace to the project and to the Form. Open the References folder in the Solution Explorer. You should see a System namespace included in the listing, but not System.IO, which is fine. The items in the References dialog represent the actual libraries (DLLs) that will be used to locate code when you are compiling your application. Each of these DLLs might actually contain multiple namespaces. This is one of those cases. The System library, or assembly, contains many namespaces. One of them is System.IO. To make life easier when coding, however, you might want to also import the namespaces you'll be using. This allows you to use shortcuts when referring to classes. For more details, see the following note. Import the System.IO namespace to save some typing. Add the line Imports System.IO to the top line, before the Public Class frmMain line.

Note

Many people starting with Visual Basic .NET are confused by References and when to use them versus when to use the Imports statement. References are added using the Solution Explorer, or the Project menu. They represent the other components that your application will use. If you are going to use code that exists in another DLL—either one of the namespaces that come with the .NET Framework that isn't automatically added, or code that was

written by another developer or company—you must add it to the
References for your project. The `Imports` statement can be thought of as a
tool for shortening your code. By using the `Imports` statement, you can
avoid having to write long class names. For example, when you add a
`TextBox` to a Form, Visual Basic .NET writes:

```
Private WithEvents txtText As System.Windows.Forms.TextBox
```

Thus, the full class name is `System.Windows.Forms.TextBox`. However, if you
add `Imports System.Windows.Forms` to the top of the file, you can shorten
this to:

```
Private WithEvents txtText As TextBox
```

When Visual Basic .NET sees the `TextBox`, it uses the namespaces added with
the `Imports` statement to search for the `TextBox` class.

So, if you use a namespace, it must be included in the `References` section. If
you want to shorten your code, use the `Imports` statement.

Next, add two new properties to the Form. Add a property to keep track of the filename
(with path) and whether anything has changed. Add the code in Listing 17.3 to the program just after the line `Inherits System.Windows.Forms.Form`.

INPUT   **LISTING 17.3**   Properties for the Note Application

```
 1    Private m_sFileName As String
 2    Private m_bDirty As Boolean
 3    Public Property FileName() As String
 4        Get
 5            Return m_sFileName
 6        End Get
 7        Set(ByVal Value As String)
 8            m_sFileName = Value
 9            Me.Text = "Note - " & m_sFileName
10        End Set
11    End Property
12    Public Property Dirty() As Boolean
13        Get
14            Return m_bDirty
15        End Get
16        Set(ByVal Value As Boolean)
17            m_bDirty = Value
18            Me.Text = "Note - " & m_sFileName & "*"
19        End Set
20    End Property
21    Public Sub NewFile()
22        Me.txtText.Text = ""
```

LISTING **17.3**   continued

```
23        Me.FileName = ""
24        Me.Dirty = False
25    End Sub
```

ANALYSIS   The code is a relatively straightforward set of property statements. The top two lines declare private fields that will hold the values for the properties. Lines 3–11 represent the FileName property. This property saves the filename for later access in the m_sFileName field. When set, the FileName is also written to the caption for the Form (line 9).

Similarly, the Dirty property (lines 12–20) stores its information in the m_bDirty field and adds an asterisk to the end of the title bar.

Next, add the About box. After all, it is the most important part of many applications: It lets people know who is to blame for the application. To make it simpler, just use a MessageBox to show the information.

Double-click on the Help, About menu item to bring up the code editor. Add the code shown in Listing 17.4.

INPUT   **LISTING 17.4**   Help, About Menu

```
1 Private Sub mnuHelpAbout_Click(ByVal sender As System.Object, _
2     ByVal e As System.EventArgs) Handles mnuHelpAbout.Click      Dim sMessage
      ➟As String
3     sMessage = "Note — a simple text editor" & ControlChars.CrLf & _
4         "Original in Teach Yourself Visual Basic .NET in 21 Days." & _
5          controlchars.CrLf & _
6         "copyright 2001. Full rights to extend provided by the author."
7     MessageBox.Show(sMessage, _
8         "Note", _
9         MessageBoxButtons.OK, MessageBoxIcon.Information)
10 End Sub
```

ANALYSIS   The About box for Note is a simple MessageBox. In the code, we create and fill a string variable (lines 3–6). Notice that we are adding new lines to the message by embedding the ControlChars.CrLf to the middle of the string. This symbol represents a Carriage-return, line-feed combination to the string, creating a new line. Finally, we display the MessageBox (line 7), including the OK button and the Information icon.

Note

> What's the deal with "Carriage-return, line-feed"? Why not just newline or something simpler? As always, the reasons are based in the long ago, dark ages of computing (maybe 30 years ago). When people first used computers, they didn't work with monitors and mice. They worked with Teletype machines, which worked remarkably like the typewriters they looked like. As anyone who has ever worked with a manual typewriter knows, when you get to the end of a line, and the bell goes ding, you push the return lever. The return lever does two things, it moves you back to the beginning of the line, and it moves you down to the next line.
>
> Carriage-return = move the carriage (the thing holding the paper and roller) back to the return (or beginning of the line). Line-feed = move to the next line. Therefore, Carriage-return, line-feed means "move to the beginning of the next line." Carriage-return, line-feed is a mouthful, even for computer people, so this tended to be shortened to CRLF. In Visual Basic .NET, this is available as `ControlChars.CrLf`.

Now it's time to put some actual functionality into the program. Start with the File menu, as in Listing 17.5.

INPUT   **LISTING 17.5**   File Menu Commands

```
 1 Private Sub mnuFileNew_Click(ByVal sender As System.Object, _
 2   ByVal e As System.EventArgs) Handles mnuFileNew.Click
 3     If Me.Dirty = True Then
 4         If MessageBox.Show( _
 5             "You have made changes to the file that will be lost. " & _
 6             "Do you want to Continue?", _
 7             "New File", _
 8             MessageBoxButtons.YesNo, MessageBoxIcon.Question) = _
 9         DialogResult().Yes Then
10             NewFile()
11         End If
12     Else
13         NewFile()
14     End If
15 End Sub

16 Private Sub mnuFileOpen_Click(ByVal sender As System.Object, _
17   ByVal e As System.EventArgs) _
18   Handles mnuFileOpen.Click
19   Dim oFile As FileStream
20   Dim oReader As StreamReader
21   If Me.dlgOpen.ShowDialog = DialogResult().OK Then
22       'OK, we can try to open and read the file
```

LISTING 17.5   continued

```
23        Try
24            Me.FileName = Me.dlgOpen.FileName
25            oFile = File.OpenRead(Me.FileName)
26            oReader = New StreamReader(oFile)
27            Me.txtText.Text = oReader.ReadToEnd
28        Catch ex As Exception
29            'just display the error for now
30            MessageBox.Show(ex.Message, _
31                "Error Opening File", _
32                MessageBoxButtons.OK, _
33                MessageBoxIcon.Error)
34        Finally
35            'remember to always close your readers and files
36            oReader.Close()
37            oFile.Close()
38        End Try
39    End If
40 End Sub

41 Private Sub mnuFileSave_Click(ByVal sender As System.Object, _
42    ByVal e As System.EventArgs) _
43    Handles mnuFileSave.Click
44        'we should only try to save this file if it has a name
45    If Me.FileName <> "Untitled" Then
46        'OK, let's try saving the file
47        Dim oFile As FileStream
48        Dim oWriter As StreamWriter
49        Try
50            oFile = File.OpenWrite(Me.FileName)
51            'convert the contents of the TextBox to an array of Bytes
52            oWriter = New StreamWriter(oFile)
53            'and write to the file
54            oWriter.Write(Me.txtText.Text)
55            'and now we're not dirty
56            Me.Dirty = False
57        Catch ex As Exception
58            'for now, just display an error on an Exception
59            MessageBox.Show(ex.Message, _
60                "Error Saving File", _
61                MessageBoxButtons.OK, _
62                MessageBoxIcon.Error)
63        Finally
64            'always remember to close all writers and streams
65            oWriter.Close()
66            oFile.Close()
67        End Try
68    Else
69        'if not, go get a name
70        mnuFileSaveAs_Click(sender, e)
```

17

LISTING 17.5   continued

```
71     End If
72 End Sub

73 Private Sub mnuFileSaveAs_Click(ByVal sender As System.Object, _
74    ByVal e As System.EventArgs) _
75    Handles mnuFileSaveAs.Click
76    If Me.dlgSave.ShowDialog = DialogResult().OK Then
77         'they've clicked OK, we can set the filename and save
78         Me.FileName = Me.dlgSave.FileName
79         'use the code already in the File, Save item to save th e file
80         mnuFileSave_Click(sender, e)
81    End If
82 End Sub

83 Private Sub mnuFileExit_Click(ByVal sender As System.Object, _
84    ByVal e As System.EventArgs) _
85    Handles mnuFileExit.Click
86    Me.Close()
87 End Sub
```

ANALYSIS This might seem like a lot of code, but let's take it a few steps at a time and see what it does, beginning with the File, New command in lines 1–15. We added the Dirty property to allow us to determine whether the text has changed at all. If it has, we want to make sure that the user doesn't accidentally destroy those changes. Therefore, if the user requests a new file after making those changes, we should warn them. This is just good behavior—protecting the user from what could be an accidental keystroke. If the file is dirty (changed), we ask whether it is all right to lose the changes (line 3–9) and to create a new file. If it is all right (line 10 in the listing), or if there have been no changes (line 13 in the listing), we create a NewFile. We will create the NewFile procedure later. Because there are a number of locations where we might create a new file, it's a good idea to put this code in a procedure by itself.

Next we see the File, Open menu item (lines 16–40). Here we begin to use the classes for working with files. We will be using a FileStream object (line 19) and a StreamReader (line 20). Remember that a FileStream is really just a special type of Stream object. After declaring these two variables, we allow the user to select a file to open (line 21) using the FileOpenDialog control added to the Form. If they have select-ed a file, we can open it. Notice that we are trying to open it in the middle of a Try...End Try block (lines 23–38). Opening files can be prone to exceptions—the file might not exist, might not be available, might be locked by another user, and so on. Any of these occurrences could lead to an exception. Therefore, whenever you want to open a file, you should use a Try...End Try block.

Do	**DON'T**
DO use a `Try...End Try` block to catch exceptions whenever you attempt to deal with files—either when opening them, deleting them, or saving them. Always use the `Finally` section of the block to close the file and any streams, readers, or writers you used to access the file.	

Within the `Try...End Try` block, we first retrieve the name of the file (including the path) to open from the dialog (line 24). This name will be displayed on the title bar of the Note window. Next (line 25), we use the `Shared` method, `OpenRead` to open the file. Recall that `Shared` methods do not need an instance of a file, but the file itself. This is one area that could lead to an exception, so it is good that it is in the `Try...End Try` block. The `oFile` variable in line 25 is of type `FileStream`; therefore, it represents a series of bytes in the file (that is, a stream). To read this stream, we pass this `FileStream` to the constructor for a `StreamReader` (line 26). This `StreamReader` (`oReader`) can be used to read all the contents of the `FileStream` (line 27) and pass it to the main `TextBox` used on the form.

If an exception occurs while opening or reading the file (most likely when opening), we catch it at line 28 and simply display it to the user at lines 30–33. An ideal exception handler would possibly try to help the user fix the exception. For example, if the user is forbidden from opening the file due to security reasons (a `SecurityException` will be thrown), you could inform the user that he must request permission from the document's owner before he tries to open the file. Finally, at lines 36 and 37, we close the `StreamReader` and `FileStream` objects. Always close these objects to ensure that they do not remain open, possibly locking out some other program from viewing or changing the file.

At the end of the File, Open menu item, we should have selected a file to edit, and the contents should be in the `TextBox`. Next, we need to deal with the two related ways of saving the file—that is the File, Save menu item and the File, Save As menu item.

Of the two menu items related to saving the file, File, Save is more complicated. In fact, as you'll see, the File, Save As menu item merely uses this menu item to perform its action. The File, Save menu item's code is shown in lines 41–72. We first test to see whether the user has previously named the file (line 45). If not, we'll call the `mnuFileSaveAs_Click` routine (that is, the File, Save As menu item) to get a name (line 70). Assuming that the file has a name, we open it for writing at line 50. When open, we create a `StreamWriter` to write to the file (line 52) and write the contents of the `TextBox` to the newly created file (line 54). Because the file no longer has any changes, we set the `Dirty` flag to `False`.

If an exception occurs when writing to the file, we catch it at line 57. Just as we did with any exceptions that might occur when reading the file, we simply display the exception (line 58–62). Again, just as we did when reading the file, it is essential to close the `StreamWriter` and `FileStream` objects (lines 65 and 66). This is even more important when writing to the file than when reading the file because changes made might not be written until the stream and file are closed.

At the end of the File, Save menu item, the contents of the `TextBox` should be written to the file requested. You can confirm by opening it in Notepad, or some other editor.

The code for the File, Save As menu item is much simpler than the code used to save the file because it leverages the work done in the other routine. This code is used to simply generate a new filename for the file. We use the `FileSaveDialog` added to the form (line 76) to allow the user to select a location and name for the file. If the user clicks OK to close the dialog, we continue by setting the `FileName` property to the new name (line 78) and then calling the `mnuFileSave_Click` routine to actually save the file (line 80). Alternatively, we could have placed the entire contents of the save code here, but this would have created a great deal of duplication.

Finally (for the File menu), the code for the File, Exit command occurs. Here we simply close the form, ending the application (line 86).

Most of the `Stream` related code is in the File menu (where you'd expect it), allowing you to open and save files. In Listing 17.6, we'll look at the code in the Edit menu that allows you to Cut, Copy, and Paste as you would in an application such as Notepad or Word.

INPUT   **LISTING 17.6**   Edit Menu Commands

```
1 Private Sub mnuEditCut_Click(ByVal sender As System.Object, _
2    ByVal e As System.EventArgs) Handles mnuEditCut.Click
3      Clipboard.SetDataObject(Me.txtText.SelectedText)
4      Me.txtText.SelectedText = ""
5 End Sub
6
7 Private Sub mnuEditCopy_Click(ByVal sender As System.Object, _
8    ByVal e As System.EventArgs) Handles mnuEditCopy.Click
9      Clipboard.SetDataObject(Me.txtText.SelectedText)
10 End Sub
```

LISTING 17.6   continued

```
11
12 Private Sub mnuEditPaste_Click(ByVal sender As System.Object, _
13    ByVal e As System.EventArgs) Handles mnuEditPaste.Click
14    Me.txtText.SelectedText = _
15       CType(Clipboard.GetDataObject.GetData(DataFormats.Text), String)
16 End Sub
```

ANALYSIS   Thankfully, the code for the Edit commands is much shorter than that for the File
commands. In addition, we see another powerful object in the .NET
Framework—the Clipboard object.

Beginning with the Edit, Cut code, we take the text selected in the TextBox and copy it
to the Clipboard (line 3). The Clipboard class is an abstraction of the Windows
Clipboard that is shared by all applications. It has methods that enable you to program-
matically assign text, graphics, or other information to the Clipboard, and to retrieve the
information from the Clipboard. Table 17.9 outlines these two methods. After copying
the information to the Clipboard, we delete the selected text in the TextBox (line 4). This
creates the expected behavior of cutting text—adding it to the Clipboard and removing it
from the form.

TABLE 17.9   Methods of the Clipboard Class

Method	Description
SetDataObject	Assigns information to the Clipboard. This method takes an object, and, therefore, you can write anything to the Clipboard. Note that there are actually two versions of this method. That is, it is an overloaded method. The second version includes a Boolean value that determines whether the contents should remain after the application ends. The normal behavior is to keep information on the Clipboard after the program ends.
GetDataObject	Used to retrieve the information on the Clipboard, or to retrieve information about the contents of the Clipboard. This method actually returns an Interface—IDataObject that is used to perform the actual retrieval. Table 17.10 outlines the important methods of the IDataObject interface.

TABLE 17.10   Methods of the IDataObject

Method	Description
GetData	Retrieves the information stored on the Clipboard. Alternate forms allow you to convert the information to a specific format.
GetFormats	Used to determine what formats are stored on the Clipboard. For example, if a graphic has been copied to the Clipboard, this method returns all the formats that it might be pasted as.

TABLE 17.10 continued

Method	Description
GetDataPresent	Determines whether any data of a particular format is stored on the Clipboard. This could be used to determine whether you want to allow the user to paste information in your application. For example, if graphical information is stored on the Clipboard, we wouldn't allow the user to paste this in our Note application.

The code for Edit, Copy is similar to that for the Edit, Cut command (line 9), except that we do not delete the selected text. Either command, however, results in copying information to the Clipboard.

The code for the Edit, Paste command seems complex but is simple when you break down lines 14–15 into a series of steps. The first step in retrieving information from the Clipboard is to retrieve the IDataObject stored on the Clipboard with GetDataObject. Next, we use the GetData method of the IDataObject to retrieve the information, requesting that it be in simple text format. Although we have requested it in text format, however, it is an object. Therefore, to assign it to the TextBox, we must convert it to a string. We could have used either the CStr or the CType functions, although here we have used the CType function. Finally, we take the resulting text and use it to replace the SelectedText of the TextBox. We use SelectedText and not Text because, if we replace the Text, then the contents of the TextBox will be only the information from the Clipboard. This is not the expected behavior of using the Clipboard. By using the SelectedText, we only replace the highlighted text. If nothing is highlighted, the text from the Clipboard will be added at the position of the text cursor.

The last of the menus we will be using is the Help menu. Listing 17.7 shows the code for the Help, About procedure.

INPUT   **LISTING 17.7**   Help, About Command

```
 1 Private Sub mnuHelpAbout_Click(ByVal sender As System.Object, _
 2     ByVal e As System.EventArgs) Handles mnuHelpAbout.Click
 3   Dim sMessage As String
 4   sMessage = "Note -- a simple text editor" & _
 5       ControlChars.CrLf & _
 6       "Original in Teach Yourself Visual Basic .NET in 21 Days." & _
 7       ControlChars.CrLf & _
 8       "copyright 2001. Full rights to extend provided by the author."
 9   MessageBox.Show(sMessage, _
10       "Note", _
11       MessageBoxButtons.OK, _
12       MessageBoxIcon.Information)
13 End Sub
```

ANALYSIS Although not needed for this example, we add the Help, About command for completeness. It is a simple routine that builds a string (lines 4–8) and displays it to the user (lines 9–12). In a more advanced application, you would have an actual form to display to the user.

Finally, Listing 17.8 shows three routines you can add to the application to round out the functionality.

LISTING 17.8 Other Code for the Note Application

```
 1 Public Sub NewFile()
 2     Me.txtText.Text = ""
 3     Me.FileName = "Untitled"
 4     Me.Dirty = False
 5 End Sub
 6
 7 Private Sub txtText_TextChanged(ByVal sender As System.Object, _
 8     ByVal e As System.EventArgs) Handles txtText.TextChanged
 9     Me.Dirty = True
10 End Sub
11
12 Private Sub frmNote_Closing(ByVal sender As System.Object, _
13     ByVal e As System.ComponentModel.CancelEventArgs) Handles MyBase.Closing
14     If Me.Dirty = True Then
15         If MessageBox.Show( _
16         "You have made changes to the file that will be lost. Continue?", _
17             "New File", _
18             MessageBoxButtons.YesNo, _
19             MessageBoxIcon.Question, _
20             MessageBoxDefaultButton.Button2) = DialogResult().No Then
21             e.Cancel = True
22         End If
23     End If
24 End Sub
```

ANALYSIS As you recall, the NewFile procedure is called by the mnuFileNew_Click procedure when creating a new file. This procedure assigns the defaults for the new file: blanking the information in the TextBox (line 2), setting the FileName property to "Untitled" (line 3), and setting the Dirty property to False (line 4).

We want the application and user to know when there have been changes to the document. This is the purpose of the Dirty property. We can take advantage of the TextChanged event to change the value of this property. If any changes occur, either by an edit, copying information from the Clipboard, or the user typing, this event is triggered, setting the Dirty flag to True.

Finally, we again want to make sure to protect the user from stray keystrokes. The Closing event occurs when the form is closing. It is an excellent time to determine whether the user wants to save information. We should only ask the user to save changes if there are any, so our first step (line 14) is to determine whether there have been changes since the last save. If not, we don't have to do anything, and the form can close. If there have been changes, however, we need to ask the user whether she wants to save changes before exiting. Lines 15–20 create and display a MessageBox with Yes and No buttons. If the user selects the No button, it implies that the user doesn't want to close the file. Therefore, we can cancel this event (and the resulting closing of the form) by setting the Cancel property of the EventArgs object (passed in to all events) to True, as in line 21.

There you have it—about 100 lines of code, and you have a functioning text editor that you can use as the basis for a more complete implementation. This version allows you to open and save files, and use the Clipboard. You have used the FileStream, StreamReader, and StreamWriter objects to manipulate the text files that it works with. Creating a similar application to open and save binary files, such as those created by the graphics classes, is almost identical.

Drawing with the Graphics Classes

Visual Basic .NET (actually the .NET Framework) has a rich set of drawing tools that help you draw lines, boxes, circles, and other shapes on virtually any surface of your forms. You access these tools by using the classes in the System.Drawing and related namespaces. These tools provide a wide range of capabilities for drawing graphics and working with various image files. System.Drawing contains many of the core classes you will need for any type of drawing, including Color, Brush, Image, and so on. We will look at these important classes shortly.

The next most important of the namespaces related to graphics is System.Drawing.Drawing2D. This is the class that contains the classes related to actually drawing lines, shapes, and so on. You also will use many of these classes today, and whenever you want to add simple shapes to a form or graphic.

Looking at the Graphics Classes

With a Windows application open, start the Object Browser (choose View, Other Windows, Object Browser). Find the System.Drawing namespace and open it, as shown in Figure 17.2. The total number of classes, structures, and enumerations might seem overwhelming at first. However, many of these classes are rarely used. Really only a few items in this namespace should be considered required knowledge. The most important of these are described in Table 17.11.

FIGURE 17.2

System.Drawing *name-space.*

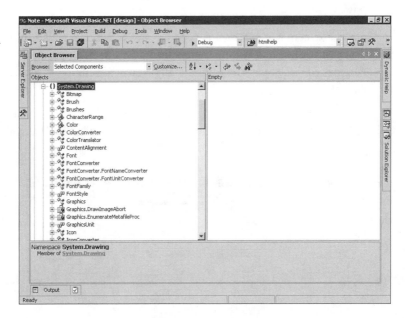

TABLE 17.11 Important Classes and Structures in the System.Drawing Namespace

Item	Type	Description
Bitmap	Class	The Bitmap representing an image, such as a GIF, BMP, or JPG. This class is used frequently when loading and working with graphics.
Brush	Class	Used when filling in areas with color. There are different types of Brush classes, including ones that use solid color and others that apply a texture. This texture is usually based on a Bitmap.
Color	Structure	The Color structure contains information about all the common, named colors as well as the capability to create new colors.
Font	Class	The Font class is used whenever you want to draw text on a graphic.
Graphics	Class	The most important of the System.Drawing classes. This is the class that contains all the methods used to draw and is the surface that will be drawn on.
Pen	Class	Used when drawing lines with color.
Point	Structure	Used to represent a location on a drawing surface. Contains X and Y coordinates for the location.
Rectangle	Structure	Represents a rectangular area at a known location. This is defined as a region starting at a point, with a known width and height.
Size	Structure	Represents a rectangular area. This area has a height and width.

17

You use the classes in Table 17.11 a great deal. For example, if you are drawing a square on the screen, it would be drawn on a `Graphics` object, with a specific `Pen`, in an assigned `Color`, and within a `Rectangle` on the screen. The `Rectangle` in turn would be composed of a `Point` and `Size`. Finally, you could fill in the square with a selected `Brush`.

To demonstrate the use of the graphics classes, we will create a simple drawing program. Figure 17.3 shows this application running. You can extend the application to create more complex graphics later.

FIGURE 17.3

Scribble program in action.

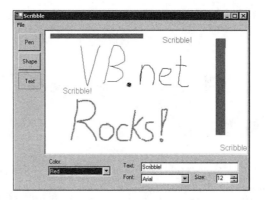

Begin by creating a new Windows application project. Name the project Scribble. As you can see from Figure 17.3, the user has three drawing tools available: a pen, shapes, and text. Each of these three tools has its own set of options that affect how it is drawn. In addition, each can be drawn in a selected color. The large white drawing area is a `PictureBox` control.

Always change the name of the Form. Close the Form designer. Change the name of the Form in the Solution Explorer to `frmScribble`. Switch to Code view and change all references to `Form1` in the form to `frmScribble`. Right-click on the project in the Solution Explorer and select Properties. On the General Properties tab, change the Startup Object to `frmScribble`. Build and run the application to ensure that all changes have been made.

Now we can begin to add controls to the form. Open the form in Design view and add the controls as shown in Table 17.12. Use Figure 17.3 to assist you, but don't worry if the controls aren't exactly in place.

TABLE 17.12 Controls on the Scribble Application

Control	Property	Value
Form	Height	332
	Width	500
	Text	Scribble
	BorderStyle	FixedSingle
Menu	Name	mnuMain
File Menu	Name	mnuFile
File, New	Name	mnuFileNew
	Shortcut	CtrlN
	Text	&New
File, Open	Name	mnuFileOpen
	Shortcut	CtrlO
	Text	&Open…
File, Save	Name	mnuFileSave
	Shortcut	CtrlS
	Text	&Save
File, Exit	Name	mnuFileExit
	Shortcut	CtrlQ
	Text	E&xit
OpenFileDialog	Name	dlgOpen
	DefaultExt	Bmp
	Filter	Bitmap files|*.bmp|PNG files|*.png
SaveFileDialog	Name	dlgSave
	DefaultExt	Bmp
	Filename	Scribble1
	Filter	Bitmap files|*.bmp|PNG files|*.png
	Dock	DockStyle.Left
	Width	64
RadioButton	Name	optPen
	Appearance	Button
	Checked	True
	Location	8,8
	Size	48,36
	Text	Pen
	TextAlign	MiddleCenter
RadioButton	Name	optShape
	Appearance	Button
	Location	8, 48

17

TABLE 17.12 continued

Control	Property	Value
RadioButton	Size	48,36
	Text	Shape
	TextAlign	MiddleCenter
RadioButton	Name	optText
	Appearance	Button
	Location	8,88
	Size	48,36
	Text	Text
	TextAlign	MiddleCenter
PictureBox	Name	picDraw
	BackColor	White
	BorderStyle	Fixed3D
	Dock	Fill
Panel	Name	pnlOptions
	Dock	Bottom
	Height	72
Label	Name	lblColor
	Location	8, 8
	Size	48, 16
	Text	Color:
ComboBox	Name	cboColors
	DropDownStyle	DropDownList
	Location	8, 24
	Width	136
Panel	Name	pnlPenOptions
	Location	160, 8
	Size	274, 56
Label	Name	lblPenWidth
	Location	8, 8
	Size	80, 16
	Text	Pen Width:
NumericUpDown	Name	updPenWidth
	Location	96, 8
	Maximum	10
	Minimum	1
	Size	48, 20
	Value	1

TABLE 17.12   continued

Control	Property	Value
Panel	Name	pnlShapeOptions
	Location	160, 8
	Size	274, 56
Label	Name	lblShapeType
	Location	8, 8
	Size	48, 16
	Text	Type:
DropDown	Name	cboShapeType
	DropDownStyle	DropDownList
	Location	64, 8
	Width	121
Label	Name	lblShapeHeight
	Location	8, 32
	Size	48, 16
	Text	Height:
NumericUpDown	Name	updShapeHeight
	Location	64, 32
	Maximum	1000
	Minimum	1
	Size	48, 20
	Value	20
Label	Name	lblShapeWidth
	Location	128, 32
	Size	48, 16
	Text	Width:
NumericUpDown	Name	updShapeWidth
	Location	184, 32
	Maximum	1000
	Minimum	1
	Size	48, 20
	Value	20
Panel	Name	pnlTextOptions
	Location	160, 8
	Size	274, 56
Label	Name	lblText
	Location	8, 8
	Size	40, 16
	Text	Text:

17

TABLE 17.12   continued

Control	Property	Value
TextBox	Name	txtText
	Location	48, 8
	Size	208, 20
	Text	Scribble!
Label	Name	lblTextFont
	Location	8, 32
	Size	40, 16
	Text	Font:
DropDown	Name	cboTextFont
	DropDownStyle	DropDownList
	Location	48, 32
	Width	104
Label	Name	lblFontSize
	Location	160, 32
	Size	40, 16
	Text	Size:
NumericUpDown	Name	updFontSize
	Location	208, 32
	Maximum	72
	Minimum	6
	Size	48, 20
	Value	12

Note

When adding the RadioButton controls to the tools Panel, remember to click on the control in the Toolbox and then drag on the panel. This ensures that the control is contained by the panel. You should also do this with the controls on the options panel.

One other point to note is that the three option panels (pnlPenOptions, pnlShapeOptions, and pnlTextOptions) are all the same size and location. At runtime, only one will be visible at a time. However, this can be difficult to assemble at design-time. The easiest way to set up this is to work on them one at a time. When one is finished, set the Location property so that it is off the screen. Setting the Left property to -10000 is an easy way to do this. When all three panels are complete, set the Location back to the original value for all three.

What Can I Draw on?

You can draw on almost all the Windows Form controls and on many of the Web Form controls as well. This means that you can easily modify one of the existing controls, or simply add a graphic or symbol to almost anything in your programs. This is both useful and flexible, allowing you to easily customize your forms and controls by adding a unique graphic and touch to them.

Your first step when drawing is always to obtain a `Graphics` object. This object can either be obtained as part of some events, such as the `Paint` event, or by using the `CreateGraphics` method. This method is shared by all controls, including forms.

Whenever Windows determines that it needs to repaint all or part of your forms or controls, it fires the `Paint` event for the item it needs to repaint. This happens when a window is first created and anytime another form is moved in front of your window. For example, if you display a `MessageBox`, when the `MessageBox` goes away, the part of your form that was under the `MessageBox` must be repainted. This causes the `Paint` event of all the covered controls, and of the form, to be called. The `Paint` event for a form would look like

```
Private Sub frmScribble_Paint(ByVal sender As Object, _
    ByVal e As System.Windows.Forms.PaintEventArgs) _
    Handles MyBase.Paint
End Sub
```

In this example, the form is called `frmScribble`. As with all events, we are passed two objects—the sender and the `EventArgs` object. In the case of the `Paint` event, we don't receive the base `EventArgs` object, but one of the children, `PaintEventArgs`, instead. `PaintEventArgs` has two read-only properties:

- `ClipRectangle`   The `Rectangle` that must be repainted. This allows you to optimize your drawing code to only update the changed area, rather than always redrawing the entire image. We won't be using this parameter in our applications.

- `Graphics`   The `Graphics` surface to draw on. This is used to draw the needed shapes.

Alternatively, you can use the `CreateGraphics` method of a control to create your own `Graphics` object for drawing.

```
Dim oGraphics As System.Drawing.Graphics
oGraphics = picDraw.CreateGraphics()
```

Whichever method you use to create a `Graphics` object, you can use it to draw various shapes.

17

In the Scribble application, we will store the Graphics object for use by the various drawing tools. In addition, we need to track the active and available tools. Add the code in Listing 17.9 to the Scribble project.

INPUT **LISTING 17.9**   Properties and General Code for the Scribble Application

```
1    Public Enum DrawingTools
2        Pen
3        Shape
4        Text
5    End Enum
6
7    Private m_sFileName As String
8    Private m_bDrawing As Boolean
9    Private m_eCurrentTool As DrawingTools
10
11   Private oGraphics As System.Drawing.Graphics
12   Private oTool As Object
13   Private sngX As Single
14   Private sngY As Single
15
16   Public Property FileName() As String
17       Get
18           Return m_sFileName
19       End Get
20       Set(ByVal Value As String)
21           m_sFileName = Value
22       End Set
23   End Property
24
25   Public Property Drawing() As Boolean
26       Get
27           Return m_bDrawing
28       End Get
29       Set(ByVal Value As Boolean)
30           m_bDrawing = Value
31       End Set
32   End Property
33
34   Public Property CurrentTool() As DrawingTools
35       Get
36           Return m_eCurrentTool
37       End Get
38       Set(ByVal Value As DrawingTools)
39           m_eCurrentTool = Value
40           'destroy the existing tool
41           If Not oTool Is Nothing Then
42               CType(oTool, IDisposable).Dispose()
43           End If
```

LISTING 17.9 continued

```
44        End Set
45    End Property
46
47    Private Sub frmScribble_Load(ByVal sender As Object, _
48        ByVal e As System.EventArgs) _
49        Handles MyBase.Load
50         'set up the Color ComboBox
51         FillLists()
52         'create the graphics we'll be drawing on
53         Me.picDraw.Image = New Bitmap(picDraw.Width, _
54            picDraw.Height, _
55            System.Drawing.Imaging.PixelFormat.Format24bppRgb)
56         Me.oGraphics = Graphics.FromImage(Me.picDraw.Image)
57         'set the background to white
58         Me.oGraphics.Clear(Color.White)
59         'set the initial tool to the Pen
60         optPen_Click(Nothing, Nothing)
61    End Sub
62
63    Private Sub optPen_Click(ByVal sender As Object, _
64        ByVal e As System.EventArgs) _
65        Handles optPen.Click
66         'set the tool to a pen
67         Me.CurrentTool = DrawingTools.Pen
68         'hide all the other tool's panels
69         pnlPenOptions.Visible = True
70         pnlShapeOptions.Visible = False
71         pnlTextOptions.Visible = False
72    End Sub
73
74    Private Sub optShape_Click(ByVal sender As Object, _
75        ByVal e As System.EventArgs) _
76        Handles optShape.Click
77         'set the tool to a Shape
78         Me.CurrentTool = DrawingTools.Shape
79         'hide all the other tool's panels
80         pnlPenOptions.Visible = False
81         pnlShapeOptions.Visible = True
82         pnlTextOptions.Visible = False
83    End Sub
84
85    Private Sub optText_Click(ByVal sender As Object, _
86        ByVal e As System.EventArgs) _
87        Handles optText.Click
88         'set the tool to Text
89         Me.CurrentTool = DrawingTools.Text
90         'hide all the other tool's panels
91         pnlPenOptions.Visible = False
92         pnlShapeOptions.Visible = False
```

17

LISTING 17.9 continued

```
 93          pnlTextOptions.Visible = True
 94    End Sub
 95
 96    Private Sub FillLists()
 97        With cboColors.Items
 98            .Add("Black")
 99            .Add("Red")
100            .Add("Green")
101            .Add("Blue")
102        End With
103        cboColors.SelectedIndex = 0
104
105        With cboShapeType.Items
106            .Add("Rectangle")
107            .Add("Ellipse")
108        End With
109        cboShapeType.SelectedIndex = 0
110
111        With cboTextFont.Items
112            .Add("Arial")
113            .Add("Times New Roman")
114            .Add("Courier New")
115        End With
116        cboTextFont.SelectedIndex = 0
117    End Sub
```

ANALYSIS We first declare a new enumeration (lines 1–5). This enumeration will be used to track the available tools and to ensure that the CurrentTool property (declared later) can only be set to one of the valid settings. If you decide to add other drawing tools later, you should add them to this enumeration.

Lines 7–9 are the member variables for the three properties exposed by the form. The three properties (lines 16–23, 25–32, and 34–45) are basically simple properties, with a single exception. In the Set part of the CurrentTool property, the lines 41–43 stand out. Drawing tools such as pens, brushes, and fonts have a special place in Windows. Only a limited number of these components are available. Therefore, you should always remember to call the Dispose method on these components to ensure that they are freed up for the next user. Normally, you can directly call Dispose on these objects. The code in line 42 is needed because oTool has been declared as an object at line 12. This is an example of one of the sacrifices made when you write generic code; sometimes it means more work later.

The Form Load event (lines 47–61) is where we set up the form, loading the DropDownLists and preparing the graphics for drawing. Line 51 calls the FillLists routine that we will write later. Next, in lines 53–55, we create a new `Bitmap` and assign it to the `PictureBox`. This is the `Bitmap` that we will be drawing on. The parameters used define the size of the new graphic, and the type of `Bitmap` to create. Here we create a 24-bit graphic. This means that we can use any of 16777216 colors when selecting a color.

Line 56 extracts the `Graphics` object from the `Bitmap` and assigns it to the form. We will use this `Graphics` object later when we are drawing. To create a nice, clean surface for drawing, we `Clear` the `Graphics` object to `White`, and to ensure we have a selected tool, select the Pen tool.

Each of the next three routines performs the same task. They are used when the user selects a new tool. The routines set the `CurrentTool` to the desired tool and ensure that the correct set of options for the current tool is visible, while the incorrect ones are not.

The `FillLists` procedure (lines 96–105) populates the `DropDownList` controls with various colors, shapes, and fonts and selects the first item of each. You can extend this if you want to include other colors, shapes, and fonts.

Drawing Shapes

After you have a `Graphics` object, you next need to know how to use it. The `Graphics` object has several methods used to draw various lines, shapes, and text onto a surface. These methods fall into two broad categories:

- Draw methods These methods are used to draw using a Pen. Generally, this just creates an empty shape.
- Fill methods These methods are used to draw using a Brush. They create a shape that is filled in with a color or texture.

Table 17.13 describes some of the more commonly used methods of the `Graphics` class.

TABLE 17.13 Methods of the `System.Drawing.Graphics` Class

Method	Description
Clear	Removes all content from the `Graphics` object, replacing it with the requested color.
DrawEllipse	Draws an ellipse or circle on the `Graphics` object using an assigned Pen. If the height and width are the same, you get a circle; otherwise, you get an oval.
DrawLine	Draws a line on the `Graphics` object using an assigned Pen.
DrawRectangle	Draws a rectangle or square on the `Graphics` object using an assigned Pen. If the height and width are the same, you get a square; otherwise, you get a rectangle.
DrawString	Draws text on the `Graphics` object.

TABLE 17.13 continued

Method	Description
FillEllipse	Fills in an oval or circular area on the Graphics object using an assigned Brush.
FillRectangle	Fills in a rectangular or square area on the Graphics object using an assigned Brush.

We are now ready to add the code to the Scribble application that does the actual drawing. When in Shape or Text mode, we will draw a rectangle or ellipse or add text wherever the user clicks. However, line drawing is slightly different. We can't actually draw a line when the user clicks the mouse button; we must wait for the mouse to move. Instead, when the mouse is down, we will simply mark it as down. Later, when the user moves the mouse, if the mouse is down, we will do the actual drawing. Listing 17.10 shows the code for the PictureBox event handlers.

INPUT   **LISTING 17.10**   PictureBox Event Handlers

```
1    Private Sub picDraw_MouseMove(ByVal sender As Object, _
2       ByVal e As System.Windows.Forms.MouseEventArgs) _
3       Handles picDraw.MouseMove
4        If Me.Drawing Then
5            'this is only true if the current tool is a pen
6            oGraphics.DrawLine(oTool, sngX, sngY, e.X, e.Y)
7            sngX = e.X
8            sngY = e.Y
9            'force a redraw
10           Me.picDraw.Refresh()
11       End If
12   End Sub
13
14   Private Sub picDraw_MouseUp(ByVal sender As Object, _
15      ByVal e As System.Windows.Forms.MouseEventArgs) _
16      Handles picDraw.MouseUp
17       'we can stop drawing now
18       Me.Drawing = False
19   End Sub
20
21   Private Sub picDraw_MouseDown(ByVal sender As Object, _
22      ByVal e As System.Windows.Forms.MouseEventArgs) _
23      Handles picDraw.MouseDown
24       'start drawing
25       'Shape and Text are stamps, Pen works on MouseMove
26       'we need to create the tool
27       'and either draw it, or get ready to draw it
28       Select Case Me.CurrentTool
```

LISTING 17.10   continued

```
29              Case DrawingTools.Shape
30                  Select Case Me.cboShapeType.Text
31                      Case "Rectangle"
32                          oGraphics.FillRectangle( _
33                              New SolidBrush( _
34                                  Color.FromName(Me.cboColors.Text)), _
35                              e.X, _
36                              e.Y, _
37                              Me.updShapeWidth.Value, _
38                              Me.updShapeHeight.Value)
39                      Case "Ellipse"
40                          oGraphics.FillEllipse( _
41                          New SolidBrush( _
42                              Color.FromName(Me.cboColors.Text)), _
43                          e.X, _
44                          e.Y, _
45                          Me.updShapeWidth.Value, _
46                          Me.updShapeHeight.Value)
47                      Case Else
48                  End Select
49                  'force a redraw
50                  Me.picDraw.Refresh()
51              Case DrawingTools.Text
52                  'create a font
53                  oTool = New System.Drawing.Font( _
54                      Me.cboTextFont.Text, Me.updFontSize.Value)
55                  'draw the text at the current mouse location
56                  oGraphics.DrawString(Me.txtText.Text, _
57                      oTool, _
58                      New SolidBrush( _
59                          Color.FromName(Me.cboColors.Text)), _
60                      e.X, e.Y)
61                  'force a redraw
62                  Me.picDraw.Refresh()
63              Case DrawingTools.Pen
64                  'create the pen (for drawing in MouseMove)
65                  oTool = New System.Drawing.Pen( _
66                      Color.FromName(Me.cboColors.Text), _
67                  Me.updPenWidth.Value)
68                  sngX = e.X
69                  sngY = e.Y
70                  Me.Drawing = True
71          End Select
72      End Sub
```

ANALYSIS   Lines are drawn during the MouseMove event of the PictureBox. We only want to draw the line if we are in drawing mode; therefore, the first step is to test the Drawing property (line 4). This property will be set to True later in the MouseDown event.

In drawing mode, the first step is to draw a line using the current Pen (line 6). The `sngX` and `sngY` variables are private, form-level variables used to record the last mouse position. Each time we draw a line, we draw it from this stored position to the current mouse position. The current mouse position is provided as properties of the `MouseEventArgs` class passed into the event handler. We copy the current position into the temporary storage at lines 7 and 8 for the next time the event is called. Finally, at line 10, we force a refresh of the `PictureBox`. This guarantees that any changes we've made will be shown to the user.

The `MouseUp` event handler (lines 14–19) is simple. It is only used to end drawing mode if we are in it. Later `MouseMove` events without `Drawing` set to `True` will not cause any drawing.

The `MouseDown` event handler is where the bulk of the processing occurs. The application will react differently based on the currently selected tool and settings. Our first step (line 28) is to determine the current tool.

If the current tool is `Shape`, we next need to determine the type of shape selected. The actual drawing code is similar. We use the `Fill` method to draw either a rectangle or ellipse at the current mouse position with the sizes selected by the `NumericUpDown` controls. The current mouse position is provided by the `MouseEventArgs` parameter of the `MouseDown` event handler.

If the current tool is `Text`, the first task we must perform is to create a new font (lines 53–54). This font is used when we draw the graphical text on the `PictureBox` (lines 56–60). The text is drawn with the created font, using a newly created Brush.

Finally, if we are drawing lines with the Pen tool, we must create the new `Pen` object (lines 65–67). This will have the selected color and pen width. Next, we store the current mouse position for later use in the `MouseMove` event handler (lines 68–69) and turn on Drawing mode (line 70).

Saving Graphics

After you have created a graphic, you use the `Save` method of the `Bitmap` object to store it as a file. This method allows you to save the graphic at a specific size and format.

A variety of different formats are supported by the `Bitmap` object. These include

- Bitmap   A common graphics format used in Windows, this graphics format is typically fairly large. Any number of colors can be supported, and the extension used is BMP.

- GIF   Short for Graphics Interchange Format, this is a common graphics format used on the Internet. Typically, GIFs are small because they are compressed;

however, they are only capable of using 256 colors per image. The extension used for these files is GIF.

- JPEG   Short for Joint Photographic Experts Group, this is another common graphics format used on the Internet. JPEG is typically used for storing photographs or other graphics that require many colors to display. The JPEG format can be compressed greatly; however, highly compressed files can lose information or quality. The extension for these files is JPG.

- PNG   Short for Portable Network Graphics, this is a relatively uncommon file format. It was created as a replacement for GIF and TIFF files. Files are relatively small, although usually not as small as with GIF or JPEG files. Support is rare, although Internet Explorer and other programs can display them. The extension for these files is PNG.

- TIFF   Short for Tagged Image File Format, this is a rarely found format that used to be common. TIFF files can be large or small, depending on which of the many TIFF variants is used to store it. The extension for these files is TIF.

17

Note

Generally, if you are going to display the graphic on a Web page, you will want to save the graphic in either GIF (if less than 256 colors) or JPEG format. Alternatively, if you are saving the graphic for use in a desktop application, you should try out each of the file formats to see which one provides the best combination of file size and quality for your needs. Typically, JPEG is good if the graphic uses many colors (like a photograph), whereas PNG or BMP are good for more simple images. For example, Table 17.14 shows the sizes of the same simple bitmap saved in each of the formats.

TABLE 17.14   Comparison of Graphics Formats

Format	File size
BMP	340,134
GIF	10,088
JPG	20,971
PNG	10,262
TIFF	15,492

We can now finish our application by adding the code to the File commands as seen in Listing 17.11.

LISTING 17.11   Menu Commands

```
1    Private Sub mnuFileNew_Click(ByVal sender As System.Object, _
2        ByVal e As System.EventArgs) Handles mnuFileNew.Click
3        Me.oGraphics.Clear(Color.White)
4        'force the refresh
5        Me.picDraw.Refresh()
6    End Sub
7
8    Private Sub mnuFileOpen_Click()
9        If Me.dlgOpen.ShowDialog = DialogResult.OK Then
10            Me.picDraw.Image.FromFile(Me.dlgOpen.FileName)
11        End If
12   End Sub
13
14   Private Sub mnuFileSave_Click(ByVal sender As Object, _
15       ByVal e As System.EventArgs) Handles mnuFileSave.Click
16       Dim sFileName As String
17       Dim oFormat As System.Drawing.Imaging.ImageFormat
18
19       'get the filename to save to
20       If dlgSave.ShowDialog = DialogResult.OK Then
21           sFileName = dlgSave.FileName
22           Select Case dlgSave.FilterIndex
23               Case 0  'save as bitmap
24                   oFormat = System.Drawing.Imaging.ImageFormat.Bmp
25               Case 1  'save as PNG
26                   oFormat = System.Drawing.Imaging.ImageFormat.Png
27               Case Else
28                   'should never happen
29           End Select
30           'possible exception on save
31           Try
32               Me.picDraw.Image.Save(sFileName, oFormat)
33
34           Catch ex As Exception
35               'just display for now
36               MessageBox.Show(ex.Message, "Error saving file", _
37                   MessageBoxButtons.OK, MessageBoxIcon.Error)
38           End Try
39       End If
40   End Sub
41
42   Private Sub mnuFileExit_Click(ByVal sender As System.Object, _
43       ByVal e As System.EventArgs) Handles mnuFileExit.Click
44       Me.Close()
45   End Sub
```

ANALYSIS   Lines 1–6 show the File, New command code. This is simple; all it does is clear the existing contents of the oGraphics object in line 3, replacing it with a nice new white background. As before, we force the `PictureBox` to refresh itself (line 5) to display the changed graphic.

Opening the file is almost as easy as clearing the image. At line 9 in the code we display the File Open dialog. If the user selects a file, we load this into the `PictureBox`'s `Image`. The `PictureBox` will determine the type of the file and display it as appropriate.

The code required to save the graphic is slightly longer but remains simple. We begin (line 20) by showing the standard File Save dialog. After the user has selected the location and type of file to save, we can continue. To shorten later lines, we save the selected filename to a variable. Our dialog allows the user to select from two different graphics formats—Bitmap or PNG. We use this selection to set another variable for the `ImageFormat` we will use to save the graphic. Finally, we are ready to save the graphic. In case of an exception, such as an out of disk space exception, we wrap the graphic in a `Try...End Try` block. Line 32 is the actual save, taking advantage of the capability of any `Image` object to save itself.

Finally, the File, Exit command simply closes the form, ending the application.

Saving graphics stored in an `Image` is relatively easy, as is loading a new `Image`. In fact, this is one of the best examples of the benefits of using objects because this takes what would be a complex task and encapsulates the required code into the `Graphics`, `Image`, and `Bitmap` objects.

Summary

Learning all the classes, structures, properties, methods, and events that make up the .NET Framework takes some time. However, learning a few fundamental classes will help you time after time, as the ideas shown by these classes are repeated throughout the Framework. After you have learned one stream, every time you see a stream, you will know what to do. Similarly, after you learn how to draw with the `Graphics` classes, you can draw anywhere.

Tomorrow, you'll see how to add the "finishing touches" to our applications.

Q&A

Q. What's Unicode?

A. One problem in the world is that there has never been one language that everyone could agree on. Many languages use the same or similar character set used in North America and Western Europe. These characters were defined as the ASCII

(American Standard Code for Information Interchange) character set. This character set uses 255 characters (one byte) to represent any character used in these languages. For example, the character "A" is represented by character 65 in all character sets that use the ASCII encoding.

However, other languages, such as Tamil, or Japanese, require many more characters. As such, the Unicode character set was defined by the International Standards Organization (ISO). Unicode uses two bytes to encode for each symbol in any of the languages on Earth (and a few non-Earth languages—there is a mapping of Klingon into Unicode (`http://anubis.dkuug.dk/jtc1/sc2/wg2/docs/n1643/n1643.htm`). For example, the Unicode character 20AC should always be the Euro. The first 256 characters in the Unicode encoding are the same as those in ASCII for convenience.

So, the short answer is a two-byte value that can identify any character used in any character set. Why should you care? At some point, you will see a bunch of characters that look like ????? and you'll wonder why. Odds are, they're Unicode, and you should look into how to convert them to ASCII, or to display the native characters.

Q. **I want to draw a complex shape. Are there commands in `System.Drawing` for drawing shapes such as octagons as well?**

A. A number of methods of the `Graphics` object can be used to create more complex shapes. These include `DrawArc`, `DrawCurve`, `DrawLines`, `DrawPath`, and `DrawPolygon`. To draw an octagon, you should use the `DrawPolygon` method, passing in the Pen to use for the drawing, and an array of `Points`. The array of `Points` describes each of the corners of the octagon.

Workshop

The Workshop is designed to help you anticipate possible questions, review what you've learned, and get you thinking about how to put your knowledge into practice. The answers to the quiz are in Appendix A, "Answers to Quizzes/Exercises."

Quiz

1. Which of the following code fragments would you use to determine whether a file exists?

A. ```
Dim oFile As New File
Dim bExists As Boolean = oFile.Exists("some file")
```

B. ```
Dim bExists As Boolean = Directory.Exists("some file")
```

C. ```
Dim bExists As Boolean = File.Exists("some file")
```

D. ```
Dim oDir As New Directory
Dim bExists As Boolean = oDir.Exists("some file")
```

2. What is the relationship between the `Stream`, `StreamReader`, and `StreamWriter` classes?

3. What graphics formats can you create (or show in an `Image` control)?

4. What is the difference between a `Point`, a `Size`, and a `Rectangle`?

Exercises

1. One of the problems with the Note program we wrote is that it allows you to use the Cut, Copy, and Paste commands without there being any selected text or text in the Clipboard. See whether you can discover an easy way of enabling and disabling these menu items before you show the menu to the user. (Hint: Add an event to the `mnuEdit` menu item.)

2. Change the format used to save graphics and compare the resulting file sizes. Which is the smallest format for simple black-and-white drawings? For photos?

DAY **18**

Finishing Touches

This book focuses on teaching you how to program with .NET, but there are many aspects to building a complete application. Today's lesson will cover some details you need to understand when creating an actual system, especially a large and complex one, including

- Documenting your application
- Using source code control

Both these topics are optional; you do not need to do them to produce a system that works, but they are part of almost every large development project.

Documenting Your Application

Sometimes when you create a system, you write all the code and deploy the system to your users and then no one ever sees that code again. That is the exception, not the rule, and likely it only occurs with small systems. It is more common that your code will be revisited again and again as the original system is modified to add functionality and fix bugs, and could even be used as the basis for completely new versions of the same system. To make modifications and reuse of your code as easy as possible for you or for other programmers, you should document your system.

This type of documenting is different than documenting your system for your users, which I will discuss later in today's lesson. This documentation provides information on the workings of your system for people who have access to your code and varies widely in the amount of detail because there is no single method to document your code. One path to good documentation is to first consider the purpose of providing this information. Documentation exists to ensure that all knowledge about a system is retained—whether business requirements or the rationale behind technical decisions—to simplify maintenance by increasing the available information about your code. Documentation can be broken down into a few key guidelines (not necessarily in order of importance), the first of which is not about documentation at all:

- Create the simplest solution that solves the problem.
- Document your system with as few assumptions as possible.
- Use your time wisely. Don't comment the obvious; focus on demystifying the complex portions of your system instead.
- Detailed explanations of your code are meaningless without an understanding of the system's overall purpose. Document the system, each of the system's components, and the code itself.

Taken together these guidelines create well-documented systems that are as maintainable as you can possibly make them. In the following sections, I will expand on each of these ideas, illustrating with code examples where useful.

Create the Simplest Solution

If the point of documenting your code is to make it easier to understand, wouldn't it be best to make it as easy as possible right from the start? Your goal should be code that is understandable without any further explanation, and commenting should fill in where you couldn't achieve that result. There are two main ways to accomplish this: writing clean code and writing simple solutions. I will cover the clean code concept first, but the deeper issue is certainly the creation of simple solutions.

Writing Clean Code

Consider Listings 18.1 and 18.2, both of which are designed to do the same thing.

LISTING 18.1 Code Can Be More Complex Than It Needs to Be

```
1 Option Explicit On
2 Option Strict On
3
```

LISTING 18.1   continued

```
 4 Imports System
 5 Imports System.IO
 6
 7 Module Module1
 8
 9    Sub Main()
10       Dim Path1 As String = "C:\file.txt"
11       Dim Path2 As String = "C:\file_new.txt"
12       Dim File1 As New StreamReader(Path1)
13       Dim File2 As New StreamWriter(Path2)
14       Dim x As String
15       x = File1.ReadLine()
16       Do Until x Is Nothing
17          File2.WriteLine(x)
18          x = File1.ReadLine()
19       Loop
20       File2.Close()
21       File1.Close()
22    End Sub
23
24 End Module
```

18

LISTING 18.2   By Making Your Code Easier to Understand, You Can Do Less Documenting

```
 1 Option Explicit On
 2 Option Strict On
 3
 4 Imports System
 5 Imports System.IO
 6
 7 Module WorkWithFiles
 8
 9    Sub CopyFiles()
10       Dim sInputFilePath As String = "C:\test.txt"
11       Dim sOutputFilePath As String = "C:\output.txt"
12       Dim fileInput As New StreamReader(sInputFilePath)
13       Dim fileOutput As New StreamWriter(sOutputFilePath)
14       Dim sLine As String
15
16       sLine = fileInput.ReadLine()
17       Do Until sLine Is Nothing
18          fileOutput.WriteLine(sLine)
19          sLine = fileInput.ReadLine()
20       Loop
21
22       fileOutput.Close()
```

LISTING **18.2**   continued

```
23          fileInput.Close()
24
25      End Sub
26
27      Sub Main()
28          CopyFiles()
29      End Sub
30
31 End Module
```

ANALYSIS   Listing 18.1 and 18.2 read a file in and write it out to a new file, but Listing 18.2 is much clearer than the same code in Listing 18.1. The first reason is the name of the Module and the Sub itself; the default values do not provide any information, whereas the procedure name CopyFiles is a fairly direct indication of the purpose of the routine. The next difference is in spacing. In Listing 18.2, blank lines are used to group related pieces of code, grouping the initialization code (lines 10–14), the file reading code (lines 16–20), and the clean-up code (lines 22–23). These blank lines will have absolutely no effect on the end result of this system—both examples will execute at the same speed and with the same results—but grouping the code increases readability.

The remaining key difference between the two code samples is in variable naming, a topic that I have touched on briefly in earlier lessons. Variables can be named anything, as long as you aren't using a keyword or other reserved value of .NET. You can think of the variable name as a built-in documenting mechanism. Listing 18.1 is an extreme example; most code you see won't be as bad about variable naming. But this attempts to illustrate the effect of poor variable names. Referring to the two files as fileInput and fileOutput (compared to File1 and File2) documents the purpose of the variables without any further commenting required. Similar choices have been made with the other variable names, and when these variables are used together (such as line 12 in Listing 18.2), the purpose of the code is almost completely explained just through the names used.

A useful and common coding practice is also used in choosing variable names; each name is prefixed with one or more characters to indicate the data type of the variable. In Listing 18.2, strings are prefixed with s, and the StreamReader/StreamWriter objects use file to indicate their usage to read and write from files. This method of naming variables is based on *Hungarian notation*, where leading characters are used to describe the data type and scope (global versus local, public versus private) of variables. I say that it is based on this type of notation, instead of saying that it "is" Hungarian Notation because I generally apply a much looser naming standard than the original set of rules described as Hungarian notation by its creator (Charles Simonyi of Microsoft). I will discuss variable naming later today in the section "Best Practices and Coding Standards."

A final point about creating clean code, one that is not illustrated in the previous example code, is how the structure of your code can make it easier to understand. I like to create my systems using many procedures, even for code that will not necessarily be reused in any way. The result of structuring your system in this way is that higher-level procedures can be read and understood while still avoiding the more complex (and more confusing) details. Listing 18.3 gives you an example.

LISTING 18.3   Procedures Are Another Way to Make Your Code Easier to Understand

```
 1 Module StartUp
 2    Public Sub Main()
 3       Dim sPassword, sData, sFilePath As String
 4       sFilePath = "C:\Input.txt"
 5       InitializeSystemVariables()
 6
 7       sPassword = GetPassword()
 8       sData = ReadData(sFilePath)
 9       sData = EncryptData(sPassword, sData)
10       WriteData(sFilePath, sData)
11    End Sub
12 End Module
```

18

Listing 18.3 does nothing on its own; the real meat of this system is contained within the procedures it references. Reading just this routine gives you a good idea of what the system is doing, and you can dive into the individual routines if needed. If you structure your code correctly, higher-level routines can act as a "Reader's Digest" view of all the lower-level routines they call. It is worth noting, though, that although you might be able to read the code from Listing 18.3 and understand what is occurring, only with proper documentation would you be sure why it is occurring!

Simplifying Your Systems

Creating clean code is one aspect of the first guideline, but it is not the most important. It is more important that the actual solution created, how you decided to achieve the system's goals, is as simple as possible.

Avoiding Assumptions

When you start documenting your code, you likely (consciously or unconsciously) will have an audience in mind for those comments. You might be writing as if you will be the only one reading these comments, or perhaps you expect that other developers from your current team will be the ones who need to understand your code to maintain it. The problem with having any target audience in mind is that you tend to write different documentation for different people.

Do not assume that the comments will be read only by people with C++ experience, or even with Visual Basic .NET experience. Do not assume that the comments will be viewed by people who understand the overall point of the system, or who have any understanding whatsoever of the business side of this discussion. Your assumptions might seem valid—perhaps you have a team full of nothing but experts—but things change. Your code could end up in the hands of a consulting company in charge of updating your code for a company that bought your current firm, or an individual piece of your code could be lifted for use in another project.

Even small assumptions, that the reader understands database terms for example, should be covered in the beginning of any documents you create. There is, of course, a limit to this rule; if you couldn't assume at least a basic knowledge of Visual Basic, then you would have to explain every single aspect of the code.

Do Not Comment the Obvious, Only the Confusing

This rule is actually related closely to the first because the simpler and cleaner you can make your code, the less commenting it requires. Consider Listings 18.1 and 18.2 and how you might comment them to ensure that they can be maintained easily. In the end, you need to spend a great deal more time commenting the first example, explaining the meaning of variables such as `Path1` and `Path2`, whereas the second example is somewhat self-documenting. A variable name of `sInputFilePath` tells you everything you need to know, without having to add any comments at all. The use of Hungarian notation, covered later in today's lesson, along with meaningful variable names adds even more information, letting you know that this is a string variable in this case and further reducing the need for comments.

Document the System, Not Just Your Code

The final point in our general principles of documenting is that you need to always focus on the goal, which is to make it easy for another person to understand your system. Documenting every variable in detail, and every loop, does not help me understand your system if I do not know what that system is supposed to accomplish. Provide documentation at several different levels, from the original vision and scope behind the system down to the details of the individual lines of code. The different documentation pieces that I would want to have available on a system include the following:

- Vision/Scope
- Requirements/Use Case
- Detailed Design
- Some form of system history/change requests

The definition of each of these types of documentation varies widely across different development methodologies and different people, but the basic intent of the document is all that I am concerned with here. Details on the general point of this documentation are provided in the following sections, but the question that you are likely to ask yourself as you read these details is "I have to write all this? I thought I was done!" That is a good question. If you do not have any of this documentation, and your system is done, there is not much chance that you will create it. But that is not how it is supposed to work. The idea is that you create this documentation before you build the system, most of it before you start writing any actual code beyond a prototype and some of it during the coding phase itself. On Day 1, "Welcome to Visual Basic .NET," I discussed the software development life cycle, but here it is again for your reference (see Figure 18.1).

FIGURE 18.1

The software development life cycle is a never-ending process, often represented as a circle that reconnects to itself to indicate an ongoing cycle.

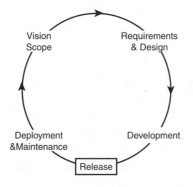

Vision/Scope

The Vision/Scope documentation states the agreed-on point and goal of the system, and should be determined at the beginning of development. As a reference for maintenance purposes, it is good to start by understanding what the point of the system is from the beginning. An example Vision Scope at its simplest level might be:

> "The Employee Skill Tracking system will maintain a listing of employees and track their level of expertise in various job-related skills for the purpose of building teams and planning projects."

Notice that this statement doesn't fill in all the details: What skills? Who will use the system? Where will it get the list of employees? These questions and others are not part of the Vision. They need to be answered, but they will be found in the other documentation.

Requirements and Use Cases

Requirement and Use Case documentation can be done separately or together. Perhaps you will only have one or the other available, but the same purpose is served regardless.

The Requirements of a system document the individual functions that the users will be performing with the system, and Use Cases attempt to describe representative interactions that will take place with the system. Either one provides a listing of functions that the system needs to be capable of doing and should give you an idea of how each of those functions should work. These documents provide a picture of the application from the user's point of view, but you will need to look further for information on how the system actually performs these functions.

Detailed Design

Many documents fall into this category—anything that provides more detail than the Requirements documentation. The intention of documents in this category is to detail how the system works: what steps it follows internally to execute on the user requirements laid out in the previous documentation. Expect to see flowcharts; state diagrams; and lists of components, procedures, and other code elements as part of this material.

Change History

If applications matched up exactly with their specifications when they shipped, it would be a miracle. If there is one constant in application development, it is that changes are made constantly. Much of the work of building a system is tracking and controlling that change, preventing it from taking the project completely off schedule. This tracking often is referred to as *change control*, and it involves recording every requested change, following some form of approval process to determine which changes make it into the system, and then documenting those decisions and the effect that each such change has on the project schedule. If the change that occurs in your system is documented, that material will be an invaluable resource for developers working on new features and maintenance of existing features, and for architects and managers planning new releases of your software.

Best Practices and Coding Standards

When it comes to documenting your code, there are few "best practices" worth using or at least considering. The first is establishing a set of common (common to at least your team) standards for naming variables, controls, and objects. The second is providing header blocks in your code—comments at the top of modules, classes, and procedures that use a common format and provide information about that code in a single location. I will discuss each of these and provide some examples of how to handle them within your team.

Variable, Control, and Object Naming

The most important issue concerning a naming standard is that it has to be a standard; everyone on your team must use the same naming conventions without exception. In fact, naming should be just one part of a larger document that details commenting, exception handling, source code control, and more—everything a developer needs to know to function as part of your team. If you can get everyone using your naming standard, establishing the actual standard is a breeze.

Hungarian notation is a form of naming, discussed briefly earlier in today's lesson, that uses prefixes to provide information about the variable, control, or object. These prefixes consist of one or more letters and are designed to convey at least the data type and sometimes also the scope of the object. The knowledge base article Q110264 (`http://support.microsoft.com/support/kb/articles/Q110/2/64.asp`) details an example set of naming conventions created for use with older versions of Visual Basic. Much of that article is still valid, but it is not updated for .NET. For my own code, I use a fairly simple set of naming conventions that are based at least in part on this article and have evolved into a set of conventions that I actually use. I will dive into some detailed coverage of conventions, but there are few general guidelines to cover first.

- I only use this notation to indicate data type; I don't add scope information, other than adding m_ to indicate a member variable (private) of a class. Not specifying scope is a matter of simplicity because I rarely use anything other than procedure or class level variables. This way I don't have to have any type of scope indicator on procedure level variables.

- All these naming conventions apply to internal names, such as private variables, controls on your form, and so on. When you are creating classes, public properties, and public methods, you are defining an external interface, and those names should be simple human-readable names. For instance, I might call an internal counter variable `iCount` (to indicate that it is an integer), but a similar property on a public class should be called just `Count`.

- The end goal is to make your code more readable, not less. In addition to the Hungarian notation, make sure that the variable name itself is meaningful!

For all the following naming examples, I use *camel case*, where the prefix is in lowercase, and the variable name is capitalized, producing more readable names.

Data Types

I generally use as few characters as possible for my data type notation, and therefore (unlike the Microsoft article reference earlier) I do not even attempt to use the same number of characters for all my data types. Remember that I am giving my notation in Table 18.1, but I have included common alternatives in brackets where appropriate. It is not realistic to cover all the .NET data types, including all the classes in the .NET Framework, so I am trying to provide enough examples to give you an idea of how I name my variables.

18

TABLE 18.1 Common Data Type Prefixes

Data Type	Hungarian Notation
String	S [str]
Integer, Int32	I [int]
Double	Dbl
Single	sng [f(for float, a C++ type)]
Long, Int64	L [lng]
Boolean	B [bool]
Date/Time	dt
System.Data.DataSet	ds
System.Data.DataColumn	dc
Object	obj

For anything that is sufficiently unusual, something I use infrequently, I often will just use a descriptive name with the obj prefix, such as objWebRequest.

Controls

The examples in Table 18.2 apply equally to Web controls used with WebForms and Windows.Forms controls.

TABLE 18.2 Common Control Prefixes

Control	Hungarian Notation
Button	btn [cmd(goes back to pre .NET VB)]
Label	lbl
Text box	txt
List box	lb
Combo box	cbo
Radio buttons	opt
Check boxes	chk
Data grid	dg
Menu items	mnu

Comment Blocks

At the top of each procedure, and each class, you can include a large multiline comment describing that set of code. These comment blocks often are used as the location for providing any form of information that applies to the entire set of code instead of to a single line or single structure. I generally include the following information in class (including module) comment headers:

- Name (of the class)
- Dependencies (references required by this class, other classes, system requirements such as SQL Server)
- Purpose
- Author (usually the original author)
- Last edited by
- Last edited date
- Comments (notes on problems, bugs found and fixed, anything that is not specific to a line within the class but is worth noting)

Listing 18.4 shows an example of a class comment block.

LISTING 18.4 Consistent Comment Blocks Are Worth the Effort

```
 1 Imports System
 2 Imports System.Data
 3 Imports System.Data.SqlClient
 4 '********************************************************
 5 'Class Name:     GetAuthors
 6 'Dependencies:   System.Data, SQL Server must be available
 7 'Purpose:        To access SQL Server and retrieve data
 8 '                from the Authors table in the Pubs
 9 '                Sample database
10 'Author:         Duncan Mackenzie
11 'Last Edited By:Duncan Mackenzie
12 'Last Edited On:08/09/2001
13 'Comments:       Modified to have SQL Server name passed in
14 '                instead of hardcoded.
15 '********************************************************
16
17 Public Class GetAuthors
18 End Class
```

For a procedure comment block, I include a slightly different set of information:

- Name (of the procedure)

18

- Dependencies (references required by this sub or function, other classes, system requirements such as SQL Server)

- Purpose

- Author (usually the original author)

- Parameters (include all possible if you have one comment block and multiple over-loaded versions, or include just the current version if you place a comment block before each overloaded version)

- Last edited by

- Last edited date

- Comments (notes on problems, bugs found and fixed, anything that is not specific to a line within the procedure but is worth noting)

It is not difficult to write an add-in for .NET that provides at least a template of a comment block for you and saves you a bit of typing, so if you have the time, you might want to build one as a weekend project.

Using Source Code Control

The source code you create is valuable; it represents the result of your work and the base for future work. Both during development and after the fact, you need to find a way to store your code. The main requirements for storing this code are that the code is secure, and changes are tracked so that you can compare between two different versions. In Visual Studio .NET, facilities are provided for you to access a source code control system, and the system available from Microsoft is essentially the same one that shipped with Visual Studio 6.0, Visual SourceSafe (VSS) 6.0c.

To enable support for VSS in .NET, simply install the server and client (or just the client, assuming that a server already exists somewhere else) onto your machine, and it will enable the proper menu commands in Visual Studio .NET. In this section, I will walk you through the basics of using source code control, covering how to check code into the source code system, how to check it out from that system, and how to roll back to an earlier change.

Checking Out Code

After you have enabled source code control in Visual Studio .NET by installing the client portion of VSS, you will have some new menu options available. On the File menu, a submenu called Source Control provides a variety of choices, depending on whether a project is currently open. If nothing is open, then you have the option of opening up a project directly from the source code control system, but for your first use of VSS, it makes more sense to open up a project and add that project into the source code system. What project you open is not really important at this point, but you might as well just make a new, empty console application for the purpose of this example. Name the application SCC Sample and place the code shown in Listing 18.5 into its module, allowing me to sneak in a little demo of accessing Web content while you learn about source control.

LISTING 18.5   Retrieving a Web Page

```
 1 Imports System.Net
 2 Imports System.IO
 3 Module SCC_Sample
 4
 5     Sub Main()
 6         Dim sOutput As String
 7         Dim sURL As String
 8         sURL = "http://msdn.microsoft.com"
 9         Try
10             Dim objNewRequest _
11                 As WebRequest = HttpWebRequest.Create(sURL)
12             Dim objResponse _
13                 As WebResponse = objNewRequest.GetResponse
14             Dim objStream _
15                 As New StreamReader(objResponse.GetResponseStream())
16             sOutput = objStream.ReadToEnd()
17         Catch eUFE As UriFormatException
18             sOutput = "Error in URL Format: [" & sURL & "]" & _
19                 System.Environment.NewLine() & eUFE.Message
20         Catch eWEB As WebException
21             sOutput = "Error With Web Request: " _
22                 & System.Environment.NewLine() & eWEB.Message
23         Catch e As Exception
24             sOutput = e.ToString
25         Finally
26             Console.Write(sOutput)
27         End Try
28         Console.ReadLine()
29     End Sub
30 End Module
```

18

Now, save all your files by selecting File, Save All from the menu. With your project started and containing some data, the next step is to add it into your source code control system. Select Microsoft Visual SourceSafe under the File, Source Control, Add Solution to Source Control menu.

Note

User IDs and passwords are required for Visual Source Safe, and you can con-figure them by running the Visual Source Safe Administrator program from the Visual Source Safe folder on the Programs menu. For now, if you are prompted to enter a userid or password, just use Admin and a blank pass-word (which are configured by default).

This brings up a dialog that allows you to choose a path within the source code system to store your solution and the projects within it (see Figure 18.2).

FIGURE **18.2**

When you check in your code, you get to choose where, within the Source Code repos-itory, it gets stored.

Your dialog likely shows nothing but the root of the source code control tree $/, but some projects already exist in my source code control system. You can create subdirecto-ries by typing the desired name and clicking Create. Make sure that the root is selected in the dialog and then type **Teach Yourself Visual Basic .NET** and click Create. Now, the new directory is selected, which is what you want, so type **Day 18** and click Create. Finally, type the name you want for your solution (SCC Sample is a good choice; see Figure 18.3) and click OK. You are prompted that the project does not already exist and asked if you want to create it automatically, which you do, so click Yes.

FIGURE **18.3**

You can create a com-plete hierarchy to store your projects based on whatever categories you want to use.

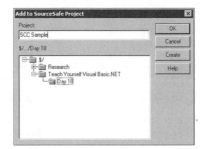

Now, Visual Studio .NET adds this project into Source Code Control and checks it in at the same time, which means that you have to check it out before you can modify it. Notice that your files are now read-only, as indicated in the Visual Studio .NET title bar and in the Solution Explorer (see Figure 18.4).

FIGURE 18.4

One of the intentions of source code control is to only allow one developer to edit code at a time. Therefore only code that is checked out can be modified.

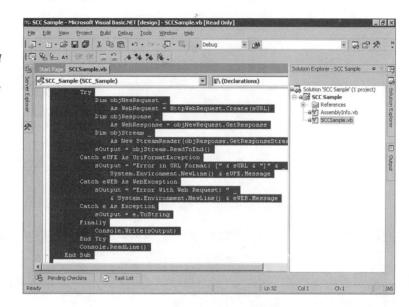

At this point, you can check out your code because you finally have it all checked in for the first time. Select the module in the Solution Explorer, which I named SCCSample.vb in my project, and right-click on it. In the context-menu that appears, you have a new option, Check Out Now (see Figure 18.5), which allows you to check out that single file and edit it. Until a file is checked out, it is read-only, and when it is checked out, it can be edited only on the machine where it was retrieved.

Another option, which might be more useful, is available if you right-click on the project or the solution, Check Out Now (Recursive) as shown in Figure 18.6, which checks out the solution or project and all the files within it. You will see this option, to check out everything all at once, only if you have selected the option Display Silent Check-Out Command in Menus. This option can be found under the Source Control folder of the options dialog, which you can bring up by selecting the Tools, Options menu item.

After a file is checked out, it indicates this status through a new icon next to its name in the Solution Explorer, as shown in Figure 18.7, and through the fact that it is no longer read-only. You can now make changes to these files as much as you want, but those changes will not be reflected in the Source Safe system until you check the files back in.

18

FIGURE **18.5**

You can check out any single file you want to work with.

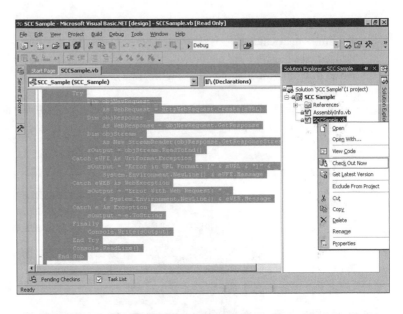

FIGURE **18.6**

Using the recursive check-out to check out all your project files at one time often is easier than checking out files one at a time.

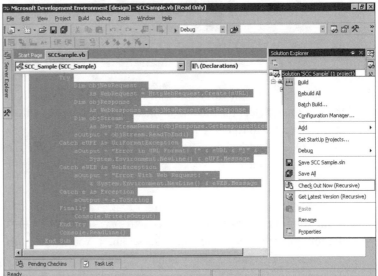

Checking In Code

While a file is checked out, other programmers using the source code system will only have access to a read-only copy of the file; you have exclusive access to the copy that you have. You do not want to keep files checked out if you are not using them, unless you intentionally want to keep those files from being modified by anyone else, so check your code back in after you have made (and usually after you have tested) your modifications.

FIGURE 18.7

The Solution Explorer indicates whether a file is checked in or out, after you have chosen to use source code control with your project.

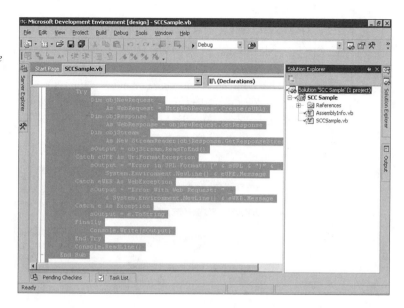

For your sample code, which is currently checked out if you have been following along, make a couple of changes to the module, such as removing the `Console.ReadLine` at line 28, and changing the URL set in line 8 to `http://www.microsoft.com`. Now, save your files and then you can check them back in to Source Safe. There are several ways to check in files, but the simplest is to just right-click on the Solution or Project (the same level you checked out at) and select Check In. This brings up a dialog (see Figure 18.8) that allows you to specify which files in the solution should be checked in and add a comment explaining what you changed and why.

18

FIGURE 18.8

When you check files back in, you can add comments to document the changes you made.

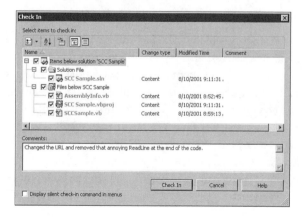

Viewing and Rolling Back Your Changes

Now, with your files checked back in, you can play with some of the neater features of using source code control. The first feature you can try is viewing the history of a file, showing every check in/check out where changes were made. Select the module in the Solution Explorer and then select File, Source Control, History from the menu. You will be given the ability to configure the history listing, but just clicking OK will bring up a listing of versions available for this file (see Figure 18.9).

FIGURE 18.9

Every time you check modified source code back into the source code control system, this new version is maintained for future reference.

Select the first version, which was the original file you checked into Source Safe, and then click on the Diff button. This brings up a dialog at which you can make sure that Visual is selected and then click OK. Now, you are shown a window (see Figure 18.10) that details the current state of the file and the file as it was in the selected version and details the differences. This visual format makes it clear what was changed, but it takes up a lot of space to illustrate changes in a large source file. The other two formats (Unix and Source Safe) provide brief summaries of the changes between two versions, which might be more to your liking.

Returning to the History window, you can roll back to an earlier version of a file, if you want to undo many changes, and you don't mind losing everything done from one version to the next. Rolling back, compared to viewing the differences and undoing a selective number of changes manually, is a radical operation, but sometimes it is the only way to return to a known working state. Select the first version of this file in the history list and then click the Rollback button. You are warned that this action cannot be undone, but go ahead and do it anyway. Now, there will be only the one version. Your local copies will be updated to that version, and if you or anyone else were to get this file from Source Safe, this is the version you would receive. You have totally removed any changes past the selected version.

FIGURE 18.10

Source Safe can provide a visual interface to detail the changes between one version and another. This makes it easy to locate the source of a problem in a specific version.

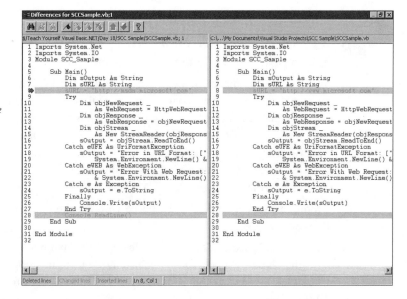

Security Considerations for Using Visual Source Safe

In the History dialog, the user who checked in the file is shown, and in this case it is always "Admin." It is important that everyone logs in as himself so that you can see who made which changes to your source code and so that passwords are set up so that no one can make changes using someone else's name. Visual Source Safe does not seem capable of integrating with Windows 2000/NT security, but you can fake it by creating users with the same names as your developers' network IDs and having them use those IDs when connecting to VSS. Using the Visual Source Safe interface, you can set project-level security based on the user's login ID, allowing you to limit access to a project as needed.

Summary

Documentation is considered by many to be a necessary evil of programming. It is often done at the end of a project in a mad rush to provide the minimum amount of commenting to be able to say that you are finished. The key to making documentation useful and much less difficult to complete is to work on it as you go. Following the guidelines in today's lesson will make your code as easy to understand as possible and commenting will fill in any understanding gaps that might exist.

18

Q&A

Q. Isn't commenting just a way to make up for unclear code? If your code is written right, it shouldn't require any comments.

A. I have heard this statement a few times, and it is partially true. The clearer your code is, the fewer comments are required. Follow this thought along and you will conclude that really clear code requires no comments. I agree, but I believe that any program consisting of more than 10 lines of code can never be that clear because the potential audience reading your code is so varied. Make your code as clear as you can, thereby minimizing comments, but some amount of commenting will likely always be required.

Q. I thought .NET included XML-based commenting, but you didn't cover it in this lesson.

A. Sadly, XML-based commenting is a feature of C# but not Visual Basic .NET (or any other .NET language for that matter). If you are interested, take a look at the C# reference materials that ship with the .NET Framework for more details on XML commenting.

Workshop

The Workshop is designed to help you anticipate possible questions, review what you've learned, and get thinking about how to put your knowledge into practice. The answers to the quiz are in Appendix A, "Answers to Quizzes/Exercises."

Quiz

1. Based on the naming standards discussed in this lesson, what do you know about a variable named sConnectionInfo?

2. Visual Source Safe provides source code control services to Visual Studio .NET. Name at least two reasons why you would want to use a source code control system.

3. What is it called when you use the source code system to go back to an earlier version of your code?

DAY 19

Deploying Your Application

After you have built an application, you have to be able to get that system to your users. The process of taking a system from production to use is known as *deployment*, and it often is considered one of the hardest phases of any development project. Today's lesson will cover the basic steps of deploying an application using Visual Studio .NET, including

- Introducing deployment
- Building a Windows setup program
- Distribution options for an install program

.NET has done a lot to reduce the difficulties surrounding application deployment, but it is still a required process and often more complicated than it seems.

Introduction to Deployment

Deploying an application is, quite simply, providing your application to the people who are going to use it. Deployment entails different things for different types of applications. For a Web application, deployment can mean placing your pages and code onto a Web server, whereas for a Windows application, it might mean getting your .exe file out to every user. Often you are dealing with several different files, and each of those files has its own requirements, complicating the entire process. A *dependency* is when one file, such as your .exe, requires another file, such as a library (.dll), to run correctly. So, your application might be dependent on one or more other files, but those files themselves also might have dependencies and so on. Deploying your single .exe file so that it works correctly could require the installation of a multitude of other files!

The most common dependency you will encounter, because it is required by every .NET application you create, is the .NET Framework. As you might remember, the .NET Framework was installed as part of installing Visual Studio .NET, and it consists of many files to hold all the class libraries, the Common Language Runtime (CLR), and other important components. To avoid having to include all these different files and their dependencies individually, a merge module has been provided.

NEW TERM   A *merge module* is a single file that is essentially an entire installation program of its own that you can include as a part of your deployment. Merge modules (which are stored as .msm files on disk) are an excellent way to package up all the required settings, dependencies, and files for a single library or application. You can create your own merge modules, if you ever create a library or other project that often will be included into other setups, but Visual Studio .NET includes many MSM's already for your use. These merge modules, stored in `\Program Files\Common Files\Merge Modules\`, include the portions of the .NET Framework required to deploy your application onto another machine.

In pre-.NET days, installing often involved registering COM components, which meant creating entries in the system registry for those components so that they could be found and created by applications that wanted to use them. In .NET, this need to modify the registry to install an application is removed; all the settings and metadata about an application or a component (such as a class library) are stored either within the file itself or as additional files in the same directory. This removal of registration allows for "X-Copy" installations, allowing applications to be completely installed simply through copying the files from one machine to another.

With this in mind, the need to create an actual install is not very clear. Often there is more to installing an application than just getting it running on the target machine: Icons need to be created on the desktop and the start menu; dependencies such as the .NET Framework need to be installed; an uninstall option needs to be provided, and sometimes even registry entries for application settings need to be created. All these actions, common features you have likely seen as part of many different application installations, are available through creating a complete setup program.

In Visual Studio .NET, deployment is handled through the creation of Windows Installer files. Windows Installer is a relatively new form of installation technology that has deeper support from the operating system and is being used by more products, including Visual Studio .NET itself, Microsoft Office, and many more. Suffice it to say that by using this technology, your setup programs can take advantage of many great features, all of which are described as part of the Platform SDK.

MSDN pages that are part of the Platform SDK have a disturbing tendency to change URLs over time, so I will walk you down the library tree instead of giving a direct link. Go to http://msdn.microsoft.com/library and then find the entry in the tree view (on the left side of the page) called Setup and System Administration. Expand this node and then continue down through Setup, Windows Installer, SDK Documentation. Finally, you end up at Windows Installer (it appears twice in the path; don't let that bother you). Excellent, detailed information is available about the Windows Installer, but perhaps the best way to learn is to try it yourself.

Creating a Simple Setup

I will stop just talking about deployment and walk you through creating a simple setup for a simple application. To make this a perfect sample, you need an additional machine (not the one you have .NET installed on), preferably one that does not have .NET on it. This second machine, if you have one, should be networked to the first, or you need some other means of moving large files such as a CD burner. Now, if you only have one machine, the process can still be followed, but the demo will not be as close to the real world in which you will end up running your real deployment programs.

The goal of this example is to create a simple .NET application, the actual contents of which are totally unimportant. Early in this book, though, you were told that we would not create any "hello world!" applications as demos. With that in mind, we need to create a real application to build our sample around. Simple is still the goal, though, so we will build a single form that connects to a SQL Server database and displays a list of authors (from the Pubs sample database). This will be contained in a single form, which is not the best way to write an application for real use, but it keeps the example simple, and we will build a more proper example a little later in this lesson. I will cover the code only briefly; for more details, return to Day 12, "Accessing Data with .NET," for coverage of working with databases and the System.Data classes.

The example is created by making a new Windows application in its own solution. I will walk through each of the relevant steps, and you can either follow along or download the completed code from this book's Web site.

19

Create the New Project and New Solution

If you currently have a solution open, select File, Close Solution from the menu to close it. Now, with nothing open, select New, Project from the File menu. The New Project dialog appears; select the Visual Basic Projects folder and the Windows Application project template. Now, make sure that the full version of this dialog is shown by clicking the More button if it is not already expanded. Name the project something appropriate, such as AuthorList, and then make sure that Create Directory For Solution is checked, which will allow you to provide a name for your Solution. Give the solution a name, such as Pubs Demo, which indicates that it could contain more than just this project. Finally, click OK to create the new solution and the new project. Create a directory for any solution that will hold more than one single project because this provides an automatic organization to your files, placing all the projects that are part of a single solution into a directory together. A new project and solution will be created with the names you choose.

Set Up the New Form

In the Windows Application project, a new form will have been created by default, currently called Form1. Rename this form to the more meaningful name of frmDisplayAuthors and then add a list box control onto the otherwise blank form. Set the new list box's name to lbAuthors, set its Dock property to Fill, and set its IntegralHeight to False. These settings make a data grid that covers the entire form, even if the form is resized by the user. The IntegralHeight setting is unique to list boxes and determines whether the control should always be sized as a multiple of the height of a single list item so that no partial list items are visible. If you don't set IntegralHeight to False, then the list box does not always completely fill the form's height, which does not look very appealing.

Add Some Code

The purpose of this application is to display a list of authors, so the code has to establish the database connection, go get that list, and show it in the list box control. All these steps are covered as part of Day 12, so I will just show you the completed code (see Listing 19.1), which is called from the form's constructor. Add the code from line 8 into the New subroutine of your form and then place the LoadAuthors routine anywhere else inside your form, except inside another procedure.

LISTING 19.1   Adding Code to the New Subroutine of Your Form

```
1     Public Sub New()
2         MyBase.New()
3
```

LISTING **19.1** continued

```
4           'This call is required by the Windows Form Designer.
5           InitializeComponent()
6
7           'Add any initialization after the InitializeComponent() call
8:          LoadAuthors()
9     End Sub
10
11    Private Sub LoadAuthors()
12          Dim sConnectionString As String
13          sConnectionString = "Data Source=(local);" & _
14              "Initial Catalog=Pubs;" & _
15              "User ID=sa;password=daneel"
16          Dim connPubs As New SqlConnection(sConnectionString)
17          Dim cmdAuthors As New SqlCommand( _
18                  "Select au_fname + ' ' + au_lname as Name from Authors", _
19                    connPubs)
20          Dim daAuthors As New SqlDataAdapter(cmdAuthors)
21          Dim dsAuthors As New DataSet("Authors")
22
23          connPubs.Open()
24          daAuthors.Fill(dsAuthors, "Authors")
25
26          lbAuthors.DataSource = dsAuthors.Tables(0).DefaultView
27          lbAuthors.DisplayMember = "Name"
28    End Sub
```

I need to take you for a little off-topic journey for a moment and discuss something that comes up when you get into the final stages of an application. There is an issue with the code shown in Listing 19.1 that will cause you problems when you deploy it. It uses (local) to specify the SQL Server name (Data Source in the connection string in Listing 19.1). This tells .NET that you want to connect to the SQL Server on the local machine, which is likely correct while you are developing, but when this code is being run on a bunch of different client machines, you probably want them all to access the same central SQL Server. There are two ways to fix this: the quick way that will hard-code the desired SQL Server name or the slightly more complicated way that will allow the server name to be changed without a recompile of the code. Of course, I want to show you both, so I will start with the easier method, where you simply change your connection string to include the real computer name of your SQL Server:

```
sConnectionString = "Data Source=Olivaw;" & _
    "Initial Catalog=Pubs;" & _
    "User ID=sa;password=daneel"
```

Nothing else has to be changed, and now, regardless of which machine this is executed on, it will attempt to locate the server based on the name "Olivaw".

19

It is possible that this server name will change or that you might choose to use a different server for this application. The server you use for development and the server used for production commonly are two different machines. It would be beneficial to be able to change the server that this application connects to without recompiling the code at all. Prior to .NET, this type of functionality would be provided using the Registry. This option is still available, but one of the major new concepts of VS .NET is that your application should be able to be installed simply by copying your application's directory onto a machine (that has the .NET Framework on it). Having information that needs to be available from the Registry can prevent that type of installation from functioning correctly.

Towards the goal of enabling easy application installations and reinstallations, .NET introduces a new system for storing your application settings, one that is more similar to the older technology of .ini files than the Registry. This new system works through the use of configuration files, XML documents that can be associated with an entire machine or with individual applications. After you complete this simple setup, I will cover the use of configuration files in the next section.

Test the Project

Now back to the original goal of creating a setup file. Edit the connection string as required to make sure that it can correctly connect to a SQL Server and find the Pubs sample database. With that complete, run the project to make sure that it works correctly and that you see a list of Author names in the list box control. If everything works, and you have provided something other than (local) for the server name in your connection string, then you have a completed application that you can build a setup program for.

Adding the Setup Project

In VS .NET, you add deployment projects to the solution containing one or more other projects that you want to deploy. In this case, we have a single project that will produce an .exe file, and the end result needs to be the installation of that file onto the target machine. To build a setup for this application, add a new project to the current solution (by selecting File, Add Project, New Project from the menu) and choose the Setup Wizard (see Figure 19.1) because it is a good starting point.

When you add this project, it automatically starts the wizard (see Figure 19.2).

This wizard understands that it is part of a solution, and its options are based on the other projects available in that solution. The default setting for installer type (see Figure 19.3) is to create an installation for a Windows application, and that is what you want to use for this example. In the next screen (see Figure 19.4) you are given the choice of what your setup program is going to deploy, and the choices reflect the various parts available from the other projects in this solution. For this example, we want to deploy the output of our simple Windows application, which is an .exe file in this case, but we also could use the installer to deploy our source, debug files, or other content. For this example, choose Primary Output from AuthorList.

FIGURE 19.1

You can use the Setup Wizard, or you can just choose Setup Project to add all the files you need individually.

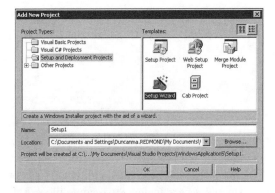

FIGURE 19.2

The Setup Wizard walks you through creating a simple installation project for your solution.

FIGURE 19.3

If you want to create a graphical install onto a Windows machine, choose the default setup for a Windows application.

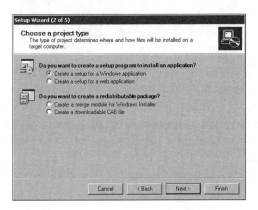

19

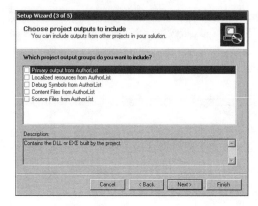

In addition to the outputs from one or more of our projects (if more than one project was
in the solution, other than the setup project, then all the projects would have been included in the outputs list), you also can choose any additional files you want to include (see
Figure 19.5). In my example, I have included a readme file, but this could be your
method for deploying almost any type of file including some XML content or even an
Access database (.mdb file).

FIGURE **19.5**

*Adding readme files,
.config files, and docu-
mentation are just a
few of the uses for the
additional files section
of the Setup project.*

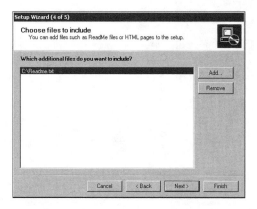

Finally, a summary screen (see Figure 19.6) is displayed, and the wizard is complete
when you click Finish. At this point, the setup project has to do some thinking to determine the dependencies of your chosen outputs, by inspecting the corresponding project
files. When this is done, you can see the Setup project in your Solution Explorer and,
within the Dependencies subfolder, the dependencies that it has discovered. Using the
properties window for the project itself and for its various files, you can modify how the
setup program will be created, but for now, I will just leave everything as it is.

FIGURE 19.6

The summary window gives you some basic information about what the Setup project will create, but the actual work does not start until you click Finish.

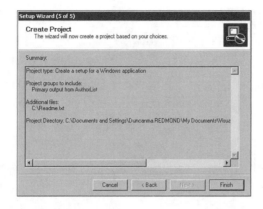

Building the Setup

Just like any other project, to create the output of this setup project, you need to build it. Press Ctrl+Shift+B, or select Build, Build Solution from the menu to build all the projects in the solution, including the new setup project. This build takes some time, and it is basically all due to the setup project, which is compressing all the required .NET redistributable files into a single .msi file. Several other files will be built and included into the output directory of your setup project, but these other files are really just support files for the Windows Installer technology.

Visual Studio .NET uses version 2.0 of Windows Installer, which might be the version currently installed on your target machine. If it is not already on the machine, these support files will allow the user to install it. If you can be sure that all users have the right version of the Windows Installer, due to their OS version for instance, or because they all have another .NET program installed, then you can choose to include nothing but the .msi file in your deployment. The settings that control the inclusion of these installs can be found by ensuring that your Setup project is selected and then selecting Properties from the Project menu (see Figure 19.7).

19

Note

The term *target machine* generally refers to the machine that will be running the application and that needs the application files installed onto it. The target is pretty clear when you are talking about Windows applications—every user's machine—but keep in mind that with Web applications (WebForms, for instance), the target machine is the Web server, not the end user's machine.

FIGURE 19.7

If you are not sure what version (if any) of the Windows Installer will be available on the target machine, make sure that you include the files required to update or install the proper version.

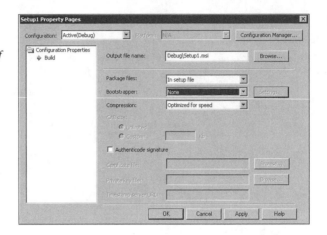

In the dependencies folder of your setup project, you will see a variety of files, all of which are required for your application to run. Now, you might know that you do not need to install a certain file or files, but the setup program will include them regardless. If you want to force the exclusion of a file, right-click on that file and select Exclude from the menu that appears. You also can view the properties for a file and change the Exclude property to True if you want; both will have the same effect. A common reason to exclude files is that you know the .NET Framework is already installed, and you want to try and reduce the size of your installation accordingly.

That completes the creation of a simple setup program, but the real test is to take that .msi file (which, at the time of this writing, is compressed to approximately 25 MB) and deploy it onto a target machine. Simply copy the file (which will be in the debug directory under your setup project's folder) across to the target, or place it onto a CD. Then on the target machine, right-click on the .msi file and select Install. At this point, you will get an error if you do not have the newest Windows Installer version on the target machine, but otherwise the install should proceed along and place the .NET Framework and your .exe onto the target machine.

You might have a bit of trouble finding what it has installed, though, but it places the files into the target machine's \Program Files\<Setup Project Author>\<Setup Title>\, which by default turns into \Program Files\Microsoft\Setup1\. Before you build a setup program for your own purposes, make sure that you change the Author and Setup Title properties, which are available through the properties window of the Setup project.

Configuration Files

Configuration files are XML documents associated with your .NET application based on name and location. These configuration files follow the simple naming format of the complete name of the applications (AuthorList.exe, for example) followed by .config (producing AuthorList.exe.config) and are located in the same directory as the applications themselves. The content of the document is standard XML, but the actual format (or *schema*, in XML terms) is dictated by .NET. Searching in the .NET Framework documentation for "configuration file schema" produces several helpful results that detail how to create your own configuration files.

A basic introduction is that the file consists of one or more sections, each of which has its own name and contains related settings. Each configuration section must be described as a row inside a set of `<configSections> </configSections>` tags. Configuration files exist at the machine level as well, though, and sections described at that level can then be used (without redescribing) in your application-specific config files. One of the main sections, `AppSettings`, is predescribed in the machine configuration file, so you can just go ahead and use it for your application configuration. I have built a configuration file for the Author List application, as an example of how you could use this type of file, and the file itself is provided below. This file contains within the `AppSettings` section, a single row with a name of `"Server"` and a value of `"Olivaw"`, representing the name of my SQL Server:

```
<configuration>
    <appSettings>
        <add key="Server" value="Olivaw" />
    </appSettings>
</configuration>
```

Now, back in my code, I need to make changes so that the hard-coded server name in the connection string is loaded from the configuration file instead. The modified version of `LoadAuthors` that has been rewritten to use the configuration file to determine the SQL Server name, is provided in Listing 19.2.

19

LISTING 19.2 Using a Configuration File to Make Your Code More Flexible

```
1      Private Sub LoadAuthors()
2          Dim sConnectionString As String
3          sConnectionString = "Data Source=" & GetServerName() & ";" & _
4              "Initial Catalog=Pubs;" & _
5              "User ID=sa;password=daneel"
6          Dim connPubs As New SqlConnection(sConnectionString)
7          Dim cmdAuthors As New SqlCommand( _
8                  "Select au_fname + ' ' + au_lname as Name from Authors", _
9                   connPubs)
10         Dim daAuthors As New SqlDataAdapter(cmdAuthors)
11         Dim dsAuthors As New DataSet("Authors")
12
13         connPubs.Open()
```

LISTING 19.2 continued

```
14          daAuthors.Fill(dsAuthors, "Authors")
15
16          lbAuthors.DataSource = dsAuthors.Tables(0).DefaultView
17          lbAuthors.DisplayMember = "Name"
18     End Sub
19
20     Private Function GetServerName() As String
21          Dim sServerName As String
22          sServerName = _
23              Configuration.ConfigurationSettings.AppSettings.Get("Server")
24          Return sServerName
25     End Function
```

ANALYSIS Line 22 does all the actual work with the configuration file, work that is made much simpler because my configuration file used only built-in sections. If I wanted to include my own sections, I would have to describe the new section as a row within the configSections block of the application or machine configuration files and then add the individual settings as rows within this new section. In this case, line 22 returns whatever data is in the value attribute of the row, as a string, and I can then use that string in the creation of my connection (line 3).

Multiproject Deployments

The sample application created earlier in today's lesson was contained completely within a single project, but it is common to build systems where some amount of the application's functionality has been placed into one or more other components. When you build these systems in Visual Studio .NET, you usually will have all the involved projects (at least those that you or your group are in control of) as part of a single solution. In such a situation, the options presented to you by the Setup Wizard will be different because the Setup Wizard doesn't really understand which project is the "main" application.

To illustrate this point, I will break that single application into two projects, by removing the data access code from the first project and placing it into a separate code library. The code, as it is now, is shown in Listing 19.2 and is encapsulated into the LoadAuthors subroutine. Add a new project to the current solution, a Visual Basic Class Library, and name it PubsDataAccess. This new project will contain a single class file, which starts out basically empty and named Class1.vb. Rename the file and the class itself to GetAuthors (GetAuthors.vb for the filename) and then replace its contents with the code from Listing 19.3.

LISTING 19.3   Using a Separate Class to Isolate Your Data Access Code

```
 1 Option Explicit On
 2 Option Strict On
 3
 4 Imports System
 5 Imports System.Data
 6 Imports System.Data.SqlClient
 7
 8 Public Class GetAuthors
 9
10     Public Function AuthorList(ByVal sServerName As String) As DataSet
11         Dim sConnectionString As String
12         sConnectionString = "Data Source=" & sServerName & ";" & _
13             "Initial Catalog=Pubs;" & _
14             "User ID=sa;password=daneel"
15         Dim connPubs As New SqlConnection(sConnectionString)
16         Dim cmdAuthors As New SqlCommand( _
17             "Select au_fname + ' ' + au_lname as Name from Authors", _
18             connPubs)
19         Dim daAuthors As New SqlDataAdapter(cmdAuthors)
20         Dim dsAuthors As New DataSet("Authors")
21
22         connPubs.Open()
23         daAuthors.Fill(dsAuthors, "Authors")
24
25         Return dsAuthors
26
27     End Function
28 End Class
```

19

ANALYSIS   Notice that the single method of this class, AuthorList (line 10), takes a server name as a parameter, allowing us to pass that information in from the main application. The original application now needs to be rewritten to use the new library, which also requires adding a reference to the project. To add the reference, you right-click on the References folder (of the original project) and select Add Reference. This brings up the Add Reference dialog, at which point you can find the new class library project under the Projects tab (see Figure 19.8). Make sure that the PubsDataAccess project is highlighted and then click OK to add a reference to the main project.

With that reference added, you can rewrite the code behind your form to use the library, creating the code in Listing 19.4.

LISTING 19.4   Adding Code to Load Values into Your Application

```
1 Dim sServerName As String
2 Private Sub LoadAuthors()
3     Dim dsAuthors As DataSet
```

LISTING 19.4   continued

```
 4      Dim objDA As New PubsDataAccess.GetAuthors()
 5
 6      dsAuthors = objDA.AuthorList(sServerName)
 7
 8      lbAuthors.DataSource = dsAuthors.Tables(0).DefaultView
 9      lbAuthors.DisplayMember = "Name"
10: End Sub
11
12 Private Sub frmDisplayAuthors_Load _
13 (ByVal sender As System.Object, _
14  ByVal e As System.EventArgs) _
15 Handles MyBase.Load
15      sServerName = _
   Configuration.ConfigurationSettings.AppSettings.Get("Server")
17 End Sub
```

FIGURE 19.8

*The Projects tab
allows you to directly
reference other pro-
jects in your solution,
or elsewhere, even if
their outputs have not
been built.*

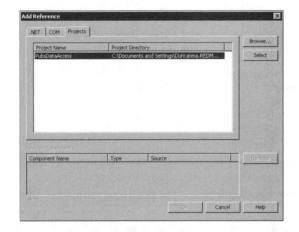

So that we can add another setup project, right-click on the setup project and select Remove to take it out of the current solution. Right-click the solution and select Add, New Project from the context menu that appears, and you will bring up the New Project dialog. Select the Setup Wizard for a project type, enter a different name than the default to avoid conflicting with the project you created earlier, and then click OK. The same Setup Wizard as last time should appear, but one of the steps, Choose Project Outputs to Include, will show you some different information than the last time you ran this wizard. This time, the output files from both the main application and your new library will be shown (see Figure 19.9).

FIGURE 19.9

When building a setup in a solution with more than one project (excluding the setup itself), all the possible outputs from all the projects will be available to your setup program.

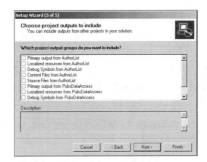

Despite the differences and all the options that are now visible in the Choose Project Outputs step, you should still choose only the primary output from the main application. In this case, that is AuthorList, the project containing the single Windows Form, so you need to select only the primary outputs from that single project. After you have selected the desired outputs, finish the wizard. The Setup Wizard then determines the dependencies of the selected output(s), and, in this case, it finds an additional dependency on the PubsDataAccess DLL. Because of this dependency, the required DLL will be installed, even though you didn't choose it as one of the desired outputs. If you were to select the outputs of both, this would not cause the installation to fail, although you would get a warning during the building of your setup file: "WARNING: Two or more objects have the same target location ('[targetdir]\pubsdataaccess.dll')".

Installing this project will seem no different to the end user, even though it will be installing an additional library, and everything is still going onto the same target machine.

Summary

Deploying systems is one of the final steps in creating an application, and it often is much more complicated than developers expect. .NET has made deployment much simpler, but only by building your application and your setup and then testing deployment to as many machines as possible will you have any certainty that your real deployment stage will succeed.

Q&A

Q. **Windows Installer technology appears to have many more options than what I can find in the Setup and Deployment projects. How can I build a setup with features like I see in commercial installations?**

A. The setup features provided by VS .NET are excellent, but they cover only the basic needs for an installation program. Although there are more features in VS .NET's setup projects than I have shown in today's lesson, to get at all the features available in the Windows Installer technology, you will want to work with a third-party installation program such as Install Shield (`http://www.installshield.com`) or Wise Installer (`http://www.wisesolutions.com`).

Q. I thought I didn't have to write installation programs with .NET, that I could just use XCOPY.

A. That is true, you do not have to provide a setup program for your application, just copying the application directory should provide the functionality you need. But the .NET Framework install is a bit more complex and will be needed on many machines before your application can run. In addition, a .bat file running an XCOPY command should work for you, but a graphical install with dialog boxes and other options is a much more professional option to show your users.

Workshop

The Workshop is designed to help you anticipate possible questions, review what you've learned, and get you thinking about how to put your knowledge into practice. The answers to the quiz are in Appendix A, "Answers to Quizzes/Exercises."

Quiz

1. If you are not sure whether the .NET Framework is available on all your target machines, do you have to build two setups (one with and one without)?

2. If you have created an application that consists of a single main project and several library projects that it uses, do you have to create multiple setups?

3. How do you set up your install to have multiple forms of a single installation, such as a Typical install, a Full install, and a Minimal install?

4. How would you include a configuration file (.config) or other additional files with your installation?

Exercises

1. Build a Windows Forms application that uses a .config file to determine what caption (`Text` property of the `Form`) to place in its Windows's title bar and then create a .config file for it and a setup program. Deploy the project and then try changing the contents of the .config file and rerunning the application.

DAY **20**

Introduction to XML

Unless you've avoided anyone who has looked at, touched, or been in the same building as a computer for the last few years, you might have heard the three-letter acronym "XML." XML (eXtensible Markup Language) is everywhere these days—even appearing in mass market news magazines. Today I will try to cut through some of the hype and examine what XML can do for your programs. In particular, this lesson will focus on

- What is XML?
- Working with XML

What Is XML?

Extensible Markup Language (XML—granted it should have been EML, but that wouldn't have been half as cool a name) is a way of adding information to text. XML is the current popular term in software—entire companies and product lines have been created or modified just to add XML to the product brochures—and there are many myths and misconceptions about what it can do and is intended to do.

Before we deal with the misconceptions, though, let's first look at what it does. XML is a way of adding information to text. What kind of information? Information about the text. It might sound like a circular argument, but I'm serious, and this has a real name—metadata. Metadata is information about information. The formal definition is

> Data about data. Metadata describes how and when and by whom a particular set of data was collected, and how the data is formatted. Metadata is essential for understanding information stored in data warehouses (from Internet.com's Webopedia).

To have one view of metadata, let's examine the book you are currently looking at. Obviously, there is one important part of the book—the information in it. This is the data. In addition, there is more information about the book—the number of lessons, the placement of section headings, and so on. Even the formatting provides more information about the text. If I **bold face** some text, you might assume that it is more important than the surrounding text. This is information about the text in the book—metadata. Metadata is a powerful idea; it gives the information a framework and purpose.

You can add metadata to data in many ways. For example, in a database, metadata is in the form of the names and sizes of the columns in the database tables. It tells you what type of data should be there, how large it is, and perhaps a name that implies the contents. HTML also provides metadata in the form of the relative importance of some text. That is, is it in a heading tag, and if so, what level. However, HTML is not a great example because it is intended to be used for formatting, not identifying information.

One thing that HTML did teach us, however, is the power of using simple tags to add formatting, to add metadata, to text. Tags are the items in angle brackets (like <this>) that you see when you look at HTML. If you have never looked at any HTML, or you just want to see what it looks like, take a look at the source of any Web page. You can do this by selecting View, Source in Internet Explorer. You should see a lot of tags. HTML uses these tags to identify what should be boldfaced text, what should be in italics, where a table or image should go, and so on. It also identifies the end of each of these sections. So, if you were to look at the source of the Web page shown in Figure 20.1, you would see

```
<html><body><strong>April 22, 1970</strong><body><html>
```

The `<strong>` tag marks everything between it and the ending `</strong>` tag as being important, and most browsers will show this in boldface. The `<strong>` tag has added information to the text, so, it's metadata.

XML is similar to HTML; in fact, they are related. Many years ago, just shortly after the dark ages (in the 1960s), a number of researchers, upset at how many ways you could identify an important point, came up with something called Standard Generalized Markup Language (SGML). SGML introduced many innovative ideas:

FIGURE 20.1

A date to remember.

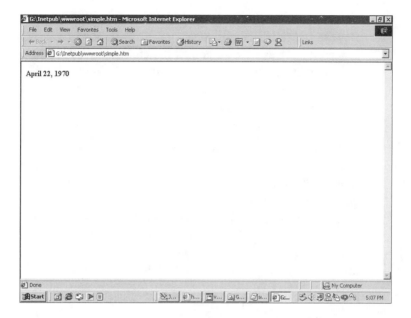

- You should mark the beginning of a section of information with a marker.

- The marker should identify itself as such by using a set of characters that rarely appear in normal writing. In their case, the SGML authors chose angle brackets (<>).

- The marker should also have some information, no matter how brief, about the contained information.

- You should mark the end of the information with another marker.

- This related marker should identify itself as being related to the previous marker by using the previous information, with the addition of a character that is unlikely to appear in the original information.

The end result could look much like this:

```
<strong>April 22, 1970</strong>
```

As you can probably guess, HTML is descended from SGML. It is one of many special-purpose uses for SGML. You see, SGML was not really a way of marking up specific documents, but instead was a way of identifying the types of tags you might add to a document, and, therefore, the way of identifying the metadata about a document. People would then create a definition of a document (that is, a list of the tags you might use) and begin to use that definition to create documents. HTML, therefore, identified a number of tags that could be used for formatting, and people used these tags to create all the lovely pages that exist on the World Wide Web (WWW).

20

XML is a cousin to HTML—that is, they both inherit a lot of ideas from SGML. However, XML is more like SGML than HTML. Rather than defining a specific type of document (such as a Web page), XML defines a way of identifying the parts of a document (like SGML did). It uses the same basic ideas of SGML; it uses tags to mark the beginning and end of a section of information. These tags are angle-bracketed words that should give information about the contained information. In other words, it looks just like the two previous chunks of HTML and SGML.

Why did the authors of XML create something so close to the two existing standards? They did this because SGML is complex, and HTML is really only intended for adding formatting information to a document. XML was intended to be a simplified SGML that could be used to create a number of industry- or technology-specific sets of tags, or languages. Many of these are available, including languages for describing mathematical equations (MathML), recipes, and even a version of HTML that is defined using XML (XHTML). Each of these languages defines the possible metadata that can be applied to information; however, they all do this while following the rules of XML.

So, what are the rules of XML? They are officially defined as:

- XML shall be straightforwardly usable over the Internet.
- XML shall support a wide variety of applications.
- XML shall be compatible with SGML.
- It shall be easy to write programs which process XML documents.
- The number of optional features in XML is to be kept to the absolute minimum, ideally zero.
- XML documents should be human-legible and reasonably clear.
- The XML design should be prepared quickly.
- The design of XML shall be formal and concise.
- XML documents shall be easy to create.
- Terseness in XML markup is of minimal importance.

So, that is what XML is. What about those misconceptions mentioned previously? There seem to be a lot of them. Many have been caused by the way various marketing departments promoted their company's use of XML; others were caused by writers giving people strange ideas about XML, but of course I'm not one of *them*.

The main misconceptions I see frequently are

- You have to choose between Visual Basic .NET and XML. Although XML is a language, it is not a programming language like Visual Basic .NET. People seem to get confused about that "language" part and start to ask questions such as, "Should

I learn Visual Basic .NET or XML?" XML is not a programming language, only a way to describe information.

- XML is complicated and difficult to read. Some people look at all the tags and end tags and get confused. Why add all this "stuff" to the document when *X* (some other technique) does the same thing? The answer is simple: It is an easy way to identify the parts of a document. For example, many people suggest that something called *Comma-separated values* (CSV) is better than XML because it is simpler, is easy to produce, and the files are smaller (see next point). However, which of these two listings tells you more about the displayed information:

```
<employees>
  <employee id="1">
      <firstname>John</firstname>
      <lastname>Bull</lastname>
  </employee>
  <employee id="2">
      <firstname>Mary</firstname>
      <lastname>Tell</lastname>
  </employee>
</employees>

1, John, Bull
2, Mary, Tell
```

Personally, I find the first (the XML) much more readable.

- XML is slow to work with (or too big). This often comes from those old-timers who feel that if you are using one character too many, you are wasting memory/processor speed/effort. Although I sometimes suffer from this affliction, XML is not one of the areas where it happens. The argument you might hear goes something like, "All those tags and end tags take up a lot of space, and take a long time to move around. We should use *X* (fill in something here that they like more) instead." Most of you who are reading this can probably remember the result of such thinking: it was called the Y2K bug. There is such a thing (in my opinion) as over-optimized code. Sometimes using a less-efficient technique that makes it easier to understand intent is far superior (again, just my opinion). XML is one of those less efficient, but more understandable techniques.

20

- The answer is XML. What is the question? XML is not going to solve world hunger, prevent war, or even make coffee for you in the morning. All it wants to do is tell you about a block of text. Many people try to make XML the solution to everything, or try to apply it where it might not, or should not, fit. If it seems like it is causing more problems than you want to solve, or even if it isn't solving any problems, don't use it. Find another, better solution.

Elements

A number of items can be used to create an XML document; however, you will find two important parts in almost every XML document—elements and attributes.

An *element* is the fundamental building block of every XML file. It consists of a start tag, the end tag, and the content in between. As an example, there are three elements in the following XML:

```
<employee id="1">
    <firstname>John</firstname>
    <lastname>Bull</lastname>
</employee>
```

One element is employee. The employee element begins with the employee tag (`<employee>`), ends with the end employee tag (`</employee>`), and contains the other two tags, `<firstname>` and `<lastname>`. The first name element begins with the `<firstname>` tag, ends with the `</firstname>` end tag, and contains the text, John.

Elements define the important "things" in the XML file. The preceding XML obviously describes an employee of a company, and that employee has a first name and a last name. To tie this into previous days' lessons—elements are similar to the objects and properties we looked at on Day 7, "Working with Objects." This could describe an employee object that has two properties.

Attributes

Although the majority of any XML file will be elements, attributes also can be in the file. Attributes are used to provide extra information about an element.

If you have used HTML in the past, you will likely know what an attribute is. For example, in the HTML fragment

```
<a href="http://msdn.microsoft.com/vbasic">Visual Basic Home Page</a>
```

the href is an attribute that defines a location for the a (or anchor) element. It defines where the anchor element should direct your browser when you click on it. For those who have not looked at HTML, the previous line of code would add a hyperlink (one of those underlined links) to a Web page.

Similarly, other attributes provide information for other elements. This leads to one of the biggest differences between attributes and elements: attributes cannot stand alone and need to be applied to elements. An attribute always appears within the opening tag of an element. In addition, it always has the following form:

```
name="value"
```

That is, an attribute is composed of two parts: a name and a value. The name must be unique within each element, although two elements can have the same attribute. In addition, an element can have many attributes.

Note

The XML community has two camps. On one side are the people who suggest that you should use elements everywhere. All bits of information should be elements contained within other elements. The reasoning can often be boiled down into, "While it might seem like a property now, later you might need to have something as a property of it." For example, think of how you might need to further define an address property into street, city, and postal code properties. These "nothing but elements" people would define our John Bull using the following XML:

```
<employee>
  <id>1</id>
  <firstname>John</firstname>
  <lastname>Bull</lastname>
</employee>
```

On the other side are those who suggest that if a piece of information is about another element (like a property to an object), it should be an attribute. This makes the XML files smaller and in some ways more readable. These people would have our Johnny written as follows:

```
<employee id="1" firstname="John" lastname="Bull" />
```

Obviously, you are free to use whichever of the two, or even a hybrid of the two, as your style. However, keep in mind a couple of points when deciding whether something should be an element or an attribute:

- An attribute cannot have children. This means that making something an attribute is a one-way street. You cannot later decide to add new information without changing the structure of a file. Elements, on the other hand, allow you to later add new child elements or attributes as needed.

- An attribute-heavy document generally is smaller than an element-heavy document. The more attributes you have in your XML compared to the number of elements, the smaller the XML. This is primarily because attributes don't have a close tag.

20

Schemas

Although schemas are not truly a part of XML, they do play an important part in using XML, and this will become more important as schemas become an official standard. As I write this, XML Schemas have just become a Recommended Standard. XML Schemas are, first and foremost, an application of XML. That is, they are written in XML, just as the files we created earlier. Just like any other XML, they are information about information (metadata—tired of hearing that term yet?). XML Schemas define a proper way of structuring an XML file. This includes the data types for each of the elements and attributes, what can be a child element of any other element, even what are valid elements for a given file.

Some of you might be wondering why schemas are even required. Didn't I say that you could build an XML file containing any combination of elements and attributes? Well, yes, I suppose so. However, there is a difference between building an XML file to contain some data and XML that defines a specific type of data. For example, if you are working with a file containing employee data, you might expect to see certain items—name, employee ID, some contact information, and so on. However, you have no idea of where in the file this information is, nor what the tags might be called. Without a schema, you would have to look at the file and write specific code to read each file. With a schema, you know the structure of the data beforehand. Not every field is required, nor even necessarily in the same spot from one file to another, but you will certainly know what the fields are called and have enough information to retrieve it either via the DOM or using an `XMLTextReader`. We will look at these objects in a moment. Figure 20.2 shows a simple XML Schema.

Note

If you have done previous reading, or if you decide to do further reading on XML, you will come across the idea of a Document Type Definition (DTD). DTDs were an earlier attempt at defining proper structure for XML files. In fact, DTDs date back to SGML. DTDs seem to perform the same task as XML Schemas; however, there are some important differences:

- XML Schemas are written using XML; DTDs are not. DTDs use a similar but non-XML format for defining the proper structure for an XML file. This is important because it means that you need one set of tools for working with DTDs, and another for dealing with the resulting XML. Because XML Schemas are XML, you can work on them with the same tools.

- DTDs do not define the types of the information. DTDs describe the structure of the information (that is, what elements can be contained by another), but not whether a given element should be an integer, string, or other type of information. XML Schemas provide the capability of adding this information.

As has been described many times already in this book, one of the core goals of Visual Basic .NET is to make working with complex technologies easier. Therefore, it shouldn't come as a surprise that Visual Basic .NET has an editor to allow you to view and edit XML Schemas. Creating schemas also has a happy side effect in that it makes working with XML documents easier, as well. Figure 20.2 shows a simple XML Schema. This is a graphical editor that allows you to create the various types and structures that XML Schemas are composed of. After you have created a schema, you can attach it to an XML file, and Visual Basic .NET will provide Intellisense for the elements and attributes defined in the schema (see Figure 20.3).

FIGURE 20.2

Creating an XML Schema with Visual Basic .NET.

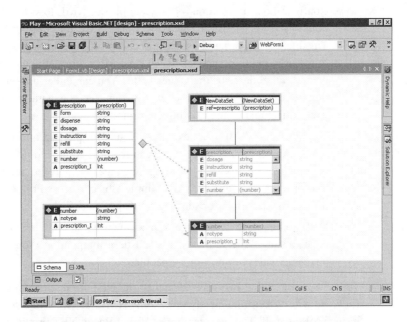

FIGURE 20.3

IntelliSense with XML.

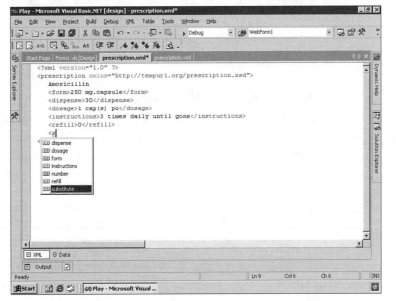

20

Working with XML

Now that you have a general understanding of just what this beast called XML is, how can you use it in your applications? XML is flexible in its use. There are many possible uses, but the most common are

- Configuration information—Many people use XML to store configuration information. In fact, Visual Basic .NET itself uses XML for configuration information. This includes information such as security settings for Web applications, locations of required modules, and so on. Using XML to format your configuration files allows you to describe the values better. You can either use the existing configuration file or create your own. Creating your own is generally safer because you won't affect any of the existing configuration.
- Data passing—XML is an excellent format for passing information between computers. Any computer receiving it can read the contained information, regardless of operating system, or programming language. We will see one example of this tomorrow as we look at SOAP (Simple Object Access Protocol); however, you can use your own format for sending XML just as easily.
- Data storage—XML is a great replacement for small databases. It allows you to create a simple file format that is self-describing, allows for relationships, and can be edited with programs or by people.

Today, we will look at two ways Visual Basic .NET makes it easy to work with XML files. We will concentrate mostly on reading XML, but we will also look at how you can write XML as well. The two techniques Visual Basic .NET provides for working with XML are

- The Document Object Model
- Readers and Writers

The Document Object Model

The Document Object Model (DOM) is an awkward way of saying, "The standard way of reading and writing XML," but that is what it is. The DOM represents the World Wide Web Consortium's (www.w3.org) recommended standard programming interface for working with XML. This is the same organization that standardized XML and all its related technologies. A version of the DOM is available on most popular operating systems, usable from most programming languages, including Visual Basic .NET. It is an Application Programming Interface (API) for querying XML files.

The idea behind the DOM is that any XML file can be described in terms of a tree of nodes. Figure 20.4 shows what this could look like conceptually, given the following XML example:

FIGURE 20.4

Logical structure of an XML file.

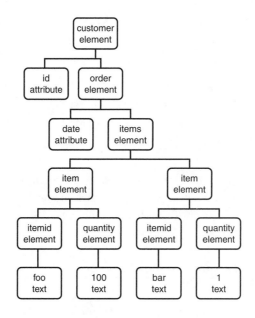

```
<?xml version="1.0"?>
<customer id="12345">
  <order date="04/01/01">
    <items>
      <item>
        <itemid>foo</itemid>
        <quantity>100</quantity>
      </item>
      <item>
        <itemid>bar</itemid>
        <quantity>1</quantity>
      </item>
    </items>
  </order>
</customer>
```

20

There are two ways of looking at any of the nodes in a DOM. In one sense, they are all nodes. However, they are also specific types of nodes. For example, the node called order represents an element node, whereas the node called date is an attribute node. Each type of node supports all the capabilities of a generic node, as well as specific methods and properties for the type of node they are. Table 20.1 describes the most commonly used types of nodes.

TABLE 20.1   Commonly Used Nodes in an XML File

Node Type	Description
XmlElement	Represents an element in an XML file.
XmlAttribute	Represents an attribute in an XML file.
XmlDocument	Represents the document as a whole.
XmlComment	Represents a comment in an XML file. Comments in XML begin with `<!--` and end with `-->`.

One benefit of having the various types of nodes inherit from a single common node is that all nodes share a common set of properties and methods. This allows you to more easily learn how to work with the DOM. Table 20.2 outlines the most frequently used of these common methods and properties.

TABLE 20.2   Common Properties and Methods of All XML Nodes

Member	Description
Properties	
Attributes	Collection of all the attributes for this node. This allows you to navigate through the list of attributes at each level in the hierarchy.
ChildNodes	Collection of all the child nodes for this node. This is one of the main ways of navigating through the DOM, by looping through the children with a `For...Next` loop.
FirstChild	Returns the first child node of the current node. This is the other main way of navigating through the DOM, by finding the first child node and then looping while `NextSibling` (discussed later in the table) returns a value.
InnerText	The text contained within each node. This includes any child nodes contained within the node.
Name	The text in the angle brackets for the current node.
NextSibling	Returns the next available node at the same level as this one. For example, in Figure 20.4, if the current node was stored in the `oNode` variable and pointing at the `item` node, and you call `oNode=oNode.NextSibling`, `oNode` will then be pointing at the next `item` node.
NodeType	Returns the type of the current node—for example, `XmlElement`, `XmlAttribute`, and so on.
Methods	
AppendChild	Adds a new child node onto the current node. This is how you extend a current set of nodes.

Using the XmlDocument to work with XML files is similar to looking at the tree of nodes in Figure 20.4. At the top of the hierarchy is a single root node, customer. This and all other nodes in the DOM have a collection of child nodes. Each of these nodes in turn has child nodes and so on. The objects have methods that assist you in navigating this hierarchy. Table 20.3 describes some of these methods and properties. In addition, the XmlDocument supports the same properties and methods of the XmlNode class.

TABLE 20.3 Methods and Properties of the XmlDocument

Member	Description
Properties	
DocumentElement	The root node for the document.
Methods	
CreateNode	Used to create new nodes to add into the document. This generic method allows you to create any type of XmlNode.
CreateElement	Similar to CreateNode; however, CreateElement is used to create elements. CreateAttribute is used to create

e into the document.

itaining XML into the document.

ocument to a file.

d XML, you generally use ChildNodes

KML, finding the nodes you are inter-

y labor intensive because only the

butes, and so on. After the particular

collection with the AppendChild

g XML files. Generally, it is useful

20

and writing XML, it does suffer from a

se is that when you load an XML doc-

e loaded into memory. At this time, the

DOM builds the entire tree describing the document, with all nodes, node lists, and so on. As you might imagine, if the XML file is large, this could take up a lot of memory.

This process also takes a lot of time, especially if all you need is one or two items from the document.

Visual Basic .NET includes another strategy for working with XML—Readers and Writers. To be more specific, `XmlTextReader` and `XmlTextWriter`. The `XmlTextReader` provides fast, forward-only access to a block of XML, whereas the `XmlTextWriter` provides a small, fast way of writing XML. Although in some ways they are not as intuitive as using the DOM, they do improve on the DOM in two main areas:

- The entire file does not need to be loaded before you begin to process the document—in fact, it does not even need to be available. This might happen if you are downloading an XML file from the Internet. By not needing the entire file in memory, `XmlTextReader` and `XmlTextWriter` can greatly reduce the overall memory requirements of your application.
- `XmlTextReader` and `XmlTextWriter` are fast. Very fast. This is due to the fact that they do not need to build up all the memory structures, such as lists of nodes, that the DOM uses.

There is one downside to working with the `XmlTextReader` and `XmlTextWriter`, however. Because they don't store the whole document in memory, it can sometimes be difficult to relate one part of the document to another. If you need to keep track of multiple parts of the document, and still want to use `XmlTextReader` and `XmlTextWriter`, you must write code yourself to do this.

With the `XmlTextReader`, you read the file by looping through the file with the `Read` method, stopping at each node in the XML document. You then determine whether you're interested in the current node and, if so, use the rest of the properties and methods for the current node. Table 20.4 shows some of the most commonly used methods and properties of the `XmlTextReader`.

TABLE 20.4 Common Properties and Methods of the `XmlTextReader`

Member	*Description*
Properties	
Name	Name of the current node.
NodeType	The type of the current node—that is element, attribute, and so on.
Methods	
Read	Reads the next node in the XML document. Each time this method is called, it moves to the next node.

The XmlTextWriter is used to build up the XML document by adding the individual start and end element tags. It can be a natural way of building up a document by calling methods to create each part. Table 20.5 describes the most commonly used properties and methods of the XmlTextWriter.

TABLE 20.5 Common Properties and Methods of the XmlTextWriter

Member	Description
Properties	
Formatting	Used to set that the resulting XML is formatted. Generally, if the resulting XML is intended to be read by a human, this should be set to Formatting.Indented because it creates a more legible document. Alternatively, if this property is not set, or set to Formatting.None, all the XML will appear on a single line.
Methods	
Close	Closes the writer. As with other writers you have seen, you should always close the writer when you are finished using it.
WriteElementString	Creates a new element in the document. This new element includes the start and end tags, as well as any text in the element. This is the method you should use when creating a standalone element that does not have any child nodes.
WriteStartElement	Creates a new element in the document. This method only creates the start tag for the element. This is the method you should use when creating elements that do have child nodes.
WriteEndElement	Writes the end tag for the current element.

Reading XML

Although you could use the IndexOf and SubString methods of the String class to read XML and determine the contents, it is not the most efficient way of reading XML. Instead, you should use either the DOM, or XmlTextReader objects to read XML. These two families of objects can more easily interpret XML files.

The DOM is more appropriate if you need to read an entire XML file into memory and work with it. As described earlier, the DOM allows you to move forward and backward through the file, relate one section to another, and alter the file as you read it. Alternatively, the XmlTextReader is most appropriate when all you need to do is read once through the file.

To see how the two sets of objects work, it would be good to see them in action in a sample. Many applications need to be customized by the users, as you might do in the

20

settings in the Tools, Options dialog. This information can be easily stored in an XML file, allowing you or your users to easily read or change settings. Putting the code for this functionality into a component allows you to more easily reuse the capability. Settings is a class that allows you to store configuration settings in a file and to read them back later. The contents of the file will look similar to Figure 20.5. Creating such a class assists you in allowing the user to customize the application to her needs. Listing 20.1 shows the basic properties and methods of this class. You will later add the capability to read and write the settings to this class.

FIGURE 20.5

Configuration file.

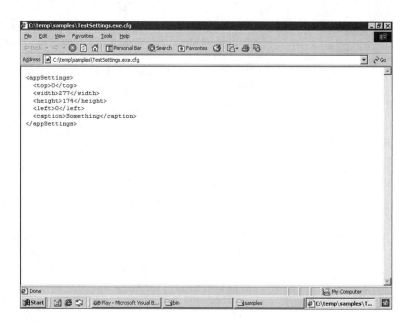

LISTING 20.1 AppSettings Class

```
1 Imports System.Xml
2
3 Public Class Settings
4     Private m_sFileName As String
5     Private m_oItems As Hashtable
6
7     Public Sub New()
8         Me.FileName = AppDomain.CurrentDomain.BaseDirectory & _
9                 AppDomain.CurrentDomain.FriendlyName & ".cfg"
10    End Sub
11
12    Public Sub New(ByVal fileName As String)
13        Me.FileName = fileName
14    End Sub
15
16    Public Property FileName() As String
```

LISTING **20.1**   continued

```
17            Get
18                Return m_sFileName
19            End Get
20            Set(ByVal Value As String)
21                m_sFileName = Value
22                LoadDOM()
23            End Set
24      End Property
25
26      Public Property Items() As Hashtable
27            Get
28                Return m_oItems
29            End Get
30            Set(ByVal Value As Hashtable)
31                m_oItems = Value
32            End Set
33      End Property
34
35 End Class
```

ANALYSIS   The class has two constructors (lines 7–10 and lines 12–14). This was done for flexibility. The programmer can create a new instance of this class by using `oSettings = New Settings()`, in which case the file used is the default, composed of the application name, followed by the extension, `.cfg`. Alternatively, the programmer can create the Settings object by naming the file containing the configuration information, such as `oSettings = New Settings("SomeFile.xml")`. Either way, the `FileName` property is set. After this is done (lines 20–23), the internal variable `m_sFileName` is set, and the `LoadDOM` method (to be written in a moment) is called. This method loads the settings defined in the desired file into the internal HashTable. A HashTable is one of the collections defined in `System.Collections`. It holds a collection of items, stored by name, similar to the `Tables` property of the DataSet. This allows you to retrieve items from the `Items` property using code similar to `oSettings.Items("SomeSetting")`.

Of course, before you can use this class, you should add the functionality to load the settings. Listing 20.2 shows doing this with the `XmlTextReader`, whereas Listing 20.3 shows how this is done with the DOM.

20

LISTING 20.2   Loading Settings Using the `XmlTextReader`

```
36      Public Sub LoadReader()
37          'loads the contents of the setting file into
38          '   the HashTable
39          m_oItems = New Hashtable()
```

LISTING 20.2 continued

```
40          Dim oReader As XmlTextReader
41          Dim sLastElement As String
42
43          Try
44              oReader = New XmlTextReader(FileName)
45              While (oReader.Read)
46                  Select Case oReader.NodeType
47                      Case XmlNodeType.Element
48                          If oReader.Name <> "appSettings" Then
49                              m_oItems.Add(oReader.Name, Nothing)
50                              sLastElement = oReader.Name
51                          End If
52                      Case XmlNodeType.Text
53                          m_oItems.Item(sLastElement) = oReader.Value
54                      Case Else
55                  End Select
56              End While
57          Catch ex As Exception
58          Finally
59              oReader.Close()
60              oReader = Nothing
61          End Try
62      End Sub
```

ANALYSIS The LoadReader method first initializes the HashTable (line 39) and declares the XmlTextReader object and a string variable that will be used during processing. Because this processing is done on a file that might or might not exist, opening and reading the file is protected by wrapping in a Try...End Try block (lines 43–61). As before, the Finally clause of this block (beginning with line 58) guarantees that the reader is closed and destroyed, even if an error occurs.

The bulk of this method is the While...End While loop in lines 45–56. This reads each of the nodes from the file. As each node is read, the code first determines the type of the node (line 46). For this code, we only care about element and text nodes because those are the only types of nodes that exist in the file. If the current node is an element but isn't the appSettings node (the root node), the code adds a new item into the HashTable (line 49) and saves the name of this newly added item to the string variable. The next Read should then return the text node associated with the element, and this is used to add the value to the last item added to the HashTable. At the end of the routine, the HashTable should contain all the settings stored in the file.

LISTING 20.3   Loading Settings Using the DOM

```
63      Public Sub LoadDOM()
64          m_oItems = New Hashtable()
65          Dim oDoc As New XmlDocument()
66          Dim oNode As XmlElement
67
68          Try
69              oDoc.Load(FileName)
70
71              oNode = oDoc.DocumentElement.FirstChild
72              Do While Not IsNothing(oNode)
73                  m_oItems.Add(oNode.Name, oNode.InnerText)
74                  oNode = oNode.NextSibling
75              Loop
76
77          Catch ex As Exception
78          Finally
79              oDoc = Nothing
80          End Try
81      End Sub
```

ANALYSIS   The code begins similarly to the previous listing by initializing the HashTable. Here, however, the code creates an XmlDocument and an XmlElement to store the nodes as the file is read. Again, a Try...End Try block is used to protect if an error occurs while reading the file. First, the file is loaded (line 69). Recall that at this stage the entire file is loaded into memory, and the DOM is constructed. At line 71, two bits of navigation are performed. First, the DocumentElement (the appSettings node) is selected; then the FirstChild of this node is selected. After this code completes, the result should be that oNode is pointing at the first node contained within the appSettings node. The code then loops through the siblings of this node, adding items into the HashTable. When there are no siblings, the NextSibling method returns Nothing, and the loop will complete. As before, the XmlDocument is set to nothing (line 79) when complete.

You can now add this class to other projects, or add it to a class library of your own and compile it into a DLL. When finished, you can use this class as shown in Listing 20.4 to configure your application.

20

LISTING 20.4   Using the Settings Class

```
1:      Private Sub frmTest_Load(ByVal sender As System.Object, _
2:          ByVal e As System.EventArgs) _
3:          Handles MyBase.Load
4:              ''comments: blah
5:              oSettings = New Settings()
6:              With Me
```

LISTING 20.4 continued

```
 7:              .Height = oSettings.Items("height")
 8:              .Width = oSettings.Items("width")
 9:              .Left = oSettings.Items("left")
10              .Top = oSettings.Items("top")
11              .Text = oSettings.Items("caption")
12          End With
13      End Sub
```

ANALYSIS To read the settings and assign them to the current application, you first initialize the Settings object (line 5). Remember that it loads the settings at this point. Then, read each of the settings and assign them to the desired property of the form, a control on the form, or use as needed (lines 6–12).

Writing XML

Just as when reading XML, it is possible to create XML by simply using strings. That is, you can create XML by adding the appropriate start and end element tags to a string variable. However, it is much more likely that you will create a correct XML file if you use the DOM or XmlTextWriter classes.

Listing 20.5 shows the code required to save the configuration information in the Settings object using the XmlTextWriter, whereas Listing 20.6 shows the same code for the XmlDocument objects. This should be added to the Settings object created earlier.

LISTING 20.5 Writing Configuration Settings with XmlTextWriter

```
82    Public Sub SaveWriter()
83        Dim oWriter As XmlTextWriter
84        Dim oItem As DictionaryEntry
85
86        oWriter = New XmlTextWriter(m_sFileName, Nothing)
87        oWriter.Formatting = Formatting.Indented
88        oWriter.WriteStartElement("appSettings")
89
90        For Each oItem In m_oItems
91            oWriter.WriteElementString(oItem.Key, oItem.Value)
92        Next
93        oWriter.WriteEndElement()
94
95        oWriter.Flush()
96        oWriter.Close()
97
98    End Sub
```

ANALYSIS The `SaveWriter` method begins by instantiating the needed variables. One variable that might seem odd is the oItem object declared on line 84. The items in a HashTable are `DictionaryEntry` items; therefore, to allow using a `For Each...Next` loop for processing the HashTable, we need one of these objects.

The writing code begins by opening the file (line 86) and assigning the formatting to be indented. Remember that this is for the benefit of the human reader and is not needed by any of the code. Next, the root node's start element is written (line 88), and each of the items is written to the XML file in the `For Each...Next` loop (lines 90–92). The `WriteElementString` method creates both the start and end tags based on the name of the item in the HashTable, as well as the text in between based on the value of the item in the HashTable. Finally, the end tag for the root node is created (line 93), and the file is closed, writing information to the actual file.

LISTING 20.6 Writing Configuration Settings with the DOM

```
 99    Public Sub SaveDOM()
100        Dim oDoc As New XmlDocument()
101        Dim oRoot As XmlElement
102        Dim oItem As DictionaryEntry
103        Dim oNode As XmlElement
104
105        oRoot = oDoc.CreateElement("appSettings")
106        oDoc.AppendChild(oRoot)
107
108        For Each oItem In m_oItems
109            oNode = oDoc.CreateElement(oItem.Key)
110            oNode.InnerText = oItem.Value
111            oRoot.AppendChild(oNode)
112        Next
113
114        oDoc.Save(m_sFileName)
115    End Sub
```

ANALYSIS The code for writing with the DOM begins by creating the root node and appending it to the document. All other nodes will be appended to this, the `appSettings` node. This is done in a `For Each...Next` loop as was done in the `SaveWriter` method. Each node is created (line 109); the text is assigned (110) and added to the `appSettings` node.

Now that the code has been added to save the settings, you can modify the program that uses it to save the settings for the next time the application is run. This is often done in the Closing event for a Form, as seen in Listing 20.7.

20

LISTING 20.7 Code to Save Settings

```
14      Private Sub frmTest_Closing(ByVal sender As Object, _
15        ByVal e As System.ComponentModel.CancelEventArgs) _
16        Handles MyBase.Closing
17          With Me
18              oSettings.Items("height") = .Height
19              oSettings.Items("width") = .Width
20              oSettings.Items("left") = .Left
21              oSettings.Items("top") = .Top
22              oSettings.Items("caption") = .Text
23          End With
24          oSettings.SaveWriter()
25      End Sub
```

ANALYSIS   Before you can save the settings to the file, they should be copied from the actual values. Typically, you would do this as you close the Tools, Options dialog, or when the application ends. When all configuration settings are copied, you can use either the `SaveWriter` or `SaveDOM` methods to save the settings to the file. When this code has been added, try running the project (see Figure 20.6). Change the size of the Form and move it to another position on the screen. Close the Form, ending the application, and rerun it. You should see the Form in the same position on the screen, the same size as you changed it to. Having your application remember Form positions like this is often appreciated by your users.

FIGURE 20.6

Testing Settings Class.

Summary

XML is one of those technologies that you can look at on many levels. It is simple, yet it has profound repercussions. You can either create it with a program, or in a simple text editor. Similarly, you can write a program to process it, while at the same time it is readable by a human. However you create or process it, XML provides a powerful way to format information. All hype aside, I think it is one of the most important innovations in computing, ranking just behind ASCII. As such, you owe it to yourself to learn at least a little of what it can do for you and your applications.

Tomorrow, we will finish our examination of Visual Basic .NET by looking at a new way of building applications—Web Services. The look at XML will be useful because Web Services use XML extensively.

Q&A

Q. **I've read about another way of processing XML, what is SAX?**

A. SAX (Simple API for XML) is yet another way of reading XML made popular by Java developers and later versions of MSXML (Microsoft's XML parser for COM). It was developed by David Megginson and the XML-DEV mailing list as a lightweight means of reading XML. It is similar to the `XmlTextReader` in that it does not load the entire document into memory. However, in use, it is in many ways the opposite of the `XmlTextReader`. Whereas the `XmlTextReader` is a "pull" model, pulling pieces of the XML out, SAX is an "event" model. As a SAX processor reads an XML file, it fires events, such as `BeginElement`, `EndElement`, `BeginDocument`, and so on. You must write the event handlers you are interested in to process the XML.

Q. **I've heard about a number of other XML related acronyms, such as XSLT, XPath, SOAP, and more. Where can I find out more information about these?**

A. There are many standards and proposed standards for dealing with XML—far too many to cover here. If you are interested in learning more about how to use these other standards, you should pick up a good XML book (there are a lot of them), or find a good community site on the Web that provides this information (`http://msdn.microsoft.com/xml` would be a great starting place).

Q. **I've heard that some languages, such as Java and C#, allow you to add comments to a source file as you are writing it and have these comments converted into documentation. Can I do this with Visual Basic .NET?**

A. Unfortunately, Visual Basic .NET does not currently support this feature. However, a simple version of how to add this to your applications is on the CD for this book (look in the DocGen chapter under today's code) and on the Web site. This application allows you to add `<summary>` tags to each of the methods properties and classes in your application, and have them added to an XML document you can use as the beginnings of documentation for your classes (see Figures 20.7 and 20.8).

20

FIGURE 20.7

XML documentation.

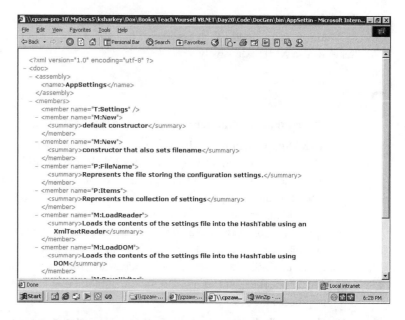

FIGURE 20.8

XML documentation with style sheet applied.

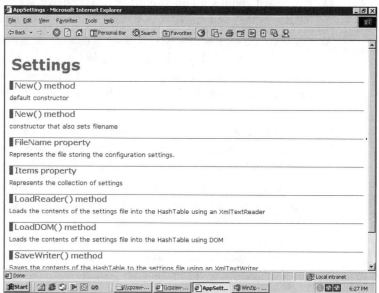

Workshop

The Workshop is designed to help you anticipate possible questions, review what you've learned, and get you thinking about how to put your knowledge into practice. The answers to the quiz are in Appendix A, "Answers to Quizzes/Exercises."

Quiz

1. How can I quickly add a new element, including the start and end tags and some text, to an XML file using an `XmlTextWriter`?

2. When would you choose to use the DOM for reading an XML file over the `XmlTextReader` class?

3. What's metadata?

Exercises

The code shown in today's lesson that tests the `Settings` class is currently hard-coded to use the `LoadDOM` method to load the settings and the `SaveWriter` method to save them. Write another test form that saves a number of settings and allows the user to select which of the two methods to use for saving and retrieving.

20

DAY 21

Creating Web Services with Visual Basic .NET

Unless you've been living under a rock (or on a South Pacific island, waiting to get voted off) for the last few years, you've probably heard of the Internet. It's this amazing thing—imagine a worldwide network—oh, you've heard of it. At any rate, the Internet is a valuable tool for developers to take advantage of. It provides an essentially free network you can use to pass information from your programs to others, wherever in the world they happen to be. So, creating programs that use the Internet is obviously very important for Visual Basic .NET developers. Today, you will learn

- What a Web Service is
- SOAP (and what it has to do with Web Services)
- How to create a Web Service in Visual Basic .NET
- How to create a Web Service client in Visual Basic .NET

What Is a Web Service?

It's obvious to anyone who has ever used the World Wide Web that there are a lot of services available on it. You use them almost everywhere; search engine services, shopping cart services, services that retrieve information, and so on. So, why have a lesson on creating Web Services in a book on Visual Basic? Today's lesson explains the difference between a service on the Web, and a Web Service.

 Note For the sake of clarity, I'll refer to regular web services in lowercase, and the Web Services created in Visual Basic .NET in mixed case.

You interact with a "normal" web service by browsing to some page on the Internet, filling in a form, and sending that information to some other Web page. It is easy, and that ease of use has definitely contributed to the growth and popularity of the Internet. However, there is no easy way to take the information you get from that web service, and use it in a program. For example, you might use a service on the Web to look up the current value of a stock you're interested in. Usually, you type in the symbol of the stock, click a button, and get a Web page that includes the current stock price. Often, you'll also get other information as well, such as the opening and closing prices, the change since the previous close, and perhaps a chart of the recent stock changes. All of this is very handy when you're browsing the Web, but, if all you wanted was to obtain the current stock price and use it in another program, you're forced to do one of two things:

- Have the user browse for the information, fill out the form, wait for the results, and then type it into your program. The problem here is fairly obvious—most users aren't going to want to do this too often. Imagine trying to do this with some value, such as the price of stocks, where the value changes frequently. Imagine trying to persuade someone to enter information into a Web page, click a button, and type the one value into your program more often than once or twice an hour.

- Have your program browse to the Web page (in the background), parse (read) the Web page, and extract the information you want. This is often known as *scrubbing* a Web page. The problem here is if the authors of the page change the layout, you are forced to change your program to parse the new layout. In addition, if you decide to change the web site you are using for your information you will likely also have to rewrite the code that parses the Web page.

So, what about Web Services? Web Services are programs that provide some service on the Internet, but that are designed to allow other programs to communicate with them, rather than have humans work with them. So now, someone could create a Web Service that allows other programmers to retrieve stock prices, do searches, and so on. One nice feature of Web Services is that they can be written on any operating system, in any programming language. They use a message format that can be read and written to easily.

Visual Basic .NET makes creating these Web Services as easy as creating any other type of application. The details of creating and reading the message are hidden from view by Visual Basic .NET itself. Similarly, Visual Basic .NET makes using Web Services as easy as calling any other object, even though it could exist across the Internet, and even be written in another programming language, or running on another operating system.

Web Services not only allow two programs to communicate over the Internet, they also allow one program to combine information from multiple Web Services into a single application, potentially increasing the value of the data. For example, a stock application could not only show the current value of a number of different stocks (possibly retrieved from multiple stock Web Services), it could also include current recommendations from analysts based on the displayed stocks, similar company types, news on the company, and so on, all retrieved from a number of different Web Services.

Web Services communicate with one another and with clients using standard Internet protocols. They can use the common HTTP protocol, the same protocol that browsers use. In that case, they use the GET and POST commands that a Web browser uses. Alternatively, a Web Service can use the SOAP to communicate with a client or other service. Using SOAP allows the communication to be richer because SOAP allows for objects to be passed between the two applications, whereas HTTP does not.

The Simple Object Access Protocol

SOAP is a relatively new protocol. It defines a way of formatting an XML message for use as a message. Web Services generally use SOAP to communicate the request and response between two programs. SOAP uses normal Internet protocols, such as HTTP, the protocol used by Web browsers, or SMTP, the protocol that enables Internet e-mail. But, SOAP allows for richer communication than would exist if you were only using simple messages.

SOAP was initially developed by a number of companies, including Microsoft, to allow for rich object-to-object communication between programs. In one sense, the goal of SOAP was to define a way of working with objects over the Internet, using only standard protocols and formats, instead of binary formats and proprietary protocols. After SOAP

21

was available for a while, the developers refined its capabilities. Now SOAP is a general messaging format that can be used by any protocol and that fits many needs beyond the creation of Web Services. However, today's lesson will be looking at SOAP only in the context of its use in creating and using Web Services. For more details on SOAP, read the specification. This is available on the Internet at `http://www.w3.org/TR/SOAP`.

The Protocol

Although the actual details of the SOAP protocol are hidden within the .NET Framework, you might be curious to find out what is happening in the background. So, let's spend a bit of time to see what a SOAP message looks like, and how it can be used to send an object across the network.

A SOAP message is an XML message using a specific format, or *schema*. The schema defines the overall structure of the message (see Day 20, "Introduction to XML," for more details on schemas). This format enables the inclusion of a great deal of information in the message, including objects and additional information about how each side of the communication should interpret the message. For example, the message might include information on security, identifying the user making the request. Listing 21.1 shows a simple SOAP request.

INPUT   **LISTING 21.1**   A Simple SOAP Request

```
 1   <?xml version="1.0" encoding="utf-8"?>
 2   <soap:Envelope
 3     xmlns:xsi="http://www.w3.org/2001/XMLSchema-instance"
 4     xmlns:xsd="http://www.w3.org/2001/XMLSchema"
 5     xmlns:soap="http://schemas.xmlsoap.org/soap/envelope/">
 6     <soap:Body>
 7       <Add xmlns="http://tempuri.org/">
 8         <X>int</X>
 9         <Y>int</Y>
10       </Add>
11     </soap:Body>
12   </soap:Envelope>
```

ANALYSIS   In this message there are three main sections. The first (in lines 2–5) is the `Envelope` tag. This is the root element for the SOAP message. The namespaces included define the structure of the message, the type of encoding, and the use of XML Schemas in the message.

The second section occurs at line 6, with the declaration of the `Body` of the message, which contains the actual request. This request, the third section, is defined in lines 7–10. In this case, it is an `Add` request, with two values, x and y.

Web Service Description Language (WSDL)

When you have a way of communicating, you next need a way to describe the message. In languages, you call this the *grammar*. Grammar defines how to construct a message, and how to identify important parts of the message.

Although SOAP defines the message format, you also need a way of describing the grammar of the SOAP messages. This allows clients and servers to automatically generate and recognize valid SOAP messages. The *Web Service Description Language* (WSDL) is a way of describing Web Services. It defines the messages (*methods*) supported by a Web Service, and the components (*parameters*) for each message. In many ways, WSDL is the "contract" that binds the client and the server.

WSDL builds on another standard, XML Schemas, which, as you learned in Day 20, define the structure for an XML message. WSDL uses schemas to define the two messages that make up the typical Web Service communication, the request and the response. The schemas for the request and the response are one part of the WSDL file. Another part of the file describes the fact that the two structures are related. Finally, the WSDL file identifies the target to which the client should send the SOAP message in order for it to be processed. Listing 21.2 shows a sample WSDL contract.

 Note

> If you had the opportunity to work with early Beta versions of Visual Basic .NET, such as the version released at the Professional Developers' Conference (PDC) or Beta 1, you might have heard of something called SDL (Service Description Language). SDL was an older format that has been replaced by WSDL.

LISTING 21.2   A WSDL Contract

```
 1: <?xml version="1.0" encoding="utf-8" ?>
 2:     <definitions xmlns:s="http://www.w3.org/2001/XMLSchema"
 3:     xmlns:http="http://schemas.xmlsoap.org/wsdl/http/"
 4:     xmlns:mime="http://schemas.xmlsoap.org/wsdl/mime/"
 5:     xmlns:tm="http://microsoft.com/wsdl/mime/textMatching/"
 6:     xmlns:soap="http://schemas.xmlsoap.org/wsdl/soap/"
 7:     xmlns:soapenc="http://schemas.xmlsoap.org/soap/encoding/"
 8:     xmlns:s0="http://tempuri.org/"
 9:     targetNamespace="http://tempuri.org/"
10:     xmlns="http://schemas.xmlsoap.org/wsdl/">
11:     <types>
12:         <s:schema attributeFormDefault="qualified"
13:         elementFormDefault="qualified"
14:         targetNamespace="http://tempuri.org/">
```

21

LISTING 21.2   continued

```
15:                    <s:element name="Add2Ints">
16:                        <s:complexType>
17:                            <s:sequence>
18:                                <s:element minOccurs="1" maxOccurs="1"
19:                                 name="X" type="s:int" />
20:                                <s:element minOccurs="1" maxOccurs="1"
21:                                 name="Y" type="s:int" />
22:                            </s:sequence>
23:                        </s:complexType>
24:                    </s:element>
25:                    <s:element name="Add2IntsResponse">
26:                        <s:complexType>
27:                            <s:sequence>
28:                                <s:element minOccurs="1" maxOccurs="1"
29:                                 name="Add2IntsResult" type="s:int" />
30:                            </s:sequence>
31:                        </s:complexType>
32:                    </s:element>
33:                    <s:element name="int" type="s:int" />
34:                </s:schema>
35:            </types>
36:            <message name="Add2IntsSoapIn">
37:                <part name="parameters" element="s0:Add2Ints" />
38:            </message>
39:            <message name="Add2IntsSoapOut">
40:                <part name="parameters" element="s0:Add2IntsResponse" />
41:            </message>
42:            <message name="Add2IntsHttpGetIn">
43:                <part name="X" type="s:string" />
44:                <part name="Y" type="s:string" />
45:            </message>
46:            <portType name="Service1Soap">
47:                <operation name="Add2Ints">
48:                    <input message="s0:Add2IntsSoapIn" />
49:                    <output message="s0:Add2IntsSoapOut" />
50:                </operation>
51:            </portType>
52:            <binding name="Service1Soap" type="s0:Service1Soap">
53:                <soap:binding transport="http://schemas.xmlsoap.org/soap/http"
54:                 style="document" />
55:                <operation name="Add2Ints">
56:                    <soap:operation soapAction="http://tempuri.org/Add2Ints"
57:                     style="document" />
58:                    <input>
59:                        <soap:body use="literal" />
60:                    </input>
61:                    <output>
62:                        <soap:body use="literal" />
63:                    </output>
```

LISTING 21.2   continued

```
64:            </operation>
65:        </binding>
66:        <service name="Service1">
67:            <port name="Service1Soap" binding="s0:Service1Soap">
68:                <soap:address
69:                    location="http://localhost/Add2Ints/Service1.asmx" />
70:            </port>
71:        </service>
72: </definitions>
```

Discovery

When you have a message, and a way of describing that message, the next feature that people want is to be able to find the Web Service. In some ways, this is similar to having a phone or fax number on a business card. By having the numbers on the card, you are essentially advertising the fact that you have the Web Service to communicate using those tools. For SOAP and Web Services, this business card is Discovery, or DISCO for short. DISCO, apart from being a dance craze of the '70s, is an XML format (could it have been anything else?) that describes the services supported by a server. Other computers can use this DISCO file to find out the capabilities of a given computer. The DISCO file is usually placed in the root directory of a Web site, enabling clients to find it easily.

Visual Basic .NET supports two types of DISCO files. The first is a manually edited one, such as the one shown in Listing 21.3. This file lists each of the services supported. You can easily create one of these files by adding a new DISCO file to a project, and manually inserting the desired services as shown in the listing.

INPUT   **LISTING 21.3**   A Simple DISCO File

```
 1  <?xml version="1.0" ?>
 2  <discovery xmlns="http://schemas.xmlsoap.org/DISCO/">
 3  <contractRef ref="/demos/Async/Add.asmx?sdl"
 4               docRef="/demos/Async/Add.asmx"
 5               xmlns="http://schemas.xmlsoap.org/DISCO/scl/" />
 6  <contractRef ref="/demos/Interop/CCValidator.asmx?sdl"
 7               docRef="/demos/Interop/CCValidator.asmx"
 8               xmlns="http://schemas.xmlsoap.org/DISCO/scl/" />
 9  <contractRef ref="/demos/WebServices/Async/99Bottles.asmx?sdl"
10               docRef="/demos/WebServices/Async/99Bottles.asmx"
11               xmlns="http://schemas.xmlsoap.org/DISCO/scl/" />
12  </discovery>
```

21

ANALYSIS Each DISCO file is composed of a number of contracts. Each *contract* (or *contractRef*) identifies a WSDL file describing a Web Service. For each Web Service listed, there are three important attributes:

- ref—The location of the WSDL file
- docRef—The location of the Web Service
- xmlns—The namespace defining the format of the WSDL file. This allows for a single DISCO file to be used with a variety of service description languages.

The second type of DISCO file Visual Basic .NET supports is a dynamic discovery file. This is the type of discovery file that is created when you start a Web Service project. To differentiate it from a manual DISCO file, it is given the extension: vsdisco. This file will search through all the directories of a Web server, finding all the Web Services exposed. It will then return this list (in simple DISCO format) to the client. This type of DISCO file is convenient because you do not need to change anything to add a new Web Service. It will be found by the dynamic DISCO file automatically. You might not want to use this type of DISCO file if you want to control more tightly the services you make available. Listing 21.4 shows an example of a dynamic DISCO file.

INPUT   **LISTING 21.4**   A Dynamic DISCO File

```
1 <?xml version="1.0" ?>
2 <dynamicDiscovery xmlns="urn:schemas-dynamicdiscovery:DISCO.2000-03-17">
3 <exclude path="_vti_cnf" />
4 <exclude path="_vti_pvt" />
5 <exclude path="_vti_log" />
6 <exclude path="_vti_script" />
7 <exclude path="_vti_txt" />
8 <exclude path="Web References" />
9 </dynamicDiscovery>
```

ANALYSIS This form of DISCO file is much easier to maintain than the simple discovery file. Rather than identifying all the Web Services (or rather, the WSDL files) supported, it lists the locations that should not be searched for WSDL files. Each of the listed <exclude path="" /> lines identifies a directory that should not be searched. This form of DISCO file is slightly slower than the manual DISCO file because it requires that the discovery engine search all the subdirectories, other than those listed in an <exclude path="" /> statement.

Now that you have your ducks in a row (or at least know about the protocols you'll be using), you can use Visual Basic .NET to create a Web Service.

Creating a Simple Web Service

You create a Web Service application by, strangely enough, adding a Web Service project to the solution, or creating a new solution containing a Web Service project (see Figure 21.1).

FIGURE 21.1

Creating a new Web Service project.

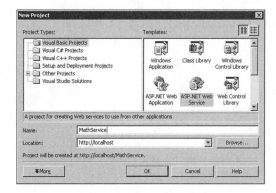

In order to see what's involved in creating and using a Web Service, you'll create a very simple Web Service—a "Math" service. This is a simple example of a Web Service. Although this is a simple service, it shows the mechanics well. Any additional functionality isn't really very different. The mechanics of creating a Web Service are the same.

Creating the Project

While in the development environment, select New Project, ASP.NET Web Service. Name the new Web Service, `MathService`.

After the project has been created, there are a number of files in the project.

- `Web.Config`   This is the file used by the ASP.NET processor for its configuration. You can use it to change the settings for the virtual directory used for this Web Service. For example, you could turn on `Tracing`, which would allow you to better monitor usage. The example won't change this file.

- `Global.asax`   This is the file used by the ASP.NET processor to hold event handlers. You can use this file to write code that will occur when important events occur in the life of a Web application. The example won't change this file.

- `MathService.vsdisco`   This is the discovery file for the Web Service. It allows a client to discover the web services exposed in this virtual directory. The DISCO file created in the project is a dynamic discovery file, so you don't have to make any changes to expose more services.

21

- Service1.asmx   This is the file you will edit to create the functionality of the Web Service.

Listing 21.5 shows the code in the Service1.asmx file.

LISTING 21.5   A Basic Service File

```
1   Imports System.Web.Services
2
3   Public Class Service1
4       Inherits System.Web.Services.WebService
5
6   #Region " Web Services Designer Generated Code "
7
8   Public Sub New()
9       MyBase.New()
10
11      'This call is required by the Web Services Designer.
12      InitializeComponent()
13
14     'Add your own initialization code after the InitializeComponent() call
15
16  End Sub
17
18  'Required by the Web Services Designer
19  Private components As System.ComponentModel.Container
20
21  'NOTE: The following procedure is required by the Web Services Designer
22  'It can be modified using the Web Services Designer.
23  'Do not modify it using the code editor.
24  <System.Diagnostics.DebuggerStepThrough()> Private Sub InitializeComponent()
25      components = New System.ComponentModel.Container()
26  End Sub
27
28  Protected Overloads Overrides Sub Dispose(ByVal disposing As Boolean)
29      'CODEGEN: This procedure is required by the Web Services Designer
30      'Do not modify it using the code editor.
31  End Sub
32
33  #End Region
34
35  ' WEB SERVICE EXAMPLE
36  ' The HelloWorld() example service returns the string Hello World.
37  ' To build, uncomment the following lines then save and build the project.
38  ' To test this web service, ensure that the .asmx file is the start page
39  ' and press F5.
40  '
41  '<WebMethod()> Public Function HelloWorld() As String
42  '      HelloWorld = "Hello World"
```

LISTING 21.5   continued

```
43   ' End Function
44
45   End Class
```

ANALYSIS The Web Service module begins like most Visual Basic .NET files, with the included namespaces. The most important included namespace in this case is the `System.Web.Services` namespace. This includes the core routines that add the Web Service functionality.

Notice on line 4 that the class inherits from `System.Web.Services.WebService`. This provides a number of properties to your Web Service, as can be seen in Table 21.1. Most of these allow it to access the ASP.NET "intrinsics." These are the `Request`, `Response`, `Session`, and `Application` properties.

TABLE 21.1 Properties of WebService

Property	Description
Application	Provides access to the variables stored in the `Application` object within ASP.NET. This is a shorthand property for `Context.Application`.
Context	Provides access to all the data provided within ASP.NET. This includes the actual `Request` and `Response` objects, the `Cache` object, and other properties of the request.
Server	Provides access to the Server object. This object is used to query the Web server hosting the Web Service, or to encode messages (for example, to convert a string into a valid Querystring, adding all the appropriate +, %20, and other characters). This is a shorthand property for `Context.Server`.
Session	Provides access to the variables stored in the Session object within ASP.NET. This is a short-hand property for `Context.Session`.
User	Provides access to information about the user making the request.

The code from lines 6–33 in Listing 21.5 are wrapped in a `#Region` area. This code is actually collapsed in the development environment (see Figure 21.2). This is a useful technique, new in Visual Basic .NET, that allows you to make your code less complex by hiding the details that might not matter. In this case, it hides the code used by the IDE itself. This is the code that allows you to drag and drop items onto the visible surface. Generally, you should not change this code manually, so it makes sense to hide it in the editor.

21

FIGURE 21.2

*The starting Web
Service.*

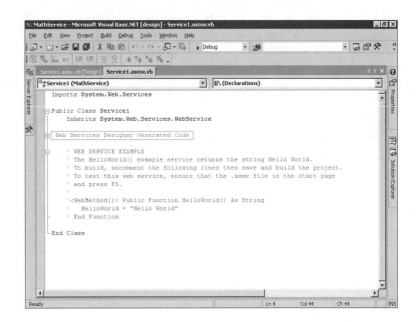

The code from lines 41–43 is an example of how you would add a new method to this
Web Service. Notice that this is commented out by default. If you want to expose this
method, simply remove the comment characters.

Adding the Code

Now that you have a base Web Service, you need to add the code that will perform your
Web Service's tasks. You do this in a Web Service by adding public methods to the Web
Service class. You could also add public properties, but this would have less meaning (as
you'll see later). The public methods in a Web Service are the same as those in any other
class, with one addition, a <WebMethod()> attribute.

The Syntax for Web Service Methods

The syntax for Web Service methods is

```
<WebMethod()> Public Function MethodName(ByVal Parameter As Type) As ReturnType
    'Code for method
End Function
```

in which *MethodName* is the name for the method, *Parameter* is the list of parameters for
the method, *Type* is the type of each parameter, and *ReturnType* is the type returned
from the Web method.

The addition to a normal method is indicated by the <WebMethod()> in the normal declaration. This is an example of an *attribute*, a .NET element that adds new behavior to a class, method, or property. In the sample syntax, the attribute adds the Web Service to "speak" SOAP to a given method. Any methods marked with this attribute are exposed publicly as part of the Web Service.

In the following example, I added a single, simple method to the Web Service by adding the code in Listing 21.6 to the Web Service project after the sample method. Alternatively, you can delete the comment and replace it with this method.

LISTING 21.6   Code for a Sample Web Service Method

```
1 <WebMethod()> Public Function Add( _
2   ByVal X As Integer, _
3   ByVal Y As Integer) As Integer
4     Return X + Y
5 End Function
```

This method simply adds two numbers, returning the sum. Although you might discount this as overly simplified, it does everything all Web Service methods usually do:

- It contains the <WebMethod()> attribute in the declaration
- It returns a value

You could add more methods, or more complex methods, at this point. However, this is not necessary. You will write a more realistic Web Service later today.

Compiling the Web Service

You compile a Web Service in the same way that you build other projects. Select Build from the Build menu. This creates a DLL (placed in the bin directory under the Web Service root directory) that contains the actual code of the Web Service. After you have the service built, you should be able to browse to the created ASMX file. Right-click on the ASMX file in the Server Explorer and select View in Browser to see it in action. An ASMX file is the file containing the functionality of a Web Service, in the same way that an .exe file is a program, or ASPX is a Web Form. Figures 21.3 and 21.4 show views of the sample project. The URL viewed is

```
http://localhost/MathService/service1.asmx
```

The first screen that you see will show the description of the Web Service, along with the names of all methods that have had the WebMethod attribute added (see Figure 21.3).

21

FIGURE 21.3

Test page for Web Service.

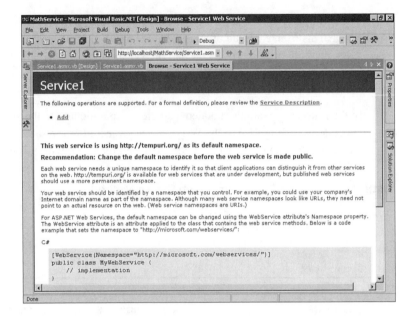

If you select one of the methods, such as the Add method just created, you should see another test page that includes a form that allows you to enter test values for the Web Service (see Figure 21.4). In addition, it includes sample SOAP messages for request and response for this method.

FIGURE 21.4

Entering values in the test page.

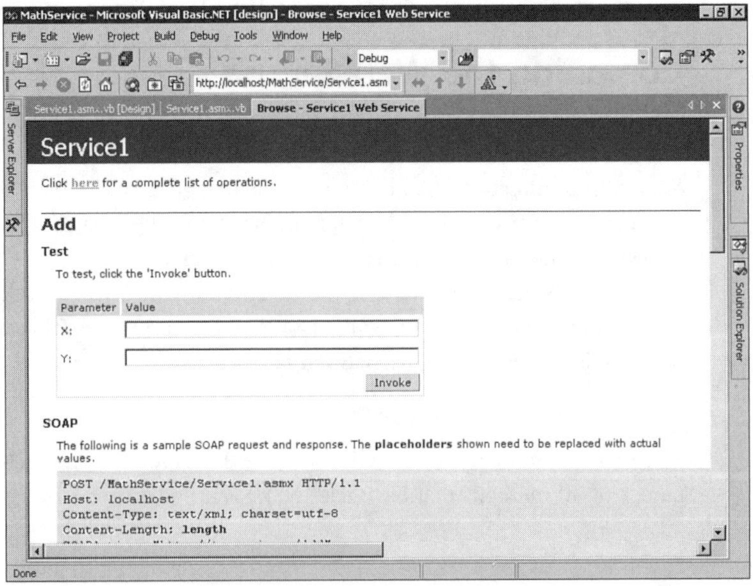

This test page is automatically generated when you view an ASMX file. It provides you with information about the methods the Web Service provides. In addition, it creates a test form for each method, allowing you to enter some values and run the function. Enter a few values into the text fields for the Add Method section, and click the Invoke button. Another browser window should open and show you the sum, as in Figure 21.5

FIGURE 21.5

Adding values with the Web Service.

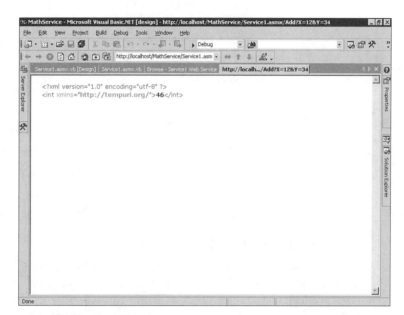

Creating a Web Service Client

Although the test page created for the ASMX file is useful for testing, you shouldn't expect your users to use it to work with your Web Service. Instead, you should create a client (either a Windows Form or Web Form) that will communicate with the Web Service. Communication between this client and the Web Service is performed with the assistance of an intermediate class, also known as a proxy.

NEW TERM In general terms, *proxy* is an authorized deputy or substitute. It is a go-between. For Web Services, a *proxy* is a small client-side component that looks like the Web Service to the client program. When the client program makes a call into the proxy, it generates the appropriate SOAP request for the Web Service and passes it on. When the Web Service responds with a SOAP response, it converts this back into the expected return value for the function, and returns this to the client. Figure 21.6 shows this process.

21

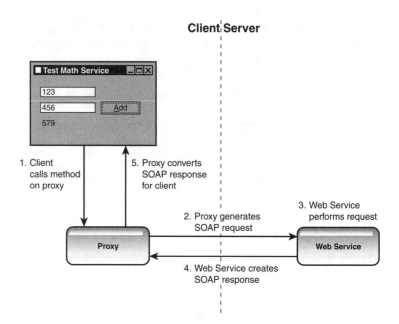

FIGURE 21.6

Flow of information between client, proxy, and Web Service.

Creating the Project

Although you could create a client using either a Windows Form, or a Web Form (or even another library or Web Service), in this section, you'll look at creating a Web Service client by creating a Windows Form. This will be an example of one possible use for Web Services, as a means to extend existing (or future) desktop clients, such as Microsoft Office. Creating a client using Web Forms is similar.

Create a new Windows Application project and call it MathClient. You might want to create it in the same solution as the MathService, to allow you to keep the two together, although this is not necessary. Select File, New, Project. In the New Project dialog, select Windows Application and enter **MathClient** in the name field. Make certain that Add to Solution is selected, and then click OK. Visual Basic .NET should create a project with a single form. Before going too far along, close the Form designer, and rename the Form1.vb file as **frmTest.vb**. Next, open the form in code view, and change all references of Form1 to **frmTest**. Next, right-click on the MathClient project and select Properties. On the General page, change the Startup Object to **frmTest** and select OK. Finally, right-click on the MathClient project again, and select Set as Startup Project. This will ensure that this project will run first when you start the solution.

Adding the Code

When you call another object in Visual Basic .NET, you generally must load a reference to that object. This allows the IDE to know about the various properties and methods in the object. You cannot do this with a Web Service, however, because it does not have all the exposed information of a local object. Instead, you must load a Web Reference, which is a pointer to a WSDL file. Recall that this file describes all the methods and their parameters of a Web Service.

Adding a web reference is easy: Right-click the MathClient project and select Add Web Reference. You should see the dialog in Figure 21.7

FIGURE 21.7

Adding a web reference.

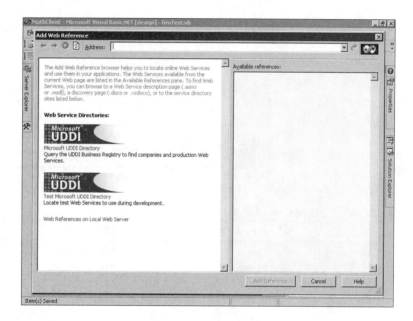

The dialog requests the URL to either a DISCO file or the location of the WSDL for the Web Service. These would normally be provided by the author of the service. In the case of the `MathService`, the URL should be:
`http://localhost/MathService/MathService.vsdisco`. Enter this URL and click the search arrow. Ideally, after a pause, it should find the Web Service, as shown in Figure 21.8.

After the web reference has been found, click the Add Web Reference button. This will add a new section to the project (Web References), which should contain three files under the Localhost section: `Service1.wsdl`, `MathService.vsdisco`, and `Reference.Map`. The compiler will use these files at compile time to add a proxy to the client program that knows how to communicate with the Web Service.

Now that your client program knows how to communicate with the Web Service, you can add the code to call the service. To do this, you'll add two text boxes, a label, and a button to the form. Set the properties as in Table 21.2.

21

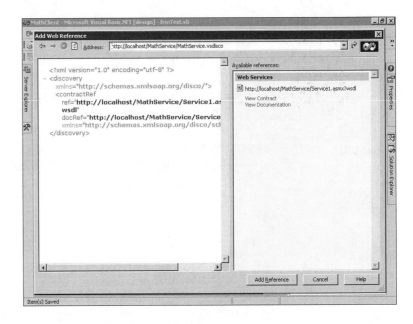

FIGURE 21.8

Locating the web reference.

TABLE 21.2 Properties for MathClient Form

Control	Property	Value
Form	Text	Test Math Service
	Size	248, 160
	BorderStyle	FixedSingle
TextBox	Name	txtX
	Text	123
	Location	16, 24
	Size	100, 20
TextBox	Name	txtY
	Text	456
	Location	16, 56
	Size	100, 20
Button	Name	cmdAdd
	Text	&Add
	Location	128, 56
	Size	75, 23
Label	Name	lblResult
	Text	0
	Location	16, 88
	Size	100, 23

Finally, you are ready to add the code in Listing 21.7, which will call the Web Service. Double-click the Add button to add this code.

INPUT   **LISTING 21.7** Calling the Web Service

```
1  Private Sub cmdAdd_Click( _

2    ByVal sender As System.Object, _
3    ByVal e As System.EventArgs) _
4    Handles cmdAdd.Click
5      Dim oMath As New localhost.Service1()
6      lblResult.Text = oMath.Add(CInt(txtX.Text), CInt(txtY.Text))
7  End Sub
```

ANALYSIS   Something that should be immediately obvious is that the code is remarkably similar to that used for normal object access. The only difference between the code in lines 5 and 6 and the same code accessing a local object is that the full name of the object is based on the server providing the Web Service, in this case, `localhost.Service1`. One important item to note is that the name of the Web Service will change based on the host for the service.

The resulting program should be able to reach across to call the Web Service, whether it exists on the same machine, as I've shown here, or across the Internet. Figure 21.9 shows the result.

FIGURE 21.9

Using the client to call the Web Service.

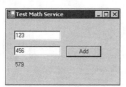

Although this added service seems trivial (and it is), as stated earlier, this includes all the mechanics of creating and using a Web Service:

- Creating a Web Service project (or adding a Web Service to an existing Web Project)
- Adding one or more public methods with the `<WebMethod()>` attribute
- Adding a Web reference to a client application that points to the WSDL for the Web Service
- Creating a new variable that points to the Web Service, and executing one or more of its methods.

21

A More Involved Web Service

To show that you have indeed seen all there is to know about creating Web Services, you'll create a Web Service that does more than just add two numbers. You'll create a Web Service that might be exposed from a store, in this case, Northwind. The Web Service will allow you to perform the following tasks:

- Retrieve a list of product categories
- Retrieve a list of products in a single category
- Order a product

One difference between this Web Service and the previous example is that the current example shows that you can retrieve objects. Any built-in or user-created object can be sent to, or returned from, a Web Service. The object is converted to XML to pass through the network, and returned to an object for the client's use.

Creating the Service

As with the simple service, you will begin by creating the Web Service. In Visual Basic .NET, create a new Web Services project. You will call this one Northwind. Figure 21.10 shows the New Project dialog.

FIGURE 21.10

Creating the Northwind Web Service.

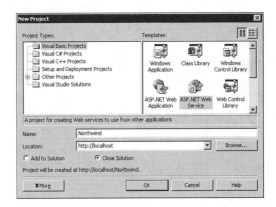

Close the designer, and change the name of the Service1.asmx file to **Products.asmx**. Open the Products.asmx file in Code view and change the line

```
Public Class Service1
```

to

```
Public Class ProductManager
```

Next, you will add the three methods. The first method will return an array containing all the categories. The second method will return a DataSet containing all the product information for a given category, and the third method will insert new information into the Categories table. Listing 21.8 shows these three methods. For more information on the data access code in these methods, see Day 12, "Accessing Data with .NET." Add this code after the region marked as "Web Services Designer Generated Code," but before the End Class line. In addition, you will need to add two Imports statements, one to import the System.Data namespace, and the other to import the System.Data.SqlClient namespace. Add these two statements just below the Imports System.Web.Service line.

INPUT **LISTING 21.8** The Code for the Products Web Service

```
1   Private Const DSN As String = _
2     "server=localhost;database=northwind;user id=sa;password=;"
3
4   <WebMethod()> Public Function GetCategories() As String()
5       Dim oCon As New SqlConnection(DSN)
6       Dim sSQL As String
7       sSQL = "SELECT CategoryName FROM Categories"
8       Dim oCmd As New SqlDataAdapter(sSQL, oCon)
9       Dim oDS As New DataSet()
10      Dim sReturn() As String
11      Dim I As Integer
12
13      oCmd.Fill(oDS, "Categories")
14      ReDim sReturn(oDS.Tables(0).Rows.Count)
15      For I = 0 To oDS.Tables(0).Rows.Count - 1
16          sReturn(I) = CStr(oDS.Tables(0).Rows(I).Item(0))
17      Next
18      Return sReturn
19  End Function
20
21  <WebMethod()> _
22  Public Function GetProducts( _
23    ByVal categoryName As String) As DataSet
24      Dim oCon As New SqlConnection(DSN)
25      Dim sSQL As String
26      sSQL = "SELECT ProductID, ProductName, UnitPrice " & _
27        "QuantityPerUnit, Discontinued, CategoryName " & _
28        "FROM Categories INNER JOIN Products " & _
29        "ON Categories.CategoryID = Products.CategoryID " & _
30        "WHERE (Discontinued=0) AND " & _
31        "(CategoryName LIKE '" & categoryName & "%')"
32      Dim oCmd As New SqlDataAdapter(sSQL, oCon)
33      Dim ods As New DataSet()
34
35      oCmd.Fill(ods, "products")
```

21

LISTING **21.8** continued

```
36      Return ods
37  End Function
38
39  <WebMethod()> _
40  Public Function InsertCategory( _
41    ByVal categoryName As String, _
42    ByVal description As String) As Boolean
43      Dim oCon As New SqlConnection(DSN)
44      Dim sSQL As String
45      sSQL = "INSERT INTO Categories" & _
46        "(CategoryName, Description) " & _
47        "VALUES('" & categoryName & "'" & _
48        ", '" & description & "')"
49      Dim oCmd As New SqlCommand(sSQL, oCon)
50      Try
51          oCon.Open()
52          oCmd.ExecuteNonQuery()
53          Return True
54      Catch
55          Return False
56      End Try
57  End Function
```

ANALYSIS   The first of the three methods, GetCategories, returns an array of strings containing the names of each of the categories of products. It could have returned a DataSet just as easily (in fact, it would have been easier), however, this was done to show that arrays could also be returned.

The connection string that will be used to access the database is created as a constant in lines 1 and 2. You will need to change this if your database is stored elsewhere, or if you need specific credentials to log into the database. The appropriate data access objects are created in lines 5–11. Here you are using the SQL database access methods. Therefore, you will need to include the System.Data.SqlClient namespace in this file. In addition, if you are going to be accessing a non-SQL database, you should use the ADO connection objects, which are stored in the System.Data.OleDb namespace. Notice that you are only retrieving a single column from the Categories table (line 7).

Line 13 retrieves the data and populates the DataSet. Lines 14–17 take the information from the DataSet and use it to populate the array. Finally, the array is returned to the calling function at line 18.

The second method, GetProducts, is simpler than the first. In it, you return a DataSet populated with all the non-discontinued products for a requested category. The most complex part of the method is the code from lines 26–31, where the SQL statement is built to retrieve the list. Ideally, this would be stored as a view or stored procedure in the database. The final string would look something like

```
SELECT ProductID, ProductName, UnitPrice, ➡
QuantityPerUnit, Discontinued, CategoryName ➡
FROM Categories INNER JOIN Products ➡
ON Categories.CategoryID = Products.CategoryID ➡
WHERE (Discontinued = 0) AND (CategoryName LIKE 'Bev%'
```

The resulting SQL statement would return all the requested fields where the product is not discontinued, and where the category name started with Bev.

The final method, `InsertCategory`, demonstrates that you can also request that the Web Service do something other than retrieval. In this case, you will insert a new category into the database.

You begin in the same way that you began the two previous methods, by creating a connection to the database, and writing your SQL statement. In this case, the final statement built in lines 45–48 will appear similar to

```
INSERT INTO Categories(CategoryName, Description) ➡
VALUES('Stuff', 'Other stuff we sell')
```

One difference in this method is that rather than creating a `SqlDataAdapter`, you create a `SqlCommand`. `SqlCommands`, as you learned in Day 12, are better suited for inserting, deleting, and changing data, rather than retrieving it. Another point worth noting is the `Try...Catch` block from lines 50–56. In this case, you attempt to execute the SQL statement. If it succeeds, you return `True` from the method. If an exception occurs, for any reason, you return `False`. An exception generally wouldn't occur in this method, unless the database was not running, or if you had run out of disk space.

Testing the Web Service

Just as you did with the simple Web Service, you can use the built-in functionality to test this Web Service. Build the project, and then open a Web browser, and navigate to `http://localhost/northwinds/products.asmx`. You should see the test page generated as in Figure 21.11.

You should test each of the three methods before continuing. Figures 21.12, 21.13, and 21.14 show the result of each of the methods in action. The second method was tested with the string `Bev`, and the third was tested with the strings `Stuff` and `Just some other stuff we sell`.

21

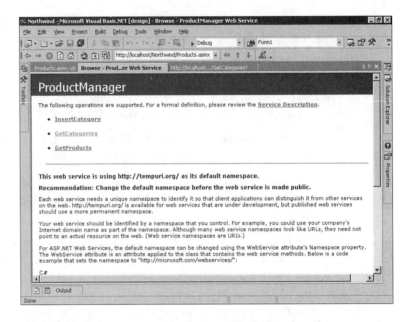

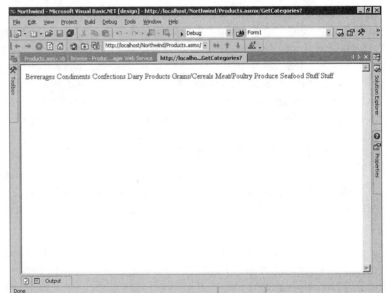

Creating the Client

Just as before, you are now ready to create a client for your Web Service. This time, however, you will create a Web Forms–based client. This could represent one Web site using a Web Service to provide it with content, but using its own layout. Alternatively, this could represent the Web Forms client for an intranet application.

FIGURE 21.13

Testing GetProducts.

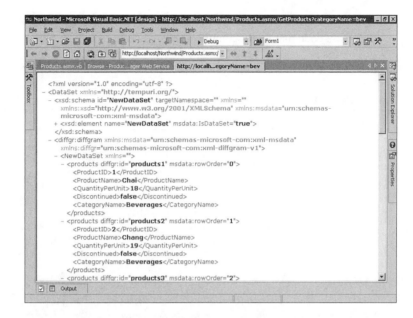

FIGURE 21.14

Testing
InsertCategory.

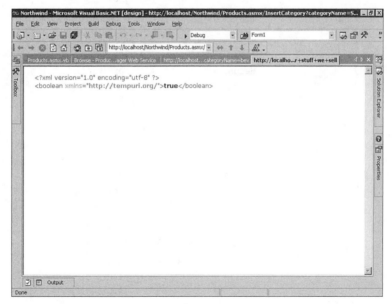

21

Begin the client project by adding a new Web application project. You'll call this one
NWClient (for Northwind client). Right-click on the project name, and select Set as
Startup Project. Close the designer and rename the WebForm1.aspx file to
Products.aspx. Finally, reopen the designer, and you will create a fairly Spartan

interface. This is mostly because I have little graphical skill, but also to limit the amount of extra code that might complicate the example.

The properties of the controls on the page are described in Table 21.3.

Table 21.3 Properties for NWClient Web Form

Control	Property	Value
Document	title	Northwind Products
Panel	(ID)	pnlNewCategory
	Height	181px
	Width	368px
Label	(ID)	lblNewCategory
	Text	New Category
Label	(ID)	lblName
	Text	Name:
TextBox	(ID)	txtName
	Height	24px
	Width	213px
Label	(ID)	lblDescription
	Text	Description:
TextBox	(ID)	txtDescription
	Height	41px
	Width	222px
	TextMode	MultiLine
Button	(ID)	cmdAdd
	Text	Add
Label	(ID)	lblResult
	Height	19px
	Width	329px
	BackColor	Silver
Label	(ID)	lblCategories
	Text	Categories
DropDownList	(ID)	cboCategory
	Height	22px
	Width	202px
	AutoPostBack	True
DataGrid	(ID)	dbgProducts
	Height	265px
	Width	438px

ANALYSIS On the form, you add a ComboBox (DropDownList) and DataGrid controls. These will be used to display the results of the GetCategories and GetProducts calls. In addition, you have a panel that contains two text boxes, a button, and a label. These will be used for the InsertCategory method.

One property of the DropDownList to notice is AutoPostBack. As you learned in Day 10, "Building a User Interface with Web Forms," AutoPostBack causes the form to be sent back to the server immediately, rather than waiting for a Submit button to be pressed. In this case, the form will be submitted whenever the user changes the contents of the DropDownList.

Following the DropDownList, the DataGrid is defined. You might also want to use the AutoFormat capability of the DataGrid designer to make it look nicer than the default.

Figure 21.15 shows what the user interface should resemble in Visual Basic .NET.

FIGURE 21.15

Northwind client.

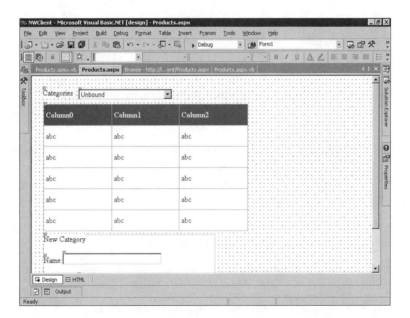

Adding the Code

Almost there. All you need to do is hook up a few routines. You want the Categories combo box filled when the user first looks at the page, and the grid populated with the results of the category. In addition, you will want that grid updated whenever the user selects a new category. Finally, you will want to add a new category when the user clicks the Add button.

21

Before you can add code, you must add a Web Reference to the Web Service. Right-click on the NWClient project, and select Add Web Reference. The DISCO file created for the Web Service is `http://localhost/Northwind/Northwind.vsdisco`. Figure 21.16 shows the result of querying that file.

FIGURE 21.16

Discovering the Northwind service.

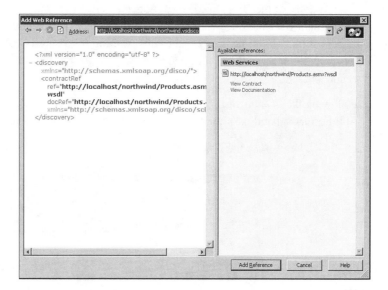

Rather than starting by populating the combo box, start with the grid. You know that you want to update the grid whenever the contents of the combo box changes. The appropriate event to add code to then is the `SelectedIndexChanged` event. Double-click on the combo box and update the event handler as shown in Listing 21.9.

INPUT **LISTING 21.9** Updating the Grid

```
1   Private Sub cboCategory_SelectedIndexChanged( _
2     ByVal sender As System.Object, _
3     ByVal e As System.EventArgs) _
4     Handles cboCategory.SelectedIndexChanged
5       Dim oProducts As New localhost.ProductManager()
6       Dim oDS As DataSet
7       oDS = oProducts.GetProducts(cboCategory.SelectedItem.Text)
8       dbgProducts.DataSource = oDS.Tables(0).DefaultView
9       dbgProducts.DataBind()
10  End Sub
```

ANALYSIS This method begins by instantiating a new `ProductManager` (the Web Service). It then retrieves the list of products (as a `DataSet`) from the Web Service, using the

GetProducts method (line 7). Finally, in lines 8 and 9, it binds the DataSet to the DataGrid and causes it to update.

When you have the grid updating itself, it's time to consider the combo box. It should be filled with the list of categories when the user first loads the page. The appropriate event to make this happen is the WebForm1_Load event. Listing 21.10 shows this method.

INPUT **LISTING 21.10** Loading the Categories

```
11  Private Sub Page_Load( _
12    ByVal sender As System.Object, _
13    ByVal e As System.EventArgs) Handles MyBase.Load
14      If Not IsPostBack Then
15          Dim oProducts As New localhost.ProductManager()
16          Dim sCategories() As String
17          sCategories = oProducts.GetCategories
18          cboCategory.DataSource = sCategories
19          cboCategory.DataBind()
20          cboCategory_SelectedIndexChanged(Me, Nothing)
21      End If
22  End Sub
```

ANALYSIS As you learned in Day 10, the IsPostBack property is used to determine whether this is the first time viewing a Web page, or whether it is returning. Generally, you only want to perform tasks such as populating controls once, so you add your code to the If Not IsPostBack section. In the page load event, you initially create a new instance of the Web Service (line 15). Next, you call the GetCategories method (line 17), which returns an array of strings.

One interesting development is used in lines 18 and 19 of the page load event. Not only can controls be bound to DataSets, but they can also be bound to Arrays (and Collections). So, you can bind a category's array directly to a combo box.

The line of code on line 20 deserves a bit of explanation. When the combo box is populated, the selected index is not considered to have changed. Therefore, you explicitly call the event handler for the combo box, to ensure that the grid will be populated when the user first visits the page.

Figure 21.17 shows the result of loading the Web page, whereas Figure 21.18 shows the result of changing the category.

21

FIGURE 21.17

Viewing the Northwind client.

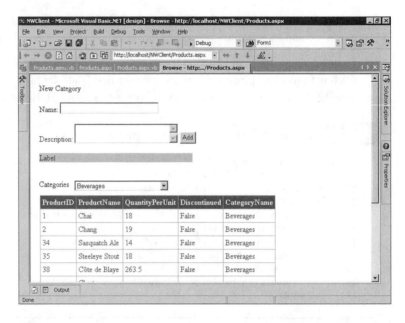

FIGURE 21.18

Changing·the selected category.

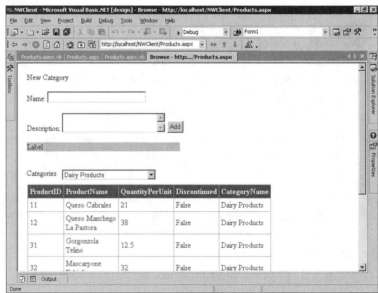

Finally, you'll add the code to make the Add button add a new category to the database. Double-click on the Add button to open the code window. Add the code in Listing 21.11 to the procedure.

INPUT   **LISTING 21.11**   The Add Button

```
23  Private Sub cmdAdd_Click( _
24    ByVal sender As System.Object, _
25    ByVal e As System.EventArgs) _
26    Handles cmdAdd.Click
27      Dim oProducts As New localhost.ProductManager()
28      If oProducts.InsertCategory(txtName.Text, txtDescription.Text) Then
29          lblResult.Text = "New category added: " & txtName.Text
30      Else
31          lblResult.Text = "Failed to add new category"
32      End If
33  End Sub
```

ANALYSIS   Hopefully, there is nothing earth-shatteringly complex here. You create a new instance of the Web Service and call the `InsertCategory` method, passing in the contents of the two fields. When it returns (either `True` or `False`), you change the contents of the `Label` with either a success or failure message. Figure 21.19 shows the result of running this method.

FIGURE 21.19

Clicking the Add button.

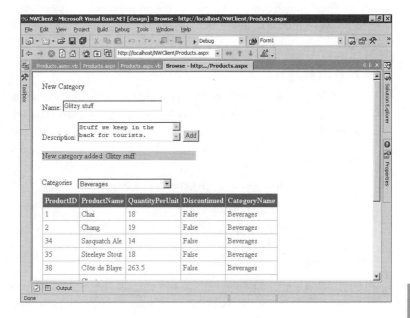

Summary

Web Services are a new way of accessing programs and components across a network or the Internet. They are useful in both Web and traditional desktop applications. They provide the ease of development and cross-platform use of Web clients with objects. One key benefit is that they can be written in any programming language, and allow interoperability with any operating system. Expect Web Services to become more significant as they become more plentiful.

Q&A

Q. Can I secure a Web Service to control who can access it?

A. Yes, Web Services fully support use of HTTPS (and SSL) for controlling access.

Q. Are Web Services only good for a solution that uses Microsoft products throughout?

A. No, Web Services can be used to communicate with any operating system. As long as the client is able to interpret the SOAP request (and build a SOAP response), it can be used to interoperate with a client or server written in Visual Basic .NET.

Q. What happens if I try to access a Web Service, and it's down?

A. Sadly, there is little that can be done in these situations. Generally, you will need to add code to your client to react appropriately to this situation. The client might fail gracefully, or cache and reuse the last response as appropriate.

Workshop

The Workshop is designed to help you anticipate possible questions, review what you've learned, and get you thinking about how to put your knowledge into practice. The answers to the quiz are in Appendix A, "Answers to Quizzes/Exercises."

Quiz

1. What is the purpose of the DISCO file?
2. What is the purpose of a proxy?
3. Why is SOAP important for Web Services?

Exercise

Try adding some more methods to either of the two Web Services we have created. For example, add `Subtract`, `Multiply`, and `Divide` methods to the `MathService`. Update your client to work with the new methods.

WEEK 3

In Review

Week 3 covered a heavy set of topics, touching on a wide variety of features that you will need to spend even more time on in the future. To start, you learned how to make your own objects in .NET, building blocks of code that could then stand on their own and be reused by other projects as necessary. Day 16 took you through some of the more advanced techniques and technologies for creating Windows-based applications using .NET, such as splitter controls and menus.

Day 17 provided coverage of two commonly needed areas of the .NET Framework: the graphics library, showing you how to manipulate images and the appearance of your application, and the file handling features of .NET, detailing how to create, open, and modify files. In Day 18, you learned how to make your application as easy to maintain and support as possible, including documenting your code and using source code control to protect your valuable work. Day 19 continued the topic of getting your application ready for distribution, including the various considerations for redistributing the required .NET files for your program to function correctly. Creating installation programs, learning about remote installation options, and providing user documentation were all part of Day 19.

Days 20 and 21 covered two technologies that are the foundation of the .NET concept: XML and Web Services. You learned how .NET provides classes for reading, writing, transforming, and building XML documents, and XML could be used within your applications. Day 21 showed you Web Services, one of the major features of .NET, and you learned how they allow you to expose the functionality of your system to the Web using the HTTP and XML standards. Building Web Services and the use of these services in your own systems was also covered, although full coverage of this topic is beyond the scope of this book.

Finally, the bonus project for Week 3, which is available on the Web at `http://www.samspublishing.com/detail_sams.cfm?item=0672320665`, showed you how the concepts covered in earlier chapters such as file usage, graphics, XML, and even some advanced Windows Forms work, can be used to create a complete program. In this case, you have built a game, but that was just a more enjoyable way to learn techniques that can be applied to almost any type of system you need to create.

With the completion of this week, you have also finished 21 days of Visual Basic .NET and have an overall understanding of the language, the underlying framework, and how you can use both to start creating your own systems. In development, learning is an ongoing process that never really ends, but you have made it through a fairly extensive introduction to an amazing new language. You should be able to escape the introductory level of study for a time and focus on building a variety of applications (sample or real, depending on your current work) to solidify all the information that you have covered over the past three weeks. Make sure that you are coding in .NET as much as you can; there is no better way to gain confidence and further understanding in a new language and in a new technology.

APPENDIX **A**

Answers for Day 1

Quiz

1. Microsoft first produced a compiler for the original BASIC language, calling that product Microsoft BASIC. The next version of that compiler, and the predecessor to Visual Basic, was Quick BASIC, or QBASIC.

2. All the .NET languages share these features because the Common Language Runtime provides them. It is through this runtime that each of these languages works with .NET.

3. This process is called compiling.

4. If you don't explicitly state an output file, using the `/out:<filename>` switch, the compiler will use the name of the source file as the name of the executable. In this case, the output would be `MySourceCode.exe`.

Exercises

1. To produce a specific exe, all you need is the `/out:<filename>` switch for the command-line compiler. To accomplish this task, go into the console (command prompt). Navigate (using the command cd) to the folder containing your work files from the previous examples, specifically `step3.vb`.

Now, run the compiler by typing **vbc step3.vb /t:exe /out:WhatOS.exe** and pressing Enter. This compiles step3, but saves the compiled result into a file named WhatOS.exe.

2. There are many different properties available through the Environment portion of the .NET Framework, so there are several different ways you could have answered this question. In the end, though, all the answers should have resembled the following solution, which outputs the version of the .NET Framework:

```
Public Class FrameworkVersion
    Shared Sub Main()
        System.Console.WriteLine(System.Environment.Version.ToString())
    End Sub
End Class
```

This code produces the following output (this output is produced when using Beta 2 of .NET; you will get different results if you use the release version):

INPUT/
OUTPUT

```
C:\TYVB\C1>vbc FrameworkVersion.vb /t:exe
Microsoft (R) Visual Basic.NET Compiler version 7.00.9254
for Microsoft (R) .NET CLR version 1.00.2914.16
Copyright (C) Microsoft Corp 2001. All rights reserved.


C:\TYVB\C1>FrameworkVersion
1.0.2914.16
```

Alternatively, you could have chosen to output the path to the System directory, or one of many other values, all of which follow the same basic pattern. An example of using the SystemDirectory value is shown here:

```
Public Class SysDir
    Shared Sub Main()
        System.Console.WriteLine(System.Environment.SystemDirectory)
    End Sub
End Class
```

INPUT/
OUTPUT

```
C:\TYVB\C1>vbc SysDir.vb /t:exe
Microsoft (R) Visual Basic.NET Compiler version 7.00.9254
for Microsoft (R) .NET CLR version 1.00.2914.16
Copyright (C) Microsoft Corp 2001. All rights reserved.


C:\TYVB\C1>SysDir
C:\WINNT\System32
```

Answers for Day 2

Quiz

1. You would use the Solution Explorer, which shows all the open projects, and all the files in each. This window can be made visible by pressing the key combination of CTRL+R.

2. By default, projects are placed under the current user's `My Documents folder\Visual Studio Projects` and into a new folder with the project's name. When you create a new project, this path is displayed in the New Project dialog, and you can change it as you want.

3. Choose an icon in the Project Properties dialog, which you can reach by right-clicking on the project in the Solution Explorer and selecting Properties from the context menu. You can also choose an .ico (icon) file under Common Properties\Build.

4. In the Command window, typing `>cmd` and pressing Return switches you into Command mode. Typing `immed` and pressing Return switches you back into Immediate mode.

Exercise

By placing a `MessageBox.Show` call into the `TextChanged` event of a text box, a message will be displayed whenever the contents of that text box are modified. Although this is a useful place for code that validates the user's text entry, displaying a message inside this event would quickly get annoying!

Answers for Day 3

Quiz

1. You should use the most appropriate size and type of variable from among the available types.

2. A and C are correct. When calling a function, you must enclose the parameters in parentheses. In addition, the function returns a value, so generally something must be done with the result. Either assign to another variable, or display it.

3. If a variable is declared using the `Private` keyword, it is available throughout the module or class in which it is declared.

Exercises

One possible solution for the payment calculator exercise would be

```
1    Module Payment
2
3        Private dblAnnualInterest As Double = 0
4        Private iYears As Integer = 0
5        Private dblLoanAmount As Double = 0
6        Private dblMonthlyDeposit As Double = 0
7
8        Sub Main()
9            Dim dblResult As Double
10
11           'get input values
12           GetInputValues()
13
14           'calculate
15           dblResult = CalculatePayment(dblLoanAmount, _
16                           dblAnnualInterest, _
17                           iYears)
18           'output result
19           DisplayResults(dblResult)
20
21       End Sub
22
23       Private Function CalculatePayment(Byval LoanAmount As Double, _
24               ByVal AnnualInterest As Double, _
25               ByVal Years As Integer) As Double
26           'divide by 1200 to make it percent and per month
27           Dim dblMonthlyInterest As Double = CDec(AnnualInterest / 1200)
28           Dim iMonths As Integer = Years * 12
29           Dim dblTemp As Double
30           Dim dblReturn As Double
31
32
33           'we'll need this value in a couple of places
34           dblTemp = CDec(((1 + dblMonthlyInterest) ^ iMonths))
35           dblReturn = LoanAmount * _
36               (dblMonthlyInterest * dblTemp / (dblTemp - 1))
37           Return dblReturn
38
39       End Function
40
41       Private Sub GetInputValues()
42           Console.WriteLine()
43           dblLoanAmount = CDec(GetValue("Loan Amount: "))
44           dblAnnualInterest = _
45             CDbl(GetValue("Annual Interest (e.g. for 5%, enter 5): "))
46           iYears = CInt(GetValue("Years of loan: "))
```

```
47              Console.WriteLine()
48         End Sub
49
50         Private Function GetValue(ByVal Prompt As String) As String
51
52              Console.Write(Prompt)
53              Return Console.ReadLine
54
55         End Function
56
57         Private Sub DisplayResults(ByVal Result As Double)
58              Console.WriteLine()
59
60              Console.WriteLine("If you borrow {0:c}, ", dblLoanAmount)
61              Console.WriteLine("at {0}% interest.", dblAnnualInterest)
62              Console.WriteLine("for {0} years", iYears)
63
64              Console.WriteLine()
65              Console.WriteLine("Your monthly payment would be: {0:c}", Result)
66
67         End Sub
68
69      End Module
```

Answers for Day 4

Quiz

1. The For loop is best suited for this type of solution, although any of the loops could be used.

2. Although any of the loops can be used to simulate any one of the others, the Do loop is the most flexible due to its support for While and Until clauses and for entry and exit positions for placing the conditional expression.

3. The inner block is the code that will be executed for every iteration of the loop, so a performance hit or the number of iterations of the loop magnifies gain inside a loop.

4. Assuming that CalculatedTotalNetWorth() is a bit more complex than the code that runs under dtCurrentDate.Hour(), you would do best to swap the two sides of the expression. This would ensure that, if the first expression, dtCurrentDate.Hour() > 12, is FALSE, then the larger, more expensive routine will not even be executed.

Exercise

1. There are many different ways you could write the NumberGuesser program, but
   the general result should resemble this:

```
Public Class GamePlayer

    Shared Sub Main()
    Dim iUpperBound As Integer
    Dim iLowerBound As Integer
    Dim iCurrentGuess As Integer
    Dim sInput As String
    Dim sGuessStatus As String

        System.Console.Write("Please enter the lower bound: ")
        sInput = System.Console.ReadLine()
        iLowerBound = CInt(sInput)

        System.Console.Write("Please enter the upper bound: ")
        sInput = System.Console.ReadLine()
        iUpperBound = CInt(sInput)

        'Ask User to Pick Number
        System.Console.WriteLine("Pick a number between " & iLowerBound & _
            " and " & iUpperBound & ", and remember it!")
        System.Console.WriteLine("Hit Return To Continue")

        System.Console.ReadLine()

        iCurrentGuess = 0
        sGuessStatus = ""

        Do Until sGuessStatus = "="
            iCurrentGuess = GetMyGuess(iLowerBound, iUpperBound)
            System.Console.WriteLine("My Guess Is: " & iCurrentGuess)
            System.Console.Write("How did I do? ")
            sGuessStatus = System.Console.ReadLine()
            sGuessStatus = sGuessStatus.ToUpper()
            Select Case sGuessStatus

                Case "H"
                    iUpperBound = iCurrentGuess - 1
                Case "L"
                    iLowerBound = iCurrentGuess + 1

            End Select
        Loop
    End Sub
```

A

```
      Shared Function GetMyGuess(iUpper As Integer, iLower As Integer)
      ➥As Integer
          If iUpper = iLower Then
              GetMyGuess = iLower
          Else
              GetMyGuess = iLower + ((iUpper - iLower - 1)\2)
          End If
      End Function
  End Class
```

Answers for Day 5

Quiz

1. There are several, but the most important is that no distribution is required before the application can be used or to update the application. Another key benefit is that applications with a Web interface can be accessed from non-Windows platforms.

2. This is still a single-tier system. The different levels of application are based on the locations where code and/or processing occur. In this example, no processing is handled by the server; it merely holds the file for use by the client application. All the logic, processing, and code occurs only on the client system.

3. The key requirement is the .NET Framework, which must be installed on any system that will be executing .NET code, including the server that runs an ASP.NET Web site.

Answers for Day 6

Quiz

1. Locals window, Watch window, Watch pop-up, Immediate window, Quickwatch window.

Exercises

1. Listing 6.11 shows one possible solution.

INPUT   **LISTING 6.11**   Finished Multiplication Table

```
1 Imports System
2 Imports Microsoft.VisualBasic.ControlChars
3
4 Module modTable
5
6     Sub Main()
```

LISTING 6.11 continued

```
 7          Dim iLow, iHigh As Integer
 8          Dim sInput As String
 9
10          'Allow multiple runs through the table generation
11          Do
12              'prompt for values
13              Console.Write("Low value (maximum of 20, 0 to end): ")
14              sInput = Console.ReadLine()
15              iLow = CInt(sInput)
16
17              If iLow <> 0 Then
18                  Console.Write("High value (maximum of 20): ")
19                  sInput = Console.ReadLine()
20                  iHigh = CInt(sInput)
21
22                  OutputTable(iLow, iHigh)
23              End If
24          Loop Until iLow = 0
25          Console.Write("Press ENTER to continue")
26          Console.ReadLine()
27      End Sub
28
29      Private Sub OutputTable(ByVal MinValue As Integer, _
30        ByVal MaxValue As Integer)
31          Dim iCount, iCount2 As Integer
32
33          Console.WriteLine()
34          Console.WriteLine("Multiplication Table ({0} to {1})", _
35            MinValue, MaxValue)
36
37          'write header
38          For iCount = MinValue To MaxValue
39              Console.Write(Tab & CStr(iCount))
40          Next
41          Console.WriteLine()
42
43          'Write each of the lines of the table
44          For iCount = MinValue To MaxValue
45              For iCount2 = MinValue To MaxValue
46                  Console.Write(Tab & CStr(iCount * iCount2))
47              Next
48              Console.WriteLine()
49          Next
50      End Sub
51
52 End Module
```

Answers for Day 7

Quiz

1. If a method within a class is marked as MustOverride, then the class must be marked as MustInherit. This is because the first requirement, that all client classes must implement their own code for that method, then forces the MustInherit keyword because the base class does not override the method.

2. The MyBase keyword allows you to call members of the class's parent or base class. You can use MyBase.New() to call the default constructor of your base class.

3. Two of the overloaded constructors are effectively the same to the Visual Basic compiler and are therefore not allowed.

```
Public Sub New(ByVal sColor As String)
    m_dtManufactured = System.DateTime.Now()
    m_sColor = sColor
End Sub

Public Sub New(ByVal sName As String)
End Sub
```

In this case, because the procedures both share the same name and have the same parameters, the Visual Basic compiler considers them the same and therefore will not allow them both to exist. The fact that one argument is named sColor and another sName is irrelevant for the purposes of this issue.

Exercises

There are many different ways you could choose to create this example, but here is one possible implementation (see Figure 7.4):

```
Namespace Biology
    Public Class Animal
        Public Overridable Property Name() As String
            Get
            End Get
            Set(ByVal Value As String)
            End Set
        End Property
        Public Overridable Property NumberOfLimbs() As Integer
            Get
            End Get
            Set(ByVal Value As Integer)
            End Set
        End Property
        Public Overridable Property Color() As String
            Get
```

```vb
            End Get
            Set(ByVal Value As String)
            End Set
        End Property
        Public Overridable Property Weight() As Single
            Get
            End Get
            Set(ByVal Value As Single)
            End Set
        End Property
        Public Overridable Property AirBreather() As Boolean
            Get
            End Get
            Set(ByVal Value As Boolean)
            End Set
        End Property
    End Class

    Public Class Reptile
        Inherits Animal
    End Class
    Public Class Mammal
        Inherits Animal
        Public Overrides Property AirBreather() As Boolean
            Get
                Return True
            End Get
            Set(ByVal Value As Boolean)
                Throw New System.Exception("All mammals breathe air")
            End Set
        End Property
    End Class

    Public Class Human
        Inherits Mammal
        Public Overrides Property NumberOfLimbs() As Integer
            Get
                Return 4
            End Get
            Set(ByVal Value As Integer)
            End Set
        End Property
    End Class
End Namespace
```

FIGURE 7.4

The Object Browser shows the classes that make up this example and their relationship to one another.

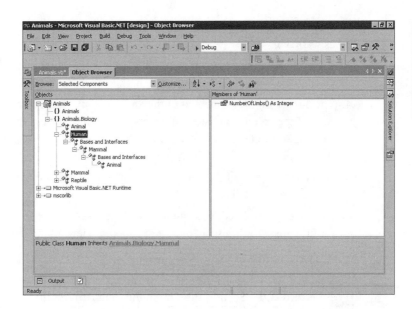

Do not be concerned if your code doesn't match up that closely with this example, as long as it runs and you have been able to use some of the object features described in Day 7's lesson.

Answers for Day 8

Quiz

1. You could redirect the output or error streams to a file for logging purposes.

2. The SortedList collection automatically sorts the items in a list as you add them, so you don't have to remember to continually call the Sort method. The ArrayList collection does not have this function.

3. A number between 2 and 12 would be displayed on the console.

Exercises

To create the console program described, you would use the GetCommandArgs method of the Environment class, and the Sort method of the ArrayList class. As such, you would need the System and System.Collections namespaces. Follow these steps:

1. Create a new console application. Mine is called SortedArgs.

2. Change the name of the module from Module1 to modMain. Save the resulting file as `Main.vb`.

3. Right-click on the project name in the Solution Explorer and select Properties. Change the Startup Object to `modMain`. Select OK to close the dialog box.

4. The `GetCommandArgs` method of the `Environment` class returns a string array of each of the arguments listed on the command-line (including the name of the application). You can use this to create a new `ArrayList`, and use the built-in sorting functionality to sort your list.

5. Because the name of the application is in your `ArrayList`, you should remove it before sorting the list.

6. After the list is sorted, you can use the `Console.WriteLine` method to display the resulting list. You'll use a `For...Next` loop to view all the items in the list.

The full source for the example is in Listing 8.4.

INPUT   **LISTING 8.4**   Sorting the Command-Line Arguments

```
1  Module modMain
2      Sub Main()
3          Dim oArgs As New ArrayList(Environment.GetCommandLineArgs())
4          Dim I As Integer
5          With oArgs
6              .RemoveAt(0)
7              .Sort()
8              For I = 0 To .Count - 1
9                  Console.WriteLine(.Item(I))
10             Next
11         End With
12     End Sub
13 End Module
```

ANALYSIS   Listing 8.4 is short, but it demonstrates a variety of techniques for manipulating collections, as well as retrieving command-line arguments.

Line 3 creates a new `ArrayList`, copying the string array returned by the `GetCommandLineArgs` method. This technique is available to many of the collections defined in `System.Collections`. It enables you to take an existing array, convert it to the collection (`ArrayList`, `Queue`, or `Stack`), and get the additional behavior of the collection. In this case, it enables you to remove the undesired item (line 6) and sort the remaining items (line 7). Finally, the code in lines 8 through 10 displays the resulting array. Running the application should produce the following output:

```
OUTPUT   1 SortedArgs Asimov Heinlein Bradley Niven _
         2 Pournelle Clarke Herbert Card LeGuin Haldeman
         3 Asimov
         4 Bradley
         5 Card
         6 Clarke
         7 Haldeman
         8 Heinlein
         9 Herbert
        10 LeGuin
        11 Niven
        12 Pournelle
```

Answers for Day 9

Quiz

1. Modal versus Nonmodal: When a Window is displayed modally, the user cannot interact with any other part of the application until the window is dismissed. In the code that displays a modal form, code execution is halted until the form is hidden or closed. When a nonmodal form is displayed, the user is not prevented from working with any other parts of the application, and the code that displayed the form will continue to run without waiting for the form to close.

2. You set the CausesValidation property to True to indicate that you want to ensure that the data entry fields contain valid data when the user moves to this control. If you set this property on a Cancel button, then the user will have to have entered valid information even when she just wants to cancel the process!

3. The Handles statement, followed by one or more specific event names, is used to indicate that a procedure is an event handler. Handles btnOpen.Click at the end of a procedure would indicate that the procedure will be called whenever the Click event of btnOpen occurs (when the user clicks btnOpen).

Exercises

1. The key to handling the three events through a single routine is to determine which particular event has occurred when the routine is called. By casting the sender parameter to a System.Windows.Forms.Control object, you can access its Name property, which will provide you the name of the control that is the source of the event. The revised event procedure, which would replace the other three, is shown in Listing 9.21.

LISTING 9.21 Event Procedures

```
 1 Private Sub DoEverything(ByVal sender As Object, _
 2 ByVal e As System.EventArgs) _
 3 Handles btnCopy.Click, btnMove.Click, btnDelete.Click
 4
 5     Dim sEventSource As String _
 6 = CType(sender, Control).Name
 7     Dim sSource As String
 8     Dim sDestination As String
 9     sSource = txtSource.Text()
10     sDestination = txtDestination.Text()
11
12     Select Case sEventSource
13       Case "btnCopy"
14         File.Copy(sSource, sDestination)
15       Case "btnMove"
16         File.Move(sSource, sDestination)
17       Case "btnDelete"
18         File.Delete(sSource)
19       Case Else
20         'do nothing
21     End Select
22 End Sub
```

Answers for Day 10

Quiz

1. `Label` controls give you the capability to dynamically change the text later.

2. `LinkButton`, `HyperLink` controls.

3. Either use the `Image` control or the `ImageButton` control (if the image is intended to be clicked on), or simply select Insert, Image from the menu.

Exercises

Because of the conditions on the form, you should use the `Validator` controls. You will add them to each of the controls. Most will be `RequiredFieldValidators`, but you will also need a `CompareValidator` to ensure that the two passwords match. In addition, you will see how to create a password field.

Create a new project (or add a new form to an existing project). Add a new table (Table, Insert, Table) to the form, with three columns and six rows. See Figure 10.9 for details.

Add three labels to the new form, one in each of the first three rows of the first column. Similarly, add four `TextBox` controls to the first four rows of the second column. The end result should look similar to Figure 10.10.

FIGURE 10.9

Insert Table dialog.

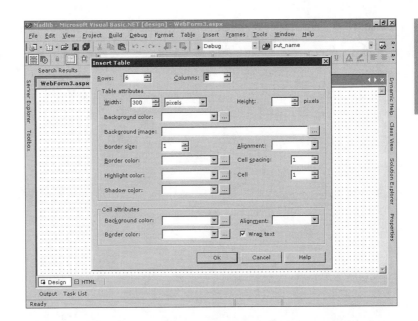

FIGURE 10.10

The Web Form in progress.

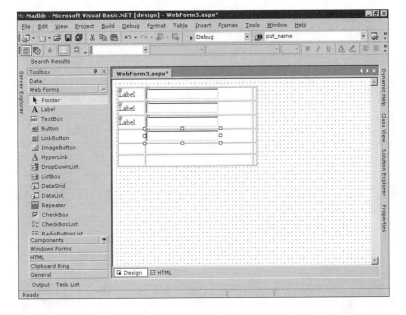

To complete the second column, add a Button and another Label control. Finally, to the third column, add (from top to bottom) three RequiredFieldValidators and a CompareValidator. Set the properties of all controls as shown in Table 10.6.

TABLE 10.6 Properties for the Registration Form

Control	Property	Value
Label	(ID)	lblName
	Text	Name:
	Font Bold	True
Label	(ID)	lblAlias
	Text	Alias:
	Font Bold	True
Label	(ID)	lblPassword
	Text	Password:
	Font Bold	True
TextBox	(ID)	txtName
TextBox	(ID)	txtAlias
	MaxLength	10
TextBox	(ID)	txtPassword1
	TextMode	Password
TextBox	(ID)	txtPassword2
	TextMode	Password
Button	(ID)	cmdRegister
	Text	Register
Label	(ID)	lblSummary
	BackColor	#E0E0E0
	BorderColor	Silver
	BorderStyle	Groove
	BorderWidth	1px
	Text	<blank>
Validator	(ID)	reqName
	ControlToValidate	txtName
	ErrorMessage	Name is a required field.
Validator	(ID)	reqAlias
	ControlToValidate	txtAlias
	ErrorMessage	Alias is a required field.
Validator	(ID)	reqPassword
	ControlToValidate	txtPassword1
	ErrorMessage	You must enter a password.
CompareValidator	(ID)	cmpPassword
	ControlToCompare	txtPassword1
	ControlToValidate	txtPassword2
	ErrorMessage	Two passwords must match.

A

Finally, you are ready to add the code. As before, you don't have to add any code for the
validation because the controls manage this. As such, you have little code to add to the
page. You only need to add code for when the user clicks on the Register button. This
will run only if all the errors are cleared. It simply displays a message in the summary
label. Double-click on the Register button and add the code in Listing 10.5.

INPUT	LISTING 10.5 Code for the Register Button

```
1    Public Sub cmdRegister_Click(ByVal sender As Object, ByVal e As
➡System.EventArgs)
2        lblSummary.Text = "Welcome, " & txtAlias.Text
3    End Sub
```

Build and run the project. When the browser is available, try entering different values for
the fields. Clear any entry you have made for the Name and Alias fields. You should see
the error messages for these controls. Enter two different passwords to see the
CompareValidator in action (see Figure 10.11). Finally, enter values for the Name,
Alias, and matching Passwords to see the final summary. See Figure 10.12.

FIGURE 10.11

*Registration form with
errors.*

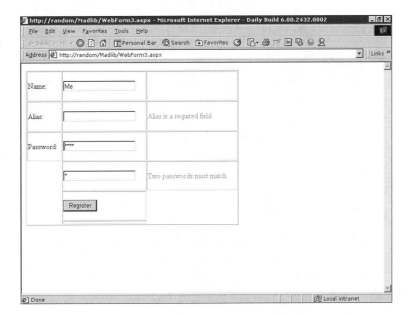

FIGURE 10.12

Registration form completed.

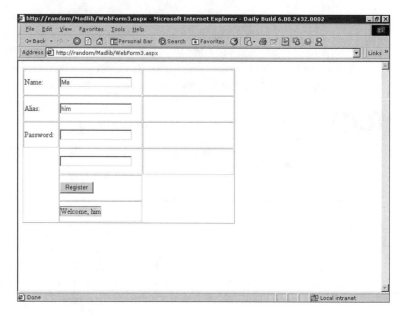

Answers for Day 11

Quiz

1. The field (or fields) used to uniquely identify a database record is called the primary key.

2. This SQL executed a LEFT OUTER JOIN between these two tables, specifying that all the records from the Make table and those records from Model that matched the join condition should be included in the output. The following results will be created:

Make	Model
Ford	Mustang
Ford	Explorer
Audi	<Null>
BMW	<Null>
Pontiac	Grand Am
Pontiac	Grand Prix
Pontiac	Aztek
Toyota	Rav 4
Toyota	Camry

A

3. This SQL statement specifies an INNER JOIN, which is the most common type of join. This will produce results with only those records from both tables where the join condition is met, as follows:

Make	Model
Ford	Mustang
Ford	Explorer
Pontiac	Grand Am
Pontiac	Grand Prix
Pontiac	Aztek
Toyota	Rav 4
Toyota	Camry

Notice that Audi and BMW, which had no records in the Model table, are not included in the output from the second SQL statement.

Exercises

1. There are many different ways you could extend your CD database to handle multiple users, but here is the most straightforward:

   First, add a User table that will include a UserID field as a primary key. What other fields are included in this table is largely irrelevant, but it will likely include information such as the user's name, e-mail address, and perhaps a password, so that you can enforce security and prevent users from modifying other people's CD collection.

   Next, you will work on the assumption that, if two users both had the same "Fields Of Gold" album by Sting, you should have only one entry in Artist for Sting, and only one entry in Disc for that particular CD. With those assumptions, what you end up with is a many-to-many relationship between User and Disc, which can be expressed as a UserDisc relationship table. The modified database is shown in Figure 11.7.

2. As ugly as the data in Orders.txt might look, it is not uncommon to be given data in this format, especially when it is coming from a spreadsheet. To place this into an efficient database, you have to break out the Customer information from the Order info, and also place the individual order items (what if a customer wanted to order four items on the same order?) into their own table. Along the way, you can also remove some calculated fields (Order Total, ItemX Total Cost) that could instead be obtained as part of a query. This database layout is shown in Figure 11.8.

FIGURE 11.7

Adding two tables is all that is needed to make your CD database into a multiuser system.

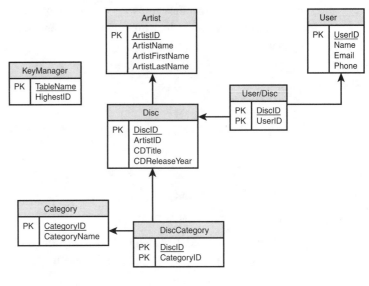

FIGURE 11.8

Restructured Order database.

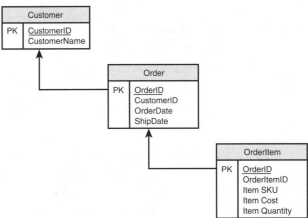

If desired, you could take this database further, creating an Items table to hold a record for each SKU with a price and item description and removing those fields from the OrderItem table. Note that in an order entry database, it is sometimes necessary to have a bit of duplication—storing item costs with order line items, for example—to allow item prices to change over time without changing the information in past orders.

Answers for Day 12

Quiz

1. The property in question is `MissingSchemaAction`, and the setting to ensure that primary key information is created is `AddWithKey`.

2. `Delete` marks the row as deleted but does not remove it from the table; it stays so that the `Update` routine knows to delete that row from the database. `Remove` simply takes that `DataRow` object right out of the `Rows` collection, but it is not removed from the database when `Update` is called.

3. This is a command that returns no records, so you should call it using the `ExecuteNoQuery` method of the Command object. Your code could look like this:

```
Sub Main()
   Dim sSQL As String
   sSQL = "DELETE FROM Artist Where ArtistID=3"
   Dim objConn As New _
      System.Data.OleDb.OleDbConnection(sConnection)
   Dim objCmd As New _
      System.Data.OleDb.OleDbCommand(sSQL, objConn)
   objConn.Open()
   objCmd.ExecuteNonQuery()
End Sub
```

Exercises

You could create an interface for your CD library database in many different ways, but the essential pieces will be the same in each case. All the code for an example interface is provided for you on this book's Web site.

Answers for Day 13

Quiz

1. Loaded Modules, Processes (and you can also get this from Management Information).

2. A service is a program that runs in the background on your computer, providing some functionality. For example, SQL Server provides database functionality.

3. The current value for the CPU % in use (% Processor Time) will be written to the Console.

Answers for Day 14

Quiz

1. `MyBase` provides the functionality desired and can be used to refer to properties or methods of the base class.

2. Creating multiple versions of the same procedure, but with different sets of parameters, is called overloading.

3. The output will be

    ```
    x.Name = Fred
    y.Name = Fred
    ```

    Both x and y refer to the same instance of `myFirstClass`, and `x.Name = y.Name` changes nothing because it is equivalent to `x.Name = x.Name`.

Exercises

One possible design choice would be to handle the various event types using an object hierarchy, instead of just using a category or type property on a single `Event` class. You could create a base `Event` class, with some common properties like the event name and perhaps the contact information for that event. Derived from that base, you could build classes such as `SportingEvent` (Inherits `Event`), `ConcertEvent`, `ComedyEvent`, `PublicSpeakingEvent`, and so on. The hierarchy could be taken down even farther, leading to classes like `BaseballGame` (Inherits `SportingEvent`), `PoliticalEvent` (Inherits `PublicSpeakingEvent`), and so on. The individual properties of the various derived classes could be described in whatever level of detail you want, but should avoid repetition. If two classes have similar properties, consider moving the common properties into a base class.

Answers for Day 15

Quiz

1. Interfaces provide this type of functionality, allowing you to indicate that many different classes share some common feature or capability. Interfaces are especially well suited to this task because a single class can implement many different interfaces.

2. `MustOverride` can be used to indicate that a particular method or property must be overridden in a derived class.

3. `MustInherit` makes a base class into an "abstract" class, one that cannot be instantiated itself, but must instead have classes derived from it.

4. Classes marked as `NotInheritable` also are known as "Sealed" classes, and they cannot be used as a base class (other classes cannot inherit from them).

Exercises

There are many different ways you could create an object hierarchy that includes `Customer`, but Figure 15.4 illustrates one example. In this case, the `Customer` class has been derived from a more generic `Person` class, and the Contact Information aspects have been broken out right in that original base class.

FIGURE **15.4**

Designing classes for reusability can sometimes create a more complex architecture.

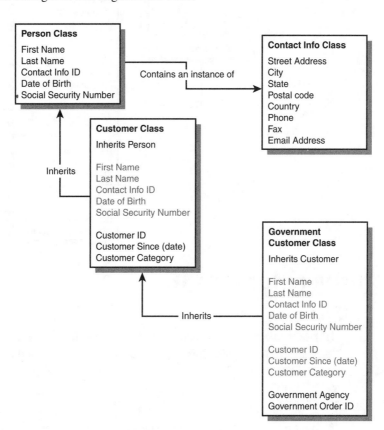

An alternative design, see Figure 15.5, illustrates how a simpler version of the same information can be structured.

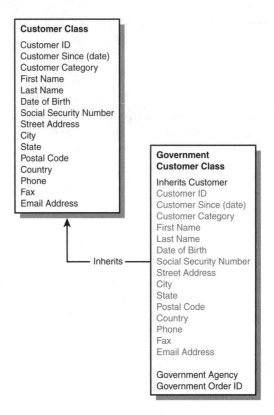

Figure 15.5

The same set of information can be modeled in multiple ways.

Answers for Day 16

Quiz

1. Use the `LayoutMdi` method of the MDI parent form to set the layout to MdiLayout.Cascade. This arranges the child windows so that all their title bars are visible.

Exercises

1. It's personal preference really. Generally, I prefer SDI because I can usually see the individual windows on the taskbar. However, for some applications that might open multiple files, such as a graphics application, I prefer MDI, to keep all the graphics in one spot.

2. The `GetAttributes` and `GetLastWriteTime` methods of the `File` class are useful when retrieving this information from a file. Both are `Shared` methods of the `File` class, therefore you don't have to create an instance of a file before using them. To

A

add this functionality, you can either modify the original Pioneer, or copy all files from the Pioneer directory to a new directory and modify that.

Change the View property of the ListView to Detail. This enables the feature where you can add multiple columns to the ListView. Add three columns to the ListView using the Columns property editor. Table 16.17 describes the properties for these columns.

TABLE 16.17   Column Properties

Column	Property	Value
First	Name	hdrName
	Text	File Name
	Width	180
Second	Name	hdrAttributes
	Text	Attributes
	TextAlign	Center
Third	Name	hdrModified
	Text	Last Modified
	TextAlign	Right
	Width	80

The only code that is needed is to add the information to the columns for the Attributes and Last Modified columns. Modify the tvwFolders_AfterSelect event handler to create these columns (see Listing 16.8).

LISTING 16.8   Creating Additional Columns

```
1    Private Sub tvwFolders_AfterSelect(ByVal sender As Object, _
2        ByVal e As System.Windows.Forms.TreeViewEventArgs) _
3        Handles tvwFolders.AfterSelect
4
5        Dim sFiles() As String = _
6          Directory.GetFiles(tvwFolders.SelectedNode.FullPath)
7        Dim sFile As String
8        Dim oItem As ListViewItem
9
10       lvwFiles.Items.Clear()
11
12       For Each sFile In sFiles
13           oItem = lvwFiles.Items.Add(StripPath(sFile))
14           If lvwFiles.Items.Count > 0 Then
```

LISTING **16.8** continued

```
15                    oItem.SubItems.Add(GetAttributeString(sFile))
16                    oItem.SubItems.Add(File.GetLastWriteTime(sFile))
17              End If
18          Next
19      End Sub
```

ANALYSIS The added code is the declaration of the ListViewItem at line 8, and the code in lines 13-17. When you add a new ListViewItem to a ListView, the item added is returned from the Add method. If you are simply adding an item to the list, as we did before, it is not important to save this into a new variable. However, because you will be adding subitems to this new item, you should store it in a variable, as shown in line 13. After adding the item, you then use the SubItems property of each ListViewItem to add new values for the columns added previously. First, the code calls the GetAttributeString function, which you will create in a moment, to add the string representing each file's attributes. Then, line 16 adds the date and time that the file was last written to into the Last Modified column.

Finally, you should create a routine that displays the attributes assigned to the file. Add the code in Listing 16.9 to add this.

LISTING **16.9** GetAttributeString Function

```
20      Private Function GetAttributeString(ByVal fileName As String) _
21         As String
22         Dim sReturn As String
23         Dim oAttr As FileAttributes = File.GetAttributes(fileName)
24
25         If (oAttr And FileAttributes.ReadOnly) = _
26            FileAttributes.ReadOnly Then
27             sReturn = "R"
28         Else
29             sReturn = "-"
30         End If
31
32         If (oAttr And FileAttributes.Hidden) = _
33            FileAttributes.Hidden Then
34             sReturn += "H"
35         Else
36             sReturn += "-"
37         End If
38
39         If (oAttr And FileAttributes.System) = _
40            FileAttributes.System Then
41             sReturn += "S"
```

LISTING 16.9 continued

```
42          Else
43              sReturn += "-"
44          End If
45
46          Return sReturn
47
48      End Function
```

ANALYSIS The GetAttributeString function retrieves the attributes for each file and converts them into a string for viewing. The return value from the File.GetAttributes method is a FileAttributes value that contains the sum of all the attributes assigned to the file (Line 23). The If statement at lines 25 and 26 tests this value to see whether it includes the ReadOnly attribute. This test uses the logical operator And to compare the full value containing all the attributes to the attribute FileAttributes.ReadOnly. If the FileAttributes.ReadOnly value is part of the whole, this test will return the value FileAttributes.ReadOnly. That is, if you join two numbers together with the And operator, the return value is the value they have in common, or 0 if they have nothing in common. For example, 33 And 1 returns 1, whereas 33 And 2 returns 0. If the file does have the ReadOnly attribute set, the code puts an R in the string; otherwise, it puts a hyphen. The tests for Hidden and System attributes are identical, except testing for the desired attribute. Finally, at line 46, the complete string is returned to add to the ListView column.

Note

The return value from GetAttributes is a bitmask of all the attributes on a file. A *bitmask* is the term applied to a value where each bit in the value is used as a flag, to mark some characteristic. For example, if you look at some of the actual values for each of the FileAttributes enumeration (see Table 16.18), you will see that there are gaps between the values.

TABLE 16.18 Possible File Attribute Values

Member	Value
ReadOnly	1
Hidden	2
System	4
Directory	16
Archive	32
Device	64

TABLE 16.18 continued

Member	Value
Normal	128
Temporary	256
Sparse File	512
Reparse Point	1024
Compressed	2048
Offline	4096
Not Content Indexed	8192
Encrypted	16384

As you can see, generally each value is 2X the previous. This means that you can pack multiple flags into the same integer (or long) variable without them affecting one another. Each uses the next power of two to represent the desired value. For example, if a file is read-only, with archive set to True, the value returned would be 33:

```
Power of 2:      7 6 5 4 3 2 1 0
Bit:             0 0 1 0 0 0 0 1
Value:               32        1
```

FileAttributes.Archive has a value of 32, whereas FileAttributes.ReadOnly is 1. Therefore, a file with both of those attributes set would return 33 from GetAttributes.

Bitmasks are a common strategy to use when you need to provide many flags in a relatively small memory space. Bit arithmetic using And, Or, and Xor takes a bit of getting used to, but is easy when you divide the task into the powers of 2.

Run the altered program. You should be able to see the status of the Hidden, ReadOnly, and System file attributes, in addition to the filenames and last modified dates (see Figure 16.18).

A

FIGURE **16.18**

Running the modified Pioneer.

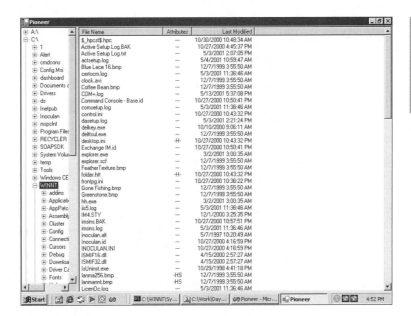

Answers for Day 17

Quiz

1. The correct answer is C. The `Exists` method is a `Shared` method of the `File` object. You do not have to create an instance of the `File` class before using the method.

2. `Stream` is an abstract class that represents a flow of information. `StreamReader` is a simple means of adding to the stream, whereas `StreamWriter` is used to write to the stream.

3. You can create and use a wide variety of file formats in the `Image` control, including BMP, GIF, JPG, PNG, and TIF files.

4. A `Point` describes a location in space. A `Size` defines height and width. A `Rectangle` is made up of a `Size` at a specific `Point`. That is, it has height and width and is at a specific location.

Exercises

1. The `Click` event for the top-level Edit menu is a great place to prepare the menu before showing it to the user, as seen in Listing 17.12. This allows you to customize the menu, setting the `Enabled` property of the Cut, Copy, and Paste commands as appropriate. Nothing is on the Clipboard, for example, the Paste command should not be enabled.

INPUT **LISTING 17.12**   Dynamically Updating the Edit menu

```
1    Private Sub mnuEdit_Click(ByVal sender As System.Object, _
2      ByVal e As System.EventArgs) _
3      Handles mnuEdit.Click
4
5      'is there any text selected?
6      If Me.txtText.SelectedText.Length > 0 Then
7        mnuEditCut.Enabled = True
8        mnuEditCopy.Enabled = True
9      Else
10       mnuEditCut.Enabled = False
11       mnuEditCopy.Enabled = False
12     End If
13
14     'is there anything on the Clipboard that we can paste here?
15     If Clipboard.GetDataObject.GetDataPresent(DataFormats.Text) Then
16       mnuEditPaste.Enabled = True
17     Else
18       mnuEditPaste.Enabled = False
19     End If
20
21   End Sub
```

ANALYSIS   The code in the mnuEdit_Click event will execute before the menu is shown. There are two parts to the routine. The first (lines 5–12) determine whether the Cut and Copy menu items should be enabled. If any selected text is in the txtText TextBox, the test at line 6 will be true. This enables the Cut and Copy menu items. The text at line 15 is more complex. Recall that the Clipboard class has two methods: GetDataObject and SetDataObject. Here, we call the GetDataObject, which returns the object that contains the data on the Clipboard. It has a method, GetDataPresent, which is used to query the data object to determine whether it contains anything in a known format. In this case, we query it to see whether it contains text. If there is, we can enable the Paste menu item because this is an acceptable format for the TextBox. If there had been something like a Word document on the Clipboard instead of plain text, this also would have been acceptable because the data object can convert between the two types. However, if there had been a graphic on the Clipboard, the GetDataPresent method would have returned False because there is no way to convert a graphic to text.

2. It is variable; however, generally GIFs and PNGs are the smallest file formats for simple graphics with few colors, whereas JPEGs are smallest when storing photographs.

A

Answers for Day 18

Quiz

1. All that the name provides is the fact that the variable is most likely related to making a database connection and that it is a string (due to the leading "s").

2. To protect your source code, to coordinate the work of multiple programmers on the same project, and to track changes made to the code over time.

3. This process is called rolling back, and it can be done to any earlier point when the code was checked in.

Answers for Day 19

Quiz

1. You only need to create a single installation, including the .NET Framework, and it will determine whether the Framework needs to be installed at runtime on the target machine.

2. If all the components of the application are to be installed onto the same target machine, one setup is perfectly fine. If the library components are going to be installed onto a server, while the main project is installed onto the user's machine, then you should create separate installs for the two groups of projects.

3. Advanced installation options and features are not available through the VS.NET Setup tools; you will need to use a third-party installer package, such as Install Shield or Wise Installer.

4. During the Setup Wizard, you are given the option of adding any additional files to your setup, and those files will be installed into the application directory by default. You also can add files after the completion of the initial wizard by just adding them to the project (right-click on the setup project and select Add, File from the context menu).

Exercises

To complete this exercise, you can follow along with me as I perform the required steps:

1. Create a new Visual Basic.NET Windows application.

2. Create a .config file and put it into the bin directory of your new project. The configuration file does not need to contain much, just a single setting that we will use for the Window's title:

```
<configuration>
   <appSettings>
      <add key="Title" value="This is my Window Title" />
   </appSettings>
</configuration>
```

3. Add the following code to the constructor of your form (the New() subroutine) to load the title value and assign it to the Text property of the Form.

```
1    Public Sub New()
2        MyBase.New()
3
4        'This call is required by the Windows Form Designer.
5        InitializeComponent()
6
7        'Add any initialization after the InitializeComponent() call
8        Me.Text = GetTitle()
9    End Sub
10
11   Private Function GetTitle() As String
12       Dim sTitle As String
13       sTitle = _
             Configuration.ConfigurationSettings.AppSettings.Get("Title")
14       Return sTitle
15   End Function
```

4. Run the project to test it.

5. Now add a Setup Wizard project to your solution and walk through the steps, accepting the defaults for everything until you get to the Additional Files step. Add the .config file as an Additional File, and it will be added to your install and deployed into the same directory as the .exe of the application.

Answers for Day 20

Quiz

1. Use the WriteElementString method of the XmlTextWriter to create a complete element:

   ```
   oWriter.WriteElementString("name", "value")
   ```

2. You should use the DOM when you need to work with different parts of an XML document, or when you need to move forward and backward through the file. In addition, you could use the DOM if you will be both reading and writing to the file.

3. Metadata is data about data, such as the size of the information, the names of any fields, and so on.

Exercises

1. Figure 20.9 and Listing 20.8 show one possible solution.

FIGURE 20.9

Test application with memory.

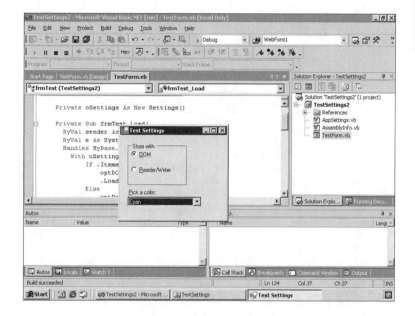

LISTING 20.8 Test Application

```
1 Public Class frmTest
2     Inherits System.Windows.Forms.Form
3
4     Private oSettings As New Settings()
5
6     Private Sub frmTest_Closing( _
7       ByVal sender As Object, _
8       ByVal e As System.ComponentModel.CancelEventArgs) _
9       Handles MyBase.Closing
10
11        'copy configuration to settings object
12        With oSettings
13            .Items("left") = Me.Left
14            .Items("top") = Me.Top
15            .Items("height") = Me.Height
16            .Items("width") = Me.Width
17            .Items("color") = cboColor.SelectedIndex
18            If optDOM.Checked Then
19                .Items("strategy") = "DOM"
20                .SaveDOM()
21            Else
22                .Items("strategy") = "ReaderWriter"
```

LISTING 20.8 continued

```
23                  .SaveWriter()
24              End If
25          End With
26      End Sub
27
28      Private Sub cboColor_SelectedIndexChanged( _
29        ByVal sender As Object, _
30        ByVal e As System.EventArgs) _
31        Handles cboColor.SelectedIndexChanged
32          Me.BackColor = Color.FromName(cboColor.Text)
33      End Sub
34
35      Private Sub frmTest_Load( _
36        ByVal sender As Object, _
37        ByVal e As System.EventArgs) _
38        Handles MyBase.Load
39          With oSettings
40              If .Items("strategy") = "DOM" Then
41                  optDOM.Checked = True
42                  .LoadDOM()
43              Else
44                  optReaderWriter.Checked = True
45                  .LoadReader()
46              End If
47              Me.Left = .Items("left")
48              Me.Top = .Items("top")
49              Me.Height = .Items("height")
50              Me.Width = .Items("width")
51              cboColor.SelectedIndex = .Items("color")
52          End With
53      End Sub
54 End Class
```

ANALYSIS The code here is similar to that in the original test application. In the Form Closing event (lines 6–26), the configuration information, including the Form position and the current values for the option buttons and DropDownList, are stored in the Settings variable, and then written using the desired technique.

Almost the exact opposite code happens in the Form Load event (lines 35–53) where first the desired reader is determined. This is possible because the creation of the Settings object actually populated the settings, so when the load happens at either line 42 or 45, this is reloading the settings. Finally, the settings are copied back to the desired variables.

The last event handler in the sample application is used to confirm when a selection is made in the DropDownList by changing the background color to the selected color.

Run the application and change the size or position of the Form, the color selected in the `DropDownList`, or the strategy selection. Close the Form and rerun. Your changes should be persistent.

Answers for Day 21

Quiz

1. The DISCO file is used by the client to discover the Web Services provided by a server.

2. The proxy is the client-side view of the Web Service. It is responsible for creating the SOAP message, and for converting the SOAP response into the appropriate data types.

3. SOAP is the message format used by Web Services. It provides the way of creating a platform and programming language independent messages.

INDEX